This entirely new translation of the *Critique of Pure Reason* is the most accurate and informative English translation ever produced of this epochal philosophical text. Though its simple and direct style will make it suitable for all new readers of Kant, the translation displays an unprecedented philosophical and textual sophistication that will enlighten Kant scholars as well.

Through the comparison of the best modern German editions to the original 1781 and 1787 versions of the text, and careful attention to the precise translation of Kant's terminology, as well as the faithful rendering of the structure and syntax of Kant's prose, this translation recreates as far as possible a text with the same interpretative nuances and richness as the original. Moreover, by including the complete text of the handwritten emendations and marginal notes made by Kant in his own personal copy of the first edition, this volume does what even no German edition has ever done: furnish the reader with a text as close as possible to the one present in Kant's own library.

The Cambridge Edition places the reader in the most independent yet best informed interpretative position by presenting entirely separate (though meticulously cross-referenced) versions of all the portions of the work that Kant revised heavily for the second edition: the prefaces, the introduction, Transcendental Aesthetic, Transcendental Deduction, the chapter on Phenomena and Noumena, and the Paralogisms of Pure Reason.

The extensive editorial apparatus includes informative annotation, detailed glossaries, a thorough but perspicuous index, and a large-scale general introduction in which two of the world's preeminent Kant scholars provide a succinct summary of the structure and argument of the *Critique* as well as a detailed account of its long and complex genesis.

THE CAMBRIDGE EDITION OF THE WORKS OF IMMANUEL KANT

IMMANUEL KANT
Critique of Pure Reason

THE CAMBRIDGE EDITION OF THE WORKS
OF IMMANUEL KANT

IMMANUEL KANT

Critique of Pure Reason

TRANSLATED AND EDITED BY

PAUL GUYER
University of Pennsylvania

ALLEN W. WOOD
Stanford University

CAMBRIDGE
UNIVERSITY PRESS

CAMBRIDGE UNIVERSITY PRESS

Cambridge, New York, Melbourne, Madrid, Cape Town, Singapore, São Paulo, Delhi

Cambridge University Press

32 Avenue of the Americas, New York, NY 10013-2473, USA

www.cambridge.org

Information on this title: www.cambridge.org/9780521657297

First published 1998
Reprinted 1998
First paperback edition 1999
15th printing 2009

Printed in the United States of America

A catalog record for this publication is available from the British Library.

Library of Congress Cataloging in Publication Data

Kant, Immanuel, 1724–1804.
[Kritik der reinen Vernunft. English]
The critique of pure reason / edited [and translated] by Paul
Guyer, Allen W Wood.
p.   cm. – (The Cambridge edition of the works of Immanuel Kant)
Includes bibliographical references and index.
ISBN 0-521-35402-1 (hardcover)
1. Knowledge, Theory of.   2. Causation.   3. Reason.   I. Guyer,
Paul, 1948–   II. Wood, Allen W.   III. Title.   IV. Series: Kant,
Immanuel, 1724–1804. Works. English, 1992.
B2778.E5G89   1998
121 – dc21   97-4959

ISBN 978-0-521-35402-8 hardback
ISBN 978-0-521-65729-7 paperback

Contents

General editors' preface

Within a few years of the publication of his *Critique of Pure Reason* in 1781, Immanuel Kant (1724–1804) was recognized by his contemporaries as one of the seminal philosophers of modern times – indeed as one of the great philosophers of all time. This renown soon spread beyond German-speaking lands, and translations of Kant's work into English were published even before 1800. Since then, interpretations of Kant's views have come and gone and loyalty to his positions has waxed and waned, but his importance has not diminished. Generations of scholars have devoted their efforts to producing reliable translations of Kant into English as well as into other languages.

There are four main reasons for the present edition of Kant's writings:

1. Completeness. Although most of the works published in Kant's lifetime have been translated before, the most important ones more than once, only fragments of Kant's many important unpublished works have ever been translated. These include the *Opus postumum*, Kant's unfinished *magnum opus* on the transition from philosophy to physics; transcriptions of his classroom lectures; his correspondence; and his marginalia and other notes. One aim of this edition is to make a comprehensive sampling of these materials available in English for the first time.

2. Availability. Many English translations of Kant's works, especially those that have not individually played a large role in the subsequent development of philosophy, have long been inaccessible or out of print. Many of them, however, are crucial for the understanding of Kant's philosophical development, and the absence of some from English-language bibliographies may be responsible for erroneous or blinkered traditional interpretations of his doctrines by English-speaking philosophers.

3. Organization. Another aim of the present edition is to make all Kant's published work, both major and minor, available in comprehensive volumes organized both chronologically and topically, so as to facilitate the serious study of his philosophy by English-speaking readers.

4. Consistency of translation. Although many of Kant's major works have been translated by the most distinguished scholars of their day, some of these translations are now dated, and there is considerable terminological disparity among them. Our aim has been to enlist some of the most accomplished Kant scholars and translators to produce new translations, freeing readers from both the philosophical and literary preconceptions of previous generations and allowing them to approach texts, as far as possible, with the same directness as present-day readers of the German or Latin originals.

In pursuit of these goals, our editors and translators attempt to follow several fundamental principles:

1. As far as seems advisable, the edition employs a single general glossary, especially for Kant's technical terms. Although we have not attempted to restrict the prerogative of editors and translators in choice of terminology, we have maximized consistency by putting a single editor or editorial team in charge of each of the main groupings of Kant's writings, such as his work in practical philosophy, philosophy of religion, or natural science, so that there will be a high degree of terminological consistency, at least in dealing with the same subject matter.

2. Our translators try to avoid sacrificing literalness to readability. We hope to produce translations that approximate the originals in the sense that they leave as much of the interpretive work as possible to the reader.

3. The paragraph, and even more the sentence, is often Kant's unit of argument, and one can easily transform what Kant intends as a continuous argument into a mere series of assertions by breaking up a sentence so as to make it more readable. Therefore, we try to preserve Kant's own divisions of sentences and paragraphs wherever possible.

4. Earlier editions often attempted to improve Kant's texts on the basis of controversial conceptions about their proper interpretation. In our translations, emendation or improvement of the original edition is kept to the minimum necessary to correct obvious typographical errors.

5. Our editors and translators try to minimize interpretation in other ways as well, for example, by rigorously segregating Kant's own footnotes, the editors' purely linguistic notes, and their more explanatory or informational notes; notes in this last category are treated as endnotes rather than footnotes.

We have not attempted to standardize completely the format of individual volumes. Each, however, includes information about the context in which Kant wrote the translated works, a German–English glossary, an English–German glossary, an index, and other aids to comprehension. The general introduction to each volume includes an explanation of specific principles of translation and, where necessary, principles of selection of works included in that volume. The pagination of the standard German edition of Kant's works, *Kant's Gesammelte Schriften*, edited by the Royal Prussian (later German) Academy of Sciences (Berlin: Georg Reimer, later Walter de Gruyter & Co., 1900–), is indicated throughout by means of marginal numbers.

Our aim is to produce a comprehensive edition of Kant's writings, embodying and displaying the high standards attained by Kant scholarship in the English-speaking world during the second half of the twentieth century, and serving as both an instrument and a stimulus for the further development of Kant studies by English-speaking readers in the century to come. Because of our emphasis on literalness of translation and on information rather than interpretation in editorial practices, we hope our edition will continue to be usable despite the inevitable evolution and occasional revolutions in Kant scholarship.

PAUL GUYER
ALLEN W. WOOD

Acknowledgments

This translation of Kant's Critique of Pure Reason is the work of both of us over many years, during which we have had the helpful input of many students, friends, and colleagues. Those who have been especially generous of their time and effort are owed special thanks. Those who helped us in one way or another in the preparation and revision of the translation are Günter Zöller, Charles Parsons, Stephan Wagner, the students in Paul Guyer's Kant classes at the University of Pennsylvania in 1994–95, and the students in Allen Wood's "German Philosophical Texts" classes at Cornell University in 1990 and 1992. Jens Timmerman made available to us detailed corrections of the Raymund Schmidt (Meiner) edition of the German text, and Georg Mohr provided us with corrections of the Ingeborg Heidemann (Reclam) edition. Several people, including Lewis White Beck, Rolf George and Martin Weatherston, offered us corrections of earlier English translations. John Cooper and Rega Wood helped us with the identification and attribution of classical quotations. The trustees of the Florence R. C. Murray Trust endowed the research fund that paid for facsimiles of the original editions of the Critique and other research materials. Finally, special thanks to Allison Crapo and Cynthia Schossberger for their generous and meticulous help with the proofreading and to Michael Rohlf, Zenon Feszczak, Ashley Vaught, Erik Watkins, Frederick Beiser, M. S. Adib-Soltani, Vilem Mudroch, Julian Wuerth, and Steven M. Bayne for their help in identifying further corrections.

Introduction to the
Critique of Pure Reason

PAUL GUYER AND ALLEN WOOD

Immanuel Kant's *Critique of Pure Reason* is one of the seminal and monumental works in the history of Western philosophy. Published in May 1781, when its author was already fifty-seven years old, and substantially revised for its second edition six years later, the book was both the culmination of three decades of its author's often very private work and the starting-point for nearly two more decades of his rapidly evolving but now very public philosophical thought. In the more than two centuries since the book was first published, it has been the constant object of scholarly interpretation and a continuous source of inspiration to inventive philosophers. To tell the whole story of the book's influence would be to write the history of philosophy since Kant, and that is beyond our intention here. After a summary of the *Critique*'s structure and argument, this introduction will sketch its genesis and evolution from Kant's earliest metaphysical treatise in 1755 to the publication of the first edition of the *Critique* in 1781 and its revision for the second edition of 1787.

I.
THE ARGUMENT OF THE *CRITIQUE*

The strategy of the *Critique*. In the conclusion to his second critique, the *Critique of Practical Reason* of 1788, Kant famously wrote, "Two things fill the mind with ever new and increasing admiration and awe the more often and more enduringly reflection is occupied with them: **the starry heavens above me and the moral law within me.**"[1] This motto could just as well have served for virtually all of Kant's philosophical works, and certainly for the *Critique of Pure Reason*. From the outset of his career, Kant had been concerned to resolve a number of the most fundamental scientific controversies of his epoch and to establish once and for all the basic principles of scientific knowledge of the world, thereby explaining our knowledge of the "starry heavens."

1

Almost as early in his career, Kant was intent on showing that human freedom, understood not only as the presupposition of morality but also as the ultimate value served and advanced by the moral law, is compatible with the truth of modern science. The *Critique of Pure Reason* was the work in which Kant attempted to lay the foundations both for the certainty of modern science and for the possibility of human freedom.

The book is complex, however, not just because of the complexity of Kant's own position, but also because he argues on several fronts against several different alternative positions represented in early modern philosophy generally and within the German Enlightenment in particular. In order to make room for his own dualistic defense of both modern science and human autonomy, Kant, like Descartes, Locke, and Hume, felt he had to rein in the pretensions of traditional metaphysics, which was represented for him by the school of Christian Wolff (1679–1754) and his followers, especially Alexander Gottlieb Baumgarten (1714–1762).[2] Their position, which Kant called "dogmatism," was compared in the Preface to the *Critique* to the despotic ministry of an absolute monarchy – Kant held dogmatism to be capricious, opinionated, faction-ridden and consequently unstable and open to the contempt of rational observers.

Yet Kant wanted to distinguish his own *critical* stance toward dogmatism from several other ways of rejecting it, which he regarded as themselves equally dangerous to the cause of reason. The first of these is *skepticism*, the position Kant took David Hume (1711–1776) to advocate.[3] Another position Kant rejected was *empiricism*, which understood the "way of ideas" described in John Locke's (1632–1704) *Essay concerning Human Understanding* (1690) as grounding knowledge solely on ideas acquired in the course of individual experience. Yet another philosophical stance Kant encountered was what he called *indifferentism*, which did not reject metaphysical assertions themselves but did reject any attempt to argue for them systematically and rigorously. Here he had in mind a number of popular philosophers who were often in substantive agreement with dogmatists on metaphysical issues such as the existence of God and the immortality of the soul, but who were unconvinced by the scholastic subtlety of the dogmatists' propositions and proofs, holding instead that the beliefs on these matters that we need for the successful conduct of human life are simply given through "healthy understanding" or common sense.[4]

Yet while he attempted to criticize and limit the scope of traditional metaphysics, Kant also sought to defend against empiricists its underlying claim of the possibility of universal and necessary knowledge – what Kant called *a priori* knowledge, knowledge originating independently of experience, because no knowledge derived from any particular experience, or *a posteriori* knowledge, could justify a claim to universal and necessary validity. He sought likewise to defend its scientific character against skeptics who dismiss its rigorous arguments as insufficient and against proponents of "common sense" who regard them as pedantic and superfluous. As Kant compared dogmatic metaphysicians to defenders of despotism, so he likened skeptics to nomads who abhor any form of permanent civil society and are prepared to disrupt or overthrow the monarchy of metaphysics, and Lockeans to calumniators who would foist a false and degrading genealogy on the monarch. Those who would pretend indifference to metaphysical inquiries he charged with being closet dogmatists, like supporters of a corrupt regime who scoff at its defects and feign ironic detachment from it but have no independent convictions of their own.

Kant's position thus required him not only to undermine the arguments of traditional metaphysics but also to put in their place a scientific metaphysics of his own, which establishes what can be known *a priori* but also limits it to that which is required for ordinary experience and its extension into natural science. Kant therefore had to find a way to limit the pretensions of the dogmatists while still defending metaphysics as a science which is both possible (as was denied by the skeptics) and necessary (as was denied by the indifferentists). Thus Kant had to fight a war on several different fronts,[5] in which he had to establish the unanswerability of many metaphysical questions against both dogmatists and empiricists but also defend parts of the positions he was attacking, such as the possibility of *a priori* cognition of the fundamental principles of natural science, against both empiricists and skeptics. And while he wanted to prove to the indifferentists that a science of metaphysics is important, he also wanted to embrace part of their position, since he thought that in regard to some insoluble metaphysical questions, indeed the most important of them, we can defend a kind of commonsense belief – in God, freedom and immortality – because our moral outlook has an inescapable stake in them.

The structure of the *Critique*. This complex program led to the enormous complexity of the structure and argument of the *Critique of Pure Reason*. To many readers, the elaborate structure or "architectonic" of the *Critique* has been a barrier to understanding it, but a brief account of the origin of the main divisions of the book can illuminate its contents. Although these contents are profoundly original, Kant actually borrowed much of the book's structure from well-known models. After the preface (which was completely rewritten for the second edition) and the introduction, the *Critique* is divided into two main parts, the "Doctrine of Elements" and the "Doctrine of Method." This distinction is a variation on a distinction common in German logic textbooks between "general logic" and "special" or applied logic;[6] in Kant's hands, it becomes a rubric to distinguish between his fundamental exposition of his theory of *a priori* cognition and its limits, in the "Doctrine of Elements," and his own reflections on the methodological implications of that theory, under the rubric of the "Doctrine of Method," where he provides contrasts between mathematical and philosophical proof and between theoretical and practical reasoning, as well as contrasts between his own critical method and dogmatic, empirical, and skeptical methods of philosophy.

The "Doctrine of Elements" in turn is divided into two main (although very disproportionately sized) parts, the "Transcendental Aesthetic" and the "Transcendental Logic," the first of which considers the *a priori* contributions of the fundamental forms of our *sensibility*, namely space and time, to our knowledge, and the second of which considers the *a priori* contributions of the intellect, both genuine and spurious, to our knowledge. This division is derived from Baumgarten's introduction of "aesthetics" as the title for the science of "lower" or "sensitive cognition" in contrast to logic as the science of higher or conceptual cognition;[7] at the time of writing the *Critique*, however, Kant rejected Baumgarten's supposition that there could be a science of *taste* (what we now call "aesthetics"), and instead appropriated the term for his theory of the contribution of the forms of sensibility to knowledge in general.[8] After a brief explanation of the distinction between "general logic" and "transcendental logic" – the former being the basic science of the forms of thought regardless of its object and the latter being the science of the basic forms for the thought *of* objects (A50–57/B74–82) – Kant then splits the "Transcendental Logic" into two main divisions, the "Transcendental Analytic" and the "Transcendental Dialectic." Kant uses this distinction, which derives from a sixteenth-century Aristotelian distinction between the logic of truth and the logic of probability, represented in eighteenth-century Germany by the Jena professor Joachim Georg Darjes (1714–1791),[9] to distinguish between the positive contributions of the understanding, working in cooperation with sensibility, to the conditions of the possibility of experience and knowledge (the "Transcendental Analytic") and the spurious attempt of reason working independently of sensibility to provide metaphysical insight into things as they are in themselves (the "Transcendental Dialectic"). The "Transcendental Analytic" is in turn divided into two books, the "Analytic of Concepts" and the "Analytic of Principles," the first of which argues for the universal and necessary validity of the pure concepts of the understanding, or the *categories*, such as the concepts of substance and causation, and the second of which argues for the validity of fundamental principles of empirical *judgment* employing those categories, such as the principles of the conservation of substance and the universality of causation.

The "Transcendental Dialectic" is also divided into two books, "On the Concepts of Pure Reason" and "On the Dialectical Inferences of Pure Reason," in which Kant explains how pure reason generates ideas of metaphysical entities such as the soul, the world as a whole, and God and then attempts to prove the reality of those ideas by extending patterns of inference which are valid within the limits of human sensibility beyond those limits. But it should be noted that the combination of the twofold division of the "Transcendental Analytic" into the "Analytic of Concepts" and "Analytic of Principles" with the main part of the Dialectic, the "Dialectical Inferences of Pure Reason," replicates the traditional division of logic textbooks into three sections on *concepts*, *judgments*, and *inferences*:[10] Kant uses this structure to argue that the *concepts* of pure understanding, when applied to the forms of *sensibility*, give rise to sound principles of *judgment*, which constitute the heart of his critical metaphysics, but that *inferences* of pure reason performed without respect to the limits of sensibility give rise only to metaphysical illusion. The treatment of inferences is in turn divided into three sections, "The Paralogisms of Pure Reason," "The Antinomy of Pure Reason," and "The Ideal of Pure Reason," which expose metaphysically fallacious arguments about the nature of the soul, about the size and origin of the world as a whole, and about the existence of God, respectively. These divisions are also derived from Kant's predecessors: Wolff and Baumgarten divided metaphysics into "general metaphysics," or "ontology," and "special metaphysics," in turn divided into "rational psychology," "rational cosmology," and "rational theology." Kant replaces their "ontology" with the constructive doctrine of his own "Transcendental Analytic" (see A 247 / B 303), and then presents his criticism of dogmatic metaphysics based on pure reason alone by demolishing the special metaphysics of rational psychology, cosmology, and theology.

Finally, Kant divides the "Doctrine of Method," in which he reflects on the consequences of his demolition of traditional metaphysics and reconstruction of some parts of it, into four chapters, the "Discipline," the "Canon," the "Architectonic," and the "History of Pure Reason."[11] The first two of these sections are much more detailed than the last two. In the "Discipline of Pure Reason," Kant provides an extended contrast between the nature of mathematical proof and philosophical argument, and offers important commentary on his own new critical or "transcendental" method. In the "Canon of Pure Reason," he prepares the way for his subsequent moral philosophy by contrasting the method of theoretical philosophy to that of practical philosophy, and giving the first outline of the argument that runs through all three critiques, namely that *practical reason* can justify metaphysical *beliefs* about God and the freedom and immortality of the human soul although *theoretical reason* can never yield *knowledge* of such things. The last two parts of the "Doctrine of Method," the "Architectonic of Pure Reason" and the

"History of Pure Reason," recapitulate the contrasts between Kant's own critical philosophical method and those of the dogmatists, empiricists, and skeptics with which he began, treating these contrasts in both systematic and historical terms. Indeed, although Kant himself never cared much about the history of philosophy as a scholarly discipline, in the few pages of his "History of Pure Reason" he outlined the history of modern philosophy as the transcendence of empiricism and rationalism by his own critical philosophy, the pattern that we still use, although of course we also have to add room to this pattern for the heirs and successors of Kant's own philosophy.

With this analysis of the organization of the *Critique of Pure Reason* in hand, we now provide a brief resumé of its contents.

"Introduction": the idea of transcendental philosophy. Although Kant himself often suggests that the negative side of his project, the critique of dogmatic metaphysics, is the most important, the *Critique* presents Kant's positive doctrine of the *a priori* elements of human knowledge first. In the introduction, Kant argues that our mathematical, physical, and quotidian knowledge of nature requires certain judgments that are "synthetic" rather than "analytic," that is, going beyond what can be known solely in virtue of the contents of the concepts involved in them and the application of the logical principles of identity and contradiction to these concepts, and yet also knowable *a priori*, that is, independently of any particular experience since no particular experience could ever be sufficient to establish the universal and necessary validity of these judgments. He entitles the question of how synthetic *a priori* judgments are possible the "general problem of pure reason" (B 19), and proposes an entirely new science in order to answer it (A 10–16/B 24–30).

This new science, which Kant calls "transcendental" (A 11/B 25), does not deal directly with objects of empirical cognition, but investigates the conditions of the possibility of our experience of them by examining the mental capacities that are required for us to have any cognition of objects at all. Kant agrees with Locke that we have no *innate* knowledge, that is, no knowledge of any particular propositions implanted in us by God or nature prior to the commencement of our individual experience.[12] But experience is the product both of external objects affecting our sensibility and of the operation of our cognitive faculties in response to this effect (A 1, B 1), and Kant's claim is that we can have "pure" or *a priori* cognition of the contributions to experience made by the operation of these faculties themselves, rather than of the effect of external objects on us in experience. Kant divides our cognitive capacities into our receptivity to the effects of external objects acting on us and giving us sensations, through which these objects are given to us in empirical intuition, and our active faculty for relating the data of intuition by thinking them under concepts, which is called understanding (A 19 / B 33), and forming judgments about them. As already suggested, this division is the basis for Kant's division of the "Transcendental Doctrine of Elements" into the "Transcendental Aesthetic," which deals with sensibility and its pure form, and the "Transcendental Logic," which deals with the operations of the understanding and judgment as well as both the spurious and the legitimate activities of theoretical reason.

"Transcendental Aesthetic": space, time, and transcendental idealism. Despite its brevity – a mere thirty pages in the first edition and forty in the second – the "Transcendental Aesthetic" argues for a series of striking, paradoxical and even revolutionary theses that determine the course of the whole remainder of the *Critique* and that have been the subject of a very large proportion of the scholarly work devoted to the *Critique* in the last two centuries.[13] In this section, Kant attempts to distinguish the contribution to cognition made by our receptive faculty of sensibility from that made solely by the objects that affect us (A 21–2 / B 36), and argues that space and time are pure forms of all intuition contributed by our own faculty of sensibility, and therefore forms of which we can have *a priori* knowledge. This is the basis for Kant's resolution of the debate about space and time that had raged between the Newtonians, who held space and time to be self-subsisting entities existing independently of the objects that occupy them, and the Leibnizians, who held space and time to be systems of relations, conceptual constructs based on non-relational properties inhering in the things we think of as spatiotemporally related.[14] Kant's alternative to both of these positions is that space and time are neither subsistent beings nor inherent in things as they are in themselves, but are rather only forms of our sensibility, hence conditions under which objects of experience can be given at all and the fundamental principle of their representation and individuation. Only in this way, Kant argues, can we adequately account for the necessary manifestation of space and time throughout all experience as single but infinite magnitudes – the feature of experience that Newton attempted to account for with his metaphysically incoherent notion of absolute space and time as the *sensorium dei* – and also explain the *a priori* yet synthetic character of the mathematical propositions expressing our cognition of the physical properties of quantities and shapes given in space and time – the epistemological certainty undercut by Leibniz's account of space and time as mere relations abstracted from antecedently existing objects (A 22–5 / B 37–41, A 30–2 / B 46–9).

Kant's thesis that space and time are pure forms of intuition leads him to the paradoxical conclusion that although space and time are *empirically real*, they are *transcendentally ideal*, and so are the objects given in them. Although the precise meaning of this claim remains subject to debate,[15] in general terms it is the claim that it is only from the human standpoint that we can speak of space, time, and the spatiotemporality of the objects of experience, thus that we cognize these things not as they are in themselves but only as they appear under the conditions of our sensibility (A26–30/B42–5, A32–48/B49–73). This is Kant's famous doctrine of *transcendental idealism*, which is employed throughout the *Critique of Pure Reason* (and the two subsequent critiques) in a variety of ways, both positively, as in the "Transcendental Aesthetic" and "Discipline of Pure Reason," to account for the possibility of synthetic *a priori* cognition in mathematics, and negatively, as in the "Transcendental Dialectic," to limit the scope of our cognition to the appearances given to our sensibility, while denying that we can have any cognition of things as they are in themselves, that is, as transcendent realities constituted as they are independently of the constitution of our cognitive capacities.

"Transcendental Analytic": the metaphysical and transcendental deductions. The longest and most varied part of the *Critique* is the "Transcendental Logic," containing the two main divisions: the constructive "Transcendental Analytic," which considers the *understanding* as the source of *a priori* concepts that yield *a priori* cognitions in conjunction with the forms of intuition already analyzed; and the primarily destructive "Transcendental Dialectic," which investigates the faculty of *reason*, in the first instance as a source of illusory arguments and metaphysical pseudo-sciences, although in the end also as the source of valuable regulative principles for the conduct of human inquiry and practical reasoning. The "Transcendental Analytic," as we saw, is in turn divided into two books, the "Analytic of Concepts," dealing with the *concepts* of the understanding, and the "Analytic of Principles," concerning the *principles* of the understanding that arise from the application of those concepts to the forms of intuition.

In the "Analytic of Concepts," Kant presents the understanding as the source of certain concepts that are *a priori* and are conditions of the possibility of any experience whatever. These twelve basic concepts, which Kant calls the *categories*, are *fundamental concepts of an object in general*, or the forms for any particular concepts of objects, and in conjunction with the *a priori* forms of intuition are the basis of all synthetic *a priori* cognition. In an initial section of the "Transcendental Analytic" (A66–81/B91–116), which he named in the second edition of the *Critique* the "metaphysical deduction" of the categories (B159), Kant derives the twelve categories from a table of the twelve *logical functions* or forms of judgments, the logically significant aspects of all judgments. Kant's idea is that just as there are certain essential features of all judgments, so there must be certain corresponding ways in which we form the concepts of objects so that judgments may be about objects.

There are four main logical features of judgments: their *quantity*, or the scope of their subject-terms; the *quality* of their predicate-terms, whose contents are realities and negations; their *relation*, or whether they assert a relation just between a subject and predicate or between two or more subject-predicate judgments; and their *modality*, or whether they assert a possible, actual, or necessary truth. Under each of these four headings there are supposed to be three different options: a judgment may be universal, particular or singular; affirmative, negative or infinite; categorical, hypothetical or disjunctive; and problematic, assertoric, or apodictic. Corresponding to these twelve logical possibilities, Kant holds there to be twelve fundamental categories for conceiving of the quantity, quality, relation, and modality of objects (A70/B95, A80/B106). The plausibility of Kant's claim that there are exactly twelve logical functions of judgment and twelve corresponding categories for conceiving of objects has remained controversial since Kant first made it.[16]

Even if Kant establishes by this argument that we have certain concepts *a priori*, it is a more ambitious claim that all of these concepts apply universally and necessarily to the objects that are given in our experience. Kant takes on this more ambitious project in the "Transcendental Deduction of the Categories," the chapter which he says in the first edition of the *Critique* cost him the most labor (Axvi), but which he then rewrote almost in its entirety for the second edition (A84–130/B116–69) after other attempts in the intervening works, the *Prolegomena to Any Future Metaphysics* (1783) and *Metaphysical Foundations of Natural Science* (1786). In both versions of the *Critique*, although not in the intervening works, Kant centers his argument on the premise that our experience can be ascribed to a single identical subject, via what he calls the "transcendental unity of apperception," only if the elements of experience given in intuition are synthetically combined so as to present us with objects that are thought through the categories. The categories are held to apply to objects, therefore, not because these objects make the categories possible, but rather because the categories themselves constitute necessary conditions for the representation of all possible objects of experience. Precisely what is entailed by the idea of the unity of apperception, however, and what the exact relation between apperception and the representation of objects is, are obscure and controversial, and continue to generate lively philosophical discussion even after two centuries of interpretation.[17]

Principles of pure understanding. Even if the transcendental deduction does establish that the categories do apply to all possible data for experience, or (in Kant's terms) all manifolds of intuition, it does so only abstractly and collectively – that is, it does not specify how each category applies necessarily to the objects given in experience or show that all of the categories must be applied to those objects. This is Kant's task in Book II of the "Transcendental Analytic," the "Analytic of Principles." This book is in turn divided into three chapters, "The Schematism of the Pure Concepts of the Understanding," the "System of All Principles of Pure Understanding," and "On the Ground of the Distinction of All Objects in General into Phenomena and Noumena." In the first of these chapters Kant shows how the logical content of the categories derived from the metaphysical deduction is to be transformed into a content applicable to the data of our senses; in the second, he demonstrates principles of judgment showing that all of the categories must be applied to our experience by means of arguments that are sometimes held to prove the objective validity of the categories independently of the prior transcendental deduction; and in the third chapter Kant draws out the consequences of the preceding two, arguing that because the categories have a determinate use only when applied to spatiotemporal data and yet the forms of space and time themselves are transcendentally ideal, the categories also have a determinate cognitive use only when applied to appearances ("phenomena"), and therefore that by means of the categories things as they are in themselves ("noumena") might be *thought* but not *known*.

In the "Schematism," Kant argues that the categories, whose content has thus far been derived solely from the logical structure of judgments, must be made applicable to objects whose form has thus far been specified solely by the pure forms of space and time. He argues that this can be done by associating each category with a "transcendental schema," a form or relation in intuition that is an appropriate representation of a logical form or relation. In particular, Kant argues that each category must be associated with a *temporal* schema, since time is the form of every sensible intuition whatever, while space is the form of outer intuitions only. For example, the schema of the logical conception of ground and consequence is the concept of *causality* as rule-governed temporal *succession*: the concept of a cause, as opposed to that of a mere ground, is the concept of "the real upon which, whenever it is posited, something else always follows," or "the succession of the manifold insofar as it is subject to a rule" (A 144/B 183). As Kant will make clearer in the second edition, however, the subsequent chapter on the "Principles" will show that although the content of the transcendental schemata for the categories may be explicated in purely temporal terms, the *use* of these schemata in turn depends upon judgments about the *spatial* properties and relations of at least some objects of empirical judgment. Thus the argument of the "Analytic of Principles" as a whole is that the categories both must and can only be used to yield knowledge of objects in space and time. The principles expressing the universal and necessary application of the categories to objects given in space and time are precisely the synthetic *a priori* judgments that are to be demonstrated by Kant's critical replacement for traditional metaphysics.

In the second chapter of the "Analytic of Principles," the "System of All Principles," Kant organizes the principles of pure understanding under four headings corresponding to the four groups of categories. For each of the first two groups of categories, those listed under "Quantity" and "Quality," Kant supplies a single "mathematical" principle meant to guarantee the application to empirical objects of certain parts of mathematics, which are in turn supposed to be associated with certain parts of the logic of judgment. The first principle, under the title "Axioms of Intuition," guarantees that the *a priori* mathematics of *extensive* magnitudes, where wholes are measured by their discrete parts, applies to empirical objects because these are given in space and time which are themselves extensive magnitudes (A162–6/B202–7). The general implication of this argument is that the empirical use of the logical quantifiers (one, some, all) depends on the division of the empirical manifold into distinct spatiotemporal regions. The second principle, under the title of the "Anticipations of Perception," guarantees that the mathematics of *intensive* magnitudes applies to the "real in space," or that properties such as color or heat, or material forces such as weight or impenetrability, must exist in a continuum of degrees because our sensations of them are continuously variable (A166–76/B207–18). Here Kant's argument is that since the use of the logical functions of affirmation and negation is dependent on the presence or absence of sensations that come in continuously varying degrees, the empirical use of the categories of "Quality" is connected with the mathematics of intensive magnitudes in a way that could not have been predicted from an analysis of the logical content of these categories themselves (another example of how a synthetic *a priori* rather than merely analytic judgment arises).

Switching from "mathematical" to "dynamical" principles, the third section of the "System," the "Analogies of Experience," concerns the necessary *relations* among what is given in space and time, and thus gives expression to the necessary conditions for the application of the categories of "Relation" to empirical objects. Many interpreters consider this the most important section of the *Critique*. In the first analogy, Kant argues that the unity of time implies that all change must consist in the alteration of states in an underlying substance, whose existence and quantity must be unchangeable or conserved (A182–6/B224–32). In the second analogy, Kant argues that we can make determinate judgments about the objective succession of events as contrasted to merely subjective successions of representations only if every objective alteration follows a necessary rule of succession, or a causal law (A186–211/B232–56). In the third analogy, Kant argues that determinate judgments that objects (or states of substance) in different regions of space exist simultaneously are possible only if such objects stand in the mutual causal relation of community or reciprocal interaction (A211–15/B256–62). The second analogy is generally supposed to supply Kant's answer to Hume's skeptical doubts about causality, while the third analogy is the basis for Kant's refutation of Leibniz's rejection of real interaction between independent substances – an essential thesis of Leibniz's "monadology." In particular, both what the second analogy is intended to prove and how the proof is supposed to proceed have been matters of exegetical controversy; they have been disputed almost as intensely as the philosophical question whether Kant's reply to Hume is successful.

In the first edition of the *Critique*, the final section of the "System of Principles," the "Postulates of Empirical Thought," provides conditions for the empirical use of the modal categories of possibility, existence, and necessity, and argues that our determinate use of the categories of both *possibility* and *necessity* is in fact confined to the sphere of the *actual*, that is, that which is actually given in experience (A218–35/B265–74, 279–87). In the second edition, however, Kant inserted a new argument, the "Refutation of Idealism" (B274–9), which attempts to show that the very possibility of our consciousness of ourselves presupposes the existence of an external world of objects that are not only represented as spatially outside us but are also conceived to exist independently of our subjective representations of them. Although the implications of this argument have been intensely debated, it seems to confirm Kant's claim in the *Prolegomena to Any Future Metaphysics* that his "transcendental idealism" is a "critical" or "formal" idealism that, unlike traditional idealism, implies the subjectivity of space and time as forms of intuition without denying the real *existence* of the objects distinct from ourselves that are represented as being in space and time.[18]

In the third chapter of the "Analytic of Principles," on phenomena and noumena, Kant emphasizes that because the categories must always be applied to data provided by sensibility in order to provide cognition, and because the data of sensibility are structured by the transcendentally ideal forms of intuition, the categories give us knowledge only of things as they appear with sensibility ("phenomena," literally "that which appears"). Although through pure understanding (*noûs* in Greek) we may *think* of objects independently of their being given in sensibility, we can never *cognize* them as such non-sensible entities ("noumena," literally "that which is thought") (A235–60/B294–315). The meaning of Kant's use of the term "phenomena" is self-evident, but the meaning of "noumena" is not, since it literally means not "things as they are independently of appearing to us" but something more like "things as they are understood by pure thought." Yet Kant appears to deny that the human understanding can comprehend things in the latter way. For this reason, Kant says it is legitimate for us to speak of noumena only "in a negative sense," meaning things as they may be in themselves independently of our representation of them, but not noumena "in a positive sense," which would be things known through pure reason alone. A fundamental point of the *Critique* is to deny that we ever have knowledge of things through pure reason alone, but only by applying the categories to pure or empirical data structured by the forms of intuition.

At this point in the *Critique* Kant has completed the largest part of his constructive project, showing how synthetic *a priori* principles of theoretical cognition are the necessary conditions of the application of the categories to sensible data structured by the pure forms of intuition. The next part of his argument is the critical demonstration that traditional metaphysics consists largely of illusions arising from the attempt to acquire knowledge of all things (the soul, the world as a whole, and God) as they are in themselves by the use of reason alone regardless of the limits of sensibility. The bulk of this argument is reserved for the "Transcendental Dialectic," but Kant makes a start on it with the interesting appendix that completes the "Transcendental Analytic" entitled the "Amphiboly of Concepts of Reflection" (A160–92/B316–49). In this appendix Kant presents his criticism of Leibniz's monadology by arguing that through a confusion (or "amphiboly") Leibniz has taken mere features of concepts through which we think things, specifically concepts of comparison or reflection such as "same" and "different" or "inner" and "outer," which are in fact never applied directly to things but only applied to them through more determinate concepts, as if they were features of the objects themselves. Kant thereby rejects the Leibnizian-Wolffian account of such metaphysical concepts as essence, identity, and possibility, and reinforces his own insistence that empirical individual judgments of real possibility require sensible conditions in addition to logical intelligibility and non-contradictoriness.

The "Transcendental Dialectic": the critique of metaphysics. The second division of the "Transcendental Logic" turns to the main destructive task of the *Critique of Pure Reason*, and that which gives it its name, the task of discrediting dogmatism and displaying the limits of metaphysics. The "Transcendental Analytic" has prepared the way for this critique of traditional metaphysics and its foundations by its argument that synthetic *a priori* principles can be established only within the limited domain of sensible experience. But Kant's aim in the "Dialectic" is not only to show the failure of a metaphysics that transcends the boundaries of possible experience. At the same time, he also wants to demonstrate that the questions that preoccupy metaphysics are inevitable, and that the arguments of metaphysics, although deceptive, should not be dismissed without sympathetic comprehension (as they are by the traditional skeptic). Kant argues that they tempt us for genuine reasons, inherent in the nature of human reason itself, and when these grounds are properly understood they can be put to good use for the causes of both human knowledge and human morality. This argument is the basis for Kant's theory of the regulative use of the ideas of reason in scientific inquiry, which Kant first suggests in the final appendix to the "Transcendental Dialectic" and then elaborates in the *Critique of Judgment*, and for his theory of the foundation of morality in the practical use of pure reason, which he first describes in the "Doctrine of Method" and elaborates in many subsequent works, but especially in the *Groundwork of the Metaphysics of Morals* and the *Critique of Practical Reason*.

The Leibnizian-Wolffian tradition, as presented in Alexander Gottlieb Baumgarten's *Metaphysica* (first edition, 1738), which Kant used as the textbook for his lectures on metaphysics for virtually his entire career, was divided into four parts: ontology, psychology, cosmology, and theology. The "Transcendental Aesthetic" and "Analytic" are Kant's critical replacement for traditional ontology. The "Transcendental Dialectic," however, is dedicated to arguing that the other three parts of the rationalist system are pseudo-sciences founded on inevitable illusions of human reason attempting to extend itself beyond the limits of sensibility. Kant does not present the three rationalistic pseudo-sciences as mere historical artifacts, but attempts to display them as inevitable products of human reason by associating them with the unconditioned use of the three traditional forms of syllogism: categorical, hypothetical, and disjunctive. Seeking the unconditioned subject to which all our thoughts relate as predicates, we generate the idea of the soul as a simple, non-empirical substance; seeking the unconditioned in respect of any of several hypothetical series arising in the world (of composition or extension, of decomposition or division, of cause and effect) leads to ideas such as that of a first event in time, an outer limit to space, a simple substance and a first cause. Finally, Kant derives the idea of a most real being or God as the ideal ground of the real properties constituting all other things. Kant's overall argument is that although these rationalist doctrines are inevitable illusions they are still pseudo-sciences, and must give way to doctrines remaining within the limits of sensibility: rational psychology gives way to empirical psychology, which Kant expounded in his lectures in the form of "anthropology"; rational cosmology gives way to the metaphysical foundations of natural science, which Kant derives by adding the sole empirical concept of motion to the principles of judgment; and rational theology gives way to what Kant will call moral theology, the doctrine that God and immortality are postulated, along with freedom of the will, solely as conditions of the possibility of human morality.

The opening book of the "Transcendental Dialectic" is therefore a derivation and even a limited defense of the *transcendental ideas,* such as the immortal soul, free will, and God, with which dogmatic metaphysics has always been preoccupied (A 293–338/B 349–96). *Reason,* traditionally thought to be the highest of our cognitive faculties, has a "logical use" in which it simply draws inferences from principles, but also a "real use" in which it seeks to base series of ordinary inferences, such as those from cause to effect, in ultimate, foundational principles, such as the idea of an uncaused first cause. The ideas of such ultimate principles are generated *a priori* by the faculty of reason when it seeks, through regressive syllogistic reasoning, for what is *unconditioned* in respect of the objects given in experience, according to the principles of understanding that govern these objects. In particular, it is the three categories of *relation* when used without regard to the limits of sensibility that give rise to the chief ideas of metaphysics: the concept of substance giving rise to the idea of the soul as the ultimate subject, the concept of causation giving rise to the idea of the world-whole as a completed series of conditions, and the concept of community giving rise to the idea of God as the common ground of all possibilities. Kant suggests that each of the three relational categories gives rise to a distinctive form of syllogistic inference, series of which can only be terminated by the idea of an unconditioned ground, but also that the attempt to acquire knowledge by means of the relational categories without sensibility gives rise directly to the idea of an unconditioned subject, series, and set of all possibilities.

The second and by far the larger book of the "Dialectic" expounds "The Dialectical Inferences of Pure Reason" in great detail. The errors of rational psychology are diagnosed under the rubric of "The Paralogisms of Pure Reason," those of rational cosmology under the rubric of "The Antinomy of Pure Reason," and those of rational theology under the rubric of "The Ideal of Pure Reason."

The "Paralogisms." Rational psychology is the topic of the "Paralogisms" (or fallacious inferences) of pure reason, which argue invalidly from the formal unity, simplicity, and identity of the *thought* of the subject of thinking or the "I" to the conclusion that the *soul* is a real and simple (hence indestructible) substance that is self-identical throughout all experience (A 341–66). In the first edition, the "Paralogisms" included a fourth part, which defends the reality of external appearance in space simply by reducing objects in space to one form of immediate representation (A 366–405). This response to idealism appears to provide only a Pyrrhic victory over it, which provoked charges of Berkeleianism against Kant, and was therefore replaced in the second edition with the "Refutation of Idealism," which as we saw argues for the real existence of objects in space and time although for the transcendental ideality of their spatial and temporal form. In the second edition, the entire chapter on the paralogisms was rewritten and simplified (B 406–22); to fill the place of the superseded fourth paralogism, Kant adds an argument that his dualism of appearance and reality undercuts the traditional dualism of mind and body, with its problem about the possibility of interaction between two fundamentally distinct kind of substances, by opening up the possibility that both mind and body are different appearances of some single though unknown kind of substance.

The "Antinomies." The longest and most painstaking part of the "Transcendental Dialectic" is the "Antinomy of Pure Reason," which deals with the topics of rational cosmology (A405–583/B432–611); indeed, as we will show below, Kant originally thought that all of the errors of metaphysics could be diagnosed in the form of these antinomies. Here Kant argues that reason's natural illusions are not merely revealed by subtle philosophical analysis but unavoidably manifest themselves in the form of actual contradictions each side of which seems naturally plausible. Kant argues that unless we accept the transcendental idealist distinction between appearances and things in themselves, we will be committed to accepting mutually incompatible arguments, arguments both that there must be a first beginning of the world in time and that there cannot be, that there must be limits to the world in space and that there cannot be (the two halves of the first antinomy), both that there must be a simple substance and that there cannot be (the second antinomy), both that there must be at least one first or uncaused cause and that there cannot be (the third antinomy), and that there must be a being whose necessary existence is the ground of all contingent beings and that there can be no necessary being (the fourth antinomy).

The only way of resolving these contradictions, Kant argues, is by accepting that the natural world is a realm of appearances constituted by the application of the categories to sensible intuitions, and not a realm of things in themselves. Regarding the first two antinomies, which he calls "mathematical" antinomies because they have to do with size and duration, Kant argues that there is no fact of the matter about the size of the world as a whole, because the natural world is never present in experience as a whole, but rather is given to us only through the progressive or regressive synthesis of spatiotemporal intuitions. We can always proceed *indefinitely* far in the progressive composition of spaces and times into ever larger or longer realms or in the regressive decomposition of space and time into ever smaller regions, but we can never reach a beginning or an end to such series, as would be possible if they were finite, nor complete any synthesis of them as infinite either. Both sides of the mathematical antinomies, therefore, turn out to be false, because both rest on the common – and false – assumption that the world is given independently of our ongoing synthesis in its representation, and that it therefore has a determinate magnitude, which must be either finite or infinite. For the third and fourth antinomies, which he calls "dynamical" because they have to do with the causation of the world and its events, Kant proposes a different solution. Here he argues that both sides may be true, if the denial of a free cause or necessary being is restricted to the natural and sensible world and their affirmation is taken to refer to what might exist in a noumenal or supersensible world of things in themselves. Just as his thinking about the antinomies generally shaped his thinking about the structure and outcome of the entire "Transcendental Dialectic," so Kant's resolution of the third antinomy will go on to play an important role in his moral philosophy and in his ultimate account of the relation between theoretical and moral philosophy.

The "Ideal of Pure Reason." Rational theology, the third and last of the metaphysical pseudo-sciences, is taken up by Kant in the final chapter of the "Transcendental Dialectic" (A 567–642 / B 595–670). If an "idea" is a pure concept generated by reason, then an "ideal" is the concept of an *individual thing* as exemplifying an idea of pure reason. It would not be natural to think of the idea of the soul, for example, as giving rise to an ideal, because we naturally think there are many souls; but it is natural (at least in the Judaeo-Christian tradition) to think of the idea of God as the idea of a single thing, and thus the idea of God is the *ideal* of pure reason. Kant argues for the inevitability of the idea of God as an *ens realissimum*, or supreme individual thing possessing all realities or perfections and thus also grounding all the possibilities realized by other particular things. Much of Kant's argument here makes use of a line of thought he developed nearly twenty years before the publication of the *Critique* in *The Only Possible Ground of Proof for a Demonstration of the Existence of God* (1763). But now Kant subjects to withering criticism his own earlier attempt to prove the existence of God as such an *ens realissimum* as well as the other traditional attempts to prove the existence of God, which were already criticized in Kant's earliest philosophical writing, the *New Elucidation of the First Principles of Metaphysical Cognition* (1755) as well as in *The Only Possible Ground.*

Kant organizes the traditional proofs of the existence of God (without attempting to explain why there should only be these three) into the *ontological* proof, based solely on the *concept* of God, the *cosmological* proof, based on the sheer fact of the *existence* of a world, and the *physico-theological* proof, based on the particular constitution of the actual world, especially its alleged exhibition of purposive design. The first of these is Kant's representation of the proof favored by St. Anselm and revived by Descartes; the second is his name for an argument from contingent existents to their necessary ground favored by Wolff and his followers; and the third is what Kant calls the argument from design favored by so many thinkers of the early Enlightenment, especially in Britain (where Hume had already subjected it to trenchant criticism in his *Dialogues concerning Natural Religion*, which, because of the delay of their translation into German, Kant had not yet seen at the time he published the *Critique*). First Kant attacks the ontological argument, holding that since existence is not a property and therefore not itself a perfection, it cannot be included among the contents of the idea of God, and cannot be inferred from that idea alone. Instead, Kant argues, the existence of an object is always the presupposition of the truth of any assertion about it, and cannot itself be assumed for the proof of such an assertion. Kant then argues that even if the cosmological and physico-theological proofs could establish the existence of *some* necessary and purposive being (which they cannot), they still could not establish the existence of a supremely perfect Deity unless the ontological proof also succeeded. Since the ontological proof is unsound, the entire metaphysical enterprise of proving the existence of God – as an object of *theoretical cognition* – must be given up as hopeless.

Regulative use of the ideas. The outcome of the "Transcendental Dialectic," therefore, seems to be entirely negative. This is a misleading conclusion, however. In an appendix to the "Dialectic," Kant begins a limited rehabilitation of the ideas of traditional metaphysics by arguing that the ideas of reason have an important function in the conduct of natural science if they are understood *regulatively*, that is, if they are taken to represent not metaphysical beings or entities whose reality is supposed to be demonstrable, but rather goals and directions of inquiry that mark out the ways in which our knowledge is to be sought for and organized. This is true of the idea of a simple soul, which stimulates us to search for a unified psychology; of the idea of a complete world-whole, which leads us constantly to expand the domain of our scientific investigations; and above all of the idea of God, for regarding the world as if it were the product of a highest intelligence leads us to look for the maximum in order and connectedness, which is beneficial for the organization of whatever empirical knowledge we do acquire. This argument, which Kant continues in the *Critique of Judgment*, is the first of Kant's constructive arguments that reason can be misleading but if wisely used is far from idle or even unnecessary. Kant's second constructive argument about reason, that its ideas have a profound practical use for the guidance and regulation of conduct, is begun in the final part of the *Critique*, the "Doctrine of Method."

"The Doctrine of Method." The second major division of the *Critique*, the "Doctrine of Method," tends to be neglected by its readers, perhaps because the "Doctrine of Elements" is so long and the arguments already surveyed are so exhausting. But the "Doctrine of

Method," in which Kant reflects upon the potential and the limits of his critical philosophy by comparing it with other methods – he compares the method of philosophy with the method of mathematics, the method of theoretical philosophy with the method of practical philosophy, and the method of critical philosophy with the methods of dogmatic, empirical, and skeptical philosophy – includes some extremely important discussions. Its first chapter, the "Discipline of Pure Reason," provides Kant's most mature treatment of the difference between philosophy and mathematics, arguing that both provide synthetic *a priori* cognition, but that mathematics provides determinate answers to its problems because its objects can be constructed in pure intuition, whereas philosophy provides only general principles because what it can construct are the conditions of possibility for the experience of objects, not particular objects (A712–38/B740–69). Then it provides an ardent defense of freedom of public communication as well as of open-mindedness in the discussion of metaphysical issues, arguing that the very existence of reason itself depends on the free give-and-take of controversy between rational beings, which requires the liberty to come to one's own conclusions honestly and to express them openly to others (A738–69/B766–97). This discussion presages Kant's impassioned defense of freedom of thought in his political writings of the 1790s. The chapter concludes with a discussion of the contrasting roles of hypotheses in science and philosophy (A769–82/B798–810) and then with a reflection upon his own style of philosophical argumentation, what he calls "transcendental proofs" (A782–94/B810–22).

The second chapter of the "Doctrine of Method," the "Canon of Pure Reason," contrasts the epistemological status of theoretical cognition with that of the principles and presuppositions of practical reason, or morality, and in so doing provides Kant's most systematic discussion of moral philosophy prior to the *Groundwork of the Metaphysics of Morals* (1785) and Kant's first systematic statement of his argument for rational faith in God on moral grounds (A795–831/B823–59), an argument that Kant was to restate and refine in the subsequent two critiques and to continue to work on until the end of his life. The third chapter, the "Architectonic of Pure Reason," continues the discussion of the contrast between philosophy and other forms of cognition, such as historical knowledge, as well as of the contrast within philosophy between theoretical and practical reason (A832–51/B860–79), while the final chapter of the "Doctrine of Method," and of the whole *Critique*, the "History of Pure Reason," orients the critical philosophy clearly in relation to the competing positions of dogmatism, empiricism, skepticism, and indifferentism, the discussion of which had opened the *Critique* (A852–56/B880–84). For all its brevity, this section has had considerable influence on subsequent conceptions of the history of philosophy.

II.

THE MESSAGE OF THE *CRITIQUE*

The *Critique of Pure Reason* is complex and many-sided. Both its overall message and its meaning for the subsequent history of philosophy defy any easy summary. The *Critique* has perhaps most often been seen as marking out a third way that combines the virtues, while avoiding the pitfalls, of both the "rationalism" of Descartes and Leibniz and the "empiricism" of Locke and Hume. This way of reading the *Critique*, however, even though to some extent suggested by Kant himself, depends on a simplified reading of the history of modern philosophy and at the very least on an incomplete assessment of the strengths and weaknesses of Kant's modern predecessors. Less controversial is the observation that the *Critique*'s main intention is to find a middle way between traditional metaphysics, especially its attempts to bolster a theistic view of the world with *a priori* rational arguments, and a skepticism that would undercut the claims of modern natural science along with those of religious metaphysics.

We see this clearly in the way that Kant defines the position of critical philosophy in contrast to dogmatism, empiricism, skepticism, and indifferentism. He seeks to carve out for theoretical philosophy a significant but limited domain, distinct from that of empirical knowledge and the opinions of common sense, but excluding the exaggerated claims that have brought metaphysics into disrepute. In this way, the *Critique of Pure Reason* belongs to a main tradition in modern philosophy, beginning with Descartes, that tries to provide an *a priori* philosophical foundation for the methods and broad features of a modern scientific view of nature by an examination of the suitability of human cognitive faculties for the kind of knowledge of nature that modern science aims to achieve. At the same time, Kant tries to save precisely what the dogmatic metaphysicians cannot, by connecting the claims of religious metaphysics not to the sphere of theory but to the sphere of moral practice, and, in the famous words of the second-edition preface, by limiting knowledge in order to make room for faith (B xxx). But Kant tries to accomplish all these goals, especially the last, in an authentically *Enlightenment* manner, always giving first place to our rational capacity to reflect on our cognitive abilities and achievements, to correct them, and to subject the pretensions of reason to *self*-limitation, so that human reason itself retains ultimate authority over all matters of human knowledge, belief, and action. The ultimate autonomy of human thought lies in the fact that it neither can nor must answer to any authority outside itself.

The originality of the *Critique* can be indicated by focusing on the way it attempts simultaneously to resolve two of the most intractable problems of early modern philosophy, the simultaneous vindication of the principle of universal causality and of the freedom of the human will. The great idea of the *Critique of Pure Reason* is that the very thing that explains the possibility of our knowledge of the fundamental principles grounding a scientific view of nature is also the key to the possibility of our freedom in both intention and action, which seems threatened by the rule of causality in that natural world. Kant argues that the principles of the scientific worldview can be known with certainty because they express the structure of our own thought. They are therefore conditions of the possibility of our experience, which we impose upon the raw data of sensation. Thus, there is a sense in which certitude about the principles of science is possible only because of human autonomy: we are not merely passive perceivers of sensible information flowing into us from external objects, but also cognitive agents who structure what we perceive in accordance with the necessary conditions of our active thought. Thus Kant argues that we can be certain of the fundamental principles of science – above all the universal law of causation, the assumption underlying all scientific inquiry that every event has a cause and can therefore be explained in accordance with a law of nature – precisely because this law is a condition of the possibility of the thought that we must impose upon our perceptions in order to have any experience at all.

In the seventeenth and eighteenth centuries, the principle of causation had been put into ever more successful use by practicing scientists, but at the same time doubt had been cast upon it by philosophers. First the principle had been supported upon theological foundations by Descartes and his follower Nicolas Malebranche, and then reduced to a mere phenomenon, as by Leibniz, or finally exposed by Hume as simply the result of mere custom. Kant, however, argues that a genuine necessary connection between events is required for their objective succession in time, and that the concept of causality in which this connection is expressed is imposed on experience by our own thought as an indispensable condition of its possibility. The human understanding, therefore, is the true lawgiver of nature, and the successes of modern science are due to its conduct of its inquiries in accordance with a plan whose ground lies *a priori* in the structure of human thought (Bxii-xviii). At the same time, nature is to be regarded as essentially an object of human sensation and thinking, and the validity of the causal principle is to be restricted to the world as it appears under the conditions of our experience of it. In this way, the same account that guarantees the certitude of the principle of causation also guarantees the freedom of the human will, which is precisely what was typically thought to be excluded by the universality of causation.

According to Kant, if we understand the principle of causality and the fundamental principles of the scientific worldview as products of our own thought imposed upon experience, this leaves open the possibility of a radical self-determination of human action when the human will is considered not as it appears but as it is in itself. In later works, such as the *Critique of Practical Reason* (1788) and the *Religion within the Boundaries of Mere Reason* (1793), Kant completes this theory with the further argument that only the inexorable awareness of our obligation to live up to the moral law, which is given spontaneously by our own reason and which we all acknowledge (even if only in the breach), can prove the reality of our freedom, which is the necessary condition of the possibility of the moral demand we make upon ourselves. Yet this further argument presupposes the first *Critique's* argument that we cannot ground the principles of natural science themselves without at the same time revealing that their scope is limited to mere appearances.

Kant's bold attempt to resolve with one stroke two of the most pressing problems of modern philosophy has seldom been accepted by his successors without qualification. Some feel that Kant's identification of the basic principles of science with the fundamental principles of human understanding itself betrays too much confidence in the specifically Newtonian mechanistic physics that prevailed at his time, leaving too little room for subsequent scientific developments, such as the theory of general relativity and quantum mechanics. Others have felt that Kant's reduction of the laws of science to the laws of human thought is not an adequate account of the truly objective validity of science. Few have felt comfortable with the idea that the possibility of freedom could be defended by placing the real arena of human decision making behind a veil of ignorance, and many have felt that the idea that human freedom is our ultimate value but that it can be realized only through adherence to law is a strange and paradoxical one. Yet at the same time, broad elements of Kant's philosophy have become indispensable and therefore often almost invisible assumptions of the modern frame of mind. No modern thinker can believe that the human mind is merely a passive recorder of external fact, or a "mirror of nature."[19] But although many hold that since we have no way of stepping outside the human point of view, it may not be as easy as Kant thought to separate out our subjective contributions to the constitution of nature, yet every modern philosophy holds in some form or other the Kantian thesis that human beings make an active contribution to their knowledge. And although few defend human freedom through a rigid Kantian distinction between phenomenal appearance and noumenal reality, even fewer have thought that the assumption of causal determinism in science precludes conceiving of ourselves as agents who make decisions according to what seem to us to be the most rational principles of value. Thus many have accepted in some form the Kantian idea that there is a fundamental difference between the standpoints of the actor and the spectator,[20] and that this difference is crucial to the solution of the problem of free will. Even those who reject Kant's solutions to the problems of grounding natural science and making sense of our moral agency must solve these problems and find a way to avoid what they find objectionable in Kant's solution to them. In this way, all modern thinkers are children of Kant, whether they are happy or bitter about their paternity.

III.
THE EVOLUTION OF THE *CRITIQUE*

The *Critique of Pure Reason* has often been represented as the product of a violent revolution in Kant's thought that took place around 1772 – a midlife crisis in which the forty-eight-year-old thinker rejected his previous adherence to the Leibnizian-Wolffian philosophy, the systematic philosophy that Christian Wolff (1679–1754) had created out of the brilliant fragments that were all that was then known of the philosophy of Gottfried Wilhelm Leibniz (1646–1716) and that had become the dominant philosophy in enlightened German universities after the 1720s. Kant himself gave rise to this legend with several of his own remarks, above all his comment in the introduction to his *Prolegomena to Any Future Metaphysics* – the short work that Kant published in 1783 to try to overcome the initially indifferent or hostile reception of the *Critique* – that "it was the recollection of David Hume that many years ago first interrupted my dogmatic slumber and gave an entirely different direction to my investigations in the field of speculative philosophy."[21] There were certainly major changes in Kant's thought both before and after the publication of his inaugural dissertation, *De mundi sensibilis atque intelligibilis forma et principiis* (On the Form and Principles of the Sensible and Intelligible World) in 1770, the last publication preceding the years of intense but unpublished work leading up to the publication of the *Critique* in 1781. Nevertheless, Kant has misled those who have supposed that all his work in the years preceding this point was slumbering in Wolffian dogmatism, and that he awoke from this slumber only through some sudden recollection of the skepticism of David Hume (1711–1776).

In fact, Kant had been chipping away at fundamental tenets of the Leibnizian-Wolffian synthesis at least since the publication of his first exclusively philosophical work, his M.A. thesis *Principiorum primorum cognitionis metaphysicae nova dilucidatio* (A New Elucidation of the First Principles of Metaphysical Cognition) in 1755. There were certainly major developments in the content of Kant's philosophical views in the period around 1769–70 leading to the publication of the inaugural dissertation, and then further developments in Kant's doctrines and his conception of philosophical method in the period beginning in 1772 and culminating in the publication of the *Critique*. Many of these were revolutionary developments both in Kant's own thought and in the history of Western philosophy. Even so, the *Critique of Pure Reason*, as well as the further "critical" works that were to follow it, have to be seen as the product of a continuous evolution at least since 1755, a process in which Kant never fully subscribed to the Wolffian orthodoxy and in which he continued revising his position both substantively and methodologically until he arrived at the *Critique*.

Moreover, even after the *Critique* was first published, Kant's thought continued to evolve: as we will see below, there are major differences between the first and second editions of the work (both presented in their entirety in the present translation). Indeed, even after the publication of the second edition, Kant continued to revise and refine both his views and his arguments, in published work such as the *Critique of Judgment* and in the manuscripts on which he was still working at the end of his life (later published as the *Opus postumum*).²² Further, it should by no means be thought that Kant's mature philosophy, as first expressed in the *Critique of Pure Reason*, represents an outright rejection of the philosophy of his predecessors, above all of the original philosophy of Leibniz. On the contrary, Kant's philosophy can be thought of as an attempt to synthesize Leibniz's vision of the preestablished harmony of the principles of nature and the principles of grace²³ with the substance of Newtonian science and the moral and political insights of Jean-Jacques Rousseau (1712–1778). To the extent that Kant was a critic of the Leibnizian-Wolffian philosophy, his criticisms came not only from Hume but even more from Wolff's Pietist critic Christian August Crusius (1715–1775). These critical forerunners led Kant to transform Leibniz's vision of a harmonious world of monads under the rule of God and Rousseau's vision of a social contract expressing a general will into ideals of human reason, neither of which can simply be asserted to exist in well-founded cognitive judgments made within the limits of human sensibility and understanding, but both of which can and must represent the ultimate even if never completely attainable goals of human theoretical and practical thought and conduct.

We cannot offer here a full account of Kant's intellectual development. But we will comment briefly on a number of the works Kant published through 1770, in order to point out some of the ideas that were incorporated into the *Critique of Pure Reason* as well as some that had to be rejected or overcome before the *Critique* could take shape. We will then comment equally briefly on some of the evidence for the development of Kant's thought in the so-called "silent decade" between 1770 and 1781. This discussion of the genesis of the *Critique* is provided to help interpret the intentions of the work as well as to cast some light on the complexities of its organization and argumentation.

Nova dilucidatio (**1755**). In his first treatise on metaphysics, Kant already took issue with some of the most fundamental tenets of the Leibnizian-Wolffian philosophy, while expressing his continued allegiance to other aspects of it. Several of the most important criticisms that Kant made in this first philosophical work will reappear in the *Critique*. The most important critical points made in the *Nova dilucidatio* are four. First, Kant rejects the assumption, to which Wolff may have been more clearly committed than Leibniz, that there is a "unique, absolutely first, universal principle of all truths."[24] What Kant argues here is a logical point, that affirmative truths rest on the principle "whatever is, is" and that negative truths rest on the principle "whatever is not, is not."[25] That is, he argues that the assumption that the negation of a true proposition is false is itself a substantive presupposition of a logical system and not something provable by any logical system itself. This is not yet the argument that there are some truths that can be demonstrated from adequate definitions by logic alone and others that require going beyond logic, which will become the distinction between analytic and synthetic judgments. But it shows that from the outset of his career Kant was dubious of the supposition that all philosophical truth could in principle be derived from a single principle that lay beneath Leibniz's theory that all true propositions can be proved by the analysis of concepts.

Second, Kant rejected the proof of the principle of sufficient reason offered by both Wolff and his disciple Baumgarten. According to Kant, their proof was that if it were assumed that something did not have a sufficient ground, then its sufficient ground would be nothing, which would then mean that nothing was something;[26] this is both circular, assuming precisely what is in question (that everything does have a ground), and also a mere play on words. Kant's alternative argument is that in every true proposition the subject must be determinate with respect to any predicate that might be asserted of an object, so that there must always be something that determines whether a given predicate is true of it.[27] This is not adequate either, since it fails to see that nothing more than the *properties* of an object are necessary to determine what *predicates* should be asserted of it. But it already reveals Kant's characteristic tendency to convert *ontological* questions into *epistemological* questions – that is, the transformation of questions about what sorts of things there must be into questions about the conditions under which it is possible for us to make claims to knowledge about things. The development of this tendency into a full-blown philosophical method will be the key to the *Critique of Pure Reason*, in which, as Kant is to say, "The proud name of ontology, which presumes to offer synthetic *a pri-*

ori cognition of things in general in a systematic doctrine . . . must give way to the modest one of a mere analytic of pure understanding" (A247/B303).

Third, Kant rejected the argument which he was later famously to dub the "ontological" argument for the existence of God. This was the proof of St. Anselm, revived by Descartes and refined by Leibniz, that the existence of God could be inferred from predicates necessarily included in the concept of God. Kant's rejection of it was based on the supposition that its proof is "ideal" rather than "real": that is, that it only unpacks what we may have included in the *concept* of God but cannot establish that there is any *object* answering to that concept.[28] At this stage, Kant offered an alternative argument that the real existence of God must be accepted as the ground of all *possibility*. He was later to reject this argument too in the *Critique of Pure Reason*,[29] but his hostility to the ontological argument and his analysis of its defect were to remain essentially unchanged. His criticism of the ontological argument was another precursor of the *Critique of Pure Reason*'s foundational distinction between analytic and synthetic judgments. In the *Critique*, Kant will argue that all substantive truths in mathematics, physical science, and philosophy itself, although necessarily true and knowable independently of appeal to any particular experience (what he will call "*a priori*"), go beyond what can be derived from the mere analysis of concepts, and therefore require the discovery of a whole new method of thought beyond the method of analysis employed by his predecessors Leibniz, Wolff, and Baumgarten.

Finally, in the *Nova dilucidatio* Kant rejects the basic principle of the monadology maintained by Leibniz and, following him, Baumgarten. This is the principle that everything true of a substance is true in virtue of the inherent nature of that substance itself, so that what would appear to be real interactions between substances are only reflections of the harmonious plan God has chosen to follow as the creator of all substances in a world that is the best of all possible ones precisely because it is harmonious. Kant maintains what he calls the "Principle of Succession," that "No change can happen to substances except insofar as they are connected with other substances; their reciprocal dependency on each other determines their reciprocal changes of state."[30] Kant used this principle to argue for the system of "physical influx," which his teacher Martin Knutzen (1713–1751) had employed against the monadology. The argument for a system of real interaction among all physical objects in space and time was to be a crucial part of the "principles of empirical thought" for which Kant would argue in the *Critique*. Further, Kant also derived from this "principle of succession" a special argument that all changes among *perceptions* would have to be explained as due to changes in *bodies*, and thus a proof of the "real existence of bodies."[31] Changed from an ontological to an epistemological key, this argument would become the basis of the "Refutation of Idealism" in the second edition of the *Critique of Pure Reason.*

So Kant's first piece of philosophy already contained some of Kant's most characteristic criticisms of his predecessors as well as some of the substantive conclusions of his mature work. What was still needed was a new philosophical method that could get him beyond his own still shaky arguments for these conclusions to a totally new foundation for them. That would take at least two more decades to discover.

Before leaving the *Nova dilucidatio*, however, we should also mention several points at which Kant still agreed with his predecessors, above all Leibniz, and that would only subsequently come in for serious criticism. The first point concerns Kant's early treatment of the freedom of the will, to which he devoted an extensive dialogue within the *Nova dilucidatio.*[32] At this stage, Kant recognized only the two traditional alternatives of determinism, according to which any event, including a human action, is entirely determined by an antecedent sequence of events, which in the case of a human action may go all the way back to earlier involuntary events in the agent's life or even to events prior to that life, and indeterminism, according to which a free human choice is in no way determined by any prior history. The latter position, which Kant called the "indifference of equilibrium," was represented for him by Crusius,[33] and firmly rejected on the ground that this position would undermine any reasonable conception of responsibility. Instead, he opted for Leibniz's position, which was a form of determinism now usually known as "compatibilism": all events, including human actions, admit of causal explanation, but some human actions are due to an inner rather than an outer cause or principle, and among those some are due to the representation of the chosen action as what would be best for the agent to do. Actions caused in this way, even though they might be necessary and predictable, are still entitled to be called spontaneous, voluntary, or free.[34] By the time of the *Critique of Practical Reason*, Kant was to reject this Leibnizian conception of freedom as the "freedom of a turnspit,"[35] and it was to be a fundamental task of the *Critique of Pure Reason*, not yet foreseen in 1755, to make way for a third alternative between traditional determinism and indeterminism. Kant was to do this by means of his "transcendental idealism," his distinction between the necessary appearance of things to human cognition and how those things, including human agents themselves, might be in themselves: this would allow him to reconcile the Leibnizian and Crusian positions by maintaining the Leibnizian position as the truth about appearances or "phenomena" while holding that the Crusian position might be true about things in themselves or "noumena."

The second point concerns another retention of Leibnizian theory.

This is what Kant calls the "Principle of Coexistence," or the thesis that "Finite substances do not, in virtue of their existence alone, stand in a relationship with each other, nor are they linked together by any interaction at all, except insofar as the common principle of their existence, namely the divine understanding, maintains them in a state of harmony in their reciprocal relations."[36] Even though the rejection of this principle follows from his "Principle of Succession," Kant did not yet recognize this, and would continue to maintain this part of Leibnizian metaphysics through the inaugural dissertation, even though that work would reject fundamental aspects of Leibniz's theory of space and time and introduce Kant's own mature theory of space and time. It would not be until the *Critique of Pure Reason* itself that Kant would recognize that thoroughgoing interaction among physical objects is a necessary condition of the unity of our own spatiotemporal experience, and that the unity of the physical world admits of no other ground than the unity of our experience; coming to this recognition would be one of the major accomplishments of the 1770s leading up to the *Critique*.

   The philosophical works of 1762–64. Around the time of the *Nova dilucidatio*, Kant published two other works in natural science that would help to provide a foundation for his later philosophy. These are the *Universal Natural History and Theory of the Heavens* (1755) and the *Metaphysicae cum geometria junctae usus in philosophia naturalis, cuius Specimem I continet Monadologiam Physicam* (The Employment in Natural Philosophy of Metaphysics combined with Geometry, of which Sample I contains the Physical Monadology) (1756). However, the next period of major philosophical publication for Kant was the years 1762 to 1764, during which time Kant published four philosophical works all of which are important stepping stones to the *Critique of Pure Reason*. Three of these works appear to have been completed in the fall of 1762, possibly in this order: the *False Subtlety of the Four Syllogistic Figures*, published in 1762; *The Only Possible Basis for a Demonstration of the Existence of God*, published in 1763; and the *Inquiry concerning the Distinctness of the Principles of Natural Theology and Morality*, the second-prize winner in a competition held by the Berlin Academy of Sciences, in which an "Essay on Evidence" by Moses Mendelssohn (1729–1785) won first prize. Finally, the *Attempt to Introduce the Concept of Negative Magnitudes into Philosophy* was completed and published by the summer of 1763.

   The essay on *False Subtlety*, which is primarily concerned to effect a simplification of the many classes of syllogism recognized in Aristotelian logic, would seem to contribute the least to the emergence of the *Critique of Pure Reason*. But in its "Concluding Reflection" Kant touches on one theme that will be crucial for both the formulation as well as the solution of virtually all the philosophical problems dealt with in the *Critique*. This is the claim that the fundamental notion in formal logic and in the analysis of the powers of the human capacity for cognition is the notion of *judgment.* Concepts, he argues, which link predicates to one another, can become distinct only by means of judgments; and inferences, which might have been thought to call upon additional powers of mind beyond the power of judgment, are in fact complex or iterated judgments.[37] Thus Kant concludes that *"understanding* and *reason,* that is to say, the faculty of cognizing distinctly and the faculty of syllogistic reasoning, are not different *fundamental faculties.* Both consist in the capacity to judge . . ."[38]

The recognition that judgment is the fundamental form of all cognitive acts will be crucial to the *Critique* in three ways: Kant will formulate the problem of the very possibility of philosophy as the problem of the possibility of synthetic *a priori* judgment, or the problem of how judgments can go beyond what can be derived from the mere analysis of concepts yet also claim universal and necessary validity. He will argue that the necessary conditions for the application of categories derived from the logical forms of judgment to the spatiotemporal form of human experience are the source of all those synthetic *a priori* judgments that theoretical (as contrasted to practical or moral) philosophy can actually prove. And he will argue, in the "Transcendental Dialectic" of the first *Critique,* that the fundamental illusion of traditional metaphysics is to think that human reason gives direct theoretical insight into the constitution of things as they are in themselves instead of simply concatenating simpler judgments of the understanding into the more complex judgments we call syllogisms or inferences. Kant's insistence on the primacy of judgment in human thought is a first step toward all these critical theses.

In a longer work, indeed a small book, *The Only Possible Basis for a Demonstration of the Existence of God,* Kant's thought advanced toward the *Critique* from a different direction. The argument of the book divides into two main parts. In the first section, as the title suggests, Kant discusses proofs of the existence of God. On the one hand, he refines his original criticism of the ontological argument, and adds to it criticisms of two other traditional arguments, the argument from the contingency of the world to the necessity of its cause, which had been popularized by Leibniz and which Kant was to dub the "cosmological" argument, and the argument from the order of the world to an intelligent author of it, or the argument from design, which was widely popular among eighteenth-century thinkers and which Kant was to call the "physico-theological" argument.[39] On the other hand, Kant refines and extends his own argument that the existence of God can be demonstrated as an actual and necessary condition of the existence of any other possibility, an argument that appeals to the premise that it would be impossible to deny that anything is possible.[40] From the concept of God as the necessary ground of possibility, Kant then proceeds to derive traditional predicates of God such as uniqueness, simplicity, immutability, and indeed even the claim that the necessary being is a mind.[41]

The introduction of God as the ground of all possibility must have seemed to Kant logically sounder than the ontological argument and theologically more orthodox than the Leibnizian conception, on which the power of God in the creation of the universe is constrained by the antecedent existence of determinate possible worlds. But in the *Critique of Pure Reason* Kant was ultimately to reject this argument as well as the three traditional ones, and to argue that both the existence and predicates of God could only be demonstrated on moral grounds, as practical beliefs rather than theoretical dogmas (A810–16/B838–44; A828–9/B856–7). Nevertheless, the underlying idea of Kant's argument, that a genuine or "real possibility" is not established just by demonstrating that a concept is free from contradiction but must have some sort of affirmative ground in actual existence, was remarkably deep-seated in Kant's thought, and would manifest itself again not just in the structure of Kant's theoretical philosophy but at crucial points in his practical philosophy as well.

The second main section of the *Only Possible Basis* shows Kant's early concern to find a proper characterization of scientific laws of nature, and reveals that Kant's complex view of teleology, or final causes, which seems to be a late accretion to the *Critique of Pure Reason*, touched on only in the appendix to the "Transcendental Dialectic" (A642–704/B670–732) and fully developed only in the *Critique of Judgment*, was actually a longstanding part of his thought. Against the background of the debate between occasionalism and preestablished harmony, Kant argues that God's purposes for the world would be expressed through unchanging natural laws valid throughout its entire history, and not through any miraculous episodic interventions: "Where nature operates in accordance with necessary laws, there will be no need for God to correct the course of events by direct intervention; for, in virtue of the necessity of the effects that occur in accordance with the order of nature, that which is displeasing to God cannot occur."[42] Thus Kant argues "That in the procedure of purified philosophy there prevails a rule which, even if it is not formally stated, is nonetheless always observed in practice . . . that in investigating the causes of certain effects one must pay careful attention to maintaining the unity of nature as far as possible."[43]

Here Kant defined an ideal of human knowledge that was to be central to the *Critique of Pure Reason* and all of his subsequent works, even as its theological foundation in a conception of God became ever more attenuated. To have knowledge of the events of an objective world beyond one's own consciousness is to subsume those events under causal laws, and to have knowledge of causal laws is to conceive of those laws as themselves part of a system of laws that, if not actually created by God, can nevertheless only be conceived by us as if they had been created by an intelligence like but more powerful than ours.[44] Though Kant did not yet see how much effort this would involve, his task in the *Critique of Pure Reason* and subsequent works would be precisely to show that knowledge of the "unity of nature" or of constant laws of nature is the necessary condition of the unity of our own experience, and to explain how knowledge of such laws of nature itself is possible.

Kant's thought about the problem of causal laws would be advanced further in the last of the four key works of 1762–63, the essay on *Negative Magnitudes*. But before we turn to that, we will consider the different steps in the direction of the *Critique* that Kant took in the third of these works, the *Inquiry concerning the Distinctness of the Principles of Natural Theology and Morality*. Kant wrote this work in the late fall of 1762 and submitted it to the Academy of Sciences in Berlin by 1 January 1763, the deadline for the Academy's competition on the question of whether metaphysics, conceived to include natural theology and ethics, had the same prospects for certitude as mathematics and could use the same method. The Academy, still dominated by Wolffians, preferred Moses Mendelssohn's elegant restatement of the fundamental tenets of Wolffianism for the first prize, but recognized the merits of Kant's essay with an honorable mention and publication along with Mendelssohn's essay (which did not take place until 1764).

In the rationalist tradition, Mendelssohn argued for the similarity of the methods of mathematics and philosophy – although with a twist, the suggestion that the certitude of metaphysics is even greater than that of mathematics. In an account of the epistemology of mathematics that would still be acceptable to many philosophers, he argued that the *proof* of mathematical theorems from their premises depends solely on the application of logical principles to mathematical concepts, but that the *truth* of mathematical propositions is an empirical matter, depending upon the incontestable but still observational fact that the basic concepts of our mathematics fit our experience. Mendelssohn then held that metaphysical argumentation proceeds for the most part along the same lines as mathematical proof, with the one difference that in two key cases the connection of the formal system of proof to reality does not have to be made empirically but is also secured on purely conceptual grounds. These two cases are the metaphysics of the soul (what Kant would later label "rational psychology") where the Cartesian *cogito* proves the existence of the soul in a non-empirical way, and the metaphysics of God (or "rational theology"), where Mendelssohn accepted the ontological argument as proving the existence of God from the mere concept of God. Since in these two paradigmatic parts of philosophy existence claims could be proved without recourse even to the most secure observation, Mendelssohn judged philosophy to have the potential for even greater certainty than mathematics.[45]

Although he wrote without prior knowledge of Mendelssohn's essay, Kant was of course familiar with the Wolffian background on which Mendelssohn was drawing, and in criticizing the methodological assumptions of Wolffianism more firmly than he had ever done before, Kant wrote an essay diametrically opposed to that of his competitor. This essay takes major steps toward the position of the *Critique of Pure Reason*, although crucial differences still remain. Kant's most radical departure from prevailing orthodoxy and his biggest step toward the *Critique* comes in his account of mathematical certainty. Instead of holding that mathematics proceeds by the two-front process of analyzing concepts on the one hand and confirming the results of those analyses by comparison with our experience on the other hand, Kant argues that in mathematics definitions of concepts, no matter how similar they may seem to those current in ordinary use, are artificially constructed by a process which he for the first time calls "synthesis," and that mathematical thinking gives itself objects "*in concreto*" for these definitions, or *constructs* objects for its own concepts from their definitions. Thus, whatever exactly the concept of a cone might signify in ordinary discourse, in mathematics the concept of a cone "is the product of the arbitrary representation of a right-angled triangle which is rotated on one of its sides."[46] Thus, we can have certain knowledge of the definition because we ourselves construct it; and we can have certain knowledge that the definition correctly applies to its objects because the true objects of mathematics are nothing but objects constructed, however that may be, in accordance with the definitions that we ourselves have constructed.

In philosophy, however, things are quite different. Philosophy does not begin from self-constructed and well-defined definitions, but from concepts, which are already given but are also given in a confused manner. Complete definitions of philosophical concepts come, if they come at all, at the end of philosophical inquiry. In fact, Kant insists, the goal of defining concepts – so central to the academic philosophy of the time – is not the goal of philosophy at all. Instead, Kant compares the proper method for philosophy to what he takes to be the method "introduced by Newton into natural science": obtaining certainty not about complete definitions but about "those characteristic marks that are certainly to be found in the concept of any general property" and can lead to "judgments about the object that are true and completely certain." The certainty of such judgments has to be grounded in something other than definitions, in the case of metaphysics in "an immediate and self-evident inner consciousness."[47] Such sources of evidence then have to be carefully analyzed for their implications, so while "geometers acquire their concepts by means of *synthesis* . . . Philosophers can acquire their concepts only by means of *analysis* – and that completely changes the method of thought."[48] Further, while from the definitions introduced into mathematics determinate objects can be constructed, this is not the case in philosophy, where the objects of knowledge are not our own constructs, and where our concepts give us only abstract and indeterminate knowledge of objects rather than determinate and concrete objects themselves. Thus "in mathematics, the object is considered under sensible signs *in concreto*, whereas in philosophy the object is only ever considered in universal abstracted concepts."[49] So mathematical knowledge is certain because it is grounded on definitions of our own construction and fully determinate because concrete objects can be constructed from those definitions, whereas philosophical knowledge is less certain because it is dependent on the analysis of given concepts and less determinate because it yields only general judgments about objects.

Kant illustrates the differences between mathematical and philosophical method with three examples. First, following Crusius, he argues that metaphysics depends not only on two distinct formal or logical principles (as Kant had already argued in 1755), but also on many "first material principles of human reason" that are "indemonstrable," such as *"a body is compound."*[50] Second, he reiterates his argument of the *Only Possible Basis* that from the argument for the existence of God as the ground of all possibility other predicates of God can be derived – this is supposed to show how from a certain though incomplete consciousness of some of a thing's characteristics other certain judgments can be derived – but also adds that in further judgments, about God's justice and goodness, only an "approximation to certainty" is possible.[51] Finally, about morality Kant argues that although we may easily be able to identify some *formal* principles of obligation, such as "I ought to advance the total greatest perfection," such principles are useless without *material* principles of obligation, which tell us what the extension of an abstract concept like perfection actually is – what courses of action actually contribute to perfection – and such material principles are themselves indemonstrable.[52]

Kant is here clearly working his way toward several of the central ideas of the *Critique of Pure Reason*. Although he does not yet speak of analytic or synthetic *judgments*, his distinction between analytic and synthetic *methods* is leading in that direction: whereas traditionally this contrast between methods was merely a contrast between direction in causal or syllogistic inference,[53] for Kant the difference has become one between constructing concepts or their definitions (the synthetic method) and unpacking concepts to get to definitions (the analytical method). This will lead to the distinction between judgments that construct fuller concepts by amplifying what is given (synthetic judgments) and those that merely explicate given concepts by showing what predicates they already contain (analytic judgments) (see A6–7/B10–11). Further, Kant's argument that both metaphysics and morality depend upon indemonstrable material principles, and not just formal or logical principles, is clearly preparing the way for the fundamental tenet of his mature theoretical and practical philosophy that the basic propositions of both are synthetic yet *a priori* judgments. But Kant's conception of philosophical method in the *Inquiry* has not yet caught up to this recognition: he is at a loss to explain how we know these "indemonstrable" principles when the method of philosophy is still considered to be analytic, rather than synthetic like the method of mathematics. Before Kant's mature work could be written, he would have to discover a philosophical method that could yield "material" or synthetic judgments. This would be the philosophical work of the 1770s that would finally pave the way for the *Critique of Pure Reason*.

Once Kant takes this further step, however, the contrast between mathematics and philosophy provided in the *Inquiry* will have to be revised. The difference between mathematics and philosophy will no longer simply be that the former uses the synthetic method and the latter the analytical method. On Kant's mature account, both mathematics and philosophy must use a synthetic method. This does not mean that the account of the *Inquiry* will be completely surrendered, but rather that the difference between the concrete constructions of mathematics and the abstract results of philosophy will have to be recast as a difference *within* the synthetic method: The use of the synthetic method in mathematics will yield synthetic yet certain results about *determinate objects*, whereas the use of the synthetic method in philosophy will yield synthetic yet certain *principles for the experience of objects*, or what Kant will call "schemata" of the pure concepts of the understanding, "the true and sole conditions for providing [these concepts] with a relation to objects" (A146/B185). Thus the *Inquiry* already contains key aspects of Kant's mature theory of mathematics, but does not yet see that both mathematics and philosophy must use synthetic methods. Once Kant sees this, however, then the *Inquiry's* distinction between the concrete results of mathematics and the abstract results of philosophy can be retained as the difference between the construction of determinate mathematical objects and the construction of philosophical principles for the possibility of the experience of objects in general.[54]

The last of the essays of 1762–63, the *Attempt to Introduce the Concept of Negative Magnitudes into Philosophy*, focuses on a substantive rather than a methodological issue. Kant considers a variety of relationships that must be construed as real opposition rather than logical contradiction: positive and negative numbers, motion in opposite directions, pleasure and pain. Asserting a proposition and its contradictory results in a contradiction, which asserts nothing at all. Combining equal motions in opposite directions does not result in a logical nonentity, but in a state of rest that is a real state of affairs. So all sorts of sciences need room for the concept of positive and negative magnitudes, not just the logical notion of contradiction. Kant's underlying thought then, already hinted at in the last part of the *Inquiry*, is that the formal, logical laws of identity and contradiction are not sufficient principles for knowledge of the objective world, and that philosophy must find room for material principles. He concludes by noting that the relation between cause and effect, although it is not a relation of opposition, is also a real rather than a logical relation, and cannot be justified by any mere analysis of concepts showing that the consequence is contained in the ground. This raises the fundamental question, "How am I to understand **the fact that, because something is, something else is?**"[55] The problem of understanding real opposition, real causation, and more generally real relations becomes the fundamental substantive problem of theoretical philosophy. Kant rejects Crusius's attempt to solve this problem,[56] and makes no mention of Hume's formulation of an empirical solution to this problem, which was already available to him in the German translation of the first *Enquiry* (1755). But he concludes with these prophetic words:

Let us see whether we can offer a distinct explanation of how it is that, *because something is, something else is canceled,* and whether we can say anything more than I have already said on the matter, namely that it simply does not take place in virtue of the law of contradiction. I have reflected upon the nature of our cognition with respect to our judgment concerning grounds and consequences, and one day I shall present a detailed account of the fruits of my reflections.[57]

This day was not to come until the publication of the *Critique of Pure Reason* in May 1781; Kant had identified a problem to which he did not yet possess a solution. But he clearly was not waiting for a recollection of Hume to awake him from dogmatic slumbers.

Kant published three more significant works during the 1760s: the *Observations on the Beautiful and Sublime* in 1764; *Dreams of a Spirit-Seer* in 1766, a devastating critique of the pretensions of Swedenborgian spiritualism as an extreme example of metaphysics that also contained some interesting anticipations of his later moral theory; and a short essay, *On the Differentiation of Directions in Space*, in 1768, which used the existence of incongruent counterparts (for example, right- and left-handed gloves or screws) to argue for a Newtonian conception of absolute space against a Leibnizian conception of space as a representation of a system of relations among objects that could in principle be captured by purely conceptual relations, which would supposedly leave out differences of *direction* between otherwise identical objects such as gloves or screws. Once again, Kant was worrying about the difference between logical and real relations, but in this brief essay he did not yet have his own theory of how we could know something like absolute space, or draw any general philosophical conclusions from this specific issue about the nature of space.

The Inaugural Dissertation (1770). This was to change in Kant's next work, also the last of his publications on the way to the *Critique* before the "silent decade" of the 1770s. This was Kant's inaugural dissertation, *De Mundi Sensibilis atque Intelligibilis Forma et Principiis* (On the Form and Principles of the Sensible and Intelligible World), defended and published in August 1770, after Kant's long-awaited ascension to the chair of logic and metaphysics in Königsberg on March 31 of that year. The work is presumed to have been written between March and August, although Kant had begun to mention the possibility of writing a systematic work on new foundations for metaphysics as early as 1765, and his publisher had even listed a forthcoming book on *The Proper Method of Metaphysics* in the autumn book fair catalogue of that year.[58] But whatever plan he may have had at that time had come to naught, and it was not until occasion demanded it in 1770 that Kant wrote another systematic work, though as it turned out an essay on the substance rather than the method of metaphysics.

This work is a milestone in Kant's progress toward the *Critique of Pure Reason* because it introduces the fundamental distinction between the sensible and the intellectual capacities of the mind, the capacity, on the one hand, to have singular and immediate representations of particular objects by means of the senses, which Kant henceforth calls "intuition";[59] and, on the other hand, the capacity to form abstract and general representations, or concepts, by means of the intellect. Further, as his title suggests, Kant argues that our capacities for intuition and conceptualization each have their own characteristic forms, principles, or laws, which can be known by us and which constitute the basis of metaphysical cognition. Moreover, Kant argues, introducing the doctrine that he will later name "transcendental idealism," the "*laws of intuitive cognition*,"[60] or the laws of the representation of things by means of the senses, characterize how things necessarily *appear* to us, but not how they actually are in themselves.[61] By contrast, at this stage, although not later, Kant holds that intellectual representations of things, or concepts, present things "*as they are.*" Thus, sensibility and intellect present us with two different accounts of objects: "phenomena," things as they appear to the senses, and "noumena," things as they really are and are known to be by the intellect (*noûs*).[62]

On this account, sensibility and the intellect operate essentially independently of one another. The fundamental stimulus to this radical distinction seems to have been Kant's discovery, perhaps made in 1769, that several paradoxes about the infinite (long known and prominently discussed by a number of eighteenth-century philosophers),[63] such as the conflict between the supposition that time appears to have no beginning yet any object and thus any universe of objects must have had a beginning, could be resolved by distinguishing between the forms of intuition as forms of appearance, on the one hand, and the forms of thought as the forms of reality, on the other: thus it could be argued, for example, that there is no contradiction between the sensible appearance that time has no beginning and the reality, known by the intellect, that all existence must have some beginning, for sensibility and intellect do not present the same things. In the *Critique of Pure Reason*, Kant was to call the set of such paradoxes, to be resolved by the distinction between phenomena and noumena, the antinomies of pure reason.

However, there is also a crucial difference between Kant's treatment of the antinomies in 1770 and his eventual treatment of them in 1781. This is connected with an equally fundamental difference in Kant's conception of the relation between the two basic mental capacities of intuition and conceptualization in the inaugural dissertation and the *Critique*. In the dissertation, Kant supposes that the intellect alone reveals the true nature of reality, and that the antinomies are to be resolved by preventing any limits inherent in the laws of sensibility from being misconstrued as limits on purely intellectual knowledge of reality. But he has in fact no adequate account of the role of concepts in knowledge of ordinary objects in space and time, and once he realizes – as he will after 1772 – that concepts of the understanding must be used in conjunction with the intuitions or data supplied by sensibility to account for the possibility of such knowledge, not independently, then he will also have to revise his account of the antinomies. He will have to revise his resolution of them by arguing that there can be no knowledge of any spatiotemporal reality at all beyond the limits of sensibility, although in cases where concepts of the understanding can be used to formulate coherent conceptions of non-spatiotemporal entities, above all God, there may be coherent *belief*, even if not any *knowledge*.

In sum, in the inaugural dissertation Kant introduces his fundamental distinction between intuitions and concepts, and uses that distinction for a resolution of the antinomies, but does not yet realize that knowledge can arise only from the conjoint use of intuitions and concepts to yield a unified experience. Once he comes to that realization, he will have to transform his resolution of the antinomies, surrendering the view that sensibility gives us knowledge of appearances and the intellect metaphysical knowledge of things as they are in themselves. Only then will the way be open for Kant's fully mature position that the limits of knowledge leave room for certain beliefs that cannot become knowledge but that can be justified on practical grounds.[64]

We will describe the contents of the inaugural dissertation in some detail, since it will be helpful in reading the *Critique* to see exactly what Kant could retain from the earlier work and what had to be fundamentally revised. Kant signals the importance of the problem of the antinomies from the outset, opening the work with the statement that "just as analysis does not come to an end until a part is reached which is not a whole, that is to say a SIMPLE, so likewise synthesis does not come to an end until we reach a whole which is not a part, that is to say a WORLD."[65] He then argues that since the world of appearances is given with space and time as its form, and space and time are continuous quantities, there can be "*no limit*" in analysis or the "*regression* from the whole to the parts" nor in synthesis or composition, "the *progression* from the parts to the given whole,"[66] and thus no satisfaction of the opening definition of a simple and a world; but since the pure concepts of the intellect give us access to a realm of things with their own principles of form, where parts are not spatiotemporal regions and the principle of composition is not that of spatiotemporal extension, but where instead the parts are substances and the principle of composition is the common dependence of substances upon God, the conditions for metaphysical knowledge of both simples and a single world of them can be satisfied. The remainder of the work is then divided into a fuller statement of the distinctions between intuition and concept and phenomena and noumena (Section 2); separate expositions of the fundamental forms of intuition or sensibility (Section 3) and of the laws of understanding (Section 4); and the concluding argument that the limits of sensibility must not be mistaken to preclude metaphysical knowledge through the intellect (Section 5). Section 3 is taken over into the *Critique of Pure Reason* without essential modification, but Section 4 will be radically revised by the mature theory of the function of the understanding in the *Critique*, and once that revision is made there must also be fundamental revision in the treatment of the antinomies in Section 5.

In Section 2, Kant first introduces his distinction between *sensibility*, which is characterized as the "*receptivity* of the subject in virtue of which it is possible for the subject's own representative state to be affected in a definite way by the presence of some object," and what he here calls "*intelligence* (or rationality)," "the *faculty* of a subject in virtue of which it has the power to represent things which cannot by their own quality come before the senses";[67] he also calls this faculty "intellect" (*intellectus*).[68] Next, he argues "that things which are thought sensitively are representations of things **as they appear,** while things which are intellectual are representations of things **as they are.**"[69] Kant's reasons for this momentous claim are far from clear. He suggests two reasons:

first, that "whatever in cognition is sensitive" should be considered as "dependent upon the subject insofar as the subject is capable of this or that modification by the presence of objects," where it is assumed that different subjects may be modified by or respond to the same objects in different ways, and thus cannot all represent the objects as they really are; and second, that "objects do not strike the senses in virtue of their form or aspect," but only in virtue of their matter, thus "the **form** of . . . representation . . . is not an outline or any kind of schema of the object, but only a certain law, which is inherent in the mind and by means of which it coordinates for itself that which is sensed from the presence of the object."[70]

Next, Kant argues that there are two uses of the intellect, a "logical" use in which it subordinates concepts, "no matter whence they are given," to one another in accord with logical rules (e.g., "the principle of contradiction"), and a "real" use, in which concepts themselves, "whether of things or relations," are given. Kant suggests that the *logical* use of intellect, or "the reflective cognition, which arises when several appearances are compared by the intellect" to produce *empirical* concepts, is sufficient to transform mere appearance into *experience.*[71] Finally, he argues that in its *real* use the intellect produces concepts, such as "possibility, existence, necessity, substance, cause, etc.," which "never enter into any sensory representation as parts," but that can instead be used "dogmatically" to lead to a "paradigm" of "NOUMENAL PERFECTION," which in the theoretical context is God and in the practical context is moral perfection.[72] Thus in its merely logical use, intellect supplies no unique concepts of its own, and merely organizes data supplied by the senses into experience or empirical knowledge; in its real use, it does supply original concepts of its own, and uses them to know a non-sensible reality as it really is or to define a non-sensible goal for our action.

This series of claims throws light on doctrines of the subsequent *Critique*, but also raises problems that the later work will need to solve. First, the characterization of sensibility as a passive power of the mind and intellect as active will remain central to many arguments in the *Critique*;[73] but Kant will also subsume sensibility under the "cognitive faculties" (*Erkenntnisvermögen*) generally, and since the term "faculty" (*facultas*, for which Kant's German equivalent is *Vermögen*) implies activity, this means that there is an active element in sensibility as well, which fits Kant's claim that the *form* of sensibility is in fact supplied by the mind. So it will be important to see that even sensibility has both a passive and an active element: our senses are acted upon by external objects, but we act upon the sensations so induced to give them form.

Further, the two arguments that Kant here gives for his claim that sensibility represents the mere appearance of things – his eventual "transcendental idealism" – are both problematic. His first argument is that different subjects might represent outer objects in different ways; but from this it does not follow that *all* those subjects represent objects other than they actually are – maybe there is one sort of subject who represents objects correctly while others do not, and maybe indeed that one sort of subject is us. His second argument is that the form of the representation of objects cannot represent the objects as they are in themselves because this form represents a "law inherent in the mind." But there are two issues here: first, there is an unstated and unargued assumption that a "law inherent in the mind" cannot *also* represent a form inherent in objects themselves; and second, since intellectual concepts also are laws inherent in the mind used to give form to our representations of things, it would seem to follow that they too give knowledge of objects only as they appear to us and not as they really are. We will see that Kant supplies further arguments for transcendental idealism both later in the dissertation and in the *Critique;* whether these arguments are independent of the initial assumptions that whatever is receptive and whatever is formal are inherently subjective rather than objectively valid will be an important question.

Finally, there are major questions about Kant's characterization of the "intellect" here. As we saw, he supposes that we need only the "logical" use of the intellect to generate empirical concepts and experience out of mere appearance, and the "real" use of the intellect, in which it generates non-empirical concepts, is sufficient to furnish knowledge of non-empirical objects. Both assumptions will be rejected after 1772. On the one hand, Kant will recognize that non-empirical concepts generated by the intellect – in fact, a list of non-empirical concepts including those mentioned here such as "possibility, existence, necessity, substance, cause, etc." – must be applied to the data given by sensibility in order to arrive at experience or empirical knowledge; mere abstraction and reflective comparison will not suffice for this purpose. On the other hand, Kant will also conclude that those concepts by themselves *cannot* be used to obtain theoretical knowledge about objects we do not sense, such as God, although they can ultimately be used to form coherent conceptions of such objects that can be validated on moral grounds.

These profound revisions in Kant's thought will call for terminological revisions as well. Here Kant speaks of a single faculty, "intelligence" or "intellect," which has both a real and a logical use. In the *Critique*, Kant will distinguish between *understanding* and *reason* as two parts or perhaps better aspects of the higher cognitive faculties of the mind.[74] Understanding will be the source of non-empirical categories or "pure concepts of the understanding" that must be applied to data furnished by the senses to yield empirical knowledge, and thus have a real use but only for empirical objects; further, since Kant continues to believe that sensibility furnishes mere appearance, the real use of the understanding will also be confined to appearance. Reason will be a further faculty, which has a legitimate logical use insofar as it links judgments constituted with concepts of the understanding into more complex, inferential structures, but has a mistaken real use if it is thought that either by means of inference or by the use of concepts of the understanding without accompanying data from sensibility it can obtain knowledge of non-empirical objects such as God. The only legitimate real use of reason will be to formulate conceptions of non-empirical objects that may be validated by moral considerations; that is, reason has a real use only as practical reason. Thus, reason will be denied the power of introducing a "paradigm" of "noumenal perfection" on theoretical grounds, though it will retain the power of introducing the practical paradigm of "moral perfection" and will be able to justify a certain non-cognitive use of theoretical ideas as what Kant will come to call "postulates of practical reason."[75]

The few paragraphs of Section 2, then, introduce fundamental assumptions of the *Critique of Pure Reason* as well as positions that will be radically revised. The three paragraphs of Section 3, by contrast, present a treatment of the forms of intuition, space, and time, that will be carried over into the *Critique* largely unaltered, though (especially in the second edition of the *Critique*) somewhat amplified. Here Kant claims that the principle of form of the world as appearance or phenomenon is "a fixed law of the mind, in virtue of which it is necessary that all the things that can be objects of the senses . . . are seen as *necessarily* belonging to the same whole."[76] He then argues that there are in fact two such laws or principles, time, the form of all that we sense, whether inner or outer, and space, the form of our outer sense, or our sensory perception of objects we take to be distinct from ourselves. Kant argues that space and time are both the *pure forms* of all intuitions, or *"formal principle[s] of the sensible world*,"[77] and themselves *pure intuitions:*[78] They are the forms in which particular objects are presented to us by the senses, but also themselves unique particulars of which we can have *a priori* knowledge, the basis of our *a priori* knowledge of both mathematics and physics.[79] But the embrace of space and time "is limited to **actual things,** insofar as they are thought capable of *falling under the senses*" – we have no ground for asserting that space and time characterize things that we are incapable of sensing.[80]

Kant makes the following claims about time:[81] (1) *"The idea of time does not arise from but is presupposed by the senses"*: this is because any concepts we can form from our experience of things already presupposes that we can represent them as either simultaneous or successive. (2) *"The idea of time is singular* and not general"*: this is because all particular times, say two particular years, are thought of as part of a single larger time, in which they each occupy a determinate position, and are not just unrelated tokens of a similar type. (3) *"The idea of time is an intuition,"* and indeed a *"pure intuition,"* precisely because it is both singular and immediately given to us in all our experience, which makes it an intuition, but also given to us as presupposed by rather than abstracted from all our experience, which makes it pure. All of these claims will be reiterated in the *Critique of Pure Reason* without revision, although the exposition of them will be somewhat amplified.[82]

Next, Kant asserts a claim that is not explicitly made in the initial discussion of time in the *Critique* but is presupposed in a number of later important parts of the work: the claim that (4) *"Time is a continuous magnitude,"* or that it consists of no simple parts but instead that between any two times, no matter how small, there is always another, smaller interval of time. Then Kant adds to the reasons already given in Section 2 for the claim that (5) *"Time is not something objective and real, nor is it a substance, nor an accident, nor a relation."* It is important to see that there is both a positive and a negative aspect to this claim (5). The positive side is the argument that we must have a pure intuition of time because it is presupposed by our perception of any particular objects or states as simultaneous or successive, the argument (1) which Kant now reiterates. This implies that we must have a pure representation of time independent of any particular empirical perception, but does not imply that time is not also "objective and real," that is, *nothing but* a form of representation. For that further, negative claim Kant suggests two sorts of reasons: a metaphysical reason, aimed against Newton and "the English philosophers," that the idea of absolute time as a substance or a property of any substance (such as the *sensorium dei*) is absurd; and an epistemological argument, aimed against Leibniz, that conceiving of time as something we abstract from perceived relations of objects would render our knowledge of it merely empirical and therefore "completely destroy" all the certitude of the fundamental rules of mathematics and physics. The full premises of this epistemological argument, however, are not spelled out before the *Critique*, and even there are only hinted at.[83] Finally, Kant adds that although (6) *"time,* posited in itself and absolutely, would be an imaginary being," nevertheless, as "the universal form of phenomena," whether inner or outer, it is "to the highest degree true" and (7) *"an absolutely first formal principle of the sensible world."*

Kant makes a series of parallel claims about space.[84] He claims (1) *"The concept of space is not abstracted from outer sensations,"* because I can "only conceive of something as placed outside me [*extra me*] by representing it as in a place which is different from [*in loco . . . diverso*] the place in which I am myself"; in other words, I cannot abstract the concept of space from my experience of objects distinct from myself because I cannot experience them as distinct without already representing them as in space. (2) Like that of time, *"the concept of space is a singular representation,"* because all regions of space are represented as parts of a single, bound-less space rather than as instances of some general sort. As before, Kant infers from these two arguments that (3) *"The concept of space is thus a pure intuition,"* an intuition because it is singular and pure because it is not "compounded from sensations" but presupposed by all "outer sensation" or experience of objects as distinct from ourselves. Here Kant skips an argument that space is a continuous quantity, though he will also assume that in the *Critique*, and instead inserts the argument from 1768 about incongruent counterparts, using it now to show that since features of di-rectionality such as a right- and left-handedness are not inferable from the concepts of objects they must be "apprehended by a certain pure in-tuition." (This argument will be omitted from the *Critique*.) Now, as in the case of time, Kant infers from these results that *"Space is not something objective and real,* nor is it a substance, nor an accident, nor a relation; it is rather, subjective and ideal; it issues from the nature of the mind." Again, he infers this from the prior arguments that it is "the scheme . . . for coordinating everything that it senses externally" and also from the two additional claims, the metaphysical claim made against "the English" that the idea of an *absolute* and boundless *receptacle* of possi-ble things is absurd" and the epistemological argument made against Leibniz that conceiving of the propositions of geometry, which are taken to describe space, as merely abstracted from an experience of relations among objects would "cast geometry down from the summit of cer-tainty, and thrust it back into the rank of those sciences of which the principles are empirical." Finally, Kant again concludes that (5) even though "the *concept of space* as some objective and real being or property be imaginary, nonetheless, *relatively to all sensible things whatever,* it is not only a concept that is in the highest degree true, it is also the foundation of all truth in outer sensibility." This is as good a statement of the doc-trine of transcendental idealism as we will find in the *Critique* itself, in-sisting on both the subjectivity yet also universality and necessity of space as a form of representation.[85]

This account of space and time as the forms and principles of the sen-sible world, as we have said, remains essentially unchanged in the *Critique*. In Section 4 of the dissertation, however, Kant gives an ac-count of the "principle of the form of the intelligible world" that is still largely unchanged from his earliest work but will disappear from the *Critique*. The content of this section is basically just the Leibnizian ar-gument that a multitude of substances can constitute a single world only in virtue of their common dependence on a single cause. This argument is based on the thoroughly Leibnizian premise that "the existence of each [necessary] substance is fully established without appealing to any dependence on anything else whatsoever,"[86] and the further inference that contingent substances, the only kind which might therefore constitute an interrelated whole, are characterized precisely by their dependence on a cause, and therefore constitute a single world in virtue of their dependence on a common cause.[87] Kant's attempt to reconcile this argument with his longstanding attraction to the theory of physical influx, or real interaction between distinct objects, is unavailing.[88] However, not only this argument but also the underlying assumption that pure concepts of the intellect, such as the concept of substance, can be used on their own to provide knowledge of things as they are in themselves will disappear from the *Critique*. This particular argument will be replaced by the argument that interaction among physical objects is a necessary condition for experiencing them as simultaneously occupying different yet determinate positions in a single space (Kant's important "Third Analogy"),[89] and the underlying metaphysics will be replaced by Kant's critical position that pure categories of the understanding lead to ideas of reason that are illusory if used for theoretical knowledge on their own, though they can serve as postulates of practical reason.

The same transformation awaits Kant's treatment of "method in metaphysics" in the concluding Section 5 of the inaugural dissertation. Kant begins by arguing that philosophy has no special method to prescribe to ordinary science, because here the use of the intellect is only logical, organizing concepts that are not themselves provided by the intellect but are instead abstracted from experience. In the case of metaphysics, however, where the intellect does have a real use, supplying original concepts, "*method precedes all science*."[90] The method of metaphysics, Kant then maintains, "amounts to this prescription: great care must be taken *lest the principles that are native to sensitive cognition transgress their limits, and affect what belongs to the understanding*."[91] The fundamental obstacle to progress in metaphysics, that is, comes from assuming that the necessary conditions and inherent limits of sensibility are limits on the possibility of intellectual knowledge as well. Kant lists three "subreptic axioms" that arise from this confusion. These unwarranted assumptions are:

1. The same sensitive condition, under which alone the *intuition* of an object is possible, is a condition of the *possibility* itself of the *object*.
2. The same sensitive condition, under which alone *it is possible to compare what is given so as to form a concept of the understanding of the object*, is also a condition of the possibility itself of the object.
3. The same sensitive condition, under which alone some *object* met with can be *subsumed under a given concept of the understanding*, is also the condition of the possibility itself of the object.[92]

In other words, at this stage Kant holds that it is a mistake to assume that the characteristic forms and limits of sensible representations and the conditions for the application of concepts to sensible representations limit our metaphysical cognition of objects as they really are. Kant gives examples of the errors that arise from this assumption: It is an error to assume that whatever exists is located in space and time;[93] it is an error to assume that "*every actual multiplicity can be given numerically,*" as multiplicities given in space and time are, and thus that "every magnitude is finite;"[94] and it is a mistake to assume that what may be an empirical criterion for the application of a concept, as non-existence at some time is a sensible criterion for the modal concept of contingency, is actually a necessary feature for any use of the concept at all.[95] The implication of Kant's argument is that paradoxes may arise in the attempt to derive metaphysical knowledge from the conditions of sensibility. One such paradox is that if the world is represented as existing in space and time, then the world must be both finite and infinite. Now Kant's argument further implies that such paradoxes can be avoided because we can have intellectual knowledge of reality independently of the concepts of space and time as conditions of "sensitive cognition."

Finally, Kant concludes the section by mentioning, almost as an afterthought, that there are certain "principles of convenience" (*principia convenientiae*) that are not principles of sensitive cognition but rather rules by means of which "it seems to the intellect itself easy and practical to deploy its own perspicacity." These are the principles that "*all things in the universe take place in accordance with the order of nature,*" that "*principles are not to be multiplied beyond what is absolutely necessary,*" and that "*nothing material at all comes into being or passes away.*"[96] This is a striking list, because it includes two principles – the principle of universal causation and the principle of the conservation of (material) substance – that Kant will later identify as "constitutive" or necessary conditions of the possibility of the experience of objects at all, but another one – the principle traditionally called "Ockham's razor" – that is more like what he will later identify as a "regulative" principle, which is not a necessary condition of the possibility of any experience at all but an assumption we make for various subjective reasons.

The fact that Kant could indiscriminately mix what he would later distinguish as constitutive and regulative principles shows that he did not yet have a clear conception of the function of the former as necessary conditions of the possibility of experience, a consequence of the fact that he did not yet have a clear understanding that the pure concepts of the understanding (such as the concepts of causation and substance mentioned in these principles) can yield knowledge only when applied to data furnished by the faculty of sensibility. Likewise, that he could argue at this stage that metaphysical illusion can be avoided by not letting the conditions of sensibility limit the use of concepts of the intellect shows that he did not yet see that the concepts of the understanding have a cognitive use only in application to sensibility and therefore within its limits, and beyond that can have only a practical use. Before he could progress from the inaugural dissertation to the *Critique of Pure Reason*, Kant would have to develop a new conception of the use of the intellect with distinctions among the sensible use of the understanding, the illusory use of pure theoretical reason, and the reliable use of pure practical reason.

IV.

THE GENESIS OF THE *CRITIQUE*

1770–72. After the publication of the dissertation, Kant fell into a prolonged silence broken only by a few minor essays[97] and a series of letters to his student Marcus Herz. Herz had participated in the public defense of Kant's dissertation[98] and was now in Berlin, studying medicine but also in contact with the prominent philosophers of the capital. Aside from what little can be gleaned from these letters, our primary source of information about Kant's thought in these years comes from surviving marginalia and notes, though presumably these are only a fragment of what Kant actually wrote during this period and have to be used with caution.[99] Fragmentary as they are, however, these materials cast considerable light on the emergence of some of the most important new arguments of the *Critique* and also explain some of its most troublesome obscurities.

In the fall of 1770, Herz went off to Berlin with copies of the dissertation for leading intellectuals such as Mendelssohn, Johann Heinrich Lambert (1728–1777) and Johann Georg Sulzer (1720–1779), and accompanying letters, of which only the letter to Lambert survives. In this letter Kant apologizes for the lapse of a prior promise of collaboration, makes a promise for the rapid publication of a work on the metaphysics of morals (a promise that would not even begin to be redeemed for another fifteen years)[100] and otherwise evinces his continuing commitment to the view of metaphysics enunciated in the dissertation.[101] By Christmas, all three Berlin philosophers had replied with letters containing essentially the same objection: how could Kant hold time to be a mere appearance with no objective reality when time is the form of inner sense and we all have immediate experience of changes in inner sense regardless of whatever external significance we might impute to those changing internal senses?[102]

Lambert initially raises a question about whether Kant's "two ways of knowing," from the senses and the intellect, "are so completely *separated* that they *never* come together,"[103] but then discusses in detail only Kant's treatment of time, accepting Kant's arguments that time is singular, continuous, and the object of a pure intuition but objecting to Kant's idealism about time:

All changes are bound to time and are inconceivable without time. *If changes are real, then time is real,* whatever it may be. *If time is unreal, then no change can be real.* I think, though, that even an idealist must grant at least that changes really exist and occur in his representations, for example, their beginning and ending. Thus time cannot be regarded as something *unreal.*[104]

Sulzer's briefer letter also raises a problem about time, asserting the position that *duration* must have "a true reality" even if the formal *concept* of time is some sort of abstraction from our experience of real duration;[105] and Mendelssohn too objects that

For several reasons I cannot convince myself that time is something merely subjective. Succession is after all at least a necessary condition of the representations that finite minds have. . . . Since we have to grant the reality of succession in a representing creature and in its alternations, why not also in the sensible objects, which are the models and prototypes of representations in the world?[106]

Kant made no immediate reply to this objection, as we know from his letter to Herz of 7 June 1771.[107] He merely asked Herz to apologize to his correspondents by saying that their letters had set him off on a long series of investigations, and then told Herz that he was now occupied with a work that "under the title *The Bounds of Sensibility and Reason* would work out in some detail the relationship of the concepts and laws determined for the sensible world together with the outline of what the nature of the theory of taste, metaphysics, and morality should contain."[108] In his next pledge, Kant said that he expected to complete the plan of the work shortly.

Kant does not appear to have written to Herz again until 21 February 1772, when he wrote what has become his most famous letter. Here Kant reviewed his plan for the work mentioned the previous June, stating that it was to consist of "two parts, a theoretical and a practical," the first of which in turn would consist of "(1) a general phenomenology and (2) metaphysics, but this only with regard to its nature and method," while the second part was to deal with "(1) the universal principles of feeling, taste, and sensuous desire and (2) the basic principles of morality."[109] However, Kant says, as he thought about the theoretical part – where the "phenomenology" was to have dealt with the limits of sensitive cognition before the purely intellectual foundations of metaphysics were expounded – "I noticed that I still lacked something essential, something that in my long metaphysical studies I, as well as others, had failed to pay attention to and that, in fact, constitutes the key to the whole secret of hitherto still obscure metaphysics." But the fundamental problem that Kant now announced had nothing to with the objection to his idealism regarding time that the Berlin savants had raised; indeed, although Kant would eventually acknowledge that objection,[110] he would in no way rethink his position about the ideality of time.

Instead, Kant raises a completely different question: "What is the ground of the relation of that in us which we call representation to the object?"[111] This is a puzzle precisely in the case of the relationship of pure concepts of the understanding to objects presented by sensible experience. It is not a puzzle in the case of entirely empirical representations, which are merely caused by their external objects, nor in the case of divine archetypes (or, we may add, human intentions), where the object is merely caused by the antecedent representation. But, Kant now holds, "the pure concepts of the understanding . . . though they must have their origin in the nature of the soul" because they are formulated by us and known "completely *a priori*," must yet apply to objects of sensible experience even though they are neither caused by nor cause the latter.[112] Kant now admits that he had completely passed over this question in the inaugural dissertation because he there failed to realize that our pure concepts as well as forms of intuition must be applied to the same objects, the objects of our experience. Thus what must now be explained is "the possibility of such concepts, with which . . . experience must be in exact agreement and which nevertheless are independent of experience." The idea that the pure concepts of the understanding provide knowledge of entities *other than* the spatiotemporal objects of sensibility suddenly disappears.

Kant did not describe how the possibility and necessity of the agreement of experience with pure concepts of the understanding is to be explained, beyond suggesting that a systematic classification of these "concepts belonging to complete pure reason" or "categories" can be reached by "following a few fundamental laws of the understanding." In spite of this obscurity, Kant was confident that he would be ready to publish the work, which he now for the first time entitled a *Critique of Pure Reason*, in only three months![113] In fact, it would be almost nine years before the work with that title appeared. Much of this delay was due to the fact that Kant did not yet have a clear idea of why the categories necessarily apply to objects of experience.

As Kant thinks further about this problem, a problem about time will play a key role, though not the problem about the reality of time but rather a problem about how we can make determinate judgments about the order of objective states of affairs or even our own experiences in time. This problem will become the focus of Kant's attention in the several years following the letter to Herz, especially in 1774–75, and will remain central in the *Critique*.

Kant's next report on his progress is in another letter to Herz, this one written toward the end of 1773.[114] Kant writes that he will not "be seduced by any author's itch into seeking fame," suggests that he is still working on "a principle that will completely solve what has hitherto been a riddle and that will bring the misleading qualities of the self-alienating understanding under certain and easily applied rules," but nevertheless promises that he will have his book, which he continues to call "a critique of pure reason," ready by the following Easter or shortly after,[115] that is, in the spring of 1774. In Kant's next surviving letter to Herz, however, written three years later in November 1776,[116] we again find him suggesting that he has been held up by difficulties surrounding the fundamental principle of his new position, though he says that he made progress with it the previous September and once again promises the completed book by the following Easter. Yet the following August still finds Kant reporting "a stone in the way of the *Critique of Pure Reason*," though once again he is optimistic that he can get by this obstacle during the following winter (1778). But April 1778 finds Kant writing that the rumor that some pages of his book are already at the press is premature, and in August of that year Kant will only say he is "still working indefatigably" on his "handbook."

So for at least five years the completion of the promised book continues to be put off, and there are repeated hints that Kant has still not found the fundamental principle he needs, presumably the one that would answer the fundamental question of 1772. From the letters to Herz, the only one of his known correspondents in this period to whom Kant says anything at all about his planned book, it might seem as if Kant was making no progress at all. But our other sources reveal that he was indeed working "indefatigably" on the *Critique* throughout this period, and that beginning by April 1774 – in other words, in the vicinity of his first promised Easter completion date – Kant did begin to explore a solution to his puzzle about why *a priori* concepts of the understanding should necessarily apply to the data presented to us by sensibility and not have any constitutive, theoretical use outside of that application.

1774–75. Using a letter sent to him on 28 April 1774 as scrap paper, Kant wrote a series of notes that were clearly part of his work on the *Critique*. Much of the material goes over claims about space and time already established in the inaugural dissertation, but Kant now adds a line of thought that had not previously appeared. He says that the unity of time implies the unity of the self and the determinate position of all objects in time; even more explicitly that the unity of space depends on the unity of the subject and on the ability of the subject to assign representations of objects determinate positions in space; and then suggests that the concepts of the understanding are necessary precisely to achieve such unification of and order among the intuitions of objects presented in the form of time and space. In his words, he asserts first:

1. Time is unique [*einig*]. Which means this: I can intuit all objects only in my-self and in representations found in my own subject, and all possible objects of my intuition stand in relation to each other in accordance with the special form of this intuition . . .
4. All things and all states of things have their determinate position in time. For through the unity of inner sense they must have their determinate relation to all other putative objects of intuition.[117]

He then makes parallel claims about space – space is not only our unique form for representing objects external to ourselves, but also uni-fied in the sense that every object must be assigned a determinate posi-tion in relation to all others in it:

Space is nothing but the intuition of mere form even without given matter, thus pure intuition. It is a single [*einzelne*] representation on account of the unity of the subject (and the capability), in which all representations of outer objects can be placed next to one another.[118]

Finally, Kant suggests that the use of concepts of the understanding or rules associated with them is the necessary condition of assigning rep-resentations or their objects their determinate positions in a unified space and/or time:

We have no intuitions except through the senses; thus no other concepts can in-habit the understanding except those which pertain to the disposition and order among these intuitions. These concepts must contain what is universal, and rules. The faculty of rules *in abstracto:* the learned understanding; *in concreto:* the common understanding. The common understanding has preference in all cases, where the rules must be abstracted *a posteriori* from the cases; but where they have their origin *a priori*, there it does not obtain at all.[119]

This remark presupposes that concepts are used only in application to intuitions, the thesis that Kant had not yet seen in 1770 but that was to become the hallmark of the *Critique of Pure Reason*, with its famous statement that "Thoughts without content are empty, intuitions with-out concepts are blind" (A 5 1 / B 7 5). It further suggests that the particu-lar function that the *a priori* concepts of the understanding play is to serve as rules for establishing "disposition and order" among intuitions of objects, though Kant does not yet explain why concepts should be necessary for this purpose or how concepts function as rules for this purpose. Finally, Kant suggests that even the ordinary use of abstraction for the production of empirical concepts depends upon the use of the *a priori* concepts of the understanding for the establishment of this "dis-position and order," even though these *a priori* concepts may seem "learned" rather than "common." This is an important point, because it implies that the theory of *a priori* concepts to be worked out in the *Critique of Pure Reason* is not, as it has sometimes been seen, a theory of the foundations of natural science considered as separate from everyday life, but rather a theory of the foundations of science as continuous with all of our knowledge.

The following series of notes shows that Kant spent much of his time in the next several years trying to work out his hunch that the categories can be shown to be *a priori* yet necessary conditions of all of our knowledge of objects by showing that their use is the necessary condition of all determinate "disposition and order" of intuitions. These notes are assigned to the year 1775 because one of them is written on another letter to Kant dated 20 May 1775. Although, as we saw, Kant had been moving toward the idea of a fundamental contrast between logical and real relations throughout the 1760s, it is only in these notes that he first clearly links his fundamental philosophical problem with the distinction between judgments that are analytic and those that are synthetic yet *a priori*. Kant asks under what conditions a predicate *b* can be predicated of an object *x* that is also subsumed under another predicate *a*. In some cases, *b* can be predicated of any *x* of which *a* is predicated because the predicate *b* is already identical to or contained in *a*, and we have no need to consider or experience any particular *x* in order to see that. In such cases, a proposition of the form "All *x*'s that are *a* are also *b*" would be true in virtue of "the principle of identity and contradiction," or a "merely logical" "principle of form rather than content," that is, it would be analytic.[120] If, however, the predicates *a* and *b* can be related to each other only through *x*, then the judgment is synthetic: "If I refer both predicates to *x* and only thereby to each other, then it is synthetic," and the predicates are in that case "not in a logical but in a real relation."[121] Kant also says that "In synthetic propositions the relation between the concepts is not really immediate (for this happens only in the case of analytic propositions), rather it is represented in the conditions of their concrete representation in the subject."[122] Kant does not say so explicitly, but he is clearly already assuming that propositions asserting that *a priori* concepts apply to the objects of sensibility will fall into this class of synthetic judgments expressing real relations.

Kant's next step is to argue that there are three different ways in which synthetic judgments may be made. The object *x* by means of which we link predicates *a* and *b* may be constructed in pure intuition, it may simply be given in empirical intuition or appearance, or it may be "the sensible condition of the subject within which a perception is to be assigned its position."[123] Or, in another passage, he writes:

x is therefore the determinable (object) that I think through the concept *a*, and *b* is its determination or the way in which it is determined. In mathematics, *x* is the construction of *a*, in experience it is the *concretum*, and with regard to an inherent representation or thought in general *x* is the function of thinking in general in the subject.[124]

It is clear enough what Kant means by the first two options. In mathematics, synthetic judgments – such as "The sum of the interior angles of a plane triangle equals two right angles" – are made or confirmed by constructing an object satisfying the first predicate ("plane triangle") in pure intuition, and then seeing that the construction satisfies the second predicate as well ("equals two right angles"); such a construction yields a determinate answer (two right angles contain 180 degrees, not 179 or 181) because it is the construction of a particular object, but it yields a result that is *a priori*, because it takes place in pure intuition, the form that determines the structure of all possible triangles or other spatial figures or objects. In ordinary experience, observation establishes synthetic and determinate but only contingent or *a posteriori* propositions because of the appeal to particular experience: a proposition like "My copy of the *Critique* is worn and dog-eared" adds information ("worn and dog-eared") that goes beyond the initial description of the object ("my copy of the *Critique*"), but that additional information can only be asserted of the particular object that is observed, because it has nothing to do with any essential form of appearance. But what does Kant mean by his third case, referred to only by such obscure phrases as "the sensible condition of a subject" or "the function of thinking in general"?

What Kant has in mind is what he hinted at in 1774, namely that there are certain rules necessary for the "disposition and order" of representations conceived of as belonging to a unified self and occupying determinate positions in the space and time in which that self places its representations, and that these rules add general conditions to the concept of any possible object of experience that go beyond the particular features of such objects we may happen to observe and by means of which we may happen to refer to them. He brings together the steps of this argument thus far in this passage:

> In analytic judgments the predicate [*b*] pertains properly to the concept *a*, in synthetic judgments to the object of the concept, since the predicate [*b*] is not contained in the concept. However, the object that corresponds to a concept has certain conditions for the application of this concept, i.e., its position *in concreto* . . . Now the condition of all concepts is sensible; thus, if the concept is also sensible, but universal, it must be considered *in concreto*, e.g., a triangle in its construction. If the concept does not signify pure intuition, but empirical, then *x* contains the condition of the relative position (*a*) in space and time, i.e., the condition for universally determining something in them.[125]

This is still somewhat obscure, but what Kant is saying is that judgments that are synthetic but also genuinely universal, that is, *a priori*, can be grounded in one of two ways: in the case of mathematics, such judgments are grounded in the construction of a mathematical object; in the other case, such judgments are grounded in the condition of determining the relative position of one object in space and time to others.

Kant also puts this point by saying that what he is looking for are the *principles of the exposition of appearances*, where that means precisely the assignment of each representation to a determinate position in the unified space and time that is the framework for all the representations belonging to a unified self. Kant introduces this concept when he writes:

The *principium* of the exposition of appearances is the general ground of the exposition of that which is given. The exposition of that which is thought depends merely on consciousness, but the exposition of that which is given, if one regards the matter as undetermined, depends on the ground of all relation and on the linkage [*Verkettung*] of representations (sensations). . . . The exposition of appearances is therefore the determination of the ground on which the nexus of sensations depends.[126]

But perhaps a clearer statement of Kant's strategy is this:

There is in the soul a *principium* of disposition as well as of affection. The appearances can have no other order and do not otherwise belong to the unity of the power of representation except insofar as they are amenable to the common *principio* of disposition. For all appearance with its thoroughgoing determination must still have unity in the mind, consequently be subjected to those conditions through which the unity of representations is possible. Only that which is requisite for the unity of representations belongs to the objective conditions. The unity of apprehension is necessarily connected with the unity of the intuition of space and time, for without this the latter would give no real representation.

The principles of exposition must be determined on the one side through the laws of apprehension, on the other side through the unity of the power of understanding. They are the standard for observation and are not derived from perceptions, but are the ground of those in their entirety.[127]

Kant's argument is that although all particular representations are given to the mind in temporal form, and all representations of outer objects are given to the mind as spatial representations, these representations cannot be linked to each other in the kind of unified order the mind demands, in which each object in space and time has a determinate relation to any other, except by means of certain principles that are inherent in the mind and that the mind brings to bear on the appearances it experiences. These principles will be, or be derived from, the pure concepts of the understanding that have a subjective origin yet necessarily apply to all the objects of our experience, and those concepts will not have any determinate use except in the exposition of appearances. This is the theory that will answer the puzzle Kant raised in his letter to Herz of February 1772, and that will eventually allow him to write the *Critique*.

But *how* exactly will the categories be shown to be the necessary conditions for the exposition of appearances? This has by no means been made clear in anything cited thus far. Kant throws out a number of tantalizing but incomplete suggestions. Perhaps it was his difficulty in choosing between as well as working out the details of these suggestions that prevented the *Critique* from taking final shape before 1779. One thing that Kant suggests is that the task of linking appearances in the orderly fashion required by a unified mind or self-consciousness imposes certain principles on those appearances because there is a certain way in which it is necessary to conceive of a unified mind – or what Kant now calls "apperception" – itself. He states that "Whatever is to be *thought* as an object of perception stands under a rule of apperception, or self-perception,"[128] and then claims that there is a "threefold dimension of *synthesis*" because there are "three functions of apperception" or three "exponents" of the way in which we conceive of ourselves: we necessarily conceive of our own thoughts as having "1. relation to a subject, 2. a relation of succession among each other, and 3. [comprising] a whole," and we therefore impose these same categories – what Kant will later identify as the categories of relation[129] – on the objects of our representations. Following this argument, Kant says that "I am the original of all objects," that is, I conceive of objects in analogy with the way in which I must conceive of myself.[130] Alternatively, Kant sometimes suggests that we necessarily conceive of *objects* by using the categories of a subject to which both a succession and a whole of properties belongs, and then conceive of our selves and the unity of our thought in analogy with the way we necessarily think of objects. Thus, in another note he argues that "All existence belongs to a substance; everything that happens is a member of a series; everything that is simultaneous belongs to a whole whose parts reciprocally determine each other," and then suggests that the way in which we conceive of ourselves, as subjective orders of experience, corresponds to these fundamental ways for conceiving of objects.[131]

In some of his most promising remarks, however, Kant suggests that there may be direct arguments showing the necessity of the use of certain categories of the understanding for certain time-determinations without any appeal to analogies between the way in which we conceive of the self and of objects in either direction. Thus, Kant argues that assigning determinate positions to events in time presupposes a framework of principles employing the same categories that in the other passages he has associated with the concept of a subject or of an object:

Something must always precede an occurrence (condition of perception).
All sorts of things can precede an occurrence, but among these there is one from which it always follows.
A reality is always attached (to a point in time and that which determines it) to something accompanying it, through which the point in time is determined (condition of perception).

All sorts of things can accompany, but among them there is something that is always there.

With regard to that which is simultaneous there is always a connection (condition of perception).

But it can be accompanied with all sorts of things; however, what is to be considered as objectively connected is a mutual determination of the manifold by one another.

If there were not something that always was, thus something permanent, *stabile*, there would be no firm point or determination of the point in time, thus no perception, i.e., determination of something in time.

If there were not something that always preceded an occurrence, then among the many things that precede there would be nothing with which that which occurs belongs in a series, it would have no determinate place in the series.

Through the rules of perception the objects of the senses are determinable in time; in intuition they are merely given as appearances. In accordance with those rules there is found an entirely different series than that in which the object was given.[132]

Here Kant suggests that what he has previously called the "exposition of appearances" is the determination of a definite order and position for occurrences in time. He does not say whether the occurrences are representations in a subject or states of objects, but in either case to order them in time is to determine whether at some particular point or period in time such occurrences succeed one another in a specific order or are simultaneous with each other. In order to determine this, Kant holds, we have to posit the existence of objects that endure through time – substances – and the existence of determinate patterns of causation and interaction among them. Thus we need to use the fundamental categories of substance, causation, and interaction for time-determination or the "exposition of appearances."

Kant does not explain in any detail *why* we must use these categories to accomplish this end – a fuller explanation of that will await the section of the published *Critique* called the "Analogies of Experience" (A176–218/B218–65). In the *Critique*, the "Analogies" follow a separate argument for the universal and necessary validity of the categories from certain more abstract conceptions of both objects and apperception, which he calls the "Transcendental Deduction of the Pure Concepts of the Understanding" (A84–130 and B116–69). Since in Kant's original sketches of the central argument of his planned *Critique* there is no separation between the discussion of apperception, objects, and the exposition of appearances, and the original discussion of the relation between apperception and objects already has the form of an analogy, it is an enduring question for the interpretation of the *Critique* whether or not these two sections have rendered asunder considerations that should have remained joined. This is a question for any reader of the

Critique to consider in trying to analyze the relation between the "Transcendental Deduction" and the "Analogies."

1776–77. These thoughts seem to be as far as Kant had gotten by 1775. In several further extensive notes from around 1776–77, we find for the first time what looks like an outline for a whole intended book. In the first of these notes, Kant divides his plan under four headings: "Dialectic of Sensibility"; "Dialectic of Understanding – Transcendental Theory of Magnitude"; "Transcendental Theory of Appearance – Reality and Negation"; and "Transcendental Theory of Experience."[133] This fourfold division does not, however, imply as elaborate a conception of the intended work as it might seem to, because the first three headings all cover the same ground, namely, Kant's theory of space and time as already stated in the inaugural dissertation. The fourth part adds to this a statement of the three principles of experience involving the concepts of substance, causation, and interaction that were first clearly listed in R 4681. Further, in spite of the fact that the first three sections all have the word "dialectic" in their titles, it is only in the fourth section that Kant explicitly states both theses and antitheses of the kind that we find in the "Dialectic" of the *Critique*, though he also hints at antinomies in the treatment of space and time.

At this point Kant is still experimenting with the organization of his planned work. But the content that he here envisages including is fairly clear: First, about space and time, he maintains that "All space and times are parts of larger ones," and that "All parts of space and time are themselves spaces" and times.[134] This implies that there are no simple parts in space and time, that space and time are continuous, and that space and time are infinite yet unitary (no matter how large a region of space or time is, it is always part of *one* larger space or time).[135] Kant implies that in order to understand these claims we also have to assume that space and time "are nothing real."[136] Under the title of "Dialectic of Understanding – Transcendental Theory of Magnitude" he further states that although the nature of our representation of space and time implies the infinitude of the possible extension or division of space and time, nevertheless "Infinite space and infinite past time are incomprehensible" [*unbegreiflich*].[137] This suggests a conflict between the nature of the intuition of space and time and the nature of an intellectual concept or comprehension of them; but Kant does not explain how this conflict is to be resolved beyond asserting that "Space and time belong only to the appearances and therefore to the world and not beyond the world."[138]

Then Kant turns to the "Transcendental Theory of Experience." Here he asserts three theses:

1. Something as substance, that is matter, neither comes into nor goes out of existence, from nothing comes nothing, i.e., matter is eternal (*ex nihilo nihil in mundo fit*) although dependent.

2. Every condition of the world is a consequence, for in the continuity of alteration everything is starting and stopping, and both have a cause.
3. All appearances together constitute a world and belong to real objects (against idealism). God as a cause does not belong to the world. For only through the agreement of representations with objects do they agree with one another and acquire the unity which perceptions that would be appearances must have.

To the first two theses he opposes what he explicitly labels "antitheses": for (1), the antithesis is that "There is no substance," and for (2), "Then there would be no first cause." Kant is not clear about the source of the conflict between theses and antitheses, although the whole note seems to suggest a conflict between the infinite structure of space and time and the needs of the understanding.

The next note gives a clear picture of the sources of dialectical conflict, while also suggesting that the whole content of the *Critique* could be organized around this conflict. Kant begins by explicitly formulating for the first time a principle that will be crucial in the *Critique:* "The principles of the possibility of experience (of distributive unity) are at the same time the principles of the possibility of the objects of experience." He then suggests that there are two classes of such principles, namely, (1) principles of "Unity of intuition," or principles of "appearance" as such, and (2) the principles of "experiences," or those in accordance with which "the existence of appearances is given." Finally, he suggests how antinomies arise: we get one set of principles from the "empirical use of reason," where the concepts of reason are applied to "space and time as conditions of appearance," and a different set from the "pure use of reason," where space and time are not taken to be conditions of the use of the concepts of reason. On this basis, Kant describes two sets of competing principles that clearly lead directly to the "Antinomy of Pure Reason" expounded in the *Critique:*

Immanent principles of the empirical use of understanding:
1. There is no bound to the composition and decomposition of appearances.
2. There is no first ground or first beginning.
3. Everything is mutable and variable, thus empirically contingent, since time itself is necessary but nothing is necessarily attached to time.
Transcendent principles of the pure use of understanding:
1. There is a first part, namely the simple as *principium* of composition, and there are limits to all appearances together.
2. There is an absolute spontaneity, transcendental freedom.
3. There is something which is necessary in itself, namely the unity of the highest reality, in which all multiplicity of possibilities can be determined through limits . . . [139]

The first pair of principles from each group stakes out the debate separated into the first two antinomies in the *Critique*, the disputes over whether or not space and time are infinite in extension and over whether or not they are infinitely divisible; the second pair corresponds to the third antinomy in the *Critique*, which debates whether all events have an antecedent cause or whether there is a first cause that has no antecedent cause of its own; and the third pair parallels the later fourth antinomy, which debates whether the whole series of events in the world is contingent or has an external ground that makes it necessary.[140]

However, the conclusion that Kant draws from this presentation of the antinomies is not yet what he will later argue. He clearly suggests that the "transcendent principles" (what will be the theses in the later antinomies) arise from using concepts of the understanding without space and time as conditions, while the "immanent principles" result from applying the concepts of the understanding to space and time and using them within the conditions imposed by the structure of our representations of space and time – using them as "principles of the exposition of appearances." But he does not reject the "transcendent" use of the concepts of the understanding. On the contrary, he still seems to hold, as he did in the inaugural dissertation, that there is a legitimate transcendent use of the concepts of the understanding unrestricted by the conditions of space and time. Thus he reiterates the three subreptic axioms of the dissertation as three "Rules of Dialectic":

1. Do not judge what does not belong to appearances in accordance with rules of appearance, e.g., God with [rules of] space and time.
2. Do not subject what does not belong to outer appearance, e.g., spirit, to its conditions.
3. Do not hold to be impossible what cannot be conceived and represented in intuition, the totality of the infinite or of infinite division.

Then he lists four "principles of the absolute unity of reason" that can apparently be maintained as long as we do not violate any of these three rules:

a. Simplicity of the thinking subject.
b. Freedom as the condition of rational actions.
c. *Ens originarium* as the *substratum* of all connection of one's representations in a whole.
d. Do not confuse the restriction [*Einschränkung*] of the world in accordance with its origin and content with its limitation [*Begrenzung*].[141]

At this point, then, it seems as if Kant envisioned for the *Critique* (1) an account of the nature and structure of space and time paralleling that in the dissertation, (2) a new account of the use of *a priori* concepts of the understanding, according to which they yield "immanent principles for the empirical use of the understanding" only when applied to the conditions of spatiotemporal representation to achieve an "exposition of appearances," but (3) continued adherence to the view of the dissertation that these concepts can also yield transcendent or metaphysical knowledge when freed of the restriction of the forms of sensibility.

Perhaps this last point was only a momentary lapse, however, for in the next preserved note Kant says that "The transcendent principles are principles of the subjective unity of cognition through reason, i.e. of the agreement of reason with itself"; "Objective principles are principles of a possible empirical use."[142] This suggests that whatever exactly the use of the transcendent principles of pure reason is, it is *not* to obtain any knowledge of external objects, which can only be achieved through the empirical use of the concepts of understanding, their application to representations in space and time for the exposition of appearances. Kant continues with this thought in the following note, where he lays out four conflicts between "principles of the exposition of appearances," or principles applied to "appearances" for the "unity of experience," on the one hand, and "principles of rationality or comprehension" on the other. These conflicts correspond precisely to the four antinomies of the *Critique.* The first set of principles is:

1. no absolute totality in composition, hence infinite *progressus,*
2. no absolute totality of decomposition, hence nothing absolutely simple,
3. no absolute totality of the series of generation, no unconditioned spontaneity,
4. no absolute necessity.

The opposing set of principles of rationality is:

1. Unconditioned totality of the dependent whole,
2. Unconditioned simple,
3. Unconditioned spontaneity of action,
4. Unconditioned necessary being.

Kant says that the latter "propositions are subjectively necessary as principles of the use of reason in the whole of cognition: unity of the whole of the manifold of cognition of the understanding. They are practically necessary with regard to . . ."[143] He does not finish the thought, or explain the practical necessity of the principles of reason. But he is clearly drawing back from the thought that reason by itself furnishes metaphysical cognition of real objects independent of our own thought.

Summing up our results thus far, then, it looks as if by 1777 Kant had come this far in planning the *Critique:* it would include (1) the account of space and time as transcendentally ideal pure forms of intuition already reached in 1770; (2) a derivation of three concepts of the understanding – substance, causation, and interaction – and their associated principles – as necessary for the exposition of appearances given through the forms of space and time and as objectively valid only in that context, and (3) a presentation in the form of a four-part antinomy pitting those principles, valid for the exposition of appearances, against four opposed transcendent principles, using the concepts of understanding but without restriction by the forms of sensibility which have no objective validity but can be used in an unspecified way for the unification of empirical knowledge and for some equally unspecified practical purpose. Such a *Critique* would basically have consisted of a theory of sensibility, a theory of experience, and an antinomy of pure reason.

Clearly Kant needed more time to understand the positive function of pure reason, which is only hinted at in these notes. But this is not the only way that the outline of the *Critique* that we can construct for the period around 1777 differs from the work as finally published. There are several other glaring differences. First, the "transcendental theory of experience," or theory of the "immanent use" of the concepts of understanding, is not yet divided into a transcendental deduction of the categories and a derivation of the principles of judgment used in the exposition of appearances, as it will be in the published work. Second, all of these notes suggest that the content of the "Dialectic" is exhausted by the four antinomies of pure reason, whereas in the published *Critique* the Dialectic is divided into three parts, the "Paralogism," "Antinomy," and "Ideal of Pure Reason." Can we learn anything about what led to these further divisions of the *Critique* before it finally took on the form Kant gave it in 1779 and 1780?

1778–80. Fortunately, some notes assigned to the period 1776–78 rather than 1775–77 survive and throw light on the final development of Kant's conception of the *Critique*. In one note that has been assigned to the later part of this period, Kant for the first time suggests that there may be a deduction of the categories as necessary conditions of apperception or the unity of consciousness that does not depend upon the temporal character of the data to be unified. Since this may be the earliest surviving sketch of a transcendental deduction conceived of as separate from and antecedent to the argument to the categories as conditions of the possibility of the exposition of appearances, or what Kant would come to call the "Analogies of Experience," it is worth quoting this passage in full:

In everything passive or what is given, apprehension must not merely be found, but it must also be necessitated in order to represent it as given, i.e., the individual apprehension must be determined by the universal. The universal is the relation to the others and to the whole of the state. By being distinguished from the arbitrary is it considered as given, and only by being subsumed under the categories is it considered as something. It must therefore be represented in accordance with a rule by which appearance becomes experience and by which the mind comprehends it as one of its actions of **self-consciousness,** within which, as in space and time, all *data* are to be encountered. The unity of the mind is the condition of thinking, and the subordination of every particular under the universal is the condition of the possibility of associating a given representation with others through an action. Even if the rule is not immediately obvious, nevertheless one must represent the object as amenable to a rule in order to conceive it as that which represents something, i.e., something which has a determinate position and function among the other determinations. . . . [144]

This note, which is very similar to a crucial passage in the version of the "Transcendental Deduction" published in the first edition of the *Critique* (A 108), is notable for two reasons.

On the one hand, it clearly suggests that there must be general rules for the unity of consciousness that can be characterized independently of specific rules for time-determination, although the way remains open for a further inference that once the temporal character of the data for consciousness is considered, then these general rules may have given rise to further rules which are themselves temporal in content. Such a separation between the most general form of rules for the unity of consciousness and the specific rules for the unity of a consciousness that is temporal in character, along with the necessity of explaining the relation between the two forms of rules, will be central to the organization of the *Critique of Pure Reason,* where Kant will offer: (1) a transcendental deduction of the pure concepts of the understanding as conditions of the possibility of any unity of consciousness in general, under the rubric of an "Analytic of Concepts"; (2) a derivation from those general rules of more specific rules for time-determination, under the rubric of a "Schematism of the Pure Concepts of the Understanding,"[145] which is in turn part of (3) the "Analytic of Principles," in which Kant argues for specific principles involving the temporally interpreted categories, such as the principles of the conservation of substance and of universal causation, as necessary conditions of objective time-determination.[146] The introduction of the concept of schematism, which Kant first records in a note from 1778–79 with the statement that "We must subject all of our pure concepts of the understanding to a schema, a way of putting the manifold together in space and time,"[147] is required precisely by the explicit separation between the transcendental deduction of the categories and the analogies of experience (and related arguments) by means of which Kant had previously derived the categories.

On the other hand, this note also reveals a fundamental ambivalence about exactly *how* the categories are to be derived from the general idea of the "unity of consciousness," an ambiguity continuing one already found in the materials from 1775. In one strategy, rules are necessary to distinguish an arbitrary series of representations from the orderly or rule-governed series of representations by means of which a determinate *object* is presented to consciousness; on this account, the "unity of consciousness" would mean the unity of consciousness characteristic of the presentation of an object. Alternatively, Kant suggests that rules are necessary for the unity of consciousness as a form of *self-consciousness*, the recognition that various representations, whatever objects they may or may not represent, all have the unity of belonging to a single *mind*. Kant does not clearly separate these two strategies, nor suggest a means for connecting them. This ambiguity will plague all of Kant's attempts to find a definitive form for the deduction of the categories. It runs throughout the first-edition version of the "Deduction," and then leads Kant to continue to experiment with the proper form for the deduction, not merely in the second edition of the *Critique*, in which he completely rewrites the "Deduction," but in the intervening period, in which he tries to resolve the ambiguity in the *Prolegomena to Any Future Metaphysics* (1783),[148] the *Metaphysical Foundations of Natural Science* (1786),[149] and a number of surviving drafts,[150] and on into the 1790s as well, where he continued to tinker with the deduction in his drafts for an essay on the *Real Progress of Metaphysics from the Time of Leibniz and Wolff.*[151] Arriving at a definitive interpretation of the transcendental deduction of the categories has been the most difficult task for Kant scholarship throughout the twentieth century, and this underlying ambivalence in Kant's conception of its strategy is a large part of the reason for this problem.[152]

Kant never resolved the issue of the fundamental strategy of the deduction of the categories, but much else about the content and structure of the *Critique* had clearly been resolved by 1778–79. Several extensive drafts from this period show that Kant had not only arrived at the final organization of the "Transcendental Analytic," but also that he had now arrived at the final organization of the "Transcendental Dialectic," which is also more complicated than the schemes he had been considering in the period 1775–77. Whereas in the notes from that period Kant presented the material of the "Dialectic" as a single set of antinomies, now he has divided the material into three main parts, the diagnosis of "three kinds of transcendental illusion" generated by "three kinds of rational inference."[153] Thus, at this point Kant envisioned the following argument.

The constructive argument of the book would consist of two main parts. The first of these would in turn be broken into two further parts: first would be the account of space and time that had been in place since 1770; in the *Critique* Kant would finally entitle this the "Transcendental Aesthetic." Then in the second, under the title of "Transcendental Analytic" that he now introduces,[154] Kant would make the argument, based on the principle that "We can have synthetic cognition *a priori* about objects of experience, if [it] consists of principles of the possibility of experience"[155] that he now explicitly formulates, in which a transcendental deduction of the categories would be linked to a demonstration of their role in empirical time-determination by means of an intervening schematism of those categories. This argument, showing that the categories must be applied to representations given in space and time in order to yield unity of consciousness and objective experience of objects, would have the consequence that by concepts "we cognize only objects of the senses," thus that the categories "do not reach to the supersensible."

It would then be the burden of the second main part of the work, which Kant had already been referring to as a "Dialectic" for some years, to show that "Even though the concepts [of the pure understanding] extend to all objects of thought in general," "they do not yield any amplification of theoretical cognition," but may nevertheless have a "practical-dogmatic" role in a "practical regard, where freedom is the condition of their use."[156] Now Kant divides this critical part of the work into three divisions. He argues that it is characteristic of pure reason to assume as a "petition" or "postulate" the principle that "All conditioned cognition not only stands under conditions, but finally under one which is itself unconditioned," or that "If the conditioned is given, then the entire series of all its conditions is also given."[157] He now argues that because there are three kinds of rational inference, from a property to its subject, from a property to another property, and from a property to its ground, there must be three dialectical inferences back to an unconditioned or absolute substance, an unconditioned or absolute whole, and an unconditioned or absolute ground. Thus reason postulates "the unconditioned subjective conditions of thinking, the unconditioned (objective) condition of appearances, and the unconditioned objective condition of all things in general."[158] These three inferences, which Kant will discuss in the *Critique* under the titles of the "Paralogism," the "Antinomy," and the "Ideal of Pure Reason," will be diagnosed as theoretically unjustified, because the underlying principle, that whenever the conditioned is given so is its ultimate condition, is theoretically unjustified. Nevertheless these three ideas of the unconditioned will be useful in a practical context.

Even in the *Critique* Kant will retain the argument that the three forms of "transcendental illusion" arise from three forms of inference,[159] but he also suggests both in these notes and in the published work that they arise directly from an unwarranted reification of the three concepts of a subject, a series, and a ground,[160] and it is easier to understand his diagnosis in these terms. Thus, the three fundamental errors of metaphysics are the assumptions (1) that because we assign all of our thoughts to our selves as subjects, we have knowledge of the soul as an absolute subject; (2) that because we place all appearances in series of ever increasing spaces and times, of ever decreasing spaces and times, of causes and effects, and of contingents necessarily dependent upon something else, we have knowledge of completed extensions in space and time, of simples in space and time, of a first cause, and of a necessary ground for all contingents; and (3) that because we must think of some ground for any possibility, we have knowledge of an absolute ground of all possibilities. In Kant's words:

> The idea of the soul is grounded on [the idea that] the understanding must relate all thoughts and inner perceptions to the self and assume this as the only permanent subject.
> The idea of the unconditioned for all conditions in appearance is grounded in reason as the prescription to seek the completeness of all cognition of the understanding in [series of] subordination.
> The idea of the unconditioned unity of all objects of thought in an *ens entium* is necessary in order to seek the relationship among all possible [things] . . . [161]

Kant suggests that it is natural for us to form these ideas, and that there is even a subjective necessity to do so, but it is a mistake to interpret them as offering theoretical knowledge of objects of a kind that could never be presented by the senses.

What led Kant to divide his diagnosis of metaphysical illusions concerning the self, the world, and God into these three parts (rational psychology, rational cosmology, and rational theology), when previously the claims about the soul were simply instances of the second and third antinomies (the simplicity of the soul was just an instance of simplicity in general, and the freedom of the self just an instance of absolute spontaneity), and an absolutely necessary ground of all contingents was the subject of the fourth antinomy?[162] The contents of the third part of the "Dialectic" in the published *Critique*, the "Ideal of Pure Reason," suggest that Kant elevated the discussion of rational theology into a separate section simply because he had too much material to treat it as a single antinomy – he recapitulates his critique of the ontological, cosmological, and physico-theological arguments from the *Only Possible Ground* of 1763 as well as criticizing his own positive argument from that work, even while retaining the arguments about God that constitute the third and fourth antinomies in the *Critique*. Kant would also have been hard put to integrate his positive account of the necessary rational genesis of an ideal of pure reason ("Transcendental Dialectic," Book II, Chapter III, Section 2; A571–83/B599–611) into any discussion that takes the form of an antinomy.

The criticism of rational psychology in the "Paralogism," however, is something new, which appears in these notes of 1778–79 for the first time. Here one can conjecture that the new "Paralogism" is Kant's response to his own new transcendental deduction of the categories –

because he has claimed that the *unity of consciousness* is an *a priori* necessity from which we can deduce the validity of the categories, he now also has to tell us to be careful what *not* to infer from this unity of consciousness, namely any metaphysical claims about the *soul*, claims that the *subject* or *bearer* of consciousness is a unitary, simple, and eternal substance. Such a "paralogism of pure reason" would really be "a transcendental subreption," an illusion in which "the unity of apperception, which is subjective, would be taken for the unity of the subject as a thing."[163] We find no such warning in Kant before we find the introduction of a separate transcendental deduction of the categories from the unity of consciousness; so we can assume that the expansion of the "Dialectic" to include paralogisms of pure reason separate from the second and third antinomies was a cautionary response to the new deduction, Kant's own warning about what not to read into his deduction. Then once the structure of the "Dialectic" had been so expanded, it would not have been unnatural for Kant to add a fuller treatment about theoretically unjustified though morally useful conceptions of God as well.

One last note, written on a matriculation record from March 1780, and thus either a last draft for the about to be written *Critique* or a memo written during its composition, recapitulates much of this outline and then adds a reference to one final section of the *Critique:*

To the *Canon:* the end of the whole of metaphysics is God and the future and the end of these [in] our conduct, not as though morality must be arranged in accordance with these, but because without these morality would be without consequences.[164]

This is cryptic, and can only be fully understood in light of the argument that Kant develops, over all three *Critique*s, that the highest good or maximization of both virtue and happiness, which we can only conceive of as being made possible by an intelligent and benevolent Author of the world prepared to give us the time necessary to perfect our virtue and to make the world suitable for the achievement of our ends, is not the motivation for virtuous action but is presupposed by its rationality. This is the practical use to which Kant will put the theoretical illusions of metaphysics. Conceiving of a "canon" of pure reason as well as its critique – that is, a doctrine of its positive practical use as well as the negative criticism of its misguided theoretical use – was thus the final stage in conceiving of the structure and content of the *Critique*, where this "canon" would be expanded into a "Doctrine of Method" that would accompany the "Doctrine of Elements," into which the "Transcendental Aesthetic," "Transcendental Analytic," and "Transcendental Dialectic" would be placed.

With all of this in place by 1779 or 1780, Kant was finally able to write the *Critique*, and to announce to Herz on 1 May 1781, after a decade of apologies and postponements, that "In the current Easter book fair there will appear a book of mine, entitled *Critique of Pure Reason.*"[165] Ten days later, he wrote to Herz these lines:

My work, may it stand or fall, cannot help but bring about a complete change of thinking in this part of human knowledge [metaphysics], a part of knowledge that concerns us so earnestly. For my part I have nowhere sought to create mirages or to advance specious arguments in order to patch up my system; I have rather let years pass by, in order that I might get to a finished insight that would satisfy me completely and at which I have in fact arrived; so that I now find nothing I want to change in the main theory (something I could never say of any of my previous writings), though here and there little additions and clarifications would be desirable.[166]

V.

THE CHANGES IN THE SECOND EDITION

For Kant himself, the *Critique of Pure Reason* was never intended to be more than a propaedeutic to the systematic metaphysics of nature and of morals that he had long intended to write, and his own intention upon the completion of the *Critique* must have been to proceed directly to these two parts of his philosophical system. He made substantial progress in this direction, publishing the *Metaphysical Foundations of Natural Science* in 1786, in which he tried to show that the application of his general principles of judgment to the empirical concept of motion yields the basic principles of Newtonian physics, and the *Groundwork of the Metaphysics of Morals* in 1785, intended to be the introduction to the detailed system of duties that would constitute the metaphysics of morals (and would not in fact appear until 1797). But the initial reception of the *Critique of Pure Reason* sorely disappointed Kant's expectation that the work could not "help but bring about a complete change of thinking," and a great deal of Kant's effort during the decade of the 1780s was devoted to the unforeseen task of clarifying the critical foundations of his system of philosophy that he thought he had completed in May 1781. This work took a number of different forms: the publication of a brief defense and attempted popularization of the *Critique* in 1783, the *Prolegomena to any Future Metaphysics;* continued work on the transcendental deduction in his private notes during 1783–84; a proposed revision of the transcendental deduction of the categories in the introduction to the 1786 *Metaphysical Foundations of Natural Science;* a substantial revision of the *Critique of Pure Reason* for its second edition in 1787; and finally the publication of two further critiques, the *Critique of Practical Reason* (1788) and the *Critique of Judgment* (1790), which were clearly not works Kant had planned at the time of the publication of the *Critique of Pure Reason* but which instead grew out of his ongoing struggle to clarify the foundations of his critical philosophy. We cannot comment on all this material here; instead, after some brief comments on the revisions to the *Critique of Pure Reason* that are implicit in the *Prolegomena* and *Metaphysical Foundations of Natural Science*, we will conclude this introduction by outlining the main changes made in the second edition of the first *Critique*.

After a year of silence, broken only by two friendly but insignificant reviews published in Frankfurt and Greifswald, the *Critique* finally received its first serious review in the first supplementary volume of the *Göttingischen Anzeigen von gelehrten Sachen* for 1782. The university at Göttingen, which had been founded in 1737 by George I of England in his continuing capacity as Georg August, elector of Hanover, was home to a group of empiricist philosophers led by J. G. H. Feder (1740–1821). The review, apparently abridged and rewritten by Feder from a much longer and more sympathetic draft by the Berlin moral philosopher Christian Garve (1742–1798), was dismissive.[167] The version of the review published by Feder omitted Garve's careful exposition of much of Kant's arguments and his quite insightful interpretation of Kant's justification of the possibility of synthetic *a priori* cognition in general, and in mathematics in particular, to focus on three objections. First, it charged that Kant's "system of the higher or... transcendental idealism" was nothing but a restatement of Berkeley's idealism, reducing all objects to our own sensations and leaving the real existence of any objects beyond our own representations entirely unknown. Second, it argued that on Kant's account there could be no differentiation "between the actual and the imagined, the merely possible," between the actual and "mere visions and fantasies." Third, it charged that Kant's argument that the unsound theoretical use of pure reason can and must be replaced by a sound practical use was entirely unnecessary, since morality already has a sound foundation in common sense.

Kant had apparently already formulated the intention to write a shorter and more popular presentation of his critical philosophy almost as soon as the *Critique* was published, but the hostile review clearly galvanized him, and he included explicit answers to some of its charges in the pages of the *Prolegomena to any Future Metaphysics* that he published in August 1783. Specifically, he differentiated his position from Berkeleian idealism by arguing that he denied the real existence of *space* and *time* and the *spatiotemporal properties* of objects, but not the real existence of *objects* themselves distinct from our representations, and for this reason he proposed renaming his transcendental idealism with the more informative name of "formal" or "critical idealism," making it clear that his idealism concerned the *form* but not the existence of external objects.[168] Further, he argued that his theory of the understanding and its principles, unlike the usual brands of idealism, offered determinate principles for establishing the coherence of veridical experience as contrasted to incoherent dreams and fantasies,[169] and that for this reason it should not be considered a form of "higher" idealism, an expression in which he detected a pejorative implication of fancifulness, but rather a philosophy firmly rooted in the "fruitful **bathos** of experience."[170] Finally, Kant rejected any comparison of his view to Berkeley's on the ground that Berkeley's empiricism leaves all knowledge of space and time *a posteriori* and contingent, whereas only Kant's own formal idealism can explain our *a priori* knowledge of space and time as the universal and necessary forms of intuition.[171]

Emphasizing that only his transcendental idealism can explain our *a priori* knowledge of mathematics and pure physics while at the same time demonstrating that as formal idealism it is entirely compatible with the real existence of external objects would both be major objectives in Kant's revisions of the *Critique* for its second edition. Vindicating his view that the illusory theoretical use of pure reason must be replaced by its sound practical use, the last point challenged by the Göttingen review although not replied to in the *Prolegomena*, would also be an aim of those revisions. But, as had been the case before with the critical response to the inaugural dissertation, Kant also revealed in the *Prolegomena* a concern that his critic had not raised: namely, a concern about the adequacy of the transcendental deduction of the categories itself. Kant expressed this worry about the deduction (and the associated paralogisms) as mildly as he could: he says that he is completely satisfied with the "content, order, and doctrine" of his work but that he is "not entirely satisfied with the presentation in some parts of the Doctrine of Elements, e.g., the deduction of the categories or the paralogisms of pure reason."[172] In fact, both of those chapters would be completely rewritten in the second edition of the *Critique*, in part to respond to the challenge to Kant's variety of idealism raised by the Göttingen review but also to respond to Kant's own concerns about their persuasiveness.

Indeed, Kant had already begun to manifest his concern about the adequacy of the deduction in the *Prolegomena* itself. Following what he claims to be the "analytic" method of the *Prolegomena* rather than the "synthetic" method of the *Critique*[173] – the difference is supposed to be between a method that analyzes the presuppositions of undisputed knowledge-claims and one that determines the consequences of fundamental claims about the human cognitive faculties,[174] but in fact the major difference between Kant's argument in the two works concerns *which* knowledge-claims it is whose conditions are analyzed – Kant replaces the transcendental deduction of the categories, which purports to analyze the necessary conditions of the possibility of the transcendental unity of apperception, with an analysis of the necessary condition of universally and necessarily valid judgments in ordinary life and science that makes no use of the concept of apperception at all. Thus, Kant argues that while mere "judgments of perception," which make no claim to necessary objective validity or the agreement of others at all, but only report how things seem to a single subject, use the logical forms of judgment, "judgments of experience," which do make claims to objective validity necessary for all, can only derive their universal and necessary validity from their use of *a priori* categories to make the otherwise indeterminate use of the forms of judgment determinate.[175] This approach is pursued even further in the Preface to the *Metaphysical Foundations of Natural Science* three years later, where Kant suggests that the categories can be derived as the necessary conditions of making the use of the logical forms of judgment determinate even without explicit reference to the alleged distinction between judgments of perception and of experience.[176] But although this strategy avoids the obscurity of some of Kant's claims about the transcendental unity of apperception, it is open to the charge of begging the question against both empiricists and skeptics, proving that the categories are necessary only by accepting an interpretation of ordinary and scientific knowledge-claims as universally and necessarily true that neither a skeptic nor an empiricist would dream of accepting.

In any case, Kant's notes from the period 1783–84 show that he continued to experiment with both the unity of apperception as well as the concept of objectively valid judgment as possible bases for the deduction of the categories.[177] However, when Kant came to rewrite the chapter on the transcendental deduction for the second edition, he returned to his original strategy of trying to combine the conditions of possibility of the unity of apperception with those of the judgment of objects to create an unshakable foundation for the objective validity of the categories.

When Kant was first notified by his publisher in April 1786 that a new edition of the *Critique* would be needed, he apparently contemplated a drastic revision that would include an extensive discussion of practical reason as well as a restatement of his work on theoretical reason. At the same time, he also assumed the rectorship of his university. At some point during the year he must have decided on the more modest though still extensive revisions that we have, enough of which were completed by January 1787 for typesetting of the new edition to begin, and all of which were apparently completed by that April, just a year after the new edition was first requested.[178] (At some point between 1781 and 1787 Kant made the annotations in his own copy of the first edition of the *Critique* that we reproduce throughout our translation, but as these notes are not closely matched by the changes in the edition of 1787, there is no reason to believe that these notes were made during 1786–87 as part of the work on the new edition.)

The main changes in the second edition, growing partly out of Kant's response to the criticism of the first and partly out of his own concerns, as we have just described, are as follows. (1) Kant replaced the preface to the first edition, which speaks in only the most general terms about the need to place the science of metaphysics on a secure footing, with a considerably longer one that describes in much more detail both the innovations of Kant's critical method – it is here that Kant introduces the famous comparison between his own anthropocentric procedure in philosophy and Copernicus's heliocentric revolution in astronomy (B xvi) – and his position that pure reason ultimately has a positive role only in its practical rather than theoretical use (B xxiv–xxxvii). The latter emphasis is clearly meant to respond to the dismissive remarks of the Göttingen review on this subject.[179] The new preface concludes with a brief comment on the changes in the new edition, and then with a long footnote (B xxix–xli) revising yet further the new "Refutation of Idealism" that is one of the most important of those changes.

(2) The introduction is considerably expanded. Its main changes are, first, a more detailed discussion of the distinction between *a priori* and *a posteriori* cognition than the first edition had included, and then an extended argument that the synthetic *a priori* cognitions of pure mathematics and physics can only be explained by his transcendental idealism, which are in fact lifted virtually without change from the *Prolegomena*.[180] Kant's inclusion of these pages shows that he is still very concerned to emphasize the difference between Berkeley's idealism and his own, since Berkeley's inability to explain *a priori* knowledge was one of Kant's chief charges in the *Prolegomena*.

(3) The "Transcendental Aesthetic" is also considerably expanded. Kant's aim in its revision seems to have been primarily to buttress the (anti-Berkeleian) argument for the necessity of his transcendental idealism to explain synthetic *a priori* cognition, rather than the argument that his form of idealism is compatible with knowledge of the real existence of external objects, which will dominate his revisions in later parts of the work. Thus, Kant divides his previously undivided discussions of space and time into what he now calls the "Metaphysical" and "Transcendental Exposition" of each, where the first of these titles subsumes the arguments that space and time are pure and *a priori* forms of intuition as well as pure intuitions in their own right, and the second separately expounds the argument that our synthetic *a priori* cognition of mathematics (especially geometry) can only be explained by transcendental idealism. The revised version of the "Aesthetic" concludes with a number of additional arguments in behalf of transcendental idealism that were not present in the first edition.

(4) The next major change comes in the "Transcendental Deduction" of the categories, which Kant rewrote almost completely for the second edition (two introductory sections are left largely unchanged, but the rest is completely rewritten, thirty-five pages in the first edition being replaced with forty completely new ones in the second). To characterize the nature of the changes that Kant made in any detail would be an interpretative venture inappropriate for this introduction, but a few points can be noted. First, in spite of his experiments with an apperception-free deduction in 1783 and 1786, Kant in fact tried to ground the entire deduction more clearly on the starting-point of the unity of apperception than he had in 1781. At the same time, trying to salvage his experiments of the intervening years, he also tried to connect the unity of apperception more unequivocally with the idea of the objective validity of judgment than he had in the earlier version. Second, Kant tried to prepare the way for the coming new "Refutation of Idealism" by stressing that the cognitive subject must be regarded as determining the structure and order of its own *self*-consciousness just as much as it does to the representation of external objects (§§ 23–5). Finally, continuing the stress on the necessity of the representation of space that was part of the *Prolegomena*'s response to the charge of Berkeleian idealism, Kant stresses that the synthetic unity of consciousness, which in the first edition had been associated exclusively with the synthesis of *time*, is responsible for the unity of both space and time, and indeed that the representation of determinate *spatial* relations is a necessary condition for the representation of a determinate *temporal* order, which is an undeniable feature of any conceivable self-consciousness (see B 156).

(5) The argument that while time is the form of all sense, the representation of space is itself the necessary condition for the representation of determinate order in time, which continues Kant's rebuttal of the charge of Berkeleian idealism, is the chief theme of all of the revisions in the "Analytic of Principles." These revisions take the form of restatements of the several principles of judgment, and of additional paragraphs at the start of each of the proofs; but Kant's most important addition to this part of the book is the new "Refutation of Idealism" that is inserted into the discussion of actuality in the "Postulates of Empirical Thought" (B 274–9). This may seem like an inauspicious location for such an addition, but Kant's intention in choosing it can only have been to show that empirically meaningful judgments about the modalities of possibility and necessity all depend upon connection to the actual in perception, and then to show what he means by the actual in perception: that which we judge to exist independently of our representation of it, even if we also know that the *form* in which we represent the independence of such objects is itself dependent upon the constitution of our own sensibility. The "Refutation of Idealism," in other

words, is Kant's ultimate attempt to prove that his idealism is *merely* formal idealism rather than the subjective realism of Berkeley.

The "Refutation of Idealism" is one of the most important of Kant's additions to the second edition, but the fact that before the new edition was even published he was already revising this revision in the new preface (presumably the last part to be rewritten) shows that Kant was hardly satisfied with his new argument. In fact, the new "Refutation" is not so much the culmination of a long-considered process of thought as the beginning of a new one, and a dozen or more further versions from the period 1788–90 survive to show that Kant continued to work on this argument even after the second edition of the *Critique* had already appeared.[181]

(6) Kant also undertook major revisions in the chapter on the distinction between phenomena and noumena. His primary concern in these revisions was to clarify the difference between using the concept of a noumenon in a negative and a positive sense. This can be regarded as a step toward clarifying his doctrine that whereas pure reason has only a negative theoretical use it does have a positive practical use, a doctrine the clarity of which had been challenged both by the Göttingen review and by Garve's original draft.

(7) Having added a new "Refutation of Idealism," Kant had no choice but to rewrite at least the fourth paralogism of the first edition, which above all other passages had given justification to the charge of Berkeleianism by insisting that we could be as certain of the objects of outer sense as of those of inner sense because objects in space are nothing but one species of representation alongside representations of inner sense (see especially A370). Kant replaced this argument with a completely different, anti-Cartesian argument that there should be no puzzle about the possibility of interaction between mind and body because the differences in their appearances that Descartes and his followers had assumed to stand in the way of interaction might be no more than different appearances of a single sort of underlying reality (B427–8). However, Kant did not confine himself to this change, but took the opportunity to rewrite and simplify the whole chapter on the paralogisms. Except for his substantive change in the fourth paralogism, this is the only part of his revisions that lives up to his pretense of merely improving his manner of exposition (B xxxvii).

Beyond the "Paralogisms of Pure Reason," Kant made no further significant changes for the second edition. We do not know if this means that he remained completely content with the remainder of the book, or only that he ran out of time and patience. His continuing restatement and refinement in the second and third *Critiques* of many important doctrines touched upon in the remainder of the book, such as his theory of the postulates of practical reason and the regulative use of the ideas of reason, suggest the latter rather than the former explanation.

In sum, then, the bulk of Kant's changes in the second edition grew out of his desire to refine and defend his transcendental idealism by showing that only it could explain our *a priori* knowledge while at the same time arguing that it was completely compatible with the real existence of external objects. Beyond this, Kant wanted to emphasize the positive role of reason in the practical rather than theoretical sphere, and he continued to try to find a clear and adequate deduction of the categories. These concerns led him to revise substantially his introduction, the "Transcendental Aesthetic," and the chapter on phenomena and noumena, as well as to revise completely his preface, the "Transcendental Deduction" of the categories, and the "Paralogisms of Pure Reason."

Note on translation

This is an entirely new translation of the *Critique of Pure Reason*. Our intention in producing this translation has been to try to give the reader of the translation an experience as close as possible to that of the reader of the German original. The criterion for success in this intention is that as much interpretative work be left for the reader of the translation as is left for the reader of the original. This intention has dictated a number of our choices.

Obviously it has required as much consistency as possible in the translation of Kant's terminology; to the extent possible, we have always used the same English word for any philosophically significant German word, and where a single English word has had to stand duty for several German words, we have noted this fact. This situation typically arises when Kant uses both a germanic and a latinate word that would be translated into English by the same word, e.g., "*Gegenstand*" and "*Object*," both of which are translated into English as "object." In some such cases it may be a matter of interpretation whether Kant means precisely the same thing or not, so we have preserved the information about his usage by marking the Latinate member of the pair in the footnotes, but have not imposed any interpretation of the distinction in the text.

Other obvious consequences of our underlying intention include the preservation of Kant's sentences as wholes, even where considerations of readability might have suggested breaking them up, and the preservation of ambiguous and obscure constructions in Kant's original text wherever possible. The latter decision means that we have refrained from accepting emendations to the German text as long as we believe some sense can be made of the unemended original, even if a proposed emendation makes easier sense out of a given passage. In those cases where we do accept emendations, we have not cited authorities earlier than Benno Erdmann's edition of the *Critique* in the *Akademie* edition (1911), cited as "Erdmann." This means that we have not reproduced the ascriptions of emendations going back to nineteenth-century editors that decorate the pages of the edition by Raymund Schmidt (1926, 1930), which was the basis for Norman Kemp Smith's English translation (1929, 1933). Our decision also means that where Kant's location of the adverbial phrase "*a priori*," which he always treats as a Latin borrowing rather than a naturalized latinate German term, is ambiguous between an adverbial modification of a verb and an adjectival modification of a noun, we have tried to leave it ambiguous, although we could not always do so.

The biggest issue that we faced, however, was how to present the variations between the first (1781 or "A") and second (1787 or "B") editions of the *Critique*. Here too our underlying intention eventually dictated a different approach from that adopted by either Erdmann or Schmidt and Kemp Smith. Erdmann treated A and B as two separate works, publishing in Volume 3 of the *Akademie* edition B in its entirety, followed by a separate edition in Volume 4 of A up through the point after which Kant made no further revisions (the "Paralogisms of Pure Reason"). This approach makes it difficult for the reader to compare particular passages in A and B. Schmidt and Kemp Smith also regarded B as the definitive text, but presented a single text that always follows the text of B on the main part of the page and relegates modified or deleted passages from A to their notes, except where Kant rewrote chapters or sections of the book in their entirety, in which case the version from A was presented in the text followed by the version from B. This often makes it difficult for the reader to follow the text, and makes it particularly difficult for the reader to get a clear sense of how the first edition read. In order to avoid this problem, we have presented both versions of those sections of the book that Kant rewrote extensively as well as completely: thus, we present two versions of the introduction, the "Transcendental Aesthetic," and the chapter on the "Distinction between Phenomena and Noumena" as well as two versions of the preface, "Transcendental Deduction," and "Paralogisms." But in order to make comparison between the two editions easier than Erdmann made it, we have also provided the pagination of both editions for all passages that Kant preserved intact or largely intact from the first edition, even in those chapters that he rewrote extensively although not completely for the second, and have noted the changes that Kant made in our footnotes. Where Kant made only minor changes in a section, we have followed the practice of Schmidt and Kemp Smith by preferring B in our main text and noting divergences in A in our footnotes (new material inserted in B is enclosed in angled brackets). In this way, we hope to make it easy for the reader to remain clearly aware of the differences between the two editions without treating them as if they were two unrelated works, as Erdmann's approach does.

Our view that we should avoid imposing our own interpretation of the *Critique* as much as possible has not meant that we should avoid referring our readers to materials that might help them in the interpretation of the text. Instead, we have provided two sorts of references that may help in the interpretation of the text. The first sort of material is Kant's notes in his own copy of the first edition of the *Critique*, which were published by Benno Erdmann in 1881 (Benno Erdmann; *Nachträge zu Kants Kritik der reinen Vernunft* [Kiel: Lipsius & Tischer, 1881]). These notes range from mere cross-outs to changes in words or phrases to extensive comments or paragraphs. Schmidt and Kemp Smith noted those places where Kant had changed a couple of words, but omitted all the rest. We have presented all of the material that Erdmann recorded in our footnotes, following Erdmann's description of the location of the notes as closely as possible. In this way, the reader can have the experience not merely of reading and interpreting Kant's original text of the first edition but that of reading Kant's own copy of that edition. (No annotated copy of the second edition has ever been known to exist.) These notes are cited thus: "E" (for Erdmann), followed by Erdmann's roman numeral and the page number in his edition; then the volume and page number of their appearance in the *Akademie* edition. Second, we have provided cross-references to many of Kant's notes in the *Handschriftliche Nachlaß* ("hand-written remains") transcribed in volumes 14 through 23 of the *Akademie* edition. Obviously we could not index all of these notes, but have tried to give references to those that throw light on specific passages in the *Critique*, especially those that seem to be either preliminary drafts or subsequent reworkings of specific passages. Since this material does not appear in the original editions of the *Critique* or Kant's own copy of the first edition, we have not referred to it, let alone reproduced it, in our footnotes on Kant's pages, but have put the references to it in our endnotes.

Our translation has not been produced from any single German edition. As do most contemporary scholars, we began by working from the edition of the *Critique* by Raymund Schmidt in the *Philosophische Bibliothek*. As we worked on the translation, however, we realized that Schmidt's edition is the least conservative twentieth-century edition of Kant's text, not only modernizing spelling and punctuation more than others do but also accepting the largest number of editorial emendations to the text. We thus began to check our translation against the three other main twentieth-century editions of the text, namely those of Erdmann in the *Akademie* edition, of Wilhelm Weischedel in the Insel Verlag, subsequently Suhrkamp Verlag *Studienausgabe* (1956), and of Ingeborg Heidemann in the Reclam *Studienausgabe* (1966). Of these, the Heidemann edition appears closest to the original editions, though it does modernize spelling. Finally, we have checked the translation against facsimiles of the original editions.

Here we can add a word about our choice of typography. The original editions were set primarily in *Fraktur* (gothic type). Latin words, including such frequently used words as "*a priori*" and "*a posteriori*" as well as "*phenomena*" and "*noumena*," which Kant did not regard as naturalized into German, were set in roman type. Emphasis was indicated, not by the modern English method of italics nor by the modern German method of *Sperrdruck* (spaced type), but by the use of larger and thicker *Fraktur* type than is used elsewhere (boldface or *Fettdruck*). To try to recreate the appearance of Kant's pages, we have therefore used bold type for emphasis and italics for the foreign words that Kant had printed in roman type. In the original, a range of *Fettdruck* sizes was used, which makes it sometimes quite easy and sometimes very difficult to tell whether a word is being emphasized – this is a source of disagreement in modern editions about which words should be emphasized. We have not tried to reproduce this range of type sizes. We should also note that Kant sometimes but not always uses *Fettdruck* to indicate that a word or sentence is being mentioned rather than used. Where he does so, we use bold type; where he does not, we have introduced quotation marks.

Now for a word about our use of previous English translations. We have followed Kemp Smith in many of his choices for translation of Kant's technical terminology, for the simple reason that Kemp Smith usually (but not always) adopted the wise procedure of letting Kant's own Latin equivalents for his German technical terms determine the English translation. (No doubt many of Kemp Smith's turns of phrase also reverberated in our minds after years of using his translation.) Nevertheless, the present work is by no means a revision of Kemp Smith, and it departs from his translation systematically and consistently throughout on many points. We have always worked directly from German texts, consulting Kemp Smith from time to time but also consulting the earlier English translations as well. Of these, we found that by Friedrich Max Müller (1881) more helpful than that by J. M. D. Meikeljohn (1855). Of surprising help was a full translation of only the second edition done by Francis Haywood (second edition, 1848). This is the earliest English translation of the *Critique* we have been able to discover, and often proved helpful because, like us, Haywood clearly made literalness in translation his primary objective.

Bibliography

In this bibliography, we list the German editions of the text of the *Critique of Pure Reason* that we have consulted, the earlier English translations we have consulted, and a selection of scholarly works including discussion of the genesis and text of the *Critique*. The last selection is not intended as even a selective guide to philosophically interesting and useful works on the interpretation of the *Critique*.

1. German texts

KANT, IMMANUEL. *Critik der reinen Vernunft*. Riga: Johann Friedrich Hartknoch, 1781. Facsimile edition: London: Routledge/Thoemmes Press, 1994.

KANT, IMMANUEL. *Critik der reinen Vernunft*. Zweyte hin und wieder verbesserte Auflage. Riga: Johann Friedrich Hartknoch, 1787. Facsimile edition: London: Routledge/Thoemmes Press, 1994.

KANT, IMMANUEL. *Kritik der reinen Vernunft. Zweite Auflage* 1787. [Edited by Benno Erdmann.] *Kant's gesammelte Schriften*, herausgegeben von der Königlich Preußischen Akademie der Wissenschaften, Band III. Berlin: Georg Reimer, 1911.

KANT, IMMANUEL. *Kritik der reinen Vernunft (1. Aufl.)*. [Edited by Benno Erdmann.] *Kant's gesammelte Schriften*, herausgegeben von der Königlich Preußischen Akademie der Wissenschaften, Band IV. Berlin: Georg Reimer, 1911. Pp. 1–252.

KANT, IMMANUEL. *Kritik der reinen Vernunft. Nach der ersten und zweiten Original-Ausgabe*. Herausgegeben von Raymund Schmidt. Dritte Auflage, mit einer Bibliographie von Heiner Klemme. Hamburg: Felix Meiner Verlag, 1990. (First and second editions, 1926, 1930.)

KANT, IMMANUEL. *Kritik der reinen Vernunft*. Herausgegeben von Wilhelm Weischedel. Werkausgabe, Bände III, IV. Frankfurt am Main: Suhrkamp, 1974. (Originally Wiesbaden: Insel Verlag, 1956.)

KANT, IMMANUEL. *Kritik der reinen Vernunft*. Herausgegeben von Ingeborg Heidemann. Stuttgart: Philipp Reclam Jun., 1966.

2. English translations

KANT, IMMANUEL. *Critick of Pure Reason*. Second edition with notes and explanation of terms. Translated by Francis Haywood. London: William Pickering, 1848.

KANT, IMMANUEL. *Critique of Pure Reason*. Translated by J. M. D. Meikeljohn, introduction by A. D. Lindsay. London: J. M. Dent, 1934. (Original edition: 1855.)

KANT, IMMANUEL. *Critique of Pure Reason. A revised and expanded translation based on Meikeljohn*. Edited by Vasilis Politis. London: J. M. Dent, 1993.

KANT, IMMANUEL. *Critique of Pure Reason*. Translated by F. Max Müller.

Garden City: Anchor Books, 1966. (Original edition: London: Macmillan, 1881.)

Immanuel Kant's Critique of Pure Reason. Translated by Norman Kemp Smith. Second impression with corrections. London: Macmillan, 1933. (First edition, 1929.)

3. Selected secondary sources

AL-AZM, SADIK. *The Origins of Kant's Arguments in the Antinomies.* Oxford: Oxford University Press, 1972.

ALLISON, HENRY E. *Kant's Transcendental Idealism: An Interpretation and Defense.* New Haven: Yale University Press, 1983.

AMERIKS, KARL. *Kant's Theory of Mind: An Analysis of the Paralogisms of Pure Reason.* Oxford: Clarendon Press, 1982.

ARNOLDT, EMIL. *"Die äussere Entstehung und die Abfassungszeit der Kritik der reinen Vernunft."* In Arnoldt, *Gesammmelte Schriften,* Band IV. Berlin: Bruno Cassirer, 1908. Pp. 119–225.

BECK, LEWIS WHITE. *Studies in the Philosophy of Kant.* Indianapolis: Bobbs-Merrill, 1965.

Early German Philosophy: Kant and his Predecessors. Cambridge, Mass.: Harvard University Press, 1969.

BEISER, FREDERICK C. *The Fate of Reason: German Philosophy from Kant to Fichte.* Cambridge, Mass.: Harvard University Press, 1987.

BENNETT, JONATHAN F. *Kant's Analytic.* Cambridge: Cambridge University Press, 1966.

Kant's Dialectic. Cambridge: Cambridge University Press, 1974.

BIRD, GRAHAM. *Kant's Theory of Knowledge: An Outline of One Central Argument in the Critique of Pure Reason.* London: Routledge & Kegan Paul, 1962.

BRANDT, REINHARD. *The Table of Judgment: Critique of Pure Reason A67–76; B92–101.* Translated by Eric Watkins. North American Kant Society Studies in Philosophy, Volume 4. Atascadero, Cal.: Ridgeview, 1995.

BROAD, C. D. *Kant: An Introduction.* Ed. C. Lewy. Cambridge: Cambridge University Press, 1978.

CARL, WOLFGANG. *Der schweigende Kant: Die Entwürfe zu einer Deduktion der Kategorien vor 1781.* Göttingen: Vandenhoeck & Ruprecht, 1989.

COHEN, HERMANN. *Kants Theorie der Erfahrung.* 2nd. ed. Berlin: F. Dümmler, 1885.

DRYER, DOUGLAS P. *Kant's Solution for Verification in Metaphysics.* London: Allen & Unwin, 1966.

ERDMANN, BENNO. *Kant's Kriticismus in der ersten und zweiten Auflage der Kritik der reinen Vernunft. Eine historische Untersuchung.* Leipzig: Leopold Voss, 1878.

Nachträge zu Kants Kritik der reinen Vernunft. Kiel: Lipsius & Tischer, 1881.

Beiträge zur Geschichte und Revision des Textes von Kants Kritik der reinen Vernunft. Berlin, 1900.

FALKENSTEIN, LORNE. *Kant's Intuitionism: A Commentary on the Transcendental Aesthetic.* Toronto: University of Toronto Press, 1995.

FRIEDMAN, MICHAEL. *Kant and the Exact Sciences.* Cambridge, Mass.: Harvard University Press, 1992.

GUYER, PAUL. *Kant and the Claims of Knowledge.* Cambridge: Cambridge University Press, 1987.

HÄRING, THEODOR. *Der Duisburg'sche Nachlaß und Kants Kritizismums um 1775.* Tübingen, 1910.

HENRICH, DIETER. *Der Ontologische Gottesbeweis.* 2nd. ed. Tübingen: J. C. B. Mohr (Paul Siebeck), 1960.

The Unity of Reason: Essays on Kant's Philosophy. Edited by Richard Velkley. Cambridge, Mass.: Harvard University Press, 1994.

HINSKE, NORBERT. *Kants Weg zur Transzendentalphilosophie: Der dreißigjährige Kant.* Stuttgart: Kohlhammer, 1970.

HOLZHEY, HELMUT. *Kants Erfahrungsbegriff: Quellengeschichtliche und bedeutungsanalytische Untersuchungen.* Basel: Schwabe, 1970.

KITCHER, PATRICIA. *Kant's Transcendental Psychology.* New York: Oxford University Press, 1990.

KLEMME, HEINER F. *Kants Philosophie des Subjekts: Systematische und entwicklungs geschichtliche Untersuchungen zum Verhältnis von Selbstbewußtsein und Selbsterkenntnis.* Kant-Forschungen, Band 7. Hamburg: Felix Meiner, 1996.

KOPPER, JOACHIM AND RUDOLF MALTER, EDS. *Materialen zu Kants Kritik der reinen Vernunft.* Frankfurt a.M.: Suhrkamp, 1975.

KREIMENDAHL, LOTHAR. *Kant – Der Durchbruch von 1769.* Köln: Dinter, 1990.

LANDAU, ALBERT, EDITOR. *Rezensionen zur Kantischen Philosophie.* Band I: 1781–1787. Bebra: Albert Landau, 1990.

LONGUENESSE, BÉATRICE. *Kant et la pouvoir de juger.* Paris: Presses Universitaires de France, 1993.

MELNICK, ARTHUR. *Kant's Analogies of Experience.* Chicago: University of Chicago Press, 1973.

Space, Time and Thought in Kant. Dordrecht: Kluwer, 1989.

PATON, H. J. *Kant's Metaphysic of Experience.* 2 vols. London: Allen & Unwin, 1936.

PRAUSS, GEROLD. *Erscheinung bei Kant.* Berlin: Walter de Gruyter, 1971.

REICH, KLAUS. *The Completeness of Kant's Table of Judgments.* Trans. Jane Kneller and Michael Losonsky. Stanford: Stanford University Press, 1992.

SALA, GIOVANNI. "Bausteine zur Entstehungsgeschichte der Kritik der reinen Vernunft." *Kant-Studien* **78** (1987): 153–69.

SCHULTZ, JOHANN. *An Exposition of Kant's Critique of Pure Reason.* Translated by James C. Morrison. Ottawa: University of Ottawa Press, 1995.

SMITH, A. H. *Kantian Studies.* Oxford: Clarendon Press, 1947.

SMITH, NORMAN KEMP. *A Commentary to Kant's "Critique of Pure Reason."* Second edition. London: Macmillan, 1923.

STRAWSON, P. F. *The Bounds of Sense: An Essay on Kant's Critique of Pure Reason.* London: Methuen, 1966.

THÖLE, BERNHARD. *Kant und das Problem der Gesetzmässigkeit der Natur.* Berlin: Walter de Gruyter, 1991.

TONELLI, GIORGIO. *Kant's Critique of Pure Reason within the Tradition of*

Modern Logic. Edited by David H. Chandler. Hildesheim: Georg Olms, 1994.

TUSCHLING, BURKHARD, ED. *Probleme der "Kritik der reinen Vernunft": Kant-Tagung Marburg 1981.* Berlin: Walter de Gruyter, 1984.

VAIHINGER, HANS. *Kommentar zur Kritik der reinen Vernunft.* 2 vols. Stuttgart: W. Spemann, 1881, and Union Deutsche Verlagsgesellschaft, 1892.

VLEESCHAUWER, HERMAN-JEAN DE. *La déduction transcendentale dans l'oeuvre de Kant.* 3 vols. Antwerp, Paris, The Hague: De Sikkel, Champion, and Martinus Nijhoff, 1934–37.

The Development of Kantian Thought. Translated by A. R. C. Duncan. Edinburgh: Thos. Nelson, 1962.

VORLÄNDER, KARL. *Immanuel Kant: Der Mann und das Werk.* 2 vols. Leipzig: Felix Meiner, 1924.

WALSH, W. H. *Kant's Criticism of Metaphysics.* Edinburgh: University of Edinburgh Press, 1975.

WASHBURN, MICHAEL. "The Second Edition of the *Critique*: Toward an Understanding of its Nature and Genesis." *Kant-Studien* **66** (1975): 277–90.

WERKMEISTER, W. H. *Kant's Silent Decade.* Tallahasee: University Presses of Florida, 1981.

Kant: The Architectonic and Development of His Philosophy. LaSalle, Ill.: Open Court, 1980.

WOLFF, MICHAEL. *Die Vollständigkeit der kantischen Urteilstafel.* Frankfurt am Main: Klostermann, 1995.

WOLFF, ROBERT PAUL. *Kant's Theory of Mental Activity: A Commentary on the Transcendental Analytic of the Critique of Pure Reason.* Cambridge, Mass.: Harvard University Press, 1963.

Critique
of
Pure Reason

by

Immanuel Kant

Professor in Königsberg

Riga

Published by Johann Friedrich Hartknoch

1781

Critique
of
Pure Reason

by

Immanuel Kant

Professor in Königsberg
Member of the Royal Academy of Sciences in Berlin

Second edition, improved here and there

Riga

Johann Friedrich Hartknoch

1787

TABLE OF CONTENTS *ᵃ*

ᵃ This Table of Contents is the editors' expansion of the less detailed one provided by Kant in the first edition. The second edition contained no Table of Contents at all. A translation of Kant's own first-edition Table of Contents follows the two versions of the preface, corresponding to its original location.
ᵇ *Principien*
ᶜ *Principien*
ᵈ *Aufgabe*

Contents

---

a *Principien*

Contents

[a] *Verhältnisse*

Contents

[a] *Aufgaben*
[b] *Princip*

Contents

^{a} *Zusammensetzung*
^{b} transcendental prototype
^{c} *Principien*

Contents

II. Transcendental doctrine of method

Instauratio Magna. Praefatio

De nobis ipsis silemus: De re autem, quae agitur, petimus: ut homines eam non Opinionem, sed Opus esse cogitent; ac pro certo habeant, non Sectae nos alicuius, aut Placiti, sed utilitatis et amplitudinis humanae fundamenta moliri. Deinde ut suis commodis aequi . . . in commune consulant . . . et ipsi in partem veniant. Praeterea ut bene sperent, neque Instaurationem nostram ut quiddam infinitum et ultra mortale fingant, et animo concipiant; quum revera sit infiniti erroris finis et terminus legitimus.[a]

[a] This motto was added in the second edition:

Bacon of Verulam

The Great Instauration. Preface

Of our own person we will say nothing. But as to the subject matter with which we are concerned, we ask that men think of it not as an opinion but as a work; and consider it erected not for any sect of ours, or for our good pleasure, but as the foundation of human utility and dignity. Each individual equally, then, may reflect on it himself . . . for his own part . . . in the common interest. Further, each may well hope from our instauration that it claims nothing infinite, and nothing beyond what is mortal; for in truth it prescribes only the end of infinite errors, and this is a legitimate end.

To his Excellency,

the Royal Minister of State,

Baron von Zedlitz[1]

a Gracious Lord,

    To further for one's own part the growth of the sciences is to labor in your Excellency's own interest; for the former is most inwardly bound up with the latter, not only through the exalted post as a protector of the sciences, but also through the more intimate relationship*b* of a lover and an enlightened connoisseur. On this account, I avail myself of the only means within my capacity to show my gratitude for the gracious trust with which your Excellency honors me, as though that could con- tribute something to this aim.

    For someone who enjoys the life of speculation the approval of an enlightened and competent judge is, given his modest wishes, a powerful encouragement to toils whose utility is great, but distant, and hence it is wholly misjudged by vulgar eyes.

    To such a judge and to his gracious attention, I now dedicate this piece of writing; to his protection I commend all the remaining business of my literary vocation; and with deepest reverence I am,

Your Excellency's humble,
most obedient servant

Immanuel Kant

Königsberg: the 29th of March, 1781

---

a As in the first edition.
b *vertrautere Verhältnis*; this last word was added later, according to Kant's letter to Biester of 8 June 1781.

^a<Gracious Lord, ^{B V}

To further for one's own part the growth of the sciences is to labor in your Excellency's own interest; for the former is most inwardly bound up with the latter, not only through the exalted post as a protector of the sciences, but also through the more intimate relationship^b of a lover and an enlightened connoisseur. On this account, I avail myself of the only means within my capacity to show my gratitude for the gracious trust with which your Excellency honors me, as though that could contribute something to this aim.

To the same gracious attention with which Your Excellency has dig- ^{B vi} nified the first edition of this work, I dedicate also this second one, and at the same time all the remaining business of my literary vocation; and with deepest reverence I am,

Your Excellency's humble,
most obedient servant,

Immanuel Kant

Königsberg, the 23rd of April, 1787>

---

^a As in the second edition.
^b *vertrautere Verhältnis;* this last word was added later, according to Kant's letter to Biester of 8 June 1781.

Human reason has the peculiar fate in one species of its cognitions that it is burdened with questions which it cannot dismiss, since they are given to it as problems[b] by the nature of reason itself, but which it also cannot answer, since they transcend every capacity[c] of human reason.

Reason falls into this perplexity through no fault of its own. It begins from principles whose use is unavoidable in the course of experience and at the same time sufficiently warranted by it. With these principles it rises (as its nature also requires) ever higher, to more remote conditions. But since it becomes aware in this way that its business must always remain incomplete because the questions never cease, reason sees itself necessitated to take refuge in principles that overstep all possible use in experience, and yet seem so unsuspicious that even ordinary common sense agrees with them. But it thereby falls into obscurity and contradictions, from which it can indeed surmise that it must somewhere be proceeding on the ground of hidden errors; but it cannot discover them, for the principles on which it is proceeding, since they surpass the bounds of all experience, no longer recognize any touchstone of experience. The battlefield of these endless controversies is called **metaphysics.**

There was a time when metaphysics was called the **queen** of all the sciences, and if the will be taken for the deed, it deserved this title of honor, on account of the preeminent importance of its object. Now, in accordance with the fashion of the age, the queen proves despised on all sides; and the matron, outcast and forsaken, mourns like Hecuba: *Modo maxima rerum, tot generis natisque potens – nunc trahor exul, inops –* Ovid, *Metamorphoses.*[d]

In the beginning, under the administration of the **dogmatists,**[2] her rule was **despotic.** Yet because her legislation still retained traces of ancient barbarism, this rule gradually degenerated through internal wars into complete **anarchy;** and the skeptics,[3] a kind of nomads who abhor all permanent cultivation of the soil, shattered civil unity from time to

---

[a] As in the first edition. Kant wrote a new preface for the second edition, given below.
[b] *aufgegeben*
[c] *Vermögen*
[d] "Greatest of all by race and birth, I now am cast out, powerless" (Ovid, *Metamorphoses* 13:508–10).

time. But since there were fortunately only a few of them, they could not prevent the dogmatists from continually attempting to rebuild, though never according to a plan unanimously accepted among themselves. Once in recent times it even seemed as though an end would be put to all these controversies, and the lawfulness*a* of all the competing claims would be completely decided, through a certain **physiology** of the human understanding (by the famous Locke);[4] but it turned out that although the birth of the purported queen was traced to the rabble of common experience and her pretensions would therefore have been rightly rendered suspicious, nevertheless she still asserted her claims, because in fact this **genealogy** was attributed to her falsely; thus meta-

A X physics fell back into the same old worm-eaten **dogmatism,** and thus into the same position of contempt out of which the science was to have been extricated. Now after all paths (as we persuade ourselves) have been tried in vain, what rules is tedium and complete **indifferentism,**[5] the mother of chaos and night in the sciences, but at the same time also the origin, or at least the prelude, of their incipient transformation and enlightenment, when through ill-applied effort they have become obscure, confused, and useless.

For it is pointless to affect **indifference** with respect to such inquiries, to whose object human nature **cannot** be **indifferent.** Moreover, however much they may think to make themselves unrecognizable by exchanging the language of the schools for a popular style, these so-called **indifferentists,** to the extent that they think anything at all, always unavoidably fall back into metaphysical assertions, which they yet professed so much to despise. Nevertheless this indifference, occurring amid the flourishing of all sciences, and directed precisely at those sciences whose results*b* (if such are to be had at all) we could least do with-

A xi out, is a phenomenon deserving our attention and reflection. This is evidently the effect not of the thoughtlessness of our age, but of its ripened **power of judgment,*** which will no longer be put off with il-

---

* Now and again one hears complaints about the superficiality of our age's way of thinking, and about the decay of well-grounded science. Yet I do not see that those sciences whose grounds are well laid, such as mathematics, physics, etc., in the least deserve this charge; rather, they maintain their old reputation for well-groundedness, and in the case of natural science, even surpass it. This same spirit would also prove itself effective in other species of cognition if only care had first been taken to correct their principles.*c* In the absence of this, indifference, doubt, and finally strict criticism are rather proofs of a well-grounded way of thinking. Our age is the genuine age of **criticism,** to which

a *Rechtmässigkeit*
b *Kenntnisse*
c *Principien*

lusory knowledge, and which demands that reason should take on anew the most difficult of all its tasks, namely, that of self-knowledge,[a] and to institute a court of justice, by which reason may secure its rightful claims while dismissing all its groundless pretensions, and this not by mere decrees but according to its own eternal and unchangeable laws; A xii and this court is none other than the **critique of pure reason** itself.[6]

Yet by this I do not understand a critique of books and systems, but a critique of the faculty of reason in general, in respect of all the cognitions after which reason[b] might strive **independently of all experience,** and hence the decision about the possibility or impossibility of a metaphysics in general, and the determination of its sources, as well as its extent and boundaries, all, however, from principles.[c]

It is on this path, the only one left, that I have set forth, and I flatter myself that in following it I have succeeded in removing all those errors that have so far put reason into dissension with itself in its nonexperiential use. I have not avoided reason's questions by pleading the incapacity of human reason as an excuse; rather I have completely specified these questions according to principles,[d] and after discovering the point where reason has misunderstood itself, I have resolved them to reason's full satisfaction. To be sure, the answer to these questions has not A xiii turned out just as dogmatically enthusiastic lust for knowledge might have expected; for the latter could not be satisfied except through magical powers in which I am not an expert. Yet this was also not the intent of our reason's natural vocation; and the duty of philosophy was to abolish the semblance arising from misinterpretation, even if many prized and beloved delusions have to be destroyed in the process. In this business I have made comprehensiveness my chief aim in view, and I make bold to say that there cannot be a single metaphysical problem that has not been solved here, or at least to the solution of which the key has not been provided. In fact pure reason is such a perfect unity that if its principle[e] were insufficient for even a single one of the questions that are set

---

everything must submit. **Religion** through its **holiness** and **legislation** through its **majesty** commonly seek to exempt themselves from it. But in this way they excite a just suspicion against themselves, and cannot lay claim to that unfeigned respect that reason grants only to that which has been able to withstand its free and public examination.

---

[a] *Selbsterkenntnis*
[b] *sie.* To agree with "faculty of reason" (*das Vernunftvermögen*) the pronoun should have been neuter; perhaps Kant was taking the antecedent to be "reason" (*die Vernunft*).
[c] *Principien*
[d] *Principien*
[e] *Princip*

for it by its own nature, then this [principle] might as well be discarded, because then it also would not be up to answering any of the other questions with complete reliability.[7]

A xiv   While I am saying this I believe I perceive in the face of the reader an indignation mixed with contempt at claims that are apparently so pretentious and immodest; and yet they are incomparably more moderate than those of any author of the commonest program who pretends to prove the simple nature of the **soul** or the necessity of a first **beginning of the world.** For such an author pledges himself to extend human cognition beyond all bounds of possible experience, of which I humbly admit that this wholly surpasses my capacity; instead I have to do merely with reason itself and its pure thinking; to gain exhaustive acquaintance with them I need not seek far beyond myself, because it is in myself that I encounter them, and common logic already also gives me an example of how the simple acts of reason may be fully and systematically enumerated; only here the question is raised how much I may hope to settle with these simple acts if all the material and assistance of experience are taken away from me.

So much for the **completeness** in reaching **each** of the ends, and for the **comprehensiveness** in reaching **all** of them together, which ends are not proposed arbitrarily, but are set up for us by the nature of cognition itself, as the **matter** of our critical investigation.

A xv   Furthermore **certainty** and **clarity,** two things that concern the **form** of the investigation, are to be viewed as essential demands, which may rightly be made on the author who ventures upon so slippery an undertaking.

As far as **certainty** is concerned, I have myself pronounced the judgment that in this kind of inquiry it is in no way allowed to **hold opinions,** and that anything that even looks like an hypothesis is a forbidden commodity, which should not be put up for sale even at the lowest price but must be confiscated as soon as it is discovered. For every cognition that is supposed to be certain *a priori* proclaims that it wants to be held for absolutely necessary, and even more is this true of a determination of all pure cognitions *a priori*, which is to be the standard and thus even the example of all apodictic (philosophical) certainty. Whether I have performed what I have just pledged in that respect remains wholly to the judgment of the reader, since it is appropriate for an author only to present the grounds, but not to judge about their effect on his judges. But in order that he should not inadvertently be the cause of weaken-

A xvi   ing his own arguments, the author may be permitted to note himself those places that, even though they pertain only to the incidental end of the work, may be the occasion for some mistrust, in order that he may in a timely manner counteract the influence that even the reader's slightest reservation on this point may have on his judgment over the chief end.

I am acquainted with no investigations more important for getting to the bottom of that faculty we call the understanding, and at the same time for the determination of the rules and boundaries of its use, than those I have undertaken in the second chapter of the Transcendental Analytic, under the title **Deduction of the Pure Concepts of the Understanding;** they are also the investigations that have cost me the most, but I hope not unrewarded, effort. This inquiry, which goes rather deep, has two sides. One side refers to the objects of the pure understanding, and is supposed to demonstrate and make comprehensible the objective validity of its concepts *a priori;* thus it belongs essentially to my ends. The other side deals with the pure understanding itself, concerning its possibility and the powers of cognition on which it itself rests; thus it considers it in a subjective relation, and although this ex-   A xvii position is of great importance in respect of my chief end, it does not belong essentially to it; because the chief question always remains: "What and how much can understanding and reason cognize free of all experience?" and not: "How is the **faculty of thinking** itself possible?"[8] Since the latter question is something like the search for the cause of a given effect, and is therefore something like a hypothesis (although, as I will elsewhere take the opportunity to show, this is not in fact how matters stand), it appears as if I am taking the liberty in this case of expressing an **opinion,** and that the reader might therefore be free to hold another **opinion.** In view of this I must remind the reader in advance that even in case my subjective deduction does not produce the complete conviction that I expect, the objective deduction that is my primary concern would come into its full strength, on which what is said at pages [A] 92–3 should even be sufficient by itself.

Finally, as regards **clarity,**[a] the reader has a right to demand first **discursive** (logical) **clarity, through concepts,** but then also **intuitive** (aesthetic) clarity, through **intuitions,** that is, through examples or   A xviii other illustrations *in concreto.* I have taken sufficient care for the former. That was essential to my undertaking but was also the contingent cause of the fact that I could not satisfy the second demand, which is less strict but still fair. In the progress of my labor I have been almost constantly undecided how to deal with this matter. Examples and illustrations always appeared necessary to me, and hence actually appeared in their proper place in my first draft. But then I looked at the size of my task and the many objects with which I would have to do, and I became aware that this alone, treated in a dry, merely **scholastic** manner, would

---

[a] *Deutlichkeit*

suffice to fill an extensive work; thus I found it inadvisable to swell it further with examples and illustrations, which are necessary only for a **popular** aim, especially since this work could never be made suitable for popular use, and real experts in this science do not have so much need for things to be made easy for them; although this would always be agreeable, here it could also have brought with it something counter-productive. The Abbé Terrasson says that if the size of a book is mea-sured not by the number of pages but by the time needed to understand it, then it can be said of many a book **that it would be much shorter if it were not so short.**⁹ But on the other hand, if we direct our view toward the intelligibility of a whole of speculative cognition that is wide-ranging and yet is connected in principle,ᵃ we could with equal right say that **many a book would have been much clearer if it had not been made quite so clear.** For the aids to clarity helpᵇ in the **parts** but often confuse in the **whole,** since the reader cannot quickly enough attain a survey of the whole; and all their bright colors paint over and make unrecognizable the articulation or structure of the system, which yet matters most when it comes to judging its unity and soundness.¹⁰

A xix

It can, as it seems to me, be no small inducement for the reader to unite his effort with that of the author, when he has the prospect of car-rying out, according to the outline given above, a great and important piece of work, and that in a complete and lasting way. Now meta-physics, according to the concepts we will give of it here, is the only one of all the sciences that may promise that little but unified effort, and that indeed in a short time, will complete it in such a way that nothing remains to posterity except to adapt it in a **didactic** manner to its in-tentions, yet without being able to add to its content in the least. For it is nothing but the **inventory** of all we possess through **pure reason,** or-dered systematically. Nothing here can escape us, because what reason brings forth entirely out of itself cannot be hidden, but is brought to light by reason itself as soon as reason's common principleᶜ has been dis-covered. The perfect unity of this kind of cognition, and the fact that it arises solely out of pure concepts without any influence that would ex-tend or increase it from experience or even **particular intuition,** which would lead to a determinate experience, make this unconditioned com-pleteness not only feasible but also necessary. *Tecum habita, et noris quam sit tibi curta supellex.* – Persius.ᵈ

A xx

A xxi

Such a system of pure (speculative) reason I hope myself to deliver

---

ᵃ *Princip*

ᵇ Kant's text reads *"fehlen"* (are missing). We follow Erdmann, reading *helfen*.

ᶜ *Princip*

ᵈ "Dwell in your own house, and you will know how simple your possessions are" (Persius, *Satires* 4:52).

under the title **Metaphysics of Nature,** which will be not half so extensive but will be incomparably richer in content than this critique, which had first to display the sources and conditions of its possibility, and needed to clear and level a ground that was completely overgrown. Here I expect from my reader the patience and impartiality of a **judge,** but there I will expect the cooperative spirit and assistance of a **fellow worker;** for however completely the **principles**[a] of the system may be expounded in the critique, the comprehensiveness of the system itself requires also that no **derivative** concepts should be lacking, which, however, cannot be estimated *a priori* in one leap, but must be gradually sought out; likewise, just as in the former the whole **synthesis** of concepts has been exhausted, so in the latter it would be additionally demanded that the same thing should take place in respect of their **analysis,** which would be easy and more entertainment than labor.

I have only a few more things to remark with respect to the book's printing. Since the beginning of the printing was somewhat delayed, I was able to see only about half the proof sheets, in which I have come upon a few printing errors, though none that confuse the sense except the one occurring at page [A] 379, fourth line from the bottom, where **specific** should be read in place of **skeptical.** The Antinomy of Pure Reason, from page [A] 425 to page [A] 461, is arranged in the manner of a table, so that everything belonging to the **thesis** always continues on the left side and what belongs to the **antithesis** on the right side, which I did in order to make it easier to compare proposition and counter-proposition with one another.

A xxii

[a] *Principien*

Preface to the second edition[a]

Whether or not the treatment of the cognitions belonging to the concern of reason travels the secure course of a science is something which can soon be judged by its success. If after many preliminaries and preparations are made, a science gets stuck as soon as it approaches its end, or if in order to reach this end it must often go back and set out on a new path; or likewise if it proves impossible for the different co-workers to achieve unanimity as to the way in which they should pursue[b] their common aim; then we may be sure that such a study is merely groping about, that it is still far from having entered upon the secure course of a science; and it is already a service to reason if we can possibly find that path for it, even if we have to give up as futile much of what was included in the end previously formed without deliberation.

That from the earliest times **logic** has traveled this secure course can be seen from the fact that since the time of Aristotle it has not had to go a single step backwards, unless we count the abolition of a few dispensable subtleties or the more distinct determination of its presentation, which improvements belong more to the elegance than to the security of that science. What is further remarkable about logic is that until now it has also been unable to take a single step forward, and therefore seems to all appearance to be finished and complete. For if some moderns have thought to enlarge it by interpolating **psychological** chapters about our different cognitive powers (about imagination, wit), or **metaphysical** chapters about the origin of cognition or the different kinds of certainty in accordance with the diversity of objects[c] (about idealism, skepticism, etc.), or **anthropological** chapters about our prejudice (about their causes and remedies), then this proceeds only from their ignorance of the peculiar nature of this science. It is not an improvement but a deformation of the sciences when their boundaries are allowed to run over into one another; the boundaries of logic, however, are determined quite precisely by the fact that logic is the science that exhaustively presents and strictly proves nothing but the formal

---

[a] This new preface, so entitled, replaces the preface from the first edition.

[b] Kant's text reads "*erfolgt*" (result or ensue), which does not make sense here because it is an intransitive verb; we follow Grillo in reading *verfolgt*.

[c] *Objecte*

rules of all thinking (whether this thinking be empirical or *a priori*, whatever origin or object*ª* it may have, and whatever contingent or natural obstacles it may meet with in our minds).

For the advantage that has made it so successful logic has solely its own limitation to thank, since it is thereby justified in abstracting – is indeed obliged to abstract – from all objects*ᵇ* of cognition and all the distinctions between them; and in logic, therefore, the understanding has to do with nothing further than itself and its own form. How much more difficult, naturally, must it be for reason to enter upon the secure path of a science if it does not have to do merely with itself, but has to deal with objects*ᶜ* too; hence logic as a propaedeutic constitutes only the outer courtyard, as it were, to the sciences; and when it comes to information, a logic may indeed be presupposed in judging about the latter, but its acquisition must be sought in the sciences properly and objectively so called.

Insofar as there is to be reason in these sciences, something in them must be cognized *a priori*, and this cognition can relate to its object in either of two ways, either merely **determining** the object and its concept (which must be given from elsewhere), or else also **making** the object **actual**. The former is **theoretical**, the latter **practical** cognition of reason. In both the **pure** part, the part in which reason determines its object*ᵈ* wholly *a priori*, must be expounded all by itself, however much or little it may contain, and that part that comes from other sources must not be mixed up with it; for it is bad economy to spend blindly whatever comes in without being able later, when the economy comes to a standstill, to distinguish the part of the revenue that can cover the expenses from the part that must be cut.

Mathematics and **physics** are the two theoretical cognitions of reason that are supposed to determine their **objects***ᵉ* *a priori*, the former entirely purely, the latter at least in part purely but also following the standards of sources of cognition other than reason.

Mathematics has, from the earliest times to which the history of human reason reaches, in that admirable people the Greeks, traveled the secure path of a science. Yet it must not be thought that it was as easy for it as for logic – in which reason has to do only with itself – to find that royal path, or rather itself to open it up; rather, I believe that mathematics was left groping about for a long time (chiefly among the Egyptians), and that its transformation is to be ascribed to a **revolution**, brought about by the happy inspiration of a single man in an at-

B x

B xi

ª *Object*
ᵇ *Objecte*
ᶜ *Objecte*
ᵈ *Object*
ᵉ *Objecte*

tempt from which the road to be taken onward could no longer be missed, and the secure course of a science was entered on and prescribed for all time and to an infinite extent. The history of this revolution in the way of thinking – which was far more important than the discovery of the way around the famous Cape[11]– and of the lucky one who brought it about, has not been preserved for us. But the legend handed down to us by Diogenes Laertius – who names the reputed inventor of the smallest elements of geometrical demonstrations, even of those that, according to common judgment, stand in no need of proof – proves that the memory of the alteration wrought by the discovery of this new path in its earliest footsteps must have seemed exceedingly important to mathematicians, and was thereby rendered unforgettable. A new light broke upon the first person who demonstrated the isosceles[a] triangle (whether he was called "Thales" or had some other name).[12] For he found that what he had to do was

B xii   not to trace what he saw in this figure, or even trace its mere concept, and read off, as it were, from the properties of the figure; but rather that he had to produce the latter from what he himself thought into the object and presented (through construction) according to *a priori* concepts, and that in order to know something securely *a priori* he had to ascribe to the thing nothing except what followed necessarily from what he himself had put into it in accordance with its concept.

It took natural science much longer to find the highway of science; for it is only about one and a half centuries since the suggestion of the ingenious Francis Bacon partly occasioned this discovery and partly further stimulated it, since one was already on its tracks – which discovery, therefore, can just as much be explained by a sudden revolution in the way of thinking. Here I will consider natural science only insofar as it is grounded on **empirical** principles.[b]

When Galileo[13] rolled balls of a weight chosen by himself down an inclined plane, or when Torricelli[14] made the air bear a weight that he had previously thought to be equal to that of a known column of water, or when in a later time Stahl[15] changed metals into calx[c] and then

B xiii   changed the latter back into metal by first removing something and

---

[a] Kant's text reads "*gleichseitig*" (equilateral); but on the basis of his correction in a letter to Schütz of 25 June 1787 (10:466), he appears to have meant "*gleichschenklig*" (isosceles).

[b] *Principien*

[c] *Kalk.* Kemp Smith translates this as "oxides," but that is anachronistic; prior to the chemical revolution of Priestley and Lavoisier, the calx was conceived to be what was left of a metal after its phlogiston had been driven off; only later was it discovered that this process was actually one of oxidation.

then putting it back again,* a light dawned on all those who study nature. They comprehended that reason has insight only into what it itself produces according to its own design; that it must take the lead with principles[a] for its judgments according to constant laws and compel nature to answer its questions, rather than letting nature guide its movements by keeping reason, as it were, in leading-strings; for otherwise accidental observations, made according to no previously designed plan, can never connect up into a necessary law, which is yet what reason seeks and requires. Reason, in order to be taught by nature, must approach nature with its principles[b] in one hand, according to which alone the agreement among appearances can count as laws, and, in the other hand, the experiments thought out in accordance with these principles[c] – yet in order to be instructed by nature not like a pupil, who has recited to him whatever the teacher wants to say, but like an appointed judge who compels witnesses to answer the questions he puts to them. Thus even physics owes the advantageous revolution in its way of thinking to the inspiration that what reason would not be able to know of itself and has to learn from nature, it has to seek in the latter (though not merely ascribe to it) in accordance with what reason itself puts into nature. This is how natural science was first brought to the secure course of a science after groping about for so many centuries. | B xiv

Metaphysics – a wholly isolated speculative cognition of reason that elevates itself entirely above all instruction from experience, and that through mere concepts (not, like mathematics, through the application of concepts to intuition), where reason thus is supposed to be its own pupil – has up to now not been so favored by fate as to have been able to enter upon the secure course of a science, even though it is older than all other sciences, and would remain even if all the others were swallowed up by an all-consuming barbarism. For in it reason continuously gets stuck, even when it claims *a priori* insight (as it pretends) into those laws confirmed by the commonest experience. In metaphysics we have to retrace our path countless times, because we find that it does not lead where we want to go, and it is so far from reaching unanimity in the assertions of its adherents that it is rather a battlefield, and indeed one that appears to be especially determined for testing one's powers in mock combat; on this battlefield no combatant has ever gained the least | B xv

---

* Here I am not following exactly the thread of the history of the experimental   B xiii
method, whose first beginnings are also not precisely known.

[a] *Principien*
[b] *Principien*
[c] *Principien*

109

bit of ground, nor has any been able to base any lasting possession on his victory. Hence there is no doubt that up to now the procedure of metaphysics has been a mere groping, and what is the worst, a groping among mere concepts.

Now why is it that here the secure path of science still could not be found? Is it perhaps impossible? Why then has nature afflicted our reason with the restless striving for such a path, as if it were one of reason's most important occupations? Still more, how little cause have we to place trust in our reason if in one of the most important parts of our desire for knowledge it does not merely forsake us but even entices us with delusions and in the end betrays us! Or if the path has merely eluded us so far, what indications may we use that might lead us to hope that in renewed attempts we will be luckier than those who have gone before us?

I should think that the examples of mathematics and natural science, which have become what they now are through a revolution brought about all at once, were remarkable enough that we might reflect on the essential element in the change in the ways of thinking that has been so advantageous to them, and, at least as an experiment, imitate it insofar as their analogy with metaphysics, as rational cognition, might permit. Up to now it has been assumed that all our cognition must conform to the objects; but all attempts to find out something about them *a priori* through concepts that would extend our cognition have, on this presupposition, come to nothing. Hence let us once try whether we do not get farther with the problems of metaphysics by assuming that the objects*ᵃ* must conform to our cognition, which would agree better with the requested possibility of an *a priori* cognition of them, which is to establish something about objects*ᵇ* before they are given to us. This would be just like the first thoughts of Copernicus,¹⁶ who, when he did not make good progress in the explanation of the celestial motions if he assumed that the entire celestial host revolves around the observer, tried to see if he might not have greater success if he made the observer revolve and left the stars at rest. Now in metaphysics we can try in a similar way regarding the **intuition** of objects. If intuition has to conform to the constitution of the objects, then I do not see how we can know anything of them *a priori*; but if the object (as an object*ᶜ* of the senses) conforms to the constitution of our faculty of intuition, then I can very well represent this possibility to myself. Yet because I cannot stop with these intuitions, if they are to become cognitions, but must refer them as representations to something as their object and determine this ob-

BxVI

BxVII

ᵃ *Objecte*
ᵇ *Objecte*
ᶜ *Object*

ject through them, I can assume either that the concepts through which I bring about this determination also conform to the objects, and then I am once again in the same difficulty about how I could know anything about them *a priori*, or else I assume that the objects, or what is the same thing, the *experience* in which alone they can be cognized (as given objects) conforms to those concepts, in which case I immediately see an easier way out of the difficulty, since experience itself is a kind of cognition requiring the understanding, whose rule I have to presuppose in myself before any object is given to me, hence *a priori*, which rule is expressed in concepts *a priori*, to which all objects of experience must therefore necessarily conform, and with which they must agree. As for B xviii objects insofar as they are thought merely through reason, and necessarily at that, but that (at least as reason thinks them) cannot be given in experience at all – the attempt to think them (for they must be capable of being thought) will provide a splendid touchstone of what we assume as the altered method of our way of thinking, namely that we can cognize of things *a priori* only what we ourselves have put into them.*

This experiment succeeds as well as we could wish, and it promises to metaphysics the secure course of a science in its first part, where it concerns itself with concepts *a priori* to which the corresponding objects appropriate to them can be given in experience. For after this alteration in B xix our way of thinking we can very well explain the possibility of a cognition *a priori*, and what is still more, we can provide satisfactory proofs of the laws that are the *a priori* ground of nature, as the sum total of objects of experience – which were both impossible according to the earlier way of proceeding. But from this deduction of our faculty of cognizing *a pri-*

---

* This method, imitated from the method of those who study nature, thus con- B xviii sists in this: to seek the elements of pure reason in that **which admits of being confirmed or refuted through an experiment.** Now the propositions of pure reason, especially when they venture beyond all boundaries of possible experience, admit of no test by experiment with their **objects**[a] (as in natural science): thus to experiment will be feasible only with **concepts** and **principles** that we assume *a priori* by arranging the latter so that the same objects can be considered from two different sides, **on the one side** as objects of the senses and the understanding for experience, and **on the other** B xix **side** as objects that are merely thought at most for isolated reason striving beyond the bounds of experience. If we now find that there is agreement with the principle[b] of pure reason when things are considered from this twofold standpoint, but that an unavoidable conflict of reason with itself arises with a single standpoint, then the experiment decides for the correctness of that distinction.

[a] *Objecte*
[b] *Princip*

ori in the first part of metaphysics, there emerges a very strange result, and one that appears very disadvantageous to the whole purpose with which the second part of metaphysics concerns itself, namely that with this faculty we can never get beyond the boundaries of possible experience, which is nevertheless precisely the most essential occupation of this science. But herein lies just the experiment providing a checkup*ᵃ* on the truth of the result of that first assessment of our rational cognition *a priori*, namely that such cognition reaches appearances only, leaving the thing*ᵇ* in itself as something actual for itself but uncognized by us. For that which necessarily drives us to go beyond the boundaries of experience and all appearances is the **unconditioned,** which reason necessarily and with every right demands in things in themselves for everything that is conditioned, thereby demanding the series of conditions as something completed. Now if we find that on the assumption that our cognition from experience conforms to the objects as things in themselves, the unconditioned **cannot be thought at all without contradiction,** but that on the contrary, if we assume that our representation of things as they are given to us does not conform to these things as they are in themselves but rather that these objects as appearances conform to our way of representing, then **the contradiction disappears;** and consequently that the unconditioned must not be present*ᶜ* in things insofar as we are acquainted with them (insofar as they are given to us), but rather in things insofar as we are not acquainted with them, as things*ᵈ* in themselves: then this would show that what we initially assumed only as an experiment is well grounded.* Now after speculative reason has been denied all advance in this field of the supersensible, what still remains for us is to try whether there are not data in reason's practical data for determining that transcendent rational concept of the unconditioned, in such a way as to reach beyond the boundaries of all possible experience, in accordance with the wishes of metaphysics, cognitions *a priori* that are possible, but only from a practical standpoint. By

---

* This experiment of pure reason has much in common with what the **chemists** sometimes call the experiment of **reduction,** or more generally the **synthetic procedure.** The **analysis of the metaphysician** separated pure *a priori* knowledge into two very heterogeneous elements, namely those of the things as appearances and the things in themselves. The **dialectic** once again combines them, in **unison** with the necessary rational idea of the **unconditioned,** and finds that the unison will never come about except through that distinction, which is therefore the true one.

ᵃ *Gegenprobe*
ᵇ *Sache*
ᶜ *angetroffen*
ᵈ *Sachen*

such procedures speculative reason has at least made room for such an extension, even if it had to leave it empty; and we remain at liberty, indeed we are called upon by reason to fill it if we can through practical data of reason.* B xxii

Now the concern of this critique of pure speculative reason consists in that attempt to transform the accepted procedure of metaphysics, undertaking an entire revolution according to the example of the geometers and natural scientists. It is a treatise on the method, not a system of the science itself; but it catalogs the entire outline of the science of metaphysics, both in respect of its boundaries and in respect of its entire internal structure. For pure speculative reason has this peculiarity B xxiii about it, that it can and should measure its own capacity*a* according to the different ways for choosing the objects*b* of its thinking, and also completely enumerate the manifold ways of putting problems*c* before itself, so as to catalog the entire preliminary sketch of a whole system of metaphysics; because, regarding the first point, in *a priori* cognition nothing can be ascribed to the objects*d* except what the thinking subject takes out of itself, and regarding the second, pure speculative reason is, in respect of principles*e* of cognition, a unity entirely separate and subsisting for itself, in which, as in an organized body, every part exists for the sake of all the others as all the others exist for its sake, and no principle*f* can be taken with certainty in **one** relation unless it has at the

---

* In the same way, the central laws of the motion of the heavenly bodies estab- B xxii lished with certainty what Copernicus assumed at the beginning only as a hypothesis, and at the same time they proved the invisible force (of Newtonian attraction) that binds the universe,*g* which would have remained forever undiscovered if Copernicus had not ventured, in a manner contradictory to the senses yet true, to seek for the observed movements not in the objects of the heavens but in their observer. In this Preface I propose the transformation in our way of thinking presented in criticism*b* merely as a hypothesis, analogous to that other hypothesis, only in order to draw our notice to the first attempts at such a transformation, which are always hypothetical, even though in the treatise itself it will be proved not hypothetically but rather apodictically from the constitution of our representations of space and time and from the elementary concepts of the understanding.

a *Vermögen*
b *Objecte*
c *Aufgaben*
d *Objecte*
e *Principien*
f *Princip*
g *Weltbau*
b in der Kritik, which could also be translated "in the *Critique*," referring to the present book as a whole.

same time been investigated in its **thoroughgoing** relation to the entire use of pure reason. But then metaphysics also has the rare good fortune, enjoyed by no other rational science that has to do with objects*^a* (for **logic** deals only with the form of thinking in general), which is that if by this critique it has been brought onto the secure course of a science, then it can fully embrace the entire field of cognitions belonging to it and thus can complete its work and lay it down for posterity as a principal framework*^b* that can never be enlarged, since it has to do solely with principles*^c* and the limitations on their use, which are determined by the principles themselves. Hence as a fundamental science, metaphysics is also bound to achieve this completeness, and we must be able to say of it: *nil actum reputans, si quid superesset agendum.*^d

B xxiv

But it will be asked: What sort of treasure is it that we intend to leave to posterity, in the form of a metaphysics that has been purified through criticism but thereby also brought into a changeless state?*^e* On a cursory overview of this work, one might believe that one perceives it to be only of **negative** utility, teaching us never to venture with speculative reason beyond the boundaries of experience; and in fact that is its first usefulness. But this utility soon becomes **positive** when we become aware that the principles with which speculative reason ventures beyond its boundaries do not in fact result in **extending** our use of reason, but rather, if one considers them more closely, inevitably result in **narrowing** it by threatening to extend the boundaries of sensibility, to which these principles really belong, beyond everything, and so even to dislodge the use of pure (practical) reason. Hence a critique that limits the speculative use of reason is, to be sure, to that extent **negative**, but because it simultaneously removes an obstacle that limits or even threatens to wipe out the practical use of reason, this critique is also in fact of **positive** and very important utility, as soon as we have convinced ourselves that there is an absolutely necessary practical use of pure reason (the moral use), in which reason unavoidably extends itself beyond the boundaries of sensibility, without needing any assistance from speculative reason, but in which it must also be made secure against any counteraction from the latter, in order not to fall into contradiction with

B xxv

---

^a Objecte

^b Hauptstuhl; Kant's metaphor seems to be drawn from weaving (cf. *Webstuhl,* a loom or frame for weaving).

^c Principien

^d "Thinking nothing done if something more is to be done." The correct quotation is: *"Caesar in omnia praeceps, nil actum credens, cum quid superesset agendum, instat atrox"* (Caesar, headlong in everything, believing nothing done while something more remained to be done, pressed forward fiercely) (Lucan, *De bello civili* 2:657).

^e beharrlichen Zustand

itself. To deny that this service of criticism*a* is of any **positive** utility would be as much as to say that the police are of no positive utility because their chief business is to put a stop to the violence that citizens have to fear from other citizens, so that each can carry on his own affairs in peace and safety.[17] In the analytical part of the critique it is proved that space and time are only forms of sensible intuition, and therefore only conditions of the existence of the things as appearances, further that we have no concepts of the understanding and hence no elements for the cognition of things except insofar as an intuition can be   B xxvi
given corresponding to these concepts, consequently that we can have cognition of no object as a thing in itself, but only insofar as it is an object*b* of sensible intuition, i.e. as an appearance; from which follows the limitation of all even possible speculative cognition of reason to mere objects of **experience**. Yet the reservation must also be well noted, that even if we cannot **cognize** these same objects as things in themselves, we at least must be able to **think** them as things in themselves.* For otherwise there would follow the absurd proposition that there is an appearance without anything that appears. Now if we were to assume that   B xxvii
the distinction between things as objects of experience and the very same things as things in themselves, which our critique has made necessary, were not made at all, then the principle of causality, and hence the mechanism of nature in determining causality, would be valid of all things in general as efficient causes. I would not be able to say of one and the same thing, e.g., the human soul, that its will is free and yet that it is simultaneously subject to natural necessity, i.e., that it is not free, without falling into an obvious contradiction; because in both propositions I would have taken the soul **in just the same meaning**,*c* namely as a thing in general (as a thing*d* in itself), and without prior critique, I

---

* To **cognize** an object, it is required that I be able to prove its possibility   B xxvi
(whether by the testimony of experience from its actuality or *a priori* through reason). But I can **think** whatever I like, as long as I do not contradict myself, i.e., as long as my concept is a possible thought, even if I cannot give any assurance whether or not there is a corresponding object*e* somewhere within the sum total of all possibilities. But in order to ascribe objective validity to such a concept (real possibility, for the first sort of possibility was merely logical) something more is required. This "more," however, need not be sought in theoretical sources of cognition; it may also lie in practical ones.

a *der Kritik*
b *Object*
c *Bedeutung;* "meaning" will translate this word for the remainder of this paragraph.
d *Sache*
e *Object*

could not have taken it otherwise. But if the critique has not erred in teaching that the object*a* should be taken in **a twofold meaning,** namely as appearance or as thing in itself;[18] if its deduction of the pure concepts of the understanding is correct, and hence the principle of causality applies only to things taken in the first sense, namely insofar as they are objects of experience, while things in the second meaning are not subject to it; then just the same will is thought of in the appearance (in visible actions) as necessarily subject to the law of nature and to this extent **not free,** while yet on the other hand it is thought of as belonging to a thing in itself as not subject to that law, and hence **free,** without any contradiction hereby occurring. Now although I cannot **cognize** my soul, considered from the latter side, through any speculative reason (still less through empirical observation), and hence I cannot **cognize** freedom as a property of any being to which I ascribe effects in the world of sense, because then I would have to cognize such an existence as determined, and yet not as determined in time (which is impossible, since I cannot support my concept with any intuition), nevertheless, I can **think** freedom to myself, i.e., the representation of it at least contains no contradiction in itself, so long as our critical distinction prevails between the two ways of representing (sensible and intellectual), along with the limitation of the pure concepts of the understanding arising from it, and hence that of the principles flowing from them. Now suppose that morality necessarily presupposes freedom (in the strictest sense) as a property of our will, citing *a priori* as **data** for this freedom certain original practical principles lying in our reason, which would be absolutely impossible without the presupposition of freedom, yet that speculative reason had proved that freedom cannot be thought at all, then that presupposition, namely the moral one, would necessarily have to yield to the other one, whose opposite contains an obvious contradiction; consequently **freedom** and with it morality (for the latter would contain no contradiction if freedom were not already presupposed) would have to give way to the **mechanism of nature.** But then, since for morality I need nothing more than that freedom should not contradict itself, that it should at least be thinkable that it should place no hindrance in the way of the **mechanism of nature** in the same action (taken in another relation), without it being necessary for me to have any further insight into it: the doctrine of morality asserts its place and the doctrine of nature its own, which, however, would not have occurred if criticism had not first taught us of our unavoidable ignorance in respect of the things in themselves and limited everything that we can **cognize** theoretically to mere appearances. Just the same sort of exposition of the positive utility of critical principles of pure reason can be

B xxviii

B xxix

a Object

116

given in respect to the concepts of **God** and of the **simple nature** of our **soul,** which, however, I forgo for the sake of brevity. Thus I cannot even **assume God, freedom and immortality** for the sake of the nec- essary practical use of my reason unless I simultaneously **deprive** speculative reason of its pretension to extravagant insights; because in order to attain to such insights, speculative reason would have to help itself to principles that in fact reach only to objects of possible experience, and which, if they were to be applied to what cannot be an object of experience, then they would always actually transform it into an appearance, and thus declare all **practical extension** of pure reason to be impossible. Thus I had to deny **knowledge** in order to make room for **faith;** and the dogmatism of metaphysics, i.e., the prejudice that without criticism reason can make progress in metaphysics, is the true source of all unbelief conflicting with morality, which unbelief is always very dogmatic. – Thus even if it cannot be all that difficult to leave to posterity the legacy of a systematic metaphysics, constructed according to the critique of pure reason, this is still a gift deserving of no small respect; to see this, we need merely to compare the culture of reason that is set on the course of a secure science with reason's unfounded groping and frivolous wandering about without critique, or to consider how much bet- ter young people hungry for knowledge might spend their time than in the usual dogmatism that gives so early and so much encouragement to their complacent quibbling about things they do not understand, and things into which neither they nor anyone else in the world will ever have any insight, or even encourages them to launch on the invention of new thoughts and opinions, and thus to neglect to learn the well-grounded sciences; but we see it above all when we take account of the way criticism puts an end for all future time to objections against morality and religion in a **Socratic** way, namely by the clearest proof of the ignorance of the opponent. For there has always been some metaphysics or other to be met with in the world, and there will always continue to be one, and with it a dialectic of pure reason, because dialectic is natural to reason. Hence it is the first and most important occupation of philosophy to deprive dialectic once and for all of all disadvantageous influence, by blocking off the source of the errors.

With this important alteration in the field of the sciences, and with the **loss** of its hitherto imagined possessions that speculative reason must suffer, everything yet remains in the same advantageous state as it was before concerning the universal human concern and the utility that the world has so far drawn from the doctrines of pure reason, and the loss touches only the **monopoly of the schools** and in no way the **interest of human beings.** I ask the most inflexible dogmatist whether the proof of the continuation of our soul after death drawn from the simplicity of substance, or the proof of freedom of the will against universal mechanism drawn from the subtle though powerless distinctions between subjective and objective practical necessity, or the proof of the existence of God drawn from the concept of a most real being (or from the contingency of what is alterable and the necessity of a first mover), have ever, after originating in the schools, been able to reach the public or have the least influence over its convictions? If that has never happened, and if it can never be expected to happen, owing to the unsuitability of the common human understanding for such subtle speculation; if rather the conviction that reaches the public, insofar as it rests on rational grounds, had to be effected by something else – namely, as regards the first point, on that remarkable predisposition of our nature, noticeable to every human being, never to be capable of being satisfied by what is temporal (since the temporal is always insufficient for the predispositions of our whole vocation) leading to the hope of a future life; in respect of the second point, the mere clear ex-

B xxxiii position of our duties in opposition to all claims of the inclinations leading to the consciousness of freedom; and finally, touching on the third point, the splendid order, beauty, and providence shown forth everywhere in nature leading to the faith in a wise and great author of the world – then this possession not only remains undisturbed, but it even gains in respect through the fact that now the schools are instructed to pretend to no higher or more comprehensive insight on any point touching the universal human concerns than the insight that is accessible to the great multitude (who are always most worthy of our respect), and to limit themselves to the cultivation of those grounds of proof alone that can be grasped universally and are sufficient from a moral standpoint. The alteration thus concerns only the arrogant claims of the schools, which would gladly let themselves be taken for the sole experts and guardians of such truths (as they can rightly be taken in many other parts of knowledge), sharing with the public only the use of such truths, while keeping the key to them for themselves (*quod mecum nescit, solus vult scire videri*).[a] Yet care is taken for a more equitable claim on the

B xxxiv part of the speculative philosopher. He remains the exclusive trustee of a science that is useful to the public even without their knowledge, namely the critique of reason; for the latter can never become popular, but also has no need of being so; for just as little as the people want to fill their heads with fine-spun arguments for useful truths, so just as little do the equally subtle objections against these truths ever enter their minds; on the contrary, because the school inevitably falls into both, as does everyone who raises himself to speculation, the critique of reason

---

[a] "What he knows no more than I, he alone wants to seem to know." The correct quotation is "*Quod mecum ignorat, solus volt scire videri*" (What is unknown to me, that alone he wants to seem to know) (Horace, *Epistles* 2.1.87).

is bound once and for all to prevent, by a fundamental investigation of the rights of speculative reason, the scandal that sooner or later has to be noticed even among the people in the disputes in which, in the absence of criticism, metaphysicians (and among these in the end even clerics) inevitably involve themselves, and in which they afterwards even falsify their own doctrines. Through criticism alone can we sever the very root of **materialism, fatalism, atheism,** of freethinking **unbelief,** of **enthusiasm** and **superstition,** which can become generally injurious, and finally also of **idealism** and **skepticism,** which are more dangerous to the schools and can hardly be transmitted to the public. If governments find it good to concern themselves with the affairs of B xxxv scholars, then it would accord better with their wise solicitude both for the sciences and for humanity if they favored the freedom of such a critique, by which alone the treatments of reason can be put on a firm footing, instead of supporting the ridiculous despotism of the schools, which raise a loud cry of public danger whenever someone tears apart their cobwebs, of which the public has never taken any notice, and hence the loss of which it can also never feel.

Criticism is not opposed to the **dogmatic procedure** of reason in its pure cognition as science (for science must always be dogmatic, i.e., it must prove its conclusions strictly *a priori* from secure principles)[a]; rather, it is opposed only to dogmatism, i.e., to the presumption of getting on solely with pure cognition from (philosophical) concepts according to principles,[b] which reason has been using for a long time without first inquiring in what way and by what right it has obtained them. Dogmatism is therefore the dogmatic procedure of pure reason, **without an antecedent critique of its own capacity.**[c] This opposition therefore must not be viewed as putting in a good word for that loquacious shallowness under the presumed name of popularity, or even of skepticism, which gives short shrift to all metaphysics; rather, criticism B xxxvi is the preparatory activity necessary for the advancement of metaphysics as a well-grounded science, which must necessarily be dogmatic, carried out systematically in accordance with the strictest requirement, hence according to scholastic rigor (and not in a popular way); for this requirement is one that it may not neglect, since it undertakes to carry out its business wholly *a priori* and thus to the full satisfaction of speculative reason. In someday carrying out the plan that criticism prescribes, i.e., in the future system of metaphysics, we will have to follow the strict method of the famous Wolff, the greatest among all dogmatic philosophers, who gave us the first example (an ex-

[a] *Principien*
[b] *Principien*
[c] *Vermögen*

119

ample by which he became the author of a spirit of well-groundedness in Germany that is still not extinguished) of the way in which the secure course of a science is to be taken, through the regular ascertainment of the principles,[a] the clear determination of concepts, the attempt at strictness in the proofs, and the prevention of audacious leaps in inferences; for these reasons he had the skills for moving a science such as metaphysics into this condition, if only it had occurred to him to prepare the field for it by a critique of the organ, namely pure reason itself:

B xxxvii a lack that is to be charged not so much to him as to the dogmatic way of thinking prevalent in his age; and for this the philosophers of his as of all previous times have nothing for which to reproach themselves. Those who reject his kind of teaching and simultaneously the procedure of the critique of pure reason can have nothing else in mind except to throw off the fetters of **science** altogether, and to transform work into play, certainty into opinion, and philosophy into philodoxy.

Concerning this second edition, I have wanted, as is only proper, not to forgo the opportunity to remove as far as possible those difficulties and obscurities from which may have sprung several misunderstandings into which acute men, perhaps not without some fault on my part, have fallen in their judgment of this book. I have found nothing to alter either in the propositions themselves or in their grounds of proof, or in the form and completeness of the book's plan; this is to be ascribed partly to the long period of scrutiny to which I subjected them prior to laying it before the public; and partly to the constitution of the matter itself, namely to the nature of a pure speculative reason, which contains a truly articulated structure of members in which each thing is an organ, that is, in which everything is for the sake of each member, and each

B xxxviii individual member is for the sake of all, so that even the least frailty, whether it be a mistake (an error) or a lack, must inevitably betray itself in its use. I hope this system will henceforth maintain itself in this unalterability. It is not self-conceit that justifies my trust in this, but rather merely the evidence drawn from the experiment showing that the result effected is the same whether we proceed from the smallest elements to the whole of pure reason or return from the whole to every part (for this whole too is given in itself through the final intention of pure reason in the practical); while the attempt to alter even the smallest part directly introduces contradictions not merely into the system, but into universal human reason. Yet in the **presentation** there is still much to do, and here is where I have attempted to make improvements in this edition, which should remove first, the misunderstanding of the Aesthetic, chiefly the one in the concept of time; second, the obscurity in the Deduction of the Concepts of the Understanding, next the supposed

[a] *Principien*

lack of sufficient evidence in the proofs of the Principles of Pure Understanding, and finally the misinterpretation of the paralogisms advanced against rational psychology. My revisions[19] of the mode of presentation* extend only to this point (namely, only to the end of the first chapter of the Transcendental Dialectic) and no further, because time

---

* The only thing I can really call a supplement, and that only in the way of proof, is what I have said at [B]273 in the form of a new refutation of psychological **idealism**, and a strict proof (the only possible one, I believe) of the objective reality of outer intuition. No matter how innocent idealism may be held to be as regards the essential ends of metaphysics (though in fact it is not so innocent), it always remains a scandal of philosophy and universal human reason that the existence of things outside us (from which we after all get the whole matter for our cognitions, even for our inner sense) should have to be assumed merely **on faith,** and that if it occurs to anyone to doubt it, we should be unable to answer him with a satisfactory proof. Because there are some obscurities in the expressions of this proof between the third and sixth lines, I ask leave to alter this passage as follows: **"But this persisting element cannot be an intuition in me. For all the determining grounds of my existence that can be encountered in me are representations, and as such they themselves need something persisting distinct from them, in relation to which their change, and thus my existence in the time in which they change, can be determined."** Against this proof one will perhaps say: I am immediately conscious to myself only of what is in me, i.e., of my **representation** of external things; consequently it still remains undecided whether there is something outside me corresponding to it or not. Yet I am conscious through inner **experience** of **my existence in time** (and consequently also of its determinability in time), and this is more than merely being conscious of my representation; yet it is identical with the **empirical consciousness of my existence,** which is only determinable through a relation to something that, while being bound up with my existence, **is outside me.** This consciousness of my existence in time is thus bound up identically with the consciousness of a relation to something outside me, and so it is experience and not fiction, sense and not imagination, that inseparably joins the outer with my inner sense; for outer sense is already in itself a relation[a] of intuition to something actual outside me; and its reality, as distinct from imagination, rests only on the fact that it is inseparably bound up with inner experience itself, as the condition of its possibility, which happens here. If I could combine a determination of my existence through **intellectual intuition** simultaneously with the **intellectual consciousness** of my existence, in the representation **I am,** which accompanies all my judgments and actions of my understanding, then no consciousness of a relation[b] to something outside me would necessarily belong to this. But now that intellectual consciousness does to be sure precede, but the inner intuition, in which alone

---

[a] *Verhältnis*
[b] *Verhältnis*

B xl was too short, and also in respect of the rest of the book no misunderstanding on the part of expert and impartial examiners has come my

B xli way, whom I have not been able to name with the praise due to them;

B xlii but the attention I have paid to their reminders will be evident to them in the appropriate passages. This improvement, however, is bound up with a small loss for the reader, which could not be guarded against without making the book too voluminous: namely, various things that are not essentially required for the completeness of the whole had to be omitted or treated in an abbreviated fashion, despite the fact that some readers may not like doing without them, since they could still be useful in another respect; only in this way could I make room for what I hope is a more comprehensible presentation, which fundamentally alters absolutely nothing in regard to the propositions or even their grounds of proof, but which departs so far from the previous edition in the method of presentation that it could not be managed through interpolations. This small loss, which in any case can be compensated for, if anyone likes, by comparing the first and second

B xli my existence can be determined, is sensible, and is bound to a condition of time; however, this determination, and hence inner experience itself, depends on something permanent, which is not in me, and consequently must be outside me, and I must consider myself in relation^a to it; thus for an experience in general to be possible, the reality of outer sense is necessarily bound up with that of inner sense, i.e., I am just as certainly conscious that there are things outside me to which my sensibility relates, as I am conscious that I myself exist determined in time. Now which given intuitions actually correspond to outer objects, which therefore belong to outer **sense**, to which they are to be ascribed rather than to the imagination – that must be decided in each particular case according to the rules through which experience in general (even inner experience) is to be distinguished from imagination; which procedure is grounded always on the proposition that there actually is outer experience. To this the following remark can be added: The representation of something **persisting** in existence is not the same as a **persisting representation**; for that can be quite variable and changeable, as all our representations are, even the representations of matter, while still being related to something permanent, which must therefore be a thing distinct from all my representations and external, the existence of which is necessarily included in the **determination** of my own existence, which with it constitutes only a single experience, which could not take place even as inner if it were not simultaneously (in part) outer. The "How?" of this can be no more explained than we can explain further how we can think at all of what abides in time, whose simultaneity with what changes is what produces the concept of alteration.

^{a} *Relation*

editions, is, as I hope, more than compensated for by greater comprehensibility. In various public writings (partly in the reviews of some
books, partly in special treatises) I have perceived with gratitude and
enjoyment that the spirit of well-groundedness has not died out in
Germany, but has only been drowned out for a short time by the fash- B xliii
ionable noise of a freedom of thought that fancies itself ingenious, and
I see that the thorny paths of criticism, leading to a science of pure reason that is scholastically rigorous but as such the only lasting and
hence the most necessary science, has not hindered courageous and
clear minds from mastering them. To these deserving men, who combine well-groundedness of insight so fortunately with the talent for a
lucid presentation (something I am conscious of not having myself), I
leave it to complete my treatment, which is perhaps defective here and
there in this latter regard. For in this case the danger is not that I will
be refuted, but that I will not be understood. For my own part, from
now on I cannot let myself become involved in controversies, although
I shall attend carefully to all hints, whether they come from friends or
from opponents, so that I may utilize them, in accordance with this
propaedeutic, in the future execution of the system. Since during these
labors I have come to be rather advanced in age (this month I will attain my sixty-fourth year), I must proceed frugally with my time if I am
to carry out my plan of providing the metaphysics both of nature and
of morals, as confirmation of the correctness of the critique both of
theoretical and practical reason; and I must await the illumination of
those obscurities that are hardly to be avoided at the beginning of this Bxliv
work, as well as the defense of the whole, from those deserving men
who have made it their own. Any philosophical treatise may find itself
under pressure in particular passages (for it cannot be as fully armored
as a mathematical treatise), while the whole structure of the system,
considered as a unity, proceeds without the least danger; when a system is new, few have the adroitness of mind[a] to gain an overview of it,
and because all innovation is an inconvenience to them, still fewer have
the desire to do so. Also, in any piece of writing apparent contradictions can be ferreted out if individual passages are torn out of their
context and compared with each other, especially in a piece of informal
discourse[b] that in the eyes of those who rely on the judgment of others
cast a disadvantageous light on that piece of writing but that can be
very easily resolved by someone who has mastered the idea of the
whole. Meanwhile, if a theory is really durable, then in time the effect

[a] *Geist*
[b] *als freie Rede fortgehenden Schrift*

of action and reaction, which at first seemed to threaten it with great danger, will serve only to polish away its rough spots, and if men of impartiality, insight, and true popularity make it their business to do this, then in a short time they will produce even the required elegance.

Königsberg, in the month of April, 1787.

Contents^a

^a Kant includes this table of contents only in the first edition.

Introduction*a,b*

I.
The idea of transcendental philosophy.

Experience is without doubt the first product that our understanding brings forth as it works on the raw material of sensible sensations.[1] It is for this very reason the first teaching, and in its progress it is so inexhaustible in new instruction that the chain of life in all future generations will never have any lack of new information that can be gathered on this terrain. Nevertheless it is far from the only field to which our understanding can be restricted. It tells us, to be sure, what is, but never that it must necessarily be thus and not otherwise.*c* For that very reason it gives us no true universality, and reason, which is so desirous of this kind of cognitions, is more stimulated than satisfied by it. Now such universal cognitions, which at the same time have the character of inner necessity, must be clear and certain for themselves, independently of experience; hence one calls them *a priori* cognitions:[2] whereas that which is merely borrowed from experience is, as it is put, cognized only *a posteriori*, or empirically.[3]

---

a We first present the introduction as it appeared in the first edition, followed by the revised version that appeared in the second edition. Considerable changes were made in the latter, including some deletions, major additions, and occasional alterations within the passages that were repeated. We will use notes and references to the marginal pagination to show what changes were made from the first to the second editions. The following two paragraphs in the first edition were replaced with the first two numbered sections of the second.

b In his copy of the first edition, Kant made the following two notes:
"1. On the possibility of a critique of pure reason.
2. On its necessity (not from other sciences).
3. On its division.
4. On its purpose, the science of all principles [*Principien*] of pure reason. (Practical)" (E I, p. 12).
"That reason has its boundaries with regard to its *a priori* principles [*Principien*], concerning both degree and scope.
Division of metaphysics into metaphysics of nature and of morals" (E II, p. 12).

c The following note is added in Kant's copy of the first edition:
"We cannot infer to any necessity *a posteriori* if we do not already have a rule *a priori*. E.g., 'If many cases are identical, there must be something that makes this agreement necessary' presupposes the *a priori* proposition that everything contingent has a cause that determines its concept *a priori*." (E IV, p. 14)

Now what is especially remarkable is that even among our experiences cognitions are mixed in that must have their origin *a priori* and that perhaps serve only to establish connection among our representations of the senses. For if one removes from our experiences everything that belongs to the senses, there still remain certain original concepts and the judgments generated from them, which must have arisen entirely *a priori*, independently of experience, because they make one able to say more about the objects that appear to the senses than mere experience would teach, or at least make one believe that one can say this, and make assertions contain true universality and strict necessity, the likes of which merely empirical cognition can never afford.

B6
A3
But what says still more is this, that certain cognitions even abandon the field of all possible experiences, and seem to expand the domain of our judgments beyond all bounds of experience through concepts to which no corresponding object at all can be given in experience.

And precisely in these latter cognitions, which go beyond the world of the senses, where experience can give neither guidance nor correction, lie the investigations of our reason that we hold to be far more
B7
preeminent in their importance and sublime in their final aim than everything that the understanding can learn in the field of appearances, and on which we would rather venture everything, even at the risk of erring, than give up such important investigations because of any sort of reservation or from contempt and indifference.*

Now it may seem natural that as soon as one has abandoned the terrain of experience, one would not immediately erect an edifice with cognitions that one possesses without knowing whence, and on the credit of principles whose origin one does not know, without having first assured oneself of its foundation through careful investigations, thus that one would have long since raised the question how the understanding could come to all these cognitions *a priori* and what domain, validity, and value they might have. And in fact nothing is more
A4
natural, if one understands by this word that which properly and
B8
reasonably ought to happen; but if one understands by it that which usually happens, then conversely nothing is more natural and comprehensible than that this investigation should long have been neglected. For one part of these cognitions, the mathematical, has long been reliable, and thereby gives rise to a favorable expectation about others as well, although these may be of an entirely different nature. Fur-

---

* Here the second edition adds two sentences characterizing the tasks of pure reason. See B7 below.

thermore, if one is beyond the circle of experience, then one is sure not to be contradicted through experience. The charm in expanding one's cognitions is so great that one can be stopped in one's progress only by bumping into a clear contradiction. This, however, one can avoid if one makes his inventions carefully, even though they are not thereby inventions any the less. Mathematics gives us a splendid example of how far we can go with *a priori* cognition independently of experience. Now it is occupied, to be sure, with objects and cognitions only so far as these can be exhibited in intuition. This circumstance, however, is easily overlooked, since the intuition in question can itself be given *a priori*, and thus can hardly be distinguished from a mere pure concept. Encouraged by such a proof of the power of reason, the drive for ex- A 5 pansion sees no bounds. The light dove, in free flight cutting through the air the resistance of which it feels, could get the idea*ª* that it could do even better in airless space. Likewise, Plato abandoned the world of B 9 the senses because it posed so many hindrances for the understanding, and dared to go beyond it on the wings of the ideas, in the empty space of pure understanding. He did not notice that he made no headway by his efforts, for he had no resistance, no support, as it were, by which he could stiffen himself, and to which he could apply his powers in order to get his understanding off the ground. It is, however, a customary fate of human reason in speculation to finish its edifice as early as possible and only then to investigate whether the ground has been adequately prepared for it. But at that point all sorts of excuses will be sought to assure us of its sturdiness or to refuse such a late and dangerous examination. What keeps us free of all worry and suspicion during the construction, however, and flatters us with apparent thoroughness, is this. A great part, perhaps the greatest part of the business of our reason consists in analyses of the concepts that we already have of objects. This affords us a multitude of cognitions that, though they are nothing more than illuminations or clarifications of that which is already thought in our concepts (though still in a con- A 6 fused way), are, at least as far as their form is concerned, treasured as if they were new insights, though they do not extend the concepts that we have in either matter or content but only set them apart from each other. Now since this procedure does yield a real *a priori* cognition, B 10 which makes secure and useful progress, reason, without itself noticing it, under these pretenses surreptitiously makes assertions of quite another sort, in which it adds something entirely alien to given concepts *a priori*, without one knowing how it was able to do this and without this question even being allowed to come to mind. I will therefore deal

ª Vorstellung

with the distinction between these two kinds of cognition right at the outset.[a]

On the difference between analytic and synthetic judgments.[4]

In all judgments in which the relation of a subject to the predicate is thought (if I consider only affirmative judgments, since the application to negative ones is easy), this relation is possible in two different ways. Either the predicate B belongs to the subject A as something that is (covertly) contained in this concept A; or B lies entirely outside the concept A, though to be sure it stands in connection with it. In the first case I call the judgment analytic, in the second synthetic. Analytic judgments (affirmative ones) are thus those in which the connection of the predicate is thought through identity, but those in which this connection is thought without identity are to be called synthetic judgments. One could also call the former judgments of clarification and the latter judgments of amplification,[b] since through the predicate the former do not add anything to the concept of the subject, but only break it up by means of analysis into its component concepts, which were already thought in it (though confusedly); while the latter, on the contrary, add to the concept of the subject a predicate that was not thought in it at all, and could not have been extracted from it through any analysis; e.g., if I say: "All bodies are extended," then this is an analytic judgment. For I do not need to go outside the concept[c] that I combine with the word "body" in order to find that extension is connected with it, but rather I need only to analyze that concept, i.e., become conscious of the manifold that I always think in it, in order to encounter this predicate therein; it is therefore an analytic judgment. On the contrary, if I say: "All bodies are heavy," then the predicate is something entirely different from that which I think in the mere concept of a body in general. The addition of such a predicate thus yields a synthetic judgment.

[d]Now from this it is clear: 1) that through analytic judgments our cognition is not amplified at all, but rather the concept, which I already

A 7

B 11

A 8

---

[a] Kant's copy of the first edition has the following note:
"On synthetic hypothetical and disjunctive judgments as well as categorical negative judgments." (E V, p. 14)

[b] *Erläuterungs-* and *Erweiterungsurteile.* These terms are emphasized in the second but not in the first edition.

[c] Kant's copy of the first edition here adds: " 'I exist' is an analytic judgment; 'A body exists' is a synthetic one." (E VI, p. 14)

[d] The next two paragraphs are replaced with a single one in the second edition, the second of which incorporates part of the present one; see B 11–12 below.

have, is set out, and made intelligible to me; 2) that in synthetic judgments I must have in addition to the concept of the subject something else (X) on which the understanding depends in cognizing a predicate that does not lie in that concept as nevertheless belonging to it.[a]

In the case of empirical judgments or judgments of experience there is no difficulty here.[b] For this X is the complete experience of the object that I think through some concept A, which constitutes only a part of this experience. For although[c] I do not at all include the predicate of weight in the concept of a body in general, the concept nevertheless designates the complete experience through a part of it, to which I can therefore add still other parts of the very same experience as belonging to the former. I can first cognize the concept of body analytically through the marks of extension, of impenetrability, of shape, etc., which are all thought in this concept. But now I amplify my cognition and, in looking back to the experience from which I had extracted this concept of body, I find that weight is also always connected with the previous marks.[d] Experience is therefore that X that lies outside the concept A and on which the possibility of the synthesis of the predicate of weight B with the concept A is grounded.

B12

But in synthetic *a priori* judgments this means of help is entirely lacking.[5] If I am to go outside the concept A in order to cognize another B as combined with it, what is it on which I depend and through which the synthesis becomes possible, since I here do not have the advantage of looking around for it in the field of experience? Take the proposition: "Everything that happens has its cause." In the concept of something that happens, I think, to be sure, of an existence which was preceded by a time, etc., and from that analytic judgments can be drawn. But the concept of a cause indicates something different from the concept of something that happens, and is not contained in the latter representation at all. How then do I come to say something quite different about that which happens in general, and to cognize the concept of cause as belonging to it even though not contained in it?[e] What is the X here on which the understanding depends when it believes itself to discover beyond the concept of A a predicate that is foreign to it and that is yet

A9
B13

---

[a] Kant's copy of the first edition adds here: "Analytic judgments could accordingly be called mere judgments of clarification, synthetic judgments, however, judgments of amplification." (E VII, p. 15)

[b] In Kant's copy of the first edition, this was changed to: "In the case of empirical judgments or judgments of experience there is no difficulty about how they are to be proved synthetically." (E VIII, p. 15)

[c] From here the remainder of the paragraph is incorporated into the second edition.

[d] The remainder of this paragraph is changed in the second edition; see B12.

[e] Kant ends this and the next sentence with periods, for which we have substituted question marks.

connected with it? It cannot be experience, for the principle that has been adduced adds the latter representations to the former not only with greater generality than experience can provide, but also with the expression of necessity, hence entirely *a priori* and from mere concepts. A 10 Now the entire final aim of our speculative *a priori* cognition rests on such synthetic, i.e., ampliative, principles; for the analytic ones are, to be sure, most important and necessary, but only for attaining that distinctness of concepts that is requisite for a secure and extended synthesis as a really new construction.*a*

*b*A certain mystery thus lies hidden here,* the elucidation of which alone can make progress in the boundless field of pure cognition of the understanding secure and reliable: namely, to uncover the ground of the possibility of synthetic *a priori* judgments with appropriate generality, to gain insight into the conditions that make every kind of them possible, and not merely to designate this entire cognition (which comprises its own species) in a cursory outline, but to determine it completely and adequately for every use in a system in accordance with its primary sources, divisions, domain, and boundaries. So much provisionally for the pecularities of synthetic judgments.

B 24 *c*Now from all of this there results the idea of a special science, which A 11 could serve for the critique of pure reason. Every cognition is called **pure,** however, that is not mixed with anything foreign to it. But a cognition is called absolutely pure, in particular, in which no experience or sensation at all is mixed in, and that is thus fully *a priori*. Now reason is the faculty that provides the principles*d* of cognition *a priori*. Hence pure reason is that which contains the principles*e* for cognizing something absolutely *a priori*. An organon of pure reason would be a sum B 25 total of those principles*f* in accordance with which all pure *a priori* cog-

---

* If it had occurred to one of the ancients even to raise this question, this alone would have offered powerful resistance to all the systems of pure reason down to our own times, and would have spared us so many vain attempts that were blindly undertaken without knowledge of what was really at issue.

a *Anbau*, changed to *Erwerb* (acquisition) in the second edition.
b The following paragraph, including the footnote, is omitted in the second edition, and replaced with Sections V and VI, B 14 through B 25.
c At this point the common text of the two editions resumes; in the second edition, however, there is here inserted the section number VII and the ensuing heading. In addition, the second and third sentences of this paragraph are omitted, and there are minor changes in the wording of the opening and fourth sentences. See B 24 below.
d *Principien*
e *Principien*
f *Principien*

nitions can be acquired and actually brought about. The exhaustive application of such an organon would create a system of pure reason. But since that requires a lot, and it is still an open question whether such an amplification of our cognition is possible at all and in what cases it would be possible, we can regard a science of the mere estimation of pure reason, of its sources and boundaries, as the propaedeutic to the system of pure reason. Such a thing would not be a doctrine, but must be called only a critique of pure reason, and its utility would really be only negative, serving not for the amplification but only for the purification of our reason, and for keeping it free of errors, by which a great deal is already won. I call all cognition **transcendental** that is occupied not so much with objects but rather with our *a priori* concepts of objects in general.[a,6] A system of such concepts would be called transcendental   A 12
philosophy. But this is again too much for the beginning. For since such a science would have to contain completely both analytic as well as synthetic *a priori* cognition, it is, as far as our aim is concerned, too broad in scope, since we need to take the analysis only as far as is indispensably necessary in order to provide insight into the principles of *a priori* synthesis in their entire scope, which is our only concern. This investi-   B 26
gation, which we can properly call not doctrine but only transcendental critique, since it does not aim at the amplification of the cognitions themselves but only at their correction, and is to supply the touchstone of the worth or worthlessness of all cognitions *a priori*, is that with which we are now concerned. Such a critique is accordingly a preparation, if possible, for an organon, and, if this cannot be accomplished, then at least for a canon, in accordance with which the complete system of the philosophy of pure reason, whether it is to consist in the amplification or the mere limitation[b] of its cognition, can in any case at least some day be exhibited both analytically and synthetically. For that this should be possible, indeed that such a system should not be too great in scope for us to hope to be able entirely to complete it, can be assessed in advance from the fact that our object is not the nature of things, which is inexhaustible, but the understanding, which judges about the   A 13
nature of things, and this in turn only in regard to its *a priori* cognition, the supply of which, since we do not need to search for it externally, cannot remain hidden from us, and in all likelihood is small enough to be completely recorded, its worth or worthlessness assessed, and subjected to a correct appraisal.[c]

---

[a] In the second edition, "but . . ." replaced with "but with our manner of cognition of objects insofar as this is to be possible *a priori*." See B 25 below.
[b] *Begrenzung*
[c] Two sentences are added here in the second edition; see B 27 below.

B27

II.
Division of Transcendental Philosophy[a]

Transcendental philosophy is here only an idea,[b] for which the critique of pure reason is to outline the entire plan **architectonically**, i.e., from principles,[c] with a full guarantee for the completeness and certainty of all the components that comprise this edifice.[d] That this critique is not itself already called transcendental philosophy rests solely on the fact that in order to be a complete system it would also have to contain an exhaustive analysis of all of human cognition *a priori*. Now our critique must, to be sure, lay before us a complete enumeration of all of the ancestral concepts[e] that comprise the pure cognition in question. Only it properly refrains from the exhaustive analysis of these concepts themselves as well as from the complete review of all of those derived from them, partly because this analysis would not be purposeful,[f] since it does not contain the difficulty that is encountered in the synthesis on account of which the whole critique is actually undertaken, partly because it would be contrary to the unity of the plan to take on responsibility for the completeness of such an analysis and derivation, from which one could after all be relieved given one's aim. This completeness of the analysis as well as the derivation from the *a priori* concepts which are to be provided in the future will nevertheless be easy to complete as long as they are present as exhaustive principles[g] of synthesis, and if nothing is lacking in them in regard to this essential aim.

A14/B28

To the critique of pure reason there accordingly belongs everything that constitutes transcendental philosophy, and it is the complete idea of transcendental philosophy, but is not yet this science itself, since it goes only so far in the analysis as is requisite for the complete estimation of synthetic *a priori* cognition.

The chief target in the division of such a science is that absolutely no concepts must enter into it that contain anything empirical, or that the *a priori* cognition be entirely pure. Hence, although the supreme prin-

---

[a] This number and title are omitted in the second edition, having been replaced by the number and title of Section VII at B24.

[b] The words "here only an idea" are replaced in the second edition with "the idea of a science"; see B27 below.

[c] *Principien*

[d] Here the second edition inserts the sentence "It is the system of all principles [*Principien*] of pure reason." In his copy of the first edition, Kant had added here: "For without this the former must also be without any touchstone, and therefore entirely groundless." (E IX, p. 15)

[e] *Stammbegriffe*

[f] *zweckmäßig*

[g] *Principien*

ciples of morality and the fundamental concepts of it are *a priori* cognitions, they still do not belong in transcendental philosophy, since the
concepts of pleasure and displeasure, of desires and inclinations, of
choice, etc., which are all of empirical origin, must there be presupposed.[a] Hence transcendental philosophy is a philosophy[b] of pure,
merely speculative reason. For everything practical, insofar as it contains motives,[c] is related to feelings, which belong among empirical
sources of cognition.

Now if one wants to set up the division of this science from the general viewpoint of a system in general, then the one that we will now present must contain first a **Doctrine of Elements** and second a **Doctrine
of Method** of pure reason. Each of these main parts will have its subdivision, the grounds for which cannot yet be expounded here. All that
seems necessary for an introduction or a preliminary is that there are
two stems of human cognition, which may perhaps arise from a common but to us unknown root, namely **sensibility** and **understanding,**
through the first of which objects are given to us, but through the second of which they are thought. Now if sensibility were to contain *a
priori* representations, which constitute the conditions under which objects are given to us, it would belong to transcendental philosophy. The
transcendental doctrine of the senses will have to belong to the first part
of the science of elements, since the conditions under which alone the
objects of human cognition are given precede those under which those
objects are thought.

A15
B29

B30

A16

---

[a] This sentence is revised in the second edition to reflect Kant's intervening argument,
beginning with the *Groundwork of the Metaphysics of Morals* of 1785, that the principle of
morality if not its application is indeed entirely *a priori*. See B28–9 below.

[b] *Weltweisheit*

[c] *Bewegungsgründe*, replaced in the second edition with *Triebfedern* (incentives) in order to
leave room for the idea that although incentives based on feelings are not adequate for
morality, there can be other, more purely rational motives for it (see *Groundwork*,
4:427).

Introduction^{*a*}

I.^{*b*}
On the difference between pure and empirical cognition.

There is no doubt whatever that all our cognition begins with experience; for how else should the cognitive faculty be awakened into exercise if not through objects that stimulate our senses and in part themselves produce representations, in part bring the activity of our understanding into motion to compare these, to connect or separate them, and thus to work up the raw material of sensible impressions into a cognition of objects that is called experience?⁷ **As far as time is concerned,** then, no cognition in us precedes experience, and with experience every cognition begins.

But although all our cognition commences **with** experience, yet it does not on that account all arise **from** experience. For it could well be that even our experiential cognition is a composite of that which we receive through impressions and that which our own cognitive faculty (merely prompted by sensible impressions) provides out of itself, which addition we cannot distinguish from that fundamental material until long practice has made us attentive to it and skilled in separating it out.

It is therefore at least a question requiring closer investigation, and one not to be dismissed at first glance, whether there is any such cognition independent of all experience and even of all impressions of the senses. One calls such **cognitions *a priori*,**^{*c*} and distinguishes them from **empirical** ones, which have their sources *a posteriori*, namely in experience.⁸

The former expression^{*d*} is nevertheless not yet sufficiently determinate to designate the whole sense of the question before us. For it is customary to say of many a cognition derived from experiential sources that we are capable of it or partake in it *a priori*, because we do not derive it

---

^{*a*} As in the second edition.
^{*b*} Sections I and II (B 1–6) replace the first two paragraphs of Section I in the first edition (A 1–2).
^{*c*} Normally set in roman type, here emphasized by Kant by the use of italics.
^{*d*} That is, "*a priori*."

immediately from experience, but rather from a general rule that we have nevertheless itself borrowed from experience. So one says of someone who undermined the foundation of his house that he could have known *a priori* that it would collapse, i.e., he need not have waited for the experience of it actually collapsing. Yet he could not have known this entirely *a priori*.⁹ For that bodies are heavy and hence fall if their support is taken away must first have become known to him through experience.

In the sequel therefore we will understand by *a priori* cognitions not those that occur independently of this or that experience, but rather those that occur *absolutely* independently of all experience. Opposed to B 3 them are empirical cognitions, or those that are possible only *a posteriori*, i.e., through experience. Among *a priori* cognitions, however, those are called **pure** with which nothing empirical is intermixed. Thus, e.g., the proposition "Every alteration has its cause" is an *a priori* proposition, only not pure, since alteration is a concept that can be drawn only from experience.¹⁰

II.
We are in possession of certain *a priori* cognitions, and even the common understanding is never without them.

At issue here is a mark by means of which we can securely distinguish a pure cognition from an empirical one.¹¹ Experience teaches us, to be sure, that something is constituted thus and so, but not that it could not be otherwise. **First,** then, if a proposition is thought along with its **necessity,** it is an *a priori* judgment; if it is, moreover, also not derived from any proposition except one that in turn is valid as a necessary proposition, then it is absolutely *a priori*. **Second:** Experience never gives its judgments true or strict but only assumed and comparative **universality** (through induction), so properly it must be said: as far as we have yet perceived, there is no exception to this or that rule. Thus if B 4 a judgment is thought in strict universality, i.e., in such a way that no exception at all is allowed to be possible, then it is not derived from experience, but is rather valid absolutely *a priori*. Empirical universality is therefore only an arbitrary increase in validity from that which holds in most cases to that which holds in all, as in, e.g., the proposition "All bodies are heavy," whereas strict universality belongs to a judgment essentially; this points to a special source of cognition for it, namely a faculty of *a priori* cognition. Necessity and strict universality are therefore secure indications*ᵃ* of an *a priori* cognition, and also belong together in-

---

ᵃ Kennzeichen

separably. But since in their use it is sometimes easier to show the empirical limitation in judgments than the contingency in them, or is often more plausible to show the unrestricted universality that we ascribe to a judgment than its necessity, it is advisable to employ separately these two criteria, each of which is in itself infallible.[12]

Now it is easy to show that in human cognition there actually are such necessary and in the strictest sense universal, thus pure *a priori* judgments. If one wants an example from the sciences, one need only look at all the propositions of mathematics; if one would have one

B 5 from the commonest use of the understanding, the proposition that every alteration must have a cause will do; indeed in the latter the very concept of a cause so obviously contains the concept of a necessity of connection with an effect and a strict universality of rule that it would be entirely lost if one sought, as Hume did, to derive it from a frequent association of that which happens with that which precedes and a habit (thus a merely subjective necessity) of connecting representations arising from that association.[13] Even without requiring such examples for the proof of the reality of pure *a priori* principles in our cognition, one could establish their indispensability for the possibility of experience itself, thus establish it *a priori*. For where would experience itself get its certainty if all rules in accordance with which it proceeds were themselves in turn always empirical, thus contingent?;[a] hence one could hardly allow these to count as first principles. Yet here we can content ourselves with having displayed the pure use of our cognitive faculty as a fact together with its indication.[b] Not merely in judgments, however, but even in concepts is an origin of some of them revealed *a priori*. Gradually remove from your experiential concept of a **body** everything that is empirical in it – the color, the hardness or softness, the weight, even the impenetrability – there still remains the **space** that was occupied by the body (which has now entirely disappeared),

B 6 and you cannot leave that out. Likewise, if you remove from your empirical concept of every object,[c] whether corporeal or incorporeal, all those properties of which experience teaches you, you could still not take from it that by means of which you think of it as a **substance** or as **dependent** on a substance (even though this concept contains more determination than that of an object[d] in general). Thus, convinced by the necessity with which this concept presses itself on you, you must concede that it has its seat in your faculty of cognition *a priori*.

---

[a] Question mark not in original.
[b] *Kennzeichen*, i.e., sign.
[c] *Objects*
[d] *Objects*

III.[a]
Philosophy needs a science that determines the possibility, the principles,[b] and the domain of all cognitions *a priori*.

But what says still more than all the foregoing[c] is this, that certain cognitions even abandon the field of all possible experiences, and seem to expand the domain of our judgments beyond all bounds of experience through concepts to which no corresponding object at all can be given in experience.

And precisely in these latter cognitions, which go beyond the world of the senses, where experience can give neither guidance nor correction, lie the investigations of our reason that we hold to be far more preeminent in their importance and sublime in their final aim than everything that the understanding can learn in the field of appearances, in which we would rather venture everything, even at the risk of erring, than give up such important investigations because of any sort of reservation or from contempt and indifference. [d]These unavoidable problems of pure reason itself are **God, freedom** and **immortality.** But the science whose final aim in all its preparations is directed properly only to the solution of these problems is called **metaphysics,** whose procedure is in the beginning **dogmatic,** i.e., it confidently takes on the execution of this task without an antecedent examination of the capacity or incapacity[e] of reason for such a great undertaking.

Now it may seem natural that as soon as one has abandoned the terrain of experience one would not immediately erect an edifice with cognitions that one possesses without knowing whence, and on the credit of principles whose origin one does not know, without having first assured oneself of its foundation through careful investigations, thus that one would all the more[f] have long since raised the question how the understanding could come to all these cognitions *a priori* and what domain, validity, and value they might have. And in fact nothing is more natural, if one understands by the word **natural**[g] that which properly and reasonably ought to happen; but if one understands by it that which usually happens, then conversely nothing is more natural and compre-

A3

B7

A4

B8

---

[a] This section number and title added in the second edition. The ensuing paragraph commences the first part of the introduction common to both editions, extending from here to B 14, though with one major interpolation in the next paragraph and another change at B 11–12.

[b] *Principien*

[c] "than all the foregoing" added in the second edition.

[d] The remainder of this paragraph added in the second edition.

[e] *des Vermögens oder Unvermögens*

[f] "*vielmehr*" added in the second edition.

[g] "*dem Wort **natürlich***" substituted for "*unter diesem Worte*" in the second edition.

hensible than that this investigation should long have been neglected.*
For one part of these cognitions, the mathematical, has long been reliable, and thereby gives rise to a favorable expectation about others as well, although these may be of an entirely different nature. Furthermore, if one is beyond the circle of experience, then one is sure of not being refuted* through experience. The charm in expanding one's cognitions is so great that one can be stopped in one's progress only by bumping into a clear contradiction. This, however, one can avoid if one makes his inventions carefully, even though they are not thereby inventions any the less. Mathematics gives us a splendid example of how far we can go with *a priori* cognition independently of experience. Now it is occupied, to be sure, with objects and cognitions only so far as these can be exhibited in intuitions. This circumstance, however, is easily overlooked, since the intuition in question can itself be given *a priori*, and thus can hardly be distinguished from a mere pure concept.

A 5 Captivated* by such a proof of the power of reason, the drive for expansion sees no bounds. The light dove, in free flight cutting through the air the resistance of which it feels, could get the idea* that it could

B 9 do even better in airless space. Likewise, Plato abandoned the world of the senses because it set such narrow limits* for the understanding, and dared to go beyond it on the wings of the ideas, in the empty space of pure understanding. He did not notice that he made no headway by his efforts, for he had no resistance, no support, as it were, by which he could stiffen himself, and to which he could apply his powers in order to put his understanding into motion. It is, however, a customary fate of human reason in speculation to finish its edifice as early as possible and only then to investigate whether the ground has been adequately prepared for it. But at that point all sorts of excuses will be sought to assure us of its sturdiness or also, even better,* to refuse such a late and dangerous examination. What keeps us free of all worry and suspicion during the construction, however, and flatters us with apparent thoroughness, is this. A great part, perhaps the greatest part, of the business of our reason consists in *analyses* of the concepts that we already have of objects. This affords us a multitude of cognitions that, although they are nothing more than illuminations or clarifications of that which is al-

A 6 ready thought in our concepts (though still in a confused way), are, at least as far as their form is concerned, treasured as if they were new in-

---

* The second edition reads "*lange*" instead of "*lange Zeit.*"

* The second edition reads "*widerlegt*" instead of "*widersprochen.*"

* The second edition reads "*eingenommen*" instead of "*aufgemuntert.*"

* *Vorstellung*

* The second edition reads "*so enge Schranken setzt*" instead of "*so vielfältige Hindernisse legt.*"

* The second edition inserts the words "*auch*" and "*lieber gar.*"

sights, though they do not extend the concepts that we have in either matter or content, but only set them apart from each other. Now since this procedure does yield a real *a priori* cognition, which makes secure and useful progress, reason, without itself noticing it, under these pretenses surreptitiously makes assertions of quite another sort, in which reason adds something entirely alien to given concepts and indeed[a] does so *a priori*, without one knowing how it was able to do this and without such a[b] question even being allowed to come to mind. I will therefore deal with the distinction between these two sorts of cognition right at the outset.

IV.[c]
On the difference between analytic and synthetic judgments.[14]

In all judgments in which the relation of a subject to the predicate is thought (if I consider only affirmative judgments, since the application to negative ones is easy) this relation is possible in two different ways. Either the predicate B belongs to the subject A as something that is (covertly) contained in this concept A; or B lies entirely outside the concept A, though to be sure it stands in connection with it. In the first case I call the judgment **analytic,** in the second **synthetic.** Analytic judgments (affirmative ones) are thus those in which the connection of the predicate is thought through identity, but those in which this connection is thought without identity are to be called synthetic judgments. One could also call the former **judgments of clarification,** and the latter **judgments of amplification,**[d] since through the predicate the former do not add anything to the concept of the subject, but only break it up by means of analysis into its component concepts, which were already thought in it (though confusedly); while the latter, on the contrary, add to the concept of the subject a predicate that was not thought in it at all, and could not have been extracted from it through any analysis. E.g., if I say: "All bodies are extended," then this is an analytic judgment. For I do not need to go beyond[e] the concept that I combine with the body[f] in order to find that extension is connected with it, but rather I need only to analyze that concept, i.e., become conscious of the manifold that I always think in it, in order to encounter this predicate therein; it is therefore an analytic judgment. On the contrary, if I say:

B 10

A 7

B 11

---

[a] The second edition adds the words "*und zwar.*"
[b] The second edition replaces "*diese*" with "*eine solche.*"
[c] Section number "IV" added in the second edition.
[d] "*Erläuterungs-*" and "*Erweiterungsurteile.*"
[e] The second edition reads "*über*" instead of "*aus.*"
[f] The second edition reads "*dem Körper*" instead of "*dem Wort Körper.*"

"All bodies are heavy," then the predicate is something entirely different from that which I think in the mere concept of a body in general. The addition of such a predicate thus yields a synthetic judgment.

Judgments of experience, as such, are all synthetic. For it would be absurd to ground an analytic judgment on experience, since I do not need to go beyond my concept at all in order to formulate the judgment, and therefore need no testimony from experience for that. That a body is extended is a proposition that is established *a priori*, and is not a judgment of experience. For before I go to experience, I already have all the conditions for my judgment in the concept, from which I merely draw out the predicate in accordance with the principle of contradiction, and can thereby at the same time become conscious of the necessity of the judgment, which experience could never teach me. On the contrary, although I *b*do not at all include the predicate of weight in the concept of a body in general, the concept nevertheless designates an object of experience*c* through a part of it, to which I can therefore add still other parts of the same experience as belonging with the former. I can first cognize the concept of body analytically through the marks of extension, of impenetrability, of shape, etc., which are all thought in this concept. But now I amplify my cognition and, looking back to the experience from which I had extracted this concept of body, I find that weight is also always connected with the previous marks, *d*and I therefore add this synthetically as predicate to that concept. It is thus experience *e*on which the possibility of the synthesis of the predicate of weight with the concept of body is grounded, since both concepts, though the one is not contained in the other, nevertheless belong together, though only contingently, as parts of a whole, namely experience, which is itself a synthetic combination of intuitions.

*f*But in synthetic *a priori* judgments this means of help is entirely lacking.[15] If I am to go beyond*g* the concept *A* in order to cognize another *B* as combined with it, what is it on which I depend and by means of which the synthesis becomes possible, since I here do not have the advantage of looking around for it in the field of experience? Take the proposition: "Everything that happens has its cause." In the concept of

B 12

A 8

A 9
B 13

---

a The first part of the following paragraph replaces two paragraphs in the first edition; see A7–8 above.

b The text common to the first edition resumes here.

c The second edition has "*einen Gegenstand der Erfahrung*" instead of the first edition's "*die vollständige Erfahrung.*"

d The remainder of this sentence is added in the second edition.

e The remainder of this sentence is modified and expanded in the second edition.

f The common text resumes here.

g "*über*" substituted in the second edition for "*ausser*" in the first.

something that happens, I think, to be sure, of an existence that was preceded by a time, etc., and from that analytic judgments can be drawn. But the concept of a cause lies entirely outside that concept, and[a] indicates something different than the concept of what happens in general, and is therefore[b] not contained in the latter representation at all. How then do I come to say something quite different about that which happens in general, and to cognize the concept of cause as belonging to it, indeed necessarily,[c] even though not contained in it?[d] What is the unknown =[e]X here on which the understanding depends when it believes itself to discover beyond the concept of A a predicate that is foreign to it yet which it nevertheless believes to be connected with it?[f] It cannot be experience, for the principle that has been adduced adds the latter representations to the former not only with greater generality than experience can provide, but also with the expression of necessity, hence entirely *a priori* and from mere concepts. Now the entire final aim of our speculative *a priori* cognition rests on such synthetic, i.e., ampliative principles; for the analytic ones are, to be sure, most important and necessary, but only for attaining that distinctness of concepts which is requisite for a secure and extended synthesis as a really new acquisition.[g]

A 10

B 14

[b]V.
Synthetic *a priori* judgments are contained as principles[i]
in all theoretical sciences of reason.

[j]1. **Mathematical judgments are all synthetic.**[16] This proposition seems to have escaped the notice of the analysts of human reason until now, indeed to be diametrically opposed to all of their conjectures, although it is incontrovertibly certain and is very important in the sequel. For since one found that the inferences of the mathematicians all proceed in accordance with the principle of contradiction (which is re-

---

[a] "*liegt ganz außer jenem Begriffe, und*" added in the second edition.

[b] "*ist also*" in the second edition instead of "*und ist*" in the first.

[c] "*und so gar notwendig*" added in the second edition.

[d] Kant ends this and the next sentence with periods, for which we have substituted question marks.

[e] "*unbekannte =*" added in the second edition.

[f] In the second edition, "*welches er gleichwohl damit verknüpft zu sein erachtet?*" substituted for "*das gleichwohl damit verknüpft sei.*"

[g] In the second edition, "*Erwerb*" replaces "*Anbau.*"

[h] At this point one paragraph from the first edition is omitted and replaced with the following Sections V and VI, B 14 through B 25.

[i] *Principien*

[j] Kant adapts the following five paragraphs from the *Prolegomena*, § 2 (4:268–9).

quired by the nature of any apodictic certainty), one was persuaded that the principles could also be cognized from the principle[a] of contradiction, in which, however, they[b] erred; for a synthetic proposition can of course be comprehended in accordance with the principle of contradiction, but only insofar as another synthetic proposition is presupposed from which it can be deduced, never in itself.

It must first be remarked that properly mathematical propositions are always *a priori* judgments and are never empirical, because they carry necessity with them, which cannot be derived from experience. But if one does not want to concede this, well then, I will restrict my proposition to **pure mathematics,** the concept of which already implies that it does not contain empirical but merely pure *a priori* cognition.

B15

To be sure, one might initially think that the proposition "$7 + 5 = 12$" is a merely analytic proposition that follows from the concept of a sum of seven and five in accordance with the principle of contradiction. Yet if one considers it more closely, one finds that the concept of the sum of 7 and 5 contains nothing more than the unification of both numbers in a single one, through which it is not at all thought what this single number is which comprehends the two of them. The concept of twelve is by no means already thought merely by my thinking of that unification of seven and five, and no matter how long I analyze my concept of such a possible sum I will still not find twelve in it. One must go beyond these concepts, seeking assistance in the intuition that corresponds to one of the two, one's five fingers, say, or (as in Segner's arithmetic)[17] five points, and one after another add the units of the five given in the intuition to the concept of seven. [c]For I take first the number 7, and, as I take the fingers of my hand as an intuition for assistance with the concept of 5, to that image of mine I now add the units that I have previously taken together in order to constitute the number 5 one after another to the number 7, and thus see the number 12 arise. That 7 **should** be added to 5 I have, to be sure, thought in the concept of a sum = $7 + 5$, but not that this sum is equal to the number 12. The arithmetical proposition is therefore always synthetic; one becomes all the more distinctly aware of that if one takes somewhat larger numbers, for it is then clear that, twist and turn our concepts as we will, without getting help from intuition we could never find the sum by means of the mere analysis of our concepts.

B16

---

[a] *Satz*

[b] Kant switches number from "*man*" to "*sie.*"

[c] This and the following sentence are substituted here for the clause "*Man erweitet also wirklich seinen Begriff durch diesen Satz 7 + 5 = 12 und thut zu dem ersteren Begriff einen neuen hinzu, der in jenem gar nicht gedacht war*" (One therefore really amplifies his concept through this proposition "$7 + 5 = 12$" and adds a new concept to the former, which was not thought in it) in the *Prolegomena* (4:269).

Just as little is any principle of pure geometry analytic. That the straight line between two points is the shortest is a synthetic proposition. For my concept of **the straight** contains nothing of quantity, but only a quality.[18] The concept of the shortest is therefore entirely additional to it, and cannot be extracted out of the concept of the straight line by any analysis. Help must here be gotten from intuition, by means of which alone the synthesis is possible.

To be sure, a few principles that the geometers presuppose are actually analytic and rest on the principle of contradiction; but they also[a] only serve, as identical propositions, for the chain of method and not as principles,[b] e.g., $a = a$, the whole is equal to itself, or $(a + b) > a$, i.e., the whole is greater than its part. And yet even these, although they are valid in accordance with mere concepts, are admitted in mathematics only because they can be exhibited in intuition.[19] What usually makes us believe here that the predicate of such apodictic judgments already lies in our concept, and that the judgment is therefore analytic, is merely the ambiguity of the expression. We **should,** namely, add a certain predicate to a given concept in thought, and this necessity already attaches to the concepts. But the question is not what we **should think** in addition to the given concept, but what we **actually think** in it, though only obscurely, and there it is manifest that the predicate certainly adheres to those concepts necessarily, though not as thought in the concept itself,[c] but by means of an intuition that must be added to the concept.

2. **Natural science (*Physica*) contains within itself synthetic *a priori* judgments as principles.**[d] I will adduce only a couple of propositions as examples, such as the proposition that in all alterations of the corporeal world the quantity of matter remains unaltered, or that in all communication of motion effect and counter-effect must always be equal. In both of these not only the necessity, thus their *a priori* origin, but also that they are synthetic propositions is clear. For in the concept of matter I do not think persistence, but only its presence in space through the filling of space. Thus I actually go beyond the concept of matter in order to add something to it *a priori* that I did not think **in it.** The proposition is thus not analytic, but synthetic, and nevertheless thought *a priori*, and likewise with the other propositions of the pure part of natural science.

3. **In metaphysics,** even if one regards it as a science that has thus far

B17

B18

---

[a] "*auch*" added to text from *Prolegomena* (4:269).
[b] *Principien*
[c] "*als im Begriffe selbst gedacht*" substituted here for the word "*unmittelbar*" in the *Prolegomena* (4:269).
[d] *Principien*

merely been sought but is nevertheless indispensable because of the nature of human reason, **synthetic *a priori* cognitions** are supposed **to be contained,** and it is not concerned merely with analyzing concepts that we make of things *a priori* and thereby clarifying them analytically, but we want to amplify our cognition *a priori;* to this end we must make use of such principles that add something to the given concepts that was not contained in them, and through synthetic *a priori* judgments go so far beyond that experience itself cannot follow us that far, e.g., in the proposition "The world must have a first beginning," and others besides, and thus metaphysics, at least as far as **its end is concerned,** consists of purely synthetic *a priori* propositions.[20]

B 19
VI.
The general problem[a] of pure reason.[21]

One has already gained a great deal if one can bring a multitude of investigations under the formula of a single problem. For one thereby not only lightens one's own task, by determining it precisely, but also the judgment of anyone else who wants to examine whether we have satisfied our plan or not. The real problem of pure reason is now contained in the question: **How are synthetic judgments *a priori* possible?**

That metaphysics has until now remained in such a vacillating state of uncertainty and contradictions is to be ascribed solely to the cause that no one has previously thought of this problem and perhaps even of the distinction between **analytic** and **synthetic** judgments. On the solution of this problem, or on a satisfactory proof that the possibility that it demands to have explained does not in fact exist at all, metaphysics now stands or falls. David Hume, who among all philosophers came closest to this problem, still did not conceive of it anywhere near determinately enough and in its universality, but rather stopped with the synthetic proposition of the connection of the effect with its cause

B 20 (*Principium causalitatis*), believing himself to have brought out that such an *a priori* proposition is entirely impossible, and according to his inferences everything that we call metaphysics would come down to a mere delusion of an alleged insight of reason into that which has in fact merely been borrowed from experience and from habit has taken on the appearance of necessity; an assertion, destructive of all pure philosophy, on which he would never have fallen if he had had our problem in its generality before his eyes, since then he would have comprehended that according to his argument there could also be no pure mathematics, since this certainly contains synthetic *a priori* propositions, an assertion

---

[a] *Aufgabe*

from which his sound understanding would surely have protected him.²²

In the solution of the above problem there is at the same time contained the possibility of the pure use of reason in the grounding and execution of all sciences that contain a theoretical *a priori* cognition of objects, i.e., the answer to the questions:

How is pure mathematics possible?

How is pure natural science possible?

About these sciences, since they are actually given, it can appropriately be asked **how** they are possible; for that they must be possible is proved through their actuality.* As far as **metaphysics** is concerned, however, its poor progress up to now, and the fact that of no metaphysics thus far expounded can it even be said that, as far as its essential end is concerned, it even really exists, leaves everyone with ground to doubt its possibility.   B 21

But now this **kind of cognition** is in a certain sense also to be regarded as given, and metaphysics is actual, if not as a science yet as a natural predisposition (*metaphysica naturalis*). For human reason, without being moved by the mere vanity of knowing it all, inexorably pushes on, driven by its own need to such questions that cannot be answered by any experiential use of reason and of principles*ᵃ* borrowed from such a use; and thus a certain sort of metaphysics has actually been present in all human beings as soon as reason has extended itself to speculation in them, and it will also always remain there. And now about this too the question is: **How is metaphysics as a natural predisposition possible?** i.e., how do the questions that pure reason raises, and which it is driven by its own need to answer as well as it can, arise from the nature of universal human reason?   B 22

But since unavoidable contradictions have always been found in all previous attempts to answer these natural questions, e.g., whether the world has a beginning or exists from eternity, etc., one cannot leave it up to the mere natural predisposition to metaphysics, i.e., to the pure faculty of reason itself, from which, to be sure, some sort of metaphysics (whatever it might be) always grows, but it must be possible to bring it

---

* Some may still doubt this last point in the case of pure natural science. Yet one need merely consider the various propositions that come forth at the outset of proper (empirical) physics, such as those of the persistence of the same quantity of matter, of inertia, of the equality of effect and counter-effect, etc., and one will quickly be convinced that they constitute a *physica pura* (or *rationalis*), which well deserves to be separately established, as a science of its own, in its whole domain, whether narrow or wide.   B 21

ᵃ *Principien*

to certainty regarding either the knowledge or ignorance of objects, i.e., to come to a decision either about the objects of its questions or about the capacity and incapacity[a] of reason for judging something about them, thus either reliably to extend our pure reason or else to set determinate and secure limits for it. This last question, which flows from the general problem above, would rightly be this: **How is metaphysics possible as science?**

The critique of reason thus finally leads necessarily to science; the dogmatic use of it without critique, on the contrary, leads to groundless
B 23   assertions, to which one can oppose equally plausible ones, thus to **skepticism.**

Further, this science cannot be terribly extensive, for it does not deal with objects[b] of reason, whose multiplicity[c] is infinite, but merely with itself, with problems that spring entirely from its own womb, and that are not set before it by the nature of things that are distinct from it but through its own nature; so that, once it has become completely familiar with its own capacity[d] in regard to the objects that may come before it in experience, then it must become easy to determine, completely and securely, the domain and the bounds of its attempted use beyond all bounds of experience.

Thus one can and must regard as undone all attempts made until now to bring about a metaphysics **dogmatically;** for what is analytic in one or the other of them, namely the mere analysis of the concepts that inhabit our reason *a priori*, is not the end at all, but only a preparation for metaphysics proper, namely extending its *a priori* cognition synthetically, and it is useless for this end, because it merely shows what is contained in these concepts, but not how we attain such concepts *a priori* in order thereafter to be able to determine their valid use in regard to the
B 24   objects of all cognition in general. It also requires only a little self-denial in order to give up all these claims, since the contradictions of reason, which cannot be denied and which are also unavoidable in dogmatic procedure, have long since destroyed the authority of every previous metaphysics. More resolution will be necessary in order not to be deterred by internal difficulty and external resistance from using another approach,[e] entirely opposed to the previous one, in order to promote the productive and fruitful growth of a science that is indispensable for human reason, and from which one can chop down every stem that has shot up without ever being able to eradicate its root.

[a] *Vermögen und Unvermögen*
[b] *Objecten*
[c] *Mannigfaltigkeit*
[d] *Vermögen*
[e] *Behandlung*

^aVII.
The idea and division of a special science under the name of a critique of pure reason.

Now from all of this there results the idea of a special science, which can be called the **critique of pure reason**.^b For^c reason is the faculty that provides the principles^d of cognition *a priori*. Hence pure reason is that which contains the principles^e for cognizing something absolutely *a priori*. An **organon** of pure reason would be a sum total of all those principles^f in accordance with which all pure *a priori* cognitions can be acquired and actually brought about. The exhaustive application of such an organon would create a system of pure reason. But since that requires a lot, and it is still an open question whether such an amplification of our knowledge is possible at all and in what cases it would be possible, we can regard a science of the mere estimation of pure reason, of its sources and boundaries, as the **propaedeutic** to the system of pure reason. Such a thing would not be a **doctrine,** but must be called only a **critique** of pure reason, and its utility in regard to speculation^g would really be only negative, serving not for the amplification but only for the purification of our reason, and for keeping it free of errors, by which a great deal is already won. I call all cognition transcendental that is occupied not so much with objects but rather with our mode of cognition of objects insofar as this is to be possible *a priori*.^{b,23} A **system** of such concepts would be called **transcendental philosophy.** But this is again too much for the beginning. For since such a science would have to contain completely both the analytic as well as the synthetic *a priori* cognition, it is, so farⁱ as our aim is concerned, too broad in scope, since we need to take the analysis only as far as is indispensably necessary in order to provide insight into the principles of *a priori* synthesis in their entire scope, which is our only concern. This investigation, which we

A 11

B 25

A 12

B 26

---

^a The section number VII and the following title are inserted at this point in the second edition, following which the text common to the two editions resumes, with minor alterations.

^b **"die Kritik der reinen Vernunft heißen kann"** *s*ubstituted in the second edition for *"die zur Kritik der reinen Vernunft dienen könne."* The next two sentences in the first edition are omitted; see A 11 above.

^c *"Denn"* substituted in the second edition for *"Nun."*

^d *Principien*

^e *Principien*

^f *Principien*

^g *"in Ansehung der Spekulation"* added in the second edition.

^b *"sondern mit unserer Erkenntnisart von Gegenständen, so fern diese* a priori *möglich sein soll"* substituted in the second edition for *"sondern mit unsern Begriffen* a priori *von Gegenständen."*

ⁱ *"so weit"* substituted for *"insofern"* in the second edition.

can properly call not doctrine but only transcendental critique, since it does not aim at the amplification of cognitions themselves but only at their correction, and is to supply the touchstone of the worth or worthlessness of all cognitions *a priori*, is that with which we are now concerned. Such a critique is accordingly a preparation, if possible, for an organon, and, if this cannot be accomplished, then at least for a canon, in accordance with which the complete system of the philosophy of pure reason, whether it is to consist in the amplification or mere limitation[a] of its cognition, can in any case at least some day be exhibited both analytically and synthetically. For that this should be possible, indeed that such a system should not be too great in scope for us to hope to be able entirely to complete it, can be assessed in advance from the fact that our object is not the nature of things, which is inexhaustible, but the understanding, which judges about the nature of things, and this in turn only in regard to its *a priori* cognition, the supply of which, since we do not need to search for it externally, cannot remain hidden from us, and in all likelihood is small enough to be completely recorded, its worth or worthlessness assessed, and subjected to a correct appraisal.

[b]Even less can one expect here a critique of the books and systems of pure reason, but rather that of the pure faculty of reason itself. Only if this is one's ground does one have a secure touchstone for appraising the philosophical content of old and new works in this specialty; otherwise the unqualified historian and judge assesses the groundless assertions of others through his own, which are equally groundless.

[c]Transcendental philosophy is here the idea of a science,[d] for which the critique of pure reason is to outline the entire plan architectonically, i.e., from principles,[e] with a full guarantee for the completeness and certainty of all the components that comprise this edifice. It is the system of all principles[f] of pure reason.[g] That this critique is not itself already called transcendental philosophy rests solely on the fact that in order to be a complete system it would also have to contain an exhaustive analysis of all of human cognition *a priori*. Now our critique must, to be sure, lay before us a complete enumeration of all of the ancestral concepts[b] that comprise the pure cognition in question. Only it properly refrains from the exhaustive analysis of these concepts themselves as well as

---

[a] *Begrenzung*

[b] The next two sentences are added in the second edition.

[c] The title **"II. Division of transcendental philosophy"** present in the first edition is omitted in the second.

[d] "*Die Idee einer Wissenschaft*" substituted in the second edition for "*hier nur eine Idee.*"

[e] *Principien*

[f] *Principien*

[g] This sentence inserted in the second edition.

[b] *Stammbegriffe*

from the complete review of all of those derived from them, partly because this analysis would not be purposeful,[a] since it does not contain the difficulty encountered in the synthesis on account of which the whole critique is actually undertaken, partly because it would be contrary to the unity of the plan to take on responsibility for the completeness of such an analysis and derivation, from which one could yet be relieved given its aim. This completeness of the analysis as well as the derivation from the *a priori* concepts that are to be provided in the future will nevertheless be easy to complete as long as they are present as exhaustive principles[b] of synthesis, and if nothing is lacking in them in regard to this essential aim.

A 14/B 28

To the critique of pure reason there accordingly belongs everything that constitutes transcendental philosophy, and it is the complete idea of transcendental philosophy, but is not yet this science itself, since it goes only so far in the analysis as is requisite for the complete estimation of synthetic *a priori* cognition.

The chief target in the division of such a science is that absolutely no concept must enter into it that contains anything empirical, or that the *a priori* cognition be entirely pure. Hence, although the supreme principles of morality and the fundamental concepts of it are *a priori* cognitions, they still do not belong in transcendental philosophy,[c] for, while they do not, to be sure, take the concepts of pleasure and displeasure, of desires and inclinations, etc., which are all of empirical origin, as the ground of their precepts, they still must necessarily include them in the composition of the system of pure morality in the concept of duty, as the hindrance that must be overcome or the attraction that ought not to be made into a motive. Hence transcendental philosophy is a philosophy[d] of pure, merely speculative reason. For everything practical, insofar as it contains incentives,[e] is related to feelings, which belong among empirical sources of cognition.

A 15
B 29

Now if one wants to set up the division of this science from the general viewpoint of a system in general, then what we will now present must contain first a **Doctrine of Elements** and second a **Doctrine of Method** of pure reason. Each of these main parts will have its subdivision, the grounds for which cannot yet be expounded. All that seems

---

[a] *zweckmäßig*

[b] *Principien*

[c] The remainder of this sentence in the second edition is substituted for the following in the first: "since the concepts of pleasure and displeasure, of desires and inclinations, of choice, etc., which are all of empirical origin, must thereby be presupposed."

[d] *Weltweisheit*

[e] *Bewegungsgründe* in the first edition is replaced in the second with *Triebfedern* to leave room for the idea that although incentives based on feelings are not adequate for morality, there can be other, more purely rational motives for it.

necessary for an introduction or preliminary is that there are two stems of human cognition, which may perhaps arise from a common but to us unknown root, namely sensibility and understanding, through the first of which objects are given to us, but through the second of which they are thought. Now if sensibility were to contain *a priori* representations, which constitute the condition*a* under which objects are given to us, it will belong to transcendental philosophy. The transcendental doctrine of the senses will have to belong to the first part of the science of elements, since the conditions under which alone the objects of human cognition are given precede those under which those objects are thought.

B 30

A 16

a "*Bedingung*" in the second edition replaces "*Bedingungen*" in the first.

I.

Transcendental Doctrine of Elements

The Transcendental Doctrine of Elements

First Part

The Transcendental Aesthetic[a,1]

In whatever way and through whatever means a cognition may relate to objects, that through which it relates immediately to them, and at which all thought as a means is directed as an end, is intuition.[b,2] This, however, takes place only insofar as the object is given to us; but this in turn, is possible only if it affects[c] the mind in a certain way. The capacity (receptivity) to acquire representations through the way in which we are affected by objects is called sensibility. Objects are therefore given to us by means of sensibility, and it alone affords us intuitions; but they are **thought** through the understanding, and from it arise concepts. But all thought, whether straightaway (*directe*) or through a detour (*indirecte*), must ultimately be related to intuitions, thus, in our case, to sensibility, since there is no other way in which objects can be given to us.

The effect of an object on the capacity for representation, insofar as we are affected by it, is **sensation**.[d] That intuition which is related to the object through sensation is called **empirical**. The undetermined object of an empirical intuition is called **appearance**.[3]

I call that in the appearance which corresponds to sensation its **matter,** but that which allows the manifold of appearance to be intuited as or-

---

[a] The "Transcendental Aesthetic" underwent major changes between the two editions of the *Critique*, including but not limited to the separation of the "Metaphysical" and "Transcendental" expositions of space and time and the addition of three sections to the concluding "General Remarks." We therefore present both versions in their entirety, using the marginal pagination and notes to show where specific changes were made. The following version from the first edition also includes the notes Kant made in his own copy of that edition.

[b] The following note is inserted in Kant's copy:
    "[intuition] is opposed to the concept, which is merely the mark of intuition.
    "The universal must be given in the particular. Through that it has significance."
(E X, p. 15; 23:21)

[c] Added in Kant's copy: "If the representation is not in itself the cause of the object [*Objects*]." (E XI, p. 15; 23:21)

[d] Added in Kant's copy: "Intuition is related to the object [*Object*], sensation merely to the subject." (E XII, p. 15; 23:21)

dered in certain relations[a] I call the **form** of appearance. Since that within which the sensations can alone be ordered and placed in a certain form cannot itself be in turn sensation, the matter of all appearance is only given to us *a posteriori*, but its form must all lie ready for it in the mind *a priori*, and can therefore be considered separately from all sensation.

I call all representations pure (in the transcendental sense) in which nothing is to be encountered that belongs to sensation. Accordingly the pure form of sensible intuitions in general is to be encountered in the mind *a priori*, wherein all of the manifold of appearances is intuited in certain relations. This pure form of sensibility itself is also called pure intuition. So if I separate from the representation of a body that which the understanding thinks about it, such as substance, force, divisibility, etc., as well as that which belongs to sensation, such as impenetrability, hardness, color, etc., something from this empirical intuition is still left for me, namely extension and form. These belong to the pure intuition, which occurs *a priori*, even without an actual object of the senses or sensation, as a mere form of sensibility in the mind.

I call a science of all principles[b] of *a priori* sensibility the **transcendental aesthetic.**[*,4] There must therefore be such a science, which constitutes the first part of the transcendental doctrine of elements, in contrast to that which contains the principles[c] of pure thinking, and is named transcendental logic.

---

* The Germans are the only ones who now employ the word "aesthetics" to designate that which others call the critique of taste. The ground for this is a failed hope, held by the excellent analyst Baumgarten, of bringing the critical estimation of the beautiful under principles of reason,[d] and elevating its rules to a science. But this effort is futile. For the putative rules or criteria are merely empirical as far as their sources are concerned, and can therefore never serve as *a priori* rules according to which our judgment of taste must be directed, rather the latter constitutes the genuine touchstone of the correctness of the former. For this reason it is advisable again to desist from the use of this term and to save it for that doctrine which is true science (whereby one would come closer to the language and the sense of the ancients, among whom the division of cognition into αἰσθητα και νοητα was very well known).

[a] *Verhältnissen.* Kant uses the term *Verhältnis* throughout the "Transcendental Aesthetic" to denote the relation among several things occupying different positions in space or time, reserving the word *Beziehung* to denote the relation between objects and the cognitive subject (in which sense it is used only four times, to be noted below, in the final section of the "Transcendental Aesthetic"). Since "relation" or its plural will thus almost always be translating *Verhältnis* or its plural, further notes of the occurrence of this term in the "Transcendental Aesthetic" will be omitted.

[b] *Principien*

[c] *Principien*

[d] *Vernunftprincipien*

In the transcendental aesthetic we will therefore first isolate sensibil- A 2 2
ity by separating off everything that the understanding thinks through
its concepts, so that nothing but empirical intuition remains. Second,
we will then detach from the latter everything that belongs to sensation,
so that nothing remains except pure intuition and the mere form of appearances, which is the only thing that sensibility can make available *a
priori*. In this investigation it will be found that there are two pure forms
of sensible intuition as principles[a] of *a priori* cognition, namely space
and time, with the assessment of which we will now be concerned.

The Transcendental Aesthetic B 37
First Section
On space.

By means of outer sense (a property of our mind) we represent to ourselves objects as outside us, and all as in space. In space their form,
magnitude, and relation to one another is determined, or determinable. Inner sense, by means of which the mind intuits itself, or its
inner state, gives, to be sure, no intuition of the soul itself, as an object;[b] yet it is still a determinate form, under which the intuition of its A 2 3
inner state is alone possible, so that everything that belongs to the
inner determinations is represented in relations of time. Time can no
more be intuited externally than space can be intuited as something in
us. Now what are space and time? Are they actual entities?[c] Are they
only determinations or relations of things, yet ones that would pertain
to them even if they were not intuited, or are they relations that only
attach to the form of intuition alone, and thus to the subjective consti- B 38
tution of our mind, without which these predicates could not be ascribed to any thing at all?[5] In order to instruct ourselves about this, we
will consider space first.[6]

1) Space is not an empirical concept that has been drawn from outer
experiences. For in order for certain sensations to be related[d] to something outside me (i.e., to something in another place in space from that
in which I find myself), thus in order for me to represent them as outside one another, thus not merely as different but as in different places,
the representation of space must already be their ground.[7] Thus the
representation of space cannot be obtained from the relations of outer

[a] *Principien*
[b] *Object*
[c] *wirkliche Wesen*
[d] *bezogen*

appearance through experience, but this outer experience is itself first possible only through this representation.^a

A 24   2)^b Space is a necessary representation, *a priori*, which is the ground of all outer intuitions.[8] One can never represent that there is no space, although one can very well think that there are no objects to be encoun-

B 39   tered in it.[9] It is therefore to be regarded as the condition of the possibility of appearances, not as a determination dependent on them, and is an *a priori* representation that necessarily grounds outer appearances.^c

3) The apodictic certainty of all geometrical principles and the possibility of their *a priori* construction are grounded in this *a priori* necessity. For if this representation of space were a concept acquired *a posteriori*, which was drawn out of general outer experience, the first principles of mathematical determination would be nothing but perceptions. They would therefore have all the contingency of perception, and it would not even be necessary that only one straight line lie between two points, but experience would merely always teach that. What is borrowed from experience always has only comparative universality, namely through induction. One would therefore only be able to say that as far as has been observed to date, no space has been found that has more than three dimensions.^{d,10}

4) Space is not a discursive or, as is said, general concept of relations

A 25   of things in general, but a pure intuition. For, first, one can only represent a single space, and if one speaks of many spaces, one understands by that only parts of one and the same unique space.[11] And these parts cannot as it were precede the single all-encompassing space as its components (from which its composition would be possible), but rather are only thought in it. It is essentially single; the manifold in it, thus also

---

^a The following note is added at the bottom of this page in Kant's copy:

"[1.] Space is not a concept, but an intuition.

2. —— – not an empirical intuition, for everything empirical one can . . .

3. It is an *a priori* intuition . . .

4. Space is the subjective form . . ." (E XIII, p. 16; 23:22)

^b Added in Kant's copy:

"Space is not a concept of external relations, as Leibniz supposed, but that which grounds the possibility of external relations.

"The necessity of the relation of our propositions to something external is a proof of the real connection^e in which we stand with external things; against idealism." (E XIV, p. 16; 23:22)

^c Inserted in Kant's copy:

"Space is not a concept derived from experience, but a ground of possible outer experience. I must have a concept of space if . . ." (E XV, p. 16; 23:22)

"Proof of the ideality of space from the synthetic *a priori* proposition. of. and of. [*sic*] This is no hypothesis . . . [*sic*]" (E XVI, p. 16; 23:22)

^d This paragraph is deleted in the second edition, and replaced by §3, "The Transcendental Exposition of the Concept of Space" (B 40–1).

^e *Verbindung*

the general concept of spaces in general, rests merely on limitations. From this it follows that in respect to it an *a priori* intuition (which is not empirical) grounds all concepts of them. Thus also all geometrical principles, e.g., that in a triangle two sides together are always greater than the third, are never derived from general concepts of line and triangle, but rather are derived from intuition and indeed derived *a priori* with apodictic certainty.

5) Space is represented as a given infinite magnitude. A general concept of space (which is common to a foot as well as an ell) can determine nothing in respect to magnitude. If there were not boundlessness in the progress of intuition, no concept of relations could bring with it a principle*[a]* of their infinity.*[b],12*

Conclusions from the above concepts. A26/B42

a) Space represents no property at all of any things in themselves nor any relation of them to each other, i.e., no determination of them that attaches to objects themselves and that would remain even if one were to abstract from all subjective conditions of intuition. For neither absolute nor relative determinations can be intuited prior to the existence of the things to which they pertain, thus be intuited *a priori*.[13]

b) Space is nothing other than merely the form of all appearances of outer sense, i.e., the subjective condition of sensibility, under which alone outer intuition is possible for us. Now since the receptivity of the subject to be affected by objects necessarily precedes all intuitions of these objects, it can be understood how the form of all appearances can be given in the mind prior to all actual perceptions, thus *a priori*, and how as a pure intuition, in which all objects must be determined, it can contain principles*[c]* of their relations prior to all experience.*[d]*

We can accordingly speak of space, extended beings, and so on, only from the human standpoint. If we depart from the subjective condition under which alone we can acquire outer intuition, namely that through which we may be affected by objects, then the representation of space

---

[a] *Principium*

[b] This paragraph is changed in the second edition; see paragraph 4, B39–40 below.

[c] *Principien*

[d] Inserted in Kant's copy: "Space and time carry with them in their representation the concept of necessity. Now this is not the necessity of a concept. For we can prove that their non-existence is not contradictory. Necessity also cannot lie in the empirical intuition. For this can, to be sure, carry with it the concept of existence, but not of necessary existence. Thus this necessity is not in the object [*Object*] – objective – at all; consequently it is only a necessary condition of the subject for all perceptions of the senses." (E XVII, p. 17; 23:22–3)

A27/B43 signifies nothing at all.*ª* This predicate is attributed to things only insofar as they appear to us, i.e., are objects of sensibility.*ᵇ,14* The constant
form of this receptivity, which we call sensibility, is a necessary condition of all the relations within which objects can be intuited as outside
us, and, if one abstracts from these objects, it is a pure intuition, which
bears the name of space. Since we cannot make the special conditions of
sensibility into conditions of the possibility of things, but only of their
appearances, we can well say that space comprehends all things that
may*ᶜ* appear to us externally, but not all things in themselves, whether
they be intuited or not, or*ᵈ* by whatever subject they may be intuited.
For we cannot judge at all whether the intuitions of other thinking beings are bound to the same conditions that limit our intuition and that
are universally valid for us. If we add the limitation*ᵉ* of a judgment to the
concept of the subject, then the judgment is unconditionally valid. The
proposition "All things are next to one another in space"*ᶠ* is valid only
under the limitation that these things be taken as objects of our sensible
intuition. If here I add the condition to the concept and say: "All things,
as outer intuitions, are next to one another in space," then this rule is
B44 valid universally and without limitation. Our expositions accordingly
A28 teach the **reality** (i.e., objective validity) of space in regard to everything
that can come before us externally as an object, but at the same time*ᵍ* the
ideality of space in regard to things when they are considered in themselves through reason, i.e., without taking account of the constitution of
our sensibility. We therefore assert the **empirical reality** of space (with
respect to all possible outer experience), though to be sure at the same
time its **transcendental ideality**, i.e., that it is nothing as soon as we
leave out the condition of the possibility of all experience, and take it as
something that grounds the things in themselves.

ª Inserted in Kant's copy: "Perhaps all created beings are bound to it, that we do not
know. This much one can know, that it is a merely sensible form. The most important
thing is that it yields a determinate concept *a priori*, and through inner intuition we
would not have sensations, thus no empirical representations and no science of objects
[*Objecte*] *a priori*." (E XVIII, p. 17; 23:23)

ᵇ Here Kant's copy inserts: "as Mendelssohn could so apodictically assert, since he still
gave space objective reality." (E XX, p. 17; 23:44)
  At about this point, this partially decipherable note also appears:
    "Field of space and of time.
  "1. Both cannot extend further than to objects of the senses, thus not to God; 2.
Even among these they are valid only of things as objects of . . ." (E XIX, p. 17; 23:23)

ᶜ Here Kant's copy inserts "ever" (*nur immer*) (E XXI, p. 18; 23:44).

ᵈ In his copy Kant crosses out "or not, or" (E XXII, p. 18; 23:44).

ᵉ Kant's copy changes "limitation" to "limiting condition" (E XXIII, p. 18; 23:45).

ᶠ In his copy Kant changes this proposition to "All things are next to one another in space
or they are somewhere" (E XXIV, p. 18; 23:45).

ᵍ In his copy Kant inserts "also" (changing "*ob zwar*" to "*aber auch*" (E XXV, p. 18; 23:45)

Besides space, however, there is no other subjective representation related*a* to something external that could be called *a priori* objective. *b*Hence this subjective condition of all outer appearances cannot be compared with any other. The pleasant taste of a wine does not belong to the objective determinations of the wine, thus of an object*c* even considered as an appearance, but rather to the particular constitution of sense in the subject that enjoys it. Colors are not objective qualities of the bodies to the intuition of which they are attached, but are also only modifications of the sense of sight, which is affected by light in a certain way. Space, on the contrary, as a condition of outer objects,*d* necessarily belongs to their appearance or intuition. Taste and colors are by no means necessary conditions under which alone the objects can be objects*e* of the senses for us. They are only combined with the appearance as contingently added effects of the particular organization. Hence they are not *a priori* representations, but are grounded on sensation, and pleasant taste is even grounded on feeling (of pleasure and displeasure) as an effect of the sensation. And no one can have *a priori* the representation either of a color or of any taste: but space concerns only the pure form of intuition, thus it includes no sensation (nothing empirical) in itself, and all kinds and determinations of space can and even must be able to be represented *a priori* if concepts of shapes as well as relations are to arise. Through space alone is it possible for things to be outer objects for us.*f*

    The aim of this remark is only to prevent one from thinking of illustrating the asserted ideality of space with completely inadequate examples, since things like colors, taste, etc., are correctly considered not as qualities of things but as mere alterations of our subject, which can even be different in different people. For in this case that which is originally itself only appearance, e.g., a rose, counts in an empirical sense as a thing in itself, which yet can appear different to every eye in regard to color. The transcendental concept of appearances in space, on the contrary, is a critical reminder that absolutely nothing that is intuited in space is a thing in itself, and that space is not a form that is proper to

A 29

B 45

A 30

---

a *bezogene*
b The remainder of this paragraph is altered in the second edition: see B 44–5 below.
c *Objects*
d *Objecte*
e *Objecte*
f Inserted in the margin of Kant's copy:
    "Pure idealism concerns the existence of things outside us. Critical idealism leaves that undecided, and asserts only that the form of their intuition is merely in us." (E XXVI, p. 18; 23:23)
    A further note adds: "An idealism, from which the possibility of an *a priori* cognition and of mathematics can be cognized." (E XXVII, p. 19; 23:23)

anything in itself, but rather that objects in themselves are not known to us at all, and that what we call outer objects are nothing other than mere representations of our sensibility, whose form is space, but whose true correlate, i.e., the thing in itself, is not and cannot be cognized through them, but is also never asked after in experience.

B 46

The Transcendental Aesthetic
Second Section
On time.[15]

1)[a] Time is not an empirical concept that is somehow drawn from an experience. For simultaneity or succession would not themselves come into perception if the representation of time did not ground them *a priori*. Only under its presupposition can one represent that several things exist at one and the same time (simultaneously) or in different times (successively).

A 31   2) Time is a necessary representation that grounds all intuitions. In regard to appearances in general one cannot remove time, though one can very well take the appearances away from time. Time is therefore given *a priori*. In it alone is all actuality of appearances possible. The latter could all disappear, but time itself, as the universal condition of their possibility, cannot be removed.

B 47   3) This *a priori* necessity also grounds the possibility of apodictic principles of the relations of time, or axioms of time in general. It has only one dimension: different times are not simultaneous, but successive (just as different spaces are not successive, but simultaneous). These principles could not be drawn from experience, for this would yield neither strict universality nor apodictic certainty. We would only be able to say: This is what common perception teaches, but not: This is how matters must stand. These principles are valid as rules under which experiences are possible at all, and instruct us prior to them, not through it.[b]

     4) Time is no discursive or, as one calls it, general concept, but a pure
A 32 form of sensible intuition. Different times are only parts of one and the same time.[16] That representation, however, which can only be given through a single object, is an intuition. Further, the proposition that different times cannot be simultaneous cannot be derived from a gen-

---

[a] The "1" is actually printed at above the center of the first line of this paragraph rather than at its beginning.

[b] The text reads "*belehren uns vor derselben, und nicht durch dieselbe.*" Earlier editors suggested emending the last word to "*dieselben*" but if the sentence is interpreted to mean "instructs us prior to experiences, not through common perception," it can be read without emendation.

eral concept. The proposition is synthetic, and cannot arise from concepts alone. It is therefore immediately contained in the intuition and representation of time.

5) The infinitude of time signifies nothing more than that every determinate magnitude of time is only possible through limitations of a single time grounding it. The original representation, time, must therefore be given as unlimited. But where the parts themselves and every magnitude of an object can be determinately represented only through limitation, there the entire representation cannot be given through concepts (for then the partial representations precede) but their immediate intuition must be the ground.[17]

B48

Conclusions from these concepts.

B49

a) Time is not something that would subsist for itself or attach to things as an objective determination, and thus remain if one abstracted from all subjective conditions of the intuition of them; for in the first case it would be something that was actual yet without an actual object. As far as the second case is concerned, however, time could not precede the objects as a determination or order attaching to the things themselves as their condition and be cognized and intuited *a priori* through synthetic propositions. But the latter, on the contrary, can very well occur if time is nothing other than the subjective condition under which all intuitions can take place in us. For then this form of inner intuition can be represented prior to the objects, thus *a priori*.[18]

A33

b) Time is nothing other than the form of inner sense, i.e., of the intuition of our self and our inner state.[19] For time cannot be a determination of outer appearances; it belongs neither to a shape or a position, etc., but on the contrary determines the relation of representations in our inner state. And just because this inner intuition yields no shape we also attempt to remedy this lack through analogies, and represent the temporal sequence through a line progressing to infinity, in which the manifold constitutes a series that is of only one dimension, and infer from the properties of this line to all the properties of time, with the sole difference that the parts of the former are simultaneous but those of the latter always exist successively. From this it is also apparent that the representation of time is itself an intuition, since all its relations can be expressed in an outer intuition.

B50

c) Time is the *a priori* formal condition of all appearances in general. Space, as the pure form of all outer intuitions, is limited as an *a priori* condition merely to outer intuitions. But since, on the contrary, all representations, whether or not they have outer things as their object, nevertheless as determinations of the mind themselves belong to the inner state, while this inner state belongs under the formal condition of inner

A34

intuition, and thus of time, so time is an *a priori* condition of all appearance in general, and indeed the immediate condition of the inner intuition (of our souls), and thereby also the mediate condition of outer

B51 appearances. If I can say *a priori*: all outer appearances are in space and determined *a priori* according to the relations of space, so from the principle[a] of inner sense I can say entirely generally: all appearances in general, i.e., all objects of the senses, are in time, and necessarily stand in relations of time.

If we abstract from our way of internally intuiting ourselves and by means of this intuition also dealing with all outer intuitions in the power of representation, and thus take objects as they may be in themselves, then time is nothing. It is only of objective validity in regard to appearances, because these are already things that we take as **objects of**

A35 **our senses;** but it is no longer objective if one abstracts from the sensibility of our intuition, thus from that kind of representation that is peculiar to us, and speaks of **things in general.** Time is therefore merely a subjective condition of our (human) intuition (which is always sensible, i.e., insofar as we are affected by objects), and in itself, outside the subject, is nothing. Nonetheless it is necessarily objective in regard to all appearances, thus also in regard to all things that can come before us in experience. We cannot say all things are in time, because with the

B52 concept of things in general abstraction is made from every kind of intuition of them, but this is the real condition under which time belongs to the representation of objects. Now if the condition is added to the concept, and the principle says that all things as appearances (objects of sensible intuition) are in time, then the principle has its sound objective correctness and *a priori* universality.

Our assertions accordingly teach the **empirical reality** of time, i.e., objective validity in regard to all objects that may ever be given to our senses. And since our intuition is always sensible, no object can ever be given to us in experience that would not belong under the condition of time. But, on the contrary, we dispute all claim of time to absolute reality, namely where it would attach to things absolutely as a condition

A36 or property even without regard to the form of our sensible intuition. Such properties, which pertain to things in themselves, can never be given to us through the senses. In this therefore consists the **transcendental ideality** of time, according to which it is nothing at all if one abstracts from the subjective conditions of sensible intuition, and cannot be counted as either subsisting or inhering in the objects in themselves (without their relation to our intuition). Yet this ideality is to be com-

B53 pared with the subreptions of sensation just as little as that of space is, because in that case one presupposes that the appearance itself, in which

[a] *Princip*

these predicates inhere, has objective reality, which is here entirely absent except insofar as it is merely empirical, i.e., the object itself is regarded merely as appearance: concerning which the above remark in the previous section is to be consulted.[a,b]

Elucidation.

Against this theory, which concedes empirical reality to time but disputes its absolute and transcendental reality, insightful men have so unanimously proposed one objection that I conclude that it must naturally occur to every reader who is not accustomed to these considerations.[20] It goes thus: Alterations are real (this is proved by the change of   A 37 our own representations, even if one would deny all outer appearances together with their alterations). Now alterations are possible only in time, therefore time is something real. There is no difficulty in answering. I admit the entire argument. Time is certainly something real,[c] namely the real form of inner intuition. It therefore has subjective reality in regard to inner experience, i.e., I really have the representation of time and of my determinations in it. It is therefore to be regarded re-   B 54 ally not as object[d] but as the way of representing myself as object.[e] But if I or another being could intuit myself without this condition of sensibility, then these very determinations, which we now represent to ourselves as alterations, would yield us a cognition in which the representation of time and thus also of alteration would not occur at all. Its empirical reality therefore remains as a condition of all our experiences. Only absolute reality cannot be granted to it according to what has been adduced above. It is nothing except the form of our inner intuition.* If

---

* I can, to be sure, say: my representations succeed one another; but that only means that we are conscious of them as in a temporal sequence, i.e., according to the form of inner sense. Time is not on that account something in itself, nor any determination objectively adhering to things.

[a] This refers to A28–30/B44–5 in § 3.

[b] Inserted in Kant's copy, before the next section: "Space and time are not merely logical forms of our sensibility, i.e., they do not consist in the fact that we represent actual relations to ourselves confusedly; for then how could we derive from them a priori synthetic and true propositions? We do not intuit space, but in a confused manner; rather it is the form of our intuition. Sensibility is not confusion of representations, but the subjective condition of consciousness." (E XXVIII, p. 20; 23:23)

[c] Kant's copy adds: "So is space. This proves that here a reality (consequently also individual intuition) is given, which yet always grounds the reality as a thing. Space and time do not belong to the reality of things, but only to our representations." (E XXIX, p. 20; 23:24)

[d] Object

[e] Objects

one removes the special condition of our sensibility from it, then the concept of time also disappears, and it does not adhere to the objects themselves, rather merely to the subject that intuits them.[21]

The cause, however, on account of which this objection is so unanimously made, and indeed by those who nevertheless know of nothing convincing to object against the doctrine of the ideality of space,[22] is this. They did not expect to be able to demonstrate the absolute reality of space apodictically, since they were confronted by idealism, according to which the reality of outer objects is not capable of any strict proof; on the contrary, the reality of the object of our inner sense (of myself and my state) is immediately clear through consciousness. The former could have been a mere illusion, but the latter, according to their opinion, is undeniably something real. But they did not consider that both, without their reality as representations being disputed, nevertheless belong only to appearance, which always has two sides, one where the object[a] is considered in itself (without regard to the way in which it is to be intuited, the constitution of which however must for that very reason always remain problematic), the other where the form of the intuition of this object is considered, which must not be sought in the object in itself but in the subject to which it appears, but which nevertheless really and necessarily pertains to the representation of this object.

Time and space are accordingly two sources of cognition, from which different synthetic cognitions can be drawn *a priori*, of which especially pure mathematics in regard to the cognitions of space and its relations

provides a splendid example.[23] Both taken together are, namely, the pure forms of all sensible intuition, and thereby make possible synthetic *a priori* propositions. But these *a priori* sources of cognition determine their own boundaries by that very fact (that they are merely conditions of sensibility), namely that they apply to objects only so far as they are considered as appearances, but do not present things in themselves. Those alone are the field of their validity, beyond which no further objective use of them takes place. This reality of space and time, further, leaves the certainty of experiential cognition untouched: for we are just as certain of that whether these forms necessarily adhere to the things in themselves or only to our intuition of these things. Those, however, who assert the absolute reality of space and time, whether they assume it to be subsisting or only inhering, must themselves come into conflict with the principles[b] of experience. For if they decide in favor of the first (which is generally the position of the mathematical investigators of nature),[24] then they must assume two eternal and infinite self-subsisting non-entities (space and time), which exist (yet without there being any-

[a] *Object*
[b] *Principien*

thing real) only in order to comprehend everything real within themselves. If they adopt the second position (as do some metaphysicians of A 40 nature), and hold space and time to be relations of appearances (next to or successive to one another) that are abstracted from experience though confusedly represented in this abstraction, then they must dispute the validity or at least the apodictic certainty of *a priori* mathematical doctrines in regard to real things (e.g., in space), since this certainty does not occur *a posteriori*, and on this view the *a priori* concepts of space and time are only creatures of the imagination, the origin of which must really be sought in experience, out of whose abstracted relations imagination has made something that, to be sure, contains what is general in them, but that cannot occur without the restrictions that nature has attached to them.[25] The first succeed in opening the field of appearances for mathematical assertions; however, they themselves become very confused through precisely these conditions if the understanding would go beyond this field. The second succeed, to be sure, with respect to the latter, in that the representations of space and time do not stand in their way if they would judge of objects not as appearances but merely in relation to the understanding; but they can neither offer any ground for the possibility of *a priori* mathematical cognitions (since they lack a true and objectively valid *a priori* intuition), nor can they bring the propositions of experience into necessary accord with those assertions. On our A 41 theory of the true constitution of these two original forms of sensibility B 58 both difficulties are remedied.[a]

Finally, that the transcendental aesthetic cannot contain more than these two elements, namely space and time, is clear from the fact that all other concepts belonging to sensibility, even that of motion, which unites both elements, presuppose something empirical.[26] For this presupposes the perception of something movable. In space considered in itself there is nothing movable; hence the movable must be something that is found **in space only through experience,** thus an empirical datum. In the same way the transcendental aesthetic cannot count the concept of alteration among its *a priori* data; for time itself does not alter, but only something that is within time. For this there is required the perception of some existence and the succession of its determinations, thus experience.[b]

---

[a] Inserted in Kant's copy: "Leibniz's system of space and time was to transform both into intellectual but confused concepts. But from this the possibility of *a priori* cognition cannot be understood, for in that case both must precede." (E XXX, p. 20; 23:24)

[b] Inserted in Kant's copy: "Conclusion: That space and time of course have objective reality, but not for what pertains to things outside of their relation [*Relation*] to our faculty of cognition, but rather only in relation to it, and thus to the form of sensibility, hence solely as appearances." (E XXXI, p. 21; 23:24)

General remarks
on the transcendental aesthetic.

A 42   It will first be necessary to explain as distinctly as possible our opinion in regard to the fundamental constitution of sensible cognition in general, in order to preclude all misinterpretation of it.

We have therefore wanted to say that all our intuition is nothing but the representation of appearance; that the things that we intuit are not in themselves what we intuit them to be, nor are their relations so constituted in themselves as they appear to us; and that if we remove our own subject or even only the subjective constitution of the senses in general, then all the constitution, all relations of objects*a* in space and time, indeed space and time themselves would disappear, and as appearances they cannot exist in themselves, but only in us. What may be the case with objects in themselves and abstracted from all this receptivity of our sensibility remains entirely unknown to us. We are acquainted with nothing except our way of perceiving them, which is peculiar to us, and which therefore does not necessarily pertain to every being, though to be sure it pertains to every human being. We are con-
B 60   cerned solely with this. Space and time are its pure forms, sensation in general its matter. We can cognize only the former *a priori*, i.e., prior to all actual perception, and they are therefore called pure intuition; the latter, however, is that in our cognition that is responsible for it being called *a posteriori* cognition, i.e., empirical intuition. The former adheres to our sensibility absolutely necessarily, whatever sort of sensa-
A 43   tions we may have; the latter can be very different. Even if we could bring this intuition of ours to the highest degree of distinctness we would not thereby come any closer to the constitution of objects in themselves. For in any case we would still completely cognize only our own way of intuiting, i.e., our sensibility, and this always only under the conditions originally depending on the subject, space and time; what the objects may be in themselves would still never be known through the most enlightened cognition of their appearance, which is alone given to us.

That our entire sensibility is nothing but the confused representation of things, which contains solely that which pertains to them in themselves but only under a heap of marks and partial representations that we can never consciously separate from one another, is therefore a falsification of the concept of sensibility and of appearance that renders the entire theory of them useless and empty. The difference between an
B 61   indistinct and a distinct representation is merely logical, and does not concern the content. Without doubt the concept of **right** that is used

a *Objecte*

168

by the healthy understanding contains the very same things that the most subtle speculation can evolve out of it, only in common and practical use one is not conscious of these manifold representations in these thoughts. Thus one cannot say that the common concept is sensible and contains a mere appearance, for right cannot appear at all; rather its concept lies in the understanding and represents a constitution (the moral constitution) of actions that pertains to them in themselves. The representation of a **body** in intuition, on the contrary, contains nothing at all that could pertain to an object in itself, but merely the appearance of something and the way in which we are affected by it; and this receptivity of our cognitive capacity is called sensibility and remains worlds apart from the cognition of the object in itself even if one might see through to the very bottom of it (the appearance). A44

The Leibnizian-Wolffian philosophy has therefore directed all investigations of the nature and origin of our cognitions to an entirely unjust point of view in considering the distinction between sensibility and the intellectual as merely logical, since it is obviously transcendental, and does not concern merely the form of distinctness or indistinctness, but its origin and content, so that through sensibility we do not cognize the constitution of things in themselves merely indistinctly, but rather not at all, and, as soon as we take away our subjective constitution, the represented object[a] with the properties that sensible intuition attributes to it is nowhere to be encountered, nor can it be encountered, for it is just this subjective constitution that determines its form as appearance.[27] B62

We ordinarily distinguish quite well between that which is essentially attached to the intuition of appearances, and is valid for every human sense in general, and that which pertains to them only contingently because it is not valid for the relation[b] to sensibility in general but only for a particular situation or organization of this or that sense. And thus one calls the first cognition one that represents the object in itself, but the second one only its appearance. This distinction, however, is only empirical. If one stands by it (as commonly happens) and does not regard that empirical intuition as in turn mere appearance (as ought to happen), so that there is nothing to be encountered in it that pertains to any thing in itself, then our transcendental distinction is lost, and we believe ourselves to cognize things in themselves, although we have nothing to do with anything except appearances anywhere (in the world of sense), even in the deepest research into its objects. Thus, we would certainly B63

---

[a] *Object*
[b] Here is where Kant switches from *Verhältnis* to *Beziehung* as his topic switches from the relation of objects in space or time to each other to the relation of space and time to us. With one exception to be noted, therefore, for the remainder of the section "relation" translates *Beziehung*.

call a rainbow a mere appearance in a sun-shower, but would call this rain the thing in itself, and this is correct, as long as we understand the latter concept in a merely physical sense, as that which in universal experience and all different positions relative to the senses is always determined thus and not otherwise in intuition. But if we consider this A46 empirical object in general and, without turning to its agreement with every human sense, ask whether it (not the raindrops, since these, as appearances, are already empirical objects)*a* represents an object in itself, then the question of the relation of the representation to the object is transcendental, and not only these drops are mere appearances, but even their round form, indeed even the space through which they fall are nothing in themselves, but only mere modifications or foundations*b* of our sensible intuition; the transcendental object,*c* however, remains unknown to us.

The second important concern of our transcendental aesthetic is that it not merely earn some favor as a plausible hypothesis, but that it be as certain and indubitable as can ever be demanded of a theory that is to serve as an organon. In order to make this certainty fully convincing we B64 will choose a case in which its validity can become obvious.

Thus, if it were to be supposed that space and time are in themselves objective and conditions of the possibility of things in themselves, then it would be shown, first, that there is a large number of *a priori* apodictic and synthetic propositions about both, but especially about space, which we will therefore here investigate as our primary example. Since the propositions of geometry are cognized synthetically *a priori* and A47 with apodictic certainty, I ask: Whence do you take such propositions, and on what does our understanding rely in attaining to such absolutely necessary and universally valid truths?*d* There is no other way than through concepts or through intuitions, both of which, however, are given, as such, either *a priori* or *a posteriori*. The latter, namely empirical concepts, together with that on which they are grounded, empirical intuition, cannot yield any synthetic proposition except one that is also merely empirical, i.e., a proposition of experience; thus it can never contain necessity and absolute universality of the sort that is nevertheless characteristic of all propositions of geometry. Concerning the first and only means for attaining to such cognitions, however, namely through mere concepts or *a priori* intuitions, it is clear that from mere concepts no synthetic cognition but only merely analytic cognition can B65 be attained. Take the proposition that with two straight lines no space

a *Objecte*
b *Grundlagen*
c *Object*
d The question mark replaces a period in the text.

at all can be enclosed, thus no figure is possible, and try to derive it from the concept of straight lines and the number two; or take the proposition that a figure is possible with three straight lines, and in the same way try to derive it from these concepts. All of your effort is in vain, and you see yourself forced to take refuge in intuition, as indeed geometry always does. You thus give yourself an object in intuition; but what kind A48
is this, is it a pure *a priori* intuition or an empirical one? If it were the latter, then no universally valid, let alone apodictic proposition could ever come from it: for experience can never provide anything of this sort. You must therefore give your object *a priori* in intuition, and ground your synthetic proposition on this. If there did not lie in you a faculty for intuiting *a priori*; if this subjective condition regarding form were not at the same time the universal *a priori* condition under which alone the object*a* of this (outer) intuition is itself possible; if the object (the triangle) were something in itself without relation to your subject: then how could you say that what necessarily lies in your subjective conditions for constructing a triangle must also necessarily pertain to the triangle in itself?*b* for you could not add to your concept (of three lines) something new (the figure) that must thereby necessarily be encoun- B66
tered in the object, since this is given prior to your cognition and not through it. If, therefore, space (and time as well) were not a mere form of your intuition that contains *a priori* conditions under which alone things could be outer objects for you, which are nothing in themselves without these subjective conditions, then you could make out absolutely nothing synthetic and *a priori* about outer objects.*c*,28 It is therefore indubitably certain, and not merely possible or even probable, that space and time, as the necessary conditions of all (outer and inner) experience, A49
are merely subjective conditions of all our intuition, in relation*d* to which therefore all objects are mere appearances and not things given for themselves in this way; about these appearances, further, much may be said *a priori* that concerns their form, but nothing whatsoever about the things in themselves that may ground them.*e*

---

a *Object*
b Question mark added.
c *Objecte*
d *Verhältnis*
e Kant adds three paragraphs and a conclusion following this point in the second edition (B 66–73). In his copy of the first edition, he here inserted the following note, which to some extent outlines the additions to be made in the second:

"On the necessity of space and time as *a priori* conditions belonging to the existence of things – On the effort nevertheless to remove both from a being that is no object of the senses, God – Mendelssohn.

"On the theory of nature: how it is to be seen from that that bodies are mere *phenomena*." (E XXXII, p. 21; 23:24)

A19/B33

The Transcendental Doctrine of Elements
First Part
The Transcendental Aesthetic[a]

<§ 1>[b]

In whatever way and through whatever means a cognition may relate to objects, that through which it relates immediately to them, and at which all thought as a means is directed as an end, is **intuition.** This, however, takes place only insofar as the object is given to us; but this in turn, <at least for us humans,> is possible only if it affects the mind in a certain way. The capacity (receptivity) to acquire representations through the way in which we are affected by objects is called **sensibility.** Objects are therefore **given** to us by means of sensibility, and it alone affords us **intuitions;** but they are **thought** through the understanding, and from it arise **concepts.** But all thought, whether straightaway (*directe*) or through a detour (*indirecte*), must, <by means of certain marks,> ultimately be related to intuitions, thus, in our case, to sensibility, since there is no other way in which objects can be given to us.

B34 The effect of an object on the capacity for representation, insofar as
A20 we are affected by it, is **sensation.** That intuition which is related to the object through sensation is called **empirical.** The undetermined object of an empirical intuition is called **appearance.**

I call that in the appearance which corresponds to sensation its **matter,** but that which allows the manifold of appearance to be ordered[c] in

[a] We here present the revised version of the "Transcendental Aesthetic" that Kant prepared for the second edition of the *Critique.* Since in addition to the major changes that he made, all of which will be noted, Kant also made numerous minor changes that it would be cumbersome to note individually, we will enclose all the changes Kant made in B within angled brackets (< . . . >), whether or not they are otherwise noted. Editorial notes on passages unchanged from A will not be repeated.

[b] In the second edition, Kant divided the "Transcendental Doctrine of Elements" from the beginning of the "Transcendental Aesthetic" through the end of the "Transcendental Deduction of the Pure Concepts of the Understanding" into twenty-seven numbered sections. In the case of some sections, new titles were also added for material otherwise taken over without other change from the first edition.

[c] In the first edition this reads "intuited as ordered in certain relations . . ."

certain relations[a] I call the **form** of appearance. Since that within which the sensations can alone be ordered and placed in a certain form cannot itself be in turn sensation, the matter of all appearance is only given to us *a posteriori*, but its form must all lie ready for it in the mind *a priori*, and can therefore be considered separately from all sensation.

I call all representations **pure** (in the transcendental sense) in which nothing is to be encountered that belongs to sensation. Accordingly the pure form of sensible intuitions in general is to be encountered in the mind *a priori*, wherein all of the manifold of appearances is intuited in certain relations. This pure form of sensibility itself is also called **pure intuition.** So if I separate from the representation of a body that which   B 35
the understanding thinks about it, such as substance, force, divisibility, etc., as well as that which belongs to sensation, such as impenetrability, hardness, color, etc., something from this empirical intuition is still left   A 21
for me, namely extension and form. These belong to the pure intuition, which occurs *a priori*, even without an actual object of the senses or sensation, as a mere form of sensibility in the mind.

I call a science of all principles[b] of *a priori* sensibility the **transcendental aesthetic.*** There must therefore be such a science, which constitutes the first part of the transcendental doctrine of elements, in   B 36
opposition to that which contains the principles[c] of pure thinking, and which is named transcendental logic.

---

* The Germans are the only ones who now employ the word "aesthetics" to des-   A 21 / B 35
ignate that which others call the critique of taste. The ground for this is a failed hope, held by the excellent analyst Baumgarten, of bringing the critical estimation of the beautiful under principles of reason,[d] and elevating its rules to a science. But this effort is futile. For the putative rules or criteria are merely empirical as far as their <most prominent> sources are concerned, and can therefore never serve as <determinate> *a priori* rules according to which our judgment of taste must be directed; rather the latter constitutes the genuine touchstone of the correctness of the former. For this reason it is advisable <either> again to desist   B 36
from the use of this term and preserve it for that doctrine which is true science (whereby one would come closer to the language and the sense of the ancients, among whom the division of cognition into ἀισθητα και νοητα was very well known), <or else to share the term with speculative philosophy and take aesthetics partly in a transcendental meaning, partly in a psychological meaning>.

---

[a] As already noted at p. 156, note *a*, with the exception of four cases in its final section, throughout the "Transcendental Aesthetic" Kant characteristically uses the term *Verhältnis*, connoting a relation among objects, rather than *Beziehung*, connoting a relation between subject and object; thus, unless otherwise noted, "relation" or its plural translates *Verhältnis* or its derivatives.

[b] *Principien*

[c] *Principien*

[d] *Vernunftprincipien*

A22 In the transcendental aesthetic we will therefore first **isolate** sensibility by separating off everything that the understanding thinks through its concepts, so that nothing but empirical intuition remains. Second, we will then detach from the latter everything that belongs to sensation, so that nothing remains except pure intuition and the mere form of appearances, which is the only thing that sensibility can make available *a priori*. In this investigation it will be found that there are two pure forms of sensible intuition as principles*a* of *a priori* cognition, namely space and time, with the assessment of which we will now be concerned.

B37

The Transcendental Aesthetic
First Section
On space.

<§ 2
Metaphysical exposition of this concept.>

By means of outer sense (a property of our mind) we represent to ourselves objects as outside us, and all as in space. In space their shape, magnitude, and relation to one another is determined, or determinable. Inner sense, by means of which the mind intuits itself, or its inner state, gives, to be sure, no intuition of the soul itself, as an object;*b* yet it is
A23 still a determinate form, under which the intuition of its inner state is alone possible, so that everything that belongs to the inner determinations is represented in relations of time. Time can no more be intuited externally than space can be intuited as something in us. Now what are space and time? Are they actual entities?*c* Are they only determinations or relations of things, yet ones that would pertain to them even if they were not intuited, or are they relations that only attach to the form of
B38 intuition alone, and thus to the subjective constitution of our mind, without which these predicates could not be ascribed to any thing at all? In order to instruct ourselves about this, we will <expound the concept of space> first.*d* <I understand by **exposition** (*expositio*) the distinct (even if not complete) representation of that which belongs to a concept; but the exposition is **metaphysical** when it contains that which exhibits the concept **as given** *a priori*.>
    1) Space is not an empirical concept that has been drawn from outer

---

a *Principien*
b *Object*
c *wirkliche Wesen*
d In the first edition: "first consider space."

experiences. For in order for certain sensations to be related[a] to something outside me (i.e., to something in another place in space from that in which I find myself), thus in order for me to represent them as outside <and next to> one another, thus not merely as different but as in different places, the representation of space must already be their ground. Thus the representation of space cannot be obtained from the relations of outer appearance through experience, but this outer experience is itself first possible only through this representation.

2) Space is a necessary representation, *a priori*, that is the ground of all outer intuitions. One can never represent that there is no space, though one can very well think that there are no objects to be encountered in it. It is therefore to be regarded as the condition of the possibility of appearances, not as a determination dependent on them, and is an *a priori* representation that necessarily grounds outer appearances.[b]

<3)> Space is not a discursive or, as is said, general concept of relations of things in general, but a pure intuition. For, first, one can only represent a single space, and if one speaks of many spaces, one understands by that only parts of one and the same unique space. And these parts cannot as it were precede the single all-encompassing space as its components (from which its composition would be possible), but rather are only thought **in it.** It is essentially single; the manifold in it, thus also the general concept of spaces in general, rests merely on limitations. From this it follows that in respect to it an *a priori* intuition (which is not empirical) grounds all concepts of it.[c] Thus also all geometrical principles, e.g., that in a triangle two sides together are always greater than the third, are never derived from general concepts of line and triangle, but rather are derived from intuition and indeed derived *a priori* with apodictic certainty.

<[d]4) Space is represented as an infinite **given** magnitude. Now one must, to be sure, think of every concept as a representation that is contained in an infinite set of different possible representations (as their common mark), which thus contains these **under itself;** but no concept, as such, can be thought as if it contained an infinite set of representations **within itself.** Nevertheless space is so thought (for all the parts of space, even to infinity, are simultaneous). Therefore the original representation of space is an *a priori* **intuition,** not **a concept.>**

A24

B39

A25

B40

---

[a] *bezogen*

[b] In the first edition there follows a paragraph (3) (at A24 above) that is replaced by the "Transcendental Exposition of the Concept of Space" in the second (see B40–1 below); the following paragraphs, (3) and (4), were thus originally numbered (4) and (5); the content of the original paragraph (5), now renumbered (4), is also changed.

[c] In the first edition: "of them," i.e., the limitations of space.

[d] As previously mentioned, the content of this paragraph is changed from the first edition.

<§ 3
Transcendental exposition of the concept of space.

I understand by a **transcendental exposition** the explanation of a concept as a principle^a from which insight into the possibility of other synthetic *a priori* cognitions can be gained. For this aim it is required 1) that such cognitions actually flow from the given concept, and 2) that these cognitions are only possible under the presupposition of a given way of explaining this concept.

Geometry is a science that determines the properties of space synthetically and yet *a priori*. What then must the representation of space be for such a cognition of it to be possible? It must originally be intuition; for from a mere concept no propositions can be drawn that go beyond the concept, which, however, happens in geometry (Introduction V). But this intuition must be encountered in us *a priori*, i.e., prior to all perception of an object, thus it must be pure, not empirical intuition. For geometrical propositions are all apodictic, i.e., combined with consciousness of their necessity, e.g., space has only three dimensions; but such propositions cannot be empirical or judgments of experience, nor inferred from them (Introduction II).

Now how can an outer intuition inhabit the mind that precedes the objects^b themselves, and in which the concept of the latter can be determined *a priori*? Obviously not otherwise than insofar as it has its seat merely in the subject, as its formal constitution for being affected by objects^c and thereby acquiring **immediate representation**, i.e., **intuition**, of them, thus only as the form of outer **sense** in general.

Thus our explanation alone makes the **possibility** of geometry as a synthetic *a priori* cognition comprehensible. Any kind of explanation that does not accomplish this, even if it appears to have some similarity with it, can most surely be distinguished from it by means of this characteristic.>[29]

B41

A26/B42   Conclusions from the above concepts.

a) Space represents no property at all of any things in themselves nor any relation of them to each other, i.e., no determination of them that attaches to objects themselves and that would remain even if one were to abstract from all subjective conditions of intuition. For neither absolute nor relative determinations can be intuited prior to the existence of the things to which they pertain, thus be intuited *a priori*.

---

^a *Princips*
^b *Objecten*
^c *Objecten*

b) Space is nothing other than merely the form of all appearances of outer sense, i.e., the subjective condition of sensibility, under which alone outer intuition is possible for us. Now since the receptivity of the subject to be affected by objects necessarily precedes all intuitions of these objects, it can be understood how the form of all appearances can be given in the mind prior to all actual perceptions, thus *a priori*, and how as a pure intuition, in which all objects must be determined, it can contain principles[a] of their relations prior to all experience.

We can accordingly speak of space, extended beings, and so on, only from the human standpoint. If we depart from the subjective condition under which alone we can acquire outer intuition, namely that through which we may be affected by objects, then the representation of space signifies nothing at all. This predicate is attributed to things only inso-   A 27/B 43
far as they appear to us, i.e., are objects of sensibility. The constant form of this receptivity, which we call sensibility, is a necessary condition of all the relations within which objects can be intuited as outside us, and, if one abstracts from these objects, it is a pure intuition, which bears the name of space. Since we cannot make the special conditions of sensibility into conditions of the possibility of things, but only of their appearances, we can well say that space comprehends all things that may appear to us externally, but not all things in themselves, whether they be intuited or not, or by whatever subject they may be intuited. For we cannot judge at all whether the intuitions of other thinking beings are bound to the same conditions that limit our intuition and that are universally valid for us. If we add the limitation of a judgment to the concept of the subject, then the judgment is unconditionally valid. The proposition: "All things are next to one another in space," is valid under the limitation that these things be taken as objects of our sensible intuition. If here I add the condition to the concept and say "All things, as outer intuitions, are next to one another in space," then this rule is valid universally and without limitation. Our expositions accordingly teach   B 44
the **reality** (i.e., objective validity) of space in regard to everything that   A 28
can come before us externally as an object, but at the same time the **ideality** of space in regard to things when they are considered in themselves through reason, i.e., without taking account of the constitution of our sensibility. We therefore assert the **empirical reality** of space (with respect to all possible outer experience), though to be sure its **transcendental ideality**, i.e., that it is nothing as soon as we leave aside the condition of the possibility of all experience, and take it as something that grounds the things in themselves.

Besides space, however, there is no other subjective representation

---

[a] *Principien*

related*a* to something **external** that could be called *a priori* objective. *b*<For one cannot derive synthetic *a priori* propositions from any such representation, as one can from intuition in space (§ 3). Strictly speaking, therefore, ideality does not pertain to them, although they coincide with the representation of space in belonging only to the subjective constitution of the kind of sense, e.g., of sight, hearing, and feeling, through the sensations of colors, sounds, and warmth, which, however, since they are merely sensations and not intuitions, do not in themselves allow any object*c* to be cognized, least of all *a priori*.>

B45   The aim of this remark is only to prevent one from thinking of illustrating the asserted ideality of space with completely inadequate examples, since things like colors, taste, etc., are correctly considered not as qualities of things but as mere alterations of our subject, which can even be different in different people. For in this case that which is originally itself only appearance, e.g., a rose, counts in an empirical sense as a

A30   thing in itself, which yet can appear different to every eye in regard to color. The transcendental concept of appearances in space, on the contrary, is a critical reminder that absolutely nothing that is intuited in space is a thing in itself, and that space is not a form that is proper to anything in itself, but rather that objects in themselves are not known to us at all, and that what we call outer objects are nothing other than mere representations of our sensibility, whose form is space, but whose true correlate, i.e., the thing in itself, is not and cannot be cognized through them, but is also never asked after in experience.

B46

The Transcendental Aesthetic
Second Section
On time.

<§ 4
Metaphysical exposition of the concept of time.>

Time is <1)> not an empirical concept that is somehow drawn from an experience. For simultaneity or succession would not themselves come into perception if the representation of time did not ground them *a priori*. Only under its presupposition can one represent that several things exist at one and the same time (simultaneously) or in different times (successively).

A31   2) Time is a necessary representation that grounds all intuitions. In regard to appearances in general one cannot remove time, though one

---

a *bezogene*

b In the first edition, the remainder of this paragraph reads differently; see A28–9 above.

c *Object*

can very well take the appearances away from time. Time is therefore given *a priori*. In it alone is all actuality of appearances possible. The latter could all disappear, but time itself (as the universal condition of their possibility)*ᵃ* cannot be removed.

3) This *a priori* necessity also grounds the possibility of apodictic principles of relations of time, or axioms of time in general. It has only one dimension: different times are not simultaneous, but successive (just as different spaces are not successive, but simultaneous). These principles could not be drawn from experience, for this would yield neither strict universality nor apodictic certainty. We would only be able to say: This is what common perception teaches, but not: This is how matters must stand. These principles are valid as rules under which alone experiences are possible at all, and instruct us prior to them, not through it.*ᵇ*

4) Time is no discursive or, as one calls it, general concept, but a pure form of sensible intuition. Different times are only parts of one and the same time. That representation, however, which can only be given through a single object, is an intuition. Further, the proposition that different times cannot be simultaneous cannot be derived from a general concept. The proposition is synthetic, and cannot arise from concepts alone. It is therefore immediately contained in the intuition and representation of time.

5) The infinitude of time signifies nothing more than that every determinate magnitude of time is only possible through limitations of a single time grounding it. The original representation **time** must therefore be given as unlimited. But where the parts themselves and every magnitude of an object can be determinately represented only through limitation, there the entire representation cannot be given through concepts, (<for they contain only partial representations)>,*ᶜ* but immediate intuition must ground them.*ᵈ*

<§ 5
Transcendental exposition of the concept of time.

I can appeal to No. 3 where, in order to be brief, I have placed that which is properly transcendental under the heading of the metaphysical exposition. Here I add further that the concept of alteration and, with

---

ᵃ These parentheses added in B.
ᵇ The text reads "*belehren uns vor derselben, und nicht durch dieselbe.*" Earlier editors suggested emending the last word to "*dieselben*"; but if the sentence is interpreted to mean "instructs us prior to experiences, not through common perception," it can be read without emendation.
ᶜ In the first edition: "for there the partial representations precede."
ᵈ B has *ihnen* instead of *ihre* here.

it, the concept of motion (as alteration of place), is only possible
through and in the representation of time – that if this representation
were not *a priori* (inner) intuition, then no concept, whatever it might
be, could make comprehensible the possibility of an alteration, i.e., of a
combination of contradictorily opposed predicates (e.g., a thing's being
in a place and the not-being of the very same thing in the same place)
in one and the same object.ᵃ Only in time can both contradictorily op-

B49 posed determinations in one thing be encountered, namely **successively.** Our concept of time therefore explains the possibility of as much
synthetic *a priori* cognition as is presented by the general theory of motion, which is no less fruitful.>³⁰

<§ 6>

A32 Conclusions from these concepts.

a) Time is not something that would subsist for itself or attach to things
as an objective determination, and thus remain if one abstracted from
all subjective conditions of the intuition of them; for in the first case it
would be something that was actual yet without an actual object. As far

A33 as the second case is concerned, however, time could not precede the
objects as a determination or order attaching to the things themselves
as their condition and be cognized and intuited *a priori* through synthetic propositions. But the latter, on the contrary, can very well occur
if time is nothing other than the subjective condition under which all
intuitions can take place in us. For then this form of inner intuition can
be represented prior to the objects, thus *a priori*.

b) Time is nothing other than the form of inner sense, i.e., of the intuition of our self and our inner state. For time cannot be a determina-

B50 tion of outer appearances; it belongs neither to a shape or a position,
etc., but on the contrary determines the relation of representations in
our inner state. And just because this inner intuition yields no shape we
also attempt to remedy this lack through analogies, and represent the
temporal sequence through a line progressing to infinity, in which the
manifold constitutes a series that is of only one dimension, and infer
from the properties of this line to all the properties of time, with the
sole difference that the parts of the former are simultaneous but those
of the latter always exist successively. From this it is also apparent that
the representation of time is itself an intuition, since all its relations can
be expressed in an outer intuition.

A34 *c*) Time is the *a priori* formal condition of all appearances in general.
Space, as the pure form of all outer intuitions, is limited as an *a priori*

ᵃ *Objecte*

condition merely to outer intuitions. But since, on the contrary, all representations, whether or not they have outer things as their object, nevertheless as determinations of the mind themselves belong to the inner state, while this inner state belongs under the formal condition of inner intuition, and thus of time, so time is an *a priori* condition of all appearance in general, and indeed the immediate condition of the inner intuition (of our souls), and thereby also the mediate condition of outer appearances. If I can say *a priori*: all outer appearances are in space and determined *a priori* according to the relations of space, so from the principle[a] of inner sense I can say entirely generally: all appearances in general, i.e., all objects of the senses, are in time, and necessarily stand in relations of time.

B 51

If we abstract from our way of internally intuiting ourselves and by means of this intuition also dealing with all outer intuitions in the power of representation, and thus take objects as they may be in themselves, then time is nothing. It is only of objective validity in regard to appearances, because these are already things that we take as **objects of our senses**; but it is no longer objective if one abstracts from the sensibility of our intuition, thus from that kind of representation that is peculiar to us, and speaks of **things in general**. Time is therefore merely a subjective condition of our (human) intuition (which is always sensible, i.e., insofar as we are affected by objects), and in itself, outside the subject, is nothing. Nonetheless it is necessarily objective in regard to all appearances, thus also in regard to all things that can come before us in experience. We cannot say all things are in time, because with the concept of things in general abstraction is made from every kind of intuition of them, but this is the real condition under which time belongs to the representation of objects. Now if the condition is added to the concept, and the principle says that all things as appearances (objects of sensible intuition) are in time, then the principle has its sound objective correctness and *a priori* universality.

A 35

B 52

Our assertions accordingly teach the **empirical reality** of time, i.e., objective validity in regard to all objects that may ever be given to our senses. And since our intuition is always sensible, no object can ever be given to us in experience that would not belong under the condition of time. But, on the contrary, we dispute all claim of time to absolute reality, namely where it would attach to things absolutely as a condition or property even without regard to the form of our sensible intuition. Such properties, which pertain to things in themselves, can never be given to us through the senses. In this therefore consists the **transcendental ideality** of time, according to which it is nothing at all if one ab-

A 36

[a] *Princip*

stracts from the subjective conditions of sensible intuition, and cannot be counted as either subsisting or inhering in the objects in themselves (without their relation to our intuition). Yet this ideality is to be compared with the subreptions of sensation just as little as that of space is, because in that case one presupposes that the appearance itself, in which these predicates inhere, has objective reality, which is here entirely absent except insofar as it is merely empirical, i.e., the object itself is regarded merely as appearance: concerning which the above remark in the previous sections is to be consulted.*a*

<§ 7>
Elucidation.

Against this theory, which concedes empirical reality to time but disputes its absolute and transcendental reality, insightful men have so unanimously proposed one objection that I conclude that it must naturally occur to every reader who is not accustomed to these considerations.[31] It goes thus: Alterations are real (this is proved by the change of our own representations, even if one would deny all outer appearances together with their alterations). Now alterations are possible only in time, therefore time is something real. There is no difficulty in answering. I admit the entire argument. Time is certainly something real, namely the real form of inner intuition. It therefore has subjective reality in regard to inner experience, i.e., I really have the representation of time and <my>*b* determinations in it. It is therefore to be regarded really not as object*c* but as the way of representing myself as object.*d* But if I or another being could intuit myself without this condition of sensibility, then these very determinations, which we now represent to ourselves as alterations, would yield us a cognition in which the representation of time and thus also of alteration would not occur at all. Its empirical reality therefore remains as a condition of all our experiences. Only absolute reality cannot be granted to it according to what has been adduced above. It is nothing except the form of our inner intuition.* If

---

* I can, to be sure, say: my representations succeed one another; but that only means that we are conscious of them as in a temporal sequence, i.e., according to the form of inner sense. Time is not on that account something in itself, nor any determination objectively adhering to things.

a This refers to A28–30/B44–5 in § 3.
b In the first edition: "of my."
c Object
d Object

one removes the special condition of our sensibility from it, then the concept of time also disappears, and it does not adhere to the objects themselves, rather merely to the subject that intuits them.   A 38

The cause, however, on account of which this objection is so unanimously made, and indeed by those who nevertheless know of nothing convincing to object against the doctrine of the ideality of space,[32] is   B 55 this. They did not expect to be able to demonstrate the absolute reality of space apodictically, since they were confronted by idealism, according to which the reality of outer objects is not capable of any strict proof: on the contrary, the reality of the object of our inner sense (of myself and my state) is immediately clear through consciousness. The former could have been a mere illusion, but the latter, according to their opinion, is undeniably something real. But they did not consider that both, without their reality as representations being disputed, nevertheless belong only to appearance, which always has two sides, one where the object[a] is considered in itself (without regard to the way in which it is to be intuited, the constitution of which however must for that very reason always remain problematic), the other where the form of the intuition of this object is considered, which must not be sought in the object in itself but in the subject to which it appears, but which nevertheless really and necessarily pertains to the representation of this object.

Time and space are accordingly two sources of cognition, from which different synthetic cognitions can be drawn *a priori*, of which es-   A 39 pecially pure mathematics in regard to the cognitions of space and its relations provides a splendid example. Both taken together are,   B 56 namely, the pure forms of all sensible intuition, and thereby make possible synthetic *a priori* propositions. But these *a priori* sources of cognition determine their own boundaries by that very fact (that they are merely conditions of sensibility), namely that they apply to objects only so far as they are considered as appearances, but do not present things in themselves. Those alone are the field of their validity, beyond which no further objective use of them takes place. This reality of space and time, further, leaves the certainty of experiential cognition untouched: for we are just as certain of that whether these forms necessarily adhere to the things in themselves or only to our intuition of these things. Those, however, who assert the absolute reality of space and time, whether they assume it to be subsisting or only inhering, must themselves come into conflict with the principles[b] of experience.

[a] *Object*
[b] *Principien*

For if they decide in favor of the first (which is generally the position of the mathematical investigators of nature),[33] then they must assume two eternal and infinite self-subsisting non-entities (space and time), which exist (yet without there being anything real) only in order to comprehend everything real within themselves. If they adopt the second position (as do some metaphysicians of nature), and hold space and time to be relations of appearances (next to or successive to one another) that are abstracted from experience though confusedly represented in this abstraction, then they must dispute the validity or at least the apodictic certainty of *a priori* mathematical doctrines in regard to real things (e.g., in space), since this certainty does not occur *a posteriori*, and on this view the *a priori* concepts of space and time are only creatures of the imagination, the origin of which must really be sought in experience, out of whose abstracted relations imagination has made something that, to be sure, contains what is general in them but that cannot occur without the restrictions that nature has attached to them.[34] The first succeed in opening the field of appearances for mathematical assertions.[a] However, they themselves become very confused through precisely these conditions if the understanding would go beyond this field. The second succeed, to be sure, with respect to the latter, in that the representations of space and time do not stand in their way if they would judge of objects not as appearances but merely in relation to the understanding; but they can neither offer any ground for the possibility of *a priori* mathematical cognitions (since they lack a true and objectively valid *a priori* intuition), nor can they bring the propositions of experience into necessary accord with those assertions. On our theory of the true constitution of these two original forms of sensibility both difficulties are remedied.

Finally, that the transcendental aesthetic cannot contain more than these two elements, namely space and time, is clear from the fact that all other concepts belonging to sensibility, even that of motion, which unites both elements, presuppose something empirical. For this presupposes the perception of something movable. In space considered in itself there is nothing movable; hence the movable must be something that is found **in space only through experience**, thus an empirical datum. In the same way the transcendental aesthetic cannot count the concept of alteration among its *a priori* data; for time itself does not alter, but only something that is within time. For this there is required the perception of some existence and the succession of its determinations, thus experience.

A40

B57

A41

B58

---

[a] A colon in the first edition is replaced with a period in the second.

<§ 8>   B 59
General remarks
on the transcendental aesthetic

<I.>*a* It will first be necessary to explain as distinctly as possible our
opinion in regard to the fundamental constitution of sensible cognition   A 42
in general, in order to preclude all misinterpretation of it.

We have therefore wanted to say that all our intuition is nothing but
the representation of appearance; that the things that we intuit are not
in themselves what we intuit them to be, nor are their relations so constituted in themselves as they appear to us; and that if we remove our
own subject or even only the subjective constitution of the senses in
general, then all constitution, all relations of objects*b* in space and time,
indeed space and time themselves would disappear, and as appearances
they cannot exist in themselves, but only in us. What may be the case
with objects in themselves and abstracted from all this receptivity of our
sensibility remains entirely unknown to us. We are acquainted with
nothing except our way of perceiving them, which is peculiar to us, and
which therefore does not necessarily pertain to every being, though to
be sure it pertains to every human being. We are concerned solely with
this. Space and time are its pure forms, sensation in general its matter.   B 60
We can cognize only the former *a priori*, i.e., prior to all actual perception, and they are therefore called pure intuition; the latter, however, is
that in our cognition that is responsible for it being called *a posteriori*
cognition, i.e., empirical intuition. The former adheres to our sensibility absolutely necessarily, whatever sort of sensations we may have; the
latter can be very different. Even if we could bring this intuition of ours A 43
to the highest degree of distinctness we would not thereby come any
closer to the constitution of objects in themselves. For in any case we
would still completely cognize only our own way of intuiting, i.e., our
sensibility, and this always only under the conditions originally depending on the subject, space and time; what the objects may be in themselves would still never be known through the most enlightened
cognition of their appearance, which alone is given to us.

That our entire sensibility is nothing but the confused representation
of things, which contains solely that which pertains to them in themselves but only under a heap of marks and partial representations that
we can never consciously separate from one another, is therefore a falsification of the concept of sensibility and of appearance that renders

---

a "I." is added in the second edition because of the addition of the further numbered paragraphs (II through IV) added at B 66–73.
b *Objecte*

the entire theory of them useless and empty. The difference between an
B61 indistinct and a distinct representation is merely logical, and does not
concern the content. Without doubt the concept of **right** that is used
by the healthy understanding contains the very same things that the
most subtle speculation can evolve out of it, only in common and practical use one is not conscious of these manifold representations in these
thoughts. Thus one cannot say that the common concept is sensible and
A44 contains a mere appearance, for right cannot appear at all; rather its
concept lies in the understanding and represents a constitution (the
moral constitution) of actions that pertains to them in themselves. The
representation of a **body** in intuition, on the contrary, contains nothing
at all that could pertain to an object in itself, but merely the appearance
of something and the way in which we are affected by it; and this receptivity of our cognitive capacity is called sensibility and remains
worlds apart from the cognition of the object in itself even if one might
see through to the very bottom of it (the appearance).

The Leibnizian-Wolffian philosophy has therefore directed all investigations of the nature and origin of our cognitions to an entirely unjust
point of view in considering the distinction between sensibility and the
intellectual as merely logical, since it is obviously transcendental, and
B62 does not concern merely the form of distinctness or indistinctness, but
its origin and content, so that through sensibility we do not cognize the
constitution of things in themselves merely indistinctly, but rather not
at all, and, as soon as we take away our subjective constitution, the represented object*a* with the properties that sensible intuition attributes to
it is nowhere to be encountered, nor can it be encountered, for it is just
this subjective constitution that determines its form as appearance.35
A45 We ordinarily distinguish quite well between that which is essentially
attached to the intuition of appearances, and is valid for every human
sense in general, and that which pertains to them only contingently because it is not valid for the relation*b* of sensibility in general but only for
a particular situation or organization of this or that sense. And thus one
calls the first cognition one that represents the object in itself, but the
second one only its appearance. This distinction, however, is only empirical. If one stands by it (as commonly happens) and does not regard
that empirical intuition as in turn mere appearance (as ought to happen), so that there is nothing to be encountered in it that pertains to
anything in itself, then our transcendental distinction is lost, and we be-

---

a Object
b As noted in the first-edition version above, here Kant switches from *Verhältnis* to
Beziehung as his topic switches from the relation of objects in space or time to each other
to the relation of space and time to us. With one exception to be noted, therefore, for
the remainder of this section (I) "relation" translates *Verhältnis*. In the new paragraphs
II through IV added below, however, Kant again reverts to *Verhältnis*.

lieve ourselves to cognize things in themselves, though we have nothing to do with anything except appearances anywhere (in the world of sense), even in the deepest research into its objects. Thus, we would certainly call a rainbow a mere appearance in a sun-shower, but would call this rain the thing in itself, and this is correct, as long as we understand the latter concept in a merely physical sense, as that which in universal experience and all different positions relative to the senses is always determined thus and not otherwise in intuition. But if we consider this empirical object in general and, without turning to its agreement with every human sense, ask whether it (not the raindrops, since these, as appearances, are already empirical objects)*a* represents an object in itself, then the question of the relation of the representation to the object is transcendental, and not only these drops are mere appearances, but even their round form, indeed even the space through which they fall are nothing in themselves, but only mere modifications or foundations*b* of our sensible intuition; the transcendental object,*c* however, remains unknown to us.

The second important concern of our transcendental aesthetic is that it not merely earn some favor as a plausible hypothesis, but that it be as certain and indubitable as can ever be demanded of a theory that is to serve as an organon. In order to make this certainty fully convincing we will choose a case in which its validity can become obvious <and that can serve to make that which has been adduced in § 3 even more clear>.

Thus, if it were to be supposed that space and time are in themselves objective and conditions of the possibility of things in themselves, then it would be shown, first, that there is a large number of *a priori* apodictic and synthetic propositions about both, but especially about space, which we will therefore here investigate as our primary example. Since the propositions of geometry are cognized synthetically *a priori* and with apodictic certainty, I ask: Whence do you take such propositions, and on what does our understanding rely in attaining to such absolutely necessary and universally valid truths? There is no other way than through concepts or through intuitions, both of which, however, are given, as such, either *a priori* or *a posteriori*. The latter, namely empirical concepts, together with that on which they are grounded, empirical intuition, cannot yield any synthetic proposition except one that is also merely empirical, i.e., a proposition of experience; thus it can never contain necessity and absolute universality of the sort that is nevertheless characteristic of all propositions of geometry. Concerning the first and only means for attaining to such cognitions, however, namely

a *Objecte*
b *Grundlagen*
c *Object*

187

through mere concepts or *a priori* intuitions, it is clear that from mere concepts no synthetic cognition but only merely analytic cognition can be attained. Take the proposition that with two straight lines no space at all can be enclosed, thus no figure is possible, and try to derive it from the concept of straight lines and the number two; or take the proposition that a figure is possible with three straight lines, and in the same way try to derive it from these concepts. All of your effort is in vain, and you see yourself forced to take refuge in intuition, as indeed geometry always does. You thus give yourself an object in intuition; but what kind is this, is it a pure *a priori* intuition or an empirical one? If it were the latter, then no universally valid, let alone apodictic proposition could ever come from it: for experience can never provide anything of this sort. You must therefore give your object *a priori* in intuition, and ground your synthetic proposition on this. If there did not lie in you a faculty for intuiting *a priori*; if this subjective condition regarding form were not at the same time the universal *a priori* condition under which alone the object[a] of this (outer) intuition is itself possible; if the object (the triangle) were something in itself without relation to your subject: then how could you say that what necessarily lies in your subjective conditions for constructing a triangle must also necessarily pertain to the triangle in itself? for you could not add to your concept (of three lines) something new (the figure) that must thereby necessarily be encountered in the object, since this is given prior to your cognition and not through it. If, therefore, space (and time as well) were not a mere form of your intuition that contains *a priori* conditions under which alone things could be outer objects for you, which are nothing in themselves without these subjective conditions, then you could make out absolutely nothing synthetic and *a priori* about outer objects.[b] It is therefore indubitably certain and not merely possible or even probable that space and time, as the necessary conditions of all (outer and inner) experience, are merely subjective conditions of all our intuition, in relation to which therefore all objects are mere appearances and not things given for themselves in this way; about these appearances, further, much may be said *a priori* that concerns their form but nothing whatsoever about the things in themselves that may ground them.

[c]<II. For confirmation of this theory of the ideality of outer as well as inner sense, thus of all objects[d] of the senses, as mere appearances, this comment is especially useful: that everything in our cognition that belongs to intuition (with the exception, therefore, of the feeling of plea-

---

[a] *Object*
[b] *Objecte*
[c] From here to the end of the "Transcendental Aesthetic" added in the second edition.
[d] *Objecte*

188

sure and displeasure and the will, which are not cognitions at all) contains nothing but mere relations,[a] of places in one intuition (extension), alteration of places (motion), and laws in accordance with which this alteration is determined (moving forces). But what is present in the place, or what it produces in the things themselves besides the alteration of place, is not given through these relations. Now through mere relations no thing in itself is cognized; it is therefore right to judge that since nothing is given to us through outer sense except mere representations of relation, outer sense can also contain in its representation only the relation of an object to the subject, and not that which is internal to the object[b] in itself.[36] It is exactly the same in the case of inner sense. It is not merely that the representations **of outer sense** make up the proper material with which we occupy our mind, but also the time in which we place these representations, which itself precedes the consciousness of them in experience and grounds the way in which we place them in mind as a formal condition, already contains relations of succession, of simultaneity, and of that which is simultaneous with succession (of that which persists). Now that which, as representation, can precede any act of thinking something is intuition and, if it contains nothing but relations, it is the form of intuition, which, since it does not represent anything except insofar as something is posited in the mind, can be nothing other than the way in which the mind is affected by its own activity, namely this positing of its representation, thus the way it is affected through itself, i.e., it is an inner sense as far as regards its form. Everything that is represented through a sense is to that extent always appearance, and an inner sense must therefore either not be admitted at all or else the subject, which is the object of this sense, can only be represented by its means as appearance, not as it would judge of itself if its intuition were mere self-activity, i.e., intellectual. Any difficulty in this depends merely on the question how a subject can internally intuit itself; yet this difficulty is common to every theory. Consciousness of itself (apperception) is the simple representation of the I, and if all of the manifold in the subject were given **self-actively** through that alone, then the inner intuition would be intellectual. In human beings this consciousness requires inner perception of the manifold that is antecedently given in the subject, and the manner in which this is given in the mind without spontaneity must be called sensibility on account of this difference. If the faculty for becoming conscious of oneself is to seek out (apprehend) that which lies in the mind, it must affect the lat-

B 67

B 68

---

[a] Here Kant reverts to the use of *Verhältnis* for the remainder of the "Transcendental Aesthetic," and it is thus this word that is translated by "relation" here and for the remainder of the section unless otherwise noted.
[b] *Objecte*

ter, and it can only produce an intuition of itself in such a way, whose form, however, which antecedently grounds it in the mind, determines the way in which the manifold is together in the mind in the representation of time; there it then intuits itself not as it would immediately self-actively represent itself, but in accordance with the way in which it is affected from within, consequently as it appears to itself, not as it is.

III. If I say: in space and time intuition represents both outer objects[a] as well as the self-intuition of the mind as each affects our senses, i.e., as it **appears,** that is not to say that these objects would be a mere **illusion.**[b,37] For in the appearance the objects,[c] indeed even properties[d] that we attribute to them, are always regarded as something really given, only insofar as this property depends only on the kind of intuition of the subject in the relation[e] of the given object to it then this object as **appearance** is to be distinguished from itself as object[f] **in itself.** Thus I do not say that bodies merely **seem**[g] to exist outside me or that my soul only **seems**[h] to be given if I assert that the quality of space and time – in accordance with which, as condition of their existence, I posit both of these – lies in my kind of intuition and not in these objects[i] in themselves. It would be my own fault if I made that which I should count as appearance into mere illusion.* But this does not happen according to

B 69

B 70

*The predicates of appearance can be attributed to the object[j] in itself, in relation to our sense, e.g., the red color or fragrance to the rose; but the illusion can never be attributed to the object as predicate, precisely because that would be to attribute to the object[k] **for itself** what pertains to it only in relation to the senses or in general to the subject, e.g., the two handles that were originally attributed to Saturn. What is not to be encountered in the object[l] in itself at all, but is always to be encountered in its relation to the subject and is inseparable from the representation of the object, is appearance, and thus the predicates of space and of time are rightly attributed to the objects of the senses as such, and there is no illusion in this. On the contrary, if I attribute the redness to the rose **in itself,** the handles to Saturn or extension to all outer objects **in themselves,** without looking to a determinate relation of these objects to the subject and limiting my judgment to this, then illusion first arises.

[a] *Objecte*
[b] *Schein*
[c] *Objecte*
[d] *Beschaffenheiten,* here and in the remainder of this paragraph.
[e] *Relation*
[f] *Object*
[g] *scheinen*
[h] *scheint*
[i] *Objecten*
[j] *Objecte*
[k] *Object*
[l] *Objecte*

our principle[a] of the ideality of all of our sensible intuitions; rather, if one ascribes **objective reality** to those forms of representation then one cannot avoid thereby transforming everything into mere **illusion.** For if one regards space and time as properties that, as far as their possibility is concerned, must be encountered in things in themselves, and reflects on the absurdities in which one then becomes entangled, because two infinite things that are neither substances nor anything really inhering in substances must nevertheless be something existing, indeed the necessary condition of the existence of all things, which also remain even if all existing things are removed; then one cannot well blame the good Berkeley if he demotes bodies to mere illusion;[38] indeed even our own existence, which would be made dependent in such a way on the self-subsisting reality of a non-entity such as time, would be transformed along with this into mere illusion; an absurdity of which no one has yet allowed himself to be guilty.

B 71

IV. In natural theology, where one conceives of an object that is not only not an object of intuition for us but cannot even be an object of sensible intuition for itself, one is careful to remove the conditions of time and space from all of its intuition (for all of its cognition must be intuition and not **thinking,** which is always proof of limitations). But with what right can one do this if one has antecedently made both of these into forms of things in themselves, and indeed ones that, as *a priori* conditions of the existence of things, would remain even if one removed the things themselves? – for as conditions of all existence in general they would also have to be conditions of the existence of God. If one will not make them into objective forms of all things, then no alternative remains but to make them into subjective forms of our kind of outer as well as inner intuition, which is called sensible because it is **not original,** i.e., one through which the existence of the object[b] of intuition is itself given (and that, so far as we can have insight, can only pertain to the original being); rather it is dependent on the existence of the object,[c] thus it is possible only insofar as the representational capacity of the subject is affected through that.[39]

B 72

It is also not necessary for us to limit the kind of intuition in space and time to the sensibility of human beings; it may well be that all finite thinking beings must necessarily agree with human beings in this regard (though we cannot decide this), yet even given such universal validity this kind of intuition would not cease to be sensibility, for the very reason that it is derived (*intuitus derivativus*),[d] not original (*intuitius orig-*

---

[a] *Princip*
[b] *Objects*
[c] *Objects*
[d] derivative intuition

inarius),[a] thus not intellectual intuition, which for the ground already adduced seems to pertain only to the original being, never to one that is dependent as regards both its existence and its intuition (which determines its existence in relation[b] to given objects);[c] although the last remark must be counted only as an illustration of our aesthetic theory and not as a ground of its proof.

B 73

Conclusion of the Transcendental Aesthetic.

Here we now have one of the required pieces for the solution of the general problem of transcendental philosophy – **how are synthetic *a priori* propositions possible?** – namely pure *a priori* intuitions, space and time, in which, if we want to go beyond the given concept in an *a priori* judgment, we encounter that which is to be discovered *a priori* and synthetically connected with it, not in the concept but in the intuition that corresponds to it; but on this ground such a judgment never extends beyond the objects of the senses and can hold only for objects[d] of possible experience.>

[a] original intuition
[b] *Beziehung*
[c] *Objecte*
[d] *Objecte*

The Transcendental Doctrine of Elements
Second Part
The Transcendental Logic

Introduction
The Idea of a Transcendental Logic
I.
On logic in general.

Our cognition arises from two fundamental sources in the mind, the first of which is the reception of representations (the receptivity of impressions), the second the faculty for cognizing an object by means of these representations (spontaneity of concepts); through the former an object is **given** to us, through the latter it is **thought** in relation to that representation (as a mere determination of the mind). Intuition and concepts therefore constitute the elements of all our cognition, so that neither concepts without intuition corresponding to them in some way nor intuition without concepts can*a* yield a cognition. Both are either pure or empirical. **Empirical,** if sensation (which presupposes the actual presence of the object) is contained therein; but **pure** if no sensation is mixed into the representation. One can call the latter the matter of sensible cognition. Thus pure intuition contains merely the form under which something is intuited, and pure concept only the form of thinking of an object in general. Only pure intuitions or concepts alone are possible *a priori*, empirical ones only *a posteriori*.

If we will call the **receptivity** of our mind to receive representations insofar as it is affected in some way **sensibility,** then on the contrary the faculty for bringing forth representations itself, or the **spontaneity** of cognition, is the **understanding.** It comes along with our nature that **intuition** can never be other than **sensible,** i.e., that it contains only the way in which we are affected by objects. The faculty for **thinking** of objects of sensible intuition, on the contrary, is the **understanding.** Neither of these properties is to be preferred to the other. Without sensibility no object would be given to us, and without understanding none would be thought. Thoughts without content are empty, intuitions

---

a The second edition has the plural verb *können*; the first had the singular *kann*.

without concepts are blind.[1] It is thus just as necessary to make the mind's concepts sensible (i.e., to add an object to them in intuition) as it is to make its intuitions understandable (i.e., to bring them under concepts). Further, these two faculties or capacities cannot exchange their functions. The understanding is not capable of intuiting anything, and the senses are not capable of thinking anything. Only from their unification can cognition arise. But on this account one must not mix up their roles, rather one has great cause to separate them carefully from each other and distinguish them. Hence we distinguish the science of the rules of sensibility in general, i.e., aesthetic, from the science of the rules of understanding in general, i.e., logic.

B 76
A 52

Now logic in turn can be undertaken with two different aims, either as the logic of the general or of the particular use of the understanding. The former contains the absolutely necessary rules of thinking, without which no use of the understanding takes place, and it therefore concerns these rules without regard to the difference of the objects to which it may be directed.[2] The logic of the particular use of the understanding contains the rules for correctly thinking about a certain kind of objects. The former can be called elementary logic, the latter, however, the organon of this or that science. In the schools the latter is often stuck before the sciences as their propaedeutic, though in the course of human reason they are certainly the latest to be reached, once the science is already long complete, and requires only the final touch for its improvement and perfection. For one must already know the objects rather well if one will offer the rules for how a science of them is to be brought about.

B 77

Now general logic is either pure or applied logic. In the former we abstract from all empirical conditions under which our understanding is exercised, e.g., from the influence of the senses, from the play of imagination,[a] the laws of memory, the power of habit, inclination, etc., hence also from the sources of prejudice, indeed in general from all causes from which certain cognitions arise or may be supposed to arise, because these merely concern the understanding under certain circumstances of its application, and experience is required in order to know these. A **general** but **pure** logic therefore has to do with strictly *a priori* principles,[b] and is a **canon of the understanding** and reason, but only in regard to what is formal in their use, be the content what it may (empirical or transcendental). A **general logic,** however, is then called **applied** if it is directed to the rules of the use of the understanding under the subjective empirical conditions that psychology teaches us. It therefore has empirical principles,[c] although it is to be sure general in-

A 53

---

[a] *Einbildung*
[b] *Principien*
[c] *Principien*

sofar as it concerns the use of the understanding without regard to the difference of objects. On this account it is also neither a canon of the understanding in general nor an organon of particular sciences, but merely a cathartic of the common understanding.   B 78

In general logic the part that is to constitute the pure doctrine of reason must therefore be entirely separated from that which constitutes applied (though still general) logic. The former alone is properly science, although brief and dry, as the scholastically correct presentation of a doctrine of the elements of the understanding requires. In this therefore logicians must always have two rules in view.   A 54

1) As general logic it abstracts from all contents of the cognition of the understanding and of the difference of its objects, and has to do with nothing but the mere form of thinking.

2) As pure logic it has no empirical principles,[a] thus it draws nothing from psychology (as one has occasionally been persuaded), which therefore has no influence at all on the canon of the understanding. It is a proven doctrine, and everything in it must be completely *a priori*.

What I call applied logic (in opposition to the common signification of this word, according to which it ought to contain certain exercises to which pure logic gives the rule) is thus a representation of the understanding and the rules of its necessary use *in concreto*, namely under the contingent conditions of the subject, which can hinder or promote this use, and which can all be given only empirically. It deals with attention, its hindrance and consequences, the cause of error, the condition of doubt, of reservation, of conviction, etc., and general and pure logic is related to it as pure morality, which contains merely the necessary moral laws of a free will in general, is related to the doctrine of virtue proper, which assesses these laws under the hindrances of the feelings, inclinations, and passions to which human beings are more or less subject, and which can never yield a true and proven science, since it requires empirical and psychological principles[b] just as much as that applied logic does.   B 79   A 55

II.
On transcendental logic.

General logic abstracts, as we have shown, from all content of cognition, i.e. from any relation[c] of it to the object,[d] and considers only the

---

[a] *Principien*
[b] *Principien*
[c] *Beziehung*. The contrast between this term and the following use of *Verhältnis* (p. 196, note *a*) shows that Kant continues to use the former to connote a relation between subject and object and the latter among objects, though in this case objects of thought rather than sensibility. Further, unnoted instances of "relation" translate *Beziehung*.
[d] *Object*

logical form in the relation[a] of cognitions to one another, i.e., the form of thinking in general. But now since there are pure as well as empirical intuitions (as the transcendental aesthetic proved), a distinction between pure and empirical thinking of objects could also well be found. In this case there would be a logic in which one did not abstract from all content of cognition; for that logic that contained merely the rules of the pure thinking of an object would exclude all those cognitions that were of empirical content. It would therefore concern the origin of our cognitions of objects insofar as that cannot be ascribed to the objects; while general logic, on the contrary, has nothing to do with this origin of cognition, but rather considers representations, whether they are originally given *a priori* in ourselves or only empirically, merely in respect of the laws according to which the understanding brings them into relation[b] to one another when it thinks, and therefore it deals only with the form of the understanding, which can be given to the representations wherever they may have originated.

And here I make a remark the import of which extends to all of the following considerations, and that we must keep well in view, namely that not every *a priori* cognition must be called transcendental, but only that by means of which we cognize that and how certain representations (intuitions or concepts) are applied entirely *a priori*, or are possible (i.e., the possibility of cognition or its use *a priori*). Hence neither space nor any geometrical determination of it *a priori* is a transcendental representation, but only the cognition that these representations are not of empirical origin at all and the possibility that they can[c] nevertheless be related *a priori* to objects of experience can be called transcendental. Likewise the use of space about all objects in general would also be transcendental; but if it is restricted solely to objects of the senses, then it is called empirical. The difference between the transcendental and the empirical therefore belongs only to the critique of cognitions and does not concern their relation to their object.

In the expectation, therefore, that there can perhaps be concepts that may be related to objects *a priori*, not as pure or sensible intuitions but rather merely as acts of pure thinking, that are thus concepts but of neither empirical nor aesthetic origin, we provisionally formulate the idea of a science of pure understanding and of the pure cognition of reason, by means of which we think objects completely *a priori*. Such a science, which would determine the origin, the domain, and the objective validity of such cognitions, would have to be called **transcendental logic**, since it has to do merely with the laws of the understanding and reason,

B 80

A 56

B 81

A 57

---

[a] *Verhältnisse*
[b] *Verhältnis*
[c] Following Erdmann, reading *können* instead of *könne*.

but solely insofar as they are related to objects *a priori* and not, as in the B82
case of general logic, to empirical as well as pure cognitions of reason
without distinction.

III.
On the division of general logic
into analytic and dialectic.

The old and famous question with which the logicians were to be driven into a corner and brought to such a pass that they must either fall
into a miserable circle*a* or else confess their ignorance, hence the van- A58
ity of their entire art, is this: **What is truth?** The nominal definition of
truth, namely that it is the agreement of cognition with its object, is
here granted and presupposed; but one demands to know what is the
general and certain criterion of the truth of any cognition.

It is already a great and necessary proof of cleverness or insight to
know what one should reasonably ask. For if the question is absurd in
itself and demands unnecessary answers, then, besides the embarrassment of the one who proposes it, it also has the disadvantage of misleading the incautious listener into absurd answers, and presenting the
ridiculous sight (as the ancients said) of one person milking a billy-goat B83
while the other holds a sieve underneath.3

If truth consists in the agreement of a cognition with its object, then
this object must thereby be distinguished from others; for a cognition
is false if it does not agree with the object to which it is related even if
it contains something that could well be valid of other objects. Now a
general criterion of truth would be that which was valid of all cognitions
without any distinction among their objects. But it is clear that since
with such a criterion one abstracts from all content of cognition (relation to its object),*b* yet truth concerns precisely this content, it would be A59
completely impossible and absurd to ask for a mark of the truth of this
content of cognition, and thus it is clear that a sufficient and yet at the
same time general sign of truth cannot possibly be provided. Since
above we have called the content of a cognition its matter, one must
therefore say that no general sign of the truth of the matter of cognition can be demanded, because it is self-contradictory.

But concerning the mere form of cognition (setting aside all content),
it is equally clear that a logic, so far as it expounds the general and nec- B84
essary rules of understanding, must present criteria of truth in these
very rules. For that which contradicts these is false, since the understanding thereby contradicts its general rules of thinking and thus con-

---

a In the second edition, *Dialexis;* in the first, *Dialele,* i.e. reasoning in a circle.
b *Object*

tradicts itself. But these criteria concern only the form of truth, i.e., of thinking in general, and are to that extent entirely correct but not sufficient. For although a cognition may be in complete accord with logical form, i.e., not contradict itself, yet it can still always contradict the object. The merely logical criterion of truth, namely the agreement of a cognition with the general and formal laws of understanding and reason, is therefore certainly the *conditio sine qua non* and thus the negative condition of all truth; further, however, logic cannot go, and the error that concerns not form but content cannot be discovered by any touchstone of logic.[4]

General logic analyzes the entire formal business of the understanding and reason into its elements, and presents these as principles[a] of all logical assessment[b] of our cognition. This part of logic can therefore be called an analytic, and is on that very account at least the negative touchstone of truth, since one must before all else examine and evaluate by means of these rules the form of all cognition before investigating its content in order to find out whether with regard to the object it contains positive truth. But since the mere form of cognition, however well it may agree with logical laws, is far from sufficing to constitute the material (objective) truth of the cognition, nobody can dare to judge of objects and to assert anything about them merely with logic without having drawn on antecedently well-founded information about them from outside of logic, in order subsequently merely to investigate its use and connection in a coherent whole according to logical laws, or, better, solely to examine them according to such laws. Nevertheless there is something so seductive in the possession of an apparent art for giving all of our cognitions the form of understanding, even though with regard to their content one may yet be very empty and poor, that this general logic, which is merely a **canon** for judging,[c] has been used as if it were an **organon** for the actual production of at least the semblance of objective assertions, and thus in fact it has thereby been misused. Now general logic, as a putative organon, is called **dialectic.**

As different as the significance of the employment of this designation of a science or art among the ancients may have been, one can still infer from their actual use of it that among them it was nothing other than the **logic of illusion** – a sophistical art for giving to its ignorance, indeed even to its intentional tricks, the air of truth, by imitating the method of thoroughness, which logic prescribes in general, and using its topics for the embellishment of every empty pretension. Now one can take it as a certain and useful warning that general logic, **consid-**

[a] *Principien*
[b] *Beurtheilung*
[c] *Beurtheilung*

ered as an organon, is always a logic of illusion, i.e., is dialectical. For since it teaches us nothing at all about the content of cognition, but only the formal conditions of agreement with the understanding, which are entirely indifferent with regard to the objects, the effrontery of using it as a tool (organon) for an expansion and extension of its information,[a] or at least the pretension of so doing, comes down to nothing but idle chatter, asserting or impeaching whatever one wants with some plausibility.   A 62

Such instruction by no means befits the dignity of philosophy. For this reason it would be better to take this designation of "dialectic" as a **critique of dialectical illusion,** which is counted as part of logic, and in such a way we would here have it be understood.

IV.   B 87

On the division of transcendental logic into
the transcendental analytic and dialectic.

In a transcendental logic we isolate the understanding (as we did above with sensibility in the transcendental aesthetic), and elevate from our cognition merely the part of our thought that has its origin solely in the understanding. The use of this pure cognition, however, depends on this as its condition: that objects are given to us in intuition, to which it can be applied. For without intuition all of our cognition would lack objects,[b] and therefore remain completely empty. The part of transcendental logic, therefore, that expounds the elements of the pure cognition of the understanding and the principles[c] without which no object can be thought at all, is the transcendental analytic, and at the same time a logic of truth. For no cognition can contradict it without at the same time losing all content, i.e., all relation to any object,[d] hence   A 63
all truth. But because it is very enticing and seductive to make use of these pure cognitions of the understanding and principles by themselves, and even beyond all bounds of experience, which however itself alone can give us the matter (objects)[e] to which those pure concepts of   B 88
the understanding can be applied, the understanding falls into the danger of making a material use of the merely formal principles[f] of pure understanding through empty sophistries, and of judging without distinction about objects that are not given to us, which perhaps indeed

---

[a] *Kenntnisse*
[b] *Objecten*
[c] *Principien*
[d] *Object*
[e] *Objecte*
[f] *Principien*

could not be given to us in any way. Since it should properly be only a canon for the assessment of empirical use, it is misused if one lets it count as the organon of a general and unrestricted use, and dares to synthetically judge, assert, and decide about objects in general with the pure understanding alone. The use of the pure understanding would in this case therefore be dialectical. The second part of the transcendental logic must therefore be a critique of this dialectical illusion, and is called transcendental dialectic, not as an art of dogmatically arousing such illusion (an unfortunately highly prevalent art among the manifold works of metaphysical jugglery), but rather as a critique of the understanding and reason in regard to their hyperphysical use, in order to uncover the false illusion of their groundless pretensions and to reduce their claims to invention and amplification, putatively to be attained through transcendental principles, to the mere assessment and evaluation of the pure understanding, guarding it against sophistical tricks.

A64

Transcendental Logic
First Division

***

The Transcendental Analytic

This Analytic is the analysis[a] of the entirety of our *a priori* cognition into the elements of the pure cognition of the understanding. It is concerned with the following points: 1.[b] That the concepts be pure and not empirical concepts. 2. That they belong not to intuition and to sensibility, but rather to thinking and understanding. 3. That they be elementary concepts, and clearly distinguished from those which are derived or composed from them. 4. That the table of them be complete, and that they entirely exhaust the entire field of pure understanding. Now this completeness of a science cannot reliably be assumed from a rough calculation of an aggregate put together by mere estimates; hence it is possible only by means of an **idea of the whole** of the *a priori* cognition of the understanding, and through[c] the division of concepts that such an idea determines and that constitutes it, thus only through their **connection in a system.** The pure understanding separates itself completely not only from everything empirical, but even from all sensibility. It is therefore a unity that subsists on its own, which is sufficient by itself, and which is not to be supplemented by any external additions. Hence the sum total of its cognition will constitute a system that is to be grasped and determined under one idea, the completeness and articulation of which system can at the same time yield a touchstone of the correctness and genuineness of all the pieces of cognition fitting into it. This whole part of the transcendental logic, however, consists of two books, the first of which contains the **concepts** of pure understanding, the second its **principles.**

A 65

B 90

[a] *Zergliederung*
[b] The numeral "1." is missing in the second edition.
[c] Added in the second edition.

Transcendental Analytic
First Book
The Analytic of Concepts.*

I understand by an analytic of concepts not their analysis, or the usual procedure of philosophical investigations, that of analyzing* the content of concepts that present themselves and bringing them to distinctness, but rather the much less frequently attempted **analysis* of the faculty of understanding** itself, in order to research the possibility of *a priori* concepts by seeking them only in the understanding as their birthplace and analyzing its pure use in general; for this is the proper business of a transcendental philosophy; the rest is the logical treatment of con-

A 66

B 91

---

* The following notes appear at this point in Kant's copy of the first edition:
"We remarked above that experience consists of synthetic propositions, and how synthetic *a posteriori* propositions are possible is not to be regarded as a question requiring a solution, since it is a fact.
"Now it is to be asked how this fact is possible.
"Experience consists of judgments, but it is to be asked whether these empirical judgments do not in the end presuppose *a priori* (pure) judgments. The analysis [*Analysis*] of experience contains, first, its analysis [*Zergliederung*] insofar as judgments are in it; second, beyond the *a posteriori* concepts also *a priori* concepts.
"The problem is: How is experience possible? 1. What does the understanding do in judgments in general? 2. What do the senses do in empirical judgments? 3. In empirical cognition, what does the understanding, applied to the representations of the senses, do in order to bring forth a cognition of objects [*Objecte*]?
"One sees at first that experience is only possible through synthetic *a priori* propositions. Hence *a priori* principles [*Principien*] are I. immanent: in accordance with use; 2. it is to be asked, whether they are also transcendent.
"The test for whether something is also experience, i.e., a fact, is as it were experimentation with the universal propositions under which the particular empirical judgment belongs. If the latter cannot stand under a universal rule for judging, if no concept can be made out of that, then it is a *vitium subreptionis* [*vicious fallacy*]. Why in superstition and credulity." (E XXXIII, pp. 21–2; 23:24–5)
* zergliedern
* Zergliederung

cepts in philosophy in general. We will therefore pursue the pure concepts into their first seeds and predispositions in the human understanding, where they lie ready, until with the opportunity of experience they are finally developed and exhibited in their clarity by the very same understanding, liberated from the empirical conditions attaching to them.

The Analytic of Concepts
First Chapter
On the Clue to the Discovery of all Pure Concepts of the Understanding

If one sets a faculty of cognition into play, then on various occasions different concepts will become prominent that will make this faculty known and that can be collected in a more or less exhaustive treatise depending on whether they have been observed for a longer time or with greater acuteness. Where this investigation will be completed can never be determined with certainty by means of this as it were mechanical procedure. Further, the concepts that are discovered only as the opportunity arises will not reveal any order and systematic unity, but will rather be ordered in pairs only according to similarities and placed in series only in accord with the magnitude of their content, from the simple to the more composite, which series are by no means systematic even if to some extent methodically produced.

A67
B92

Transcendental philosophy has the advantage but also the obligation to seek its concepts in accordance with a principle,^{a} since they spring pure and unmixed from the understanding, as absolute unity, and must therefore be connected among themselves in accordance with a concept or idea. Such a connection, however, provides a rule by means of which the place of each pure concept of the understanding and the completeness of all of them together can be determined *a priori*, which would otherwise depend upon whim or chance.

On the Transcendental Clue for the Discovery of all Pure Concepts of the Understanding
First Section
On the logical use of the understanding in general.

The understanding has been explained above only negatively, as a non-

A68

sensible faculty of cognition. Now we cannot partake of intuition inde-

---

^{a} *Princip*

pendently of sensibility. The understanding is therefore not a faculty of intuition. But besides intuition there is no other kind of cognition than through concepts. Thus the cognition of every, at least human, understanding is a cognition through concepts, not intuitive but discursive. All intuitions, as sensible, rest on affections, concepts therefore on functions. By a function, however, I understand the unity of the action of ordering different representations under a common one. Concepts are therefore grounded on the spontaneity of thinking, as sensible intuitions are grounded on the receptivity of impressions. Now the understanding can make no other use of these concepts than that of judging by means of them. Since no*a* representation pertains to the object immediately except intuition alone, a concept is thus never immediately related to an object, but is always related to some other representation of it (whether that be an intuition or itself already a concept).*b* Judgment is therefore the mediate cognition of an object, hence the representation of a representation of it. In every judgment there is a concept that holds of many, and that among this many also comprehends a given representation, which is then related immediately to the object.[5] So in the judgment, e.g., **"All bodies are divisible,"***c* the concept of the divisible is related to various other concepts; among these, however, it is here particularly related to the concept of body, and this in turn is related to certain appearances*d* that come before us. These objects are therefore mediately represented by the concept of divisibility. All judgments are accordingly functions of unity among our representations, since instead of an immediate representation a higher one, which comprehends this and other representations under itself, is used for the cognition of the object, and many possible cognitions are thereby drawn together into one. We can, however, trace all actions of the understanding back to judgments, so that the **understanding** in general can be represented as a **faculty for judging.** For according to what has been said above it is a faculty for thinking. Thinking is cognition through concepts. Concepts, however, as predicates of possible judgments, are related to some representation of a still undetermined object. The concept of body thus signifies something, e.g., metal, which can be cognized through that concept. It is therefore a concept only because other representations are contained under it by means of which it can be re-

B93

A69
B94

---

a In his copy of the first edition, Kant inserts here the word "other" (E XXIV, p. 23; 23:45).

b Kant's copy of the first edition replaces this parenthetical aside with the following words, without parentheses: "which itself contains intuition only mediately or immediately" (E XXXV, p. 23; 23:45).

c *Teilbar,* rather than *veränderlich,* following the fourth edition.

d Kant's copy of the first edition changes "appearances" to "intuitions" (E XXXVI, p. 23; 23:45).

lated to objects. It is therefore the predicate for a possible judgment, e.g., "Every metal is a body." The functions of the understanding can therefore all be found together if one can exhaustively exhibit the functions of unity in judgments. The following section will make it evident that this can readily be accomplished.

On the Clue to the Discovery of all Pure Concepts of the Understanding
Second Section

<§ 9.> *
On the logical function of the understanding in judgments.

If we abstract from all content of a judgment in general, and attend only to the mere form of the understanding in it, we find that the function of thinking in that can be brought under four titles, each of which contains under itself three moments. They can suitably be represented in the following table.[6]

I.
Quantity of Judgments
Universal
Particular
Singular

2.	**3.**
Quality	**Relation**[b]
Affirmative	Categorical
Negative	Hypothetical
Infinite	Disjunctive

4.
Modality
Problematic
Assertoric
Apodictic

Since this division seems to depart in several points, although not essential ones, from the customary technique of the logicians, the following protests against a worrisome misunderstanding are not unnecessary.

---

a Here Kant resumes the numbering of paragraphs begun in the "Transcendental Aesthetic" in the second edition. This will continue through the end of the "Transcendental Deduction."

b Here Kant uses the latinate word *Relation* instead of either *Beziehung* or *Verhältnis*.

Section II. On the logical function in judgments

1. The logicians rightly say that in the use of judgments in syllogisms singular judgments can be treated like universal ones. For just because they have no domain at all, their predicate is not merely related to some of what is contained under the concept of the subject while being excluded from another part of it. The predicate therefore holds of that concept without exception, just as if the latter were a generally valid^a concept with a domain with the predicate applying to the whole of what is signified.^b If, on the contrary, we compare a singular judgment with a generally valid one, merely as cognition, with respect to quantity,^c then the former^d relates to the latter as unity relates to infinity, and is therefore in itself essentially different from the latter. Therefore, if I consider a singular judgment (*judicium singulare*) not only with respect to its internal validity, but also, as cognition in general, with respect to the quantity^e it has in comparison with other cognitions, then it is surely different from generally valid judgments (*judicia communia*), and deserves a special place in a complete table of the moments of thinking in general (though obviously not in that logic that is limited only to the use   B 97
of judgments with respect to each other).

2. Likewise, in a transcendental logic **infinite judgments** must also be distinguished from **affirmative** ones, even though in general logic   A 72
they are rightly included with the latter and do not constitute a special member of the classification. General logic abstracts from all content of the predicate (even if it is negative), and considers only whether it is attributed to the subject or opposed to it. Transcendental logic, however, also considers the value or content of the logical affirmation made in a judgment by means of a merely negative predicate, and what sort of gain this yields for the whole of cognition. If I had said of the soul that it is not mortal, then I would at least have avoided an error by means of a negative judgment. Now by means of the proposition "The soul is nonmortal" I have certainly made an actual affirmation as far as logical form is concerned, for I have placed the soul within the unlimited domain of undying beings. Now since that which is mortal contains one part of the whole domain of possible beings, but that which is undying^f the other,

---

^a *gemeingültiger.* While this would normally be translated "commonly valid," in this context it clearly refers to the universal (*allgemein*) judgment; we have used "generally" to preserve this reference while still marking the difference from *allgemein.*

^b *von dessen ganzer Bedeutung*; here Kant uses *Bedeutung*, as Frege was later to use it, to mean the reference or denotation of a concept; more typically, he uses it to mean something closer to what Frege called *Sinn* or sense, that is, the connotation.

^c *Größe*

^d The text has *sie* rather than *es*, but in spite of the shift in gender there is nothing for the pronoun to refer to except "a singular judgment."

^e *Größe*

^f In the second edition, *Nichtsterbende*; in the first, *Nichtsterbliche*, or "immortal."

207

nothing is said by my proposition but that the soul is one of the infinite multitude of things that remain if I take away everything that is mortal. But the infinite sphere of the possible is thereby limited only to the extent that that which is mortal is separated from it, and the soul is placed B98 in the remaining space of its domain.*ᵃ* But even with this exception this space still remains infinite, and more parts could be taken away from it A73 without the concept of the soul growing in the least and being affirmatively determined. In regard to logical domain, therefore, this infinite judgment is merely limiting with regard to the content of cognition in general, and to this extent it must not be omitted from the transcendental table of all moments of thinking in judgments, since the function of understanding that is hereby exercised may perhaps be important in the field of its pure *a priori* cognition.[7]

3. All relations*ᵇ* of thinking in judgments are those *a*) of the predicate to the subject, *b*) of the ground to the consequence, and *c*) between the cognition that is to be divided and*ᶜ* all of the members of the division. In the first kind of judgment only two concepts are considered to be in relation to each other, in the second, two judgments, and in the third, several judgments. The hypothetical proposition "If there is perfect justice, then obstinate evil will be punished" really contains the relation of two propositions, "There is a perfect justice" and "Obstinate evil is punished." Whether both of these propositions in themselves are true remains unsettled here. It is only the implication that is thought by means B99 of this judgment. Finally, the disjunctive judgment contains the relations of two or more propositions to one another, though not the relation of sequence, but rather that of logical opposition, insofar as the sphere of one judgment excludes that of the other, yet at the same time the relation of community, insofar as the judgments together exhaust the sphere A74 of cognition proper; it is therefore a relation of the parts of the sphere of a cognition where the sphere of each part is the complement of that of the others in the sum total of the divided cognition, e.g., "The world exists either through blind chance, or through inner necessity, or through an external cause." Each of these propositions occupies one part of the sphere of the possible cognition about the existence of a world in general, and together they occupy the entire sphere. To remove the cognition from one of these spheres means to place it in one of the

---

ᵃ Following the first edition, *Raum ihres Umfangs*, rather than the second, *Umfangs ihres Raums*.

ᵇ *Verhältnisse;* although he is now speaking of the functions of judgment the table had listed under the latinate heading *Relation*, Kant now reverts to *Verhältnis*, and in the remainder of this paragraph *Verhältnis* is translated by "relation." Kant's reversion to *Verhältnis* here is consistent with his use of this term elsewhere, since he is talking of the relation of parts of judgments to each other rather than to us.

ᶜ Kant's copy of the first edition replaces "and" with "of" (E XXXVII, p. 23; 23:45).

others, and to place it in one sphere, on the contrary, means to remove it from the others. In a disjunctive judgment there is therefore a certain community of cognitions, consisting in the fact that they mutually exclude each other, yet thereby determine the true cognition **in its entirety**, since taken together they constitute the entire content of a particular given cognition.[8] And this is also all that I find it necessary to remark upon for the sake of what follows.[a]

4. The modality of judgments is a quite special function of them, which is distinctive in that it contributes nothing to the content of the judgment (for besides quantity, quality, and relation[b] there is nothing more that constitutes the content of a judgment), but rather concerns only the value of the copula in relation to thinking in general.[9] **Problematic** judgments are those in which one regards the assertion or denial as merely **possible** (arbitrary). **Assertoric** judgments are those in which it is considered **actual** (true). **Apodictic** judgments are those in which it is seen as **necessary**.* Thus the two judgments whose relation constitutes the hypothetical judgment (*antecedens* and *consequens*), as well as those in whose reciprocal relation[c] the disjunctive judgment consists (the members of the division), are all merely problematic. In the above example the proposition "There is a perfect justice" is not said assertorically, but is only thought of as an arbitrary judgment that it is possible that someone might assume, and only the implication is assertoric. Thus such judgments can be obviously false and yet, if taken problematically, conditions of the cognition of truth. Thus the judgment **"The world exists through blind chance"** is of only problematic significance in the disjunctive judgment, that is, someone might momentarily assume this proposition, and yet it serves (like the designation of the false path among the number of all of those one can take) to find the true one. The problematic proposition is therefore that which only expresses logical possibility (which is not objective), i.e., a free choice to allow such a proposition to count as valid, a merely arbitrary assumption of it in the understanding. The assertoric proposition speaks of logical actuality or truth, as say in a hypothetical syllogism the antecedent in the major premise is problematic, but that in the minor premise assertoric, and in-

B 100

A 75

B 101

A 76

---

* It is just as if in the first case thought were a function of the **understanding**, in the second of the **power of judgment**, and in the third of **reason**. This is a remark the elucidation of which can be expected only in the sequel.

[a] The following note occurs in Kant's copy of the first edition: "Judgments and propositions are different. That the latter are *verbis expressa* [explicit words], since they are assertoric" (E XXXVIII, p. 23; 23:25).
[b] *Verhältnis*
[c] *Wechselwirkung*

dicates that the proposition is already bound to the understanding according to its laws; the apodictic proposition thinks of the assertoric one as determined through these laws of the understanding itself, and as thus asserting *a priori*, and in this way expresses logical necessity. Now since everything here is gradually incorporated into the understanding, so that one first judges something problematically, then assumes it assertorically as true, and finally asserts it to be inseparably connected with the understanding, i.e., asserts it as necessary and apodictic, these three functions of modality can also be called so many moments of thinking in general.

B 102

On the Clue to the Discovery of all Pure
Concepts of the Understanding
Third Section

<§ 10.>
On the pure concepts of the understanding
or categories.

As has already been frequently said, general logic abstracts from all content of cognition, and expects that representations will be given to it from elsewhere, wherever this may be, in order for it to transform them into concepts analytically. Transcendental logic, on the contrary, has a manifold of sensibility that lies before it *a priori*, which the transcen-

A 77 dental aesthetic has offered to it, in order to provide the pure concepts of the understanding with a matter, without which they would be without any content, thus completely empty. Now space and time contain a manifold of pure *a priori* intuition, but belong nevertheless among the conditions of the receptivity of our mind, under which alone it can receive representations of objects, and thus they must always also affect the concept of these objects. Only the spontaneity of our thought requires that this manifold first be gone through, taken up, and combined in a certain way in order for a cognition to be made out of it. I call this action synthesis.

B 103 By **synthesis** in the most general sense, however, I understand[a] the action of putting different representations together with each other and comprehending their manifoldness in one cognition. Such a synthesis is **pure** if the manifold is given not empirically but *a priori* (as is that in space and time). Prior to all analysis of our representations these must first be given, and no concepts can arise analytically as far as **the con-**

---

[a] In his copy of the first edition, Kant changes this sentence to this point to "I understand by **synthesis,** however, the action through which synthetic judgments come to be, in the general sense, . . ." (E XXXIX, p. 23; 23:45). Kant also adds the words "Combination, composition, and nexus" (E XL, p. 24).

tent is concerned. The synthesis of a manifold, however, (whether it be given empirically or *a priori*) first brings forth a cognition, which to be sure may initially still be raw and confused, and thus in need of analysis; yet the synthesis alone is that which properly collects the elements for cognitions and unifies them into a certain content; it is therefore the first thing to which we have to attend if we wish to judge about the first origin of our cognition.

A 78

Synthesis in general is, as we shall subsequently see, the mere effect of the imagination, of a blind though indispensable function of the soul,[b] without which we would have no cognition at all, but of which we are seldom even conscious. Yet to bring this synthesis **to concepts** is a function that pertains to the understanding, and by means of which it first provides cognition in the proper sense.[c]

Now **pure synthesis, generally represented,** yields the pure concept of the understanding. By this synthesis, however, I understand that which rests on a ground of synthetic unity *a priori*; thus our counting (as is especially noticeable in the case of larger numbers) is a **synthesis in accordance with concepts,** since it takes place in accordance with a common ground of unity (e.g., the decad). Under this concept, therefore, the synthesis of the manifold becomes necessary.

B 104

Different representations are brought **under** one concept analytically (a business treated by general logic). Transcendental logic, however, teaches how to bring under concepts not the representations but the **pure synthesis** of representations. The first thing that must be given to us *a priori* for the cognition of all objects is the **manifold** of pure intuition; the **synthesis** of this manifold by means of the imagination is the second thing, but it still does not yield cognition. The concepts that give this pure synthesis **unity,** and that consist solely in the representation of this necessary synthetic unity, are the third thing necessary for cognition of an object that comes before us, and they depend on the understanding.[10]

A 79

The same function that gives unity to the different representations **in a judgment** also gives unity to the mere synthesis of different representations **in an intuition,** which, expressed generally, is called the pure concept of understanding.[11] The same understanding, therefore, and indeed by means of the very same actions through which it brings the logical form of a judgment into concepts by means of the analytical unity, also brings a transcendental content into its representations by means of

B 105

---

[a] In the first edition, the right-hand running head is "Section III. On the pure concepts of understanding or categories"

[b] In his copy of the first edition Kant replaces this clause with "of a function of the understanding" (E XLI, p. 24; 23:45).

[c] *in eigentlicher Bedeutung*

the synthetic unity of the manifold in intuition in general, on account of which they are called pure concepts of the understanding that pertain to objects*a* *a priori;* this can never be accomplished by general logic.

In such a way there arise exactly as many pure concepts of the understanding, which apply to objects of intuition in general *a priori,* as there were logical functions of all possible judgments in the previous table: for the understanding is completely exhausted and its capacity*b* entirely measured by these functions.*c* Following Aristotle we will call

A 80 these concepts **categories,** for our aim is basically identical with his although very distant from it in execution.*d*

B 106

Table of Categories[12]

I.

Of Quantity

Unity

Plurality

Totality

2. **Of Quality** Reality Negation Limitation	3. **Of Relation***e* Of Inherence and Subsistence (*substantia et accidens*) Of Causality and Dependence (cause and effect) Of Community (reciprocity between agent and patient)

4.

Of Modality

Possibility – Impossibility

Existence – Non-existence

Necessity – Contingency

---

a *Objecte*

b *Vermögen*

c *gedachte Functionen*

d The following notes precede the ensuing table of the categories in Kant's copy of the first edition:

"Logical functions are only forms for the relation of concepts in thinking. Categories are concepts, through which certain intuitions are determined in regard to the synthetic unity of their consciousness as contained under these functions; e.g., what must be thought as subject and not as predicate." (E XLII, p. 24; 23:25)

"On the use of the categories in the division of a system.

"On the analytic of the categories and the predicables.

"On a characteristic of concepts; of intellectual, empirical, and pure sensible representations.

" – *Lex originaria:* concept of the understanding." (E XLIII, p. 24; 23:25)

e *Relation*

Section III. On the pure concepts of the understanding

Now this is the listing of all original pure concepts of synthesis[a] that the understanding contains in itself *a priori*, and on account of which it is only a pure understanding; for by these concepts alone can it understand something in the manifold of intuition, i.e., think an object[b] for it. This division is systematically generated from a common principle,[c] namely the faculty for judging (which is the same as the faculty for thinking), and has not arisen rhapsodically from a haphazard search for pure concepts, of the completeness of which one could never be certain, since one would only infer it through induction, without reflecting that in this way one would never see why just these and not other concepts should inhabit the pure understanding. Aristotle's search for these fundamental concepts was an effort worthy of an acute man. But since he had no principle,[d] he rounded them up as he stumbled on them, and first got up a list of ten of them, which he called **categories** (predicaments). Subsequently he believed that he had found five more of them, which he added under the name of post-predicaments. But his table still had holes. Further, it also included several *modi* of pure sensibility (*quando, ubi, situs,* as well as *prius, simul,*)[e] as well as an empirical one (*motus*),[f] which do not belong in this ancestral registry[g] of the understanding; derivative concepts were also included among the primary ones (*actio, passio*),[h] and several of the latter were entirely missing.

For the sake of the primary concepts it is therefore still necessary to remark that the categories, as the true **ancestral concepts**[i] of pure understanding, also have their equally pure **derivative**[j] **concepts,** which could by no means be passed over in a complete system of transcendental philosophy, but with the mere mention of which I can be satisfied in a merely critical essay.

Let me be allowed to call these pure but derivative concepts the **predicables** of pure understanding (in contrast to the predicaments). If one has the original and primitive concepts, the derivative and subalternate ones can easily be added, and the family tree[k] of pure understanding fully illustrated. Since I am concerned here not with the

---

[a] The words "of synthesis" are stricken in Kant's copy of the first edition (E XLIV, p. 24; 23:46).

[b] *Object*

[c] *Princip*

[d] *Principium*

[e] That is, the concepts of when, where, and position, and the relations of priority and simultaneity.

[f] motion

[g] *Stammregister*

[h] action, passion

[i] *Stammbegriffe*

[j] Clearly emphasized only in the first edition.

[k] *Stammbaum*

completeness of the system but rather only with the principles*a* for a system, I reserve this supplementation for another job. But one could readily reach this aim if one took the ontological textbooks in hand, and, e.g., under the category of causality, subordinated the predicables of force, action, and passion; under that of community, those of presence and resistance; under the predicaments of modality those of generation, corruption, alteration, and so on. The categories combined either with the *modis* of sensibility or with each other yield a great multitude of derivative *a priori* concepts, to take note of which and, as far as possible, completely catalogue would be a useful and not unpleasant but here dispensable effort.

I deliberately spare myself the definitions of these categories in this treatise, although I should like to be in possession of them.[13] In the sequel I will analyze these concepts to the degree that is sufficient in relation to the doctrine of method that I am working up. In a system of pure reason one could rightly demand these of me; but here they would only distract us from the chief point of the investigation by arousing doubts and objections that can well be referred to another occasion without detracting from our essential aim. In any case, from the little that I have here adduced it becomes clear that a complete lexicon with all the requisite definitions should be not only possible but even easy to produce. The headings already exist; it is merely necessary to fill them out, and a systematic topic, such as the present one, will make it easy not to miss the place where every concept properly belongs and at the same time will make it easy to notice any that is still empty.*b*

A 83

B 109

<§ 11.*c*

Subtle considerations about this table of categories could be made, which could perhaps have considerable consequences with regard to the scientific form of all cognitions of reason. For that this table is uncommonly useful, indeed indispensable in the theoretical part of philosophy for completely outlining **the plan for the whole of a science** insofar as it rests on *a priori* concepts, and **dividing** it mathematically **in accordance with determinate principles**,*d* is already self-evident from the fact that this table completely contains all the elementary concepts

---

a *Principien*
b Inserted in Kant's copy of the first edition:
  "What are categories? – – That they extend only to objects of experience.
  "1. Whence do they arise?
  "2. How are they valid *a priori* of objects of experience?" (E XLV, pp. 24–5; 23:25)
c Sections 11 and 12 were added in the second edition. This explains how Kant can refer to the *Metaphysical Foundations of Natural Science*, not published until 1786.
d *Principien*

of the understanding, indeed even the form of a system of them in the B 110 human understanding, consequently that it gives instruction about all the **moments,** indeed even of their **order,** of a planned speculative science, as I have elsewhere given proof.* Now here are several of these remarks.

The first is that this table, which contains four classes of concepts of the understanding, can first be split into two divisions, the first of which is concerned with objects of intuition (pure as well as empirical), the second of which, however, is directed at the existence of these objects (either in relation to each other or to the understanding).

I will call the first class the **mathematical** categories, the second, the **dynamical** ones. As one sees, the first class has no correlates, which are to be met with only in the second class. Yet this difference must have a ground in the nature of the understanding.

Second remark: that each class always has the same number of categories, namely three, which calls for reflection, since otherwise all *a priori* division by means of concepts must be a dichotomy. But here the third category always arises from the combination of the first two in its class.

Thus **allness** (totality) is nothing other than plurality considered as a B 111 unity, **limitation** is nothing other than reality combined with negation, community is the **causality** of a substance in the reciprocal determination of others, finally **necessity** is nothing other than the existence that is given by possibility itself. But one should not think that the third category is therefore a merely derivative one and not an ancestral concept of pure understanding. For the combination of the first and second in order to bring forth the third concept requires a special act of the understanding, which is not identical with that act performed in the first and second. Thus the concept of a **number** (which belongs to the category of allness) is not always possible wherever the concepts of multitude and of unity are (e.g., in the representation of the infinite); or **influence,** i.e., how one substance can be the cause of something in another substance, is not to be understood immediately by combining the concept of a **cause** and that of a **substance.** From this it is clear that a special act of the understanding is requisite for this; and likewise in the other cases.

Third remark: The agreement of a single category, namely that of **community,** which is to be found under the third title, with the form of a disjunctive judgment, which is what corresponds to it in the table B 112 of logical functions, is not as obvious as in the other cases.

In order to be assured of this agreement one must note that in all disjunctive judgments the sphere (the multitude of everything that is con-

* *Metaphysical Foundations of Natural Science.* B 110

tained under it) is represented as a whole divided into parts (the subordinated concepts), and, since none of these can be contained under any other, they are thought of as **coordinated** with one another, not **subordinated,** so that they do not determine each other **unilaterally,** as in a **series,** but **reciprocally,** as in an **aggregate** (if one member of the division is posited, all the rest are excluded, and vice versa).

Now a similar connection is thought of in **an entirety of things,** since one is not **subordinated,**[a] as effect, under another, as the cause of its existence, but is rather **coordinated**[b] with the other simultaneously and reciprocally as cause with regard to its determination (e.g., in a body, the parts of which reciprocally attract yet also repel each other), which is an entirely different kind of connection from that which is to be found in the mere relation[c] of cause to effect (of ground to consequence), in which the consequence does not reciprocally determine the ground and therefore does not constitute a whole with the latter (as the world-creator with the world). The understanding follows the same procedure when it represents the divided sphere of a concept as when it thinks of a thing as divisible, and just as in the first case the members of the division exclude each other and yet are connected in one sphere, so in the latter case the parts are represented as ones to which existence (as substances) pertains to each exclusively of the others, and which are yet connected in one whole.

BII3

§ 12.

But there is also yet another chapter in the transcendental philosophy of the ancients that contains pure concepts of the understanding that, although they are not reckoned among the categories, nevertheless according to them should also count as *a priori* concepts of objects, in which case, however, they would increase the number of the categories, which cannot be. These are expounded in the proposition, so famous among the scholastics: *quodlibet ens est unum, verum, bonum.*[d] Now although the use of this principle[e] for inferences has turned out to be very meager (they have yielded merely tautological propositions), so that in modern times it has been customary to grant it a place in metaphysics almost solely by courtesy, nevertheless a thought that has sustained itself so long, no matter how empty it seems, always deserves an investigation of its origin, and justifies the conjecture that it must have its

[a] *untergeordnet*
[b] *beygeordnet*
[c] *Verhältnis*
[d] Every being is one, true, and good.
[e] *Princips*

ground in some rule of the understanding, which, as so often happens, has merely been falsely interpreted. These supposedly transcendental predicates of **things** are nothing other than logical requisites and crite- B 114 ria of all **cognition of things** in general, and ground it in the categories of quantity, namely, the categories of **unity, plurality,** and **totality;** yet these categories must really have been taken as material, as belonging to the possibility of things itself, when in fact they should have been used in a merely formal sense, as belonging to the logical requirements for every cognition; thus these criteria of thinking were carelessly made into properties of things in themselves. In every cognition of an object[a] there is, namely, **unity** of the concept, which one can call **qualitative unity** insofar as by that only the unity of the comprehension[b] of the manifold of cognition is thought, as, say, the unity of the theme in a play, a speech, or a fable. Second, **truth** in respect of the consequences. The more true consequences from a given concept, the more indication of its objective reality. One could call this the **qualitative plurality** of the marks that belong to a concept as a common ground (not thought of in it as a magnitude). Third, finally, **perfection,** which consists in this plurality conversely being traced back to the unity of the concept, and agreeing completely with this one and no other one, which one can call **qualitative completeness** (totality). From this it is obvious that these logical criteria of the possibility of cognition in general transform the B 115 three categories of magnitude,[c] in which the unity in the generation of the magnitude[d] must be assumed to be completely homogeneous, into a principle[e] with the quality of a cognition for the connection of **heterogeneous** elements of cognition into one consciousness also. Thus the criterion of the possibility of a concept (not of its object)[f] is the definition, in which the **unity** of the concept, the **truth** of everything that may initially be derived from it, and finally the **completeness** of everything that is drawn from it, constitute everything that is necessary for the production of the entire concept; or the **criterion of a hypothesis** is also the intelligibility of the assumed **ground of explanation** or its **unity** (without auxiliary hypotheses), the **truth** (agreement with itself and with experience) of the consequences that are derived from it, and finally the **completeness** of the ground of explanation of these consequences, which do not refer us back to anything more or less than was already assumed in the hypothesis, and which merely analytically give back *a posteriori* and agree with that which was thought synthetically *a*

---

[a] *Objects*
[b] *Zusammenfassung*
[c] *Größe*
[d] *Quantum*
[e] *Princips*
[f] *Objects*

priori. – The transcendental table of the categories is thus not completed with the concepts of unity, truth, and perfection, as if it were lacking something, but rather, the relation[a] of these concepts to objects[b] being entirely set aside, our procedure with these concepts is only being thought under general logical rules for the agreement of cognition with itself.>

B 116

[a] *Verhältnis*
[b] *Objecte*

The Transcendental Analytic
Second Chapter
On the Deduction of the Pure Concepts of the Understanding

First Section
<§ 13.>*
On the
principles*b* of a transcendental deduction in general.[14]

'Jurists, when they speak of entitlements and claims, distinguish in a legal matter between the questions about what is lawful*d* (*quid juris*) and

---

a Paragraph number added in the second edition. In the first edition, the second chapter of the "Transcendental Analytic," the "Transcendental Deduction," is divided into three main sections, the first of which is in turn subdivided into two subsections. Apart from a few minor changes in wording, which will be noted, and the addition of the section numbers themselves, the two subsections of the first section are retained in the second edition and are identical until the last paragraph of their second subsection, which is replaced by three new paragraphs in the second edition. The second and third sections of the chapter in the first edition are then replaced by an entirely new second section in the second edition, which is broken up into numbered paragraphs § 15 through § 27. We will present all of this material in the following sequence: the first section as it appeared in both editions, with the last paragraph of the first-edition version followed by the last three paragraphs that replaced it in the second edition; the second and third sections as they appeared in the first edition; then the second section, consisting of numbered parts § 15 through § 27, as it appeared in the second edition.
b *Principien*
c The following notes are inserted here in Kant's copy of the first edition:
"Consciousness and inner sense are different. 'I think' is spontaneity and does not depend on any object. The representation, however, with which I think, must be given to me antecedently in intuition (through imagination). With regard to it I am affected." (E XLVI, p. 25; 23:26)
"It must be proved that if there were no sensible intuition *a priori*, and if this were not the form of sensibility in the subject, with which all appearances must be in accord, then:
"1. No categories would have significance.
"2. From mere categories no synthetic *a priori* propositions at all would be possible." (E XLVII, p. 25; 23:26)
d *was Rechtens ist*

that which concerns the fact (*quid facti*), and since they demand proof of both, they call the first, that which is to establish the entitlement or the legal claim, the **deduction.**[15] We make use of a multitude of empirical concepts without objection from anyone, and take ourselves to be justified in granting them a sense and a supposed signification even without any deduction, because we always have experience ready at hand to prove their objective reality. But there are also concepts that have been usurped, such as **fortune** and **fate,** which circulate with almost universal indulgence, but that are occasionally called upon to establish their claim by the question *quid juris*, and then there is not a little embarrassment about their deduction because one can adduce no clear legal ground for an entitlement to their use either from experience or from reason.

Among the many concepts, however, that constitute the very mixed fabric of human cognition, there are some that are also destined[a] for pure use *a priori* (completely independently of all experience), and these always require a deduction of their entitlement, since proofs from experience are not sufficient for the lawfulness of such a use, and yet one must know how these concepts can be related to objects[b] that they do not derive from any experience. I therefore call the explanation of the way in which concepts can relate to objects *a priori* their **transcendental deduction,** and distinguish this from the **empirical** deduction, which shows how a concept is acquired through experience and reflection on it, and therefore concerns not the lawfulness but the fact from which the possession has arisen.

Now we already have two sorts of concepts of an entirely different kind,[c] which yet agree with each other in that they both relate to objects completely *a priori*, namely the concepts of space and time, as forms of sensibility, and the categories, as concepts of the understanding. To seek an empirical deduction of them would be entirely futile work, for what is distinctive in their nature is precisely that they are related to their objects without having borrowed anything from experience for their representation. Thus if a deduction of them is necessary, it must always be transcendental.

Nevertheless, in the case of these concepts, as in the case of all cognition, we can search in experience, if not for the principle[d] of their possibility, then for the occasional causes of their generation, where the impressions of the senses provide the first occasion for opening the en-

---

[a] *bestimmt*

[b] *Objecte*

[c] Kant's copy of the first edition inserts: "They are not borrowed from experience" (E XLVIII, p. 25; 23:46).

[d] *Principium*

tire power of cognition to them and for bringing about experience, which contains two very heterogeneous elements, namely a **matter** for cognition from the senses and a certain **form** for ordering it from the inner source of pure intuiting and thinking, which, on the occasion of the former, are first brought into use and bring forth concepts. Such a tracing of the first endeavors of our power of cognition to ascend from individual perceptions to general concepts is without doubt of great B119 utility, and the famous Locke is to be thanked for having first opened the way for this. Yet a **deduction** of the pure *a priori* concepts can never be achieved in this way; it does not lie down this path at all, for in regard to their future use, which should be entirely independent of experience, an entirely different birth certificate than that of an ancestry from experiences must be produced. I will therefore call this attempted physiological derivation,[16] which cannot properly be called a deduction A87 at all because it concerns a *quaestio facti,*[a] the explanation of the **possession** of a pure cognition. It is therefore clear that only a transcendental and never an empirical deduction of them can be given, and that in regard to pure *a priori* concepts empirical deductions are nothing but idle attempts, which can occupy only those who have not grasped the entirely distinctive nature of these cognitions.

But now even if the sole manner of a possible deduction of pure *a priori* cognition is conceded, namely that which takes the transcendental path, it is still not obvious that it is unavoidably necessary. We have above traced the concepts of space and time to their sources by means of a transcendental deduction, and explained and determined their *a priori* B120 objective validity. Geometry nevertheless follows its secure course through strictly *a priori* cognitions without having to beg philosophy for any certification of the pure and lawful pedigree of its fundamental concept of space. Yet the use of the[b] concept in this science concerns only the external world of the senses, of which space is the pure form of its intuition, and in which therefore all geometrical cognition is immediately evident because it is grounded on intuition *a priori*, and the objects are given through the cognition itself *a priori* in intuition (as far as their A88 form is concerned). With the **pure concepts of the understanding,** however, there first arises the unavoidable need to search for the transcendental deduction not only of them but also of space, for since they speak of objects not through predicates of intuition and sensibility but through those of pure *a priori* thinking, they relate to objects generally without any conditions of sensibility; and since they are not grounded in experience and cannot exhibit any object[c] in *a priori* intuition on which

[a] As in the first edition; the second, declining *quaestio*, prints *quaestionem.*
[b] The first edition here reads *"dieses"* instead of the second's *"des."*
[c] *Object*

to ground their synthesis prior to any experience, they not only arouse suspicion about the objective validity and limits of their use but also make the **concept of space** ambiguous by inclining us to use it beyond the conditions of sensible intuition, on which account a transcendental deduction of it was also needed above. Thus the reader must be convinced of the unavoidable necessity of such a transcendental deduction before he has taken a single step in the field of pure reason; for he would otherwise proceed blindly, and after much wandering around would still have to return to the ignorance from which he had begun. But he must also clearly understand from the outset its inevitable difficulty, so that he will not complain of obscurity where the subject-matter itself is deeply veiled or become annoyed too soon over the removal of hindrances, since we must either surrender completely all claims to insights of pure reason in its favorite field, namely that beyond the boundaries of all possible experience, or else perfect this critical investigation.

In the case of the concepts of space and time, we were able above to make comprehensible with little effort how these, as *a priori* cognitions, must nevertheless necessarily relate to objects, and made possible a synthetic cognition of them independent of all experience. For since an object can appear to us only by means of such pure forms of sensibility, i.e., be an object*a* of empirical intuition, space and time are thus pure intuitions that contain *a priori* the conditions of the possibility of objects as appearances, and the synthesis in them has objective validity.

The categories of the understanding, on the contrary, do not represent to us the conditions under which objects are given in intuition at all, hence objects can indeed appear to us without necessarily having to be related to functions of the understanding, and therefore without the understanding containing their *a priori* conditions.[17] Thus a difficulty is revealed here that we did not encounter in the field of sensibility, namely how **subjective conditions of thinking** should have **objective validity,** i.e., yield conditions of the possibility of all cognition of objects; for appearances can certainly be given in intuition without functions of the understanding. I take, e.g., the concept of cause, which signifies a particular kind of synthesis, in which given something *A* something entirely different *B* is posited according to a rule.*b* It is not clear *a priori* why appearances should contain anything of this sort (one cannot adduce experiences for the proof, for the objective validity of this *a priori* concept must be able to be demonstrated), and it is therefore *a priori* doubtful whether such a concept is not perhaps entirely empty and finds no object anywhere among the appearances. For that

a *Object*

b Emended in Kant's copy of the first edition to "posited according to an *a priori* rule, i.e., necessarily" (E XLIX, p. 25; 23:46).

objects of sensible intuition must accord with the formal conditions of sensibility that lie in the mind *a priori* is clear from the fact that other- B123 wise they would not be objects for us; but that they must also accord with the conditions that the understanding requires for the synthetic unity*a* of thinking is a conclusion that is not so easily seen.*b* For appearances could after all be so constituted that the understanding would not find them in accord with the conditions of its unity, and everything would then lie in such confusion that, e.g., in the succession of appearances nothing would offer itself that would furnish a rule of synthesis and thus correspond to the concept of cause and effect, so that this concept would therefore be entirely empty, nugatory, and without significance. Appearances would nonetheless offer objects to our intuition, for A91 intuition by no means requires the functions of thinking.

If one were to think of escaping from the toils of these investigations by saying that experience constantly offers examples of a regularity of appearances that give sufficient occasion for abstracting the concept of cause from them, and thereby at the same time thought to confirm the objective validity of such a concept, then one has not noticed that the concept of cause cannot arise in this way at all, but must either be grounded in the understanding completely *a priori* or else be entirely surrendered as a mere fantasy of the brain. For this concept always re- B124 quires that something *A* be of such a kind that something else *B* follows from it **necessarily** and **in accordance with an absolutely universal rule**. Appearances may well offer cases from which a rule is possible in accordance with which something usually happens, but never a rule in accordance with which the succession is **necessary**; thus to the synthesis of cause and effect there attaches a dignity that can never be expressed empirically, namely, that the effect does not merely come along with the cause, but is posited **through** it and follows **from** it. The strict universality of the rule is therefore not any property of empirical rules, which cannot acquire anything more through induction than compara- A92 tive universality, i.e., widespread usefulness. But now the use of the pure concepts of the understanding would be entirely altered if one were to treat them only as empirical products.

---

a Following Erdmann in reading *"Einheit"* for *"Einsicht"*; Kant uses *"Einheit"* in a parallel fashion in the next sentence.

b Inserted in Kant's copy of the first edition: "If I were simply to say that without the connection of causes and effects I would not grasp the sequence of alterations, it would not at all follow from this that this must be precisely as an understanding needs it to be to grasp it, but I would not be able to explain whence they continuously follow one another. Only I would not raise this question if I did not already have the concept of cause and of the necessity of such persistence. A subjective necessity, habit, would make it worse. An implanted necessity would not prove necessity." (E L, pp. 25–6; 23:26)

[a]Transition
to the transcendental deduction of the categories.

There are only two possible cases in which synthetic representation and its objects can come together, necessarily relate to each other, and, as it were, meet each other: Either if the object alone makes the representa-

B 125 tion possible, or if the representation alone makes the object possible. If it is the first, then this relation is only empirical, and the representation is never possible *a priori*. And this is the case with appearance in respect of that in it which belongs to sensation. But if it is the second, then since representation in itself (for we are not here talking about its causality by means of the will) does not produce its object as far as its **existence** is concerned, the representation is still determinant of the object *a priori* if it is possible through it alone to **cognize something as an object.** But there are two conditions under which alone the cognition of an object is possible: first, **intuition,** through which it is given, but only as appearance; second, **concept,** through which an object is thought that corresponds to this intuition. It is clear from what has

A 93 been said above, however, that the first condition, namely that under which alone objects can be intuited, in fact does lie[b] in the mind *a priori* as the ground of the form of objects.[c] All appearances therefore necessarily agree with this formal condition of sensibility, because only through it can they appear, i.e., be empirically intuited and given. The question now is whether *a priori* concepts do not also precede, as conditions under which alone something can be, if not intuited, nevertheless thought as object in general, for then all empirical cognition of

B 126 objects is necessarily in accord with such concepts, since without their presupposition nothing is possible as **object[d] of experience.** Now, however, all experience contains in addition to the intuition of the senses, through which something is given, a **concept** of an object that is given in intuition, or appears;[18] hence concepts of objects in general lie at the ground of all experiential cognition as *a priori* conditions; consequently the objective validity of the categories, as *a priori* concepts, rests on the fact that through them alone is experience possible (as far as the form of thinking is concerned). For they then are related necessarily and *a priori* to objects of experience, since only by means of them can any object of experience be thought at all.

[a] No section number appears here in the second edition, but "§ 14" should have been added to avoid an unnumbered section between § 13 and § 15.
[b] Following Erdmann in reading *"liegt"* for *"liegen"*; Kant seems to have confused the singular antecedent (*Bedingung*) with the plural, perhaps because of the intervening occurrence of the plural "objects."
[c] *Objecten*
[d] *Object*

Section I. On the principles of a transcendental deduction

The transcendental deduction of all *a priori* concepts therefore has a principle^a toward which the entire investigation must be directed, namely this: that they must be recognized as *a priori* conditions of the possibility of experiences (whether of the intuition that is encountered in them, or of the thinking).[19] Concepts that supply the objective ground of the possibility of experience are necessary just for that reason. The unfolding of the experience in which they are encountered, however, is not their deduction (but their illustration), since they would thereby be only contingent. Without this original relation to possible experience, in which all objects of cognition are found, their relation to any object^b could not be comprehended at all.

^c[There are, however, three original sources (capacities or faculties of the soul), which contain the conditions of the possibility of all experience, and cannot themselves be derived from any other faculty of the mind, namely **sense, imagination,** and **apperception.** On these are grounded 1) the **synopsis** of the manifold *a priori* through sense; 2) the **synthesis** of this manifold through the imagination; finally 3) the **unity** of this synthesis through original apperception. In addition to their empirical use, all of these faculties have a transcendental one, which is concerned solely with form, and which is possible *a priori*. We have discussed this **with regard to the senses** in the first part above, however, we will now attempt to understand the nature of the two other ones.]

^d<The famous Locke, from neglect of this consideration, and because he encountered pure concepts of the understanding in experience, also derived them from this experience, and thus proceeded so **inconsistently** that he thereby dared to make attempts at cognitions that go far beyond the boundary of all experience. David Hume recognized that in order to be able to do the latter it is necessary that these concepts would have to have their origin *a priori*. But since he could not explain at all how it is possible for the understanding to think of concepts that in themselves are not combined in the understanding as still necessarily combined in the object, and it never occurred to him that perhaps the understanding itself, by means of these concepts, could be the originator of the experience in which its objects are encountered, he thus, driven by necessity, derived them from experience (namely from a subjective necessity arisen from frequent association in experience, which is subsequently falsely held to be objective, i.e., **custom**);^e however he

A94

B127

A95

B127

---

^a *Principium*

^b *Object*

^c This paragraph in the first edition is omitted in the second and replaced by three that here follow it.

^d The next three paragraphs are added in the second edition, replacing the previous one.

^e *Gewohnheit*

subsequently proceeded quite consistently in declaring it to be impossible to go beyond the boundary of experience with these concepts and the principles that they occasion. The **empirical** derivation, however,

B 128 to which both of them resorted, cannot be reconciled with the reality of the scientific cognition *a priori* that we possess, that namely of **pure mathematics** and **general natural science,** and is therefore refuted by the fact.[a]

The first of these two famous men opened the gates wide to **enthusiasm,** since reason, once it has authority on its side, will not be kept within limits by indeterminate recommendations of moderation; the second gave way entirely to **skepticism,** since he believed himself to have discovered in what is generally held to be reason a deception of our faculty of cognition. – We are now about to make an attempt to see whether we cannot successfully steer human reason between these two cliffs, assign its determinate boundaries, and still keep open the entire field of its purposive activity.

I will merely precede this with the **explanation of the categories.** They are concepts of an object in general, by means of which its intuition is regarded as **determined** with regard to one of the **logical functions** for judgments.[20] Thus, the function of the **categorical** judgment was that of the relationship of the subject to the predicate, e.g., "All bodies are divisible." Yet in regard to the merely logical use of the understanding it would remain undetermined which of these two concepts

B 129 will be given the function of the subject and which will be given that of the predicate. For one can also say: "Something divisible is a body." Through the category of substance, however, if I bring the concept of a body under it, it is determined that its empirical intuition in experience must always be considered as subject, never as mere predicate; and likewise with all the other categories.>

A 95

The Deduction of the Pure Concepts of the
Understanding
Second Section

[b]On the *a priori* grounds for the possibility
of experience.

It is entirely contradictory and impossible that a concept should be generated completely *a priori* and be related to an object although it

---

[a] *das Factum*

[b] What follows is the version of the "Transcendental Deduction" as it appeared in the first edition, where it is divided into the second and third sections of the present chapter. In the second edition, these two sections will be replaced by a single second section, divided into subsections numbered from § 15 to § 27. See B 129–69 below.

neither belongs itself within the concept of possible experience nor consists of elements of a possible experience. For it would then have no content, since no intuition would correspond to it though intuitions in general, through which objects can be given to us, constitute the field or the entire object of possible experience. An *a priori* concept that was not related[a] to the latter would be only the logical form for a concept, but not the concept itself through which something would be thought.

If there are pure *a priori* concepts, therefore, they can certainly contain nothing empirical; they must nevertheless be strictly *a priori* conditions for a possible experience, as that alone on which its objective reality can rest.

Hence if one wants to know how pure concepts of the understanding are possible, one must inquire what are the *a priori* conditions on which the possibility of experience depends and that ground it even if one abstracts from everything empirical in the appearances. A concept that expresses this formal and objective condition of experience universally and sufficiently would be called a pure concept of the understanding. Once I have pure concepts of the understanding, I can also think up objects that are perhaps impossible, or that are perhaps possible in themselves but cannot be given in any experience since in the connection of their concepts something may be omitted that yet necessarily belongs to the condition of a possible experience (the concept of a spirit), or perhaps pure concepts of the understanding will be extended further than experience can grasp (the concept of God). But the **elements** for all *a priori* cognitions, even for arbitrary and absurd fantasies, cannot indeed be borrowed from experience (for then they would not be *a priori* cognitions), but must always contain the pure *a priori* conditions of a possible experience and of an object of it, for otherwise not only would nothing at all be thought through them, but also without data they would not even be able to arise in thinking at all.

Now these concepts, which contain *a priori* the pure thinking in every experience, we find in the categories, and it is already a sufficient deduction of them and justification of their objective validity if we can prove that by means of them alone an object can be thought. But since in such a thought there is more at work than the single faculty of thinking, namely the understanding, and the understanding itself, as a faculty of cognition that is to be related to objects,[b] also requires an elucidation of the possibility of this relation, we must first assess not the empirical but the transcendental constitution of the subjective sources that comprise the *a priori* foundations for the possibility of experience.

If every individual representation were entirely foreign to the other, as

A 96

A 97

---

[a] *bezöge*
[b] *Objecte*

it were isolated and separated from it, then there would never arise anything like cognition, which is a whole of compared and connected representations. If therefore I ascribe a synopsis to sense, because it contains a manifold in its intuition, a synthesis must always correspond to this, and **receptivity** can make cognitions possible only if combined with **spontaneity.** This is now the ground of a threefold synthesis, which is necessarily found in all cognition: that, namely, of the **apprehension** of the representations, as modifications of the mind in intuition; of the **reproduction** of them in the imagination; and of their **recognition** in the concept.[21] Now these direct us toward three subjective sources of cognition, which make possible even the understanding and, through the latter, all experience as an empirical product of understanding.

A 98

Preliminary reminder

The deduction of the categories is connected with so many difficulties, and necessitates such deep penetration into the primary grounds of the possibility of our cognition in general, that in order to avoid the long-windedness of a complete theory and nevertheless not to omit anything in such a necessary inquiry, I have found it more advisable to prepare than to instruct the reader in the following four numbers, and only then to represent the exposition of these elements of the understanding systematically in the immediately following third section.[a] For this reason the reader should until then not be deterred by the obscurity that is initially unavoidable in a path that is thus far entirely unexplored, but which will, as I hope, be completely illuminated in that section.

I.
On the synthesis
of apprehension in the intuition.

Wherever our representations may arise, whether through the influence of external things or as the effect of inner causes, whether they have originated *a priori* or empirically as appearances – as modifications of the mind they nevertheless belong to inner sense, and as such all of our cognitions are in the end subjected to the formal condition of inner sense, namely time, as that in which they must all be ordered, connected, and brought into relations. This is a general remark on which one must ground everything that follows.[22]

A 99

Every intuition contains a manifold in itself, which however would not be represented as such if the mind did not distinguish the time in the succession of impressions on one another; for **as contained in one**

---

[a] The third section, beginning at A 115.

moment no representation can ever be anything other than absolute unity. Now in order for **unity** of intuition to come from this manifold (as, say, in the representation of space), it is necessary first to run through and then to take together this manifoldness, which action I call the **synthesis of apprehension,** since it is aimed directly at the intuition, which to be sure provides a manifold but can never effect this as such, and indeed as contained **in one representation,** without the occurrence of such a synthesis.

Now this synthesis of apprehension must also be exercised *a priori,* i.e., in regard to representations that are not empirical. For without it we could have *a priori* neither the representations of space nor of time, since these can be generated only through the synthesis of the manifold   A 100 that sensibility in its original receptivity provides. We therefore have a **pure** synthesis of apprehension.

2.

On the synthesis
of reproduction in the imagination.

It is, to be sure, a merely empirical law in accordance with which representations that have often followed or accompanied one another are finally associated with each other and thereby placed in a connection in accordance with which, even without the presence of the object, one of these representations brings about a transition of the mind to the other in accordance with a constant rule. This law of reproduction, however, presupposes that the appearances themselves are actually subject to such a rule, and that in the manifold of their representations an accompaniment or succession takes place according to certain rules; for without that our empirical imagination would never get to do anything suitable to its capacity,*a* and would thus remain hidden in the interior of the mind, like a dead and to us unknown faculty. If cinnabar were now red, now black, now light, now heavy, if a human being were now changed into this animal shape, now into that one, if on the longest day the land were covered now with fruits, now with ice and snow, then my   A 101 empirical imagination would never even get the opportunity to think of heavy cinnabar on the occasion of the representation of the color red; or if a certain word were attributed now to this thing, now to that, or if one and the same thing were sometimes called this, sometimes that, without the governance of a certain rule to which the appearances are already subjected in themselves, then no empirical synthesis of reproduction could take place.

There must therefore be something that itself makes possible this re-

---

a *Vermögen*

production of the appearances by being the *a priori* ground of a necessary synthetic unity of them. One soon comes upon this if one recalls that appearances are not things in themselves, but rather the mere play of our representations, which in the end come down to determinations of the inner sense. Now if we can demonstrate that even our purest *a priori* intuitions provide no cognition except insofar as they contain the sort of combination of the manifold that makes possible a thoroughgoing synthesis of reproduction, then this synthesis of the imagination would be grounded even prior to all experience on *a priori* principles,[a] and one must assume a pure transcendental synthesis of this power, which grounds even the possibility of all experience (as that which the reproducibility of the appearances necessarily presupposes). Now it is obvious that if I draw a line in thought, or think of the time from one noon to the next, or even want to represent a certain number to myself, I must necessarily first grasp one of these manifold representations after another in my thoughts. But if I were always to lose the preceding representations (the first parts of the line, the preceding parts of time, or the successively represented units) from my thoughts and not reproduce them when I proceed to the following ones, then no whole representation and none of the previously mentioned thoughts, not even the purest and most fundamental representations of space and time, could ever arise.

A 102

The synthesis of apprehension is therefore inseparably combined with the synthesis of reproduction. And since the former constitutes the transcendental ground of the possibility of all cognition in general (not only of empirical cognition, but also of pure *a priori* cognition), the reproductive synthesis of the imagination belongs among the transcendental actions of the mind, and with respect to this we will also call this faculty the transcendental faculty of the imagination.

A 103

3.
On the synthesis
of recognition in the concept.

Without consciousness that that which we think is the very same as what we thought a moment before, all reproduction in the series of representations would be in vain. For it would be a new representation in our current state, which would not belong at all to the act[b] through which it had been gradually generated, and its manifold would never constitute a whole, since it would lack the unity that only consciousness can obtain for it. If, in counting, I forget that the units that now hover

[a] *Principien*
[b] *Actus;* up to this point Kant has been using the word *Handlung.*

before my senses were successively added to each other by me, then I would not cognize the generation of the multitude*a* through this successive addition of one to the other, and consequently I would not cognize the number; for this concept consists solely in the consciousness of this unity of the synthesis.

The word "concept" itself could already lead us to this remark. For it is this **one** consciousness that unifies the manifold that has been successively intuited, and then also reproduced, into one representation. This consciousness may often only be weak, so that we connect it with the generation of the representation only in the effect, but not in the act*b* itself, i.e., immediately; but regardless of these differences one consciousness must always be found, even if it lacks conspicuous clarity, and without that concepts, and with them cognition of objects, would be entirely impossible.   A 104

And here then it is necessary to make understood what is meant by the expression "an object of representations." We have said above that appearances themselves are nothing but sensible representations, which must not be regarded in themselves, in the same way, as objects (outside the power of representation). What does one mean, then, if one speaks of an object corresponding to and therefore also distinct from the cognition? It is easy to see that this object must be thought of only as something in general = X, since outside of our cognition we have nothing that we could set over against this cognition as corresponding to it.

We find, however, that our thought of the relation of all cognition to its object carries something of necessity with it, since namely the latter is regarded as that which is opposed to our cognitions being determined at pleasure or arbitrarily rather than being determined *a priori*, since insofar as they are to relate to an object our cognitions must also necessarily agree with each other in relation to it, i.e., they must have that   A 105
unity that constitutes the concept of an object.[23]

It is clear, however, that since we have to do only with the manifold of our representations, and that X which corresponds to them (the object), because it should be something distinct from all of our representations, is nothing for us, the unity that the object makes necessary can be nothing other than the formal unity of the consciousness in the synthesis of the manifold of the representations. Hence we say that we cognize the object if we have effected synthetic unity in the manifold of intuition. But this is impossible if the intuition could not have been produced through a function of synthesis in accordance with a rule that makes the reproduction of the manifold necessary *a priori* and a concept in which this manifold is united possible. Thus we think of a triangle as

a Menge
b Actus

an object by being conscious of the composition of three straight lines in accordance with a rule according to which such an intuition can always be exhibited. Now this **unity of rule** determines every manifold, and limits it to conditions that make the unity of apperception possible, and the concept of this unity is the representation of the object = X, which I think through those predicates of a triangle.

A 106   All cognition requires a concept, however imperfect or obscure it may be; but as far as its form is concerned the latter is always something general, and something that serves as a rule. Thus the concept of body serves as the rule for our cognition of outer appearances by means of the unity of the manifold that is thought through it. However, it can be a rule of intuitions only if it represents the necessary reproduction of the manifold of given intuitions, hence the synthetic unity in the consciousness of them. Thus in the case of the perception of something outside of us the concept of body makes necessary the representation of extension, and with it that of impenetrability, of shape, etc.

Every necessity has a transcendental condition as its ground. A transcendental ground must therefore be found for the unity of the consciousness in the synthesis of the manifold of all our intuitions, hence also of the concepts of objects[a] in general, consequently also of all objects of experience, without which it would be impossible to think of any object for our intuitions; for the latter is nothing more than the something for which the concept expresses such a necessity[b] of synthesis.

Now this original and transcendental condition is nothing other than
A 107   the **transcendental apperception.**[24] The consciousness of oneself in accordance with the determinations of our state in internal perception is merely empirical, forever variable; it can provide no standing or abiding self in this stream of inner appearances, and is customarily called **inner sense** or **empirical apperception.** That which should **necessarily** be represented as numerically identical cannot be thought of as such through empirical data. There must be a condition that precedes all experience and makes the latter itself possible, which should make such a transcendental presupposition valid.

Now no cognitions can occur in us, no connection and unity among them, without that unity of consciousness that precedes all data of the intuitions, and in relation to which all representation of objects is alone possible. This pure, original, unchanging consciousness I will now name **transcendental apperception.** That it deserves this name is already obvious from this, that even the purest objective unity, namely that of the *a priori* concepts (space and time) is possible only through the relation of the intuitions to it. The numerical unity of this apper-

---

[a] *Objecte*
[b] Following Erdmann, reading *Nothwendigkeit* for *Nothwendig*.

ception therefore grounds all concepts *a priori*, just as the manifoldness of space and time grounds the intuitions of sensibility.

Just this transcendental unity of apperception, however, makes out of all possible appearances that can ever come together in one experience a connection of all of these representations in accordance with laws.[25] For this unity of consciousness would be impossible if in the cognition of the manifold the mind could not become conscious of the identity of the function by means of which this manifold is synthetically combined into one cognition. Thus the original and necessary consciousness of the identity of oneself is at the same time a consciousness of an equally necessary unity of the synthesis of all appearances in accordance with concepts, i.e., in accordance with rules that not only make them necessarily reproducible, but also thereby determine an object for their intuition, i.e., the concept of something in which they are necessarily connected; for the mind could not possibly think of the identity of itself in the manifoldness of its representations, and indeed think this *a priori*, if it did not have before its eyes the identity of its action, which subjects all synthesis of apprehension (which is empirical) to a transcendental unity, and first makes possible their connection in accordance with *a priori* rules. Further, we are now also able to determine our concepts of an **object** in general more correctly. All representations, as representations, have their object, and can themselves be objects of other representations in turn. Appearances are the only objects that can be given to us immediately, and that in them which is immediately related to the object is called intuition. However, these appearances are not things in themselves, but themselves only representations, which in turn have their object, which therefore cannot be further intuited by us, and that may therefore be called the non-empirical, i.e., transcendental object = X.[26]

The pure concept of this transcendental object (which in all of our cognitions is really always one and the same = X) is that which in all of our empirical concepts in general can provide relation to an object, i.e., objective reality. Now this concept cannot contain any determinate intuition at all, and therefore concerns nothing but that unity which must be encountered in a manifold of cognition insofar as it stands in relation to an object. This relation, however, is nothing other than the necessary unity of consciousness, thus also of the synthesis of the manifold through a common function of the mind for combining it in one representation. Now since this unity must be regarded as necessary *a priori* (since the cognition would otherwise be without an object), the relation to a transcendental object, i.e., the objective reality of our empirical cognition, rests on the transcendental law that all appearances, insofar as objects are to be given to us through them, must stand under *a priori* rules of their synthetic unity, in accordance with which their re-

A 108

A 109

A 110

lation*a* in empirical intuition is alone possible, i.e., that in experience they must stand under conditions of the necessary unity of apperception just as in mere intuition they must stand under the formal conditions of space and time; indeed, it is through those conditions that every cognition is first made possible.

4.
Provisional explanation of the possibility of the categories as *a priori* cognitions.

There is only **one** experience, in which all perceptions are represented as in thoroughgoing and lawlike connection, just as there is only one space and time, in which all forms of appearance and all relation*b* of being or non-being take place. If one speaks of different experiences, they are only so many perceptions insofar as they belong to one and the same universal experience. The thoroughgoing and synthetic unity of perceptions is precisely what constitutes the form of experience, and it is nothing other than the synthetic unity of the appearances in accordance with concepts.

A111 Unity of synthesis in accordance with empirical concepts would be entirely contingent, and, were it not grounded on a transcendental ground of unity, it would be possible for a swarm of appearances to fill up our soul without experience ever being able to arise from it. But in that case all relation of cognition to objects would also disappear, since the appearances would lack connection in accordance with universal and necessary laws, and would thus be intuition without thought, but never cognition, and would therefore be as good as nothing for us.

The *a priori* conditions of a possible experience in general are at the same time conditions of the possibility of the objects of experience. Now I assert that the **categories** that have just been adduced are nothing other than the **conditions of thinking in a possible experience,** just as **space** and **time** contain the **conditions of the intuition** for the very same thing. They are therefore also fundamental concepts for thinking objects*c* in general for the appearances, and they therefore have *a priori* objective validity, which was just what we really wanted to know.

However, the possibility, indeed even the necessity of these categories rests on the relation that the entire sensibility, and with it also all possible appearances, have to the original apperception, in which everything is necessarily in agreement with the conditions of the thorough-

---

a *Verhältnis*
b *Verhältnis*
c *Objecte*

going unity of self-consciousness, i.e., must stand under universal functions of synthesis, namely of the synthesis in accordance with concepts, as that in which alone apperception can demonstrate *a priori* its thoroughgoing and necessary identity. Thus the concept of a cause is nothing other than a synthesis (of that which follows in the temporal series with other appearances) **in accordance with concepts;** and without that sort of unity, which has its rule *a priori*, and which subjects the appearances to itself, thoroughgoing and universal, hence necessary unity of consciousness would not be encountered in the manifold perceptions. But these would then belong to no experience, and would consequently be without an object,[a] and would be nothing but a blind play of representations, i.e., less than a dream.

All attempts to derive these pure concepts of the understanding from experience and to ascribe to them a merely empirical origin are therefore entirely vain and futile. I will not mention that, e.g., the concept of a cause brings the trait of necessity with it, which no experience at all can yield, for experience teaches us that one appearance customarily follows another, but not that it must necessarily follow that, nor that an inference from a condition to its consequence can be made *a priori* and entirely universally. But that empirical rule of **association,** which one must assume throughout if one says that everything in the series of occurrences stands under rules according to which nothing happens that is not preceded by something upon which it always follows – on what, I ask, does this, as a law of nature, rest, and how is this association even possible? The ground of the possibility of the association of the manifold, insofar as it lies in the object,[b] is called the **affinity** of the manifold. I ask, therefore, how do you make the thoroughgoing affinity of the appearances (by means of which they stand under constant laws and **must** belong under them) comprehensible to yourselves?

On my principles it is easily comprehensible. All possible appearances belong, as representations, to the whole possible self-consciousness. But from this, as a transcendental representation, numerical identity is inseparable, and certain *a priori*, because nothing can come into cognition except by means of this original apperception. Now since this identity must necessarily enter into the synthesis of all the manifold of appearances insofar as they are to become empirical cognition, the appearances are thus subject to *a priori* conditions with which their synthesis (of apprehension) must be in thoroughgoing accord. Now, however, the representation of a universal condition in accordance with which a certain manifold (of whatever kind) **can** be posited is called a **rule,** and, if it **must** be so posited, a **law.** All appearances therefore stand in a thoroughgoing con-

---

[a] *Object*
[b] *Objecte*

A114 nection according to necessary laws, and hence in a **transcendental affinity,** of which the **empirical** affinity is the mere consequence.

That nature should direct itself according to our subjective ground of apperception, indeed in regard to its lawfulness even depend on this, may well sound quite contradictory and strange. But if one considers that this nature is nothing in itself but a sum of appearances, hence not a thing in itself but merely a multitude of representations of the mind, then one will not be astonished to see that unity on account of which alone it can be called object*a* of all possible experience, i.e., nature, solely in the radical faculty of all our cognition, namely, transcendental apperception; and for that very reason we can cognize this unity *a priori*, hence also as necessary, which we would certainly have to abandon if it were given **in itself** independently of the primary sources of our thinking. For then I would not know whence we should obtain the synthetic propositions of such a universal unity of nature, since in this case one would have to borrow them from the objects of nature itself. But since this could happen only empirically, from that nothing but merely contingent unity could be drawn, which would fall far short of the necessary connection that one has in mind when one speaks of nature.

A115   Of the Deduction of the Pure Concepts of the Understanding
Third Section

On the relation*b* of the understanding to objects
in general and the
possibility of cognizing these *a priori*.

What we have expounded separately and individually in the previous section we will now represent as unified and in connection. The possibility of an experience in general and cognition of its objects rest on three subjective sources of cognition: **sense, imagination,** and **apperception;** each of these can be considered empirically, namely in application to given appearances, but they are also elements or foundations *a priori* that make this empirical use itself possible. **Sense** represents the appearances empirically in **perception,** the **imagination** in association (and reproduction), and **apperception** in the **empirical consciousness** of the identity of these reproductive representations with the appearances through which they were given, hence in **recognition.**

But pure intuition (with regard to it as representation, time, the form of inner intuition) grounds the totality of perception *a priori*; the pure
A116 synthesis of the imagination grounds association *a priori*; and pure ap-

---

a Object
b Verhältnisse

perception, i.e., the thoroughgoing identity of oneself in all possible representations, grounds empirical consciousness *a priori*.[27]

Now if we wish to follow the inner ground of this connection of representations up to that point in which they must all come together in order first to obtain unity of cognition for a possible experience, then we must begin with pure apperception. All intuitions are nothing for us and do not in the least concern us if they cannot be taken up into consciousness, whether they influence it directly or indirectly, and through this alone is cognition possible.[28] We are conscious *a priori* of the thoroughgoing identity of ourselves with regard to all representations that can ever belong to our cognition, as a necessary condition of the possibility of all representations (since the latter represent something in me only insofar as they belong with all the others to one consciousness, hence they must at least be capable of being connected in it). This principle[a] holds *a priori*, and can be called **the transcendental principle**[b] **of the unity** of all the manifold of our representations (thus also in intuition). Now the unity of the manifold in a subject is synthetic; pure apperception therefore yields a principle[c] of the synthetic unity of the manifold in all possible intuition.*   A 117

This synthetic unity, however, presupposes a synthesis, or includes it,   A 118
and if the former is to be necessary *a priori* then the latter must also be

---

* One should attend carefully to this proposition, which is of great importance.   A 117
All representations have a necessary relation to a **possible** empirical consciousness: for if they did not have this, and if it were entirely impossible to become conscious of them, that would be as much as to say that they did not exist at all. All empirical consciousness, however, has a necessary relation to a transcendental consciousness (preceding all particular experience), namely the consciousness of myself, as original apperception. It is therefore absolutely necessary that in my cognition all consciousness belong to one consciousness (of myself). Now here is a synthetic unity of the manifold (of consciousness) that is cognized *a priori*, and that yields the ground for synthetic *a priori* propositions concerning pure thinking in exactly the same way that space and time yield such propositions concerning the form of mere intuition. The synthetic proposition that every different **empirical consciousness** must be combined into a single self-consciousness is the absolutely first and synthetic principle of our thinking in general. But it should not go unnoticed that the mere representation **I** in relation to all others (the collective unity of which it makes possible) is the transcendental consciousness. Now it does not matter here whether this representation be clear (empirical consciousness) or obscure, even whether it be actual; but the possibility of the logical form of all cognition necessarily rests on the relationship to this apperception **as a faculty.**

---

a *Princip*
b *Princip*
c *Principium*

a synthesis *a priori*. Thus the transcendental unity of apperception is related to the pure synthesis of the imagination, as an *a priori* condition of the possibility of all composition of the manifold in a cognition. But only the **productive synthesis of the imagination** can take place *a priori*; for the **reproductive** synthesis rests on conditions of experience. The principle[a] of the necessary unity of the pure (productive) synthesis of the imagination prior to apperception is thus the ground of the possibility of all cognition, especially that of experience.[29]

Now we call the synthesis of the manifold in imagination transcendental if, without distinction of the intuitions, it concerns nothing but the connection of the manifold *a priori*, and the unity of this synthesis is called transcendental if it is represented as necessary *a priori* in relation to the original unity of apperception. Now since this latter is the ground of the possibility of all cognitions, the transcendental unity of the synthesis of the imagination is the pure form of all possible cognition, through which, therefore, all objects of possible experience must be represented *a priori*.

A 119   **The unity of apperception in relation to the synthesis of the imagination** is the **understanding,** and this very same unity, in relation to the **transcendental synthesis** of the imagination, is the **pure understanding.** In the understanding there are therefore pure *a priori* cognitions that contain the necessary unity of the pure synthesis of the imagination in regard to all possible appearances.[30] These, however, are the **categories,** i.e., pure concepts of the understanding; consequently the empirical power of cognition of human beings necessarily contains an understanding, which is related to all objects of the senses, though only by means of intuition, and to their synthesis by means of imagination, under which, therefore, all appearances as data for a possible experience stand. Now since this relation of appearances to possible experience is likewise necessary (since without it we could not obtain any cognition at all through them, and they would thus not concern us at all), it follows that the pure understanding, by means of the categories, is a formal and synthetic principle[b] of all experiences, and that appearances have a **necessary relation to the understanding.**

Now we will set the necessary connection of the understanding with the appearances by means of the categories before our eyes by beginning from beneath, namely with what is empirical. The first thing that A 120   is given to us is appearance, which, if it is combined with consciousness, is called perception (without the relation[c] to an at least possible consciousness appearance could never become an object of cognition for us,

---

[a] *Principium*
[b] *Principium*
[c] *Verhältnis*

and would therefore be nothing for us, and since it has no objective reality in itself and exists only in cognition it would be nothing at all). But since every appearance contains a manifold, thus different perceptions by themselves are encountered dispersed and separate in the mind, a combination of them, which they cannot have in sense itself, is therefore necessary. There is thus an active faculty of the synthesis of this manifold in us, which we call imagination, and whose action exercised immediately upon perceptions I call apprehension.* For the imagination is to bring the manifold of intuition into an **image;**[a] it must therefore antecedently take up the impressions into its activity, i.e., apprehend them.

It is, however, clear that even this apprehension of the manifold alone   A121
would bring forth no image and no connection of the impressions were there not a subjective ground for calling back a perception, from which the mind has passed on to another, to the succeeding ones, and thus for exhibiting entire series of perceptions, i.e., a reproductive faculty of imagination, which is then also merely empirical.

Since, however, if representations reproduced one another without distinction, just as they fell together, there would in turn be no determinate connection but merely unruly heaps of them, and no cognition at all would arise, their reproduction must thus have a rule in accordance with which a representation enters into combination in the imagination with one representation rather than with any others. This subjective and **empirical** ground of reproduction in accordance with rules is called the **association** of representations.

But now if this unity of association did not also have an objective ground, so that it would be impossible for appearances to be apprehended by the imagination otherwise than under the condition of a possible synthetic unity of this apprehension, then it would also be entirely contingent whether appearances fit into a connection of human cognitions. For even though we had the faculty for associating perceptions, it would still remain in itself entirely undetermined and contingent   A122
whether they were also associable; and in case they were not, a multitude of perceptions and even an entire sensibility would be possible in which much empirical consciousness would be encountered in my mind, but separated, and without belonging to **one** consciousness of

---

* No psychologist has yet thought that the imagination is a necessary ingredi-   A120
ent of perception itself. This is so partly because this faculty has been limited to reproduction, and partly because it has been believed that the senses do not merely afford us impressions but also put them together, and produce images of objects, for which without doubt something more than the receptivity of impressions is required, namely a function of the synthesis of them.

[a] *Bild*

myself, which, however, is impossible. For only because I ascribe all perceptions to one consciousness (of original apperception) can I say of all perceptions that I am conscious of them. There must therefore be an objective ground, i.e., one that can be understood *a priori* to all empirical laws of the imagination, on which rests the possibility, indeed even the necessity of a law extending through all appearances, a law, namely, for regarding them throughout as data of sense that are associable in themselves and subject to universal laws of a thoroughgoing connection in reproduction. I call this objective ground of all association of appearances their **affinity**. But we can never encounter this anywhere except in the principle of the unity of apperception with regard to all cognitions that are to belong to me. In accordance with this principle all appearances whatever must come into the mind or be apprehended in such a way that they are in agreement with the unity of apperception, which would be impossible without synthetic unity in their connection, which is thus also objectively necessary.

A123   The objective unity of all (empirical) consciousness in one consciousness (of original apperception) is thus the necessary condition even of all possible perception, and the affinity of all appearances (near or remote) is a necessary consequence of a synthesis in the imagination that is grounded *a priori* on rules.

The imagination is therefore also a faculty of a synthesis *a priori*, on account of which we give it the name of productive imagination, and, insofar as its aim in regard to all the manifold of appearance is nothing further than the necessary unity in their synthesis, this can be called the transcendental function of the imagination. It is therefore certainly strange, yet from what has been said thus far obvious, that it is only by means of this transcendental function of the imagination that even the affinity of appearances, and with it the association and through the latter finally reproduction in accordance with laws, and consequently experience itself, become possible; for without them no concepts of objects at all would converge into an experience.

For the standing and lasting I (of pure apperception) constitutes the correlate of all of our representations, so far as it is merely possible to become conscious of them, and all consciousness belongs to an all-embracing pure apperception just as all sensible intuition as representation

A124   belongs to a pure inner intuition, namely that of time. It is this apperception that must be added to the pure imagination in order to make its function intellectual. For in itself the synthesis of the imagination, although exercised *a priori*, is nevertheless always sensible, for it combines the manifold only as it **appears** in intuition, e.g., the shape of a triangle. Through the relation*a* of the manifold to the unity of apperception,

---

a *Verhältnis*

however, concepts that belong to the understanding can come about, but only by means of the imagination in relation to the sensible intuition.

We therefore have a pure imagination, as a fundamental faculty of the human soul, that grounds all cognition *a priori*. By its means we bring into combination the manifold of intuition on the one side and the condition of the necessary unity of apperception on the other. Both extremes, namely sensibility and understanding, must necessarily be connected by means of this transcendental function of the imagination, since otherwise the former would to be sure yield appearances but no objects of an empirical cognition, hence there would be no experience. Actual experience, which consists in the apprehension, the association (the reproduction), and finally the recognition of the appearances, contains in the last and highest (of the merely empirical elements of experience) concepts that make possible the formal unity of experience and with it all objective validity (truth) of empirical cognition. These grounds of the recognition of the manifold, so far as they concern **merely the form of an experience in general,** are now those **categories.** On them is grounded, therefore, all formal unity in the synthesis of the imagination, and by means of the latter also all of its empirical use (in recognition, reproduction, association, and apprehension) down to the appearances, since the latter belong to our consciousness at all and hence to ourselves only by means of these elements of cognition.

Thus we ourselves bring into the appearances that order and regularity in them that we call **nature,**[31] and moreover we would not be able to find it there if we, or the nature of our mind, had not originally put it there. For this unity of nature should be a necessary, i.e., *a priori* certain unity of the connection of appearances. But how should we be able to establish a synthetic unity *a priori* if subjective grounds of such a unity were not contained *a priori* among the original sources of cognition in our mind, and if these subjective conditions were not at the same time objectively valid, being the grounds of the possibility of cognizing any object*[a]* in experience at all?*[b]*

A 125

A 126

---

[a] *Object*

[b] Question mark added. At this point, the following note is inserted in Kant's copy of the first edition:

"That the laws of nature really have their origin in the understanding, and are just as little to be encountered outside it as space and time are, is already proved by the in any case already acknowledged assertion that we cognize them *a priori* and as necessary; for if, on the contrary, they had to be borrowed from outside, we could only cognize them as contingent. But then what sort of laws are those? No greater and no less than is necessary in order to bring appearances into a general connection with one consciousness, only in order to cognize objects as such − for that is the form of their intuition and at the same time the condition of their unity in apperception given, and given *a priori*." (E LI, pp. 26–7; 23:26–7)

Erdmann observes that this is the only substantial note in Kant's copy of the first-

We have above explained the **understanding** in various ways – through a spontaneity of cognition (in contrast to the receptivity of the sensibility), through a faculty for thinking, or a faculty of concepts, or also of judgments – which explanations, if one looks at them properly, come down to the same thing. Now we can characterize it as the **faculty of rules.** This designation is more fruitful, and comes closer to its essence. Sensibility gives us forms (of intuition), but the understanding gives us rules. It is always busy poring through the appearances with the aim of finding some sort of rule in them. Rules, so far as they are objective*a* (and thus necessarily pertain to the cognition of objects) are called laws. Although we learn many laws through experience, these are only particular determinations of yet higher laws, the highest of which (under which all others stand) come from the understanding itself *a priori*, and are not borrowed from experience, but rather must provide the appearances with their lawfulness and by that very means make experience possible. The understanding is thus not merely a faculty for making rules through the comparison of the appearances; it is itself the legislation for nature, i.e., without understanding there would not be any nature at all,

A 127 i.e., synthetic unity of the manifold of appearances in accordance with rules; for appearances, as such, cannot occur outside us, but exist only in our sensibility. The latter, however, as the object of cognition in an experience, with everything it may contain, is possible only in the unity of apperception. The unity of apperception, however, is the transcendental ground of the necessary lawfulness of all appearances in an experience. This very same unity of apperception with regard to a manifold of representations (that namely of determining it out of a single one) is the rule, and the faculty of these rules is the understanding. All appearances as possible experiences, therefore, lie *a priori* in the understanding, and receive their formal possibility from it, just as they lie in the sensibility as mere intuitions, and are only possible through the latter as far as their form is concerned.

Thus as exaggerated and contradictory as it may sound to say that the understanding is itself the source of the laws of nature, and thus of the formal unity of nature, such an assertion is nevertheless correct and appropriate to the object, namely experience. To be sure, empirical laws, as such, can by no means derive their origin from the pure understanding, just as the immeasurable manifoldness of the appearances cannot be adequately conceived through the pure form of sensible intuition.

A 128 But all empirical laws are only particular determinations of the pure

---

edition deduction, from which he infers that Kant in fact very early gave up hope of improving the deduction by minor changes.

a Changed to "Rules, so far as they [represent] existence as necessary . . ." in Kant's copy of the first edition (E LII, p. 27; 23:46).

laws of the understanding, under which and in accordance with whose norm they are first possible, and the appearances assume a lawful form, just as, regardless of the variety of their empirical form, all appearances must nevertheless always be in accord with the pure form of sensibility.

The pure understanding is thus in the categories the law of the synthetic unity of all appearances, and thereby first and originally makes experience possible as far as its form is concerned. But we did not have to accomplish more in the transcendental deduction of the categories than to make comprehensible this relation*a* of the understanding to sensibility and by means of the latter to all objects of experience, hence to make comprehensible the objective validity of its pure *a priori* concepts, and thereby determine their origin and truth.

Summary representation
of the correctness and unique possibility of this
deduction
of the pure concepts of the understanding.

If the objects with which our cognition has to do were things in themselves, then we would not be able to have any *a priori* concepts of them at all. For whence should we obtain them? If we take them from the object*b* (without even investigating here how the latter could become known to us), then our concepts would be merely empirical and not *a priori* concepts. If we take them from ourselves, then that which is merely in us cannot determine the constitution of an object distinct from our representations, i.e., be a ground why there should be a thing that corresponds to something we have in our thoughts, and why all this representation should not instead be empty. But if, on the contrary, we have to do everywhere only with appearances, then it is not only possible but also necessary that certain *a priori* concepts precede the empirical cognition of objects. For as appearances they constitute an object that is merely in us, since a mere modification of our sensibility is not to be encountered outside us at all. Now even this representation – that all these appearances and thus all objects with which we can occupy ourselves are all in me, i.e., determinations of my identical self – expresses a thoroughgoing unity of them in one and the same apperception as necessary. The form of all cognition of objects (through which the manifold is thought as belonging to one object),*c* however, also consists in this unity of possible consciousness. Thus the way in which the manifold of sensible representation (intuition) belongs to a

A 129

---

a *Verhältnis*
b *Object*
c *zu Einem Object*

A130 consciousness precedes all cognition of the object, as its intellectual form, and itself constitutes an *a priori* formal cognition of all objects in general, insofar as they are thought (categories). Their synthesis through the pure imagination, the unity of all representations in relation to original apperception, precede all empirical cognition. Pure concepts of the understanding are therefore possible, indeed necessary *a priori* in relation to experience, only because our cognition has to do with nothing but appearances, whose possibility lies in ourselves, whose connection and unity (in the representation of an object) is encountered merely in us, and thus must precede all experience and first make it possible as far as its form is concerned. And from this ground, the only possible one among all, our deduction of the categories has been conducted.

Of the Deduction of the Pure Concepts of the Understanding B129
Second Section
Transcendental deduction of the pure concepts of the understanding[a,32]

<§ 15.
On the possibility of a combination in general.

The manifold of representations can be given in an intuition that is merely sensible, i.e., nothing but receptivity, and the form of this intuition can lie *a priori* in our faculty of representation without being anything other than the way in which the subject is affected. Yet the **combination** (*conjunctio*) of a manifold in general can never come to us through the senses, and therefore cannot already be contained in the pure form of sensible intuition; for it is an act[b] of the spontaneity of the B130
power of representation, and, since one must call the latter understanding, in distinction from sensibility, all combination, whether we are conscious of it or not, whether it is a combination of the manifold of intuition or of several concepts, and in the first case either of sensible or non-sensible intuition, is an action of the understanding, which we would designate with the general title **synthesis** in order at the same time to draw attention to the fact that we can represent nothing as combined in the object[c] without having previously combined it ourselves, and that among all representations **combination** is the only one that is not given through objects[d] but can be executed only by the subject itself, since it is an act[e] of its self-activity. One can here easily see that this action must originally be unitary[f] and equally valid for all combination,

[a] In the second edition, the following § 15 through § 27 replace the second and third sections of the "Transcendental Deduction" in the first edition (A95 to A130).

[b] *Actus*

[c] *Object*

[d] *Objecte*

[e] *Actus*

[f] *einig;* in modern German this is used only in idioms connoting being in agreement or harmony; perhaps Kant meant to write *einzig*, i.e., unique.

and that the dissolution (**analysis**) that seems to be its opposite, in fact always presupposes it; for where the understanding has not previously combined anything, neither can it dissolve anything, for only **through it** can something have been given to the power of representation as combined.

But in addition to the concept of the manifold and of its synthesis, the concept of combination also carries with it the concept of the unity of the manifold. Combination is the representation of the **synthetic** unity of the manifold.* The representation of this unity cannot, therefore, arise from the combination; rather, by being added to the representation of the manifold, it first makes the concept of combination possible.[33] This unity, which precedes all concepts of combination *a priori*, is not the former category of unity (§ 10); for all categories are grounded on logical functions in judgments, but in these combination, thus the unity of given concepts, is already thought. The category therefore already presupposes combination. We must therefore seek this unity (as qualitative, § 12) someplace higher, namely in that which itself contains the ground of the unity of different concepts in judgments, and hence of the possibility of the understanding, even in its logical use.

B 131

§ 16.
On the original-synthetic unity of apperception.

The **I think** must **be able** to accompany all my representations; for otherwise something would be represented in me that could not be thought at all, which is as much as to say that the representation would either be impossible or else at least would be nothing for me. That representation that can be given prior to all thinking is called **intuition.** Thus all manifold of intuition has a necessary relation to the **I think** in the same subject in which this manifold is to be encountered. But this representation is an act[a] of **spontaneity,** i.e., it cannot be regarded as belonging to sensibility. I call it the **pure apperception,** in order to distinguish it from the **empirical** one, or also the **original apperception,** since it is that self-consciousness which, because it produces the representation **I think,** which must be able to accompany all others and

B 132

B 131   * Whether the representations themselves are identical, and whether therefore one could be thought through the other analytically, does not come into consideration here. The **consciousness** of the one, as far as the manifold is concerned, is still always to be distinguished from the consciousness of the other, and it is only the synthesis of this (possible) consciousness that is at issue here.

   [a] *Actus*

which in all consciousness is one and the same, cannot be accompanied by any further representation. I also call its unity the **transcendental unity** of self-consciousness in order to designate the possibility of *a priori* cognition from it. For the manifold representations that are given in a certain intuition would not all together be **my** representations if they did not all together belong to a self-consciousness; i.e., as my representations (even if I am not conscious of them as such) they must yet necessarily be in accord with the condition under which alone they **can** stand together in a universal self-consciousness, because otherwise they would not throughout belong to me. From this original combination much may be inferred. B 133

Namely, this thoroughgoing identity of the apperception of a manifold given in intuition contains a synthesis of the representations, and is possible only through the consciousness of this synthesis. For the empirical consciousness that accompanies different representations is by itself dispersed and without relation to the identity of the subject. The latter relation therefore does not yet come about by my accompanying each representation with consciousness, but rather by my **adding** one representation to the other and being conscious of their synthesis. Therefore it is only because I can combine a manifold of given representations **in one consciousness** that it is possible for me to represent the **identity of the consciousness in these representations** itself, i.e., the **analytical** unity of apperception is only possible under the presupposition of some **synthetic** one.*,34 The thought that these representations given in intuition all together belong **to me** means, accordingly, the same as that I unite them in a self-consciousness, or at least can unite them therein, and although it is itself not yet the consciousness of the **synthesis** of the representations, it still presupposes the possibility of the latter, i.e., only because I can comprehend their manifold in a consciousness do I call them all together **my** representations; for otherwise I would have as multicolored, diverse a self as I have representa- B 134

---

* The analytical unity of consciousness pertains to all common concepts as such, e.g., if I think of **red** in general, I thereby represent to myself a feature that (as a mark) can be encountered in anything, or that can be combined with other representations; therefore only by means of an antecedently conceived possible synthetic unity can I represent to myself the analytical unity. A representation that is to be thought of as common to **several** must be regarded as belonging to those that in addition to it also have something **different** in themselves; consequently they must antecedently be conceived in synthetic unity with other (even if only possible representations) before I can think of the analytical unity of consciousness in it that makes it into a *conceptus communis*. And thus the synthetic unity of apperception is the highest point to which one must affix all use of the understanding, even the whole of logic and, after it, transcendental philosophy; indeed this faculty is the understanding itself. B 133

B 134

tions of which I am conscious. Synthetic unity of the manifold of intuitions, as given *a priori*, is thus the ground of the identity of apperception itself, which precedes *a priori* all **my** determinate thinking. Combination does not lie in the objects, however, and cannot as it were be borrowed from them through perception and by that means first B 135 taken up into the understanding, but is rather only an operation of the understanding, which is itself nothing further than the faculty of combining *a priori* and bringing the manifold of given representations under unity of apperception, which principle is the supreme one in the whole of human cognition.[35]

Now this principle of the necessary unity of apperception is, to be sure, itself identical, thus an analytical proposition, yet it declares as necessary a synthesis of the manifold given in an intuition, without which that thoroughgoing identity of self-consciousness could not be thought. For through the I, as a simple representation, nothing manifold is given; it can only be given in the intuition, which is distinct from it, and thought through **combination** in a consciousness. An understanding, in which through self-consciousness all of the manifold would at the same time be given, would **intuit**; ours can only **think** and must seek the intuition in the senses. I am therefore conscious of the identical self in regard to the manifold of the representations that are given to me in an intuition because I call them all together **my** representations, which constitute **one**. But that is as much as to say that I am conscious *a priori* of their necessary synthesis, which is called the original synthetic unity of apperception, under which all representations given B 136 to me stand, but under which they must also be brought by means of a synthesis.

§ 17.

The principle of the synthetic unity of apperception
is the supreme principle of all use of the understanding.

The supreme principle of the possibility of all intuition in relation to sensibility was, according to the Transcendental Aesthetic, that all the manifold of sensibility stand under the formal conditions of space and time. The supreme principle of all intuition in relation to the understanding is that all the manifold of intuition stand under conditions of the original synthetic unity of apperception.*[,36] All the manifold repre-

---

* Space and time and all their parts are **intuitions,** thus individual representations along with the manifold that they contain in themselves (see the Transcendental Aesthetic), thus they are not mere concepts by means of which the same consciousness is contained in many representations, but rather are many representations that are contained in one and in the consciousness of it; they are thus found to be composite, and consequently the unity of con-

sentations of intuition stand under the first principle insofar as they are **given** to us, and under the second insofar as they must be capable of being **combined** in one consciousness; for without that nothing could   B 137
be thought or cognized through them, since the given representations would not have in common the act*ᵃ* of apperception, **I think,** and thereby would not be grasped together in a self-consciousness.

    Understanding is, generally speaking, the faculty of **cognitions.** These consist in the determinate relation of given representations to an object.*ᵇ* An **object,***ᶜ* however, is that in the concept of which the manifold of a given intuition is **united.**[37] Now, however, all unification of representations requires unity of consciousness in the synthesis of them. Consequently the unity of consciousness is that which alone constitutes the relation of representations to an object, thus their objective validity, and consequently is that which makes them into cognitions and on which even the possibility of the understanding rests.

    The first pure cognition of the understanding, therefore, on which the whole of the rest of its use is grounded, and that is at the same time also entirely independent from all conditions of sensible intuition, is the principle of the original **synthetic** unity of apperception. Thus the mere form of outer sensible intuition, space, is not yet cognition at all; it only gives the manifold of intuition *a priori* for a possible cognition. But in order to cognize something in space, e.g., a line, I must **draw** it, and thus synthetically bring about a determinate combination of the   B 138
given manifold, so that the unity of this action is at the same time the unity of consciousness (in the concept of a line), and thereby is an object*ᵈ* (a determinate space) first cognized. The synthetic unity of consciousness is therefore an objective condition of all cognition, not merely something I myself need in order to cognize an object*ᵉ* but rather something under which every intuition must stand in **order to become an object***ᶠ* **for me,** since in any other way, and without this synthesis, the manifold would **not** be united in one consciousness.

    This last proposition is, as we said, itself analytic, although, to be sure, it makes synthetic unity into the condition of all thinking; for it says nothing more than that all **my** representations in any given intuition must stand under the condition under which alone I can ascribe

sciousness, as **synthetic** and yet as original, is to be found in them. This **singularity** of theirs is important in its application (see § 25).

ᵃ Actus
ᵇ Object
ᶜ Object
ᵈ Object
ᵉ Object
ᶠ Object

them to the identical self as **my** representations, and thus can grasp them together, as synthetically combined in an apperception, through the general expression **I think.**

This principle, however, is not a principle[a] for every possible understanding, but only for one through whose pure apperception in the representation **I am** nothing manifold is given at all. That understanding through whose self-consciousness the manifold of intuition would at the same time be given, an understanding through whose representation the objects[b] of this representation would at the same time exist, would not require a special act[c] of the synthesis of the manifold for the unity of consciousness, which the human understanding, which merely thinks, but does not intuit, does require. But for the human understanding it is unavoidably the first principle, so that the human understanding cannot even form for itself the least concept of another possible understanding, either one that would intuit itself or one that, while possessing a sensible intuition, would possess one of a different kind than one grounded in space and time.

B 139

§ 18.
What objective unity of self-consciousness is.

The **transcendental unity** of apperception is that unity through which all of the manifold given in an intuition is united in a concept of the object.[d] It is called **objective** on that account, and must be distinguished from the **subjective unity** of consciousness, which is a **determination of inner sense**, through which that manifold of intuition is empirically given for such a combination. Whether I can become **empirically** conscious of the manifold as simultaneous or successive depends on the circumstances, or empirical conditions. Hence the empirical unity of consciousness, through association of the representations, itself concerns an appearance, and is entirely contingent. The pure form of intuition in time, on the contrary, merely as intuition in general, which contains a given manifold, stands under the original unity of consciousness, solely by means of the necessary relation of the manifold of intuition to the one **I think,** thus through the pure synthesis of the understanding, which grounds *a priori* the empirical synthesis. That unity alone is objectively valid; the empirical unity of apperception, which we are not assessing here, and which is also derived only from the former, under given conditions *in concreto*, has

B 140

[a] *Princip*
[b] *Objecte*
[c] *Actus*
[d] *Object*

merely subjective validity. One person combines the representation of a certain word with one thing, another with something else; and the unity of consciousness in that which is empirical is not, with regard to that which is given, necessarily and universally valid.

§ 19.
The logical form of all judgments consists in the objective unity of the apperception of the concepts contained therein.[38]

I have never been able to satisfy myself with the explanation that the logicians give of a judgment in general: it is, they say, the representation of a relation[a] between two concepts. Without quarreling here about what is mistaken in this explanation, that in any case it fits only **categorical** but not hypothetical and disjunctive judgments (which latter two do not contain a relation[b] of concepts but of judgments themselves) (though from this error in logic many troublesome consequences have arisen),[*,39] I remark only that it is not here determined wherein this **relation**[c] consists.

B 141

If, however, I investigate more closely the relation[d] of given cognitions in every judgment, and distinguish that relation, as something belonging to the understanding, from the relation[e] in accordance with laws of the reproductive imagination (which has only subjective validity), then I find that a judgment is nothing other than the way to bring given cognitions to the **objective** unity of apperception.[40] That is the aim of the copula[f] **is** in them: to distinguish the objective unity of given representations from the subjective. For this word designates the relation of the representations to the original apperception and its **necessary unity,** even if the judgment itself is empirical, hence contingent,

B 142

---

* The widespread doctrine of the four syllogistic figures concerns only the categorical inferences, and, although it is nothing more than an art for surreptitiously producing the illusion of more kinds of inference than that in the first figure by hiding immediate inferences (*consequentiae immediatiae*) among the premises of a pure syllogism, still it would not have achieved any special success by this alone if it had not succeeded in focusing attention exclusively on categorical judgments as those to which all others have to be related, which according to § 9, however, is false.

B 141

---

[a] *Verhältnisses*
[b] *Verhältnis*
[c] *Verhältnis*
[d] Here Kant uses *Beziehung* when he might have used *Verhältnis.*
[e] *Verhältnisse*
[f] *Verhältniswörtchen*

e.g., "Bodies are heavy." By that, to be sure, I do not mean to say that these representations **necessarily** belong **to one another** in the empirical intuition, but rather that they belong to one another **in virtue of the necessary unity** of the apperception in the synthesis of intuitions, i.e., in accordance with principles*ª* of the objective determination of all representations insofar as cognition can come from them, which principles*ᵇ* are all derived from the principle of the transcendental unity of apperception. Only in this way does there arise from this relation*ᶜ* **a judgment,** i.e., a relation that is **objectively valid,** and that is sufficiently distinguished from the relation of these same representations in which there would be only subjective validity, e.g., in accordance with laws of association. In accordance with the latter I could only say "If I carry a body, I feel a pressure of weight," but not "It, the body, **is** heavy," which would be to say that these two representations are combined in the object,*ᵈ* i.e., regardless of any difference in the condition of the subject, and are not merely found together in perception (however often as that might be repeated).

§ 20.
All sensible intuitions stand under the
categories, as conditions under which alone
their manifold can come together in one consciousness.

The manifold that is given in a sensible intuition necessarily belongs under the original synthetic unity of apperception, since through this alone is the **unity** of the intuition possible (§ 17). That action of the understanding, however, through which the manifold of given representations (whether they be intuitions or concepts) is brought under an apperception in general, is the logical function of judgments (§ 19). Therefore all manifold, insofar as it is given in **one**ᵉ empirical intuition, is **determined** in regard to one of the logical functions for judgment, by means of which, namely, it is brought to a consciousness in general. But now the **categories** are nothing other than these very functions for judging, insofar as the manifold of a given intuition is determined with regard to them (§ 13).⁴¹ Thus the manifold in a given intuition also necessarily stands under categories.

ª *Principien*
ᵇ *Principien*
ᶜ *Verhältnisse;* the further occurrences of "relation" in this sentence translate further occurrences of *Verhältnis.*
ᵈ *Object*
ᵉ *Einer.* Not ordinarily capitalized, suggesting the translation "one" instead of merely "an."

§ 21.
Remark.

A manifold that is contained in an intuition that I call mine is repre-sented as belonging to the **necessary** unity of self-consciousness through the synthesis of the understanding, and this takes place by means of the category.* This indicates, therefore, that the empirical consciousness of a given manifold of one*ᵃ* intuition stands under a pure *a priori* self-consciousness, just as empirical intuitions stand under a pure sensible one, which likewise holds *a priori*. – In the above proposi-tion, therefore, the beginning of a **deduction** of the pure concepts of the understanding has been made, in which, since the categories arise **independently from sensibility** merely in the understanding, I must abstract from the way in which the manifold for an empirical intuition is given, in order to attend only to the unity that is added to the intu-ition through the understanding by means of the category. In the sequel (§ 26) it will be shown from the way in which the empirical intuition is given in sensibility that its unity can be none other than the one the cat-egory prescribes to the manifold of a given intuition in general accord-ing to the preceding § 20; thus by the explanation of its*ᵇ* *a priori* validity in regard to all objects of our senses the aim of the deduction will first be fully attained.

In the above proof, however, I still could not abstract from one point, namely, from the fact that the manifold for intuition must already be **given** prior to the synthesis of understanding and independently from it; how, however, is here left undetermined. For if I wanted to think of an understanding that itself intuited (as, say, a divine understanding, which would not represent given objects, but through whose represen-tation the objects would themselves at the same time be given, or pro-duced), then the categories would have no significance at all with regard to such a cognition. They are only rules for an understanding whose en-tire capacity*ᶜ* consists in thinking, i.e., in the action of bringing the syn-thesis of the manifold that is given to it in intuition from elsewhere to the unity of apperception, which therefore **cognizes** nothing at all by

---

* The ground of proof rests on the represented **unity of intuition** through   B 144
  which an object is given, which always includes a synthesis of the manifold
  that is given for an intuition, and already contains the relation of the latter to
  unity of apperception.

ᵃ *Einer,* again capitalized.
ᵇ The antecedent is probably "the category" in the preceding clause, but it could also be
  "the unity," and thus the translation has been left ambiguous.
ᶜ *Vermögen*

itself,[a] but only combines and orders the material for cognition, the intuition, which must be given to it through the object.[b] But for the peculiarity of our understanding, that it is able to bring about the unity of apperception *a priori* only by means of the categories and only through precisely this kind and number of them, a further ground may be offered just as little as one can be offered for why we have precisely these and no other functions for judgment or for why space and time are the sole forms of our possible intuition.

B 146

§ 22.
The category has no other use for
the cognition of things than its application
to objects of experience.

To **think** of an object and to **cognize** an object are thus not the same. For two components belong to cognition: first, the concept, through which an object is thought at all (the category), and second, the intuition, through which it is given; for if an intuition corresponding to the concept could not be given at all, then it would be a thought as far as its form is concerned, but without any object, and by its means no cognition of anything at all would be possible, since, as far as I would know, nothing would be given nor could be given to which my thought could be applied. Now all intuition that is possible for us is sensible (Aesthetic), thus for us thinking of an object in general through a pure concept of the understanding can become cognition only insofar as this concept is related to objects of the senses. Sensible intuition is either pure intuition (space and time) or empirical intuition of that which, through sensation, is immediately represented as real in space and time. Through determination of the former we can acquire *a priori* cognitions of objects (in mathematics), but only as far as their form is concerned, as appearances; whether there can be things that must be intuited in this form is still left unsettled. Consequently all mathematical concepts are not by themselves cognitions, except insofar as one presupposes that there are things that can be presented to us only in accordance with the form of that pure sensible intuition. **Things in space** and **time,** however, are only given insofar as they are perceptions (representations accompanied with sensation), hence through empirical representation. The pure concepts of the understanding, consequently, even if they are applied to *a priori* intuitions (as in mathematics), provide cognition only insofar as these *a priori* intuitions, and by means of them also the concepts of the understanding, can be applied to empirical intuitions. Con-

B 147

---

[a] *für sich*
[b] *Object*

sequently the categories do not afford us cognition of things by means of intuition except through their possible application to **empirical intuition,** i.e., they serve only for the possibility of **empirical cognition.** This, however, is called **experience.** The categories consequently have no other use for the cognition of things except insofar as these are taken as objects of possible experience.   B 148

§ 23.

The above proposition is of the greatest importance, for it determines the boundaries of the use of the pure concepts of the understanding in regard to objects, just as the Transcendental Aesthetic determined the boundaries of the use of the pure form of our sensible intuition. Space and time are valid, as conditions of the possibility of how objects can be given to us, no further than for objects of the senses, hence only for experience. Beyond these boundaries they do not represent anything at all, for they are only in the senses and outside of them have no reality. The pure concepts of the understanding are free from this limitation and extend to objects of intuition in general, whether the latter be similar to our own or not, as long as it is sensible and not intellectual. But this further extension of concepts beyond **our** sensible intuition does not get us anywhere. For they are then merely empty concepts of objects,*a* through which we cannot even judge whether the latter are possible or not – mere forms of thought without objective reality – since we have available no intuition to which the synthetic unity of apperception, which they alone contain, could be applied, and that could thus determine an object. **Our** sensible and empirical intuition alone can   B 149
provide them with sense and significance.

Thus if one assumes an object*b* of a **non-sensible** intuition as given, one can certainly represent it through all of the predicates that already lie in the presupposition that **nothing belonging to sensible intuition pertains to it:** thus it is not extended, or in space, that its duration is not a time, that no alteration (sequence of determinations in time) is to be encountered in it, etc. But it is not yet a genuine cognition if I merely indicate what the intuition of the object*c* **is not,** without being able to say what is then contained in it; for then I have not represented the possibility of an object*d* for my pure concept of the understanding at all, since I cannot give any intuition that would correspond to it, but could only say that ours is not valid for it. But what is most important here is that not even a single category could be applied to such a thing, e.g., the

---

a *Objecten*
b *Object*
c *Object*
d *Objects*

concept of a substance, i.e., that of something that could exist as a subject but never as a mere predicate; for I would not even know whether there could be anything that corresponded to this determination of thought if empirical intuition did not give me the case for its application. But more of this in the sequel.

B150

§ 24.
On the application of the categories to objects of the senses in general.

The pure concepts of the understanding are related through the mere understanding to objects of intuition in general, without it being determined whether this intuition is our own or some other but still sensible one, but they are on this account mere **forms of thought,** through which no determinate object is yet cognized. The synthesis or combination of the manifold in them was related merely to the unity of apperception, and was thereby the ground of the possibility of cognition *a priori* insofar as it rests on the understanding, and was therefore not only transcendental but also merely purely intellectual. But since in us a certain form of sensible intuition *a priori* is fundamental, which rests on the receptivity of the capacity for representation (sensibility), the understanding, as spontaneity, can determine the manifold of given representations in accord with the synthetic unity of apperception, and thus think *a priori* synthetic unity of the apperception of the manifold of **sensible intuition,** as the condition under which all objects of our (human) intuition must necessarily stand, through which then the categories, as mere forms of thought, acquire objective reality, i.e., applica-

B151 tion to objects that can be given to us in intuition, but only as appearances; for of these alone are we capable of intuition *a priori.*

This **synthesis** of the manifold of sensible intuition, which is possible and necessary *a priori,* can be called **figurative** (*synthesis speciosa*), as distinct from that which would be thought in the mere category in regard to the manifold of an intuition in general, and which is called combination of the understanding (*synthesis intellectualis*); both are **transcendental,** not merely because they themselves proceed *a priori* but also because they ground the possibility of other cognition *a priori.*

Yet the figurative synthesis, if it pertains merely to the original synthetic unity of apperception, i.e., this transcendental unity, which is thought in the categories, must be called, as distinct from the merely intellectual combination, the **transcendental synthesis of the imagination.** *Imagination*[a] is the faculty for representing an object even **without its presence** in intuition. Now since all of our intuition is sensible,

---

[a] Here Kant uses both large type and spacing for extra emphasis.

the imagination, on account of the subjective condition under which alone it can give a corresponding intuition to the concepts of understanding, belongs to **sensibility;** but insofar as its synthesis is still an exercise of spontaneity, which is determining and not, like sense, merely determinable, and can thus determine the form of sense *a priori* in accordance with the unity of apperception, the imagination is to this extent a faculty for determining the sensibility *a priori*, and its synthesis of intuitions, **in accordance with the categories,** must be the transcendental synthesis of the **imagination,** which is an effect of the understanding on sensibility and its first application (and at the same time the ground of all others) to objects of the intuition that is possible for us. As figurative, it is distinct from the intellectual synthesis without any imagination merely through the understanding. Now insofar as the imagination is spontaneity, I also occasionally call it the **productive** imagination, and thereby distinguish it from the **reproductive** imagination, whose synthesis is subject solely to empirical laws, namely those of association, and that therefore contributes nothing to the explanation of the possibility of cognition *a priori*, and on that account belongs not in transcendental philosophy but in psychology.

B152

* * *

Here is now the place to make intelligible the paradox that must have struck everyone in the exposition of the form of inner sense (§ 6): namely how this presents even ourselves to consciousness only as we appear to ourselves, not as we are in ourselves, since we intuit ourselves only as we are internally **affected,** which seems to be contradictory, since we would have to relate to ourselves passively; for this reason it is customary in the systems of psychology to treat **inner sense** as the same as the faculty of **apperception** (which we carefully distinguish).[42]

B153

That which determines the inner sense is the understanding and its original faculty of combining the manifold of intuition, i.e., of bringing it under an apperception (as that on which its very possibility rests). Now since in us humans the understanding is not itself a faculty of intuitions, and even if these were given in sensibility cannot take them up **into itself,** in order as it were to combine the manifold of **its own** intuition, thus its synthesis, considered in itself[a] alone, is nothing other than the unity of the action of which it is conscious as such even without sensibility, but through which it is capable of itself determining sensibility internally with regard to the manifold that may be given to it in accordance with the form of its intuition. Under the designation of a **transcendental synthesis of the imagination,** it therefore exer-

---

[a] *für sich*

257

B154 cises that action on the **passive** subject, whose **faculty** it is, about which we rightly say that the inner sense is thereby affected. Apperception and its synthetic unity is so far from being the same as the inner sense that the former, rather, as the source of all combination, applies, prior to all sensible intuition of objects*a* in general, to the manifold of **intuitions in general**, under the name of the categories; inner sense, on the contrary, contains the mere **form** of intuition, but without combination of the manifold in it, and thus it does not yet contain any **determinate** intuition at all, which is possible only through the consciousness of the determination of the manifold through the transcendental action of the imagination (synthetic influence of the understanding on the inner sense), which I have named the figurative synthesis.

We also always perceive this in ourselves. We cannot think of a line without **drawing** it in thought, we cannot think of a circle without **describing** it, we cannot represent the three dimensions of space at all without **placing** three lines perpendicular to each other at the same point, and we cannot even represent time without, in **drawing** a straight line (which is to be the external figurative representation of time), attending merely to the action of the synthesis of the manifold through which we successively determine the inner sense, and thereby attending to the succession of this determination in inner sense. B155 Motion, as action of the subject (not as determination of an object),*,b* consequently the synthesis of the manifold in space, if we abstract from this manifold in space and attend solely to the action in accordance with which we determine the form of **inner sense**, first produces the concept of succession at all. The understanding therefore does not **find** some sort of combination of the manifold already in inner sense, but **produces** it, by **affecting** inner sense. But how the I that I think is to differ from the I that intuits itself (for I can represent other kinds of intuition as at least possible) and yet be identical with the latter as the same subject, how therefore I can say that **I** as intelligence and **think-**

---

* Motion of an **object***c* in space does not belong in a pure science, thus also not in geometry; for that something is movable cannot be cognized *a priori* but only through experience. But motion, as **description** of a space, is a pure act*d* of the successive synthesis of the manifold in outer intuition in general through productive imagination, and belongs not only to geometry but even to transcendental philosophy.

a *Objecte*
b *Objects*
c *Objects*
d *Actus*

ing subject cognize my self as an object*ᵃ* that is **thought,** insofar as I am also given to myself in intuition, only, like other phenomena, not as I am for the understanding but rather as I appear to myself, this is no more and no less difficult than how I can be an object*ᵇ* for myself in general and indeed one of intuition and inner perceptions. But that it B 156 really must be so can be clearly shown, if one lets space count as a mere pure form of the appearances of outer sense, from the fact that time, although it is not itself an object of outer intuition at all, cannot be made representable to us except under the image of a line, insofar as we draw it, without which sort of presentation we could not know the unity of its measure at all, or likewise from the fact that we must always derive the determination of the length of time or also of the positions in time for all inner perceptions from that which presents external things to us as alterable; hence we must order the determinations of inner sense as appearances in time in just the same way as we order those of outer sense in space; hence if we admit about the latter that we cognize objects*ᶜ* by their means only insofar as we are externally affected, then we must also concede that through inner sense we intuit ourselves only as we are internally affected **by our selves,** i.e., as far as inner intuition is concerned we cognize our own subject only as appearance but not in accordance with what it is in itself.*,43

§ 25.   B 157

In the transcendental synthesis of the manifold of representations in general, on the contrary, hence in the synthetic original unity of apperception, I am conscious of myself not as I appear to myself, nor **as** I am in myself, but only **that** I am. This **representation** is a **thinking,** not an **intuiting.** Now since for the **cognition** of ourselves, in addition to the action of thinking that brings the manifold of every possible intuition to the unity of apperception, a determinate sort of intuition, through which this manifold is given, is also required, my own existence

---

* I do not see how one can find so many difficulties in the fact that inner sense   B 156
is affected by ourselves. Every act*ᵈ* of **attention** can give us an example of this.   B 157
In such acts the understanding always determines the inner sense, in accordance with the combination that it thinks, to the inner intuition that corresponds to the manifold in the synthesis of the understanding. How much the mind is commonly affected by this means, everyone will be able to perceive in himself.

ᵃ *Object*
ᵇ *Object*
ᶜ *Objecte*
ᵈ *Actus*

B158 is not indeed appearance (let alone mere illusion), but the determination of my existence*,44 can only occur in correspondence with the form of inner sense, according to the particular way in which the manifold that I combine is given in inner intuition, and I therefore have **no cognition** of myself **as I am,** but only as I **appear** to myself. The consciousness of oneself is therefore far from being a cognition of oneself, regardless of all the categories that constitute the thinking of an **object**^{a} **in general** through combination of the manifold in an apperception. Just as for the cognition of an object^b distinct from me I also need an intuition in addition to the thinking of an object^c in general (in the category), through which I determine that general concept, so for the cognition of myself I also need in addition to the consciousness, or in addition to that which I think myself, an intuition of the manifold in me, through which I determine this thought; and I exist as an intelligence that is merely conscious of its faculty for combination but which, B159 in regard to the manifold that it is to combine, is subject to a limiting condition that it calls inner sense, which can make that combination intuitable only in accordance with temporal relations^d that lie entirely outside of the concepts of the understanding proper, and that can therefore still cognize itself merely as it appears to itself with regard to an intuition (which is not intellectual and capable of being given through the understanding itself), not as it would cognize itself if its **intuition** were intellectual.

B157 * The **I think** expresses the act^e of determining my existence. The existence is thereby already given, but the way in which I am to determine it, i.e., the manifold that I am to posit in myself as belonging to it, is not yet thereby given. For that self-intuition is required, which is grounded in an *a priori* given form, i.e., time, which is sensible and belongs to the receptivity of the determinable. B158 Now I do not have yet another self-intuition, which would give the **determining** in me, of the spontaneity of which alone I am conscious, even before the act^f of **determination,** in the same way as time gives that which is to be determined, thus I cannot determine my existence as that of a self-active being, rather I merely represent the spontaneity of my thought, i.e., of the determining, and my existence always remains only sensibly determinable, i.e., determinable as the existence of an appearance. Yet this spontaneity is the reason I call myself an **intelligence.**

^{a} *Object*
^{b} *Objects*
^{c} *Object*
^{d} *Zeitverhältnissen*
^{e} *Actus*
^{f} *Actus*

§ 26.
Transcendental deduction of the universally possible use of the pure concepts of the understanding in experience.

In the **metaphysical deduction**[45] the origin of the *a priori* categories in general was established through their complete coincidence with the universal logical functions of thinking, in the **transcendental deduction,** however, their possibility as *a priori* cognitions of objects of an intuition in general was exhibited (§§ 20, 21). Now the possibility of cognizing *a priori* **through categories** whatever objects **may come before our senses,** not as far as the form of their intuition but rather as far as the laws of their combination are concerned, thus the possibility of as it were prescribing the law to nature and even making the latter possible, is to be explained. For if the categories did not serve in this way, it would not become clear why everything that may ever come before our senses must stand under the laws that arise *a priori* from the understanding alone.

First of all I remark that by the **synthesis of apprehension** I understand the composition of the manifold in an empirical intuition, through which perception, i.e., empirical consciousness of it (as appearance), becomes possible.

We have **forms** of outer as well as inner sensible intuition *a priori* in the representations of space and time, and the synthesis of the apprehension of the manifold of appearance must always be in agreement with the latter, since it can only occur in accordance with this form. But space and time are represented *a priori* not merely as **forms** of sensible intuition, but also as **intuitions** themselves (which contain a manifold), and thus with the determination of the **unity** of this manifold in them (see the Transcendental Aesthetic).*,[46] Thus even **unity of the synthe-**

B 160

B 161

* Space, represented as **object** (as is really required in geometry), contains more than the mere form of intuition, namely the **comprehension**^a of the manifold given in accordance with the form of sensibility in an **intuitive** representation, so that the **form of intuition** merely gives the manifold, but the **formal intuition** gives unity of the representation. In the Aesthetic I ascribed this unity merely to sensibility, only in order to note that it precedes all concepts, though to be sure it presupposes a synthesis, which does not belong to the senses but through which all concepts of space and time first become possible. For since through it (as the understanding determines the sensibility) space or time are first **given** as intuitions, the unity of this *a priori* intuition belongs to space and time, and not to the concept of the understanding (§ 24).

B 160

B 161

^a *Zusammenfassung*

sis of the manifold, outside or within us, hence also a **combination** with which everything that is to be represented as determined in space or time must agree, is already given *a priori*, along with (not in) these intuitions, as condition of the synthesis of all **apprehension.** But this synthetic unity can be none other than that of the combination of the manifold of a given **intuition in general** in an original consciousness, in agreement with the categories, only applied to our **sensible intuition.** Consequently all synthesis, through which even perception itself becomes possible, stands under the categories, and since experience is cognition through connected perceptions, the categories are conditions of the possibility of experience, and are thus also valid *a priori* of all objects of experience.

* * *

B 162   Thus if, e.g., I make the empirical intuition of a house into perception through apprehension of its manifold, my ground is the **necessary unity** of space and of outer sensible intuition in general, and I as it were draw its shape in agreement with this synthetic unity of the manifold in space. This very same synthetic unity, however, if I abstract from the form of space, has its seat in the understanding, and is the category of the synthesis of the homogeneous in an intuition in general, i.e., the category of **quantity,**[a] with which that synthesis of apprehension, i.e., the perception, must therefore be in thoroughgoing agreement.*

If (in another example) I perceive the freezing of water, I apprehend two states (of fluidity and solidity) as ones standing in a relation[b] of time to each other. But in time, on which I ground the appearance as **inner**

B 163 **intuition,** I represent necessary synthetic **unity** of the manifold, without which that relation[c] could not be **determinately** given in an intuition (with regard to the temporal sequence). But now this synthetic unity, as the *a priori* condition under which I combine the manifold of an **intuition in general,** if I abstract from the constant form of **my** inner intuition, time, is the category of **cause,** through which, if I apply it to my sensibility, I **determine everything that happens in time in**

B 162 * In such a way it is proved that the synthesis of apprehension, which is empirical, must necessarily be in agreement with the synthesis of apperception, which is intellectual and contained in the category entirely *a priori.* It is one and the same spontaneity that, there under the name of imagination and here under the name of understanding, brings combination into the manifold of intuition.

[a] *Größe*
[b] *Relation*
[c] *Relation*

general as far as its relation^{*a*} **is concerned**. Thus the apprehension in such an occurrence, hence the occurrence itself, as far as possible perception is concerned, stands under the concept of the **relation**^{*b*} of effects and causes, and so in all other cases.

* * *

Categories are concepts that prescribe laws *a priori* to appearances, thus to nature as the sum total of all appearances (*natura materialiter spectata*),^{*c*} and, since they are not derived from nature and do not follow it as their pattern (for they would otherwise be merely empirical), the question now arises how it is to be conceived that nature must follow them, i.e., how they can determine *a priori* the combination of the manifold of nature without deriving from the latter. Here is the solution to this riddle.

It is by no means stranger that the laws of appearances in nature must   B 164
agree with the understanding and its *a priori* form, i.e., its faculty of **combining** the manifold in general, than that the appearances themselves must agree with the form of sensible intuition *a priori*. For laws exist just as little in the appearances, but rather exist only relative to the subject in which the appearances inhere, insofar as it has understanding, as appearances do not exist in themselves, but only relative to the same being, insofar as it has senses. The lawfulness of things in themselves would necessarily pertain to them even without an understanding that cognizes them. But appearances are only representations of things that exist without cognition of what they might be in themselves. As mere representations, however, they stand under no law of connection at all except that which the connecting faculty prescribes. Now that which connects the manifold of sensible intuition is imagination, which depends on understanding for the unity of its intellectual synthesis and on sensibility for the manifoldness of apprehension. Now since all possible perception depends on the synthesis of apprehension, but the latter itself, this empirical synthesis, depends on the transcendental one, thus on the categories, all possible perceptions, hence everything that can ever reach empirical consciousness, i.e., all appearances of nature, as far   B 165
as their combination is concerned,⁴⁷ stand under the categories, on which nature (considered merely as nature in general) depends, as the original ground of its necessary lawfulness (as *natura formaliter spectata*).^{*d*} The pure faculty of understanding does not suffice, however, to

---

^{*a*} *Relation*
^{*b*} *Verhältnisses*
^{*c*} "Nature regarded materially," i.e., nature in the sense of its material.
^{*d*} "Nature formally regarded," i.e., nature considered with regard to its form rather than its matter.

prescribe to the appearances through mere categories *a priori* laws beyond those on which rests a **nature in general,** as lawfulness of appearances in space and time. Particular laws, because they concern empirically determined appearances, **cannot** be **completely derived** from the categories, although they all stand under them. Experience must be added in order to come to know particular laws **at all;** but about experience in general, and about what can be cognized as an object of experience, only those *a priori* laws offer instruction.

§ 27.
Result of this deduction of the concepts of the understanding.

We cannot **think** any object except through categories; we cannot **cognize** any object that is thought except through intuitions that correspond to those concepts. Now all our intuitions are sensible, and this cognition, so far as its object is given, is empirical. Empirical cognition, B 166   however, is experience. Consequently **no *a priori*** cognition is possible for us except solely of objects of possible experience.*

But this cognition, which is limited merely to objects of experience, is not on that account all borrowed from experience; rather, with regard to the pure intuitions as well as the pure concepts of the understanding, there are elements of cognition that are to be encountered in us *a priori*. Now there are only two ways in which a **necessary** agreement of experience with the concepts of its objects can be thought: either the experience makes these concepts possible or these concepts make the B 167   experience possible. The first is not the case with the categories (nor with pure sensible intuition); for they are *a priori* concepts, hence independent of experience (the assertion of an empirical origin would be a sort of *generatio aequivoca*).[a] Consequently only the second way remains

B 166   * So that one may not prematurely take issue with the worrisome and disadvantageous consequences of this proposition, I will only mention that the categories are not restricted in **thinking** by the conditions of our sensible intuition, but have an unbounded field, and only the **cognition** of objects that we think, the determination of the object,[b] requires intuition; in the absence of the latter, the thought of the object[c] can still have its true and useful consequences for the **use** of the subject's **reason,** which, however, cannot be expounded here, for it is not always directed to the determination of the object, thus to cognition, but rather also to that of the subject and its willing.

[a] The generation of one sort of thing out of something essentially different, e.g., the supposed generation of flies from rotting meat.
[b] *Object*
[c] *Object*

(as it were a system of the **epigenesis**[48] of pure reason): namely that the categories contain the grounds of the possibility of all experience in general from the side of the understanding. But more about how they make experience possible, and which principles of its possibility they yield in their application to appearances, will be taught in the following chapter on the transcendental use of the power of judgment.

If someone still wanted to propose a middle way between the only two, already named ways, namely, that the categories were neither **self-thought** *a priori* first principles[a] of our cognition nor drawn from experience, but were rather subjective predispositions for thinking, implanted in us along with our existence by our author in such a way that their use would agree exactly with the laws of nature along which experience runs (a kind of **preformation-system**[49] of pure reason), then (besides the fact that on such a hypothesis no end can be seen to how far one might drive the presupposition of predetermined predispositions for future judgments) this would be decisive against the supposed middle way: that in such a case the categories would lack the **necessity** that is essential to their concept. For, e.g., the concept of cause, which asserts the necessity of a consequent under a presupposed condition, would be false if it rested only on a subjective necessity, arbitrarily implanted in us, of combining certain empirical representations according to such a rule of relation.[b] I would not be able to say that the effect is combined with the cause in the object[c] (i.e., necessarily), but only that I am so constituted that I cannot think of this representation otherwise than as so connected; which is precisely what the skeptic wishes most, for then all of our insight through the supposed objective validity of our judgments is nothing but sheer illusion, and there would be no shortage of people who would not concede this subjective necessity (which must be felt) on their own; at least one would not be able to quarrel with anyone about that which merely depends on the way in which his subject is organized.

B 168

Brief concept of this deduction.

It is the exhibition of the pure concepts of the understanding (and with them of all theoretical cognition *a priori*) as principles[d] of the possibility of experience, but of the latter as the **determination** of appearances in space and time **in general** – and the latter, finally, from the

B 169

---

[a] *Principien*
[b] *Verhältnisses*
[c] *Objecte*
[d] *Principien*

principle^a of the **original** synthetic unity of apperception, as the form of the understanding in relation to space and time, as original forms of sensibility.

* * *

I hold the division into paragraphs to be necessary only this far, because we have been dealing with the elementary concepts. Now that we will represent their use, the exposition may proceed in a continuous fashion, without this division.>

---

^a *Princip*

The Transcendental Analytic
Second Book
The Analytic of Principles

General logic is constructed on a plan that corresponds quite precisely with the division of the higher faculties of cognition. These are: **understanding, the power of judgment,** and **reason.** In its analytic that doctrine accordingly deals with **concepts, judgments,** and **inferences,** corresponding exactly to the functions and the order of those powers of mind, which are comprehended under the broad designation of understanding in general.

Since merely formal logic, so conceived, abstracts from all content of cognition (whether it be pure or empirical), and concerns itself merely with the form of thinking (of discursive cognition) in general, it can also include in its analytical part the canon for reason, the form of which has its secure precept, into which there can be *a priori* insight through mere analysis of the actions of reason into their moments, without taking into consideration the particular nature of the cognition about which it is employed.

Transcendental logic, since it is limited to a determinate content, namely that of pure *a priori* cognitions alone, cannot imitate general logic in this division. For it turns out that the **transcendental use of reason** is not objectively valid at all, thus does not belong to the **logic of truth,** i.e., the analytic, but rather, as a **logic of illusion,** requires a special part of the scholastic edifice, under the name of the transcendental **dialectic.**

Understanding and the power of judgment accordingly have their canon of objectively valid, thus true use in transcendental logic, and therefore belong in its analytical part. Only **reason** in its attempts to make out something about objects *a priori* and to extend cognition beyond the bounds of possible experience is wholly and entirely **dialectical,** and its illusory assertions do not fit into a canon of the sort that the analytic ought to contain.

The **analytic of principles** will accordingly be solely a canon for the **power of judgment** that teaches it to apply to appearances the concepts of the understanding, which contain the condition for rules *a pri-*

ori. For this reason,[a] as I take the actual **principles of the understanding** as my theme I will make use of the designation of a **doctrine of the power of judgment,** through which this enterprise may be more precisely designated.

Introduction
On the transcendental power of judgment
in general.

If the understanding in general is explained as the faculty of rules, then the power of judgment is the faculty of **subsuming** under rules, i.e., of determining whether something stands under a given rule (*casus datae legis*)[b] or not. General logic contains no precepts at all for the power of judgment, and moreover cannot contain them. For **since it abstracts from all content of cognition,** nothing remains to it but the business of analytically dividing the mere form of cognition into concepts, judgments, and inferences, and thereby achieving formal rules for all use of the understanding. Now if it wanted to show generally how one ought to subsume under these rules, i.e., distinguish whether something stands under them or not, this could not happen except once again through a rule. But just because this is a rule, it would demand another instruction for the power of judgment, and so it becomes clear that although the understanding is certainly capable of being instructed and equipped through rules, the power of judgment is a special talent that cannot be taught but only practiced. Thus this is also what is specific to so-called mother-wit, the lack of which cannot be made good by any school; for,[c] although such a school can provide a limited understanding with plenty of rules borrowed from the insight of others and as it were graft these onto it, nevertheless the faculty for making use of them correctly must belong to the student himself, and in the absence of such a natural gift no rule that one might prescribe to him for this aim is safe from misuse.*,[d] A physician therefore, a judge, or a statesman, can have

A 133 / B 172

A 134 / B 173

A 133 / B 172

A 134 / B 173

* The lack of the power of judgment is that which is properly called stupidity, and such a failing is not to be helped. A dull or limited head, which is lacking nothing but the appropriate degree of understanding and its proper concepts, may well be trained through instruction, even to the point of becoming learned. But since it would usually still lack the power of judgment (the *secunda Petri*),[e] it is not at all uncommon to encounter very learned men who in

[a] *Ursache*
[b] case of the given law
[c] In the first edition, "since."
[d] Kant struck this footnote from his copy of the first edition (E, p. 27), but nevertheless let it remain in the second.
[e] the companion of Peter

many fine pathological, juridical, or political rules in his head, of which he can even be a thorough teacher, and yet can easily stumble in their application, either because he is lacking in natural power of judgment (though not in understanding), and to be sure understands the universal *in abstracto* but*ᵃ* cannot distinguish whether a case *in concreto* belongs under it, or also because he has not received adequate training for this judgment through examples and actual business. This is also the sole and great utility of examples: that they sharpen the power of judgment. For as far as the correctness and precision of the insight of the understanding is concerned, examples more usually do it some damage, since they only seldom adequately fulfill the condition of the rule (as *casus in terminis*)*ᵇ* and beyond this often weaken the effort of the understanding to gain sufficient insight into rules in the universal and independently of the particular circumstances of experience, and thus in the end accustom us to use those rules more like formulas than like principles. Thus examples are the leading-strings of the power of judgment, which he who lacks the natural talent for judgment*ᶜ* can never do without.⁵⁰   B174

But now although **general logic** can give no precepts to the power   A135
of judgment, things are quite different with **transcendental** logic, so that it even seems that the latter has as its proper business to correct and secure the power of judgment in the use of the pure understanding through determinate rules. For although for expansion of the role of the understanding in the field of pure cognitions *a priori*, hence as a doctrine, philosophy seems entirely unnecessary or rather ill-suited, since after all its previous attempts little or no territory has been won, yet as critique, in order to avoid missteps in judgment (*lapsus judici*)*ᵈ* in the use of the few pure concepts of the understanding that we have, philosophy with all of its perspicacity and art of scrutiny is called up (even though its utility is then only negative).

But the peculiar thing about transcendental philosophy is this: that in addition to the rule (or rather the general condition for rules), which is given in the pure concept of the understanding, it can at the same time indicate *a priori* the case to which the rules ought to be applied. The   B175
cause of the advantage that it has in this regard over all other didactic sciences (except for mathematics) lies just here: that it deals with con-

---

the use of their science frequently give glimpses of that lack, which is never to be ameliorated.

ᵃ "but" added in the second edition.
ᵇ I.e., as a limiting case.
ᶜ Following Erdmann in reading "*derselben*" instead of "*desselben*," thus taking "the power of judgment" as its antecedent.
ᵈ lapses of judgment

cepts that are to be related to their objects *a priori*, hence its objective validity cannot be established *a posteriori*, for that would leave that dignity of theirs entirely untouched; rather it must at the same time offer a general but sufficient characterization of the conditions under which objects in harmony with those concepts can be given, for otherwise they would be without all content, and thus would be mere logical forms and not pure concepts of the understanding.

This **transcendental doctrine of the power of judgment** will contain two chapters: the **first,** which deals with the sensible condition under which alone pure concepts of the understanding can be employed, i.e., with the schematism of the pure understanding; and the **second,** which deals with those synthetic judgments that flow *a priori* from pure concepts of the understanding under these conditions and ground all other cognitions *a priori*, i.e., with the principles of pure understanding.

The Transcendental Doctrine of the Power of Judgment (or Analytic of Principles) First Chapter On the schematism[b] of the pure concepts of the understanding[51]

In all subsumptions of an object under a concept the representations of the former must be **homogeneous** with the latter, i.e., the concept must contain that which is represented in the object that is to be subsumed under it, for that is just what is meant by the expression "an object is contained under a concept." Thus the empirical concept of a **plate** has homogeneity with the pure geometrical concept of a **circle,** for the roundness that is thought in the former can be intuited in the latter.

Now pure concepts of the understanding, however, in comparison with empirical (indeed in general sensible) intuitions, are entirely unhomogeneous, and can never be encountered in any intuition. Now

---

[a] The following notes pertaining to the general argument of the next section are all inserted on A137 in Kant's copy of the first edition:

"We cannot think any intuitions or relations [*Verhältnisse*] of intuitions for the categories, rather they must be given in experience. Thus all principles pertain merely to possible experience, since this is possible only in accordance with the form of the unity of understanding." (E LIII, p. 27; 23:27)

"The incomprehensibility of the categories stems from the fact that we cannot have insight into the synthetic unity of apperception." (E LIV, p. 27; 23:27)

"The schema of time a line." (E LV, p. 27; 23:27)

"The possibility of an object [*Objects*] of the concept of the understanding, e.g., a cause or *commercium*, cannot be thought *a priori*, consequently only an experience can be thought with the conditions under which it can become experience in combination with the concept of the understanding." (E LVI, p. 27; 23:27)

[b] Kant's copy of the first edition adds this note: "The synthesis of the understanding is called thus if it determines the inner sense in accordance with the unity of apperception." (E LVII, p. 27; 23:27)

how is the **subsumption** of the latter under the former, thus the **application** of the category to appearances possible, since no one would say that the category, e.g., causality, could also be intuited through the senses and is contained in the appearance? This question, so natural and important, is really the cause which makes a transcendental doctrine of the power of judgment necessary, in order, namely, to show the possibility of applying **pure concepts of the understanding** to appearances in general. In all other sciences, where the concepts through which the object is thought in general are not so different and heterogeneous from those that represent it *in concreto*, as it is given, it is unnecessary to offer a special discussion of the application of the former to the latter.

A138/B177

Now it is clear that there must be a third thing, which must stand in homogeneity with the category on the one hand and the appearance on the other, and makes possible the application of the former to the latter. This mediating representation must be pure (without anything empirical) and yet **intellectual** on the one hand and **sensible** on the other. Such a representation is the **transcendental schema**.

The concept of the understanding contains pure synthetic unity of the manifold in general. Time, as the formal condition of the manifold of inner sense, thus of the connection of all representations, contains an *a priori* manifold in pure intuition. Now a transcendental time-determination is homogeneous with the **category** (which constitutes its unity) insofar as it is **universal** and rests on a rule *a priori*. But it is on the other hand homogeneous with the **appearance** insofar as **time** is contained in every empirical representation of the manifold. Hence an application of the category to appearances becomes possible by means of the transcendental time-determination which, as the schema of the concept of the understanding, mediates the subsumption of the latter under the former.

B178
A139

After what has been shown in the deduction of the categories, hopefully no one will be in doubt about how to decide the question, whether these pure concepts of the understanding are of merely empirical or also of transcendental use, i.e., whether, as conditions of a possible experience, they relate *a priori* solely to appearances, or whether, as conditions of the possibility of things in general, they can be extended to objects in themselves (without any restriction to our sensibility). For we have seen there that concepts are entirely impossible,[a] and cannot have any significance, where an object is not given either for them themselves or at least for the elements of which they consist, consequently they cannot pertain to things in themselves (without regard to how and whether they may be given to us) at all; that, further, the modification of our sensibil-

---

[a] Altered in Kant's copy of the first edition to "are for us without sense" (E LVIII, p. 28; 23:46).

ity is the only way in which objects are given to us; and, finally, that pure concepts *a priori*, in addition to the function of the understanding in the category, must also contain *a priori* formal conditions of sensibility (namely of the inner sense) that contain the general condition under which alone the category can be applied to any object. We will call this formal and pure condition of the sensibility, to which the use of the concept of the understanding is restricted, the **schema** of this concept of the understanding, and we will call the procedure of the understanding with these schemata the **schematism** of the pure understanding.

B 179
A 140

The schema is in itself always only a product of the imagination; but since the synthesis of the latter has as its aim no individual intuition but rather only the unity in the determination of sensibility, the schema is to be distinguished from an image. Thus, if I place five points in a row, ... , this is an image of the number five. On the contrary, if I only think a number in general, which could be five or a hundred, this thinking is more the representation of a method for representing a multitude (e.g., a thousand) in an image in accordance with a certain concept than the image itself, which in this case I could survey and compare with the concept only with difficulty. Now this representation of a general procedure of the imagination for providing a concept with its image is what I call the schema for this concept.

B 180

In fact it is not images of objects but schemata that ground our pure sensible concepts.[52] No image of a triangle would ever be adequate to the concept of it. For it would not attain the generality of the concept, which makes this valid for all triangles, right or acute, etc., but would always be limited to one part of this sphere. The schema of the triangle can never exist anywhere except in thought, and signifies a rule of the synthesis of the imagination with regard to pure shapes in space. Even less does an object of experience or an image of it ever reach the empirical concept, rather the latter is always related immediately to the schema of the imagination, as a rule for the determination of our intuition in accordance with a certain general concept. The concept of a dog signifies a rule in accordance with which my imagination can specify the shape of a four-footed animal in general, without being restricted to any single particular shape that experience offers me or any possible image that I can exhibit *in concreto*. This schematism of our understanding with regard to appearances and their mere form is a hidden art in the depths of the human soul, whose true operations we can divine from nature and lay unveiled before our eyes only with difficulty. We can say only this much: the **image** is a product of the empirical faculty of productive imagination, the **schema** of sensible concepts (such

A 141

B 181

---

[a] In the first edition the right-hand heading here changes to "On the Schematism of the Categories."

A 142   as figures in space) is a product and as it were a monogram of pure *a priori* imagination, through which and in accordance with which the images first become possible, but which must be connected with the concept, to which they are in themselves never fully congruent, always only by means of the schema that they designate. The schema of a pure concept of the understanding, on the contrary, is something that can never be brought to an image at all, but is rather only the pure synthesis, in accord with a rule of unity according to concepts in general, which the category expresses, and is a transcendental product of the imagination, which concerns the determination of the inner sense in general, in accordance with conditions of its*ᵃ* form (time) in regard to all representations, insofar as these are to be connected together *a priori* in one concept in accord with the unity of apperception.

Rather than pausing now for a dry and boring analysis of what is required for transcendental schemata of pure concepts of the understanding in general, we would rather present them according to the order of the categories and in connection with these.

B 182   The pure image of all magnitudes (*quantorum*) for outer sense is space; for all objects of the senses in general, it is time. The pure **schema of magnitude** (*quantitatis*), however, as a concept of the understanding, is **number,** which is a representation that summarizes the successive addition of one (homogeneous) unit to another. Thus num-

A 143   ber is nothing other than the unity of the synthesis of the manifold of a homogeneous intuition in general, because*ᵇ* I generate time itself in the apprehension of the intuition.[53]

Reality*ᶜ* is in the pure concept of the understanding that to which a sensation*ᵈ* in general corresponds, that, therefore, the concept of which in itself indicates a being (in time). Negation is that the concept of which represents a non-being (in time). The opposition of the two thus takes place in the distinction of one and the same time as either a filled or an empty time. Since time is only the form of intuition, thus of objects as appearances, that which corresponds to the sensation in these is the transcendental matter of all objects, as things in themselves (thing-

---

ᵃ In his copy of the first edition, Kant changed this from "*ihrer*" to "*seiner,*" perhaps thereby intending to change its antecedent from "determination" to "inner sense" (E LIX, p. 28; 23:46).

ᵇ *dadurch, daß*

ᶜ *Realität*

ᵈ Inserted in Kant's copy of the first edition:

     "Sensation is that which is really empirical in our cognition, and the real of the representations of inner sense in contrast to their form, time. Sensation therefore lies outside all *a priori* cognition. Only therein, how one sensation differs from another with regard to quality, beyond the *a priori* degrees, but not of their quantity. [*sic*]" (E LX, p. 28; 23:27)

hood,^{a} reality). Now every sensation has a degree or magnitude, through which it can more or less fill the same time, i.e., the inner sense in regard to the same representation of an object, until it ceases in nothingness (= o = *negatio*). Hence there is a relation^b and connection between, or rather a transition from reality to negation, that makes every reality representable as a quantum, and the schema of a reality, as the quantity of something insofar as it fills time, is just this continuous and uniform generation of that quantity in time, as one descends in time from the sensation that has a certain degree to its disappearance or gradually ascends from negation to its magnitude.

B183

The schema of substance is the persistence of the real in time, i.e., the representation of the real as a substratum of empirical time-determination in general, which therefore endures while everything else changes. (Time itself does not elapse, but the existence of that which is changeable elapses in it. To time, therefore, which is itself unchangeable and lasting, there corresponds in appearance that which is unchangeable in existence, i.e., substance, and in it alone can the succession and simultaneity of appearances be determined in regard to time.)

A144

The schema of the cause and of the causality^c of a thing in general is the real upon which, whenever it is posited, something else always follows. It therefore consists in the succession of the manifold insofar as it is subject to a rule.

The schema of community (reciprocity), or of the reciprocal causality of substances with regard to their accidents, is the simultaneity of the determinations of the one with those of the other, in accordance with a general rule.

B184

The schema of possibility is the agreement of the synthesis of various representations with the conditions of time in general (e.g., since opposites cannot exist in one thing at the same time, they can only exist one after another), thus the determination of the representation of a thing to some time.

The schema of actuality^d is existence at a determinate time.

A145

The schema of necessity is^e the existence of an object at all times.[54]

Now one sees from all this that the schema of each category contains and makes representable: in the case of magnitude, the generation (synthesis) of time itself, in the successive apprehension of an object; in the case of the schema of quality, the synthesis of sensation (perception) with the representation of time, or the filling of time; in the case of the

---

^{a} *Sachheit*
^{b} *Verhältnis*
^{c} *der Ursache und der Causalität*
^{d} *Wirklichkeit*
^{e} "is" added in the second edition.

schema of relation,[a] the relation[b] of the perceptions among themselves to all time (i.e., in accordance with a rule of time-determination); finally, in the schema of modality and its categories, time itself, as the correlate of the determination of whether and how an object belongs to time. The schemata are therefore nothing but *a priori* **time-determinations** in accordance with rules, and these concern, according to the order of the categories, the **time-series**, the **content of time**, the **order of time**, and finally the **sum total of time**[c] in regard to all possible objects.

From this it is clear that the schematism of the understanding through the transcendental synthesis of imagination comes down to nothing other than the unity of all the manifold of intuition in inner sense, and thus indirectly to the unity of apperception, as the function that corresponds to inner sense (to a receptivity). Thus the schemata of the concepts of pure understanding are the true and sole conditions for providing them with a relation to objects,[d] thus with **significance**, and hence the categories are in the end of none but a possible empirical use, since they merely serve to subject appearances to general rules of synthesis through grounds of an *a priori* necessary unity (on account of the necessary unification of all consciousness in an original apperception), and thereby to make them fit for a thoroughgoing connection in one experience.

All of our cognitions, however, lie in the entirety of all possible experience, and transcendental truth, which precedes all empirical truth and makes it possible, consists in the general relation to this.

But it is also obvious that, although the schemata of sensibility first realize the categories, yet they likewise also restrict them, i.e., limit them to conditions that lie outside the understanding (namely, in sensibility). Hence the schema is really only the phenomenon, or the sensible concept of an object, in agreement with the category. (***Numerus** est quantitas phaenomenon,* **sensatio** *realitas phaenomenon,* **constans** *et perdurabile rerum substantia phaenomenon –* **aeternitas,** *necessitas phaenomena etc.*).[e] Now if we leave aside a restricting condition, it may seem as if we amplify the previously limited concept; thus the categories in their pure significance, without any conditions of sensibility, should hold for things in general, **as they are,** instead of their schemata merely representing them **how they appear,** and they would therefore have a sig-

B185

A146

B186

A147

---

[a] *Relation*
[b] *Verhältnis*
[c] *Zeitinbegriff*
[d] *Objecte*
[e] "*Number* is the quantity [of the] phenomenon, *sensation* the reality [of the] phenomenon, *constancy* and the endurance of things the substance [of the] phenomenon, *eternity* the necessity [of] phenomena, etc."

nificance independent of all schemata and extending far beyond them. In fact, even after abstraction from every sensible condition, significance, but only a logical significance of the mere unity of representations, is left to the pure concepts of the understanding, but no object and thus no significance is given to them that could yield a concept[a] of the object.[b] Thus, e.g., if one leaves out the sensible determination of persistence, substance would signify nothing more than a something that can be thought as a subject (without being a predicate of something else). Now out of this representation I can make nothing, as it shows me nothing at all about what determinations the thing that is to count as   B 187 such a first subject is to have. Without schemata, therefore, the categories are only functions of the understanding for concepts, but do not represent any object. This significance comes to them from sensibility, which realizes the understanding at the same time as it restricts it.

[a] Changed in Kant's copy of the first edition to "cognition" (E LXI, p. 28; 23:46).
[b] *Object*

Transcendental Doctrine of the Power of Judgment (or Analytic of Principles) Second Chapter System of all principles of pure understanding

In the previous chapter we have considered the transcendental power of judgment only in accordance with the general conditions under which alone it is authorized to use the pure concepts of the understanding for synthetic judgments. Now our task is to exhibit in systematic combination the judgments that the understanding actually brings about *a priori* subject to this critical warning, for which our table of the categories must doubtless give us natural and secure guidance. For it is precisely these whose relation to possible experience must constitute all pure cognition of the understanding *a priori*, and whose relation*a* to sensibility in general will, on that very account, display all

transcendental principles of the use of the understanding completely and in a system.

A priori principles bear this name not merely because they contain in themselves the grounds of other judgments, but also because they are not themselves grounded in higher and more general cognitions. Yet

this property does not elevate them beyond all proof. For although this could not be carried further objectively, but rather grounds all cognition of its object,*b* yet this does not prevent a proof from the subjective sources of the possibility of a cognition of an object in general from being possible, indeed even necessary, since otherwise the proposition would raise the greatest suspicion of being a merely surreptitious assertion.

Second, we will limit ourselves merely to those principles that are re-

---

a *Verhältnis*
b *Objects*

lated to the categories. The principles*ᵃ* of the transcendental aesthetic, therefore, according to which space and time are the conditions of the possibility of all things as appearances, as well as the restriction of these principles, namely that they cannot be related to things in themselves, do not belong within our confined field of investigation. Likewise the mathematical principles do not constitute any part of this system, since they are drawn only from intuition, not from the pure concept of the understanding; yet their possibility, since they are likewise synthetic *a priori* judgments, necessarily finds a place here, not in order to prove their correctness and apodictic certainty, which is not at all necessary, but only to make comprehensible and to deduce the possibility of such evident cognitions *a priori*.   B189

But we must also speak of the principle of analytic judgments, in contrast, to be sure, to that of synthetic judgments, with which we are properly concerned, since precisely this contrast will free the theory of the latter from all misunderstanding and lay their particular nature clearly before our eyes.   A150

The System of the Principles of Pure Understanding
First Section

On the supreme principle
of all analytic judgments.⁵⁵

Whatever the content of our cognition may be, and however it may be related to the object,*ᵇ* the general though to be sure only negative condition of all of our judgments whatsoever is that they do not contradict themselves; otherwise these judgments in themselves (even without regard to the object)*ᶜ* are nothing. But even if there is no contradiction within our judgment, it can nevertheless combine concepts in a way not entailed by the object, or even without any ground being given to us either *a priori* or *a posteriori* that would justify such a judgment, and thus, for all that a judgment may be free of any internal contradiction, it can still be either false or groundless.   B190

Now the proposition that no predicate pertains to a thing that contradicts it is called the principle*ᵈ* of contradiction, and is a general though merely negative criterion of all truth, but on that account it also belongs merely to logic, since it holds of cognitions merely as cogni-   A151

ᵃ Principien
ᵇ Object
ᶜ Object
ᵈ Satz: ordinarily translated as "proposition," it will be translated as "principle" in the phrase *"Satz des Widerspruchs"* throughout this section.

tions in general, without regard to their content, and says that contradiction entirely annihilates and cancels them.

But one can also make a positive use of it, i.e., not merely to ban falsehood and error (insofar as it rests on contradiction), but also to cognize truth. For, **if the judgment is analytic,** whether it be negative or affirmative, its truth must always be able to be cognized sufficiently in accordance with the principle of contradiction. For the contrary of that which as a concept already lies and is thought in the cognition of the object[a] is always correctly denied, while the concept itself must necessarily be affirmed of it, since its opposite would contradict the object.[b]

Hence we must also allow the **principle of contradiction** to count as the universal and completely sufficient **principle[c] of all analytic cognition;** but its authority and usefulness does not extend beyond this, as a sufficient criterion of truth. For that no cognition can be opposed to it without annihilating itself certainly makes this principle[d] into a *conditio sine qua non*, but not into a determining ground of the truth of our cognition. Since we now really have to do only with the synthetic part of our cognition, we will, to be sure, always be careful not to act contrary to this inviolable principle, but we cannot expect any advice from it in regard to the truth of this sort of cognition.

There is, however, still one formula of this famous principle, although denuded of all content and merely formal, which contains a synthesis that is incautiously and entirely unnecessarily mixed into it. This is: "It is impossible for something to be and not to be **at the same time.**" In addition to the fact that apodictic certainty is superfluously appended to this (by means of the word "impossible"), which must yet be understood from the proposition itself, the proposition is affected by the condition of time, and as it were says: "A thing = A, which is something = B, cannot at the same time be *non-B*, although it can easily be both (B as well as *non-B*) in succession." E.g., a person who is young cannot be old at the same time, but one and the same person can very well be young at one time and not young, i.e., old, at another. Now the principle of contradiction, as a merely logical principle, must not limit its claims to temporal relations.[e] Hence such a formula is entirely contrary to its aim. The misunderstanding results merely from our first abstracting a predicate of a thing from its concept and subsequently connecting its opposite with this predicate, which never yields a contradiction with the subject, but only with the predicate that is combined with it synthetically, and indeed only when both the first and the sec-

B 191

A 152

B 192

A 153

---

[a] *Objects*
[b] *Objecte*
[c] *Principium*
[d] *Satz*
[e] *Zeitverhältnisse*

ond predicate are affirmed at the same time. If I say "A person who is unlearned is not learned," the condition **at the same time** must hold; for one who is unlearned at one time can very well be learned at another time. But if I say that "No unlearned person is learned," then the proposition is analytic, since the mark (of unlearnedness) is now comprised in the concept of the subject, and then the negative proposition follows immediately from the principle of contradiction, without the condition **at the same time** having to be added. This is also then the cause why I have above so altered the formula of it that the nature of an   B 193
analytic proposition is thereby clearly expressed.

Of the System of the Principles of Pure Understanding   A 154
Second Section

On the supreme principle of all synthetic judgments.[56]

The explanation of the possibility of synthetic judgments is a problem with which general logic has nothing to do, indeed whose name it need not even know. But in a transcendental logic it is the most important business of all, and indeed the only business if the issue is the possibility of synthetic *a priori* judgments and likewise the conditions and the domain of their validity. For by completing this task transcendental logic can fully satisfy its goal of determining the domain and boundaries of pure understanding.

In the analytic judgment I remain with the given concept in order to discern something about it. If it is an affirmative judgment, I only ascribe to this concept that which is already thought in it; if it is a negative judgment, I only exclude the opposite of this concept from it. In synthetic judgments, however, I am to go beyond the given concept in order to consider something entirely different from what is thought in it as in a relation*a* to it, a relation*b* which is therefore never one of either   B 194
identity, or contradiction, and one where neither the truth nor the error   A 155
of the judgment can be seen in the judgment itself.

If it is thus conceded that one must go beyond a given concept in order to compare it synthetically with another, then a third thing is necessary in which alone the synthesis of two concepts can originate. But now what is this third thing, as the medium of all synthetic judgments? There is only one totality*c* in which all of our representations are contained, namely inner sense and its *a priori* form, time. The synthesis of representations rests on the imagination, but their synthetic unity (which is requisite for judgment), on the unity of apperception. Herein

a *Verhältnis*
b *Verhältnis*
c *Inbegriff*

therefore is to be sought the possibility of synthetic judgments, and, since all three contain the sources of *a priori* representations, also the possibility of pure synthetic judgments, indeed on these grounds they will even be necessary if a cognition of objects is to come about which rests solely on the synthesis of the representations.

If a cognition is to have objective reality, i.e., to be related to an object, and is to have significance and sense in that object, the object must be able to be given in some way. Without that the concepts are empty, and through them one has, to be sure, thought but not in fact cognized anything through this thinking, but rather merely played with representations. To give an object, if this is not again meant only mediately, but it is rather to be exhibited immediately in intuition, is nothing other than to relate its representation to experience (whether this be actual or still possible). Even space and time, as pure as these concepts are from everything empirical and as certain as it is that they are represented in the mind completely *a priori*, would still be without objective validity and without sense and significance if their necessary use on the objects of experience were not shown; indeed, their representation is a mere schema, which is always related to the reproductive imagination that calls forth the objects of experience, without which they would have no significance; and thus it is with all concepts without distinction.

The **possibility of experience** is therefore that which gives all of our cognitions *a priori* objective reality. Now experience rests on the synthetic unity of appearances, i.e., on a synthesis according to concepts of the object of appearances in general, without which it would not even be cognition but rather a rhapsody of perceptions, which would not fit together in any context in accordance with rules of a thoroughly connected (possible) consciousness, thus not into the transcendental and necessary unity of apperception. Experience therefore has principles[a] of its form which ground it *a priori*, namely general rules of unity in the synthesis of appearances, whose objective reality, as necessary conditions, can always be shown in experience, indeed in its possibility. But apart from this relation synthetic *a priori* propositions are entirely impossible, since they would then have no third thing, namely a pure object,[b] in which the synthetic unity of their concepts could establish objective reality.

Thus although in synthetic judgments we cognize *a priori* so much about space in general or about the shapes that the productive imagination draws in it that we really do not need any experience for this, still this cognition would be nothing at all, but an occupation with a mere figment of the brain, if space were not to be regarded as the condition

B 195

A 156

B 196

A 157

---

[a] *Principien*

[b] *reinen Gegenstand*; Erdmann suggests *keinem Gegenstand*, i.e., "no object."

of the appearances which constitute the matter of outer experience; hence those pure synthetic judgments are related, although only mediately, to possible experience, or rather to its possibility itself, and on that alone is the objective validity of their synthesis grounded.

Thus since experience, as empirical synthesis, is in its possibility the only kind of cognition that gives all other synthesis reality, as *a priori* cognition it also possesses truth (agreement with the object)^a only insofar as it contains nothing more than what is necessary for the synthetic unity of experience in general.

B 197

A 158

The supreme principle^b of all synthetic judgments is, therefore: Every object stands under the necessary conditions of the synthetic unity of the manifold of intuition in a possible experience.

In this way synthetic *a priori* judgments are possible, if we relate the formal conditions of *a priori* intuition, the synthesis of the imagination, and its necessary unity in a transcendental apperception to a possible cognition of experience in general, and say: The conditions of the **possibility of experience** in general are at the same time conditions of the **possibility of the objects of experience,** and on this account have objective validity in a synthetic judgment *a priori*.^{c}

Of the System of the Principles of Pure Understanding
Third Section

Systematic representation of all synthetic principles of pure understanding.

That there are principles anywhere at all is to be ascribed solely to the pure understanding, which is not only the faculty of rules in regard to that which happens, but is rather itself the source of the principles in accordance with which everything (that can even come before us as an object) necessarily stands under rules, since, without such rules, appearances could never amount to cognition of an object corresponding to them. Even laws of nature, if they are considered as principles of the empirical use of the understanding, at the same time carry with them an expression of necessity, thus at least the presumption of determination by grounds that are *a priori* and valid prior to all experience.[57] But with-

B 198

A 159

---

^{a} *Object*
^{b} *Principium*
^{c} The following two notes are entered in Kant's copy at A158:
    "How are the objects determined in accordance with the concept *a priori?*" (E LXII, p. 28; 23:28)
    "The [principles] can never be proved from mere concepts, as if they dealt with things in themselves, but can only be proved from the possibility of the perception of things." (E LXIII, p. 29; 23:28)

out exception all laws of nature stand under higher principles of the understanding, as they only apply the latter to particular cases of appearance. Thus these higher principles alone provide the concept, which contains the condition and as it were the exponents for a rule in general, while experience provides the case which stands under the rule.

There can really be no danger that one will regard merely empirical principles as principles of the pure understanding, or vice versa; for the necessity according to concepts that distinguishes the latter, and whose lack in every empirical proposition, no matter how generally it may hold, is easily perceived, can easily prevent this confusion. There are, however, pure principles *a priori* that I may nevertheless not properly ascribe to the pure understanding, since they are not derived from pure concepts but rather from pure intuitions (although by means of the understanding); the understanding, however, is the faculty of concepts. Mathematics has principles of this sort, but their application to experience, thus their objective validity, indeed the possibility of such synthetic *a priori* cognition (its deduction) still always rests on the pure understanding.

Hence I will not count among my principles those of mathematics, but I will include those on which the possibility and objective *a priori* validity of the latter are grounded, and which are thus to be regarded as the principle of these principles,[a] and that proceed **from concepts** to the intuition but not **from the intuition** to concepts.

In the application of the pure concepts of understanding to possible experience the use of their synthesis is either **mathematical**[58] or **dynamical:** for it pertains partly merely to the **intuition,** partly to the **existence** of an appearance in general. The *a priori* conditions of intuition, however, are necessary throughout in regard to a possible experience, while those of the existence of the objects[b] of a possible empirical intuition are in themselves only contingent. Hence the principles of the mathematical use will be unconditionally necessary, i.e., apodictic, while the principles of the dynamical use, to be sure, also carry with them the character of an *a priori* necessity, but only under the condition of empirical thinking in an experience, thus only mediately and indirectly; consequently these do not contain the immediate evidence that is characteristic of the former (though their universal certainty in relation to experience is not thereby injured). Yet this will be better judged at the conclusion of this system of principles.

The table of categories gives us entirely natural direction for the table of principles, since these principles are nothing other than rules of

B 199
A 160

B 200

A 161

---

[a] *als Principium dieser Grundsätze*, i.e., as the general principle giving objective validity to the propositions of mathematics which are themselves synthetic *a priori* according to the "Transcendental Aesthetic."

[b] *Objecte*

the objective use of the categories. All principles of the pure understanding are, accordingly,[59]

1.
Axioms
of intuition.

2.
Anticipations
of perception.

3.
Analogies
of experience.

4.
Postulates
of empirical thinking
in general.[a]

I have chosen these titles with care, in order not to leave unnoted the distinctions with respect to the evidence and the exercise of these principles. But it will soon be shown that as far as the evidence as well as the   B 201
a priori determination of appearances according to the categories of **magnitude** and **quality** are concerned (if one attends solely to the form of the latter), their principles are importantly distinct from those of the   A 162
two others; while the former are capable of an intuitive certainty, the latter are capable only of a discursive certainty, though in both cases they are capable of a complete certainty. I will therefore call the former the **mathematical** and the latter the **dynamical** principles.*,[b],[60] But one

---

* [Note added in the second edition:] <All **combination** (*conjunctio*) is either   B 201
  composition[c] (*compositio*) or **connection**[d] (*nexus*). The former is the syn-

---

[a] The following note is inserted in Kant's copy of the first edition:
  "1. Axioms of Intuition. *Formal.*
    pure mathematics – *pura*
    applied mathematics – *dynamics.*
                   Mathematics
  2. Anticipations of Perception. *Real.*
    Perception is the consciousness
    of an appearance (before any concept)
  3. Analogies of Experience   1. *Physical*
                 Physiology
  4. Postulates of empirical   2. *Metaphysical*
    Thinking in general
              Sensation not beyond
              experience"
            (E LXIV, p. 29; 23:28)
[b] Changed in Kant's copy of the first edition to: "the **physiological** principles" (E LXV, p. 29; 23:46), though obviously this change was not incorporated into the second edition.
[c] *Zusammenhang*
[d] *Verknüpfung*

should note well that I here have in mind the principles of mathematics just as little in the one case as the principles of general (physical) dynamics in the other, but rather have in mind only the principles of the pure understanding in relation*a* to the inner sense (without distinction of the representations which are given therein), through which the former principles all acquire their possibility. I am therefore titling them more with respect to their application than on account of their content, and I now proceed to the consideration of them in the same order in which they are represented in the table.

B 202

I.

<Axioms of Intuition.>*b*

[In the first edition:]

Principle of pure understanding: All appearances are, as regards their intuition, **extensive magnitudes.**

[In the second edition:]
<Their principle is: **All intuitions are extensive magnitudes.**>*c,d,*61

e<Proof

All appearances contain, as regards their form, an intuition in space and time, which grounds all of them *a priori.* They cannot be appre-

---

thesis of a manifold of what **does not necessarily** belong **to each other,** as e.g., the two triangles into which a square is divided by the diagonal do not of themselves necessarily belong to each other, and of such a sort is the synthesis of the **homogeneous** in everything that can be considered **mathematically** (which synthesis can be further divided into that of **aggregation** and of **coalition,** of which the first is directed to **extensive** magnitudes and the second to **intensive** magnitudes). The second combination (*nexus*) is the synthesis of that which is manifold insofar as they **necessarily** belong **to one another,** as e.g., an accident belongs to some substance, or the effect to the cause – thus also as represented as **unhomogeneous** but yet as combined *a priori,* which combination, since it is not arbitrary, I call **dynamical,** since it concerns the combination of the **existence** of the manifold (which can again be divided into the

B 202

physical combination of the appearances with one another and the **metaphysical,** their combination in the *a priori* faculty of cognition).>

---

a *Verhältnis*

b In the first edition: "On the Axioms of Intuition."

c *Größen.* In this section, Kant uses the word "*Größe*" as the German equivalent for both *quantitas* and *quantum,* as is shown by his parenthetical inclusion of the Latin words. According to C. C. E. Schmid's *Wörterbuch zum leichteren Gebrauch der Kantischen Schriften* (Jena: Cröcker, 1798), *Größe* as *quantitas* refers primarily to the pure concept

hended, therefore, i.e., taken up into empirical consciousness, except through the synthesis of the manifold through which the representations of a determinate space or time are generated, i.e., through the composition of that which is homogeneous *a* and the consciousness of the synthetic unity of this manifold (of the homogeneous). Now the consciousness of the homogeneous manifold *b* in intuition in general, insofar as through it the representation of an object *c* first becomes possible, is the concept of a magnitude (*Quanti*). Thus even the perception of an object,*d* as appearance, is possible only through the same synthetic unity of the manifold of given sensible intuition through which the unity of the composition of the homogeneous manifold is thought in the concept of a **magnitude,** i.e., the appearances are all magnitudes, and indeed **extensive magnitudes,** since as intuitions in space or time they must be represented through the same synthesis as that through which space and time in general are determined.>

I call an extensive magnitude that in which the representation of the parts makes possible the representation of the whole (and therefore necessarily precedes the latter).[62] I cannot represent to myself any line, no matter how small it may be, without drawing it in thought, i.e., successively generating all its parts from one point, and thereby first sketching this intuition. It is exactly the same with even the smallest time. I think therein only the successive progress from one moment to another, where through all parts of time and their addition a determi-

B 203

A 162

A 163

---

of quantity, while *Größe* as *quantum* refers to "*eine Größe* in concreto" (pp. 298, 300). This distinction can be marked in English as that between "quantity" and "magnitude." However, we will follow our practice in earlier sections, using "magnitude" as the translation of *Größe* and reserving "quantity" for *Quantität*.

d The following notes are inserted in Kant's copy of the first edition at the start of this section:

"One must subsume the perceptions under the categories. But one can infer nothing from those categories themselves, but only from the possibility of perception, which can only happen through the determination of time and in time, in which the act [*Actus*] that determines the intuition is possible only in accordance with a category." (E LXVI, p. 29; 23:28)

"Since we can all arrange perceptions only through apprehension in time, but this is a synthesis of the homogeneous, which the concept of magnitude corresponds to in the unity of consciousness, we cannot cognize the objects of outer and inner sense otherwise than as magnitudes in experience. Limitation of the concept of magnitude." (E LXVII, p. 30; 23:28–9)

c The heading "Proof" and the following paragraph were added in the second edition.

a *Gleichartigen*, syntactically singular but semantically plural, thus meaning "homogeneous units"; see the expression *Gleichartigen (der Einheiten)* at A 164/ B 205 below.

b *des mannigfaltigen Gleichartigen*

c Objects

d Objects

nate magnitude of time is finally generated.[a] Since the mere intuition in all appearances is either space or time, every appearance as intuition is an extensive magnitude, as it can only be cognized through successive synthesis (from part to part) in apprehension. All appearances are accordingly already intuited as aggregates (multitudes of antecedently given parts),[b] which is not the case with every kind of magnitude, but rather only with those that are represented and apprehended by us as **extensive**.[c]

On this successive synthesis of the productive imagination, in the generation of shapes, is grounded the mathematics of extension (geometry) with its axioms, which express the conditions of sensible intuition *a priori*, under which alone the schema of a pure concept of outer appearance can come about; e.g., between two points only one straight line is possible; two straight lines do not enclose a space, etc. These are the axioms that properly concern only magnitudes (*quanta*) as such.

But concerning magnitude (*quantitas*), i.e., the answer to the question "How big is something?", although various of these propositions are synthetic and immediately certain (*indemonstrabilia*), there are nevertheless no axioms in the proper sense. For that equals added to or subtracted from equals give an equal are analytic propositions, since I am immediately conscious of the identity of one generation of a magnitude with the other; but axioms ought to be synthetic *a priori* propositions. The self-evident propositions of numerical relation,[d] on the contrary, are to be sure, synthetic, but not general, like those of geometry, and for that reason also cannot be called axioms, but could rather be named numerical formulas. That $7 + 5 = 12$ is not an analytic proposition. For I do not think the number 12 either in the representation of 7 nor in that of 5 nor in the representation of the combination[e] of the two (that I ought to think this in the **addition of the two** is not here at issue; in the case of an analytic proposition the question is only

---

[a] Inserted in Kant's copy of the first edition: "Hence the concept of an extensive magnitude does not pertain merely to that wherein there is extension, i.e., merely to our intuition. Satisfaction has extensive magnitude in accordance with the length of the time that is agreeably spent, although it also has magnitude *intensive* [intensively] according to the degree of this agreeableness." (E LXVIII, p. 30; 23:29)

[b] These words are stricken in Kant's copy of the first edition (E LXIX, p. 30; 23:46).

[c] Inserted in Kant's copy of the first edition: "We can never take up a manifold as such in perception without doing so in space and time. But since we do not intuit these for themselves, we must take up the homogeneous manifold in general in accordance with concepts of magnitude." (E LXX, p. 30; 23:29)

[d] *Zahlverhältnis*

[e] *Zusammensetzung*

whether I actually think the predicate in the representation of the subject). Although it is synthetic, however, it is still only a singular proposition. Insofar as it is only the synthesis of that which is homogeneous (of units) that is at issue here, the synthesis here can take place only in a single way, even though the subsequent **use** of these numbers is general. If I say: "With three lines, two of which taken together are greater than the third, a triangle can be drawn," then I have here the mere function of the productive imagination, which draws the lines greater or smaller, thus allowing them to abut at any arbitrary angle. The A 165 number 7,[a] on the contrary, is possible in only a single way, and likewise the number 12, which is generated through the synthesis of the former with 5. Such propositions must therefore not be called axioms (for otherwise there would be infinitely many of them) but rather nu- B 206 merical formulas.

This transcendental principle of the mathematics of appearances yields a great expansion of our *a priori* cognition. For it is this alone that makes pure mathematics in its complete precision applicable to objects of experience, which without this principle would not be so obvious, and has indeed caused much contradiction. Appearances are not things in themselves. Empirical intuition is possible only through the pure intuition (of space and time); what geometry says about the latter is therefore undeniably valid of the former, and evasions, as if objects of the senses did not have to be in agreement with the rules of construction in space (e.g., the rules of the infinite divisibility of lines or angles), must cease. For one would thereby deny all objective validity to space, and with it at the same time to all mathematics, and would no longer know why and how far they are to be applied to appearances. The synthesis of spaces and times, as the essential form of all intuition, is that which at the same time makes possible the apprehension of the appearance, thus every outer experience, consequently also all cognition of its ob- A 166 jects, and what mathematics in its pure use proves about the former is also necessarily valid for the latter. All objections to this are only the chicanery of a falsely instructed reason, which erroneously thinks of B 207 freeing the objects of the senses from the formal condition of our sensibility, and, though they are mere appearances, represents them as objects in themselves, given to the understanding; in which case, certainly, nothing synthetic could be cognized of them *a priori* at all, thus not even through pure concepts of space, and the science that they determine, namely geometry, would not itself be possible.

---

[a] Inserted in Kant's copy of the first edition: "in the proposition 7 + 5 = 12" (E LXXI, pp. 30–1; 23:46).

2.

<Anticipations of Perception.>*a*

[In the first edition:]

The **principle,** which anticipates all perceptions, as such,
runs thus: In all appearances the sensation, and the **real,**
which corresponds to it in the object (*realitas
phaenomenon*), has an **intensive magnitude,** i.e., a degree.

[In the second edition:]

<Its principle*b* is: **In all appearances the real, which is an object
of the sensation, has intensive magnitude,** i.e., a degree.>[63]

c<Proof

Perception is empirical consciousness, i.e., one in which there is at the
same time sensation. Appearances, as objects of perception, are not
pure (merely formal) intuitions, like space and time (for these cannot be
perceived in themselves). They therefore also contain in addition to the
intuition the materials for some object*d* in general (through which
something existing in space or time is represented), i.e., the real of the
sensation, as merely subjective representation, by which one can only
be conscious that the subject is affected, and which one relates to an ob-
B 208 ject*e* in general. Now from the empirical consciousness to the pure consciousness a gradual alteration is possible, where the real in the former
entirely disappears, and a merely formal (*a priori*) consciousness of the
manifold in space and time remains;[64] thus there is also possible a synthesis of the generation of the magnitude of a sensation from its beginning, the pure intuition = o, to any arbitrary magnitude. Now since
sensation in itself is not an objective representation, and in it neither
the intuition of space nor that of time is to be encountered, it has, to be
sure, no extensive magnitude, but yet it still has a magnitude (and indeed through its apprehension, in which the empirical consciousness
can grow in a certain time from nothing = o to its given measure), thus
it has an **intensive magnitude,** corresponding to which all objects*f* of
perception, insofar as they contain sensation, must be ascribed an **intensive magnitude,** i.e., a degree of influence on sense.>
A 166 One can call all cognition through which I can cognize and determine *a priori* what belongs to empirical cognition an anticipation, and

---

a In the first edition: "The Anticipations of Perception."
b *Princip*
c The heading "Proof" and the following paragraph were added in the second edition.
d *Objecte*
e *Object*
f *Objecten*

without doubt this is the significance with which Epicurus used his ex-   A167
pression προλημψις.[65] But since there is something in the appearances
that is never cognized *a priori*, and which hence also constitutes the real
difference between empirical and *a priori* cognition, namely the sensation (as matter of perception), it follows that it is really this that cannot   B209
be anticipated at all. On the contrary, we would call the pure determinations in space and time, in regard to shape as well as magnitude, anticipations of appearances, since they represent *a priori* that which may
always be given *a posteriori* in experience. But if it were supposed that
there is something which can be cognized *a priori* in every sensation, as
sensation in general (without a particular one being given), then this
would deserve to be called an anticipation in an unusual sense, since it
seems strange to anticipate experience precisely in what concerns its
matter, which one can draw out of it. And this is actually how things
stand.

Apprehension, merely by means of sensation, fills only an instant (if I
do not take into consideration the succession of many sensations). As
something in the appearance, the apprehension of which is not a successive synthesis, proceeding from the parts to the whole representation, it
therefore has no extensive magnitude; the absence of sensation in the
same moment would represent this as empty, thus = 0. Now that in the   A168
empirical intuition which corresponds to the sensation is reality (*realitas
phaenomenon*); that which corresponds to its absence is negation = 0.
Now, however, every sensation is capable of a diminution, so that it can   B210
decrease and thus gradually disappear.[66] Hence between reality in appearance and negation there is a continuous nexus of many possible intermediate sensations, whose difference from one another is always
smaller than the difference between the given one and zero, or complete
negation. That is, the real in appearance always has a magnitude, which
is not, however, encountered in apprehension, as this takes place by
means of the mere sensation in an instant and not through successive
synthesis of many sensations, and thus does not proceed from the parts
to the whole; it therefore has a magnitude, but not an extensive one.

Now I call that magnitude which can only be apprehended as a unity,
and in which multiplicity can only be represented through approximation to negation = 0, **intensive magnitude.** Thus every reality in the
appearance has intensive magnitude, i.e., a degree. If one regards this
reality as cause (whether of the sensation or of another reality in appearance, e.g., an alteration), then one calls the degree of reality as
cause a "moment," e.g., the moment of gravity, because, indeed, the degree designates only that magnitude the apprehension of which is not   A169
successive but instantaneous. But I touch on this here only in passing,
for at present I am not yet dealing with causality.

Accordingly every sensation, thus also every reality in appear-   B211 ance,[a] however small it may be, has a degree, i.e., an intensive magnitude, which can still always be diminished, and between reality and negation there is a continuous nexus of possible realities, and of possible smaller perceptions. Every color, e.g., red, has a degree, which, however small it may be, is never the smallest, and it is the same with warmth, with the moment of gravity, etc.

The property of magnitudes on account of which no part of them is the smallest (no part is simple) is called their continuity. Space and time are *quanta continua*,[b] because no part of them can be given except as enclosed between boundaries (points and instants), thus only in such a way that this part is again a space or a time. Space therefore consists only of spaces, time of times. Points and instants are only boundaries, i.e., mere places of their limitation; but places always presuppose those intuitions that limit or determine them, and from mere places, as components that could be given prior to space or time, neither space nor time can be composed. Magnitudes of this sort can also be called **flowing,** since the synthesis (of the productive imagination) in their generation is a progress in time, the continuity of which is customarily designated by the expression "flowing" ("elapsing").

All appearances whatsoever are accordingly continuous magnitudes, either in their intuition, as extensive magnitudes, or in their mere perception (sensation and thus reality), as intensive ones. If the synthesis of the manifold of appearance is interrupted, then it is an aggregate of many appearances, and not really appearance as a quantum, which is not generated through the mere continuation of productive synthesis of a certain kind, but through the repetition of an ever-ceasing synthesis. If I call thirteen dollars a quantum of money, I do so correctly insofar as I mean by that an amount of a mark of fine silver, which is to be sure a continuous magnitude, in which no part is the smallest but each part could constitute a coin that would always contain material for still smaller ones. But if by the term "thirteen round dollars" I mean so many coins (whatever their amount of silver might be), then it would not be suitable to call this a quantum of dollars, but it must instead be called an aggregate, i.e., a number of coins. Now since there must still be a unity grounding every number, appearance as unity is a quantum, and is as such always a continuum.

Now if all appearances, considered extensively as well as intensively, are continuous magnitudes, then the proposition that all alteration[c] (transi-

A 170

B 212

A 171

---

[a] Inserted in Kant's copy of the first edition: "I do not say that all reality has a degree any more than that every thing has an extensive magnitude." (E LXXII, p. 31; 23:29)

[b] continuous magnitudes

[c] Inserted in Kant's copy of the first edition: "[The] possibility of which, just like that of all other objects [*Objecte*] of pure concepts of the understanding, cannot be given otherwise than in sensible intuition. It is not cognizable in itself." (E LXXIII, p. 31; 23:29)

tion of a thing from one state into another) is also continuous could be   B213
proved here easily and with mathematical self-evidence, if the causality of
an alteration in general did not lie entirely beyond the boundaries of a
transcendental philosophy and presuppose empirical principles.[a] For the
understanding gives us no inkling *a priori* that a cause is possible which
alters the state of things, i.e., determines them to the opposite of a certain
given state, not merely because it simply does not give us insight into the
possibility of this (for this insight is lacking in many *a priori* cognitions),
but rather because alterability concerns only certain determinations of
appearances, about which experience alone can teach us, while their cause
is to be found in the unalterable. But since we have before us here nothing that we can use except the pure fundamental concepts of all possible
experience, in which there must be nothing at all empirical, we cannot
anticipate general natural science, which is built upon certain fundamental experiences, without injuring the unity of the system.   A172

Nevertheless, we are not lacking proofs of the great influence that
our principle has in anticipating perceptions, and even in making good
their absence insofar as it draws the bolt against all the false inferences
that might be drawn from that.

If all reality in perception has a degree, between which and negation   B214
there is an infinite gradation of ever lesser degrees, and if likewise every
sense must have a determinate degree of receptivity for the sensations,
then no perception, hence also no experience, is possible that, whether
immediately or mediately (through whatever detour in inference one
might want), would prove an entire absence of everything real in appearance, i.e., a proof of empty space or of empty time can never be
drawn from experience. For, first, the entire absence of the real in sensible intuition cannot itself be perceived, and, second, it cannot be deduced from any single appearance and the difference in the degree of its
reality, nor may it ever be assumed for the explanation of that. For even
if the entire intuition of a determinate space or time is real through and
through, i.e., no part of it is empty, yet, since every reality has its degree
that can decrease to nothing (emptiness) through infinite steps while the   A173
extensive magnitude of the appearance remains unaltered, it must yield
infinitely different degrees with which space or time is filled, and the intensive magnitude in different appearances can be smaller or greater
even though the extensive magnitude of the intuition remains identical.

We will give an example of this. Nearly all natural philosophers,[b] since   B215
they perceive a great difference in the quantity of matter of different
sorts in the same volumes (partly through the moment of gravity, or
weight, partly through the moment of resistance against other, moved

[a] *Principien*
[b] *Naturlehrer*

matter), unanimously infer from this that this volume (extensive magnitude of the appearance) must be empty in all matter, although to be sure in different amounts. But who among these for the most part mathematical and mechanical students of nature ever realized that their inference rested solely on a metaphysical presupposition, which they make so much pretense of avoiding? – for they assume that the **real** in space (I cannot call it here impenetrability or weight, since these are empirical concepts), is **everywhere one and the same,** and can be differentiated only according to its extensive magnitude, i.e., amount.[a] Against this presupposition, for which they can have no ground in experience and which is therefore merely metaphysical, I oppose a transcendental proof,

A174 which, to be sure, will not explain the variation in the filling of space, but which still will entirely obviate the alleged necessity of the presupposition that the difference in question cannot be explained except by the assumption of empty spaces, and which has the merit of at least granting the understanding the freedom also to think of this difference in another

B216 way, if the explanation of nature should make some hypothesis necessary for this end. For there we see that, although equal spaces can be completely filled with different matters in such a way that in neither of them is there a point in which the presence of matter is not to be encountered, nevertheless everything real has for the same quality its degree (of resistance or of weight) which, without diminution of the extensive magnitude or amount,[b] can become infinitely smaller until it is transformed into emptiness and disappears. Thus an expansion that fills a space, e.g. warmth, and likewise every other reality (in appearance) can, without in the least leaving the smallest part of this space empty, decrease in degree infinitely, and nonetheless fill the space with this smaller degree just as well as another appearance does with a larger one. My aim here is by no means to assert that this is how it really is concerning the specific gravity of the variety of matters, but only to establish, on the basis of a prin-

A175 ciple of pure understanding, that the nature of our perceptions makes an explanation of this sort possible, and that it is false to assume that the real in appearance is always equal in degree and differs only in aggregation and its extensive magnitude, especially when this is allegedly asserted on the basis of a principle of understanding *a priori*.

B217 Nevertheless there must always be something striking about this anticipation of perception for a researcher who has become accustomed to transcendental consideration and thereby become cautious, and some reservation is aroused about the fact that the understanding can anticipate a synthetic proposition of the sort which that concerning the degree of everything real in appearance is, and thus about the possibility

[a] *Menge*
[b] *Menge*

of the inner variation of the sensation itself if one abstracts from its empirical quality, and it is therefore a question not unworthy of solution, how the understanding can assert something synthetic *a priori* about appearances, and indeed anticipate them in that which is really merely empirical, namely what pertains to sensation.

The **quality** of sensation is always merely empirical and cannot be represented *a priori* at all (e.g. colors, taste, etc.). But the real, which corresponds to sensations in general, in opposition to the negation = o, only represents something whose concept in itself contains a being, and does not signify anything except the synthesis in an empirical consciousness   A176
in general. In inner sense, namely, the empirical consciousness can be raised from o up to any greater degree, so that the very same extensive magnitude of intuition (e.g., an illuminated surface) can excite as great a sensation as an aggregate of many other (less illuminated) surfaces taken together. One can therefore abstract entirely from the extensive magnitude of appearance and yet represent in the mere sensation in one mo-   B218
ment a synthesis of uniform increase from o up to the given empirical consciousness. All sensations are thus, as such, given only *a posteriori*,[a] but their property of having a degree can be cognized *a priori*. It is remarkable that we can cognize *a priori* in magnitudes in general only a single **quality**, namely continuity, but that in all quality (the real of appearances) we can cognize *a priori* nothing more than their intensive **quantity**,[b] namely that they have a degree, and everything else is left to experience.

3.
\<Analogies of Experience.\>[c,67]

[In the first edition:]
Their general **principle** is: As regards their existence, all appearances stand *a priori* under rules of the determination of their relation to each other in **one** time.

[In the second edition:]
\<Their principle[d] is: **Experience is possible only through the representation of a necessary connection of perceptions.**\>

[e]**\<Proof**

Experience is an empirical cognition, i.e., a cognition that determines an object[f] through perceptions. It is therefore a synthesis of perceptions,

---

[a] Following Erdmann, reading "*a posteriori*" instead of "*a priori*."
[b] *Quantität*
[c] In the first edition: "The Analogies of Experience."
[d] *Princip*
[e] The heading "Proof" and the following paragraph were added in the second edition.
[f] *Object*

which is not itself contained in perception but contains the synthetic unity of the manifold of perception in one consciousness, which constitutes what is essential in a cognition of **objects**ᵃ of the senses, i.e., of ex-

B219 perience (not merely of the intuition or sensation of the senses). Now in experience, to be sure, perceptions come together only contingently, so that no necessity of their connection is or can become evident in the perceptions themselves, since apprehension is only a juxtapositionᵇ of the manifold of empirical intuition, but no representation of the necessity of the combined existence of the appearances that it juxtaposes in space and time is to be encountered in it. But since experience is a cognition of objectsᶜ through perception, consequently the relationᵈ in the existence of the manifold is to be represented in it not as it is juxtaposed in time but as it is objectively in time, yet since time itself cannot be perceived, the determination of the existence of objectsᵉ in time can only come about through their combination in time in general, hence only through *a priori* connecting concepts. Now since these always carry necessity along with them, experience is thus possible only through a representation of the necessary connection of the perceptions.>

A177 ᶠThe three *modi* of time are **persistence, succession,** and **simultaneity.** Hence three rules of all temporal relations of appearances, in accordance with which the existenceᵍ of each can be determined with regard to the unity of all time, precede all experience and first make it possible.

B220 The general principle of all three analogies rests on the necessary **unity** of apperception with regard to all possible empirical consciousness (of perception) **at every time,** consequently, since that is an *a priori* ground, it rests on the synthetic unity of all appearances according to their relations in time. For the original apperception is related to inner sense (the sum of all representations), and indeed related *a priori*

ᵃ *Objecte*

ᵇ *Zusammenstellung*

ᶜ *Objecte*

ᵈ Throughout this section of the work, "relation" will translate *Verhältnis* unless otherwise noted.

ᵉ *Objecte*

ᶠ The text common to the two editions resumes here, although in his copy of the first edition Kant had struck out the next two paragraphs and instead written the following two notes:

"For the proposition that I myself am simultaneous with all time in me so far as I think it, i.e., with the whole time that I think, or its form, would be tautologous." (E LXXIV, p. 31; 23:29)

"The principle of persistence does not concern things in themselves, hence the subject of the representations of things as itself, i.e., apperception, but only appearances. For the concept of time does not apply to anything else, not even to the subject of time itself." (E LXXV, p. 31; 23:29)

ᵍ In Kant's copy of the first edition, "existence" is replaced with "the relation [*Verhältnis*] of the real in appearance" (E LXXVI, p. 31; 23:47).

to its form, i.e., the relation of the manifold empirical consciousness in time. Now in the original apperception all of this manifold, so far as its temporal relations are concerned, is to be unified; for this is what its transcendental unity, under which everything stands that is to belong to my (i.e., my united)^a cognition, and thus can become an object for me, asserts *a priori.* This **synthetic unity** in the temporal relation of all perceptions, **which is determined *a priori,*** is thus the law that all empirical time-determinations must stand under rules of general time-determination, and the analogies of experience, with which we will now A178 deal, must be rules of this sort.

These principles have the peculiarity that they do not concern the appearances and the synthesis of their empirical intuition, but merely their **existence** and their **relation** to one another with regard to this their existence. Now the way in which something is apprehended in appearance can be determined *a priori* so that the rule of its synthesis at the same time yields this intuition *a priori* in every empirical example, i.e., can bring the former about from the latter. Yet the existence of appearances cannot be cognized *a priori,* and even if we could succeed on this path in inferring to some existence or other, we still would not be able to cognize it determinately, i.e., be able to anticipate that through which its empirical intuition is differentiated from others.

The preceding two principles, which I named the mathematical ones in consideration of the fact that they justified applying mathematics to appearances, pertained to appearances with regard to their mere possibility, and taught how both their intuition and the real in their perception could be generated in accordance with rules of a mathematical synthesis, hence how in both cases numerical magnitudes and, with them, the determination of the appearance as magnitude, could be used. E.g., I would be able to compose and determine *a priori,* i.e., construct the de- A179 gree of the sensation of sunlight out of about 200,000 illuminations from the moon. Thus we can call the former principles constitutive.

Things must be entirely different with those principles that are to bring the existence of appearances under rules *a priori.* For, since this existence cannot be constructed, these principles can concern only the rela- B222 tion^b of existence, and can yield nothing but merely **regulative** principles.^{c} Here therefore neither axioms nor intuitions are to be thought of; rather, if a perception is given to us in a temporal relation to others (even though indeterminate), it cannot be said *a priori* **which** and **how great** this other perception is, but only how it is necessarily combined with the first, as regards its existence, in this *modus* of time. In philosophy analogies signify something very different from what they represent in mathe-

---

^{a} *einigen*
^{b} *Verhältnis*
^{c} *Principien*

297

matics. In the latter they are formulas that assert the identity of two relations of magnitude,[a] and are always **constitutive,** so that if two members of the proportion are given the third is also thereby given, i.e., can be constructed. In philosophy, however, analogy is not the identity of two **quantitative** but of two **qualitative** relations, where from three given members I can cognize and give *a priori* only the **relation** to a fourth member but not **this** fourth **member** itself, although I have a rule for seeking it in experience and a mark for discovering it there. An analogy of experience will therefore be only a rule in accordance with which unity of experience is to arise from perceptions (not as a perception itself, as empirical intuition in general), and as a principle it will not be valid of the objects (of the appearances) **constitutively** but merely **regulatively.**[68]

The very same thing will also hold for the postulates of empirical thinking in general, which together concern the synthesis of mere intuition (of the form of appearance), of perception (of its matter), and of experience (of the relation of these perceptions), namely that they are only regulative principles, and that they differ from the mathematical principles, which are constitutive, not, to be sure, in their certainty, which is established *a priori* in both cases, but yet in the manner of their evidence, i.e., with regard to their intuitiveness (thus also their demonstration).

But what must be remembered about all synthetic principles and especially noted here is this: that these analogies have their sole significance and validity not as principles of the transcendental use of the understanding but merely as principles of its empirical use, hence they can be proven only as such; consequently the appearances must not be subsumed under the categories per se, but only under their schemata. For if the objects to which these principles were to be related were things in themselves, then it would be entirely impossible to cognize anything about them synthetically *a priori.* Now it is nothing but appearances whose complete cognition, to which in the end all *a priori* principles must come down, is only possible experience, and consequently those principles can have as their goal nothing but the conditions of the unity of empirical cognition in the synthesis of the appearances; but these conditions are thought only in the schema of the pure concept of the understanding, and the category contains the function, unrestricted by any sensible condition, of their unity, as of a synthesis in general. These principles, therefore, justify us in compounding the appearances only in accord with an analogy with the logical and general unity of concepts, and hence in the principle itself we make use of the category, but in its execution (its application to appearances) we set its schema in its place, as the key to its use, or rather we set the latter alongside the former, as its restricting condition, under the name of its formula.

---

[a] *Größenverhältnisse*

A.

A 182

First Analogy.
Principle of the persistence <of substance.>[a],[69]

[*In the first edition:*]
All appearances contain that which persists **(substance)** as the object itself, and that which can change[b] as its mere determination, i.e., a way in which the object exists.[c]

[*In the second edition:*]
<In all change of appearances substance persists, and its quantum is neither increased nor diminished in nature.>

[d]<Proof

[a] *der Substanz* added in the second edition.

[b] *das Wandelbare*

[c] The following series of notes is entered at the beginning of the "First Analogy" in Kant's copy of the first edition:

"Here it must be shown that this proposition does not pertain to any other substances than those whose alteration is effected only through moving causes, and also consists only in movement, consequently in alteration of relations [*Relationen*]." (E LXXVII, p. 31; 23:30)

"All arising and perishing is only the alteration of that which endures (the substance), and this does not arise and perish (thus the world also does not)." (E LXXVIII, p. 32; 23:30)

"Change can only be perceived through that which persists and its alteration. For the difference of the times in which things are can only be perceived in them as parts of one and the same time. All change is only the division of time. Hence there must be something that exists throughout the entire time, since the whole is always the ground of the division. Hence substance is the substratum, and that which is changing is only the way in which this exists." (E LXXIX, p.32; 23:30)

"Here the proof must be so conducted that it applies only to substances as phenomena of outer sense, consequently from space, which exists at all time along with its determination.

"In space all alteration is movement; for if there were something else in the relations [*Relationen*], then in accordance with the concept of alteration the subject would persist. Therefore everything in space would have to disappear at the same time." (E LXXX, p. 32; 23:30)

"If the substance persists, while the accidents change, but the substance, if all *accidentia* are taken away, is the empty *substantiale*, then what is it that persists? Now everything that can be distinguished from that which changes in experience is quantity [*grösse*], and this can only be assessed through the magnitude of the merely relative effect in the case of equal external relations [*Relationen*] and therefore applies only to bodies." (E LXXXI, p. 32; 23:30–1)

"Here alterations must be discussed." (E LXXXII, p. 32; 23:31)

[d] The heading "Proof" and the following first paragraph in the second edition replace the heading "Proof of this first Analogy" and this opening paragraph in the first edition:

"All appearances are in time. This can determine the relation [*Verhältnis*] **in their existence** in two ways, insofar as they **exist** either **successively** or **simultaneously**. In the case of the former time is considered as **temporal series**, with regard to the latter as **temporal domain**."

All appearances are in time, in which, as substratum (as persistent form of inner intuition), both **simultaneity** as well as **succession** can alone be represented. The time, therefore, in which all change of appearances is to be thought, lasts and does not change; since it is that in which succession or simultaneity can be represented only as determinations of it. Now time cannot be perceived by itself.*a* Consequently it is in the objects of perception, i.e., the appearances, that the substratum must be encountered that represents time in general and in which all change or simultaneity can be perceived in apprehension through the relation of the appearances to it. However, the substratum of everything real, i.e., everything that belongs to the existence*b* of things, is **substance,** of which everything that belongs to existence can be thought only as a determination. Consequently that which persists, in relation to which alone all temporal relations of appearances can be determined, is substance in the appearance, i.e., the real in the appearance, which as the substratum of all change always remains the same. Since this, therefore, cannot change in existence, its quantum in nature can also be neither increased nor diminished.>

Our **apprehension** of the manifold of appearance is always successive, and is therefore always changing. We can therefore never determine from this alone whether this manifold, as object of experience, is simultaneous or successive, if something does not ground it **which always exists,** i.e., something **lasting** and **persisting,** of which all change and simultaneity are nothing but so many ways (*modi* of time) in which that which persists exists. Only in that which persists, therefore, are temporal relations possible (for simultaneity and succession are the only relations in time), i.e., that which persists is the **substratum** of the empirical representation of time itself, by which alone all time-determination is possible. Persistence gives general expression to time as the constant correlate of all existence of appearances, all change and all accompaniment.*c* For change does not affect time itself, but only the appearances in time (just as simultaneity is not a *modus* for time itself, in which no parts are simultaneous but rather all succeed one another). If one were to ascribe such a succession to time itself, one would have to think yet another time in which this succession would be possible.*d*

B225

A182

B226

A183

---

a *für sich*

b *Existenz*

c *Begleitung*, here connoting the accompaniment of one state of affairs by another, i.e., what Kant is here otherwise calling "simultaneity" or coexistence.

d The following notes are added here in Kant's copy of the first edition:

"The perception of endurance is not possible through the perception of successive determinations and of the relation of their series to time, thus also not through the relation to another sequence of determinations, which itself requires a temporal space, but

Only through that which persists does **existence** in different parts of the temporal series acquire a **magnitude,** which one calls **duration.** For in mere sequence alone existence is always disappearing and beginning, and never has the least magnitude. Without that which persists there is therefore no temporal relation. Now time cannot be perceived in itself; thus this persisting thing in the appearances is the substratum of all time-determination, consequently also the condition of the possibility of all synthetic unity of perceptions, i.e., of experience, and in this persisting thing all existence and all change in time can only be re-   B 227 garded as a *modus* of the existence[a] of that which lasts and persists. Therefore in all appearances that which persists is the object itself, i.e., the substance (*phaenomenon*), but everything that changes or that can change belongs only to the way in which this substance or substances   A 184 exists, thus to their determinations.

    I find that at all times not merely the philosopher but even the common understanding has presupposed this persistence as a substratum of all change in the appearances, and has also always accepted it as indubitable, only the philosopher expresses himself somewhat more determinately in saying that in all alterations in the world the **substance** remains and only the **accidents** change. But I nowhere find even the attempt at a proof of this so obviously synthetic proposition, indeed it only rarely stands, as it deserves to, at the head of the pure and completely *a priori* laws of nature. In fact the proposition that substance persists is tautological. For only this persistence is the ground for our application of the category of substance to appearance, and one should have proved that in all appearances there is something that persists, of which that which changes[b] is nothing but the determination of its existence. But since such a proof can never be conducted dogmatically, i.e., from concepts, because it concerns a synthetic *a priori* proposition, and   B 228 it was never considered that such propositions are valid only in relation[c] to possible experience, hence that they can be proved only through a

---

through something whose existence is not a series of successions, but which includes these in itself as its determinations, consequently *per durabilitatem* [through the durability] of substance.

    "This proof, like all synthetic ones, is proved only from the possibility of perception. It is valid where I cannot perceive substance outside of its alterations; but where I cannot perceive it except through these alterations themselves, it is not valid, and I can estimate its endurance and in general the time of its alteration only through outer things, as I, since I think, think my own existence; my persistence is therefore not proved." (E LXXXIII, pp. 32–3; 23:31)

    "No quantum of substance is possible in the soul. Hence also nothing that one could determine through any predicate and call persistent." (E LXXXIV, p.32; 23;31)

[a] *Existenz*
[b] *das Wandelbare*
[c] *Beziehung*

A 185 deduction of the possibility of the latter, it is no wonder that it has, to be sure, grounded all experience (for one feels the need for it in empirical cognition), but has never been proved.

A philosopher was asked: How much does the smoke weigh? He replied: If you take away from the weight of the wood that was burnt the weight of the ashes that are left over, you will have the weight of the smoke. He thus assumed as incontrovertible that even in fire the matter (substance) never disappears but rather only suffers an alteration in its form.*a* Likewise the proposition "Nothing comes from nothing" is only another consequence of the principle of persistence, or rather of the everlasting existence of the proper subject in the appearances. For if that in the appearance which one would call substance is to be the proper substratum of all time-determination, then all existence in the past as well as in future time must be able to be determined in it and it alone. Hence we can grant an appearance the name of substance only if we presuppose its existence at all time, which is not even perfectly expressed through the word "persistence" since this pertains more to fu-

B 229 ture time. Nevertheless the inner necessity of persisting is inseparably connected with the necessity of always having existed, and the expres-

A 186 sion may therefore stand. *Gigni de nihilo nihil, in nihilum nil posse reverti,*b are two propositions which the ancients connected inseparably, and which are now sometimes separated only out of misunderstanding, because one imagines that they pertain to things in themselves, and that the former would be opposed to the dependence of the world on a supreme cause (even as far as its substance is concerned); but this worry is unnecessary, for here the issue is only appearances in the field of experience, the unity of which would never be possible if we were to allow new things (as far as their substance is concerned) to arise. For then everything would disappear that alone can represent the unity of time, namely the identity of the substratum in which alone all change has its thoroughgoing unity. This persistence is therefore nothing more than the way in which we represent the existence of things (in appearance).

The determinations of a substance that are nothing other than particular ways for it to exist are called **accidents**. They are always real, since they concern the existence of the substance (negations are merely determinations that express the non-being of something in the substance).

B 230 Now if one ascribes a particular existence to this real in substance (e.g., motion, as an accident of matter), then this existence is called "inherence," in contrast to the existence of the substance, which is called "sub-

A 187 sistence." Yet many misinterpretations arise from this, and it is more

---

a Inserted in Kant's copy of the first edition: "Whence does he know this? Not from experience." (E LXXXV, p. 34; 23:47)

b Nothing comes out of nothing, and nothing can revert into nothing.

precise and correct if one characterizes the accident only through the way in which the existence of a substance is positively determined.[70] Nevertheless, thanks to the conditions of the logical use of our understanding, it is still unavoidable for us to abstract out, as it were, that which can change in the existence of a substance while the substance remains, and to consider it in relation to what is really persistent and fundamental;[a] thus this category also stands under the title of relations, but more as their condition than as itself containing a relation.

Now on this persistence there is also grounded a correction of the concept of **alteration.** Arising and perishing are not alterations of that which arises or perishes. Alteration is a way of existing that succeeds another way of existing of the very same object. Hence everything that is altered is **lasting,** and only its **state changes.**[71] Thus since this change concerns only the determinations that can cease or begin, we can say, in an expression that seems somewhat paradoxical, that only what persists (the substance) is altered, while that which is changeable[b] does not suffer any alteration but rather a **change,** since some determinations cease and others begin.

B231

Alteration can therefore be perceived only in substances, and arising or perishing per se cannot be a possible perception unless it concerns merely a determination of that which persists, for it is this very thing that persists that makes possible the representation of the transition from one state into another, and from non-being into being, which can therefore be empirically cognized only as changing determinations of that which lasts.[72] If you assume that something simply began to be, then you would have to have a point of time in which it did not exist. But what would you attach this to, if not to that which already exists? For an empty time that would precede is not an object of perception; but if you connect this origination to things that existed antecedently and which endure until that which arises, then the latter would be only a determination of the former, as that which persists. It is just the same with perishing: for this presupposes the empirical representation of a time at which there is no longer an appearance.

A188

Substances (in appearance) are the substrata of all time-determinations. The arising of some of them and the perishing of others would itself remove the sole condition of the empirical unity of time, and the appearances would then be related to two different times, in which existence flowed side by side, which is absurd. For there is **only one** time, in which all different times must not be placed simultaneously but only one after another.

B232

A189

Persistence is accordingly a necessary condition under which alone

---

[a] *das eigentliche Beharrliche und Radikale*
[b] *das Wandelbare*

appearances, as things or objects, are determinable in a possible experience. As to the empirical criterion of this necessary persistence and with it of the substantiality of appearances, however, what follows will give us the opportunity to note what is necessary.[73]

B.
Second Analogy.
<Principle of temporal sequence according to the law of causality.>[a,74]

[*In the first edition:*]
Everything that happens (begins to be) presupposes something which it follows in accordance with a rule.

[*In the second edition:*]
<All alterations occur in accordance with the law of the connection of cause and effect.>

Proof

<[b](That all appearances of the temporal sequence are collectively only **alterations,** i.e., a successive being and not-being of the determinations of the substance that persists there, consequently that the being of the substance itself, which succeeds its not-being, or its not-being, which succeeds its being, in other words, that the arising or perishing of the substance does not occur, the previous principle has shown. This could also have been expressed thus: **All change (succession) of appearances is only alteration;** for the arising or perishing of substance are not alterations of it, since the concept of alteration presupposes one and the same subject as existing with two opposed determinations, and thus as persisting. – After this preliminary reminder the proof follows.)

I perceive that appearances succeed one another, i.e., that a state of things exists at one time the opposite of which existed in the previous state. Thus I really connect two perceptions in time. Now connection is not the work of mere sense and intuition, but is here rather the product of a synthetic faculty of the imagination, which determines inner sense with regard to temporal relations. This, however, can combine the two states in question in two different ways, so that either one or the other precedes in time; for time cannot be perceived in itself, nor can what precedes and what follows in objects[c] be as it were empirically determined in relation[d] to it. I am therefore only conscious that my

B233

---

[a] In the first edition: "Principle of Generation."
[b] The following two paragraphs were added in the second edition.
[c] *Objecte*
[d] *Beziehung*

imagination places one state before and the other after, not that the one state precedes the other in the object;*a* or, in other words, through the mere perception the **objective relation** of the appearances that are succeeding one another remains undetermined. Now in order for this to be cognized as determined, the relation between the two states must be thought in such a way that it is thereby necessarily determined which of them must be placed before and which after rather than vice versa. The concept, however, that carries a necessity of synthetic unity with it can only be a pure concept of understanding, which does not lie in the perception, and that is here the concept of the **relation of cause and effect,** the former of which determines the latter in time, as its consequence,*b* and not as something that could merely precede in the imagination*c* (or not even be perceived at all). Therefore it is only because we subject the sequence of the appearances and thus all alteration to the law of causality that experience itself, i.e., empirical cognition of them, is possible; consequently they themselves, as objects of experience, are possible only in accordance with this law.>

 *d*The apprehension of the manifold of appearance is always successive. The representations of the parts succeed one another. Whether they also succeed in the object is a second point for reflection, which is not contained in the first. Now one can, to be sure, call everything, and even every representation, insofar as one is conscious of it, an object;*e* only what this word is to mean in the case of appearances, not insofar as they are (as representations) objects,*f* but rather only insofar as they designate an object,*g* requires a deeper investigation. Insofar as they are, merely as representations, at the same time objects of consciousness, they do not differ from their apprehension, i.e., from their being taken up into the synthesis of the imagination, and one must therefore say that the manifold of appearances is always successively generated in the mind. If appearances were things in themselves, then no human being would be able to assess from the succession of representations how the manifold is combined in the object.*b* For we have to do only with our representations; how things in themselves may be (without regard to

B234

A189

B235
A190

---

a *Objecte*
b *Folge*
c *in der Einbildung*
d Although the text common to the two editions resumes here, in his copy of the first edition Kant crossed out the next fourteen paragraphs, through A201/B246, suggesting that at one point he had contemplated an extensive revision of the second analogy that he did not in the end undertake (E, p. 34).
e *Object*
f *Objecte*
g *Object*
b *Object*

representations through which they affect us) is entirely beyond our cognitive sphere. Now although the appearances are not things in themselves, and nevertheless are the only thing that can be given to us for cognition, I still have to show what sort of combination in time pertains to the manifold in the appearances itself even though the representation of it in apprehension is always successive. Thus, e.g., the apprehension of the manifold in the appearance of a house that stands before me is successive. Now the question is whether the manifold of this house itself is also successive, which certainly no one will concede. Now, however, as soon as I raise my concept of an object to transcendental significance, the house is not a thing in itself at all but only an appearance, i.e., a representation, the transcendental object of which is unknown; therefore what do I understand by the question, how the manifold may be combined in the appearance itself (which is yet nothing in itself)? Here that which lies in the successive apprehension is considered as representation, but the appearance that is given to me, in spite of the fact that it is nothing more than a sum of these representations, is considered as their object, with which my concept, which I draw from the representations of apprehension, is to agree. One quickly sees that, since the agreement of cognition with the object^a is truth, only the formal conditions of empirical truth can be inquired after here, and appearance, in contradistinction to the representations of apprehension, can thereby only be represented as the object^b that is distinct from them if it stands under a rule that distinguishes it from every other apprehension, and makes one way of combining the manifold necessary. That in the appearance which contains the condition of this necessary rule of apprehension is the object.^{c}

B 236
A 191

Now let us proceed to our problem. That something happens, i.e., that something or a state comes to be that previously was not, cannot be empirically perceived except where an appearance precedes that does not contain this state in itself; for a reality that would follow on an empty time, thus an arising not preceded by any state of things, can be apprehended just as little as empty time itself. Every apprehension of an occurrence is therefore a perception that follows another one. Since this is the case in all synthesis of apprehension, however, as I have shown above in the case of the appearance of a house, the apprehension of an occurrence is not yet thereby distinguished from any other. Yet I also note that, if in the case of an appearance that contains a happening I call the preceding state of perception A and the following one B, then B can only follow A in apprehension, but the perception A cannot fol-

B 237
A 192

---

^{a} *Object*
^{b} *Object*
^{c} *Object*

low but only precede *B*. E.g., I see a ship driven downstream. My perception of its position downstream follows the perception of its position upstream, and it is impossible that in the apprehension of this appearance the ship should first be perceived downstream and afterwards upstream. The order in the sequence of the perceptions in apprehension is therefore here determined, and the apprehension is bound to it. In the previous example of a house my perceptions could have begun at its rooftop and ended at the ground, but could also have begun below and ended above; likewise I could have apprehended the manifold of empirical intuition from the right or from the left. In the series of these perceptions there was therefore no determinate order that made it necessary when I had to begin in the apprehension in order to combine the manifold empirically. But this rule is always to be found in the perception of that which happens, and it makes the order of perceptions that follow one another (in the apprehension of this appearance) **necessary.**

In our case I must therefore derive the **subjective sequence** of apprehension from the **objective sequence** of appearances, for otherwise the former would be entirely undetermined and no appearance would be distinguished from any other. The former alone proves nothing about the connection of the manifold in the object,[a] because it is entirely arbitrary. This connection must therefore consist in the order of the manifold of appearance in accordance with which the apprehension of one thing (that which happens) follows that of the other (which precedes) **in accordance with a rule.** Only thereby can I be justified in saying of the appearance itself, and not merely of my apprehension, that a sequence is to be encountered in it, which is to say as much as that I cannot arrange the apprehension otherwise than in exactly this sequence.

In accordance with such a rule there must therefore lie in that which in general precedes an occurrence the condition for a rule, in accordance with which this occurrence always and necessarily follows; conversely, however, I cannot go back from the occurrence and determine (through apprehension) what precedes. For no appearance goes back from the following point of time to the preceding one, but it is related merely to **some preceding point or other;** on the contrary, the progress from a given time to the determinately following one is necessary. Hence, since there is still something that follows, I must necessarily relate it to something else in general that precedes, and on which it follows in accordance with a rule, i.e., necessarily, so that the occurrence, as the conditioned, yields a secure indication of some condition, but it is the latter that determines the occurrence.

If one were to suppose that nothing preceded an occurrence that it must follow in accordance with a rule, then all sequence of perception

B238

A193

B239

A194

[a] *Object*

307

would be determined solely in apprehension, i.e., merely subjectively, but it would not thereby be objectively determined which of the perceptions must really be the preceding one and which the succeeding one. In this way we would have only a play of representations that would not be related to any object[a] at all, i.e., by means of our perception no appearance would be distinguished from any other as far as the temporal relation is concerned, since the succession in the apprehending is always the same, and there is therefore nothing in the appearance that determines it so that a certain sequence is thereby made necessary as objective. I would therefore not say that in appearance two states follow one another, but rather only that one apprehension follows the other, which is something merely **subjective,** and determines no object,[b] and thus cannot count as the cognition of any object (not even in the appearance).

If, therefore, we experience that something happens, then we always presuppose that something else precedes it, which it follows in accordance with a rule. For without this I would not say of the object[c] that it follows, since the mere sequence in my apprehension, if it is not, by means of a rule, determined in relation to something preceding, does not justify any sequence in the object.[d] Therefore I always make my subjective synthesis (of apprehension) objective with respect to a rule in accordance with which the appearances in their sequence, i.e., as they occur, are determined through the preceding state, and only under this presupposition alone is the experience of something that happens even possible.

To be sure, it seems as if this contradicts everything that has always been said about the course of the use of our understanding, according to which it is only through the perception and comparison of sequences of many occurrences on preceding appearances that we are led to discover a rule, in accordance with which certain occurrences always follow certain appearances, and are thereby first prompted to form the concept of cause. On such a footing this concept would be merely empirical, and the rule that it supplies, that everything that happens has a cause, would be just as contingent as the experience itself: its universality and necessity would then be merely feigned, and would have no true universal validity, since they would not be grounded *a priori* but only on induction. But the case is the same here as with other pure *a priori* representations (e.g., space and time) that we can extract as clear concepts from experience only because we have put them into experience, and

---

[a] *Object*
[b] *Object*
[c] *Object*
[d] *Objecte*

experience is hence first brought about through them. Of course the logical clarity of this representation of a rule determining the series of occurrences, as that of a concept of cause, is only possible if we have made use of it in experience, but a consideration of it, as the condition of the synthetic unity of the appearances in time, was nevertheless the ground of experience itself, and therefore preceded it *a priori*.

It is therefore important to show by an example that even in experience we never ascribe sequence (of an occurrence, in which something happens that previously did not exist) to the object,[a] and distinguish it from the subjective sequence of our apprehension, except when a rule is the ground that necessitates us to observe this order of the perceptions rather than another, indeed that it is really this necessitation that first makes possible the representation of a succession in the object.[b] B242 A197

We have representations in us, of which we can also become conscious. But let this consciousness reach as far and be as exact and precise as one wants, still there always remain only representations, i.e., inner determinations of our mind in this or that temporal relation. Now how do we come to posit an object[c] for these representations, or ascribe to their subjective reality, as modifications, some sort of objective reality? Objective significance cannot consist in the relation[d] to another representation (of that which one would call the object), for that would simply raise anew the question: How does this representation in turn go beyond itself and acquire objective significance in addition to the subjective significance that is proper to it as a determination of the state of mind? If we investigate what new characteristic is given to our representations by the **relation[e] to an object,** and what is the dignity that they thereby receive, we find that it does nothing beyond making the combination of representations necessary in a certain way, and subjecting them to a rule; and conversely that objective significance is conferred on our representations only insofar as a certain order in their temporal relation is necessary. B243

In the synthesis of the appearances the manifold representations always follow one another. Now by this means no object[f] at all is represented; since through this sequence, which is common to all apprehensions, nothing is distinguished from anything else. But as soon as I perceive or anticipate that there is in this sequence a relation[g] to the A198

---

[a] *Object*
[b] *Object*
[c] *Object*
[d] *Beziehung*
[e] *Beziehung*
[f] *Object*
[g] *Beziehung*

preceding state, from which the representation follows in accordance with a rule, I represent something as an occurrence, or as something that happens, i.e., I cognize an object that I must place in time in a determinate position, which, after the preceding state, cannot be otherwise assigned to it. Thus if I perceive that something happens, then the first thing contained in this representation is that something precedes, for it is just in relation*a* to this that the appearance acquires its temporal relation, that, namely, of existing after a preceding time in which it did not. But it can only acquire its determinate temporal position in this relation through something being presupposed in the preceding state on which it always follows, i.e., follows in accordance with a rule: from which it results, first, that I cannot reverse the series and place that which happens prior to that which it follows; and, second, that if the state that precedes is posited, then this determinate occurrence inevitably and necessarily follows. Thereby does it come about that there is an order among our representations, in which the present one (insofar as it has come to be) points to some preceding state as a correlate, to be sure still undetermined, of this event that is given, which is, however, determinately related to the latter, as its consequence, and necessarily connected with it in the temporal series.

B 244

A 199

Now if it is a necessary law of our sensibility, thus **a formal condition** of all perceptions, that the preceding time necessarily determines the following time (in that I cannot arrive at the following time except by passing through the preceding one), then it is also an indispensable **law of the empirical representation** of the temporal series that the appearances of the past time determine every existence in the following time, and that these, as occurrences, do not take place except insofar as the former determine their existence in time, i.e., establish it in accordance with a rule. For **only in the appearances can we empirically cognize this continuity in the connection***b* of times.

Understanding belongs to all experience and its possibility, and the first thing that it does for this is not to make the representation of the objects distinct, but rather to make the representation of an object possible at all. Now this happens through its conferring temporal order on the appearances and their existence by assigning to each of these, as a consequence, a place in time determined *a priori* in regard to the preceding appearances, without which it would not agree with time itself, which determines the position of all its parts *a priori*. Now this determination of position cannot be borrowed from the relation of the appearances to absolute time (for that is not an object of perception), but, conversely, the appearances themselves must determine their positions

B 245

A 200

---

a *Beziehung*
b *Zusammenhange*

in time for each other, and make this determination in the temporal order necessary, i.e., that which follows or happens must succeed that which was contained in the previous state in accordance with a general rule, from which arises a series of appearances, in which by means of the understanding the very same order and constant connection*a* in the series of possible perceptions is produced and made necessary as would be encountered *a priori* in the form of inner experience (time), in which all perceptions would have to have their place.

That something happens, therefore, is a perception that belongs to a possible experience, which becomes actual if I regard the position of the appearance as determined in time, thus if I regard it as an object*b* that can always be found in the connection*c* of perceptions in accordance with a rule. This rule for determining something with respect to its temporal sequence, however, is that in what precedes, the condition is to be encountered under which the occurrence always (i.e., necessarily) follows. Thus the principle of sufficient reason*d* is the ground of possible experience, namely the objective cognition of appearances with regard to their relation in the successive series*e* of time.

B 246

A 201

The ground of proof of this proposition, however, rests solely on the following moments. To all empirical cognition there belongs the synthesis of the manifold through the imagination, which is always successive; i.e., the representations always follow each other in it. But the order of the sequence (what must precede and what must follow) is not determined in the imagination at all, and the series of successive*f* representations can be taken backwards just as well as forwards. But if this synthesis is a synthesis of apprehension (of the manifold of a given appearance), then the order in the object*g* is determined, or, to speak more precisely, there is therein an order of the successive synthesis that determines an object,*h* in accordance with which something would necessarily have to precede and, if this is posited, the other would necessarily have to follow. If, therefore, my perception is to contain the cognition of an occurrence, namely that something actually happens, then it must be an empirical judgment in which one thinks that the sequence is determined, i.e., that it presupposes another appearance in time which it follows necessarily or in accordance with a rule. Contrariwise, if I were to posit that which precedes and the occurrence did not follow it nec-

B 247

---

a *Zusammenhang*
b *Object*
c *Zusammenhang*
d *der Satz vom zureichenden Grunde*
e *Reihenfolge*
f Following Erdmann, reading *der einander folgender* instead of *der einen der folgenden.*
g *Object*
h *Object*

311

A202

essarily, then I would have to hold it to be only a subjective play of my imaginings, and if I still represented something objective by it I would have to call it a mere dream. Thus the relation of appearances (as possible perceptions) in accordance with which the existence of that which succeeds (what happens) is determined in time necessarily and in accordance with a rule by something that precedes it, consequently the relation of cause to effect, is the condition of the objective validity of our empirical judgments with regard to the series of perceptions, thus of their empirical truth, and therefore of experience. Hence the principle of the causal relation in the sequence of appearances is valid for all objects of experience (under the conditions of succession), since it is itself the ground of the possibility of such an experience.

Here, however, there is a reservation that must be resolved. The principle of causal connection among appearances is, in our formula, limited to the succession[a] of them, although in the use of this principle it turns out that it also applies to their accompaniment,[b] and cause and effect can be simultaneous. E.g., there is warmth in a room that is not to

B248

be encountered in the outside air. I look around for the cause, and find a heated stove. Now this, as the cause, is simultaneous with its effect, the warmth of the chamber; thus here there is no succession[c] in time between cause and effect, rather they are simultaneous, yet the law still

A203

holds. The majority of efficient causes[d] in nature are simultaneous with their effects, and the temporal sequence of the latter is occasioned only by the fact that the cause cannot achieve its entire effect in one instant. But in the instant in which the effect first arises, it is always simultaneous with the causality of its cause, since if the cause had ceased to be an instant before then the effect would never have arisen. Here one must note that it is the **order** of time and not its **lapse** that is taken account of; the relation remains even if no time has elapsed. The time between the causality of the cause and its immediate effect can be **vanishing** (they can therefore be simultaneous), but the temporal relation of the one to the other still remains determinable. If I consider a ball that lies on a stuffed pillow and makes a dent in it as a cause, it is simultaneous with its effect. Yet I still distinguish the two by means of the temporal relation of the dynamical connection. For if I lay the ball on the pillow the dent follows its previously smooth shape; but if (for whatever rea-

B249

son) the pillow has a dent, a leaden ball does not follow it.

The temporal sequence is accordingly the only empirical criterion of the effect in relation[e] to the causality of the cause that precedes it. The

[a] *Reihenfolge*
[b] *Begleitung*, here meaning simultaneous occurrence, as earlier at A183/B226.
[c] *Reihenfolge*
[d] Following the fourth edition, reading "*Ursachen*" instead of "*Ursache*."
[e] *Beziehung*

glass is the cause of the rising of the water above its horizontal plane,   A204
though both appearances are simultaneous. For as soon as I draw the
water into the glass from a larger vessel, something follows, namely the
alteration of the horizontal state which the water had there into a con-
cave state that it assumes in the glass.

This causality leads to the concept of action, this to the concept of
force, and thereby to the concept of substance.[75] Since I will not crowd
my critical project, which concerns solely the sources of synthetic *a priori* cognition, with analyses that address merely the elucidation (not the
amplification) of concepts, I leave the detailed discussion of these concepts to a future system of pure reason – especially since one can already
find such an analysis in rich measure even in the familiar textbooks of
this sort. Yet I cannot leave untouched the empirical criterion of a substance, insofar as it seems to manifest itself better and more readily
through action than through the persistence of the appearance.

Where there is action, consequently activity and force, there is also   B250
substance, and in this alone must the seat of this fruitful source of appearances be sought. That is quite well said; but if one would explain
what one understands by substance, and in so doing avoid a vicious circle, then the question is not so easily answered. How will one infer di-   A205
rectly from the action to the **persistence** of that which acts, which is yet
such an essential and singular characteristic of the substance (*phaenomenon*)? Yet given what we have already said, the solution of the question
is not subject to such a difficulty, though after the usual fashion (proceeding merely analytically with its concepts) it would be entirely insoluble. Action already signifes the relation of the subject of causality to the
effect. Now since all effect consists in that which happens, consequently
in the changeable, which indicates succession in time, the ultimate subject of the changeable is therefore **that which persists,** as the substratum of everything that changes, i.e., the substance. For according to the
principle of causality actions are always the primary ground of all
change of appearances, and therefore cannot lie in a subject that itself
changes, since otherwise further actions and another subject, which determines this change, would be required. Now on this account action, as
a sufficient empirical criterion, proves substantiality without it being
necessary for me first to seek out its persistence through compared per-   B251
ceptions, a way in which the completeness that is requisite for the quantity*a* and strict universality of the concept could not be attained. For that
the primary subject of the causality of all arising and perishing cannot
itself arise and perish (in the field of appearances) is a certain inference,
which leads to empirical necessity and persistence in existence, conse-   A206
quently to the concept of a substance as appearance.

---

a *Größe*

If something happens, the mere arising, without regard to that which comes to be, is already in itself an object of investigation. It is already necessary to investigate the transition from the non-being of a state to this state, assuming that this state contained no quality in the appearance. This arising concerns, as was shown in section A,[a] not the substance (for that does not arise), but its state. It is therefore merely alteration, and not an origination out of nothing. If this origination is regarded as the effect of a foreign cause, then it is called creation, which cannot be admitted as an occurrence among the appearances, for its possibility alone would already undermine the unity of experience, though if I consider all things not as phenomena but rather as things in themselves and as objects of mere understanding, then, though they are substances, they can be regarded as dependent for their existence on a foreign cause; which, however, would introduce entirely new meanings for the words and would not apply to appearances as possible objects of experience.

Now how in general anything can be altered, how it is possible that upon a state in one point of time an opposite one could follow in the next – of these we have *a priori* not the least concept. For this acquaintance with actual forces is required, which can only be given empirically, e.g., acquaintance with moving forces, or, what comes to the same thing, with certain successive appearances (as motions) which indicate such forces. But the form of such an alteration, the condition under which alone it, as the arising of another state, can occur (whatever the content, i.e., the state, that is altered might be), consequently the succession of the states itself (that which has happened), can still be considered *a priori* according to the law of causality and the conditions of time.*

If a substance passes out of a state a into another state b, then the point in time of the latter is different from the point in time of the first state and follows it. Likewise the second state as a reality (in the appearance) is also distinguished from the first, in which it did not yet exist, as b is distinguished from zero; i.e., if the state b differs from the state a even only in magnitude, then the alteration would be an arising of $b-a$, which did not exist in the prior state, and with regard to which the latter = o.

B252

A207

B253

A208

A207/B252 * Note well that I am not talking about the alteration of certain relations[b] in general, but rather of the alteration of the state. Hence if a body is moved uniformly, then it does not alter its state (of motion) at all, although it does if its motion increases or diminishes.

[a] That is, in the "First Analogy."
[b] *Relationen*

Section III. Systematic representation of all synthetic principles

The question therefore arises, how a thing passes from one state = a into another one = b. Between two instants there is always a time, and between two states in those instances there is always a difference that has a magnitude (for all parts of appearances are always in turn magniudes). Thus every transition from one state into another happens in a time that is contained between two instants, of which the former determines the state from which the thing proceeds and the second the state at which it arrives. Both are therefore boundaries of the time of an alteration, consequently of the intermediate state between two states, and as such they belong to the whole alteration. Now every alteration has a cause, which manifests its causality in the entire time during which the alteration proceeds. Thus this cause does not produce its alteration suddenly (all at once or in an instant), but rather in a time, so that as the time increases from the initial instant a to its completion in b, the magnitude of the reality ($b–a$) is also generated through all the smaller degrees that are contained between the first and the last. All alteration is therefore possible only through a continuous action of causality, which, insofar as it is uniform, is called a moment. The alteration does not consist of these moments, but it is generated through them as their effect. A 209

B 254

That is, now, the law of the continuity of all alteration, the ground of which is this: That neither time nor appearance in time consists of smallest parts, and that nevertheless in its alteration the state of the thing passes through all these parts, as elements, to its second state. **No difference** of the real in appearance is **the smallest**, just as no difference in the magnitude of times is, and thus the new state of reality grows out of the first, in which it did not exist, through all the infinite degrees of reality, the differences between which are all smaller than that between o and a.

What utility this proposition may have in research into nature does not concern us here. But how such a proposition, which seems to amplify our cognition of nature so much, is possible completely *a priori*, very much requires our scrutiny, even though it is obvious that it is real and correct, and one might therefore believe oneself to be relieved of the question how it is possible. For there are so many unfounded presumptions of the amplification of our cognition through pure reason that it must be adopted as a general principle to be distrustful of them all and not to believe and accept even the clearest dogmatic proof of this sort of proposition without documents that could provide a well-grounded deduction. B 210

B 255

All growth of empirical cognitions and every advance in perception is nothing but an amplification of the determination of inner sense, i.e., a progress in time, whatever the objects may be, either appearances or pure intuitions. This progress in time determines everything, and is not itself determined by anything further: i.e., its parts are only in time, and given through the synthesis of it, but they are not given before it. For this reason every transition in perception to something that follows in time is a determination of time through the generation of this perception and, since that is always and in all its parts a magnitude, the generation of a perception as a magnitude through all degrees, of which none is the smallest, from zero to its determinate degree. It is from this that the possibility of cognizing *a priori* a law concerning the form of alter-

B 256 ations becomes obvious. We anticipate only our own apprehension, the formal condition of which, since it is present in us prior to all given appearance, must surely be able to be cognized *a priori*.

In the same way, then, that time is the *a priori* sensible condition of the possibility of a continuous progress of that which exists to that which follows it, the understanding, by means of the unity of apperception, is the

A 211 *a priori* condition of the possibility of a continuous determination of all positions for the appearances in this time, through the series of causes and effects, the former of which inevitably draw the existence of the latter after them and thereby make the empirical cognition of temporal relations (universally) valid for all time, thus objectively valid.

C.
Third Analogy.
<Principle of simultaneity, according to the law of interaction, or community.>*ᵃ*

[*In the first edition:*]
All substances, insofar as they are **simultaneous**, stand in thoroughgoing community (i.e., interaction with one another).

[*In the second edition:*]
<All substances, insofar as they can be perceived in space as simultaneous, are in thoroughgoing interaction.>⁷⁶

Proof

ᵇ<Things are **simultaneous** if in empirical intuition the perception of

B 257 one can follow the perception of the other **reciprocally** (which in the temporal sequence of appearances, as has been shown in the case of the second principle, cannot happen). Thus I can direct my perception first to the moon and subsequently to the earth, or, conversely, first to the earth and then subsequently to the moon, and on this account, since the perceptions of these objects can follow each other reciprocally, I say that they exist simultaneously. Now simultaneity is the existence of the manifold at the same time. But one cannot perceive time itself and thereby

---

ᵃ In the first edition: **"Principle of community."**
ᵇ This paragraph added in the second edition.

derive from the fact that things are positioned at the same time that their perceptions can follow each other reciprocally. The synthesis of the imagination in apprehension would therefore only present each of these perceptions as one that is present in the subject when the other is not, and conversely, but not that the objects*a* are simultaneous, i.e., that if the one is then the other also is in the same time, and that this is necessary in order for the perceptions to be able to succeed each other reciprocally. Consequently, a concept of the understanding of the reciprocal sequence of the determinations of these things simultaneously existing externally to each other is required in order to say that the reciprocal sequence of perceptions is grounded in the object,*b* and thereby to represent the simultaneity as objective. Now, however, the relation of substances in which the one contains determinations the ground of which is contained in the other is the relation of influence, and, if the latter reciprocally contains the ground of the determinations of the former, it is the relation of community or interaction. Thus the simultaneity of substances in space cannot be cognized in experience otherwise than under the presupposition of an interaction among them; this is therefore also the condition of the possibility of the things themselves as objects of experience.>   B258

*c*Things are simultaneous insofar as they exist at one and the same time. But how does one cognize that they exist at one and the same time? If the order in the synthesis of the apprehension of this manifold is indifferent, i.e., if it can proceed from A through B, C, and D to E, but also conversely from E to A. For if they existed*d* in time one after the other (in the order that begins with A and ends at E), then it would be impossible to begin the apprehension at the perception of E and proceed backwards to A, since A would belong to past time, and thus can no longer be an object of apprehension.*e*,77   A211

Now if you assume that in a manifold of substances as appearances   A212

---

a Objecte
b Objecte
c The text common to the two editions resumes here.
d Reading *sie wären* instead of *sie wäre*, so that the antecedent can be plural; even so, it remains unclear whether Kant intends the antecedent to be the "things" referred to at the beginning of the paragraph, or the representations A through E constituting the manifold.
e In his copy of the first edition, Kant struck out the preceding paragraph and inserted the following note: "Space makes community possible. Now since the thinking being with all its faculties, whose effects belong merely to inner sense, is not a relation [*Relation*] of space, the *commercium* of the soul with the body is therefore not comprehensible. The community of things in themselves must either have a third substance, in which they exist as *accidentia* and are in relation to one another – Spinozism – or, since this won't do, it remains incomprehensible. Space is itself the *phaenomenon* of possible community. If I consider bodies merely as *phaenomena* that are in me, the cognitive faculty of inner sense may well stand in community with those of outer sense." (E LXXXVI, p. 34; 23:31–2)

each of them would be completely isolated, i.e., none would affect any other nor receive a reciprocal influence from it, then I say that their **simultaneity** would not be the object of a possible perception, and that the existence of the one could not lead to the existence of the other by any path of empirical synthesis. For if you thought that they were separated by a completely empty space, then the perception that proceeds from one to the other in time would certainly determine the existence of the latter by means of a succeeding perception, but would not be able to distinguish whether that appearance objectively follows the former or is rather simultaneous with it.

In addition to the mere existence there must therefore be something through which A determines the position of B in time, and conversely also something by which B does the same for A, since only under this condition can those substances be empirically represented as **existing simultaneously.** Now only that determines the position of another in time which is the cause of it or its determinations. Thus each substance (since it can be a consequence[a] only with regard to its determinations) must simultaneously contain the causality of certain determinations in the other and the effects of the causality of the other, i.e., they must stand in dynamical community (immediately or mediately) if their simultaneity is to be cognized in any possible experience. But now everything in regard to objects of experience is necessary without which the experience of these objects itself would be impossible. Thus it is necessary for all substances in appearance, insofar as they are simultaneous, to stand in thoroughgoing community of interaction with each other.

The word "community"[b] is ambiguous in our language, and can mean either *communio* or *commercium*.[c] We use it here in the latter sense, as a dynamical community, without which even the local community (*communio spatii*)[d] could never be empirically cognized. From our experiences it is easy to notice that only continuous influence in all places in space can lead our sense from one object to another, that the light that plays between our eyes and the heavenly bodies effects a mediate community between us and the latter and thereby proves the simultaneity of the latter, and that we cannot empirically alter any place (perceive this alteration) without matter everywhere making the perception of our position possible; and only by means of its reciprocal influence can it establish their simultaneity and thereby the coexistence of even the most distant objects (though only mediately). Without community

B259

A213

B260

---

[a] *Folge*

[b] *Gemeinschaft*

[c] I.e., "community" or "commerce," the former connoting membership in a common whole but not necessarily interaction among the parts, the latter connoting interaction.

[d] "Community of spaces," that is, a single spatial order or relationship among multiple objects.

every perception (of appearance in space) is broken off from the others, A214
and the chain of empirical representations, i.e., experience, would have
to start entirely over with every new object*a* without the previous one B261
being in the least connected or being able to stand in a temporal relation with it. I do not in the least hereby mean to refute empty space;
that may well exist where perceptions do not reach, and thus where no
empirical cognition of simultaneity takes place; but it is then hardly an
object*b* for our possible experience at all.

The following can serve as an elucidation. In our mind all appearances, as contained in a possible experience, must stand in a community
(*communio*) of apperception, and insofar as the objects are to be represented as being connected by existing simultaneously, they must reciprocally determine their position in one time and thereby constitute a
whole. If this subjective community is to rest on an objective ground, or
is to be related to appearances as substances, then the perception of one,
as ground, must make possible the perception of the other, and conversely, so that the succession that always exists in the perceptions, as
apprehensions, will not be ascribed to the objects,*c* but these can instead
be represented as existing simultaneously. But this is a reciprocal influence, i.e., a real community (*commercium*) of substances, without which
the empirical relation of simultaneity could not obtain in experience. A215
Through this commerce*d* the appearances, insofar as they stand outside
one another and yet in connection, constitute a composite*e* (*compositum* B262
reale*), and composites*f* of this sort are possible in many ways. Hence the
three dynamical relations, from which all others arise, are those of inherence, of consequence, and of composition.*g*

* * *

These, then, are the three analogies of experience. They are nothing
other than principles of the determination of the existence of appearances in time, in accordance with all three of its *modi:* that of the relation to time itself, as a magnitude (the magnitude of existence, i.e.,
duration); that of the relation in time, as a series (one after another); and
finally that in time as a sum of all existence (simultaneous). This unity
of time-determination is through and through dynamical, i.e., time is
not regarded as that within which experience immediately determines

a *Object*
b *Object*
c *Objecten*
d *Commercium*, printed as a German rather than Latin word.
e *Zusammengesetztes*
f *Composita*, printed as a German rather than Latin word.
g *Composition*

the position of each existence, which is impossible, since absolute time is not an object of perception by means of which appearances could be held together; rather the rule of the understanding, through which alone the existence of appearances can acquire synthetic unity in temporal relations, determines the position of each of them in time, thus *a priori* and validly for each and every time.

A 216/B 263   By nature (in the empirical sense) we understand the combination of appearances as regards their existence, in accordance with necessary rules, i.e., in accordance with laws. There are therefore certain laws, and indeed *a priori*, which first make a nature possible; the empirical laws can only obtain and be found by means of experience, and indeed in accord with its original laws, in accordance with which experience itself first becomes possible. Our analogies therefore really exhibit the unity of nature in the combination of all appearances under certain exponents, which express nothing other than the relation of time (insofar as it comprehends all existence in itself) to the unity of apperception, which can only obtain in synthesis in accordance with rules. Thus together they say: All appearances lie in one nature, and must lie therein, since without this *a priori* unity no unity of experience, thus also no determination of the objects in it, would be possible.

About the method of proof, however, which we have employed in the case of these transcendental laws of nature, and about its singularity, one remark is to be made, which must be very important as a precept for every other attempt to prove intellectual and at the same time synthetic *a priori* propositions. If we had wanted to prove these analogies dogmatically, i.e., from concepts – namely, that everything that exists

B 264
A 217   will only be encountered in that which persists; that every occurrence presupposes something in the previous state, which it follows in accordance with a rule; finally, that in the manifold that is simultaneous the states are simultaneous in relation*[a]* to each other in accordance with a rule (stand in community) – then all effort would have been entirely in vain. For one cannot get from one object and its existence to the existence of another or its way of existing through mere concepts of these things, no matter how much one analyzes them. So what is left for us? The possibility of experience, as a cognition in which in the end all objects must be able to be given to us if their representation is to have objective reality for us. In this third thing, now, the essential form of which consists in the synthetic unity of the apperception of all appearances, we found *a priori* conditions of the thoroughgoing and necessary time-determination of all existence in appearance, without which even empirical time-determination would be impossible, and we found rules of synthetic *a priori* unity by means of which we could anticipate expe-

[a] *Beziehung*

320

rience. In the absence of this method, and in the delusion of wanting to prove dogmatically synthetic propositions that the empirical use of the understanding recommends as its principles,[a] a proof of the principle of sufficient reason was often sought, but always in vain. No one ever even thought of the other two analogies, though one always tacitly employed them,* since the clue of the categories was missing, which alone can uncover and make noticeable every gap of the understanding, in concepts as well as in principles.

B 265

A 218

4.
The postulates
of empirical thinking in general.[78]

1. Whatever agrees with the formal conditions of experience (in accordance with intuition and concepts) is **possible.**
2. That which is connected[b] with the material conditions of experience (of sensation) is **actual.**
3. That whose connection[c] with the actual is determined in accordance with general conditions of experience is (exists) **necessarily.**[d]

B 266

---

* The unity of the world-whole, in which all appearances are to be connected, is obviously a mere conclusion from the tacitly assumed principle of the community of all substances that are simultaneous: for, were they isolated, they would not as parts constitute a whole, and were their connection (interaction of the manifold) not already necessary on account of simultaneity, then one could not infer from the latter, as a merely ideal relation, to the former, as a real one. Nevertheless we have shown, in its proper place, that community is really the ground of the possibility of an empirical cognition of coexistence, and that one therefore really only infers from the latter back to the former, as its condition.

A 218/B 265

---

[a] *Principien*
[b] *zusammenhängt*
[c] *Zusammenhang*
[d] The following notes are entered in Kant's copy of the first edition following A218:
   "The contingency of the alterable is only inferred from the fact that in accordance with the second analogy every state of its existence always requires a ground, and not vice versa, that it always requires a ground because it is contingent. We call absolutely contingent that which has no sufficient ground; never here, since it is never complete." (E LXXXVII, p. 35; 23:32)
   "On possibility: That the concept of which can be given in a corresponding intuition is possible." (E LXXXVIII, p. 35; 23:32)
   "What can be thought indeterminately in any time [is possible]." (E LXXXIX, p. 35; 23:32)
   "That which is determined in time [is actual]." (E XC, p. 36; 23:32)
   "That which is determined through the concept of time itself [is (exists) necessarily]." (E XCI, p. 36; 23:32)

A 2 1 9   Elucidation

The categories of modality have this peculiarity: as a determination of the object *a* they do not augment the concept to which they are ascribed in the least, but rather express only the relation *b* to the faculty of cognition. If the concept of a thing is already entirely complete, I can still ask about this object whether it is merely possible, or also actual, or, if it is the latter, whether it is also necessary? No further determinations in the object *c* itself are hereby thought; rather, it is only asked: how is the object itself (together with all its determinations) related to the understanding and its empirical use, to the empirical power of judgment, and to reason (in its application to experience)?

For this very reason the principles of modality are also nothing further than definitions of the concepts of possibility, actuality, and necessity in their empirical use, and thus at the same time restrictions of all categories to merely empirical use, without any permission and allowance for their transcendental use. For if the categories are not to
B 267   have a merely logical significance and analytically express the form of **thinking**, but are to concern **things** and their possibility, actuality, and necessity, then they must pertain to possible experience and its synthetic unity, in which alone objects of cognition are given.
A 2 2 0   The postulate of the possibility of things thus requires that their con-

---

"That which is determined in time and space is actual. Against idealism." (E XCII, p. 36; 23:32)

"Everything actual is necessary, either absolutely or hypothetically. That, however, holds only of *noumena;* for absolute contingency of things in themselves cannot be thought." (E XCIII, p. 36; 23:32)

"That which exists, thus in other things outside our thoughts, is thoroughly determined. This proposition is the principle [*Princip*] of the concept of an *ens realissimus* [most real being] as *conceptus originarii* [concept of the origin]. Whence the concept of the absolute necessity of this?

"Therein also belongs the proposition that all negations are limitations. This is the synthetic method of **reason.**" (E XCIV, p. 36; 23:32–3)

"We do not attribute contingency to substances, but only to the alterable accidents. Causes." (E XCV, p. 36; 23:33)

"The three criteria of hypotheses, always only in relation to experience. The possibility of the hypothesis, the reality of that which is thought up in behalf of the hypothesis. Its necessity must be certain." (E XCVI, p. 36; 23:33)

a *Objects*

b In this section, as in the preceding, Kant continues the frequent use of *Verhältnis* rather than *Beziehung,* even here where he is speaking about a relation between the cognitive faculty and its object rather than among objects, and thus by the usage of the "Transcendental Aesthetic" the latter term might have been expected. Unless otherwise noted, our "relation" translates *Verhältnis.*

c *Objecte*

cept agree with the formal conditions of an experience in general. This, however, namely the objective form of experience in general, contains all synthesis that is requisite for the cognition of objects.[a] A concept that includes a synthesis in it is to be held as empty, and does not relate to any object, if this synthesis does not belong to experience, either as borrowed from it, in which case it is an **empirical concept,** or as one on which, as *a priori* condition, experience in general (its form) rests, and then it is a **pure concept,** which nevertheless belongs to experience, since its object[b] can be encountered only in the latter. For whence will one derive the character of the possibility of an object that is thought by means of a synthetic *a priori* concept, if not from the synthesis that constitutes the form of the empirical cognition of objects?[c] That in such a concept no contradiction must be contained is, to be sure, a necessary logical condition; but B268 it is far from sufficient for the objective reality of the concept, i.e., for the possibility of such an object as is thought through the concept.[79] Thus in the concept of a figure that is enclosed between two straight lines there is no contradiction, for the concepts of two straight lines and their intersection contain no negation of a figure; rather the impossibility rests not A221 on the concept in itself, but on its construction in space, i.e., on the conditions of space and its determinations; but these in turn have their objective reality, i.e., they pertain to possible things, because they contain in themselves *a priori* the form of experience in general.

We shall now make obvious the extensive utility and influence of this postulate of possibility. If I represent to myself a thing that persists, so that everything that changes merely belongs to its states, I can never cognize from such a concept alone that such a thing is possible. Or, if I represent something to myself that is so constituted that if it is posited something else always and inevitably succeeds it, this may well be able to be so thought without contradiction; but whether such a property (as causality) will be encountered in any possible thing cannot thereby be judged. Finally, I can represent various things (sub- B269 stances) to myself that are so constituted that the state of one is followed by a consequence in the state of the other, and conversely; but whether such a relation can pertain to any things cannot be derived from these concepts, which contain a merely arbitrary synthesis. Thus only from the fact that these concepts express *a priori* the relations of the perceptions in every experience does one cognize their objective reality, i.e., their transcendental truth, and, to be sure, independently A222 of experience, but yet not independently of all relation[d] to the form of

[a] *Objecte*
[b] *Object*
[c] *Objecte*
[d] *Beziehung*

an experience in general and the synthetic unity in which alone objects can be empirically cognized.

But if one wanted to make entirely new concepts of substances, of forces, and of interactions from the material that perception offers us, without borrowing the example of their connection from experience itself, then one would end up with nothing but figments of the brain, for the possibility of which there would be no indications at all, since in their case one did not accept experience as instructress nor borrow these concepts from it. Invented concepts of this sort cannot acquire the character of their possibility *a priori*, like the categories, as conditions on which all experience depends, but only *a posteriori*, as ones given through experience itself, and their possibility must either be cognized

B270   *a posteriori* and empirically or not cognized at all. A substance that was persistently present in space yet without filling it (like that intermediate thing between matter and thinking beings, which some would introduce),[80] or a special fundamental power of our mind to *intuit* the future (not merely, say, to deduce it), or, finally, a faculty of our mind to stand in a community of thoughts with other men (no matter how dis-

A223   tant they may be)[81] – these are concepts the possibility of which is entirely groundless, because it cannot be grounded in experience and its known laws, and without this it is an arbitrary combination of thoughts that, although it contains no contradiction, still can make no claim to objective reality, thus to the possibility of the sort of object that one would here think. As far as reality is concerned, it is evidently intrinsically forbidden to think it *in concreto* without getting help from experience, because it can only pertain to sensation, as the matter of experience, and does not concern the form of the relation that one can always play with in fictions.[a]

But I leave aside everything the possibility of which can only be derived from actuality in experience, and consider here only the possibility of things through concepts *a priori*, about which I proceed to

B271   assert that it can never occur by itself solely from such concepts, but always only as formal and objective conditions of an experience in general.

It may look, to be sure, as if the possibility of a triangle could be cognized from its concept in itself (it is certainly independent of experience); for in fact we can give it an object entirely *a priori*, i.e., construct it. But since this is only the form of an object, it would still always re-

A224   main only a product of the imagination, the possibility of whose object would still remain doubtful, as requiring something more, namely that such a figure be thought solely under those conditions on which all objects of experience rest. Now that space is a formal *a priori* condition of

[a] *Erdichtungen*

outer experiences, that this very same formative *a* synthesis by means of which we construct a figure in imagination is entirely identical with that which we exercise in the apprehension of an appearance in order to make a concept of experience of it – it is this alone that connects with this concept the representation of the possibility of such a thing. And thus the possibility of continuous magnitudes, indeed even of magnitudes in general, since the concepts of them are all synthetic, is never clear from the concepts themselves, but only from them as formal conditions of the determination of objects in experience in general; and where should one want to seek objects that correspond to the concepts, if not in the experience through which alone objects are given to us? – although without anticipating experience itself we can cognize and characterize the possibility of things solely in relation to the formal conditions under which something can be determined as an object in experience at all, thus fully *a priori* but only in relation*b* to these conditions and within their boundaries.[82]

B272

The postulate for cognizing the **actuality** of things requires **perception,** thus sensation of which one is conscious – not immediate perception of the object itself the existence of which is to be cognized, but still its connection with some actual perception in accordance with the analogies of experience, which exhibit all real connection in an experience in general.

A225

In the **mere concept** of a thing no characteristic of its existence can be encountered at all. For even if this concept is so complete that it lacks nothing required for thinking of a thing with all of its inner determinations, still existence has nothing in the least to do with all of this, but only with the question of whether such a thing is given to us in such a way that the perception of it could in any case precede the concept. For that the concept precedes the perception signifies its mere possibility; but perception, which yields the material for the concept, is the sole characteristic of actuality. However, one can also cognize the existence of the thing prior to the perception of it, and therefore cognize it comparatively *a priori*, if only it is connected*c* with some perceptions in accordance with the principles of their empirical connection*d* (the analogies). For in that case the existence of the thing is still connected*e* with our perceptions in a possible experience, and with the guidance of the analogies we can get from our actual perceptions to the thing in the series of possible perceptions. Thus we cognize the existence of a magnetic mat-

B273

A226

---

a *bildende*
b *Beziehung*
c *zusammenhängt*
d *Verknüpfung*
e *hängt . . . zusammen*

ter penetrating all bodies from the perception of attracted iron filings, although an immediate perception of this matter is impossible for us given the constitution of our organs. For in accordance with the laws of sensibility and the context of our perceptions we could also happen upon the immediate empirical intuition of it in an experience if our senses, the crudeness of which does not affect the form of possible experience in general, were finer. Thus wherever perception and whatever is appended to it in accordance with empirical laws reaches, there too reaches our cognition of the existence of things. If we do not begin with experience, B274 or proceed in accordance with laws of the empirical connection[a] of appearances, then we are only making a vain display of wanting to discover or research the existence of any thing. [b]<However, a powerful objection against these rules for proving existence mediately is made by **idealism,** the refutation of which belongs here.

* * *

Refutation of Idealism[83]

Idealism (I mean **material** idealism) is the theory that declares the existence of objects in space outside us to be either merely doubtful and **indemonstrable,** or else false and **impossible; the former** is the **problematic** idealism of Descartes, who declares only one empirical assertion (*assertio),* namely **I am,** to be indubitable; the **latter** is the **dogmatic** idealism of Berkeley, who declares space, together with all the things to which it is attached as an inseparable condition, to be something that is impossible in itself, and who therefore also declares things in space to be merely imaginary.[84] Dogmatic idealism is unavoidable if one regards space as a property that is to pertain to the things in themselves; for then it, along with everything for which it serves as a condition, is a non-entity. The ground for this idealism, however, has been undercut by us in the Transcendental Aesthetic. Problematic idealism, B275 which does not assert anything about this, but rather professes only our incapacity for proving an existence outside us from our own by means of immediate experience, is rational and appropriate for a thorough philosophical manner of thought, allowing, namely, no decisive judgment until a sufficient proof has been found. The proof that is demanded must therefore establish that we have **experience** and not merely **imagination** of outer things, which cannot be accomplished unless one can prove that even our **inner experience,** undoubted by Descartes, is possible only under the presupposition of outer experience.

[a] *Zusammenhanges*
[b] The following sentence, the ensuing "Refutation of Idealism," and its proof and the subsequent remarks are all added in the second edition (B274–9).

Theorem

The mere, but empirically determined, consciousness of my own existence proves the existence of objects in space outside me.

Proof

I am conscious of my existence as determined in time. All time-determination presupposes something **persistent** in perception. This persistent thing, however, cannot be something in me, since my own existence in time can first be determined only through this persistent thing.[a] Thus the perception of this persistent thing is possible only through a **thing** outside me and not through the mere **representation** of a thing outside me. Consequently, the determination of my existence in time is possible only by means of the existence[b] of actual things that I perceive outside myself. Now consciousness in time is necessarily   B276 combined with the consciousness of the possibility of this time-determination: Therefore it is also necessarily combined with the existence[c] of the things outside me, as the condition of time-determination; i.e., the consciousness of my own existence is at the same time an immediate consciousness of the existence of other things outside me.

Note 1. One will realize that in the preceding proof the game that idealism plays has with greater justice been turned against it. Idealism assumed that the only immediate experience is inner experience, and that from that outer things could only be **inferred,** but, as in any case in which one infers from given effects to **determinate** causes, only unreliably, since the cause of the representations that we perhaps falsely ascribe to outer things can also lie in us. Yet here it is proved that outer experience is really immediate,* that only by means of it is possible not,   B277

---

* The **immediate** consciousness of the existence of outer things is not presupposed but proved in the preceding theorem, whether we have insight into the possibility of this consciousness or not. The question about the latter would be whether we have only an inner sense but no outer one, rather merely outer imagination. But it is clear that in order for us even to imagine something as external, i.e., to exhibit it to sense in intuition, we must already have an outer sense, and by this means immediately distinguish the mere receptivity of an   B277

   B276

[a] According to the revised preface (B xxxix), this sentence is to be replaced by the following: "This persistent thing, however, cannot be an intuition in me. For all grounds of determination of my existence that can be encountered in me are representations, and as such require something persistent that is distinct even from them, in relation to which their change, thus my existence in the time in which they change, can be determined."

[b] *Existenz*

[c] *Existenz*

to be sure, the consciousness of our own existence, but its determination in time, i.e., inner experience. Of course, the representation **I am,** which expresses the consciousness that can accompany all thinking, is that which immediately includes the existence*a* of a subject in itself, but not yet any **cognition** of it, thus not empirical cognition, i.e., experience; for to that there belongs, besides the thought of something existing, intuition, and in this case inner intuition, i.e., time, in regard to which the subject must be determined, for which outer objects are absolutely requisite, so that inner experience itself is consequently only mediate and possible only through outer experience.[85]

Note 2. All use of our faculty of cognition in experience for the determination of time agrees with this completely. Not only can we perceive*b* all time-determination only through the change in outer relations (motion) relative to that which persists in space (e.g., the motion of the sun with regard to the objects on the earth);[86] we do not even have anything persistent on which we could base the concept of a substance, as intuition, except merely **matter,** and even this persistence is not drawn from outer experience, but rather presupposed *a priori* as the necessary condition of all time-determination, thus also as the determination of inner sense in regard to our own existence through the existence*c* of outer things. The consciousness of myself in the representation **I** is no intuition at all, but a merely **intellectual** representation of the self-activity of a thinking subject. And hence this **I** does not have the least predicate of intuition that, as **persistent,** could serve as the correlate for time-determination in inner sense, as, say, **impenetrability** in matter, as **empirical** intuition, does.[87]

Note 3. From the fact that the existence*d* of outer objects is required for the possibility of a determinate consciousness of our self it does not follow that every intuitive representation of outer things includes at the same time their existence, for that may well be the mere effect of the imagination (in dreams as well as in delusions); but this is possible merely through the reproduction of previous outer perceptions, which, as has been shown, are possible only through the actuality of outer objects. Here it had to be proved only that inner experience in general is possible only through outer experience in general. Whether this or that

outer intuition from the spontaneity that characterizes every imagining. For even merely to imagine an outer sense would itself annihilate the faculty of intuition, which is to be determined through the imagination.

a *Existenz*
b Following Erdmann, reading *"wahrnehmen"* instead of *"vornehmen."*
c *Existenz*
d *Existenz* here and in the remainder of this sentence.

putative experience is not mere imagination must be ascertained according to its particular determinations and through its coherence with the criteria of all actual experience.

* * *>

^aFinally, as far as the third postulate is concerned, it pertains to material necessity in existence, not the merely formal and logical necessity in the connection of concepts.[88] Now since no existence^b of objects of the senses can be cognized fully *a priori*, but always only comparatively *a priori* relative to another already given existence, but since nevertheless even then we can only arrive at an existence^c that must be contained somewhere in the nexus of experience of which the given perception is a part, the necessity of existence^d can thus never be cognized from concepts but rather always only from the connection with that which is perceived, in accordance with general laws of experience. Now there is no existence that could be cognized as necessary under the condition of other given appearances except the existence of effects from given causes in accordance with laws of causality. Thus it is not the existence of things (substances) but of their state of which alone we can cognize the necessity, and moreover only from other states, which are given in perception, in accordance with empirical laws of causality. From this it follows that the criterion of necessity lies solely in the law of possible experience that everything that happens is determined *a priori* through its cause in appearance. Hence we cognize only the necessity of **effects** in nature, the causes of which are given to us, and the mark of necessity in existence does not reach beyond the field of possible experience, and even in this it does not hold of the existence^e of things, as substances, since these can never be regarded as empirical effects, or as something that happens and arises. Necessity therefore concerns only the relations of appearances in accordance with the dynamical law of causality, and the possibility grounded upon it of inferring *a priori* from some given existence (a cause) to another existence (the effect). Everything that happens is hypothetically necessary; that is a principle that subjects alteration in the world to a law, i.e., a rule of necessary existence, without which not even nature itself would obtain. Hence the proposition "Nothing happens through a mere accident" (*in mundo non datur casus*)^f

A226

A227

B280

A228

---

^a The text common to the two editions resumes here.
^b *Existenz*
^c *Existenz*
^d *Existenz*
^e *Existenz*
^f In the world there is no chance.

is an *a priori* law of nature; likewise the proposition "No necessity in nature is blind, but is rather conditioned, consequently comprehensible

B 281 necessity" (*non datur fatum*).*a* Both are laws of the sort through which the play of alterations is subjected to a **nature of things** (as appearances), or, what is the same thing, to the unity of the understanding, in which alone they can belong to an experience, as the synthetic unity of appearances. Both of these belong to the dynamical principles. The first is properly a consequence of the principle of causality (under the analogies of experience). The second belongs to the principles of modality, which adds to the causal determination the concept of necessity, which, however, stands under a rule of understanding. The principle of continuity forbade any leap in the series of appearances (alterations) (*in*

A 229 *mundo non datur saltus*),*b* but also any gap or cleft between two appearances in the sum of all empirical intuitions in space (*non datur hiatus*);*c* for one can express the proposition thus: "Nothing can enter experience that proves a *vacuum*d or even permits it as a part of empirical synthesis." For as far as concerns the void that one might think of outside of the field of possible experience (the world), this does not belong to the jurisdiction of the mere understanding, which only decides about questions concerning the use of given appearances for empirical cognition, and it is a problem for ideal reason, which goes beyond the sphere of a

B 282 possible experience and would judge about what surrounds and bounds this, and must therefore be considered in the transcendental dialectic. We could easily represent the order of these four propositions (*in mundo non datur hiatus, non datur saltus, non datur casus, non datur fatum*)*e* in accordance with the order of the categories, just like all principles of transcendental origin, and show each its position, but the already practiced reader will do this for himself or easily discover the clue to it. However, they are all united simply in this, that they do not permit anything in empirical synthesis that could violate or infringe the understanding and the continuous connection*f* of all appearances, i.e., the unity of its con-

A 230 cepts. For it is in this alone that the unity of experience, in which all perceptions must have their place, is possible.

Whether the field of possibility is greater than the field that contains everything actual, and whether the latter is in turn greater than the set*g* of that which is necessary, are proper questions, and can, to be sure, be

---

a There is no fate.

b In the world there is no leap.

c There is no hiatus.

d Inserted in Kant's copy of the first edition: "The *vacuum physicum* is different from the *vacuum metaphysicum*, in which there is no effect at all." (E XCVII, p. 36; 23:33)

e In the world there is no hiatus, there is no leap, there is no chance, there is no fate.

f *Zusammenhange*

g *Menge*

solved synthetically, though they also fall under the jurisdiction of reason alone; for they mean, roughly, to ask whether all things, as appearances, belong together in the sum total and the context of a single experience, of which each given perception is a part which therefore could not be combined with any other appearances, or whether my perceptions could belong to more than one possible experience (in their general connection).[a] The understanding gives *a priori* to experience in general only the rule, in accordance with the subjective and formal conditions of sensibility as well as of apperception, which alone make it possible. Even were they possible, we could still not conceive of and make comprehensible other forms of intuition (than space and time) or other forms of understanding (than the discursive form of thinking, or that of cognition through concepts); and even if we could, they would still not belong to experience, as the sole cognition in which objects are given to us. Whether other perceptions than those which in general belong to our entire possible experience and therefore an entirely different field of matter can obtain cannot be decided by the understanding, which has to do only with the synthesis of that which is given. Otherwise the poverty of our usual inferences through which we bring forth a great realm of possibility, of which everything actual (every object of experience) is only a small part, is very obvious. "Everything actual is possible" – from this there follows naturally, in accordance with the logical rules of conversion, the merely particular proposition, "Something possible is actual," which then seems to mean as much as "Much is possible that is not actual." It certainly looks as if one could increase the number of that which is possible beyond that of the actual, since something must be added to the former to constitute the latter. But I do not acknowledge this addition to the possible. For that which would have to be added to the possible would be impossible. All that can be added to my understanding is something beyond agreement with the formal conditions of experience, namely connection with some perception or other; but whatever is connected with this in accordance with empirical laws is actual, even if it is not immediately perceived. However, that another series of appearances in thoroughgoing connection with that which is given to me in perception, thus more than a single all-encompassing experience, is possible, cannot be inferred from that which is given, and even less without anything being given at all; for without matter[b] nothing at all can be thought. That which is possible only under conditions that are themselves merely possible is not possible **in all respects.** But this is the way the question is taken when

B283

A231

B284

A232

---

[a] *Zusammenhange*

[b] *Stoff*, i.e., matter as contrasted to form, rather than matter in a specifically physical sense.

one wants to know whether the possibility of things extends further than experience can reach.[89]

I have only mentioned these questions in order not to leave a gap in what according to common opinion belongs among the concepts of the understanding. In fact, however, absolute possibility (which is valid in every respect) is no mere concept of the understanding, and can in no way be of empirical use, rather it belongs solely to reason, which goes beyond all possible empirical use of the understanding. Hence we have had to satisfy ourselves here with a merely critical remark, but otherwise left the matter in obscurity pending further treatment later on.

Since I would now conclude this fourth section, and with it at the same time the system of all principles of the pure understanding, I must still provide the reason[a] why I have called the principles[b] of modality "postulates." I will not here take this expression in the significance that, contrary to the usage[c] of mathematics, to whom it nevertheless properly belongs, some recent philosophical writers[90] have used it, namely that postulation means the same as putting a proposition forth as immediately certain without justification or proof; for if we were to allow that synthetic propositions, no matter how evident they might be, could claim unconditional acceptance without any deduction, merely on their own claim, then all critique of the understanding would be lost, and, since there is no lack of audacious pretensions that common belief does not refuse (which is, however, no credential),[d] our understanding would therefore be open to every delusion, without being able to deny its approval to those claims that, though unjustifiable, demand to be admitted as actual axioms in the very same confident tone. When, therefore, a determination is added *a priori* to the concept of a thing, then for such a proposition if not a proof then at least a deduction of the legitimacy of its assertion must unfailingly be supplied.

The principles of modality are not, however, objective-synthetic, since the predicates of possibility, actuality, and necessity do not in the least augment the concept of which they are asserted in such a way as to add something to the representation of the object. But since they are nevertheless always synthetic, they are so only subjectively, i.e., they add to the concept of a thing (the real), about which they do not otherwise say anything, the cognitive power whence it arises and has its seat, so that, if it is merely connected in the understanding with the formal conditions of experience, its object is called possible; if it is in connection[e] with per-

---

[a] *Grund*
[b] *Principien*
[c] *Sinn*
[d] *Kreditiv*
[e] *Beziehung*

ception (sensation, as the matter of the senses), and through this determined by means of the understanding, then the object^a is actual; and if it is determined through the connection^b of perceptions in accordance with concepts, then the object is called necessary. The principles of modality therefore do not assert of a concept anything other than the action of the cognitive faculty through which it is generated. Now in mathematics a postulate is the practical proposition that contains nothing except the synthesis through which we first give ourselves an object and generate its concept, e.g., to describe a circle with a given line from a given point on a plane; and a proposition of this sort cannot be proved, since the procedure that it demands is precisely that through which we first generate the concept of such a figure. Accordingly we can postulate the principles of modality with the very same right, since they do not augment* their concept of things in general, but rather only indicate the way in which in general it is combined with the cognitive power.^c

B 287

A 235

✳ ✳ ✳

* **Through the actuality** of a thing I certainly posit more than possibility, but not **in the thing;** for that can never contain more in actuality than what was contained in its complete possibility. But while possibility was merely a positing^d of a thing in relation^e to the understanding (to its empirical use), actuality is at the same time its connection with perception.

A 234/ B 287
A 235

^e *Zusammenhange*
^a *Object*
^b *Zusammenhang*
^c The following series of notes is inserted in Kant's copy of the first edition at A 234–5, presumably constituting notes made for the "General Remark" that he adds at this point in the second edition:

"Now comes the proposition: how are synthetic *a priori* propositions possible." (E XCVIII, p. 37; 23:33)

"Finally: How are synthetic *a priori* propositions possible through concepts, how are they possible through the construction of concepts?" (E XCIX, p. 37; 23:33)

"On the possibility of an *ars characteristica vel combinatoria.*" (E C, p. 37; 23:33)

"It is remarkable that for these postulates we must always have a mechanical medium[:] either a model as a string that lies, or the motion of this string around a point." (E CI, p. 37; 23:33)

"That all principles and synthetic *a priori* propositions in general do not go further than objects of experience, and that if we would still go beyond them then no intuition can correspond to them." (E CII, p. 38; 23:33–4)

"That the pure laws of understanding also teach nothing further than the laws under which alone experience in general is possible, not the particular laws of the objects of experience. But that the laws of appearances (which are merely in us) thus have their seat and origin in the understanding, therefore also in us, is not to be marveled at. Indeed it is not possible to cognize a law with its necessity in such a way that we could have cognized it otherwise than in our own understanding. The chemical laws are not laws so much as rules of nature." (E CIII, p. 38; 23:34)

^d *Position*
^e *Beziehung*

B 288   *<General Note on the System of Principles

It is very remarkable that we cannot have insight into the possibility of any thing in accordance with the mere categories, but we must always have available an intuition in order for it to display the objective reality of the pure concept of the understanding. Take, e.g., the categories of relation.*[b] How 1) something can exist only as **subject,** not as mere determination of other things, i.e., can be **substance;** or how 2) because something is, something else must be, thus how something can be a cause at all; or 3) how, if several things exist, from the existence of one of them something about the others follows and vice versa, and in this way a community of substances can obtain – insight into these cannot be had from mere concepts at all. The same thing also holds of the other categories, e.g., how a thing can be one with a number of others taken together, i.e., be a magnitude, etc. Thus as long as intuition is lacking, one does not know whether one thinks an object*[c] through the categories, and whether there can ever be any object*[d] that even fits them; and so it is confirmed that the categories are not by themselves **cognitions,** but mere **forms of thought** for making cognitions out of

B 289 given intuitions. – In the same way it follows that no synthetic proposition can be made out of mere categories – e.g., in all existence there is substance, i.e., something that can exist only as subject and never as mere predicate; or, everything is a quantum, etc. – if there is nothing that we can use in order to go beyond a given concept and thereby connect it with another. Hence also no one has ever succeeded in proving a synthetic proposition merely from pure concepts of the understanding, e.g., the proposition "Every contingently existing thing has a cause." One could never get further than to prove that without this relation*[e] we could **not comprehend** the existence*[f] of the contingent at all, i.e., cognize the existence of such a thing *a priori* through the understanding; from which, however, it does not follow that this is also the condition of the possibility of things themselves. Hence if one will look back on our proof of the principle of causality, one will become aware that we could prove it only of objects*[g] of possible experience: "Everything that happens (every occurrence) presupposes a cause"; and indeed we could prove it only as a principle*[h] of the possibility of expe-

---

*[a] This note was added in its entirety in the second edition.
*[b] *Relation*
*[c] *Object*
*[d] *Object*
*[e] *Beziehung*
*[f] *Existenz,* here and in the next clause.
*[g] *Objecten*
*[h] *Princip*

rience, hence of the **cognition** of an object*^a* given in **empirical intuition,** and not from mere concepts. That the proposition "Everything contingent must have a cause" may be evident to everyone from mere concepts is not to be denied; but then the concept of the contingent is already taken in such a way that it contains, not the category of modality (as something, the non-existence of which **can be thought**), but that of relation*^b* (as something that can only exist as the consequence of something else), and then it is, of course, an identical proposition: "What can only exist as a consequence has its cause." In fact, when we are to give examples of contingent existence, we always appeal to **alterations** and not merely to the possibility of **the thought of the opposite.***,91 Alteration, however, is an occurrence that is possible as such only through a cause, the non-being of which is thus possible in itself; and thus one cognizes contingency from the fact that something can exist only as the effect of a cause; thus if a thing is assumed to be contingent, it's an analytic proposition to say that it has a cause.

It is even more remarkable, however, that in order to understand the possibility of things in accordance with the categories, and thus to establish the **objective reality** of the latter, we do not merely need intuitions, but always **outer intuitions.** If we take, e.g., the pure concept of **relation,***^c* we find that 1) in order to give something that **persists** in intuition, corresponding to the concept of **substance** (and thereby to establish the objective reality of this concept), we need an intuition **in space** (of matter), since space alone persistently determines, while time, however, and thus everything that is in inner sense, constantly flows. 2) In order to exhibit **alteration** as the intuition corresponding to the concept of **causality,** we must take motion, as alteration in space, as our example, indeed only by that means can we make alterations, the possibility of which cannot be comprehended by any pure understand-

B 290

B 291

* * One can easily think of the not-being of matter, but the ancients did not infer its contingency from that. And even the change from the being to the non-being of a given state of a thing, in which all alteration consists, does not prove the contingency of this state at all, as it were, from the actuality of its opposite; e.g., the rest of the body that follows its motion still does not prove the contingency of its motion just because the former is the opposite of the latter. For this opposite is here **opposed** to the other only logically, not *realiter.* In order to prove the contingency of the motion of the body, one would have to prove that **instead** of the motion in the preceding point of time, the body could have been at rest **then,** not that it rests **later;** for in the later case the two opposites are perfectly consistent.

B 290

^a *Objects*
^b *Relation*
^c **Relation**

ing, intuitable. Alteration is the combination of contradictorily opposed determinations in the existence of one and the same thing. Now how it B 292 is possible that from a given state an opposed state of the same thing should follow not only cannot be made comprehensible by reason without an example, but cannot even be made understandable without intuition, and this intuition is the motion of a point in space, the existence of which in different places (as a sequence of opposed determinations) first makes alteration intuitable to us; for in order subsequently to make even inner alterations thinkable, we must be able to grasp time, as the form of inner sense, figuratively through a line, and grasp the inner alteration through the drawing of this line (motion), and thus grasp the successive existence^a of ourself in different states through outer intuition; the real ground of which is that all alteration presupposes something that persists in intuition, even in order merely to be perceived as alteration, but there is no persistent intuition to be found in inner sense. – Finally, the possibility of the category of **community** is not to be comprehended at all through mere reason, and thus it is not possible to have insight into the objective reality of this concept without intuition, and indeed outer intuition in space. For how would one conceive^b the possibility that if several substances exist, the existence^c of the one can follow reciprocally from the existence of the other (as an effect), and thus that because there is something in the former, there must B 293 on that account also be something in the other that cannot be understood from the existence of the latter alone? For this is requisite for community, but is not even comprehensible among things each of which is entirely isolated from the others through its subsistence. Hence Leibniz, who ascribed a community to the substances of the world only as conceived by the understanding alone, needed a divinity for mediation; for from their existence alone this community rightly seemed to him incomprehensible.[92] But we can readily grasp the possibility of community (of substances as appearances) if we represent them in space, thus in outer intuition. For this already contains in itself *a priori* formal outer relations as conditions of the possibility of the real (in effect and countereffect, thus in community). – It can just as easily be established that the possibility of things as **magnitudes,** and thus the objective reality of the category of magnitude, can also be exhibited only in outer intuition, and that by means of that alone can it subsequently also be applied to inner sense. But in order to avoid being longwinded I must leave the examples of this to the reader's further thought.

This entire remark is of great importance, not only in order to con-

---

^{a} *Existenz*

^{b} *denken*

^{c} *Existenz*, used throughout this sentence.

firm our preceding refutation of idealism, but, even more, when we come to talk of **self-cognition** from mere inner consciousness and B 294 the determination of our nature without the assistance of outer empirical intuitions, to indicate to us the limits of the possibility of such a cognition.[93]

The final conclusion of this entire section is thus: All principles of the pure understanding are nothing further than *a priori* principles[a] of the possibility of experience, and all synthetic *a priori* propositions are related to the latter alone, indeed their possibility itself rests entirely on this relation.>[b]

---

[a] *Principien*
[b] *Beziehung*

The Transcendental Doctrine
of the Power of Judgment
(Analytic of Principles)
Third Chapter
On the ground of the distinction of all objects
in general into phenomena and noumena[a,b]

We have now not only traveled through the land of pure understanding, and carefully inspected each part of it, but we have also surveyed it,

<hr/>

[a] As in the first edition. For the second edition, Kant made extensive additions and some deletions in the body of this chapter prior to the appendix on the "Amphiboly of the Concepts of Reflection." We will present each version of the chapter up to the appendix in its entirety, repeating those passages that were not changed. The marginal pagination and notes will mark where the changes were made.

[b] The following notes appear at the start of this chapter in Kant's copy of the first edition:
"Here is the question: How far does the possibility of synthetic cognition *a priori* extend? If there is talk of a thing through categories that is determined merely through reason, hence also through categories, then such propositions are analytic, and yield no cognition." (E CIV, p. 38; 23:34)
"1. **On appearance and illusion.**
"2. How can one say that bodies are appearances. They consist of pure relations [*lauter Relationen*]; soul consists of pure [*lauter*] synthesis and analysis of these representations. The I is *noumenon*; I as intelligence." (E CV, p. 38; 23:34)
"Being of sense – being of understanding; *sensibilia – intelligibilia*." (E CVI, p. 38; 23:34)
"We can only think *noumena*, not cognize them." (E CVII, p. 38; 23:34)
"One must think things in themselves through the concept of a most-real being, since this excludes all experience." (E CVIII, p. 39; 23:34)
"*Mundus phaenomenon* or a whole of substances in space may readily be thought, but not as *noumenon*, since they are isolated." (E CIX, p. 39; 23:35)
"The same things as beings of sense or understanding. I myself am the only thing that does not intuit itself." (E CX, p. 39; 23:35)
"Categories do not serve to cognize things for themselves, but only to order intuitions in space and time, i.e., appearances." (E CXI, p. 39; 23:35)
"Until now one believed that through categories one actually already cognized something; now we see that they are only forms of thought for bringing the manifold of intuitions to synthetic unity of apperception." (E CXII, p. 39; 23:35)

and determined the place for each thing in it.[94] This land, however, is an island, and enclosed in unalterable boundaries by nature itself. It is the land of truth (a charming name), surrounded by a broad and stormy ocean, the true seat of illusion, where many a fog bank and rapidly melting iceberg pretend to be new lands and, ceaselessly deceiving with empty hopes the voyager looking around for new discoveries, entwine him in adventures from which he can never escape and yet also never bring to an end. But before we venture out on this sea, to search through all its breadth and become certain of whether there is anything to hope for in it, it will be useful first to cast yet another glance at the map of the land that we would now leave, and to ask, first, whether we could not be satisfied with what it contains, or even must be satisfied with it out of necessity, if there is no other ground on which we could build; and, second, by what title we occupy even this land, and can hold it securely against all hostile claims. Although we have already adequately answered these questions in the course of the Analytic, a summary overview of their solutions can still strengthen conviction by unifying their various moments in one point.

We have seen, namely, that everything that the understanding draws out of itself, without borrowing it from experience, it nevertheless has solely for the sake of use in experience. The principles of pure understanding, whether they are *a priori* constitutive (like the mathematical principles) or merely regulative (like the dynamical principles), contain nothing but only the pure schema, as it were, for possible experience; for this has its unity only from the synthetic unity that the understanding originally and from itself imparts to the synthesis of the imagination in relation to apperception, and in relation[a] to and agreement with which the appearances, as data for possible cognition, must already stand *a priori*.[b] But now even if these rules of the understanding are not only true *a priori* but are rather even the source of all truth, i.e., of the agreement of our cognition with objects,[c] in virtue of containing the ground of the possibility of experience, as the sum total of all cognition in which ob-

B295

A236

B296

A237

"*Noumena*: beings that themselves have understanding, also causality with regard to the objects [*Objecten*] of their understanding through the understanding itself, i.e., will and then all other categories, i.e., pure intelligences. But since we take all sensible conditions from them, we cannot think them determinately. The possibility of something like that is not clear." (E CXIII, p. 39; 23:35)

[a] *Beziehung*. The term *Verhältnis* does not occur again until the appendix to this chapter, so further occurrences of *Beziehung* will not be noted.

[b] Added in Kant's copy of the first edition: "We cannot have insight into the possibility of a cause without an example from experience, thus it is not a concept that one can use outside of experience. It is to be regarded as possible in experience alone and only in it can it be assumed." (E CXV, p. 40; 23:35)

[c] *Objecten*

jects^a may be given to us, still it does not seem enough to us merely to have expounded what is true, but also that which one has desired to know.^{b} If, therefore, through this critical investigation we learn nothing more than what we should in any case have practiced in the merely empirical use of the understanding, even without such subtle inquiry, then it would seem the advantage that one will draw from it would hardly be worth the expense and preparation. Now to this, to be sure, one can reply that no curiosity is more disadvantageous to the expansion of our knowledge^c than that which would always know its utility in advance, before one has entered into the investigations, and before one could have the least concept of this utility even if it were placed before one's eyes. But there is one advantage, which can be made both comprehensible and interesting to even the dullest and most reluctant student of such transcendental investigation, namely this: That the understanding occupied merely with its empirical use, which does not reflect on the sources of its own cognition, may get along very well, but cannot accomplish one thing, namely, determining for itself the boundaries of its use and knowing what may lie within and what without its whole sphere; for to this end the deep inquiries that we have undertaken are requisite. But if the understanding cannot distinguish whether certain questions lie within its horizon or not, then it is never sure of its claims and its possession, but must always reckon on many embarrassing corrections when it continually oversteps the boundaries of its territory (as is unavoidable) and loses itself in delusion and deceptions.

That the understanding can therefore make only empirical use of all its *a priori* principles, indeed of all its concepts, but never transcendental use, is a proposition that, if it can be recognized^d with conviction, points to important consequences.^{e} The transcendental use of a concept in any sort of principle consists in its being related to things **in general** and **in themselves;**^{f} its empirical use, however, in its being related merely to **appearances,** i.e., objects of a possible **experience.** But that it is only the latter that can ever take place is evident from the following. For every concept there is requisite, first, the logical form of a concept (of thinking) in general, and then, second, the possibility of giving it an object to which it is to be related. Without this latter it has no

---

^{a} *Objecte*

^{b} Emended in Kant's copy of the first edition to: "what is true, as little as it may be, but also to expand his cognition" (E CXVI, p. 40; 23:47).

^{c} *Erkenntnis*

^{d} *erkannt*

^{e} Added in Kant's copy of the first edition: "against enthusiasm" (E CXVII, p. 40; 23:47).

^{f} Kant's copy of the first edition changes "things **in general** and **in themselves**" to "objects, which are not given to us in an intuition, thus are not sensible objects" (E CXVII, p. 40; 23:47).

sense, and is entirely empty of content, even though it may still contain the logical function for making a concept out of whatever sort of *data* there are. Now the object cannot be given to a concept otherwise than in intuition, and, even if a pure intuition[a] is possible *a priori* prior to the object, then even this can acquire its object, thus its objective validity, only through empirical intuition, of which it is the mere form. Thus all concepts and with them all principles, however *a priori* they may be, are nevertheless related to empirical intuitions, i.e., to *data* for possible experience. Without this they have no objective validity at all, but are rather a mere play, whether it be with representations of the imagination or of the understanding. One need only take as an example the concepts of mathematics, and first, indeed, in their pure intuitions. Space has three dimensions, between two points there can be only one straight line, etc. Although all these principles, and the representation of the object with which this science occupies itself, are generated in the mind completely *a priori*, they would still not signify anything at all if we could not always exhibit their significance in appearances (empirical objects). Hence it is also requisite for one **to make** an abstract concept **sensible**, i.e., display the object[b] that corresponds to it in intuition, since without this the concept would remain (as one says) without **sense**, i.e., without significance. Mathematics fulfills this requirement by means of the construction of the figure,[c] which is an appearance present to the senses (even though brought about *a priori*). In the same science, the concept of magnitude seeks its standing and sense in number, but seeks this in turn in the fingers, in the beads of an abacus, or in strokes and points that are placed before the eyes. The concept is always generated *a priori*, together with the synthetic principles or formulas from such concepts; but their use and relation to supposed objects can in the end be sought nowhere but in experience, the possibility of which (as far as its form is concerned) is contained in them *a priori*.

B 299

A 240

That this is also the case with all categories, however, and the principles spun out from them,[d] is also obvious from this: That we cannot even define a single one of them without immediately descending to conditions of sensibility, thus to the form of the appearances, to which, as their sole objects, they must consequently be limited, since, if one removes this condition, all significance, i.e., relation to the object[e] disappears, and one cannot grasp through an example what sort of thing is

B 300

A 241

---

[a] Altered in Kant's copy of the first edition to: "even if a pure sensible intuition" (E CXVIII, p. 41; 23:47).

[b] *Object*

[c] *Gestalt*

[d] In his copy of the first edition, Kant adds the remark: "We cannot explain their possibility" (E CXIX, p. 41; 23:47).

[e] *Object*

really intended by concepts of that sort.^{a} Above, in the presentation of the table of the categories, we spared ourselves the definitions of each of them, on the ground that our aim, which pertains solely to their synthetic use, does not make that necessary, and one must not make oneself responsible for unnecessary undertakings that one can spare oneself. This was no excuse, but a not inconsiderable rule of prudence, not immediately to venture a definition and seek or pretend to completeness or precision in the determination of the concept if one can make do with one or another of its marks, without requiring a complete derivation of everything that constitutes the entire concept. But now it turns out that the ground of this precaution lies even deeper, namely, that we could not define them even if we wanted to,^{*,b} but rather, if one

A 242 does away with all conditions of sensibility that distinguish them as concepts of a possible empirical use, and takes them for concepts of things in general (thus of transcendental use), then that is to do nothing more than to regard the logical functions of judgments as the condition of the possibility of things themselves, without in the least being able to show whence they could have their application and their object,^{c} thus how in pure understanding without sensibility they could have any significance

B 300 and objective validity. ^{d}No one can define the concept of magnitude in general except by something like this: That it is the determination of a thing through which it can be thought how many units are posited in it. Only this how-many-times is grounded on successive repetition, thus on time and the synthesis (of the homogeneous) in it. Reality, in contrast to negation, can be defined only if one thinks of a time (as the sum total of all being) that is either filled by it or empty. If I leave out per-

---

A 241 * I mean here the real definition,^{e} which does not merely supply other and more intelligible words for the name of a thing, but rather contains in itself a clear **mark** by means of which the **object** (*definitum*) can always be securely cog-

A 242 nized, and that makes the concept that is to be explained usable in application. A real definition^f would therefore be that which does not merely make distinct a concept but at the same time its **objective reality**. Mathematical definitions, which exhibit the object in accordance with the concept **in intuition,** are of the latter sort.

^{a} The next three sentences, as well as Kant's footnote, are omitted in the second edition.
^{b} Before he dropped this note from the second edition, Kant had drafted an additional sentence for it in his copy of the first: "Instead of **define** [*erklären*]one could also use the expression **to substantiate through an example**" (E CXX, p. 41; 23:47).
^{c} *Object*
^{d} The text common to the two editions resumes here, although in the second edition Kant here begins a new paragraph.
^{e} *Realdefinition*
^{f} *Realerklärung*

sistence (which is existence at all times), then nothing is left in my concept of substance except the logical representation of the subject, which I try to realize by representing to myself something that can occur solely as subject (without being a predicate of anything). But then it is not only the case that I do not even know of any conditions under which this logical preeminence can be attributed to any sort of thing;*a* it is also the case that absolutely nothing further is to be made of it, and not even the least consequence is to be drawn from it, because by its means no object*b* whatever of the use of this concept is determined, and one therefore does not even know whether the latter means anything at all. From the concept of a cause as a pure category (if I leave out the time in which something follows something else in accordance with a rule), I will not find out anything more than that it is something that allows an inference to the existence of something else; and in that case not only would there be nothing through which cause and effect could be distinguished, but further, since the possibility of drawing this inference also requires conditions about which I would know nothing, the concept would not even have any determination through which to apply to any object.*c* The supposed principle "Everything contingent has a cause" steps forth rather gravely, as if it had its own dignity in itself. Yet if I ask what you mean by "contingent," and you answer, "that the not-being of which is possible," then I would gladly know by what means you intend to cognize the possibility of this not-being, if you do not represent a succession in the series of appearances and in this succession an existence, which follows on the not-being (or conversely), and thus a change; for that the not-being of a thing does not contradict itself is a lame appeal to a logical condition, which is certainly necessary for the concept but far from sufficient for real possibility; for I can suspend any existing substance in thought without contradicting myself, but I cannot at all infer from that to the objective contingency of its existence, i.e., the possibility of its*d* not-being in itself. As far as the concept of community is concerned, it is easy to appreciate that since the pure categories of substance as well as causality do not admit of any definition determining the object,*e* reciprocal causality in the relation of substances to each other (*commercium*) will be just as little susceptible of it. No one has ever been able to define possibility, existence, and necessity except through obvious tautologies if he wanted to draw their definition solely from the pure understanding. For the deception of substituting

A 243
B 301

A 244
B 302

---

a Here Kant adds in his copy of the first edition: "See general remark" (E CXX; 23:47).
b *Object*
c *Object*
d Following Erdmann, reading *ihres* for *seines*.
e *Object*

the logical possibility of the **concept** (since it does not contradict itself) for the transcendental[a] possibility of **things** (where an object corresponds to the concept) can deceive and satisfy only the inexperienced.[b]

[c]There is something strange and even nonsensical in there being a concept that must have some significance but is not capable of definition. Only in the case of the categories is there this special circumstance, that they can have a determinate significance and relation to any object only by means of the general **sensible condition,** but that this condition is omitted from the pure category, since this can contain nothing but the logical function for bringing the manifold under a concept. From this function, i.e., the form of the concept alone, however, nothing can be cognized and distinguished about which object[d] belongs under it, since abstraction has been made from just the sensible condition under which objects can belong under it at all. Hence the categories require, beyond the pure concept of the understanding, determinations of their application to sensibility in general (schema), and without these are not concepts through which an object can be cognized and distinguished from others, but only so many ways of thinking of an object for possible intuitions and of giving it its significance in accordance with some function of the understanding (under the requisite conditions), **i.e., of defining it:** they themselves cannot therefore be defined. The logical functions of judgment in general – unity and multiplicity, affirmation and negation, subject and predicate – cannot be defined without falling into a circle, since the definition would itself have to be a judgment and therefore already contain these functions of judgment. The pure categories, however, are nothing other than the representations of things in general insofar as the manifold of their intuition must be thought through one or another of these logical functions: Magnitude is the determination that must be thought only through a judgment that has quantity (*judicium commune*[e]); reality, that which can be thought only through an affirmative judgment; substance, that which, in relation to the intuition, must be the ultimate subject of all other determinations. But now what sorts of things those are in regard to which one must use one function rather than another remains hereby entirely undetermined: thus without the condition of sensible intuition, the synthesis of which they contain, the categories have no relation at all to any determinate object,[f] thus they cannot de-

A 245

A 246

---

[a] Altered in Kant's copy of the first edition to "real" (*realen*) (E CXXI, p. 41; 23:48).
[b] At this point the second edition adds a footnote; see B 302–3n.
[c] This paragraph is omitted in the second edition.
[d] *Object*
[e] general judgment
[f] *Object*

fine one, and consequently they do not have in themselves any validity of concepts.

*a*Now from this it follows irrefutably that the pure concepts of the understanding can **never** be of **transcendental,** but **always** only of **empirical** use,*b* and that the principles of pure understanding can be related to objects of the senses only in relation to the general conditions of a possible experience, but never to things in general*c* (without taking regard of the way in which we might intuit them).*d*   B 303

The Transcendental Analytic accordingly has this important result: That the understanding can never accomplish *a priori* anything more than to anticipate the form of a possible experience in general, and, since that which is not appearance cannot be an object of experience, it can never overstep the limits of sensibility, within which alone objects are given to us. Its principles are merely principles*e* of the exposition of appearances, and the proud name of an ontology, which presumes to offer synthetic *a priori* cognitions of things in general in a systematic doctrine (e.g., the principle of causality), must give way to the modest one of a mere analytic of the pure understanding.   A 247

Thinking is the action of relating given intuitions to an object. If the manner of this intuition is not given in any way, then the object is merely transcendental, and the concept of the understanding has none other than a transcendental use, namely the unity of thought of a manifold*f* in general. Now through a pure category, in which abstraction is made from any condition of sensible intuition as the only one that is possible for us, no object*g* is determined,*h* rather only the thought of an object*i* in general is expressed in accordance with different *modi*. Now to the use of a concept there also belongs a function of the power of judgment, whereby an object is subsumed under it, thus at least the formal condition under which something can be given in intuition. If this condition of the power of judgment (schema) is missing, then all subsumption disappears; for nothing would be given that could be subsumed under the concept. The merely transcendental use of the cate-   B 304

---

a The text common to the two editions resumes here.

b Added in Kant's copy of the first edition: "i.e., no principles from mere categories" (E CXXII, p. 41; 23:48).

c Inserted in Kant's copy of the first edition: "synthetically" (E CXXIII, p. 41; 23:48).

d Kant's copy of the first edition adds here: "if they are to produce cognition" (E CXXIV, p. 41; 23:48).

e *Principien*

f In his copy of the first edition Kant adds here: "of a possible intuition" (E CXXV, p. 41; 23:48).

g *Object*

h Added in Kant's copy of the first edition: "hence nothing is cognized" (E CXXVI, p. 41; 23:48).

i *Objects*

A 248

gories is thus in fact no use at all,^{a} and has no determinate or even, as far as its form is concerned, determinable object. From this it also follows that the pure category does not suffice for any synthetic *a priori* principle, and that the principles of the pure understanding are only of empirical but never of transcendental use; but nowhere beyond the field

B 305

of possible experience can there be any synthetic *a priori* principles.

It may therefore be advisable to express ourselves thus: The pure categories, without formal conditions of sensibility, have merely transcendental significance, but are not of any transcendental use, since this is impossible in itself, for they are lacking all conditions of any use (in judgments), namely the formal condition of the subsumption of any sort of supposed object under these concepts. Thus since (as merely pure categories) they are not supposed to have empirical use, and cannot have transcendental use, they do not have any use at all if they are separated from all sensibility, i.e., they cannot be applied to any supposed object at all; rather they are merely the pure form of the use of the understanding in regard to objects in general and of thinking, yet without any sort of object^b being able to be thought or determined through them alone.^{c}

---

^{a} Kant's copy of the first edition inserts here: "for the cognition of anything" (E CXXVII, p. 41; 23:48).

^{b} *Object*

^{c} The following notes are inserted in Kant's copy of the first edition at A 248, presumably drafts of the changes that were to be made at this point in the second edition:

"One can give the possibility of a thing only through intuition, either empirical or *a priori* intuition. The former is empirical, the latter at least sensible. Both therefore pertain to *phaenomena*. No theoretical cognition of *noumenon* at all, but practical relation to a subject, insofar as it is not *phaenomenon*." (E CXXVIII, p. 42; 23:35–6)

"If something is found, not to be sure in the sensible world, but yet in our pure consciousness of reason, which is absolutely contrary to laws of the former, e.g., that of causality, then we belong to the *noumenon*, but can have to that extent no knowledge of ourselves, but yet can at least concede the possibility of it." (E CXXIX, p. 42; 23:36)

"Beings of understanding are properly those to which nothing but intellectual intuition corresponds. Now since our understanding is not able to intuit, this intellectual intuition is nothing for us. Thus nothing is left for us but concepts of the understanding. But these are merely forms of thought, so that if one would apply them alone to an object [*Object*], without an example for sensible intuition that something can correspond to them, they cannot be comprehended at all." (E CXXX, p. 42; 23:36)

"Objects of a non-sensible intuition are either given in a sensible intuition or not. If the first, then they are certainly appearances, but one cannot know whether they could be cognized in some other way, and whether intellectual intuition is possible. Since I have no intellectual intuition, I cannot even cognize the possibility of objects that cannot be given in any sensible intuition at all, and objects of an intuition of the understanding would be mere problematical beings, and all *noumena* or beings of the understanding are to be regarded as such. N.B." (E CXXXI, pp. 42–3; 23:36)

^{a}Appearances, to the extent that as objects they are thought in accordance with the unity of the categories, are called *phaenomena*. If,   A249
however, I suppose there to be things that are merely objects of the understanding and that, nevertheless, can be given to an intuition, although not to sensible intuition (as *coram intuiti intellectuali*),^{b} then
such things would be called *noumena* (*intelligibilia*).

Now one might have thought that the concept of appearances, limited by the Transcendental Aesthetic, already yields by itself the objective reality of the *noumena*^{c} and justifies the division of objects into
phenomena and *noumena*, thus also the division of the world into a world
of the senses and of the understanding (*mundus sensibilis & intelligibilis*),
indeed in such a way that the difference here would not concern merely
the logical form of the indistinct or distinct cognition of one and the
same thing, but rather the difference between how they can originally
be given to our cognition, in accordance with which they are in themselves different species. For if the senses merely represent something to
us **as it appears,** then this something must also be in itself a thing, and
an object of a non-sensible intuition, i.e., of the understanding, i.e., a
cognition must be possible in which no sensibility is encountered, and
which alone has absolutely objective reality, through which, namely,
objects are represented to us **as they are,** in contrast to the empirical
use of our understanding, in which things are only cognized **as they**   A250
appear. Thus there would be, in addition to the empirical use of the
categories (which is limited to sensible conditions), a pure and yet objectively valid one, and we could not assert, what we have previously
maintained, that our pure cognitions of the understanding are in general nothing more than principles^d of the exposition^e of appearances
that do not go *a priori* beyond the formal possibility of experience, for
here an entirely different field would stand open before us, as it were a
world thought in spirit (perhaps also even intuited), which could not
less but even more nobly occupy our understanding.

All our representations are in fact related to some object^f through
the understanding, and, since appearances are nothing but representa-

---

"We have seen at the end of the Principles that the concept of causality serves to determine the relation [*Verhältnis*] of the temporal sequence in the course of its appearances *a priori*; if we take time away, then it is for nothing." (E CXXXII, p. 43; 23:36)

^{a} The next seven paragraphs (A249–53) are replaced with four paragraphs in the second
edition (B306–9).

^{b} by means of intellectual intuition

^{c} Kant uses the Latin plural genitive *noumenorum*.

^{d} *Principien*

^{e} Kant altered this to "synthesis of the manifold" in his copy of the first edition (E
CXXXIII, p. 43; 23:48).

^{f} *Object*

tions, the understanding thus relates them to a **something,** as the object of sensible intuition: but this something[a] is to that extent only the transcendental object.[b] This signifies, however a something = X, of which we know nothing at all nor can know anything in general (in accordance with the current constitution of our understanding), but is rather something that can serve only as a correlate of the unity of apperception for the unity of the manifold in sensible intuition, by means of which the understanding unifies that in the concept of an object. This transcendental object[c] cannot even be separated from the sensible

A251 *data,* for then nothing would remain through which it would be thought. It is therefore no object of cognition in itself, but only the representation of appearances under the concept of an object in general, which is determinable through the manifold of those appearances.[d,95]

Just for this reason, then, the categories do not represent any special object[e] given to the understanding alone, but rather serve only to determine the transcendental object[f] (the concept of something in general) through that which is given in sensibility, in order thereby to cognize appearances empirically under concepts of objects.

But the cause on account of which, not yet satisfied through the substratum of sensibility, one must add *noumena* that only the pure understanding can think to the *phaenomena,* rests solely on this. Sensibility and its field, namely that of appearances, are themselves limited by the understanding, in that they do not pertain to things in themselves, but only to the way in which, on account of our subjective constitution, things appear to us. This was the result of the entire Transcendental Aesthetic, and it also follows naturally from the concept of an appearance in general that something must correspond to it which is not in itself appearance, for appearance can be nothing for itself and outside of

A252 our kind of representation; thus, if there is not to be a constant circle, the word "appearance" must already indicate a relation to something the immediate representation of which is, to be sure, sensible, but which in itself, without this constitution of our sensibility (on which the form of our intuition is grounded), must be something, i.e., an object independent of sensibility.

Now from this arises[g] the concept of a *noumenon,* which, however, is

---

[a] Altered in Kant's copy of the first edition to "this something as object of an intuition in general" (E CXXXIV, p. 43; 23:48).

[b] *Object*

[c] *Object*

[d] Kant's copy of the first edition adds: "only forms of thought, but not cognition" (E CXXXV, p. 43; 23:48).

[e] *Object*

[f] *Object*

[g] Kant's copy of the first edition inserts "to be sure" here (E CXXXVI, p. 43; 23:48).

not at all positive and does not signify a determinate cognition of any sort of thing, but rather only the thinking of something in general, in which I abstract from all form of sensible intuition. But in order for a noumenon[a] to signify a true object, to be distinguished from all phenomena,[b] it is not enough that I **liberate** my thoughts from all conditions of sensible intuition, but I must in addition have ground to **assume** another kind of intuition than this sensible one, under which such an object could be given; for otherwise my thought is empty, even though free of contradiction. To be sure, above we were able to prove not that sensible intuition is the only possible intuition, but rather that it is the only one possible **for us;** but we also could not prove that yet another kind of intuition is possible, and, although our thinking can abstract from that sensibility, the question still remains whether it is not then a mere form of a concept and whether any object[c] at all is left over after this separation.[d]

A 2 5 3

The object[e] to which I relate appearance in general is the transcendental object, i.e., the entirely undetermined thought of something in general. This cannot be called the **noumenon;**[f] for I do not know anything about what it is in itself, and have no concept of it except merely that of the object of a sensible intuition in general, which is therefore the same for all appearances. I cannot think it through any categories; for these hold of empirical intuition, in order to bring it under a concept of the object in general. To be sure, a pure use of the category is possible,[g] i.e., without contradiction, but it has no objective validity, since it pertains to no intuition that would thereby acquire unity of the object;[h] for the category is a mere function of thinking, through which no object is given to me, but rather only that through which what may be given in intuition is thought.

[i]If I take all thinking (through categories) away from an empirical

B 309

---

[a] Not printed in roman type.
[b] Not printed in roman type.
[c] *Object*
[d] For the last part of this sentence, beginning with "whether it is not . . . ," Kant's copy of the first edition substitutes: "whether it is not then a mere form of a concept **or whether** after this separation **a possible intuition** is still left over, for nobody can establish the possibility of an intellectual intuition, and it could therefore easily be that no such manner of cognition obtained with respect to which we would consider something as an object. Thus the positive concept of a *noumenon* asserts something the possibility of which it cannot prove." (E CXXXVII, pp. 43–4; 23:49)
[e] *Object*
[f] Here Kant uses emphasis but not roman type.
[g] Emended in Kant's copy of the first edition to "logically possible" (E CXXXVIII, p. 44; 23:49).
[h] *Objects*
[i] From here to the end of the chapter, the text of the first edition is preserved in the second with only one further change on B 311 and one added footnote on B 312.

cognition, then no cognition of any object at all remains; for through mere intuition nothing at all is thought, and that this affection of sensibility is in me does not constitute any relation of such representation to any object[a] at all. But if, on the contrary, I leave out all intuition, then there still remains the form of thinking, i.e., the way of determining an object for the manifold of a possible intuition. Hence to this extent the categories extend further than sensible intuition, since they think objects[b] in general without seeing to the particular manner (of sensibility) in which they might be given. But they do not thereby determine a greater sphere of objects, since one cannot assume that such objects can be given without presupposing that another kind of intuition than the sensible kind is possible, which, however, we are by no means justified in doing.

A254

B310

I call a concept problematic that contains no contradiction but that is also, as a boundary for given concepts, connected with other cognitions, the objective reality of which can in no way be cognized. The concept of a **noumenon**,[c] i.e., of a thing that is not to be thought of as an object of the senses but rather as a thing in itself (solely through a pure understanding), is not at all contradictory; for one cannot assert of sensibility that it is the only possible kind of intuition. Further, this concept is necessary in order not to extend sensible intuition to things in themselves, and thus to limit the objective validity of sensible cognition (for the other things, to which sensibility does not reach, are called noumena[d] just in order to indicate that those cognitions cannot extend their domain to everything that the understanding thinks). In the end, however, we have no insight into the possibility of such *noumena*,[e] and the domain outside of the sphere of appearances is empty (for us), i.e., we have an understanding that extends farther than sensibility **problematically,** but no intuition, indeed not even the concept of a possible intuition, through which objects outside of the field of sensibility could be given, and about which the understanding could be employed **assertorically.** The concept of a noumenon[f] is therefore merely a **boundary concept,** in order to limit the pretension of sensibility, and therefore only of negative use. But it is nevertheless not invented arbitrarily, but is rather connected with the limitation of sensibility, yet without being able to posit anything positive outside of the domain of the latter.

A255

B311

The division of objects into *phaenomena* and *noumena*, and of the

---

[a] *Object*
[b] *Objecte*
[c] Here Kant uses emphasis (boldface) rather than roman type.
[d] Not in roman type.
[e] Here Kant prints the Latin genitive *noumenorum*.
[f] Not in roman type.

world into a world of sense and a world of understanding, can therefore not be permitted at all, although concepts certainly permit of division into sensible and intellectual ones; for one cannot determine any object for the latter, and therefore also cannot pass them off as objectively valid. If one abandons the senses, how will one make comprehensible that our categories (which would be the only remaining concepts for noumena)[a] still signify anything at all, since for their relation to any object something more than merely the unity of thinking must be given, namely a possible intuition, to which they can be applied? Nevertheless the concept of a *noumenon*,[b] taken merely problematically, remains not only admissible, but even unavoidable, as a concept setting limits to sensibility. But in that case it is not a special **intelligible object** for our understanding; rather an understanding to which it would belong is itself a problem, namely, that of cognizing its object not discursively through categories but intuitively in a non-sensible intuition, the possibility of which we cannot in the least represent. Now in this way our understanding acquires a negative expansion, i.e., it is not limited by sensibility, but rather limits it by calling things in themselves (not considered as appearances) *noumena*. But it also immediately sets boundaries for itself, not cognizing these things through categories, hence merely thinking them under the name of an unknown something.

Yet I find in the writings of the moderns an entirely different use of the expressions of a *mundi sensibilis* and *intelligibilis*,[c] which entirely diverges from the sense of the ancients, which is not itself a problem, but which is also nothing but an empty trafficking with words. In accordance with this usage some have been pleased to call the sum total of appearances, so far as it is intuited, the world of sense, but the connection[d] of them insofar as it is thought in accordance with general laws of the understanding, the world of understanding. Theoretical astronomy, which expounds the mere observation of the starry heavens, would be the former, contemplative astronomy on the contrary (explained, say, according to the Copernican world-system or even according to Newton's laws of gravitation) would be the latter, making an intelligible world representable. But such a perversion of words is a merely sophistical evasion for escaping from a difficult question by reducing its sense to a commonplace. With regard to appearances, to be sure, both understanding and reason can be used; but it must be asked whether they would still have any use if the object were not appearance (*noumenon*), and one takes it in this sense if one thinks of it as merely intelligible, i.e., as given to

A256

B312

A257

B313

---

[a] Not in roman type.
[b] Here Kant uses the Latin singular genitive *Noumeni*.
[c] "sensible and intelligible worlds." At this point the second edition adds a note; see B312.
[d] *Zusammenhang*

the understanding alone and not to the senses at all. The question is thus: whether beyond the empirical use of the understanding (even in the Newtonian representation of the cosmos) a transcendental one is also possible, pertaining to the noumenon[a] as an object – which question we have answered negatively.

A 258   If, therefore, we say: The senses represent objects to us **as they appear,** but the understanding, **as they are,** then the latter is not to be taken in a transcendental but in a merely empirical way, signifying, namely, how they must be represented as objects of experience, in the
B 314   thoroughgoing connection[b] of appearances, and not how they might be outside of the relation to possible experience and consequently to sense in general, thus as objects of pure understanding. For this will always remain unknown to us, so that it even remains unknown whether such a transcendental (extraordinary) cognition is possible at all, at least as one that stands under our customary categories. With us **understanding** and **sensibility** can determine an object **only in combination.** If we separate them, then we have intuitions without concepts, or concepts without intuitions, but in either case representations that we cannot relate to any determinate object.

If after all this discussion anyone still has reservations about denying the categories a merely transcendental use, then he should test them in any synthetic assertion. For an analytic one takes the understanding no further, and since it is occupied only with that which is already thought in the concept, it leaves it undecided whether the concept even has any
A 259   relation to objects, or only signifies the unity of thinking in general (which entirely abstracts from the way in which an object might be given); it is enough for him to know what lies in its concept; what the concept might pertain to is indifferent to him. He should accordingly
B 315   test it with some synthetic and allegedly transcendental principle, such as: "Everything that is, exists as substance, or a determination dependent on it," "Everything contingent exists as the effect of another thing, namely its cause," etc. Now I ask: Whence will he derive these synthetic propositions, since the concepts are not to hold of possible experience but rather of things in themselves (*noumena*)? Where is the third thing[c] that is always requisite for a synthetic proposition in order to connect with each other concepts that have no logical (analytical) affinity? He will never prove his proposition, indeed, what is more, he will not even be able to justify the possibility of such a pure assertion, without taking account of the empirical use of the understanding, and thereby entirely

---

[a] Not in roman type.
[b] *Zusammenhang*
[c] Kant's copy of the first edition inserts "of intuition" (E CXXXIX, p. 44; 23:49).

renouncing the pure and sense-free judgment. Thus the concept^{*a*} of pure, merely intelligible objects is entirely devoid of all principles of its application, since one cannot think up^{*b*} any way in which they could be given, and the problematic thought, which leaves a place open for them, only serves, like an empty space, to limit the empirical principles, with-out containing and displaying any other object^{*c*} of cognition beyond the sphere of the latter.

A260

---

^{*a*} In his copy of the first edition Kant expands this to "the positive concept, the possible **cognition**" (E CXLX, p. 44; 23:49).

^{*b*} *ersinnen,* a neat pun on the fact that objects must be given by sense and not mere thought.

^{*c*} *Object*

The Transcendental Doctrine
of the Power of Judgment
(Analytic of Principles)
Third Chapter
On the ground of the distinction of all objects
in general into phenomena and noumena[a]

We have now not only traveled through the land of pure understanding, and carefully inspected each part of it, but we have also surveyed it, and determined the place for each thing in it. But this land is an island, and enclosed in unalterable boundaries by nature itself. It is the land of truth (a charming name), surrounded by a broad and stormy ocean, the true seat of illusion, where many a fog bank and rapidly melting iceberg pretend to be new lands and, ceaselessly deceiving with empty hopes the voyager looking around for new discoveries, entwine him in adventures from which he can never escape and yet also never bring to an end. But before we venture out on this sea, to search through all its breadth and become certain of whether there is anything to hope for in it, it will be useful first to cast yet another glance at the map of the land that we would now leave, and to ask, first, whether we could not be satisfied with what it contains, or even must be satisfied with it out of necessity, if there is no other ground on which we could build; and, second, by what title we occupy even this land, and can hold it securely against all hostile claims. Although we have already adequately answered these questions in the course of the Analytic, a summary overview of their solutions can still strengthen conviction by unifying their various moments in one point.

We have seen, namely, that everything that the understanding draws

---

[a] We here present the extensively though not entirely revised version of this chapter as it appeared in the second edition. The divergences from the first will be marked with notes and brackets. The emendations that Kant made in his own copy of the first edition but did not incorporate into the new text in the second will not be reproduced here, having been presented above, nor will the editorial notes to the first edition be repeated.

out of itself, without borrowing it from experience, it nevertheless has solely for the sake of use in experience. The principles of pure under- B 296 standing, whether they are *a priori* constitutive (like the mathematical principles) or merely regulative (like the dynamical principles), contain nothing but only the pure schema, as it were, for possible experience; A 237 for this has its unity only from the synthetic unity that the under- standing originally and from itself imparts to the synthesis of the imag- ination in relation to apperception, and in relation to and agreement with which the appearances, as data for possible cognition, must al- ready stand *a priori*. But now even if these rules of the understanding are not only true *a priori* but are rather even the source of all truth, i.e., of the agreement of our cognition with objects,[a] in virtue of containing the ground of the possibility of experience, as the sum total of all cog- nition in which objects[b] may be given to us, still it does not seem enough to us merely to have expounded what is true, but also that which one has desired to know. If, therefore, through this critical in- vestigation we learn nothing more than what we should in any case have practiced in the merely empirical use of the understanding, even without such subtle inquiry, then it would seem that the advantage that one will draw from it would hardly be worth the expense and prepara- tion. Now to this, to be sure, one can reply that no curiosity is more disadvantageous to the expansion of our knowledge[c] than that which would always know its utility in advance, before one has entered into B 297 the investigations, and before one could have the least concept of this utility even if it were placed before one's eyes. But there is one advan- tage, which can be made both comprehensible and interesting to even A 238 the dullest and most reluctant student of such transcendental investi- gation, namely this: That the understanding occupied merely with its empirical use, which does not reflect on the sources of its own cogni- tion, may get along very well, but cannot accomplish one thing, namely, determining for itself the boundaries of its use and knowing what may lie within and what without its whole sphere; for to this end the deep inquiries that we have undertaken are requisite. But if the un- derstanding cannot distinguish whether certain questions lie within its horizon or not, then it is never sure of its claims and its possession, but must always reckon on many embarrassing corrections when it contin- ually oversteps the boundaries of its territory (as is unavoidable) and loses itself in delusion and deceptions.

That the understanding can therefore make only empirical use of all its *a priori* principles, indeed of all its concepts, but never transcenden-

[a] *Objecten*
[b] *Objecte*
[c] *Erkenntnis*

B 298

A 239

tal use, is a proposition that, if it can be recognized[a] with conviction, points to important consequences. The transcendental use of a concept in any sort of principle consists in its being related to things **in general** and **in themselves;** its empirical use, however, in its being related merely to **appearances,** i.e., objects of a possible **experience.** But that it is only the latter that can ever take place is evident from the following. For every concept there is requisite, first, the logical form of a concept (of thinking) in general, and then, second, the possibility of giving it an object to which it is to be related. Without this latter it has no sense, and is entirely empty of content, even though it may still contain the logical function for making a concept out of whatever sort of *data* there are. Now the object cannot be given to a concept otherwise than in intuition, and, even if a pure intuition is possible *a priori* prior to the object, then even this can acquire its object, thus its objective validity, only through empirical intuition, of which it is the mere form. Thus all concepts and with them all principles, however *a priori* they may be, are nevertheless related to empirical intuitions, i.e., to *data* for possible experience. Without this they have no objective validity at all, but are rather a mere play, whether it be with representations of the imagination or of the understanding. One need only take as an example the

B 299

concepts of mathematics, and first, indeed, in their pure intuitions. Space has three dimensions, between two points there can be only one straight line, etc. Although all these principles, and the representation of the object with which this science occupies itself, are generated in the

A 240

mind completely *a priori*, they would still not signify anything at all if we could not always exhibit their significance in appearances (empirical objects). Hence it is also requisite for one **to make** an abstract concept **sensible,** i.e., to display the object[b] that corresponds to it in intuition, since without this the concept would remain (as one says) without **sense,** i.e., without significance. Mathematics fulfills this requirement by means of the construction of the figure,[c] which is an appearance present to the senses (even though brought about *a priori*). In the same science the concept of magnitude seeks its standing and sense in number, but seeks this in turn in the fingers, in the beads of an abacus, or in strokes and points that are placed before the eyes. The concept is always generated *a priori*, together with the synthetic principles or formulas from such concepts; but their use and relation to supposed objects can in the end be sought nowhere but in experience, the possibility of which (as far as its form is concerned) is contained in them *a priori*.

B 300

That this is also the case with all categories, however, and the princi-

---

[a] *erkannt*
[b] *Object*
[c] *Gestalt*

ples spun out from them, is also obvious from this: That we cannot even give a real definition of a single one of them, i.e., make intelligible the possibility of their object,[a] without immediately descending to conditions of sensibility, thus to the form of the appearances, to which, as their sole objects, they must consequently be limited, since, if one removes this condition, all significance, i.e., relation to the object,[b] disappears, and one cannot grasp through an example what sort of thing is really intended by concepts of that sort.[c]

A 241

[d]No one can define the concept of magnitude in general except by something like this: That it is the determination of a thing through which it can be thought how many units are posited in it. Only this how-many-times is grounded on successive repetition, thus on time and the synthesis (of the homogeneous) in it. Reality, in contrast to negation, can only be defined if one thinks of a time (as the sum total of all being) that is either filled by it or empty. If I leave out persistence (which is existence at all times), then nothing is left in my concept of substance except the logical representation of the subject, which I try to realize by representing to myself something that can occur solely as subject (without being a predicate of anything). But then it is not only the case that I do not even know of any conditions under which this logical preeminence can be attributed to any sort of thing; it is also the case that absolutely nothing further is to be made of it, and not even the least consequence is to be drawn from it, because by its means no object[e] whatever of the use of this concept is determined, and one therefore does not even know whether the latter means anything at all. From the concept of a cause as a pure category (if I leave out the time in which something follows something else in accordance with a rule), I will not find out anything more than that it is something that allows an inference to the existence of something else; and in that case not only would there be nothing through which cause and effect could be distinguished, but further, since the possibility of drawing this inference also requires conditions about which I would know nothing, the concept would not even have any determination through which to apply to any object.[f] The supposed principle "Everything contingent has a cause" steps forth rather gravely, as if it had its own dignity in itself. Yet if I ask what you mean by "contingent," and you answer, "that the not-being of which is possible," then I would gladly know by what means you intend to cognize the possibility of this not-being, if you do not represent a

A 242

A 243
B 301

---

[a] *Objects*
[b] *Object*
[c] At this point material from the first edition is deleted; see A 241–2.
[d] The text common to the two editions resumes here.
[e] *Object*
[f] *Object*

A 244
B 302

A 246 / B 303

A 247

succession in the series of appearances and in this succession an existence, which follows on the not-being (or conversely), and thus a change; for that the not-being of a thing does not contradict itself is a lame appeal to a logical condition, which is certainly necessary for the concept but far from sufficient for real possibility; for I can suspend any existing substance in thought without contradicting myself, but I cannot at all infer from that to the objective contingency of its existence, i.e., the possibility of its*a* not-being in itself. As far as the concept of community is concerned, it is easy to appreciate that since the pure categories of substance as well as causality do not admit of any definition determining the object,*b* reciprocal causality in the relation of substances to each other (*commercium*) will be just as little susceptible of it. No one has ever been able to define possibility, existence, and necessity except through obvious tautologies if he wanted to draw their definition solely from the pure understanding. For the deception of substituting the logical possibility of the **concept** (since it does not contradict itself) for the transcendental possibility of **things** (where an object corresponds to the concept) can deceive and satisfy only the inexperienced.*,c*

Now from this it follows irrefutably that the pure concepts of the understanding can **never** be of **transcendental,** but always only of **empirical** use, and that the principles of pure understanding can be related to objects of the senses only in relation to the general conditions of a possible experience, but never to things in general (without taking regard of the way in which we might intuit them).

The Transcendental Analytic accordingly has this important result: That the understanding can never accomplish *a priori* anything more than to anticipate the form of a possible experience in general, and, since that which is not appearance cannot be an object of experience, it can never overstep the limits of sensibility, within which alone objects are given to us. Its principles are merely principles*d* of the exposition of appearances, and the proud name of an ontology, which presumes to offer synthetic *a priori* cognitions of things in general in a systematic

B 302

B 303

* <In a word, all of these concepts could not be **vouched for** and their **real** possibility thereby established, if all sensible intuition (the only one we have) were taken away, and there then remained only **logical** possibility, i.e., that the concept (thought) is possible is not the issue; the issue is rather whether it relates to an object*e* and therefore signifies anything.>

a Following Erdmann, reading "*ihres*" for "*seines.*"
b *Object*
c Footnote added in the second edition; following this point, a paragraph present in the first edition (A 244–6) is omitted in the second.
d *Principien*
e *Object*

doctrine (e.g., the principle of causality), must give way to the modest one of a mere analytic of the pure understanding.

Thinking is the action of relating given intuitions to an object. If the manner of this intuition is not given in any way, then the object is merely transcendental, and the concept of the understanding has none other than a transcendental use, namely the unity of thought of a manifold in general. Now through a pure category, in which abstraction is made from any condition of sensible intuition as the only one that is possible for us, no object*a* is determined, rather only the thought of an object*b* in general is expressed in accordance with different *modi*. Now to the use of a concept there also belongs a function of the power of judgment, whereby an object is subsumed under it, thus at least the formal condition under which something can be given in intuition. If this condition of the power of judgment (schema) is missing, then all subsumption disappears; for nothing would be given that could be subsumed under the concept. The merely transcendental use of the categories is thus in fact no use at all, and has no determinate or even, as far as its form is concerned, determinable object. From this it also follows that the pure category does not suffice for any synthetic *a priori* principle, and that the principles of the pure understanding are only of empirical but never of transcendental use; but nowhere beyond the field of possible experience can there be any synthetic *a priori* principles.

It may therefore be advisable to express ourselves thus: The pure categories, without formal conditions of sensibility, have merely transcendental significance, but are not of any transcendental use, since this is impossible in itself, for they are lacking all conditions of any use (in judgments), namely the formal conditions of the subsumption of any sort of supposed object under these concepts. Thus since (as merely pure categories) they are not supposed to have empirical use, and cannot have transcendental use, they do not have any use at all if they are separated from all sensibility, i.e., they cannot be applied to any supposed object at all; rather they are merely the pure form of the employment of the understanding in regard to objects in general and of thinking, yet without any sort of object*c* being able to be thought or determined through them alone.

d<Nevertheless, this is grounded on a deception that is difficult to avoid. As far as their origin is concerned, the categories are not grounded on sensibility, as are the **forms of intuition,** space and time;

B 304

A 248

B 305

---

a *Object*
b *Objects*
c *Object*
d The next four paragraphs were substituted in the second edition for seven paragraphs from A 249 to A 253.

they therefore seem to allow an application extended beyond all objects of the senses. But for their part they are in turn nothing other than **forms of thought,** which contain merely the logical capacity*a* for uni-

B 306 fying the manifold given in intuition in a consciousness *a priori;* thus if one takes away from them the only sensible intuition possible for us, they have even less significance than those pure sensible forms, through which at least an object*b* is given, whereas a kind of combination of the manifold that is proper to our understanding signifies nothing at all if that intuition in which alone the manifold can be given is not added to it. – Nevertheless, if we call certain objects, as appearances, beings of sense (*phaenomena*), because we distinguish the way in which we intuit them from their constitution in itself, then it already follows from our concept that to these we as it were oppose, as objects thought merely through the understanding, either other objects conceived in accordance with the latter constitution, even though we do not intuit it in them, or else other possible things, which are not objects*c* of our senses at all, and call these beings of understanding (*noumena*). Now the question arises: Whether our pure concepts of understanding do not have significance in regard to the latter, and whether they could be a kind of cognition of them?

But right at the outset here there is an ambiguity, which can occasion great misunderstanding: Since the understanding, when it calls an object in a relation mere phenomenon,*d* simultaneously makes for itself, beyond this relation, another representation of an **object in itself** and

B 307 hence also represents itself as being able to make **concepts** of such an object, and since the understanding offers nothing other than the categories through which the object in this latter sense must at least be able to be thought, it is thereby misled into taking the entirely **undetermined** concept of a being of understanding, as a something in general outside of our sensibility, for a **determinate** concept of a being that we could cognize through the understanding in some way.

If by a noumenon*e* we understand a thing **insofar as it is not an object*f* of our sensible intuition,** because we abstract from the manner of our intuition of it, then this is a noumenon in the **negative** sense.*g* But if we understand by that an **object*h* of a non-sensible intuition,**

---

a *Vermögen*

b *Object*

c *Objecte*

d Not in roman type.

e The word "noumenon" is not set in roman type here or in the remainder of this and the following paragraph.

f *Object*

g *Verstande*

h *Object*

then we assume a special kind of intuition, namely intellectual intuition, which, however, is not our own, and the possibility of which we cannot understand, and this would be the noumenon in a **positive** sense.[a]

Now the doctrine of sensibility is at the same time the doctrine of the noumenon in the negative sense, i.e., of things that the understanding must think without this relation to our kind of intuition, thus not merely as appearances but as things in themselves, but about which, however, it also understands that in this abstraction[b] it cannot consider   B 308 making any use of its categories, since they have significance only in relation to the unity of intuitions in space and time, and can even determine this unity *a priori* through general concepts of combination only on account of the mere ideality of space and time. Where this temporal unity cannot be encountered, thus in the case of the noumenon, there the entire use, indeed even all significance of the categories completely ceases; for then we could not have insight even into the possibility of the things that would correspond to the categories; on this score I need only appeal to that which I adduced right at the beginning of the general remark to the previous chapter.[96] Now, however, the possibility of a thing can never be proved merely through the non-contradictoriness of a concept of it, but only by vouching for it with an intuition corresponding to this concept. If, therefore, we wanted to apply the categories to objects that are not considered as appearances, then we would have to ground them on an intuition other than the sensible one, and then the object would be a noumenon in a **positive sense.**[c] Now since such an intuition, namely intellectual intuition, lies absolutely outside our faculty of cognition, the use of the categories can by no means reach beyond the boundaries of the objects of experience; and although beings of understanding certainly correspond to the beings of sense, and there may even be beings of understanding to which   B 309 our sensible faculty of intuition has no relation at all, our concepts of understanding, as mere forms of thought for our sensible intuition, do not reach these in the least; thus that which we call noumenon must be understood to be such only in a **negative** sense.[d]>

[e]If I take all thinking (through categories) away from an empirical   A 253 cognition, then no cognition of any object at all remains; for through mere intuition nothing at all is thought, and that this affection of sensibility is in me does not constitute any relation of such representation

---

[a] *Bedeutung*

[b] *Absonderung*

[c] *Bedeutung*

[d] *Bedeutung*

[e] From this point on the text of the first edition is preserved in the second with only one change on B 311 and one added footnote on B 312.

to any object^a at all. But if, on the contrary, I leave out all intuition, then there still remains the form of thinking, i.e., the way of determining an object for the manifold of a possible intuition. Hence to this extent the categories extend further than sensible intuition, since they think objects^b in general without seeing to the particular manner (of sensibility) in which they might be given. But they do not thereby determine a greater sphere of objects, since one cannot assume that such objects can be given without presupposing that another kind of intuition than the sensible kind is possible, which, however, we are by no means justified in doing.

I call a concept problematic that contains no contradiction but that is also, as a boundary for given concepts, connected with other cognitions, the objective reality of which can in no way be cognized. The concept of a **noumenon,**^c i.e., of a thing that is not to be thought of as an object of the senses but rather as a thing in itself (solely through a pure understanding), is not at all contradictory; for one cannot assert of sensibility that it is the only possible kind of intuition. Further, this concept is necessary in order not to extend sensible intuition to things in themselves, and thus to limit the objective validity of sensible cognition (for the other things, to which sensibility does not reach, are called noumena^d just in order to indicate that those cognitions cannot extend their domain to everything that the understanding thinks). In the end, however, we have no insight into the possibility of such *noumena,*^e and the domain outside of the sphere of appearances is empty (for us), i.e., we have an understanding that extends farther than sensibility **problematically,** but no intuition, indeed not even the concept of a possible intuition, through which objects outside of the field of sensibility could be given, and about which the understanding could be employed **assertorically.** The concept of a noumenon^f is therefore merely a **boundary concept,** in order to limit the pretension of sensibility, and therefore only of negative use. But it is nevertheless not invented arbitrarily, but is rather connected with the limitation of sensibility, yet without being able to posit anything positive outside of the domain of the latter.

The division of objects into *phaenomena* and *noumena,* and of the world into a world of sense and a world of understanding, can therefore not be permitted at all <in a positive sense>,^g although concepts cer-

A254

B310

A255

B311

---

^a *Object*
^b *Objecte*
^c Not in roman type.
^d Not in roman type.
^e Here Kant prints the Latin genitive *Noumenorum.*
^f Not in roman type.
^g The words "in a positive sense" added in the second edition.

tainly permit of division into sensible and intellectual ones; for one cannot determine any object for the latter, and therefore also cannot pass
them off as objectively valid. If one abandons the senses, how will one
make comprehensible that our categories (which would be the only re-   A 2 5 6
maining concepts for noumena)*a* still signify anything at all, since for
their relation to any object something more than merely the unity of
thinking must be given, namely a possible intuition, to which they can
be applied? Nevertheless the concept of a *noumenon*,*b* taken merely
problematically, remains not only admissible, but even unavoidable, as
a concept setting limits to sensibility. But in that case it is not a special
intelligible object for our understanding; rather an understanding to
which it would belong is itself a problem, that, namely, of cognizing its
object not discursively through categories but intuitively in a non-   B 3 1 2
sensible intuition, the possibility of which we cannot in the least represent. Now in this way our understanding acquires a negative expansion,
i.e., it is not limited by sensibility, but rather limits it by calling things
in themselves (not considered as appearances) *noumena*. But it also immediately sets boundaries for itself, not cognizing these things through
categories, hence merely thinking them under the name of an unknown
something.

Yet I find in the writings of the moderns an entirely different use of
the expressions of a *mundi sensibilis* and *intelligibilis*,*,*c* which entirely diverges from the sense of the ancients, which is not itself a problem, but   A 2 5 7
which is also nothing but empty trafficking with words. In accordance
with this usage some have been pleased to call the sum total of appearances, so far as it is intuited, the world of sense, but the connection*d* of
them insofar as it is thought in accordance with general laws of the understanding, the world of understanding. Theoretical astronomy, which   B 3 1 3
expounds the mere observation of the starry heavens, would be the former, contemplative astronomy on the contrary (explained, say, according to the Copernican world-system or even according to Newton's
laws of gravitation) would be the latter, making an intelligible world

---

* <In place of this expression one must not use that of an **intellectual** world, as   B 3 1 2
is customary in German; for only **cognitions** are intellectual or sensitive. But
that which can only be an **object** of the one mode of intuition or the other,
the objects*e* therefore, must be called intelligible or sensible (regardless of how
harsh it sounds).>

a Not in roman type.
b Here Kant uses the Latin singular genitive *Noumeni*.
c "sensible and intelligible worlds." The footnote attached here is an addition in the second edition.
d *Zusammenhang*
e *Objecte*

representable. But such a perversion of words is a merely sophistical evasion for escaping from a difficult question by reducing its sense to a commonplace. With regard to appearances, to be sure, both understanding and reason can be used; but it must be asked whether they would still have any use if the object were not appearance (*noumenon*), and one takes it in this sense if one thinks of it as merely intelligible, i.e., as given to the understanding alone and not to the senses at all. The question is thus: whether beyond the empirical use of the understanding (even in the Newtonian representation of the cosmos) a transcendental one is also possible, pertaining to the noumenon as an object – which question we have answered negatively.

A258   If, therefore, we say: The senses represent objects to us **as they appear,** but the understanding, **as they are,** then the latter is not to be taken in a transcendental but in a merely empirical way, signifying, namely, how they must be represented as objects of experience, in the

B314 thoroughgoing connection*a* of appearances, and not how they might be outside of the relation to possible experience and consequently to sense in general, thus as objects of pure understanding. For this will always remain unknown to us, so that it even remains unknown whether such a transcendental (extraordinary) cognition is possible at all, at least as one that stands under our customary categories. With us **understanding** and **sensibility** can determine an object **only in combination.** If we separate them, then we have intuitions without concepts, or concepts without intuitions, but in either case representations that we cannot relate to any determinate object.

    If after all this discussion anyone still has reservations about denying the categories a merely transcendental use, then he should test them in any synthetic assertion. For an analytic one takes the understanding no further, and since it is occupied only with that which is already thought in the concept, it leaves it undecided whether the concept even has any

A259 relation to objects, or only signifies the unity of thinking in general (which entirely abstracts from the way in which an object might be given); it is enough for him to know what lies in its concept; what the concept might pertain to is indifferent to him. He should accordingly

B315 test it with some synthetic and allegedly transcendental principle, such as: "Everything that is, exists as substance, or a determination dependent on it," "Everything contingent exists as the effect of another thing, namely its cause," etc. Now I ask: Whence will he derive these synthetic propositions, since the concepts are not to hold of possible experience but rather of things in themselves (*noumena*)? Where is the third thing that is always requisite for a synthetic proposition in order to connect with each other concepts that have no logical (analytical) affinity? He

---

a *Zusammenhang*

will never prove his proposition, indeed, what is more, he will not even be able to justify the possibility of such a pure assertion, without taking account of the empirical use of the understanding, and thereby fully renouncing the pure and sense-free judgment. Thus the concept of pure, merely intelligible objects is entirely devoid of all principles of its application, since one cannot think up*a* any way in which they could be given, and the problematic thought, which leaves a place open for them, only serves, like an empty space, to limit the empirical principles, without containing and displaying any other object*b* of cognition beyond the sphere of the latter.

A 260

a *ersinnen*
b *Object*

^aAppendix
On the amphiboly of the concepts
of reflection^b through the confusion of the
empirical use of the understanding with
the transcendental.

Reflection^c (*reflexio*) does not have to do with objects themselves, in order to acquire concepts directly from them, but is rather the state of mind in which we first prepare ourselves to find out the subjective conditions under which we can arrive at concepts.[97] It is the consciousness of the relation^d of given representations to our various sources of cognition, through which alone their relation among themselves can be correctly determined. The first question prior to all further treatment of our representation is this: In which cognitive faculty do they belong together? Is it the understanding or is it the senses before which they are connected or compared? Many a judgment is accepted out of habit, or connected through inclination: but since no reflection preceded or at least critically succeeded it, it counts as one that has received its origin in the understanding. Not all judgments require an **investigation,** i.e., attention to the grounds of truth; for if they are immediately certain, e.g., between two points there can be only one straight line, then no further mark of truth can be given for them than what they themselves express. But all judgments, indeed all comparisons, require a **reflection,** i.e., a distinction of the cognitive power to which the given con-

---

^a There are only minor differences between the versions of this section in the two editions, mostly changes in orthography that do not affect the translation. Thus only one version of the section will be presented here.
^b *Reflexion*
^c *Überlegung*; since the following parenthesis shows that Kant treats this Germanic term as synonymous with the Latinate *Reflexion*, we will not mark any distinction between occurrences of *Überlegung* and *Reflexion*.
^d *Verhältnisses*. Since *Beziehung* occurs only three times in this section, we will note only when "relation" is used to translate that term rather than the far more frequent occurrences of *Verhältnis*.

cepts belong.*a* The action through which I make the comparison of representations in general with the cognitive power in which they are situated, and through which I distinguish whether they are to be compared to one another as belonging to the pure understanding or to pure intuition, I call **transcendental reflection**. The relation, however, in which the concepts in a state of mind can belong to each other are those of **identity** and **difference**, of **agreement** and **opposition**, of the **inner** and the **outer**, and finally of the **determinable** and the **determination** (matter and form). The correct determination of this relation depends on the cognitive power in which they **subjectively** belong to each other, whether in sensibility or in understanding. For the difference in the latter makes a great difference in the way in which one ought to think of the former.

Prior to all objective judgments we compare the concepts, with regard to **identity***b* (of many representations under one concept) for the sake of **universal** judgments, or their **difference**, for the generation of **particular** ones, with regard to **agreement**, for **affirmative** judgments, or **opposition**,*c* for negative ones, etc. On this ground it would seem that we ought to call these concepts concepts of comparison (*conceptus comparationis*). But since, if it is not the logical form but the content of concepts that is concerned, i.e., whether the things themselves are identical or different, in agreement or in opposition, etc., the things can have a twofold relation to our power of cognition, namely to sensibility and to understanding, yet it is this place **in which** they belong that concerns **how** they ought to belong to each other: then it is transcendental reflection, i.e., the relation of given representations to one or the other kind of cognition, that can alone determine their relation among themselves, and whether the things are identical or different, in agreement or in opposition, etc., cannot immediately be made out from the concepts themselves through mere comparison (*comparatio*), but rather only through the distinction of the kind of cognition to which they belong, by means of a transcendental reflection (*reflexio*). To be sure, one could

A 262

B 318

---

a Inserted in Kant's copy of the first edition: "The judgment in accordance with concepts of reflection is, with regard to things in themselves, analytic, only the consciousness to determine, in appearances, is synthetic." (E CXLI, p. 44; 23:37)

b **Einerleyheit.** The following note is inserted in Kant's copy of the first edition: "Whether identical concepts of things prove one and the same thing, and therefore no multiplicity, or whether in spite of complete identity of concepts there can yet be many things, on account of the difference in places – this belongs to logical quantity." (E CXLII, p. 44; 23:37)

c **Widerstreit.** Inserted in Kant's copy of the first edition: "Mutually non-contradictory concepts of realities are in agreement. Can I therefore say that the things are in agreement, which consist in those very things together? Conversely, can two opposed determinations in an alteration be in opposition to each other in the thing in itself, but in agreement in the *phaenomenon?*" (E CXLIII, pp. 44–5; 23:37)

therefore say that **logical reflection** is a mere comparison, for in its case there is complete abstraction from the cognitive power to which the given representations belong, and they are thus to be treated the same as far as their seat in the mind is concerned; **transcendental reflection,** however, (which goes to the objects themselves) contains the ground of the possibility of the objective comparison of the representations to each other, and is therefore very different from the other, since the cognitive power to which the representations belong is not precisely the same. This transcendental reflection is a duty from which no one can escape if he would judge anything about things *a priori.* We will now take it in hand, and will draw from it not a little illumination of the determination of the proper business of the understanding.[a]

1. **Identity** and **difference.**[98] If an object is presented to us several times, but always with the same inner determinations (*qualitas et quantitas*), then it is always exactly the same if it counts as an object of pure understanding, not many but only one[b] thing (*numerica identitas*);[c] but if it is appearance, then the issue is not the comparison of concepts, but rather, however identical everything may be in regard to that, the difference of the places of these appearances at the same time is still an adequate ground for the **numerical difference** of the object (of the senses) itself. Thus, in the case of two drops of water one can completely abstract from all inner difference (of quality and quantity), and it is enough that they be intuited in different places at the same time in order for them to be held to be numerically different. Leibniz[99] took the appearances for things in themselves, thus for *intelligibilia,* i.e., objects of the pure understanding (although on account of the confusion of their representations he labeled them with the name of phenomena),[d] and there his principle of **non-discernibility** (*principium identitatis indiscernibilium*)[e] could surely not be disputed,[100] but since they are objects of sensibility, and the understanding with regard to them is not of pure but of empirical use, multiplicity and numerical difference are already given by space itself as the condition of outer appearances. For a part of space, even though it might be completely similar and equal to another, is nevertheless outside of it, and is on that account a different part from that which is added to it in order to constitute a larger space; and this must therefore hold of everything that exists simultaneously in

[a] Inserted in Kant's copy of the first edition: "These propositions obviously teach that space and time hold only of things, and among them also of ourselves, as appearances; for otherwise they would not yield entirely opposed propositions, like those we assert of things in themselves." (E CXLIV, p. 45; 23:37)
[b] In the first edition, "many" (*viel*) and "only one" (*nur Ein*) were emphasized.
[c] numerical identity
[d] Not in roman type.
[e] principle of the identity of indiscernibles

the various positions in space, no matter how similar and equal they might otherwise be.

2. **Agreement** and **opposition.** If reality is represented only through the pure understanding (*realitas noumenon*), then no opposition between realities can be thought, i.e., a relation such that when they are bound together in one subject they cancel out their consequences, as in $3 - 3 = 0$.[a,101] Realities[b] in appearance (*realitas phaenomenon*), on the contrary, can certainly be in opposition with each other and, united in the same subject, one can partly or wholly destroy the **consequence of the other,** like two moving forces in the same straight line that either push or pull a point in opposed directions, or also like an enjoyment that balances the scale against a pain.[c]

3.[d] The **inner** and the **outer.** In an object of the pure understanding only that is internal that has no relation[e] (as far as the existence is concerned) to anything that is different from it. The inner determinations of a *substantia phaenomenon*[f] in space, on the contrary, are nothing but relations, and it is itself entirely a sum total of mere relations.[g,h] We know substance in space only through forces that are efficacious in it, whether in drawing others to it (attraction) or in preventing penetration of it (repulsion and impenetrability); we are not acquainted with other properties constituting the concept of the substance that appears in space and which we call matter. As object[i] of the pure understanding, on the contrary, every substance must have inner determinations and forces that pertain to its inner reality. Yet what can I think of as inner accidents except for those which my inner sense offers me? – namely that which is either itself **thinking** or which is analogous to one. Thus because he represented them as *noumena*, taking away in thought everything that might signify outer relation,[j] thus even **composition,** Leibniz made out of all substances, even the constituents of matter, simple subjects gifted with powers of representation, in a word, **monads.**[102]

4. **Matter** and **form.** These are two concepts that ground all other re-

A 265

B 321

A 266

B 322

---

[a] Kant's copy of the first edition adds: "for reality is opposed to mere negation = 0." (E CXLV, p. 45; 23:49)

[b] *Das Reale*

[c] Inserted in Kant's copy of the first edition: "This misunderstanding causes one to place all ill and evil in the world, all vice and pain, in mere negations, and to value reality so highly." (E CXLVI, p. 45; 23:37)

[d] Added in Kant's copy of the first edition: "Idealism and dualism." (E CXLVII, p. 45)

[e] *Beziehung*

[f] phenomenal substance

[g] *Relationen*

[h] Inserted in Kant's copy of the first edition: "In space there are solely outer relations, in time purely inner ones; the absolute is absent." (E CXLVIII, p. 45; 23:37)

[i] *Object*

[j] *Relation*

flection, so inseparably are they bound up with every use of the understanding. The former signifies the determinable in general, the latter its determination*a* (both in the transcendental sense,*b* since one abstracts from all differences in what is given and from the way in which that is determined). The logicians formerly called the universal the matter, but the specific difference the form. In every judgment one can call the given concepts logical matter (for judgment), their relation (by means of the copula) the form of the judgment. In every being its components (*essentialia*) are the matter; the way in which they are connected in a thing, the essential form. Also, in respect to things in general, unbounded reality is regarded as the matter of all possibility, but its limitation (negation) as

A267

that form through which one thing is distinguished from another in accordance with transcendental concepts. The understanding, namely, de-

B323

mands first that something be given (at least in the concept) in order to be able to determine it in a certain way. Hence in the concept of pure understanding matter precedes form, and on this account Leibniz first assumed things (monads) and an internal power of representation in them, in order subsequently to ground on that their outer relation and the community of their states (namely of the representations) on that. Hence space and time were possible, the former only through the relation of substances, the latter through the connection of their determinations as grounds and consequences.[103] And so would it in fact have to be if the pure understanding could be related to objects immediately, and if space and time were determinations of the things in themselves. But if it is only sensible intuitions in which we determine all objects merely as appearances, then the form of intuition (as a subjective constitution of sensibility) precedes all matter (the sensations), thus space and time precede all appearances and all *data* of appearances, and instead first make the latter possible. The intellectualist philosopher could not bear it that form should precede the things and determine their possibility; a quite appropriate criticism, if he assumed that we intuit things as they are

A268

(though with confused representation). But since sensible intuition is an

B324

entirely peculiar subjective condition, which grounds all perception *a priori*, and the form of which is original, thus the form is given for itself alone, and so far is it from being the case that the matter (or the things themselves, which appear) ought to be the ground (as one would have to judge according to mere concepts), that rather their possibility presupposes a formal intuition (of space and time) as given.

---

a Inserted in Kant's copy of the first edition: "The thoroughgoing determination as principle [*Princip*] is grounded on the unity of consciousness: existence determined in space and time. Hence in *noumena* the highest reality contains the matter and the form contains the perfection. The *formale* is the best." (E CXLIX, p. 45; 23:37)

b *Verstande*

Remark
to the amphiboly of the concepts of reflection.

Allow me to call the position that we assign to a concept either in sensibility or in pure understanding its **transcendental place.** In the same way, the estimation of this position that pertains to every concept in accordance with the difference in its use, and guidance for determining this place for all concepts in accordance with rules, would be the **transcendental topic,** a doctrine that would thoroughly protect against false pretenses of the pure understanding and illusions arising therefrom by always distinguishing to which cognitive power the concepts properly belong. One can call every concept, every title under which many cognitions belong, a **logical place.** On this is grounded the **logical topics** of Aristotle, which schoolteachers and orators could use in order to hunt up certain titles of thinking to find that which best fits their current matter and rationalize or garrulously chatter about it with an appearance of thoroughness.[104] A 269 B 325

The transcendental topic, on the contrary, contains nothing more than the four titles for all comparison and distinction introduced above, which are distinguished from categories by the fact that what is exhibited through them is not the object in accordance with what constitutes its concept (magnitude, reality), but rather only the comparison of representations, in all their manifoldness, which precedes the concepts of things. This comparison, however, first requires a reflection, i.e., a determination of the place where the representations of the things that are compared belong, thus of whether they are thought by the pure understanding or given in appearance by sensibility.

The concepts can be compared logically without worrying about where their objects[a] belong, whether as noumena[b] to the understanding or as phenomena[c] to sensibility. But if we would get to the objects with these concepts, then transcendental reflection about which cognitive power they are objects for, whether for the pure understanding or for sensibility, is necessary first of all. Without this reflection I can make only a very insecure use of these concepts, and there arise allegedly synthetic principles, which critical reason cannot acknowledge and that are grounded solely on a transcendental amphiboly, i.e., a confusion of the pure object of the understanding[d] with the appearance. A 270/ B 326

Lacking such a transcendental topic, and thus deceived by the amphiboly of the concepts of reflection, the famous Leibniz constructed

---

[a] *Objecte*
[b] Not in roman type.
[c] Not in roman type.
[d] *Verstandesobjects*

an **intellectual system of the world,** or rather believed himself able to cognize the inner constitution of things by comparing all objects only with the understanding and the abstract formal concepts of its thinking. Our table of the concepts of reflection gives us the unexpected advantage of laying before our eyes that which is distinctive in his theory in all its parts and the leading ground of this peculiar way of thinking, which rests on nothing but a misunderstanding. He compared all things with each other solely through concepts, and found, naturally, no other differences than those through which the understanding distinguishes its pure concepts from each other. The conditions of sensible intuition, which bring with them their own distinctions, he did not regard as original; for sensibility was only a confused kind of representation for him, and not a special source of representations; for him appearance was the representation **of the thing in itself,** although distinguished from cognition through the understanding in its logical form, since with its customary lack of analysis the former draws a certain mixture of subsidiary representations into the concept of the thing, from which the understanding knows how to abstract. In a word, Leibniz **intellectualized** the appearances, just as Locke totally **sensitivized** the concepts of understanding in accordance with his system of **noogony** (if I am permitted this expression), i.e., interpreted them as nothing but empirical or abstracted concepts of reflection.[105] Instead of seeking two entirely different sources of representation in the understanding and the sensibility, which could judge about things with objective validity **only in conjunction,**[a] each of these great men holds on only to one of them, which in his opinion is immediately related to things in themselves, while the other does nothing but confuse or order the representations of the first.

A 271
B 327

Leibniz accordingly compared the objects of the senses with each other as things in general, merely in the understanding,[b] **first,** so far as they are to be judged by the understanding as identical or different. Since he therefore had before his eyes solely their concepts, and not their position in the intuition in which alone the objects can be given, and left entirely out of consideration the transcendental place of these concepts (whether the object[c] is to be counted among appearances or among things in themselves), it could not have turned out otherwise but that he extended his principle of indiscernibles,[d] which holds merely of concepts of things in general, to the objects of the senses (*mundus phaenomenon*),[e] and thereby believed himself to have made no little ad-

A 272
B 328

---

[a] *Verknüpfung*
[b] Using a comma as in the first edition rather than a period as in the second.
[c] *Object*
[d] That is, the principle of the identity of indiscernibles.
[e] phenomenal world

vance in the cognition of nature. Of course, if I know a drop of water as a thing in itself according to all of its inner determinations, I cannot let any one drop count as different from another if the entire concept of the former is identical with that of the latter. But if it is an appearance in space, then it has its place not merely in the understanding (under concepts), but also in the sensible outer intuition (in space), and since the physical places are entirely indifferent with regard to the inner determinations of the things, a place = b can just as readily accept a thing that is fully similar and equal to another in a place = a as it could if the former were ever so internally different from the latter. Without further conditions, the difference in place already makes the multiplicity and distinction of objects as appearances not only possible in itself but also necessary. Thus that putative law is no law of nature. It is simply an analytical rule or comparison of things through mere concepts.

Second, the principle that realities (as mere affirmations) never logically oppose each other is an entirely true proposition about the relations of concepts, but signifies nothing at all either in regard to nature nor overall in regard to anything in itself (of this we have no concept). For real opposition always obtains where $A - B = 0$, i.e., where one reality, if combined in one subject with another, cancels out the effect of the latter, which is unceasingly placed before our eyes by all hindrances and countereffects in nature, which, since they rest on forces, must be called *realitates phaenomena.*[a] General mechanics can even provide the empirical condition of this opposition in an *a priori* rule by looking to the opposition of directions – a condition about which the transcendental concept of reality knows nothing at all.[106] Although Herr von Leibniz did not exactly announce this proposition with the pomp of a new principle, he nevertheless used it for new assertions, and his successors expressly incorporated it into their Leibnizian-Wolffian doctrine. According to this principle, e.g., all ills are nothing but consequences of the limits of created beings, i.e., negations, since these are the only opposing things in reality (this is really so in the concept of a thing in general, but not in things as appearances).[107] Similarly, its adherents find it not merely possible but also natural to unite all reality in one being without any worry about opposition, since they do not recognize any opposition except that of contradiction (through which the concept of a thing would itself be canceled out),[108] and do not recognize the opposition of reciprocal destruction, where one real ground cancels out the effect of another, the conditions for the representation of which we find only in sensibility.

Third, the Leibnizian monadology has no ground at all other than the fact that this philosopher represented the distinction of the inner

A273
B329

B330
A274

[a] phenomenal realities

373

and outer merely in relation to the understanding. Substances in general must have something **inner,** which is therefore free of all outer relations, consequently also of composition. The simple is therefore the foundation of the inner in things in themselves. But that which is inner in their state cannot consist in place, shape, contact, or motion (which determinations are all outer relations), and we can therefore attribute to the substances no other inner state than that through which we internally determine our sense itself, namely **the state of representations.** This completes the monads, which are to constitute the fundamental matter of the entire universe, the active power of which, however, consists merely in representations, through which they are properly efficacious merely within themselves.

For this very reason, however, his principle*a* of the possible **community of substances** among themselves also had to be **predetermined harmony** and could not be a physical influence.[109] For since everything is only internal, i.e., occupied with its own representations, the state of the representations of one substance could not stand in any efficacious connection at all with that of another, but some third cause influencing all of them had to make their states correspond to one another, not, to be sure, through occasional assistance specially brought about in each case (*systema assistentiae*),*b* but rather through the unity of the idea of one cause valid for all, from which, in accordance with general laws, they must all together acquire their existence and persistence, thus also their reciprocal correspondence with each other.

Fourth, Leibniz's famous **doctrine** of **space** and **time,** in which he intellectualized these forms of sensibility, arose solely from this very same deception of transcendental reflection. If I would represent outer relations of things through the mere understanding, this can be done only by means of a concept of their reciprocal effect, and should I connect one state of the one and the same thing with another state, then this can only be done in the order of grounds and consequences. Thus Leibniz thought of space as a certain order in the community of substances, and thought of time as the dynamic sequence of their states.[110] The uniqueness and independence from things, however, which both of these seem to have in themselves, he ascribed to the **confusion** of these concepts, which made that which is a mere form of dynamical relations be taken for an intuition subsisting by itself and preceding the things themselves. Thus space and time became the intelligible form of the connection of the things (substances and their states) in themselves. The things, however, were intelligible substances (*substantiae noumena*). Nevertheless he wanted to make these concepts valid for appearances,

B 331
A 275

B 332
A 276

---

a *Principium*

b "System of assistance," i.e., the occasionalism of Nicolas Malebranche.

since he conceded to sensibility no kind of intuition of its own, but rather sought everything in the understanding, even the empirical representation of objects, and left nothing for the senses but the contemptible occupation of confusing and upsetting the representations of the former.

But even if we could say anything synthetically **about things in themselves** through the pure understanding (which is nevertheless impossible), this still could not be related to appearances at all, which do not represent things in themselves. In this latter case, therefore, I will always have to compare my concepts in transcendental reflection only under the conditions of sensibility, and thus space and time will not be determinations of things in themselves, but of appearances; what the things may be in themselves I do not know, and also do not need to know, since a thing can never come before me except in appearance. A277 B333

I proceed in the same way with the other concepts of reflection. Matter is *substantia phaenomenon.*[a] What pertains to it internally I seek in all parts of space that it occupies and in all effects that it carries out, and which can certainly always be only appearances of outer sense. I therefore have nothing absolutely but only comparatively internal, which itself in turn consists of outer relations. Yet the absolutely internal in matter, according to pure understanding, is a mere fancy, for it is nowhere an object for the pure understanding; the transcendental object,[b] however, which might be the ground of this appearance that we call matter, is a mere something, about which we would not understand what it is even if someone could tell us. For we cannot understand anything except that which has something corresponding to our words in intuition. If the complaints "**That we have no insight into the inner in things**"[111] are to mean that we do not understand through pure reason what the things that appear to us might be in themselves, then they are entirely improper and irrational; for they would have us be able to cognize things, thus intuit them, even without senses, consequently they would have it that we have a faculty of cognition entirely distinct from the human not merely in degree but even in intuition and kind, and thus that we ought to be not humans but beings that we cannot even say are possible, let alone how they are constituted. Observation and analysis of the appearances penetrate into what is inner in nature, and one cannot know how far this will go in time. Those transcendental questions, however, that go beyond nature, we will never be able to answer, even if all of nature is revealed to us, since[c] it is never given to A278 B334

[a] phenomenal substance
[b] *Object*
[c] Following the second edition, reading *da* instead of *und*. In his copy of the first edition, Kant substituted *weil* for *und* (E, p. 45).

us to observe our own mind with any other intuition that that of our inner sense. For in that lies the mystery of the origin of our sensibility. Its relation^a to an object, ^{b} and what might be the transcendental ground of this unity, undoubtedly lie too deeply hidden for us, who know even ourselves only through inner sense, thus as appearance, to be able to use such an unsuitable tool of investigation to find out anything except always more appearances, even though we would gladly investigate their non-sensible cause.

What makes this critique of the inferences from the mere actions of reflection useful above all is that it clearly establishes the nullity of all inferences about objects that one simply compares with each other in the understanding, and at the same time confirms what we have chiefly emphasized: that although appearances cannot be comprehended among the objects^c of pure understanding as things in themselves, they are nevertheless the only things by means of which our cognition can have objective reality, namely, where intuition corresponds to the concepts.

A279/B335

If we reflect merely logically, then we simply compare our concepts with each other in the understanding, seeing whether two of them contain the very same thing, whether they contradict each other or not, whether something is contained in the concept internally or is added to it, and which of them should count as given and which as a manner of thinking of that which is given. But if I apply these concepts to an object in general (in the transcendental sense),^{d} without further determining whether this is an object of sensible or intellectual intuition, then limitations (which do not flow from this concept) immediately show up, which pervert all empirical use of them, and by that very means prove that the representation of an object as a thing in general is not merely **insufficient** but rather, without sensible determinations of it and independent of an empirical condition, **contradictory** in itself, thus that one must either abstract from any object (in logic), or else, if one assumes an object, then one must think it under conditions of sensible intuition; thus the intelligible would require an entirely special intuition, which we do not have, and in the absence of this would be nothing **for us,** though on the contrary appearances also cannot be objects in themselves. For, if I think of mere things in general, then the difference in the outer relations certainly does not constitute a difference in the things^e themselves, but rather presupposes this, and, if the concept of the one is not internally distinct from that of the other, then I merely

B336
A280

---

^{a} *Beziehung*
^{b} *Object*
^{c} *Objecten*
^{d} *Verstande*
^{e} *Sachen*

posit one and the same thing in different relations. Further, through the addition of one mere affirmation (reality) to another the positive is increased, and nothing is taken away from it or canceled out; hence the real in things in general cannot contradict each other, etc.

* * *

As we have shown, through a certain misinterpretation the concepts of reflection have had such an influence on the use of the understanding that they have even been able to seduce one of the most acute of all philosophers into a supposed system of intellectual cognition, which undertakes to determine its object without supplementation by the senses. For just this reason the exposition of the deceptive cause of the amphiboly of these concepts, as the occasion of false principles, is of great utility in reliably determining and securing the boundaries of the understanding.

One must say, to be sure, that whatever pertains to or contradicts a concept in general also pertains to or contradicts everything particular that is contained under that concept (*dictum de Omni et Nullo*);[a],[112] but it would be absurd to alter this logical principle so that it would read: "Whatever is not contained in a general concept is also not contained in the particular ones that stand under it"; for the latter are particular concepts precisely because they contain more than is thought in the general concept. Yet Leibniz's entire intellectual system is really built on the latter principle: it therefore falls together with it, along with all of the ambiguity in the use of the understanding that arises from it.

The principle of indiscernibles is really based on the presupposition that if a certain distinction is not to be found in the concept of a thing in general, then it is also not to be found in the things themselves; consequently all things are completely identical (*numero eadem*)[b] that are not already distinguished from each other in their concepts (as to quality or quantity). But since in the mere concept of anything abstraction is made from many necessary conditions of an intuition, it is with peculiar haste that that from which abstraction has been made is taken as something that is not to be encountered at all, and nothing conceded to the thing except what is contained in its concept.

The concept of a cubic foot of space, wherever and however often I think it, is in itself always completely the same. Yet two cubic feet are nevertheless distinguished in space merely through their locations (*numero diversa*);[c] these are conditions of the intuition in which the object[d]

B337
A281

B338
A282

---

[a] principle of All or Nothing
[b] "the same in number," i.e., even numerically identical.
[c] numerically diverse
[d] *Object*

of this concept is given, which do not belong to the concept but to the entire sensibility. In the same way, there is no contradiction at all in the concept of a thing if nothing negative is connected with something affirmative, and merely affirmative concepts cannot, in combination, effect any cancellation. Yet in the sensible intuition in which reality (e.g., motion) is given, there are conditions (opposed directions), from which one had abstracted in the concept of motion in general, that make possible a conflict, which is certainly not a logical one, that produces a zero = o out of that which is entirely positive; and one could not say that all reality is in agreement just because no conflict^a is to be found among its concepts.* According to mere concepts the inner is the substratum of all relation or outer determinations. If, therefore, I abstract from all conditions of intuition, and restrict myself solely to the concept of a thing in general, then I can abstract from every outer relation, and yet there must remain a concept of it, that signifies no relation but merely inner determinations. Now it seems as if it follows from this that in every thing (substance) there is something that is absolutely internal and precedes all outer determinations, first making them possible, thus that this substratum is something that contains no more outer relations in itself, consequently that it is **simple** (for corporeal things are still always only relations, at least of the parts outside one another); and since we are not acquainted with any absolutely inner determinations except through our inner sense, this substratum would be not only simple, but also (according to the analogy with our inner sense) determined through **representations,** i.e., all things would really be **monads,** or simple beings endowed with representations.[113] And this would all be correct, were it not that something more than the concept of a thing in general belongs to the conditions under which alone objects of outer intuition can be given to us, and from which the pure concept abstracts. For these show that a persistent appearance in space (impenetrable extension) contains mere relations and nothing absolutely internal, and nevertheless can be the primary substratum of all outer perception. Through mere concepts, of course, I cannot think of something external without anything

B 339
A 283

B 340

A 284

---

* If one wanted to make use of the usual escape here, that at least *realitates noumena* cannot act in opposition to each other, one would still have to introduce an example of such pure and non-sensible reality in order to understand whether such a reality represents something or nothing at all. But no example can be derived from anywhere except experience, which never offers more than *phaenomena,* and thus this proposition signifies nothing more than that a concept that contains only affirmations does not contain anything negative: a proposition that we have never doubted.

^{a} *Widerstreit*

inner, for the very reason that relational concepts absolutely presuppose given things and are not possible without these. But since something is contained in the intuition that does not lie at all in the mere concept of a thing in general, and this yields the substratum that cannot be cognized through mere concepts, namely a space that, along with everything that it contains, consists of purely formal or also real relations, I cannot say that since without something absolutely inner no thing can be represented **through mere concepts,** there is also nothing outer that does not have something absolutely internal as its ground in the things themselves that are contained under these concepts and in **their intuition.** For if we have abstracted from all conditions of intuition, then of course there remains nothing in the mere concept except the inner in general, and its relation in that, through which alone the outer is possible. But this necessity, which is grounded only on abstraction, does not obtain in the case of things insofar as they are given in intuition with determinations that express mere relations without having anything inner at their ground, since these are not things in themselves but simply appearances. And whatever we can cognize only in matter is pure relations (that which we call their inner determinations is only comparatively internal); but there are among these some self-sufficient and persistent ones, through which a determinate object is given to us. The fact that if I abstract from these relations I have nothing further to think at all does not cancel out the concept of a thing as appearance, nor the concept of an object *in abstracto,* but does cancel all possibility of such an object determinable in accordance with mere concepts, i.e., a concept of a noumenon.[a] It is certainly startling to hear that a thing should consist entirely of relations, but such a thing is also mere appearance, and cannot be thought at all through pure categories; it itself consists in the mere relation of something in general to the senses. In the same way, if one begins with mere concepts one cannot very well think of the relations of things *in abstracto* except by thinking that one is the cause of the determinations in the other; for that is our concept of the understanding of relations itself. Yet since in this case we abstract from all intuition, an entire way in which the manifold can determine its place, namely the form of sensibility (space) disappears, which yet precedes all empirical causality.

If by merely intelligible objects we understand those things that are thought[b] through pure categories, without any schema of sensibility, then things of this sort are impossible. For the condition of the objective use of all our concepts of understanding is merely the manner of our sensible intuition, through which objects are given to us, and, if we

B 341

A 285

B 342

A 286

---

[a] Not in roman type.
[b] Altered in Kant's copy of the first edition to "are cognized by us" (E CL, p. 46; 23:49).

abstract from the latter, then the former have no relation[a] at all to any sort of object.[b] Indeed, even if one would assume another sort of intuition than this our sensible one, our functions for thinking would still be without any significance in regard to it. If we understand thereby only objects of a non-sensible intuition, of which our categories are certainly not valid, and of which we can therefore never have any cognition at all (neither intuition nor concept), then *noumena* in this merely negative sense must of course be allowed: for they would then not say anything but that our manner of intuition does not pertain to all things, but only to objects of our senses, consequently that their objective validity is bounded, and room thus remains for some other sort of intuition and therefore also for things as its objects.[c] But in that case the concept of a *noumenon* is problematic, i.e., the representation of a thing of which we can say neither that it is possible nor that it is impossible, since we are acquainted with no sort of intuition other than our own sensible one and no other sort of concepts than the categories, neither of which, however, is suited to an extrasensible object. Hence we cannot thereby positively expand the field of the objects of our thinking beyond the conditions of our sensibility, and assume beyond appearances objects of pure thinking, i.e., *noumena*, since those do not have any positive significance that can be given. For one must concede that the categories alone are not sufficient for the cognition of things in themselves, and without the *data* of sensibility they would be merely subjective forms of the unity of the understanding, but without any object. Thinking in itself, to be sure, is not a product of the senses, and to this extent is also not limited by them, but it is not on that account immediately of any independent and pure use, without assistance from sensibility, for it is in that case without an object.[d] And one cannot call the noumenon[e] such an **object**,[f] for this signifies precisely the problematic concept of an object for an entirely different intuition and an entirely different understanding than our own, which is thus a problem itself. The concept of the noumenon[g] is therefore not the concept of an object,[h] but rather the problem, unavoidably connected with the limitation of our sensibility, of whether there may not be objects entirely exempt from the intuition of our sensibility, a question that can only be given

B 343

A 287

B 344

A 288

---

[a] *Beziehung*
[b] *Object*
[c] *Objecte*
[d] *Object*
[e] Not in roman type.
[f] **Object**
[g] Not in roman type.
[h] *Object*

the indeterminate answer that since sensible intuition does not pertain to all things without distinction room remains for more and other objects; they cannot therefore be absolutely denied, but in the absence of a determinate concept (for which no category is serviceable) they also cannot be asserted as objects for our understanding.

The understanding accordingly bounds sensibility without thereby expanding its own field, and in warning sensibility not to presume to reach for things in themselves but solely for appearances it thinks of an object in itself, but only as a transcendental object,[a] which is the cause of appearance (thus not itself appearance), and that cannot be thought of either as magnitude or as reality or as substance, etc. (since these concepts always require sensible forms in which they determine an object); it therefore remains completely unknown whether such an object is to be encountered within or without us, whether it would be canceled out along with sensibility or whether it would remain even if we took sensibility away. If we want to call this object[b] a noumenon[c] because the representation of it is nothing sensible, we are free to do so. But since we cannot apply any of our concepts of the understanding to it, this representation still remains empty for us, and serves for nothing but to designate the boundaries of our sensible cognition and leave open a space that we can fill up neither through possible experience nor through the pure understanding.

The critique of this pure understanding thus does not allow us to create a new field of objects beyond those that can come before it as appearances, and to indulge in intelligible worlds, or even in the concept of them. The mistake that most obviously leads to this, and can certainly be excused though not justified, lies in this: that the use of the understanding, contrary to its vocation,[d] is made transcendental, and the objects, i.e., possible intuitions, are made to conform themselves to concepts, but concepts are not made to conform themselves to possible intuitions (on which alone rests their objective validity). The cause of this, however, is in turn that apperception and, with it, thinking precede all possible determination of the arrangement of representations. We therefore think something in general, and on the one side determine it sensibly, only we also distinguish the object represented in general and *in abstracto* from this way of intuiting it; thus there remains to us a way of determining it merely through thinking that is, to be sure, a merely logical form without content, but that nevertheless seems to us to be a

B 345

A 289

B 346

---

[a] *Object*
[b] *Object*
[c] Not in roman type.
[d] *Bestimmung*

way in which the object*a* exists in itself (*noumenon*), without regard to the intuition to which our sensibility is limited.

A 290   * * *

Before we leave the Transcendental Analytic behind, we must add something that, although not in itself especially indispensable, nevertheless may seem requisite for the completeness of the system. The highest concept with which one is accustomed to begin a transcendental philosophy is usually the division between the possible and the impossible.[114] But since every division presupposes a concept that is to be divided, a still higher one must be given, and this is the concept of an object in general (taken problematically, leaving undecided whether it is something or nothing). Since the categories are the only concepts that relate to objects in general, the distinction of whether an object is something or nothing must proceed in accordance with the order and guidance of the categories.*b*,[115]

B 347   1) To the concepts of all, many, and one there is opposed the concept of that which cancels everything out, i.e., **none**, and thus the object of a concept to which no intuition that can be given corresponds is = nothing, i.e., a concept without an object, like the *noumena*, which cannot be counted among the possibilities although they must not on that ground be asserted to be impossible (*ens rationis*),*c* or like something such as certain new fundamental

A 291   forces, which one thinks, without contradiction, to be sure, but also without any example from experience even being thought, and which must therefore not be counted among the possibilities.

2) Reality is **something**, negation is **nothing**, namely, a concept of the absence of an object, such as a shadow or cold (*nihil privativum*).*d*

3) The mere form of intuition, without substance, is in itself not an object, but the merely formal condition of one (as appearance), like pure space and pure time, which are to be sure something, as the forms for intuiting, but are not in themselves objects that are intuited (*ens imaginarium*).*e*

B 348   4) The object of a concept that contradicts itself is nothing because the concept is nothing, the impossible, like a rectilinear figure with two sides (*nihil negativum*).*f*

---

a *Object*

b Inserted in Kant's copy of the first edition: "the highest concept is that of the object in general" (E CLI, p. 46; 23:38).

c being of mere reason

d A privative nothing, i.e., a condition consisting solely in the absence of something else.

e An imaginary being; in the first edition, this expression is inserted after "pure time."

f a negative nothing

The table of this division of the concept of **nothing** (for the similar division of "something" follows of itself) must therefore be laid out thus:

A 292

Nothing,
as

1.
Empty concept without object,
ens rationis.

2.		**3.**
Empty object		**Empty intuition**
of a concept,		**without an object,**
nihil privativum.		*ens imaginarium.*

4.
Empty object without concept,
nihil negativum.

One sees that the thought-entity (No. 1) is distinguished from the non-entity (No. 4) by the fact that the former may not be counted among the possibilities because it is a mere invention (although not self-contradictory), whereas the latter is opposed to possibility because even its concept cancels itself out. Both, however, are empty concepts. The *nihil privativum* (No. 2) and the *ens imaginarium* (No. 3), on the contrary, are empty *data* for concepts. If light were not given to the senses, then one would also not be able to represent darkness, and if extended beings were not perceived, one would not be able to represent space. Negation as well as the mere form of intuition are, without something real, not objects.[a]

B 349

---

[a] *Objecte*

Transcendental Logic
Second Part
Transcendental Dialectic[1]

Introduction[a]
I
Transcendental illusion.

Above we have called dialectic in general a **logic of illusion**.[b] That does not mean that it is a doctrine of **probability**;[c] for that is truth, but cognized through insufficient grounds, so that the cognition of it is defective, but not therefore deceptive, and so it need not be separated from the analytical part of logic.[2] Still less may we take **appearance**[d] and **illusion** for one and the same. For truth and illusion are not in the object, insofar as it is intuited, but in the judgment about it insofar as it is thought. Thus it is correctly said that the senses do not err; yet not because they always judge correctly, but because they do not judge at all. Hence truth, as much as error, and thus also illusion as leading to the latter, are to be found only in judgments, i.e., only in the relation[e] of the object to our understanding. In a cognition that thoroughly agrees with the laws of the understanding there is also no error. In a representation of sense (because it contains no judgment at all) there is no error. No force of nature can of itself depart from its own laws. Hence neither the understanding by itself (without the influence of another cause), nor the senses by themselves, can err; the first cannot, because while it acts merely according to its own laws, its effect (the judgment) must necessarily agree with these laws.[3] But the formal aspect of all truth consists in agreement with the laws of the understanding. In the senses there is no judgment at all, neither a true nor a false one. Now because we have

[a] "We have previously proved that we can think only through categories and the concepts derived from them, but that our cognition (*a priori*) with them can reach no farther than to objects of possible experience. Now sciences come forward – psychology, cosmology, theology – that promise this." (E CLII, p. 46; 23:38)
[b] *Schein*
[c] *Wahrscheinlichkeit*
[d] *Erscheinung*
[e] *Verhältnis*

no other sources of cognition besides these two, it follows that error is effected only through the unnoticed influence of sensibility on understanding, through which it happens that the subjective grounds*a* of the judgment join with the objective ones, and make the latter deviate from their destination*,*b* just as a moved body would of itself always stay in a straight line in the same direction, but starts off on a curved line if at the same time another force influences it in another direction. In order to distinguish the proper action of the understanding from the force that meddles in, it will thus be necessary to regard the erroneous judgment of the understanding as a diagonal between two forces that determine the judgment in two different directions, enclosing an angle, so to speak, and to resolve the composite effect into the simple effects of the understanding and of sensibility; in pure judgments *a priori* this must happen through transcendental reflection, through which (as already shown) every representation is assigned its place in the faculty of cognition proper to it, and hence also the influence of the latter is distinguished from it.

B 351

A 295

Our concern here is not to treat of empirical (e.g. optical) illusion, which occurs in the empirical use of otherwise correct rules of the understanding, and through which the faculty of judgment is misled through the influence of the imagination; rather, we have to do only with **transcendental illusion,** which influences principles whose use is not ever meant for experience, since in that case we would at least have a touchstone for their correctness, but which instead, contrary to all the warnings of criticism, carries us away beyond the empirical use of the categories, and holds out to us the semblance of extending the **pure understanding.** We will call the principles whose application stays wholly and completely within the limits of possible experience **immanent,** but those that would fly beyond these boundaries **transcendent** principles. But by the latter I do not understand the **transcendental** use or misuse of categories, which is a mere mistake of the faculty of judgment when it is not properly checked by criticism, and thus does not attend enough to the boundaries of the territory in which alone the pure understanding is allowed its play; rather, I mean principles that actually incite us to tear down all those boundary posts and to lay claim to a wholly new territory

B 352

A 296

---

* Sensibility, subordinated to understanding, as the object*c* to which the latter applies its function, is the source of real cognitions. But this same sensibility, insofar as it influences the action of the understanding and determines it to judgments, is the ground of error.

A 294 / B 351

a In the first edition: "that subjective grounds."
b *Bestimmung*
c *Object*

that recognizes no demarcations anywhere. Hence **transcendental** and **transcendent** are not the same. The principles of pure understanding we presented above should be only of empirical and not of transcendental use, i.e., of a use that reaches out beyond the boundaries of experience. But a principle that takes away these limits, which indeed bids us to overstep them, is called **transcendent**. If our critique can succeed in discovering the illusion in these supposed principles, then those principles that are of merely empirical use can be called, in opposition to them, **immanent** principles of pure understanding.

Logical illusion, which consists in the mere imitation of the form of reason (the illusion of fallacious inferences) arises solely from a failure of attentiveness to the logical rule. Hence as soon as this attentiveness is focused on the case before us, logical illusion entirely disappears. Transcendental illusion, on the other hand, does not cease even though it is uncovered and its nullity is clearly seen into by transcendental criticism (e.g., the illusion in the proposition: "The world must have a beginning in time"). The cause of this is that in our reason (considered subjectively as a human faculty of cognition) there lie fundamental rules and maxims for its use, which look entirely like objective principles, and through them it comes about that the subjective necessity of a certain connection of our concepts on behalf of the understanding is taken for an objective necessity, the determination of things in themselves. [This is] an **illusion** that cannot be avoided at all, just as little as we can avoid it that the sea appears higher in the middle than at the shores, since we see the former through higher rays of light than the latter, or even better, just as little as the astronomer can prevent the rising moon from appearing larger to him, even when he is not deceived by this illusion.[4]

The transcendental dialectic will therefore content itself with uncovering the illusion in transcendental judgments, while at the same time protecting us from being deceived by it; but it can never bring it about that transcendental illusion (like logical illusion) should even disappear and cease to be an illusion. For what we have to do with here is a **natural** and unavoidable **illusion**[a] which itself rests on subjective principles and passes them off as objective, whereas logical dialectic in its dissolution of fallacious inferences has to do only with an error in following principles or with an artificial illusion that imitates them.[5] Hence there is a natural and unavoidable dialectic of pure reason, not one in which a bungler might be entangled through lack of acquaintance, or one that some sophist has artfully invented in order to confuse rational people, but one that irremediably attaches to human reason, so that even after we have exposed the mirage[b] it will still not cease to lead

B 353
A 297
B 354
A 298

---

[a] *Illusion*
[b] *Blendwerk*

our reason on with false hopes, continually propelling it into momen- B355
tary aberrations that always need to be removed.

II
On pure reason as the seat of transcendental illusion

A.
On reason in general.

All our cognition starts from the senses, goes from there to the understanding, and ends with reason, beyond which there is nothing higher
to be found in us to work on the matter of intuition and bring it under
the highest unity of thinking. Since I am now to give a definition*(a) of   A299
this supreme faculty of cognition, I find myself in some embarrassment.
As in the case of the understanding, there is in the case of reason a
merely formal, i.e., logical use, where reason abstracts from all content
of cognition, but there is also a real use, since reason itself contains the
origin of certain concepts and principles, which it derives neither from
the senses nor from the understanding. The first faculty has obviously
long since been defined by the logicians as that of drawing inferences
mediately (as distinct from immediate inferences, *consequentis immedi-
atis*); but from this we get no insight into the second faculty, which itself generates concepts.[6] Now since a division of reason into a logical
and a transcendental faculty occurs here, a higher concept of this source   B356
of cognition must be sought that comprehends both concepts under itself, while from the analogy with concepts of the understanding, we can
expect both that the logical concept will put in our hands the key to the
transcendental one and that the table of functions of the former will
give us the family tree of the concepts of reason.

In the first part of our transcendental logic we defined the understanding as the faculty of rules; here we will distinguish reason from understanding by calling reason the **faculty of principles.**(b)

The term "a principle" is ambiguous, and commonly signifies only a   A300
cognition that can be used as a principle even if in itself and as to its own
origin it is not a principle.(c) Every universal proposition, even if it is

---

(a) *Erklärung*

(b) *Principien;* in section II of this introduction, "principle" always translates *Princip* unless
otherwise noted. In addition to the German term *Grundsatz,* Kant employs not only
the Latin derivative *Princip,* but also occasionally the even more Latinate *Principium,*
whose occurrence will be noted; the plural of both terms, however, is *Principien,* which
will therefore be translated as "principles" with no note. Outside the present section,
"principle" (without a note) always translates *Grundsatz,* and the Latin terms are always
noted.

(c) *Principium*

taken from experience (by induction) can serve as the major premise in a syllogism;[a] but it is not therefore itself a principle.[b] The mathematical axioms (e.g., that there can be only one straight line between any two points) are even universal cognitions *a priori*, and thus they are correctly called principles relative to the cases that can be subsumed under them. But I cannot therefore say that in general and in itself I cognize

B 357 this proposition about straight lines from principles, but only that I cognize it in pure intuition.

I would therefore call a "cognition from principles" that cognition in which I cognize the particular in the universal through concepts. Thus every syllogism is a form of derivation of a cognition from a principle. For the major premise always gives a concept such that everything subsumed under its condition can be cognized from it according to a principle. Now since every universal cognition can serve as the major premise in a syllogism, and since the understanding yields such universal propositions *a priori*, these propositions can, in respect of their possible use, be called principles.

A 301 But if we consider these principles[c] of pure understanding in themselves as to their origin, then they are anything but cognitions from concepts. For they would not even be possible *a priori* if we did not bring in pure intuition (in mathematics) or the conditions of a possible experience in general. That everything that happens has a cause cannot at all be inferred from the concept of what happens in general; rather, it is this principle[d] that shows how one can first get a determinate experiential concept of what happens.

Thus the understanding cannot yield synthetic cognitions from con-

B 358 cepts at all, and it is properly these that I call principles absolutely; nevertheless, all universal propositions in general can be called principles comparatively.

It is an ancient wish – who knows how long it will take until perhaps it is fulfilled – that in place of the endless manifold of civil laws, their principles may be sought out; for in this alone can consist the secret, as one says, of simplifying legislation. But here the laws are only limitations of our freedom to conditions under which it agrees thoroughly with itself; hence they apply to something that is wholly our own work, and of which we can be the cause through that concept. But that ob-

A 302 jects in themselves, as well as the nature of things, should stand under principles and be determined according to mere concepts is something

---

[a] *Vernunftschluß* might equally be translated "inference of reason"; and occasionally it will be so translated below.
[b] *Principium*
[c] *Grundsätze*
[d] *Grundsatz*

that, if not impossible, is at least very paradoxical[a] in what it demands. But however that may be (for the investigation of this still lies before us), this much at least is clear; cognition from principles (in themselves) is something entirely different from mere cognition of the understanding, which can of course precede other cognitions in the form of a principle, but in itself (insofar at it is synthetic) still neither rests on mere thought nor contains in itself a universal according to concepts.

If the understanding may be a faculty of unity of appearances by means of rules, then reason is the faculty of the unity of the rules of understanding under principles.[7] Thus it[b] never applies directly to experience or to any object, but instead applies to the understanding, in order to give unity *a priori* through concepts to the understanding's manifold cognitions, which may be called "the unity of reason," and is of an altogether different kind than any unity that can be achieved by the understanding.

B359

This is the universal concept of the faculty of reason, as far as that concept can be made comprehensible wholly in the absence of examples (such as those that are to be given only in what follows).

B.
On the logical use of reason.

A303

We draw a distinction between what is cognized immediately and what is only inferred. That there are three angles in a figure enclosed by three straight lines is immediately cognized, but that these angles together equal two right angles is only inferred. Because we constantly need inferences and so in the end become wholly accustomed to them, it happens at last that we no longer even take notice of this distinction, and often, as in so-called deceptions of sense, we take as immediate what we have only inferred. In every inference there is a proposition that serves as a ground, and[c] another, namely the conclusion, that is drawn from the former, and[d] finally the inference (consequence) according to which the truth of the conclusion is connected unfailingly with the truth of the first proposition. If the inferred judgment already lies in the first one, so that it can be derived from it without the mediation of a third representation, then this is called an "immediate inference" (*consequentia immediata*); I would rather call it an inference of the understanding.[8] But if, in addition to the cognition that serves as a ground, yet another judgment is necessary to effect the conclusion,

B360

---

[a] *Widersinniges*
[b] I.e., reason. In the first edition: "It"; in the second edition: "Thus it . . . ."
[c] The word "and" added in the second edition.
[d] The word "and" added in the second edition.

then the inference is called a "syllogism."[a] In the proposition **All humans are mortal** there lie already the propositions "Some humans are mortal," "Some[b] mortal beings are human beings," "Nothing[c] immortal is a human being," and these propositions are thus immediate conclusions from the first one. On the other hand, the proposition "All scholars are mortal" does not lie in the underlying judgment (for the concept "scholar" does not occur in it at all), and can be concluded from it only by means of an intermediate judgment.

In every syllogism I think first a **rule** (the *major*) through the understanding. Second, I **subsume** a cognition under the condition of the rule (the *minor*) by means of the **power of judgment.** Finally, I determine my cognition through the predicate of the rule (the *conclusio*),[d] hence *a priori* through **reason.** Thus the relation[e] between a cognition and its condition, which the major premise represents as the rule, constitutes the different kinds of syllogisms. They are therefore threefold – just as are all judgments in general – insofar as they are distinguished by the way they express the relation[f] of cognition to the understanding: namely, **categorical** or **hypothetical** or **disjunctive** syllogisms.[9]

If, as happens for the most part, the conclusion is a judgment given as the problem,[g] in order to see whether it flows from already given judgments, through which, namely, a wholly different object is thought, then I seek whether the assertion of this conclusion is not to be found in the understanding under certain conditions according to a universal rule. Now if I find such a condition and if the object[h] of the conclusion can be subsumed under the given condition, then this conclusion is derived from the rule that **is also valid for other objects of cognition.** From this we see that reason, in inferring, seeks to bring the greatest manifold of cognition of the understanding to the smallest number of principles (universal conditions), and thereby to effect the highest unity of that manifold.

C.
On the pure use of reason.

Can we isolate reason, and is it then a genuine[i] source of concepts and judgments that arise solely from it and thereby refer it to objects; or is

---

[a] *Vernunftschluß* (literally, an "inference of reason")
[b] In the first edition: "or some."
[c] In the first edition: "or nothing."
[d] conclusion
[e] *Verhältnis*
[f] *Verhältnis*
[g] *aufgegeben*
[h] *Object*
[i] *eigener*

reason only a merely subordinate[a] faculty that gives to given cognitions a certain form, called "logical" form, through which cognitions of the understanding are subordinated to one another, and lower rules are subordinated to higher ones (whose condition includes the condition of the lower rules in its sphere), as far as this can be effected through comparing them? This is the question with which we will now concern ourselves, though only provisionally. In fact the manifold of rules and the unity of principles is a demand of reason, in order to bring the understanding into thoroughgoing connection with itself, just as the understanding brings the manifold of intuition under concepts and through them into connection.[10] Yet such a principle[b] does not prescribe any law to objects,[c] and does not contain the ground of the possibility of cognizing and determining them as such in general, but rather is merely a subjective law of economy for the provision of our understanding, so that through comparison of its concepts it may bring their universal use to the smallest number, without justifying us in demanding of objects themselves any such unanimity as might make things easier for our understanding or help it extend itself, and so give objective validity to its maxims as well. In a word, the question is: Does reason in itself, i.e., pure reason, contain *a priori* synthetic principles[d] and rules, and in what might such principles consist?

The formal and logical procedure of reason in syllogisms already gives us sufficient guidance as to where the ground of its transcendental principle[e] will rest in synthetic cognition through pure reason.

First, the syllogism does not deal with intuitions, in order to bring them under rules (as does the understanding with its categories), but rather deals with concepts and judgments. If, therefore, pure reason also deals with objects, yet it has no immediate reference to them and their intuition, but deals only with the understanding and its judgments, which apply directly to the senses and their intuition, in order to determine their object. The unity of reason is therefore not the unity of a possible experience, but is essentially different from that, which is the unity of understanding. That everything which happens must have a cause is not a principle[f] cognized and prescribed through reason at all. It makes the unity of experience possible and borrows nothing from reason, which could not have imposed any such synthetic unity from mere concepts without this reference to possible experience.

Second, reason in its logical use seeks the universal condition of its

A 306

B 363

A 307

B 364

---

[a] *subalternes*
[b] *Grundsatz*
[c] *Objecte*
[d] *Grundsätze*
[e] *Principium*
[f] *Grundsatz*

judgment (its conclusion), and the syllogism is nothing but a judgment mediated by the subsumption of its condition under a universal rule (the major premise). Now since this rule is once again exposed to this same attempt of reason, and the condition of its condition thereby has to be sought (by means of a prosyllogism) as far as we may, we see very well that the proper principle^a of reason in general (in its logical use) is to find the unconditioned for conditioned cognitions of the understanding, with which its unity will be completed.

But this logical maxim cannot become a principle^b of **pure reason** unless we assume that when the conditioned is given, then so is the whole series of conditions subordinated one to the other, which is itself unconditioned, also given (i.e., contained in the object and its connection).

A 308

Such a principle^c of pure reason, however, is obviously **synthetic**; for the conditioned is analytically related to some condition, but not to the unconditioned. Different synthetic propositions must arise from it, of which the pure understanding knows nothing, since it has to do only with objects of a possible experience, whose cognition and synthesis are always conditioned. But the unconditioned, if it actually occurs, is^d particularly to be considered according to all the determinations that distinguish it from everything conditioned, and must thereby give us material for many synthetic propositions a priori.

B 365

The principles^e arising from this supreme principle of pure reason will, however, be **transcendent** in respect of all appearances, i.e., no adequate empirical use can ever be made of that principle. It will therefore be entirely distinct from all principles^f of the understanding (whose use is completely **immanent**, insofar as it has only the possibility of experience as its theme). But whether the principle^g that the series of conditions (in the synthesis of appearances, or even in the thinking of things in general) reaches to the unconditioned, has objective correctness or not; what consequences flow from it for the empirical use of the understanding, or whether it rather yields no such objectively valid propositions at all, but is only a logical prescription in the ascent to ever higher conditions to approach completeness in them and thus to bring the highest possible unity of reason into our cognition; whether, I say, this need of reason has, through a misunderstanding, been taken for a transcendental principle^b of reason, which overhastily

A 309

B 366

---

^{a} Grundsatz
^{b} Principium
^{c} Grundsatz
^{d} Reading with the fourth edition, *wird* for *kann*.
^{e} Grundsätze
^{f} Grundsätze
^{g} Grundsatz
^{b} Grundsatz

postulates such an unlimited completeness in the series of conditions in the objects themselves; but in this case what other kinds of misinterpretations and delusions[a] may have crept into the inferences of reason whose major premise (and that perhaps more a petition than a postulate) is taken from pure reason and ascends from experience to its conditions: All this will be our concern in the transcendental dialectic, which we will now develop from its sources hidden deep in human reason. We will divide it into two main parts, the **first** of which will treat of the **transcendent concepts** of pure reason, and the **second** of reason's transcendent and **dialectical inferences of reason.**[b]

---

[a] *Verblendungen*
[b] *dialektischen Vernunftschlüßen*, which (once again) could also be translated "dialectical syllogisms."

Transcendental Dialectic
First Book
On the concepts of pure reason.

However it may be with the possibility of concepts from pure reason, they are not merely reflected concepts but inferred concepts. Concepts of the understanding are also thought *a priori* before experience and on behalf of it; but they contain nothing beyond the unity of reflection on appearances, insofar as these appearances are supposed to belong necessarily to a possible empirical consciousness. Through them alone is cognition, and determination of an object, possible. They also first give material for inferring, and no *a priori* concepts of objects precede them, from which they could be inferred. On the contrary, their objective reality is founded solely on the fact that because they constitute the intellectual form of all experience, it must always be possible to show their application in experience.

The term "a concept of reason," however, already shows in a provisional way that such a concept will not let itself be limited to experience, because it deals with a cognition (perhaps the whole of possible experience or its empirical synthesis) of which the empirical is only one part; no actual experience is fully sufficient for it, but every experience belongs to it. Concepts of reason serve for **comprehension,** just as concepts of the understanding serve for **understanding** (of perceptions). If they contain the unconditioned, then they deal with something under which all experience belongs, but that is never itself an object of experience; something to which reason leads through its inferences, and by which reason estimates and measures the degree of its empirical use, but that never constitutes a member of the empirical synthesis. If despite this such concepts have objective validity, then they can be called *conceptus ratiocinati*ᵃ (correctly inferred concepts); but if not, they have at least been obtained by a surreptitious illusion of inference, and so might be called *conceptus ratiocinantes*ᵇ (sophistical concepts). Since, however, this can be made out only in the chapter on dialectical infer-

ᵃ reasoned concepts
ᵇ ratiocinated concepts

ences, we will not take account of it yet, but just as we called the concepts of understanding "categories," we will ascribe a new name to the concepts of pure reason and call them "transcendental ideas," which term we now elucidate and justify.

First book of the transcendental dialectic   A 312
First section
On the ideas in general.

In the great wealth of our languages, the thinking mind nevertheless often finds itself at a loss for an expression that exactly suits its concept, and lacking this it is able to make itself rightly intelligible neither to others nor even to itself. Coining new words is a presumption to legis-   B 369 late in language that rarely succeeds, and before we have recourse to this dubious means it is advisable to look around in a dead and learned language to see if an expression occurs in it that is suitable to this concept; and even if the ancient use of this expression has become somewhat unsteady owing to the inattentiveness of its authors, it is better to fix on the meaning*^{a}* that is proper to it (even if it is doubtful whether it always had exactly this sense) than to ruin our enterprise by making ourselves unintelligible.

For this reason, if there perhaps occurs only one single word for a certain concept that, in one meaning already introduced, exactly suits this concept, and if it is of great importance to distinguish it from other   A 313 related concepts, then it is advisable not to be prodigal with that word or use it merely as a synonym or an alternative in place of other words, but rather to preserve it carefully in its proper meaning; for it may otherwise easily happen that when the expression does not particularly occupy our attention but is lost in a heap of others having very divergent meaning, the thought which it alone can preserve may get lost as well.

Plato made use of the expression **idea** in such a way that we can read-   B 370 ily see that he understood by it something that not only could never be borrowed from the senses, but that even goes far beyond the concepts of the understanding (with which Aristotle occupied himself), since nothing encountered in experience could ever be congruent to it.[11] Ideas for him are archetypes of things themselves, and not, like the categories, merely the key to possible experiences. In his opinion they flowed from the highest reason, through which human reason partakes in them; our reason, however, now no longer finds itself in its original state, but must call back with toil the old, now very obscure ideas through a recollection (which is called philosophy).[12] I do not wish to

---

^{a} *Bedeutung;* for the remainder of Book I of the "Dialectic," "meaning" will translate this word; *bedeuten,* however, will continue to be translated "signify."

395

A314

go into any literary investigation here, in order to make out the sense which the sublime philosopher combined with his word. I note only that when we compare the thoughts that an author expresses about a subject, in ordinary speech as well as in writings, it is not at all unusual to find that we understand him even better than he understood himself, since he may not have determined his concept sufficiently and hence sometimes spoke, or even thought, contrary to his own intention.

B371

Plato noted very well that our power of cognition feels a far higher need than that of merely spelling out appearances according to a synthetic unity in order to be able to read them as experience, and that our reason naturally exalts itself to cognitions that go much too far for any object that experience can give ever to be congruent, but that nonetheless have their reality and are by no means merely figments of the brain.

A315

Plato found his ideas preeminently in everything that is practical,* i.e., in what rests on freedom, which for its part stands under cognitions that are a proper product of reason. Whoever would draw the concepts of virtue from experience, whoever would make what can at best serve as an example for imperfect illustration into a model for a source of cognition (as many have actually done), would make of virtue an ambiguous non-entity, changeable with time and circumstances, useless for any sort of rule. On the contrary, we are all aware that when someone is

B372

represented as a model of virtue, we always have the true original in our own mind alone, with which we compare this alleged model and according to which alone we estimate it. But it is this that is the idea of virtue, in regard to which all possible objects of experience do service as examples (proofs of the feasibility, to a certain degree, of what the concept of reason requires), but never as archetypes. That no human being will ever act adequately to what the pure idea of virtue contains does not prove in the least that there is something chimerical in this thought. For it is only by means of this idea that any judgment of moral worth or unworth is possible; and so it necessarily lies at the ground of every approach to moral perfection, even though the obstacles in human nature, as yet to be determined as to their degree, may hold us at a distance from it.

A314 / B371
* Of course he also extended his concept to speculative cognitions, whenever they were pure and given wholly *a priori*, and even to mathematics, even though mathematical cognitions have their object nowhere except in **possible** experience. Now I cannot follow him in this, just as little as I can in the mystical deduction of these ideas or in the exaggerated way in which he hypostatized them, as it were; although the lofty language that served him in this field is surely quite susceptible of a milder interpretation, and one that accords better with the nature of things.

The **Platonic republic** has become proverbial as a supposedly strik- A316
ing example of a dream of perfection that can have its place only in the
idle thinker's brain; and Brucker[13] finds it ridiculous for the philosopher
to assert that a prince will never govern well unless he participates in
the ideas. But we would do better to pursue this thought further, and (at
those points where the excellent man leaves us without help) to shed
light on it through new endeavors, rather than setting it aside as useless
under the very wretched and harmful pretext of its impracticability. A B373
constitution providing for the **greatest human freedom** according to
laws that permit **the freedom of each to exist together with that of
others** (not one providing for the greatest happiness, since that would
follow of itself) is at least a necessary idea, which one must make the
ground not merely of the primary plan of a state's constitution but of all
the laws too; and in it we must initially abstract from the present obstacles, which may perhaps arise not so much from what is unavoidable in
human nature as rather from neglect of the true ideas in the giving of
laws. For nothing is more harmful or less worthy of a philosopher than
the vulgar appeal to allegedly contrary experience, which would not
have existed at all if institutions had been established at the right time
according to the ideas, instead of frustrating all good intentions by A317
using crude concepts in place of ideas, just because these concepts were
drawn from experience. The more legislation and government agree
with this idea, the less frequent punishment will become, and hence it
is quite rational to assert (as Plato does) that in perfect institutional
arrangements nothing of the sort would be necessary at all.[14] Even
though this may never come to pass, the idea of this maximum is nevertheless wholly correct when it is set forth as an archetype, in order to B374
bring the legislative constitution of human beings ever nearer to a possible greatest perfection. For whatever might be the highest degree of
perfection at which humanity must stop, and however great a gulf must
remain between the idea and its execution, no one can or should try to
determine this, just because it is freedom that can go beyond every proposed boundary.

But Plato was right to see clear proofs of an origin in ideas not only
where human reason shows true causality, and where ideas become efficient causes (of actions and their objects), namely in morality, but also
in regard to nature itself.[15] A plant, an animal, the regular arrangement
of the world's structure (presumably thus also the whole order of nature) – these show clearly that they are possible only according to ideas; A318
although no individual creature, under the individual conditions of its
existence, is congruent with the idea of what is most perfect of its
species (as little as a human being is congruent with the idea of humanity that he bears in his soul as the archetype of his actions), nevertheless
these ideas are in the highest understanding individual, unalterable,

thoroughly determined, and the original causes of things, and only the
whole of its combination in the totality of a world is fully adequate to
its idea. If we abstract from its exaggerated expression, then the philosopher's spiritual flight, which considers the physical copies*a* in the world
order, and then ascends to their architectonic connection according to
ends, i.e., ideas, is an endeavor that deserves respect and imitation; but
in respect of that which pertains to principles*b* of morality, legislation
and religion where the ideas first make the experience (of the good) itself possible, even if they can never be fully expressed in experience,
perform a wholly unique service, which goes unrecognized precisely because it is judged according to empirical rules, whose validity as principles*c* should be cancelled by those very ideas. For when we consider
nature, experience provides us with the rule and is the source of truth;
but with respect to moral laws, experience is (alas!) the mother of illusion, and it is most reprehensible to derive the laws concerning what I
ought to do from what **is done,** or to want to limit it to that.

But instead of these matters, the prosecution of which in fact makes
up the proper dignity of philosophy, we now concern ourselves with a
labor less spectacular but nevertheless not unrewarding: that of making
the terrain for these majestic moral edifices level and firm enough to be
built upon; for under this ground there are all sorts of passageways,
such as moles might have dug, left over from reason's vain but confident
treasure hunting, that make every building insecure. It is the transcendental use of pure reason, of its principles*d* and ideas, whose closer acquaintance we are now obligated to make, in order properly to
determine and evaluate the influence and the worth of pure reason. Yet
before I conclude this provisional introduction, I entreat those who take
philosophy to heart (which means more than is commonly supposed), if
they find themselves convinced by this and the following discussion, to
take care to preserve the expression **idea** in its original meaning, so that
it will not henceforth fall among the other expressions by which all sorts
of representations are denoted in careless disorder, to the detriment of
science. We are not so lacking in terms properly suited to each species
of representation that we have need for one to encroach on the property of another. Here is their progression:*e* The genus is **representation** in general (*repraesentatio*). Under it stands the representation with
consciousness (*perceptio*). A **perception***f* that refers to the subject as a
modification of its state is a **sensation** (*sensatio*); an objective percep-

B 375

A 319

B 376

A 320

---

a *von der copeilichen Betrachtung des Physischen*
b *Principien*
c *Principien*
d *Principien*
e *Stufenleiter*
f *Perception*

tion *a* is a **cognition** (*cognitio*). The latter is either an **intuition** or a **con** B377
cept (*intuitus vel conceptus*). The former is immediately related to the
object and is singular; the latter is mediate, by means of a mark, which
can be common to several things. A concept is either an **empirical** or a
pure concept, and the pure concept, insofar as it has its origin solely in
the understanding (not in a pure image of sensibility), is called *notio*.*b* A
concept made up of notions, which goes beyond the possibility of experience, is an **idea** or a concept of reason. Anyone who has become
accustomed to this distinction must find it unbearable to hear a representation of the color red called an idea. It is not even to be called a notion (a concept of the understanding).[16]

First book of the transcendental dialectic   A321
Second section
On the transcendental ideas.*c*

The transcendental analytic gave us an example of how the mere logical form of our cognition can contain the origin of pure concepts *a pri*
ori, which represent objects prior to all experience, or rather which
indicate the synthetic unity that alone makes possible an empirical cog   B378
nition of objects. The form of judgments (transformed into a concept
of the synthesis of intuitions) brought forth categories that direct all use
of the understanding in experience. In the same way, we can expect that
the form of the syllogisms, if applied to the synthetic unity of intuitions
under the authority of the categories, will contain the origin of special
concepts *a priori* that we may call pure concepts of reason or **transcen**
dental ideas, and they will determine the use of the understanding according to principles*d* in the whole of an entire experience.

The function of reason in its inferences consisted in the universality
of cognition according to concepts, and the syllogism is itself a judgment determined *a priori* in the whole domain of its condition. I can   A322
draw the proposition "Caius is mortal" from experience merely through
the understanding. But I seek a concept containing the condition under
which the predicate (the assertion in general) of this judgment is given
(i.e., here, the concept "human"), and after I have subsumed [the predicate] under this condition, taken in its whole domain ("all humans are

---

a *Perception*
b notion
c In his copy of the first edition, Kant inserted these comments:
    "In experience we can [encounter] no concepts of reason, e.g., of the simple, which
cannot exhibit any experience, the [absolutely] unconditioned of every kind.
    "The cosmological ideas, to be sure, pertain to objects [*Objecte*] of the sensible
world, but . . . ." (the end of the manuscript is missing) (E CLII, p. 46; 23:38)
d *Principien*

mortal"), I determine the cognition of my object according to it ("Caius is mortal").

Accordingly, in the conclusion of a syllogism we restrict a predicate to a certain object, after we have thought it in the major premise in its whole domain under a certain condition. This complete magnitude of the domain, in relation to such a condition, is called **universality** (*universalitas*). In the synthesis of intuition this corresponds to **allness** (*universitas*), or the **totality** of conditions. So the transcendental concept of reason is none other than that of the **totality of conditions** to a given conditioned thing. Now since the **unconditioned** alone makes possible the totality of conditions, and conversely the totality of conditions is always itself unconditioned, a pure concept of reason in general can be explained*a* through the concept of the unconditioned, insofar as it contains a ground of synthesis for what is conditioned.[17]

A323   There will be as many concepts of reason as there are species of relation*b* represented by the understanding by means of the categories; and so we must seek an **unconditioned, first,** for the **categorical** synthesis in a **subject, second** for the **hypothetical** synthesis of the members of a **series,** and **third** for the **disjunctive** synthesis of the parts in a **system.**[18]

There are, therefore, just as many species of syllogism, and in each of them prosyllogisms proceed to the unconditioned: one, to a subject that is no longer a predicate, another to a presupposition that presupposes nothing further, and the third to an aggregate of members of a division such that nothing further is required for it to complete the division of a concept. Hence the pure rational concepts of the totality in a synthesis of conditions are necessary at least as problems of extending the unity of the understanding, if possible, to the unconditioned, and they are grounded in the nature of human reason, even if these transcendental concepts lack a suitable use *in concreto* and have no other utility than to point the understanding in the right direction so that it may be thoroughly consistent with itself when it extends itself to its uttermost extremes.

A324   However, while we are speaking here about the totality of conditions and the unconditioned, as the common title of all concepts of reason, we once again run up against an expression with which we cannot dispense and at the same time cannot safely use because of an ambiguity it has acquired through long misuse. The term **absolute** is one of the few words that in its original meaning was suited to one concept that by and large no other word in the same language precisely suits, and so its loss, or what is the same thing, its vacillating use, must carry with it the loss of the concept itself, but this is indeed a concept with which we cannot dis-

    a *erklärt*
    b *Verhältnis*

pense except at great disadvantage to all transcendental estimations.[a] The word **absolute** is now more often used merely to indicate that something is valid of a thing[b] considered **in itself** and thus **internally.** In this meaning, "absolutely possible" would signify what is possible in itself (internally), which is in fact the **least** one can say of an object. On the contrary, however, it is also sometimes used to indicate that something is valid in every relation (unlimitedly) (e.g., absolute dominion); and in this meaning **absolutely possible** would signify what is **possible in all respects in every relation,** which is again the **most** that I can say about the possibility of a thing. Now sometimes, to be sure, these two   A 325
meanings coincide. So, for example, what is internally impossible is also impossible in every relation, and hence absolutely impossible. But in most cases they are infinitely far apart from each other, and so I can by no means infer that because something is possible in itself it is therefore also possible in every relation, hence absolutely possible. Indeed, in what follows I will show about absolute necessity that it by no means depends in all cases on what is internal, and so must not be regarded as signifying the same as what is internal. That whose opposite is internally   B 382
impossible, that whose opposite is clearly also impossible in all respects, is therefore itself absolutely necessary; but I cannot infer conversely that what is absolutely necessary is something whose opposite is **internally** impossible, i.e., that the **absolute** necessity of a thing is an **internal** necessity; for this "internal necessity" is in certain cases a wholly empty expression, with which we cannot connect the least concept; on the contrary, the concept of the necessity of a thing in every relation (to everything possible) carries with it very special determinations. Now because the loss of a concept that has great application in speculative philosophy can never be a matter of indifference to the philosopher, I hope he will also not be indifferent to carefully preserving the determination and the expression on which the concept depends.

It is in this extended meaning that I will make use of the word **ab-**   A 326
solute, opposing it to what is merely comparative, or valid in some particular respect; for the latter is restricted to conditions, while the former is valid without any restriction.

Now a transcendental concept of reason always goes to the absolute totality in the synthesis of conditions, and never ends except with the absolutely unconditioned, i.e., what is unconditioned in every relation. For pure reason leaves to the understanding everything that relates directly to objects of intuition or rather to their synthesis in imagination.   B 383
It reserves for itself only the absolute totality in the use of concepts, and seeks to carry the synthetic unity, which is thought in the categories, all

---

[a] *Beurteilungen;* in the third edition, this word is in the singular.
[b] *Sache*

the way to the absolutely unconditioned. We can therefore call this the **unity of reason** in appearances, just as that which the category expresses can be called the **unity of understanding.** Thus reason relates itself only to the use of the understanding, not indeed insofar as the latter contains the ground of possible experience (for the absolute totality of conditions is not a concept that is usable in an experience, because no experience is unconditioned), but rather in order to prescribe the direction toward a certain unity of which the understanding has no concept, proceeding to comprehend all the actions of the understanding in respect of every object into an **absolute whole.** Hence the objective use of the pure concepts of reason is always **transcendent,** while that of the pure concepts of understanding must by its nature always be **immanent,** since it is limited solely to possible experience.

By the idea of a necessary concept of reason, I understand one to which no congruent object can be given in the senses. Thus the pure concepts of reason we have just examined are **transcendental ideas.** They are concepts of pure reason; for they consider all experiential cognition as determined through an absolute totality of conditions. They are not arbitrarily invented, but given as problems[a] by the nature of reason itself, and hence they relate necessarily to the entire use of the understanding. Finally, they are transcendent concepts, and exceed the bounds of all experience, in which no object adequate to the transcendental idea can ever occur. When we call something an idea, we are saying a great deal about its object[b] (as an object of pure understanding), but just for this reason very little about the subject (i.e., in respect of its actuality under empirical conditions), since, as the concept of a maximum, nothing congruent to it can ever be given *in concreto.* Now because in the merely speculative use of reason the latter is really the whole aim, and approaching a concept that will, however, never be reached in execution, is the same as simply lacking that concept, it is said of a concept of this sort that it is **only** an idea. Thus we might say that the absolute whole of appearances **is only** an **idea,** since, because we can never project it in an image, it remains a **problem**[c] without any solution. On the contrary, because in the practical use of understanding it is only a matter of execution according to rules, an idea of practical reason can always be actually given *in concreto,* though only in part; indeed, it is the indispensable condition of every practical use of reason. Its execution is always bounded and defective, but within bounds that cannot be determined, hence always under the influence of the concept of an absolute completeness. Accordingly, the practical idea is

A327

B384

A328

B385

[a] *aufgegeben*
[b] *Object*
[c] *Problem*

always fruitful in the highest degree and unavoidably necessary in respect of actual actions. In it practical reason even has the causality actually to bring forth what its concept contains; and hence of such wisdom we cannot likewise say disparagingly: **It is only an idea;** rather just because it is the idea of a necessary unity of all possible ends, it must serve as a rule, the original and at least limiting condition, for everything practical.

Although we have to say of the transcendental concepts of reason: **They are only ideas,** we will by no means regard them as superfluous and nugatory. For even if no object can be determined through them, they can still, in a fundamental and unnoticed way, serve the understanding as a canon for its extended and self-consistent use, through which it cognizes no more objects than it would cognize through its concepts, yet in this cognition it will be guided better and further. Not to mention the fact that perhaps the ideas make possible a transition from concepts of nature to the practical, and themselves generate support for the moral ideas and connection with the speculative cognitions of reason. About all this we must expect to be informed in due course.

But given our present aims, we will set aside the practical ideas, and hence consider reason only in its speculative use, and in this even more narrowly, namely only in its transcendental use. Here we must strike out on the same path as we took above in the deduction of the categories; that is, we must consider the logical form of rational cognition, and see whether in this way reason will not perhaps also be a source of concepts, regarding objects*a* in themselves as determined synthetically *a priori* in respect of one or another function of reason.

Reason, considered as the faculty of a certain logical form of cognition, is the faculty of inferring, i.e., of judging mediately (through the subsumption of a condition of a possible judgment under the condition of something given). The given judgment is the universal rule (major premise, *major*). The subsumption of the condition of another possible judgment under the condition of the rule is the minor premise (*minor*). The actual judgment that expresses the assertion of the rule **in the subsumed case***b* is the conclusion (*conclusio*). The rule says something universal under a certain condition. Now in a case that comes before us the condition of the rule obtains. Thus what is valid universally under that condition is also to be regarded as valid in the case before us (which carries this condition with it). We easily see that reason attains to a cognition through actions of the understanding that constitute a series of conditions. Thus suppose I arrive at the proposition "All bodies are alterable" only by beginning with the more remote cognition (in which

A 329

B 386

A 330

B 387

---

a *Objecte*
b The fourth edition reads "to the subsumed case."

the concept of a body does not occur, but that contains the condition of this concept) that "Everything composite is **alterable**," and go from this to a closer proposition standing under the condition of the former: "Bodies are composite"; and then from this finally to a third proposition, conjoining the more distant cognition ("alterable") with the one lying before us: "Consequently, bodies are alterable"; then I arrive at a cognition (a conclusion) through a series of conditions (premises). Now every series whose exponent (whether that of the categorical or the hypothetical judgment) is given may be continued; hence the very same action of reason leads to a *ratiocinatio prosyllogistica,*[a] which is a series of inferences, that can be continued to an indeterminate extent either on the side of the conditions (*per prosyllogismos*)[b] or on the side of the conditioned (*per episyllogismos*).[c]

But we soon come to be aware that the chain or series of prosyllogisms, i.e., of inferred cognitions on the side of the grounds, or of the conditions of a given cognition – in other words, the **ascending series** of syllogisms – has to be related to the faculty of reason differently from the **descending series**, i.e., the progression of reason on the side of that which is conditioned through episyllogisms. For since in the first case the cognition (the *conclusio*) is given only as conditioned, we cannot reach it by means of reason except at least on the presupposition that all members of the series are given on the side of the conditions (totality in the series of premises), because only under this presupposition is the judgment before us possible *a priori*; on the contrary, on the side of that which is conditioned or of the consequences, there is thought only a series that **becomes**, and that is not already presupposed or **given** as a **whole**, and so only a potential progression. Hence if a cognition is regarded as conditioned, reason is necessitated to regard the series of conditions in an ascending line as completed and given in their totality. But if the very same cognition is at the same time regarded as a condition of other cognitions that constitute a series of consequences in a descending line, then reason can be entirely indifferent about how far this progression stretches *a parte posteriori*, and whether a totality of these conditions is even possible at all; for it does not need a series of the same sort for the conclusion that lies before us, since this conclusion is already sufficiently determined and secured through its grounds *a parte priori*. Now it may or may not be that on the side of the conditions, the series of premises has a **first** [member] as the supreme condition, and hence that it is without bound *a parte priori*; nevertheless it must still

---

[a] "Prosyllogistic reasoning," that is, reasoning through a series of syllogisms to arrive at a desired conclusion.

[b] by prosyllogisms

[c] by episyllogisms

contain the totality of the condition, assuming that we could never succeed in grasping it; and the whole series must be unconditionally true if the conditioned, which is regarded as a consequence arising from it, is supposed to count as true. This is a demand of reason, which declares its cognition to be determined *a priori* and necessary either as it is in itself – in which case it needs no grounds – or else – if it is derived – as a member of a series of grounds that is itself unconditionally true.

The first book of the transcendental dialectic
Third section
The system of the transcendental ideas.

A 333 / B 390

What we have to do with here is not a logical dialectic that abstracts from every content of cognition and merely discovers false illusion in the form of syllogisms, but rather a transcendental dialectic, that, fully *a priori*, is supposed to contain both the origin of certain cognitions from pure reason and inferred concepts, whose object cannot be given empirically at all, and so lies wholly outside the faculty of the pure understanding. We have gathered from the natural relation that the transcendental use of our cognition must have in its inferences as well as in its judgments that there will be only three species of dialectical inferences, relating to the three species of inference by which reason can arrive at cognitions from principles;[a] and that in everything the concern of reason is to ascend from the conditioned synthesis, to which the understanding always remains bound, toward the unconditioned, which the understanding can never reach.

Now what is universal in every relation that our representations can have is 1) the relation to the subject, 2) the relation to objects,[b] and indeed either as[c] appearances, or as objects of thinking in general. If we combine this subdivision with the above division, then all the relation[d] of representations of which we can make either a concept or an idea are of three sorts: 1) the relation[e] to the subject, 2) to the manifold of the object[f] in appearance, and 3) to all things in general.[19]

B 391
A 334

Now all pure concepts have to do generally with the synthetic unity of representations, but concepts of pure reason (transcendental ideas) have to do with the unconditioned synthetic unity of all conditions in general. Consequently, all transcendental ideas will be brought under

---

[a] *Principien*
[b] *Objecte*
[c] In the first edition: *entweder erstlich als*, which could be translated "either firstly as," or "either only as."
[d] *Verhältnis*
[e] *Verhältnis*
[f] *Object*

three classes, of which the **first** contains the absolute (unconditioned) **unity** of the **thinking subject,** the **second** the absolute **unity** of the series of **conditions of appearance,** the **third** the absolute **unity** of the **condition of all objects of thought** in general.

The thinking subject is the object of **psychology,** the sum total of all appearances (the world) is the object of **cosmology,** and the thing that contains the supreme condition of the possibility of everything that can be thought (the being of all beings) is the object of **theology.**[20] Thus pure reason provides the ideas for a transcendental doctrine of the soul (*psychologia rationalis*),[a] a transcendental science of the world (*cosmologia rationalis*),[b] and finally also a transcendental cognition of God (*theologia transcendentalis*).[c] Even so much as the mere sketch of these sciences is not prescribed by the understanding, even if it is combined with the highest logical use of reason, i.e., with all the inferences through which we can think of progressing from an object of the understanding (appearance) to all other objects, even to the most distant members of the empirical synthesis; rather, such a project is exclusively a pure and genuine product or problem[d] of pure reason.

What *modi* of pure rational concepts stand under these three titles of transcendental ideas will be finally displayed in the following sections. They run along the thread of the categories. For pure reason is never related directly to objects, but instead to concepts of them given by the understanding. Likewise, it can be made clear only in the complete execution how reason, exclusively through the synthetic use of the same function it employs in the categorical syllogism, must necessarily come to the concept of the absolute unity of the **thinking subject,** how the logical procedure in hypothetical syllogisms[e] [leads to] the ideas of the absolutely unconditioned **in a series** of given conditions, and finally how the mere form of the disjunctive syllogism necessarily carries with it the highest rational concept of a **being of all beings;** a thought which at first glance appears extremely paradoxical.

No **objective deduction** of these transcendental ideas is really possible, such as we could provide for the categories. For just because they are ideas, they have in fact no relation to any object[f] that could be given congruent to them. But we can undertake a subjective introduction to[g]

B392
A335

B393
A336

---

[a] rational psychology
[b] rational cosmology
[c] transcendental theology
[d] *Problem*
[e] The text here seems garbled. It reads "*in hypothetischen Ideen die vom Schlechthinunbedingten . . . .*" (in the first edition: "*. . . die Idee vom . . . .*". We follow Erdmann in inserting the word *Vernunftschlüssen.*
[f] *Object*
[g] *Anleitung;* Erdmann reads *Ableitung* (derivation of).

them from the nature of our reason, and this is to be accomplished in the present section.

We easily see that pure reason has no other aim than the absolute totality of synthesis **on the side of conditions** (whether they are conditions of inherence, dependence, or concurrence), and that reason has nothing to do with absolute completeness **from the side of the conditioned.** For it needs only the former series in order to presuppose the whole series of conditions and thereby give it to the understanding *a priori.* But once a complete (and unconditioned) given condition exists, then a concept of reason is no longer needed in respect of the progress of the series; for the understanding by itself makes every step downwards from the condition to the **conditioned.** In this way, the transcendental ideas serve only for **ascending** in the series of conditions to the unconditioned, i.e., to the principles.*a* But regarding **descent** to the conditioned, there is a very extensive logical use that our reason makes of the laws of the understanding, but no transcendental use and if we make ourselves an idea of absolute totality of such a synthesis (of a progressive one), e.g., an idea of the whole series of all **future** alterations in the world, then this is just a thing of thought (an *ens rationis*),*b* which is thought up only arbitrarily, and not presupposed necessarily by reason. For the possibility of something conditioned presupposes the totality of its conditions, but not the totality of its consequences. Consequently such a concept is not a transcendental idea, which is what exclusively concerns us here.

Finally we also come to be aware that a certain connection and unity showing itself among the transcendental ideas themselves and that pure reason by means of it brings all its cognitions into a system. To progress from the cognition of oneself (of the soul) to cognition of the world and, by means of this, to the original being, is so natural that this progression appears similar to the logical advance of reason from premises to a conclusion.* Whether there is actually here an affinity of the same

B 394

A 337

B 395

* *c*<Metaphysics has as the proper end of its investigation only three ideas: **God, freedom, and immortality;** so that the second concept, combined with the first, should lead to the third as a necessary conclusion. Everything else with which this science is concerned serves merely as a means of attaining these ideas and their reality. It does not need them for the sake of natural science, but instead to get beyond nature. The insight into these ideas would make **theology, morals,** and, through their combination, **religion,** thus the highest ends of our existence, dependent solely on the faculty of speculative reason and on nothing else. In a systematic representation of those ideas, the suggested order,

B 395

a *Principien*
b being of reason
c This note was added in the second edition.

kind that grounds the logical and transcendental procedures is one of the questions we must expect to answer in the course of our investiga-

tion. We have provisionally reached our end already, since we have removed from this ambiguous position the transcendental concepts of reason, which are usually mixed with other concepts in the theories of philosophers who do not distinguish them from concepts of the understanding, and thereby provided their determinate number, since there can never be any more of them, and we have been able to represent them in a systematic connection, through which a special field of pure reason has been marked out and its limits have been set.

which is a **synthetic** one, would be the most appropriate; but in working through them, which must necessarily be done first, the **analytic** order, which inverts this one, is more suitable to the end of completing our great project, proceeding from what experience makes immediately available to us from the **doctrine of the soul,** to the **doctrine of the world** and from there all the way to the cognition of **God.**>

The Transcendental Dialectic
Book Two
The dialectical inferences of pure reason

It can be said that the object of a merely transcendental idea is some-thing of which we have no concept, even though this idea is generated in an entirely necessary way by reason according to its original laws. For in fact no concept of the understanding is possible for an object that is to be adequate to the demand of reason, i.e., an object such as can be shown and made intuitive in a possible experience. But we would ex-press ourselves better and with less danger of misunderstanding if we said that we can have no acquaintance with an object*a* that corresponds to an idea, even though we can have a problematic concept of it.

Now at least the transcendental (subjective) reality of pure concepts of reason rests on the fact that we are brought to such ideas by a neces-sary syllogism. Thus there will be syllogisms containing no empirical premises, by means of which we can infer from something with which we are acquainted to something of which we have no concept, and yet to which we nevertheless, by an unavoidable illusion, give objective re-ality. In respect of their result, such inferences are thus to be called **so-phistical** rather than rational inferences;*b* even though they might lay claim to the latter term on account of what occasions them, because they are not thought up, nor do they arise contingently, but have sprung from the nature of reason. They are sophistries*c* not of human beings but of pure reason itself, and even the wisest of all human beings can-not get free of them; perhaps after much effort he may guard himself from error, but he can never be wholly rid of the illusion, which cease-lessly teases and mocks him.

There are, therefore, only three species of these dialectical syllo-gisms, as many as there are ideas in which their conclusions result. In the **first class** of syllogisms, from the transcendental concept of a sub-ject that contains nothing manifold I infer the absolute unity of this

---

a Object
b vernünftelnde, als Vernunftschlüsse, which could also be translated "rationalizing rather than rational inferences" or "sophistical inferences rather than syllogisms."
c Sophistikationen

subject itself, even though in this way I have no concept at all of it. This dialectical inference I will call a transcendental **paralogism.** The **second** class of sophistical inference is applied in general to the transcendental concept of absolute totality in the series of conditions for a given appearance; and from the fact that I always have a self-contradictory concept of the unconditioned synthetic unity in the series on one side, I infer the correctness of the opposite unity, even though I also have no concept of it. I will call the condition of reason with regard to these dialectical inferences the **antinomy** of pure reason. Finally, in the **third** kind of sophistical inference, from the totality of conditions for thinking objects in general insofar as they can be given to me I infer the absolute synthetic unity of all conditions for the possibility of things in general; i.e., from things with which I am not acquainted as to their merely transcendental concept, I infer a being of all beings, with which I am even less acquainted through its transcendental[a] concept, and of whose unconditioned necessity I can make for myself no concept at all. This dialectical syllogism I will call the **ideal** of pure reason.

[a] Reading, with the fourth edition, *transcendentalen* for *transcendenten.*

Second Book of the Transcendental Dialectic
First Chapter
The paralogisms of pure reason*a*

A logical paralogism consists in the falsity of a syllogism due to its form, whatever its content may otherwise be. A transcendental paralogism, however, has a transcendental ground for inferring falsely due to its form.²¹ Thus a fallacy of this kind will have its ground in the nature of human reason, and will bring with it an unavoidable, although not insoluble, illusion.

Now we come to a concept that was not catalogued above in the general list of transcendental concepts, and nevertheless must be assigned to it, yet without altering that table in the least and declaring it defective. This is the concept – or rather, if one prefers, the judgment – **I think.** But one will easily see that this concept is the vehicle of all concepts whatever, and hence also of transcendental concepts, and is thus always comprehended among them, and hence is likewise transcendental, but that it can have no special title, because it serves only to intro-

---

a Note added to Kant's copy of the first edition: "The question is whether, if I cognize a transcendental object [*Object*] (I) through pure categories, without otherwise having any properties of it, I thereby actually cognize it or have only a negative concept of it. Further, whether these categories could be cognized through perception regarding this object, or whether they lie *a priori* in thinking in general. Third, whether through these cognition would be extended." (E CLIV, p. 47; 23:38; cf. A 592 / B 620)

"A paralogism is a syllogism that is false *in forma*. Now it also belongs to the form that the major is a universal proposition, and also that the premises are not tautological. But here the major is a singular judgment and contains a tautology in itself. Consequently, the syllogism has only two *termini*." (E CLV, p. 47, 23:38)

"The paralogisms begin from existence as modality: 'I am'; proceed to relation [*Relation*] in order to determine existence not in time, which would be empirical. Therefore: I am as substance, simple as to quality, identical in my duration. The time of my duration is thus the time of my own self-determination." (E CLVI, p. 47; 23:38–9; cf. B 418)

"The proposition 'a exists,' is a simple substance, always the same, must in other cases be cognized through marks: 1. of perception, at least in time; 2. through properties that are persisting; 3. through demonstration of their [parts] in space and time; 4. through perception. Here I, as it were, [have sensation of] the categories or know them *a priori*." (E CLVII, p. 48; 23:39)

B400
A342

duce*a* all thinking as belonging to consciousness. Meanwhile, however pure from the empirical (from impressions of sense) it may be, it still serves to distinguish two kinds of objects through the nature of our power of representation. **I**, as thinking, am an object of inner sense, and am called "soul." That which is an object of outer sense is called "body." Accordingly, the expression "I," as a thinking being, already signifies the object of a psychology that could be called the rational doctrine of the soul, if I do not seek to know anything about the soul beyond what, independently of all experience (which always determines me more closely and *in concreto*), can be inferred from this concept **I** insofar as it occurs in all thinking.

Now the **rational** doctrine of the soul[22] is really an undertaking of this kind; for if the least bit of anything empirical in my thinking, any particular perception of my inner state, were mixed among the grounds of cognition of this science, then it would no longer be a rational but rather an **empirical** doctrine of the soul. We have thus already before us a putative science, which is built on the single proposition **I think**; and we can, in accordance with the nature of a transcendental philosophy, quite appropriately investigate its ground or groundlessness. One should not be brought up short by the fact that I have an inner experience of this proposition, which expresses the perception of oneself, and hence that the rational doctrine of the soul that

B401
A343

is built on it is never pure but is grounded in part on an empirical principle.*b* For this inner perception is nothing beyond the mere apperception **I think**, which even makes all transcendental concepts possible, which say "I think substance, cause, etc."*c* For inner experience in general and its possibility, or perception in general and its relation*d* to another perception, without any particular distinction or empirical determination being given in it, cannot be regarded as empirical cognition, but must be regarded as cognition of the empirical in general, and belongs to the investigation of the possibility of every experience, which is of course transcendental. The least object*e* of perception (e.g., pleasure or displeasure), which might be added to the general repre-

---

a *aufführen*
b *Principium*
c Added in Kant's copy of the first edition: "The propositions of rational psychology all are grounded on the 'I am.' For if even time should be added to them, then it would be an object of experience that they were treating of, and everything that would be produced through this would not have to reach any further than to this life." (E CLVIII, p. 48; 23:39)

   "[The] I, object and subject of thoughts, is identical, exists, [substance, reality], but as unity in itself . . . of the subject in all its consciousness – these are purely identical propositions." (E CLIX, p. 48; 23:39)
d *Verhältnis*
e *Object*

sentation of self-consciousness, would at once transform rational psychology into an empirical psychology.

I think[a] is thus the sole text of rational psychology, from which it is to develop its entire wisdom. One easily sees that this thought, if it is to be related to an object (myself), can contain nothing other than its transcendental predicates; because the least empirical predicate would corrupt the rational purity and independence of the science from all experience.

Here, however, we have merely to follow the guide of the categories; A344/B402 only since here first a thing, I as a thinking being, is given, we will not, to be sure, alter the above order of the categories to one another as represented in their table, but we will begin here with the category of substance, and thus go backwards through the series. The topics of the rational doctrine of the soul, from which everything else that it may contain has to be derived, are therefore the following:

1.
The soul is
substance[b]

2.
In its quality,
simple

3.
In the different times
in which it exists,
numerically identical
i.e., **unity** (not plurality)

4.
In relation[c]
to **possible** objects in space*

---

* The reader, who will not so easily guess from these expressions in their transcendental abstraction, their psychological sense and why the ultimate attribute of the soul belongs to the category of **existence**, will find this ade- B403 quately explained and justified in what follows. Besides, on account of the A345 Latin expressions that, contrary to good taste in writing, have inundated us here in place of equivalent German ones, in this section as well as in the whole work, I must adduce the following by way of apology: I would rather lose something by way of elegance of language than make scholastic usage even more difficult through the least unintelligibility.

[a] Note in Kant's copy of the first edition: "[This] is a proposition *a priori*, is a mere category of the subject, intellectual representation without anywhere or at any time, hence not empirical. Whether the category of reality lies in it, whether objective inferences are to be drawn from it." (E CLX, p. 48; 23:39)

[b] Kant's copy of the critique contains the revision: "The soul exists as substance" (E CLXI, p. 49).

[c] *Verhältnis*

A345/B403   From these elements, at least through composition, spring all the concepts of the pure doctrine of the soul, without any other principle*a* being cognized in the least. This substance, merely as an object of inner sense, gives us the concept of **immateriality;** as simple substance, it gives us that of **incorruptibility;** its identity, as an intellectual substance, gives us **personality;** all these points together give us **spirituality;** the relation*b* to objects in space gives us the **interaction**c with bodies; thus it represents the thinking substance as the principle*d* of life in matter, i.e., as a soul (*anima*) and as the ground of **animality,** and this – limited by spirituality – is **immortality.**

    Now to these concepts four paralogisms of a transcendental doctrine of the soul are related, which are falsely held to be a science of pure rea-
B404 son about the nature of our thinking being. At the ground of this doctrine we can place nothing but the simple and in content for itself
A346 wholly empty representation **I,** of which one cannot even say that it is a concept, but a mere consciousness that accompanies every concept. Through this I, or He, or It (the thing), which thinks, nothing further is represented than a transcendental subject of thoughts = *x,*e which is recognized only through the thoughts that are its predicates, and about which, in abstraction, we can never have even the least concept; because of which we therefore turn in a constant circle, since we must always already avail ourselves of the representation of it at all times in order to judge anything about it; we cannot separate ourselves from this inconvenience, because the consciousness in itself is not even a representation distinguishing a particular object,*f* but rather a form of representation in general, insofar as it is to be called a cognition; for of it*g* alone can I say that through it I think anything.

    But right at the start it must seem strange that the condition under which I think in general, and which is therefore merely a property*h* of my subject, is at the same time to be valid for everything that thinks, and that on an empirical-seeming proposition we can presume to ground an apodictic and universal judgment, namely, that everything that thinks is constituted as the claim of self-consciousness asserts of me. But the cause
B405 of this lies in the fact that we must necessarily ascribe to things *a priori*

---

a *Principium*
b *Verhältnis*
c *das Commercium*
d *Principium*
e In the first and third editions, this letter is capitalized.
f *Object*
g *sie,* which probably refers to "cognition," but would also agree grammatically with "representation."
h *Beschaffenheit;* elsewhere in the passage, "property" translates *Eigenschaft.*

all the properties that constitute the conditions under which alone we   A 347
think them. Now I cannot have the least representation of a thinking
being through an external experience, but only through self-consciousness. Thus such objects are nothing further than the transference of this
consciousness of mine to other things, which can be represented as
thinking beings only in this way. The proposition "I think" is, however,
taken here only problematically; not insofar as it may contain a perception of an existence (the Cartesian *cogito, ergo sum*),[a] but only in its mere
possibility, in order to see which properties might flow from so simple a
proposition as this for its subject (whether or not such a thing might now
exist).

If more than the *cogito*[b] were the ground of our pure rational cognition of thinking beings in general; if we also made use of observations
about the play of our thoughts and the natural laws of the thinking self
created from them: then an empirical psychology would arise, which
would be a species of the **physiology** of inner sense, which would perhaps explain the appearances of inner sense, but could never serve to reveal such properties as do not belong to possible experience at all (as
properties of the simple), nor could it serve to teach **apodictically**   B 406
about thinking beings in general something touching on their nature;
thus it would be no **rational** psychology.

Now since the proposition **I think** (taken problematically) contains   A 348
the form of every judgment of understanding whatever and accompanies all categories as their vehicle, it is clear that the conclusions from
this can contain a merely transcendental use of the understanding,
which excludes every admixture of experience; and of[c] whose progress,
after what we have shown above, we can at the start form no advantageous concept. Thus we will follow it through all the predications of the
pure doctrine of the soul with a critical eye.[d]

First paralogism
of substantiality.

That the representation of which is the **absolute subject** of our judgments, and hence cannot be used as the determination of another thing,
is **substance**.

I, as a thinking being, am the **absolute subject** of all my possible

---

[a] I think, therefore I am.
[b] I think.
[c] In the first edition: "in."
[d] From this point on, Kant completely rewrote the remainder of the chapter for the second edition. The first-edition version follows immediately; the remainder of the chapter as rewritten for the second edition follows below.

judgments, and this representation of Myself[a] cannot be used as the predicate of any other thing.

Thus I, as thinking being (soul), am **substance.**[23]

Criticism of the first paralogism
of pure psychology.

We have shown in the analytical part of the Transcendental Logic that pure categories (and among them also the category of substance) have in themselves no objective significance at all unless an intuition is subsumed under[b] them, to the manifold of which they can be applied as functions of synthetic unity. Without that they are merely functions of a judgment without content. Of any thing in general I can say that it is a substance, insofar as I distinguish it from mere predicates and determinations of things. Now in all our thinking the **I** is the subject, in which thoughts inhere only as determinations, and this I cannot be used as the determination of another thing. Thus everyone must necessarily regard Himself as a substance, but regard his thinking only as accidents of his existence and determinations of his state.

But now what sort of use am I to make of this concept of a substance?[c] That I, as a thinking being, **endure**[d] for myself, that naturally I **neither arise** nor **perish** – this I can by no means infer, and yet it is for that alone that the concept of the substantiality of my thinking subject can be useful to me; without that I could very well dispense with it altogether.

So much is lacking for us to be able to infer these properties solely from the pure category of substance, that we must rather ground the persistence of a given object on experience if we would apply to that object the empirically usable concept of a **substance.** But now we have not grounded the present proposition on any experience, but have merely inferred [it] from the concept of the relation that all thought has to the I as the common subject in which it inheres. Nor would we be able to establish such a persistence through any secure observation, even if we supposed one. For the I is, to be sure, in all thoughts; but not the least intuition is bound up with this representation, which would distinguish it from other objects of intuition. Therefore one can, to be sure, perceive that this representation continually recurs with every thought, but

A349

A350

---

[a] *Mir selbst*, the capitalization is nonstandard, suggesting that "*Mir*" is a noun rather than a pronoun; changed to *mir selbst* in fourth edition. Below capitalizations of "Me," "Myself," "Self," "Himself," etc., will be used to translate similar nonstandard capitalizations in Kant's German.

[b] *untergelegt*; fourth edition: *unterlegt*, "an intuition underlies them".

[c] Kant ends this sentence with a period.

[d] *fortdaure*

not that it is a standing and abiding intuition, in which thoughts (as variable) would change.

From this it follows that the first syllogism of transcendental psychology imposes on us an only allegedly new insight when it passes off the constant logical subject of thinking as the cognition of a real subject of inherence, with which we do not and cannot have the least acquaintance, because consciousness is the one single thing that makes all representations into thoughts, and in which, therefore, as in the transcendental subject, our perceptions must be encountered; and apart from this logical significance of the I, we have no acquaintance with the subject in itself that grounds this I as a substratum, just as it grounds all thoughts. Meanwhile, one can quite well allow the proposition **The soul is substance** to be valid, if only one admits that this concept of ours leads no further, that it cannot teach us any of the usual conclusions of the ratio-   A 3 5 1 nalistic doctrine of the soul, such as, e.g., the everlasting duration of the soul through all alterations, even the human being's death, thus that it signifies a substance only in the idea but not in reality.

Second paralogism
of simplicity.

That thing whose action can never be regarded as the concurrence of many acting things, is **simple.**

Now the soul, or the thinking I, is such a thing.

Thus etc.[24]

Criticism of the second paralogism
of transcendental psychology.

This is the Achilles of all the dialectical inferences of the pure doctrine of the soul, nothing like a mere sophistical play that a dogmatist devised in order to give his assertions a fleeting plausibility,[a] but an inference that seems[b] to withstand even the sharpest testing and the greatest scruples of inquiry. Here it is.

Every **composite** substance is an aggregate of many, and the action of a composite, or of that which inheres in it as such a composite, is an aggregate of many actions or accidents, which is distributed among the multitude[c] of substances. Now of course an effect that arises from the concurrence of many acting substances is possible if this effect is merely   A 3 5 2 external (as, e.g., the movement of a body is the united movement of all

---

[a] *Schein*
[b] *scheint*
[c] *Menge*

its parts). Yet with thoughts, as accidents belonging inwardly to a thinking being, it is otherwise. For suppose that the composite were thinking; then every part of it would be a part of the thought, but the parts would first contain the whole thought only when taken together. Now this would be contradictory. For because the representations that are divided among different beings (e.g., the individual words of a verse) never constitute a whole thought (a verse), the thought can never inhere in a composite as such.[25] Thus it is possible only in **one** substance, which is not an aggregate of many, and hence it is absolutely simple.*

The so-called *nervus probandi*[a] of this argument lies in the proposition that many representations have to be contained in the absolute unity of the thinking subject in order to constitute one thought. But no one can prove this proposition from **concepts.** For how could he set about to

A 353 accomplish this? The proposition "A thought can be only the effect of the absolute unity of a thinking being" cannot be treated as analytic. For the unity of a thought consisting of many representations is collective, and, as far as mere concepts are concerned, it can be related to the collective unity of the substances cooperating in it (as the movement of a body is the composite movement of all its parts) just as easily as to the absolute unity of the subject. Thus there can be no insight into the necessity of presupposing a simple substance for a composite thought according to the rule of identity. But that this same proposition should be cognized synthetically and fully *a priori* from sheer concepts – that answer no one will trust himself to give when he has insight into the ground of the possibility of synthetic propositions *a priori* as we have established it above.

But now it is also impossible to derive this necessary unity of the subject, as a condition of the possibility of every thought, from experience. For experience gives us cognition of no necessity, to say nothing of the fact that the concept of absolute unity is far above its sphere. Where, then, will we get this proposition, on which the whole psychological syllogism rests?

It is obvious that if one wants to represent a thinking being, one must put oneself in its place, and thus substitute one's own subject for the ob-

A 354 ject[b] one wants to consider (which is not the case in any other species of investigation); and it is also obvious that we demand absolute unity for the subject of a thought only because otherwise it could not be said:

A 352   * It is very easy to give this proof the usual dress of scholastic precision. Yet it is sufficient for my purpose to lay before our eyes the mere ground of proof, though in a popular manner.

[a] the nub (literally, "nerve") of what is to be proved
[b] *Object*

"I think" (the manifold in a representation). For although the whole of the thought could be divided and distributed among many subjects, the subjective **I** cannot be divided or distributed, and this **I** we presuppose in all thinking.

Here, therefore, as in the previous paralogism, the formal proposition of apperception, **I think,** remains the entire ground on which rational psychology ventures to extend its cognitions; this proposition is of course obviously not an experience, but rather the form of apperception, on which every experience depends and which precedes it, yet it must nevertheless always be regarded only in regard[a] to a possible cognition in general, as its **merely subjective condition,** which we unjustly make into a condition of the possibility of the cognition of objects, namely into a **concept** of a thinking being in general, because we are unable to represent this being without positing ourselves along with the formula of our consciousness, in the place of every other intelligent being.

But the simplicity of my self (as soul) is not really **inferred** from the proposition "I think," but rather the former lies already in every thought itself. The proposition **I am simple** must be regarded as an immediate expression of apperception, just as the supposed Cartesian inference *cogito, ergo sum*[b] is in fact tautological, since the *cogito (sum cogitans)*[c] immediately asserts the reality. But **I am simple** signifies no more than that this representation **I** encompasses not the least manifoldness within itself, and that it is an absolute (though merely logical) unity.

Thus the so famous psychological proof is grounded merely on the indivisible unity of a representation, which governs the verb only in regard to a person. But it is obvious that the subject of inherence is designated only transcendentally through the I that is appended to thoughts, without noting the least property of it, or cognizing or knowing anything at all about it. It signifies only a Something in general (a transcendental subject), the representation of which must of course be simple, just because one determines nothing at all about it; for certainly nothing can be represented as more simple than that which is represented through the concept of a mere Something. But the simplicity of the representation of a subject is not therefore a cognition of the simplicity of the subject itself, since its properties are entirely abstracted from if it is designated merely through the expression "I," wholly empty of content (which I can apply to every thinking subject).

This much is certain: through the I, I always think[d] an absolute but

---

[a] *nur in Ansehung . . . angesehen*
[b] I think, therefore I am.
[c] I think (I am thinking).
[d] *gedenke*

logical unity of the subject (simplicity), but I do not cognize the real simplicity of my subject. Just as the proposition "I am substance" signifies nothing but the pure category, of which I can make no (empirical) use *in concreto*, so is it permitted to me to say, "I am a simple substance," i.e., a substance the representation of which never contains a synthesis of the manifold; but this concept, or even this proposition, teaches us not the least bit in regard to myself as an object of experience, because the concept of substance is used only as a function of synthesis, without an intuition being subsumed under it, hence without an object; [a] and it is valid only of the condition of our cognition, but not of any particular object that is to be specified. We will perform an experiment concerning the supposed usefulness of this proposition.

Everyone must admit that the assertion of the simple nature of the soul is of unique value only insofar as through it I distinguish this subject from all matter, and consequently except it from the perishability to which matter is always subjected.[26] It is really only to this use that the above proposition is applied, hence it is often expressed thus: the soul is not corporeal. Now if I can show that even if one concedes all objective validity to this cardinal proposition of the rational doctrine of the soul (that everything which thinks is a simple substance) in its pure significance as a merely rational judgment (from pure categories), nevertheless not the least use of this proposition can be made in respect of its dissimilarity to or affinity with matter, then this would be the same as if I had consigned this supposed psychological insight to the field of mere ideas, which lack the reality of an objective use.

A 357

In the transcendental aesthetic we have undeniably proved that bodies are mere appearances of our outer sense, and not things in themselves. In accord with this, we can rightfully say that our thinking subject is not corporeal, meaning that since it is represented as an object of our inner sense, insofar as it thinks it could not be an object of outer sense, i.e., it could not be an appearance in space. Now this is to say as much as that thinking beings, **as such,** can never come before us among outer appearances, or: we cannot intuit their thoughts, their consciousness, their desires, etc. externally; for all this belongs before inner sense. In fact this argument seems to be the natural and popular one, by which even the commonest understanding seems always to have been pleased and thereby to have begun very early to consider souls as beings wholly distinct from their bodies.

A 358

But now although extension, impenetrability, composition and motion – in short, everything our outer senses can transmit to us – are [b] not thoughts, feelings, inclinations or decisions, and cannot contain them,

---

[a] *Object*

[b] *sein*, which makes no grammatical sense. Following Erdmann, we read *sind*.

as these are never objects of outer intuition, yet that same Something that grounds outer appearances and affects our sense so that it receives the representations of space, matter, shape, etc. – this Something, considered as noumenon (or better, as transcendental object) could also at the same time be the subject of thoughts, even though we receive no intuition of representations, volitions, etc. in the way we are affected through outer sense, but rather receive merely intuitions of space and its determinations. But this Something is not extended, not impenetrable, not composite, because these predicates pertain only to sensibility and its intuition, insofar as we are affected by such objects *a* (otherwise unknown to us). These expressions, however, do not give us cognition of what kind of object it is, but only that, since it is considered in itself without relation to outer sense, it is such that these predicates of outer appearances cannot be applied to it. Yet the predicates of inner sense,   A 359 representation and thought, do not contradict it. Accordingly, even through the conceded simplicity of its nature the human soul is not at all sufficiently distinguished from matter in regard to its substratum, if one considers matter (as one should) merely as appearance.

If matter were a thing in itself, then as a composite being it would be completely distinguished from the soul as a simple being. But it is merely an outer appearance, whose substratum is not cognized through any specifiable predicates; hence I can well assume about this substratum that in itself it is simple, even though in the way it affects our outer senses it produces in us the intuition of something extended and hence composite; and thus I can also assume that in the substance in itself, to which extension pertains in respect of our outer sense, thoughts may also be present, which may be represented with consciousness through their own inner sense. In such a way the very same thing that is called a body in one relation would at the same time be a thinking being in another, whose thoughts, of course, we could not intuit, but only their signs in appearance. Thereby the expression that only souls (as a particular species of substances) think would be dropped; and instead it would be said, as usual, that human beings think, i.e., that the same   A 360 being that as outer appearance is extended is inwardly (in itself) a subject, which is not composite, but is simple and thinks.

But without allowing such hypotheses, one can remark generally that if by a "soul" I understand a thinking being in itself, then it is already in itself an unsuitable question to ask whether or not it is of the same species as matter (which is not a thing in itself at all, but only a species of representations in us); for it is already self-evident that a thing in itself is of another nature than the determinations that merely constitute its state.

a *Objecte*

But if we compare the thinking I not with matter but with the intelligible that grounds the outer appearance we call matter, then because we know nothing at all about the latter, we cannot say that the soul is inwardly distinguished from it in any way at all.

Accordingly, the simplicity of consciousness[a] is thus no acquaintance with the simple nature of our subject, insofar as this subject is supposed thereby to be distinguished from matter as a composite being.

If this concept still does not serve to determine it[b] what is proper and distinctive to its nature even in the one case where it is useful, namely in the comparison of my self with objects of outer experience, one may still pretend to know that the thinking **I**, the soul (a name for the transcendental object of inner sense), is simple; nevertheless on this account this expression has no use at all that reaches to real objects, and hence it cannot extend our cognition in the least.

A 361

Accordingly, the whole of rational psychology collapses along with its chief supports, and here as elsewhere we can have little hope of broadening our insight through mere concepts without any relation to possible experience (still less through the mere subjective form of all our concepts, our consciousness); above all, since even the fundamental concept **of a simple nature** is of such a kind as cannot be encountered anywhere in experience, and hence there is thus no path at all by which to reach it as an objectively valid concept.

Third paralogism
of personality.

What is conscious of the numerical identity of its Self[c] in different times, is to that extent a **person.**

Now the soul is etc.

Thus it is a person.[27]

Criticism of the third paralogism
of transcendental psychology.

If I want to cognize through experience the numerical identity of an external object, then I will attend to what is persisting in its appearance, to which, as subject, everything else relates as a determination, and I will notice the identity of the former in the time in which the latter changes. But now I am an object of inner sense and all time is merely the form of inner sense. Consequently, I relate each and every one of

A 362

---

[a] *das einfache Bewusstsein*

[b] *ihn* – a masculine accusative pronoun whose antecedent and grammatical function in the sentence both remain unclear; it cannot grammatically refer to either "subject" or "consciousness" in the previous sentence, since both those nouns are neuter.

[c] In the fourth edition: "*seiner selbst.*"

my successive determinations to the numerically identical Self in all time, i.e., in the form of the inner intuition of my self. On this basis the personality of the soul must be regarded not as inferred but rather as a completely identical proposition of self-consciousness in time, and that is also the cause of its being valid *a priori*. For it really says no more than that in the whole time in which I am conscious of myself, I am conscious of this time as belonging to the unity of my Self, and it is all the same whether I say that this whole time is in Me, as an individual unity, or that I am to be found with numerical identity, in all of this time.

The identity of person is therefore inevitably to be encountered in my own consciousness. But if I consider myself from the standpoint of another (as an object of his outer intuition), then it is this external observer who originally considers*a* **me** as **in time;** for in apperception **time** is properly represented only **in me.** Thus from the I that accompanies – and indeed with complete identity – all representations at every A 363 time in **my** consciousness, although he admits this I, he will still not infer the objective persistence of my Self. For just as the time in which the observer posits me is not the time that is encountered in my sensibility but that which is encountered in his own, so the identity that is necessarily combined with my consciousness is not therefore combined with his consciousness, i.e., with the outer intuition of my subject.

The identity of the consciousness of Myself in different times is therefore only a formal condition of my thoughts and their connection, but it does not prove at all the numerical identity of my subject, in which – despite the logical identity of the I – a change can go on that does not allow it to keep its identity; and this even though all the while the identical-sounding "I" is assigned to it, which in every other state, even in the replacement of the subject, still keeps in view the thought of the previous subject, and thus could also pass it along to the following one.*

---

* An elastic ball that strikes another one in a straight line communicates to the latter its whole motion, hence its whole state (if one looks only at their positions in space). Now assuming substances, on the analogy with such bodies, in which representations, together with consciousness of them, flow from one to A 364 another, a whole series of these substances may be thought, of which the first would communicate its state, together with its consciousness, to the second, which would communicate its own state, together with that of the previous substance, to a third substance, and this in turn would share the states of all previous ones, together with their consciousness and its own. The last substance would thus be conscious of all the states of all the previously altered substances as its own states, because these states would have been carried over to it, together with the consciousness of them; and in spite of this it would not have been the very same person in all these states.[28]

a *allererst . . . erwägt*

A 364   Even if the saying of some ancient schools, that everything is **transitory** and nothing in the world is **persisting** and abiding,[29] cannot hold as soon as one assumes substances, it is still not refuted through the unity of self-consciousness. For we cannot judge even from our own consciousness whether as soul we are persisting or not, because we ascribe to our identical Self only that of which we are conscious; and so we must necessarily judge that we are the very same in the whole of the time of which we are conscious. But from the standpoint of someone else we cannot declare this to be valid because, since in the soul we encounter no persisting appearance other than the representation "I," which accompanies and connects all of them, we can never make out whether this I (a mere thought) does not flow as well as all the other thoughts that are linked to one another through it.

A 365   It is remarkable, however, that personality, and its presupposition, persistence, hence the substantiality of the soul, must be proved only now for the first time. For if we could presuppose these, then what would of course follow is not the continuous duration of consciousness, but rather the possibility of a continuing consciousness in an abiding subject, which is already sufficient for personality, since that does not cease at once just because its effect is perhaps interrupted for a time. This persistence, however, is not given to us through anything prior to the numerical identity of our Self, which we conclude from identical apperception, but rather is concluded for the first time from it (and, if things went rightly, we would have to conclude from this first of all the concept of substance, which is usable only empirically). Now since this identity of person in no way follows from the identity of the I in the consciousness of all the time in which I cognize myself, even the substantiality of the soul cannot be grounded on it above.

    Meanwhile, the concept of personality, just like the concepts of substance and of the simple, can remain (insofar as it is merely transcendental, i.e., a unity of the subject which is otherwise unknown to us, but in whose determinations there is a thoroughgoing connection of apperception), and to this extent this concept is also necessary and sufficient

A 366 for practical use; but we can never boast of it as an extension of our self-knowledge[a] through pure reason, which dazzles us with the uninterrupted continuous duration of the subject drawn from the mere concept of the identical self, since this concept merely revolves in a circle around itself and brings us no farther in regard to even one single question about synthetic cognition. What matter is, as a thing in itself (transcendental object),[b] is of course entirely unknown to us; nevertheless its persistence will be observed as appearance as long as it is represented to

---

[a] *Selbsterkenntnis*
[b] *Object*

us as something external. But since I want to observe the mere I through the change in all my representations, I have once again no correlate other than Myself for my comparisons with the general conditions of my consciousness; I can therefore give nothing but tautological answers to all questions, because I substitute my concept and its unity for the properties pertaining to my self as an object,[a] and thus merely presuppose what one demanded to know.

The fourth paralogism
of the ideality
(of outer relation).[b]

That whose existence can be inferred only as a cause of given perceptions has only a **doubtful existence:**

Now all outer appearances are of this kind: their existence cannot be   A 367
immediately perceived, but can be inferred only as the cause of given perceptions:

Thus the existence of all objects of outer sense is doubtful. This uncertainty I call the ideality of outer appearances, and the doctrine of this ideality is called **idealism,** in comparison with which the assertion of a possible certainty of objects of outer sense is called **dualism.**

Criticism of the fourth paralogism
of transcendental psychology.

First we will subject the premises to examination. We can rightly assert that only what is in ourselves can be immediately perceived, and that my own existence alone could be the object of a mere perception. Thus the existence of a real object outside me (if this last word is taken in an intellectual signification) is never given directly in perception, but can only be added in thought to what is a modification of inner sense as its external cause, and hence can only be inferred. Therefore Descartes also rightly limited all perception in the narrowest sense to the proposition "I (as a thinking being) am."[30] Thus it is clear that since the external is   A 368
not in me, I cannot encounter it in my apperception, hence not in any perception, which is properly only a determination of apperception.

Thus I cannot really perceive external things, but only infer their existence from my inner perception, insofar as I regard this as the effect of which something external is the proximate cause. But now the inference from a given effect to its determinate cause is always uncertain, since the effect can have arisen from more than one cause. Accordingly,

[a] *Object*
[b] *Verhältnisses*

in the relation of perception to its cause, it always remains doubtful whether this cause is internal or external, thus whether all so-called outer perceptions are not a mere play of our inner sense, or whether they are related to actual external objects as their cause. At least the existence of the latter is only inferred, and runs the risk of all inferences; by contrast, the object of inner sense (I myself with all my representations) is immediately perceived, and its existence suffers no doubt at all.

By an **idealist,** therefore, one must understand not someone who denies the existence of external objects of sense, but rather someone who only does not admit that it is cognized through immediate perception and infers from this that we can never be fully certain of their reality from any possible experience.

A 369

Now before I display our paralogism in its deceptive illusion, I must first remark that one would necessarily have to distinguish a twofold idealism. I understand by the **transcendental idealism** of all appearances the doctrine*ᵃ* that they are all together to be regarded as mere representations and not as things in themselves, and accordingly that space and time are only sensible forms of our intuition, but not determinations given for themselves or conditions of objects*ᵇ* as things in themselves. To this idealism is opposed **transcendental realism,** which regards space and time as something given in themselves (independent of our sensibility). The transcendental realist therefore represents outer appearances (if their reality is conceded) as things in themselves, which would exist independently of us and our sensibility and thus would also be outside us according to pure concepts of the understanding. It is really this transcendental realist who afterwards plays the empirical idealist; and after he has falsely presupposed about objects of the senses that if they are to exist they must have their existence in themselves even apart from sense, he finds that from this point of view all our representations of sense are insufficient to make their reality certain.

A 370

The transcendental idealist, on the contrary, can be an empirical realist, hence, as he is called, a **dualist,** i.e., he can concede the existence of matter without going beyond mere self-consciousness and assuming something more than the certainty of representations in me, hence the *cogito, ergo sum.ᶜ* For because he allows this matter and even its inner possibility to be valid only for appearance – which, separated from our sensibility, is nothing – matter for him is only a species of representations (intuition), which are called external, not as if they related to objects that are **external in themselves** but because they relate perceptions to space, where all things are external to one another, but that space itself is in us.

ᵃ Lehrbegriff
ᵇ Objecte
ᶜ I think, therefore I am.

Chapter I. On the paralogisms of pure reason <A>

Now we have already declared ourselves for this transcendental idealism from the outset. Thus our doctrine[a] removes all reservations about assuming the existence of matter based on the testimony of our mere self-consciousness, and it declares this to be proved in the same way as the existence of myself as a thinking being. For I am indeed conscious to myself of my representations; thus these exist, and I myself, who has these representations. But now external objects (bodies) are merely appearances, hence also nothing other than a species of my representations, whose objects are something only through these representations, but are nothing separated from them. Thus external things exist as well as my self, and indeed both exist on the immediate testimony of my self-consciousness, only with this difference: the representation of my Self, as the thinking subject, is related merely to inner sense, but the representations that designate extended beings are also related to outer sense. I am no more necessitated to draw inferences in respect of the reality of external objects than I am in regard to the reality of the objects of my inner sense (my thoughts), for in both cases they are nothing but representations, the immediate perception (consciousness) of which is at the same time a sufficient proof of their reality.

A371

Thus the transcendental idealist is an empirical realist, and grants to matter, as appearance, a reality which need not be inferred, but is immediately perceived. In contrast, transcendental realism necessarily falls into embarrassment, and finds itself required to give way to empirical idealism, because it regards the objects of outer sense as something different from the senses themselves and regards mere appearances as self-sufficient beings that are found external to us; for here, even with our best consciousness of our representation of these things, it is obviously far from certain that if the representation exists, then the object corresponding to it would also exist; but in our system, on the contrary, these external things – namely, matter in all its forms and alterations – are nothing but mere representations, i.e., representations in us, of whose reality we are immediately conscious.

A372

Now since as far as I know all those psychologists who cling to empirical idealism are transcendental realists, they have obviously proceeded very consistently in conceding great importance to empirical idealism as one of the problems from which human reason knows how to extricate itself only with difficulty. For in fact if one regards outer appearances as representations that are effected in us by their objects, as things in themselves found outside us, then it is hard to see how their existence could be cognized in any way other than by an inference from effect to cause, in which case it must always remain doubtful whether the cause is in us or outside us. Now one can indeed admit that something

[a] *Lehrbegriff*

that may be outside us in the transcendental sense is the cause of our outer intuitions, but this is not the object we understand by the representation of matter and corporeal things; for these are merely appearances, i.e., mere modes of representation, which are always found only in us, and their reality, just as much as that of my own thoughts, rests on immediate consciousness. The transcendental object is equally unknown in regard to inner and to outer sense. But we are talking not about that, but about the empirical object, which is called an **external** object if it is **in space** and an **inner** object if it is represented simply in the **relation**[a] **of time;** but space and time are both to be encountered only **in us.**

A 373

But since the expression **outside us** carries with it an unavoidable ambiguity, since it sometimes signifies something that, **as a thing in itself,** exists distinct from us and sometimes merely something that belongs to outer **appearance,** then in order to escape uncertainty and use this concept in the latter significance – in which it is taken in the proper psychological question about the reality of our outer intuition – we will distinguish **empirically external** objects from those that might be called "external" in the transcendental sense, by directly calling them "things **that are to be encountered in space.**"[31]

Space and time are of course representations *a priori*, which dwell in us as forms of our sensible intuition before any real object has even determined our inner sense through sensation in such a way that we represent it under those sensible relations.[b] This material or real entity, however, this Something that is to be intuited in space, necessarily presupposes perception, and it cannot be invented by any power of imagination or produced independently of perception, which indicates the reality of something in space. Thus sensation is that which designates a reality in space and time, according to whether it is related to the one or the other mode of sensible intuition. Once sensation is given (which, if it is applied to an object in general without determining it, is called perception), then through its manifold many an object can be invented[c] in imagination that has no empirical place outside imagination in space or time. Whether we take sensations, pleasure and pain, or even external sensations, such as colors, warmth, etc., it is certain beyond doubt that it is perception through which the material must first be given for thinking objects of sensible intuition. This perception thus represents (staying for now only with outer intuitions) something real in space. For first, perception is the representation of a reality, just as space is the representation of a mere possibility of coexistence.[d] Second, this reality is

A 374

---

[a] *Verhältnis*
[b] *Verhältnisse*
[c] *gedichtet*
[d] *Beisammenseins*

represented before outer sense, i.e., in space. Third, space is nothing other than a mere representation, hence only what is represented* in it can count as real, and conversely, what is given in it, i.e., represented through perception, is also real in it; for if it were not real in space, i.e., immediately given through empirical intuition, then it could not also be invented,^{a} because one cannot just think up the real in intuition *a priori*.^{b}

A 375

Every outer perception therefore immediately proves something real in space, or rather is itself the real; to that extent, empirical realism is beyond doubt, i.e., to our outer intuitions there corresponds something real in space. Of course space itself with all its appearances, as representations, is only in me; but in this space the real, or the material of all objects of outer intuition is nevertheless really given, independently of all invention; and it is also impossible that in this space anything outside us (in the transcendental sense) should be given, since space itself is nothing apart from our sensibility. Thus the strictest ^{c} idealist cannot demand that one prove that the object outside us (in the strict^d sense) corresponds to our perception. For if there were such a thing, then it still could not be represented and intuited outside us, because this would presuppose space; and reality in space, as a mere representation, is nothing other than perception itself. The real in outer appearances is thus actual only in perception, and cannot be actual in any other way.

A 376

Now cognition of objects can be generated from perceptions, either through a mere play of imagination or by means of experience. And then of course there can arise deceptive representations, to which objects do not correspond, and where the deception is sometimes to be attributed to a semblance of the imagination (in dreams), sometimes to a false step of judgment (in the case of so-called sense-deceptions). In order to avoid the false illusion here, one proceeds according to the

---

* One must note well this paradoxical but correct proposition, that nothing is in space except what is represented in it. For space itself is nothing other than representation; consequently, what is in it must be contained in representation, and nothing at all is in space except insofar as it is really represented in it. A proposition which must of course sound peculiar is that a thing can exist only in the representation of it; but it loses its offensive character here, because the things with which we have to do are not things in themselves but only appearances, i.e., representations.

A 374

A 375

^{a} *erdichtet*
^{b} Note in Kant's copy of the second edition: "Objects of outer senses contain the ground of time-determination of inner sense, consequently, however, also of inner experience, though not the ground of consciousness, [even if . . .]" (the end of the sentence is missing in the manuscript). (E CLXII, p. 49; 23:39)
^{c} *strengste*
^{d} *strikter*

rule: **Whatever is connected with a perception according to empirical laws, is actual.**[32] Only this deception, as much as the measures taken against it, concerns idealism as much as dualism, since here it is only a question of the form of experience. In order to refute empirical idealism, as a false scruple concerning the objective reality of our outer perceptions, it is already sufficient that outer perception immediately proves a reality in space, which space, though in itself it is only a mere form of representations, nevertheless has objective reality in regard to all outer appearances (which are also nothing but mere representations); and it is likewise sufficient to refute empirical idealism that without perception even fictions and dreams are not possible, so our outer senses, as regards the *data* from which experience can arise, have actual corresponding objects in space.

A 377

The **dogmatic idealist** would be one who **denies** the existence of matter, the **skeptical idealist** one who **doubts** it because he holds it to be unprovable.[33] The former can be so only because he believes he can find contradictions in the possibility of a matter in general, and just now we are not yet dealing with that. The following section on dialectical inferences, which represents reason in its internal conflict regarding the concepts belonging to the possibility of the connection of experience, will also help us out of this difficulty.[34] The skeptical idealist, however, who impugns merely the grounds of our assertion of the existence of matter and declares insufficient our persuasion of it, which is grounded on immediate perception, is a benefactor to human reason, since he requires us to open our eyes well even in the smallest steps of common experience, and not immediately to take for a well-earned possession what we perhaps obtain only surreptitiously. The utility created by these idealistic projects is now clearly before our eyes. They drive us forcefully – if we do not want to become tangled in confusions in our commonest assertions – to regard all perceptions, whether they are called inner or outer, merely as a consciousness of something that depends on our sensibility, and to regard their external objects not as things in themselves but only as representations, of which we can become immediately conscious like any other representation, but which are called external because they depend on that sense which we call outer sense; its intuition is space, but it is itself nothing other than an inner mode of representation, in which certain perceptions are connected with one another.

A 378

If we let outer objects count as things in themselves, then it is absolutely impossible to comprehend how we are to acquire cognition of their reality outside us, since we base this merely on the representation, which is in us. For one cannot have sensation outside oneself, but only in oneself, and the whole of self-consciousness therefore provides nothing other than merely our own determinations. Skeptical idealism thus requires us to take the only refuge remaining to us, namely to grasp the ideality of all appearances, which we have already established in the Transcendental Aesthetic independently of these consequences, which we could not then have foreseen. Now if one asks whether dualism alone holds in the doctrine of the soul, then the answer is: Of course, but only in the empirical sense, i.e., in the connection of experience matter as substance in appearance is really given to outer sense, just as the thinking I is given to inner sense, likewise as substance in appearance; and in the connection of our outer as well as our inner perceptions, appearances on both sides must be connected among themselves into one experience according to the rules that the category of substance brings in. But if one wants to broaden the concept of dualism as it is usually applied and take it in a transcendental sense, then neither it, nor the **pneumatism** that is opposed to it on the one side, nor the **materialism** on the other side, have the least ground, since then one's concepts would lack determination, and one would take the difference in the mode of representing objects, which are unknown to us as to what they are in themselves, for a difference in these things themselves. I, represented through inner sense in time, and objects in space outside me, are indeed specifically*a* wholly distinct appearances, but they are not thereby thought of as different things. The **transcendental object***b* that grounds both outer appearances and inner intuition is neither matter nor a thinking being in itself, but rather an unknown ground of those appearances that supply us with our empirical concepts of the former as well as the latter.

If, therefore, as the present critique obviously requires of us, we remain true to the rule established earlier not to press our questions beyond that with which possible experience and its object*c* can supply us, then it will not occur to us to seek information about what the objects of our senses may be in themselves, i.e., apart from any relation to the senses. But if a psychologist takes appearances for things in themselves, then as a materialist he may take up matter into his doctrine, or as a spiritualist he may take up merely thinking beings (namely, according to the form of our inner sense) as the single and sole thing existing in itself, or as a dualist he may take up both; yet through misunderstanding he will always be confined to sophistical reasonings about the way in which that which is no thing in itself, but only the appearance of a thing in general, might exist in itself.

---

a The text of the first edition reads *skeptisch*, but in the preface (A xxii), Kant corrects it to *specifisch*.

b *Object*

c *Object*

Observation[a] on
the sum of the pure doctrine of the soul,
following these paralogisms.

If we compare the **doctrine of the soul,** as the physiology of inner sense, with the **doctrine of bodies,** as a physiology of the objects of outer sense, then we will find that aside from the fact that in both doctrines much can be cognized empirically, there is nevertheless this remarkable difference, that in the latter science much can be cognized *a priori* from the mere concept of an extended impenetrable being, but in the former science nothing at all can be cognized *a priori* from the concept of a thinking being. The cause is this: Although both are appearances, the appearance before outer sense has something standing and abiding in it, which supplies a substratum grounding the transitory determinations, and thus also a synthetic concept, namely that of space and of an appearance in it; whereas time, which is the only form of our inner intuition, has in it nothing abiding, and hence gives cognition only of a change of determinations, but not of the determinable object. For in that which we call the soul, everything is in continual flux, and it has nothing abiding, except perhaps (if one insists)[b] the I, which is simple only because this representation has no content, and hence no manifold, on account of which it seems to represent a simple object,[c] or better put, it seems to designate one. This **I** would have to be an intuition, which, since it would be presupposed in all thinking in general (prior to all experience), would, as an intuition, supply *a priori* synthetic propositions if it were to be possible to bring about a pure rational cognition of the nature of a thinking being in general. Yet this I is no more an intuition than it is a concept of any object; rather, it is the mere form of consciousness,[d] which accompanies both sorts of representations and which can elevate them to cognitions only insofar as something else is given in intuition, which provides the material for the representation of an object. Thus the whole of rational psychology, as a science transcending all the powers of human reason, collapses, and nothing is left except to

---

[a] *Betrachtung*
[b] Kant later indicated that "perhaps (if one insists)" was to be omitted (E CLXIII p. 49; 23:50).
[c] *Object*
[d] Kant corrects this to: " . . . the (unknown to us) object [*Object*] of consciousness, . . . " (E CLXIV p. 49; 23:50).

study our soul following the guideline*a* of experience, and to remain within the limit of those questions that do not go beyond that whose content can be provided by possible inner experience.

But if it has no utility as an extension of our cognition, but so regarded is rather composed of mere paralogisms, it still cannot be denied an important negative utility even if it is to count for nothing more than a critical treatment of our dialectical inferences, those of common and natural reason.

Why do we have need of a doctrine of the soul grounded merely on pure rational principles?*b* Without doubt chiefly with the intent of securing our thinking Self from the danger of materialism. But this is achieved by the rational concept of our thinking Self that we have given. For according to it, so little fear remains that if one took matter away then all thinking and even the existence of thinking beings would be abolished, that it rather shows clearly that if I were to take away the thinking subject, the whole corporeal world would have to disappear, as this is nothing but the appearance in the sensibility of our subject and one mode of its representations.

A 383

Thereby of course I obviously cognize this thinking Self no better as to its properties, nor can I have any insight into its persistence, or even the independence of its existence from whatever transcendental substratum of outer appearances there may be, for this is just as unknown to me as the self is. But since it is likewise possible that I may find cause, drawn from somewhere else than mere speculative grounds, to hope for an existence of my thinking nature that is self-sufficient and persisting through all possible changes of my state, much is still won if, through the free confession of my ignorance, I can nevertheless repel the dogmatic attacks of a speculative opponent, and show him that he can never know more in which to deny my expectations about the nature of my subject than I can in order to hold to them.

A 384

On this transcendental illusion of our psychological concepts, then, three dialectical questions are grounded, which constitute the proper goal of rational psychology, and cannot be decided otherwise than by the above investigations. These questions are, namely: 1) about the possibility of the community of the soul with an organic body, i.e., the animality and the state of the soul in the life of the human being; 2) about the beginning of this community, i.e., of the soul in and before the birth of the human being; and 3) as to the end of this community, i.e., of the soul in and after the death of the human being (the question concerning immortality).

a Leitfaden
b Principien

Now I assert that all the difficulties one believes he finds in these questions, and with which, as dogmatic objections, one seeks to give the appearance of having a deeper insight into the nature of things than the common understanding can have, rest on a mere semblance, according to which one hypostatizes what exists merely in thoughts, and – assuming it to be a real object outside the thinking subject – takes the same quality, namely extension, which is nothing but appearance, for a property of external things subsisting even apart from our sensibility, and

A 385 takes motion for its effect, which really takes place in itself outside our senses. For matter, whose community with the soul excites such great reservations, is nothing other than a mere form, or a certain mode of representation of an unknown object, through that intuition that one calls outer sense. Thus there may very well be something outside us, which we call matter, corresponding to this appearance; but in the same quality as appearance it is not outside us, but is merely as a thought in us, even though this thought, through the sense just named, represents it as being found outside us. Matter thus signifies not a species of substances quite different and heterogeneous from the object of inner sense (the soul), but rather only the heterogeneity of the appearances of substances (which in themselves are unknown to us), whose representations we call external in comparison with those that we ascribe to inner sense, even though they belong as much to the thinking subject as other thoughts do; only they have in themselves this deceptive feature, that since they represent objects in space, they seem to cut themselves loose from the soul, as it were, and hover outside it; although space itself, in which they are intuited, is nothing but a representation, whose counterpart in the same quality outside the soul cannot be encountered at all. Now the question is no longer

A 386 about the community of the soul with other known but different substances outside us, but merely about the conjunction of representations in inner sense with the modifications of our outer sensibility, and how these may be conjoined with one another according to constant laws, so that they are connected into one experience.[35]

As long as we keep inner and outer appearances together with one another, as mere representations in experience, we find nothing absurd and nothing that makes the community of both modes of sense appear strange. But as soon as we hypostatize outer appearances, no longer relating them to our thinking subject as representations but rather relating them to it **in the same quality as they are in us** as **things external to us and subsisting by themselves,** and relating their actions, which show themselves as appearances in relation[a] to one another, to our thinking subject, then we have a characteristic of the efficient causes

---

[a] *Verhältnis*

outside us that is not coherent with their effects in us, because the character of the cause relates merely to outer sense, while the effects relate to inner sense; which senses, although united in one subject, are nevertheless most unlike each other. There we have no other external effects except alterations of place, and no powers except efforts that result in relations *a* in space as their effects. But in us the effects are thoughts, among which no relations *b* of place, motion, shape or spatial determination occur, and we wholly lose the guidance of causes in the effects which they are to exhibit in inner sense. But we should consider that bodies are not objects in themselves that are present to us, but rather a mere appearance of who knows what unknown object; that motion is not the effect of this unknown cause, but merely the appearance of its influence on our senses; that consequently neither of these is something outside us, but both are merely representations in us, hence that it is not the motion of matter that causes representations in us, but that motion itself (hence also the matter that makes itself knowable through it) is a mere representation; and finally that the whole self-made difficulty comes to this: How and through what cause do the representations of our sensibility stand in combination with one another, so that those representations that we call outer intuitions can be represented according to empirical laws as objects outside us? – a question that does not in the least contain the supposed difficulty of explaining the origin of representations by entirely different sorts of efficient causes found outside us, as when we take the appearance of an unknown cause for the cause outside us, which can occasion nothing but confusion. In judgments in which a misinterpretation is deeply rooted through long habit, it is impossible to correct them immediately with that lucidity that can be furthered in other cases, where our concept is not confused by such an unavoidable illusion. Hence our liberation of reason from sophistical theories can hardly have the clarity necessary for complete satisfaction.

A387

A388

I believe I can further it in the following way.

All **objections** can be divided into **dogmatic, critical** and **skeptical** ones. A dogmatic objection is one that is directed against a proposition, but a critical one is directed against its **proof.** The former requires an insight into the constitution of the nature of the object, in order to be able to assert the opposite of what the proposition claims about the object; it is itself dogmatic, therefore, and claims to have better acquaintance with the constitution of the object being talked about than its opposite has. The critical objection, because it leaves the proposition untouched in its worth or worthlessness, and impugns only the proof,

---

a *Verhältnisse*
b *Verhältnisse*

does not at all need to have better acquaintance with the object or to pretend to better acquaintance with it; it shows only that the assertion is groundless, not that it is incorrect. The skeptical objection puts the proposition and its opposite over against one another, as objections of equal weight, each alternatively a dogma with the other as an objection to it; thus on both opposed sides it is dogmatic in appearance,[a] in order to annihilate entirely every judgment about the object. Thus both, the dogmatic as well as the skeptical objection, must claim as much insight into its object as is necessary to assert something about it either affirmatively or negatively. The critical objection alone is of such a kind that it overturns a theory merely by showing that one assumes on behalf of its assertion something that is nugatory and merely imagined, thereby withdrawing from it the presumed foundation without otherwise wanting to decide anything about the constitution of the object.

A 389

Now according to the common concepts of our reason in regard to the community in which our thinking subject stands to things outside us we are dogmatic, and regard these things as objects truly subsisting independently of us, according to a certain transcendental dualism that does not count those outer appearances as representations of the subject but rather displaces them, as the sensible intuition that provides them to us, outside us as objects,[b] separating them entirely from the thinking subject. Now this subreption is the foundation of all theories about the community between soul and body, and it is never asked whether this objective reality of appearances is completely correct, but rather this is taken for granted, and the sophistry is only about the way this is to be explained and comprehended. The three usual systems that have been thought up about this, really the only possible ones, are those of **physical influence**, of **preestablished harmony**, and of **supernatural assistance**.[36]

A 390

The last two ways of explaining the community of the soul with matter are grounded on objections to the first, which is the conception[c] of the common understanding; they object, namely, that what appears as matter could not, through its immediate influence, be the cause of representations, since these are an entirely heterogeneous species of effects. However, they cannot combine what they understand as the object of outer sense with the concept of matter, which is nothing but an appearance, thus in itself a mere representation caused by some external object or other, for then they would be saying that the representations of external objects (appearances) could not be external causes of representations in our mind; that would be a wholly senseless objection, because it

[a] *dem Scheine nach*
[b] *Objecte*
[c] *Vorstellung*

would never occur to anyone to take as an external cause what he has already recognized as a mere representation. According to our principles they would therefore have to direct their theory at this: that what is the true (transcendental) object of our outer sense could not be the cause of those representations (appearances) that we understand under the name of matter. Now since no one can claim with good ground to be acquainted with anything of the transcendental cause of our representations of outer sense, any assertion about it is entirely groundless. But if the supposed improvers of the doctrine of physical influence, in accordance with the common way of representing a transcendental dualism, want to regard matter as such as a thing in itself (and not as the mere appearance of an unknown thing), and to direct their objection to showing that such an external object, which exhibits in itself no other causality than that of motion, could never be the efficient cause of representations, but rather that a third being must mediate between them in order to establish, if not reciprocity, then at least correspondence and harmony, then in that case they would have to begin their refutation by assuming in their dualism the πρωτον ψευδος[a] of physical influence, and thus their objection would refute not so much the natural influence as their own dualistic presupposition. For all the difficulties that concern the combination of thinking nature with matter arise without exception solely from the surreptitious dualistic notion[b] that matter as such is not an appearance, i.e., a mere representation of the mind, which corresponds to an unknown object, but is rather an object in itself, as it exists outside us and independently of all sensibility.

Thus no dogmatic objection can be made against the physical influence that is commonly assumed. For if the opponent assumes that matter and its motion are mere appearances and thus themselves only representations, then he can place the difficulty only in the fact that the unknown object of our sensibility could not be the cause of representations in us; a claim, however, for which he has not the least justification, because no one can decide about an unknown object what it can or cannot do. But according to our proof above, he must necessarily admit this transcendental idealism, unless he wants to hypostatize what are obviously representations and displace them outside himself, as true things.

Nonetheless, a well-grounded **critical objection** can be made against the common doctrinal opinion[c] of physical influence. The sort of community that is claimed to occur between two species of substances, thinking and extended, is grounded on a crude dualism, and makes the latter substances, which are nothing but mere representations of the

A391

A392

---

[a] primary falsity
[b] *Vorstellung*
[c] *Lehrmeinung*

thinking subject, into things subsisting for themselves. Thus the misunderstood physical influence can be completely thwarted by revealing the argument for it to be nugatory and surreptitious.

Thus if one separates out everything imaginary, the notorious question about the community between what thinks and what is extended would merely come to this: **How is outer intuition** – namely, that of space (the filling of it by shape and motion) – **possible at all in a thinking subject?** But it is not possible for any human being to find an answer to this question, and no one will ever fill this gap in our knowledge, but rather only indicate it, by ascribing outer appearances to a transcendental object that is the cause of this species of representations, with which cause, however, we have no acquaintance at all, nor will we ever get a concept of it. In all the tasks that may come before us in the field of experience, we treat those appearances as objects in themselves, without worrying ourselves about the primary ground of their possibility (as appearances). But if we go beyond their boundary, then the concept of a transcendental object becomes necessary.

An immediate consequence of these considerations[a] concerning the community between thinking and extended beings is the decision of all disputes or objections concerning the state of the thinking nature prior to this community (to life) or after such a community is terminated (in death). The opinion that the thinking subject could have thought prior to all community with bodies would be expressed this way: that before the beginning of the kind of sensibility through which something appears to us in space, the same transcendental objects that appear as bodies in the present state could have been intuited in a wholly different way. But the opinion that the soul could still continue to think after all community with the corporeal world has been terminated would be expressed in this form: that if the mode of sensibility through which transcendental (and for now entirely unknown) objects appear as a material world should cease, then not all intuition would thereby be terminated, and it might well be possible for the very same unknown object to continue to be cognized by the thinking subject, even though obviously not in the quality of bodies.

Now of course no one can adduce the least ground for such an assertion from speculative principles,[b] nor even indeed establish its possibility, but rather it can only be presupposed; yet just as little can anyone make any valid dogmatic objection against it. For whoever he may be, he knows just as little as I or anyone else about the absolute and inner cause of external and corporeal appearances. Therefore he cannot claim to know what the reality of outer appearances rests on in the present

[a] *Erinnerungen*
[b] *Principien*

state (in life), hence he also cannot claim to know that the condition of all outer intuition, or even of the thinking subject itself, will cease after this state (after death). A395

Thus every dispute about the nature of our thinking being and its conjunction with the corporeal world is merely a consequence of the fact that one fills the gaps regarding what one does not know with paralogisms of reason, making thoughts into things and hypostatizing them; from this arises an imagined science, both in regard to affirmative and negative assertions, in that everyone either presumes to know something about objects about which no human being has any concept, or else makes his own representations into objects, and thus goes round and round in an eternal circle of ambiguities and contradictions. Nothing but the sobriety of a strict but just criticism can liberate us from these dogmatic semblances, which through imagined happiness hold so many subject to theories and systems, and limit all our speculative claims merely to the field of possible experience, not by stale mockery at attempts that have so often failed, or by pious sighing over the limits of our reason, but by means of a complete determination of reason's boundaries according to secure principles, which with the greatest reliability fastens its *nihil ulterius*^{a} on those Pillars of Hercules^{37} that nature has erected, so that the voyage of our reason may proceed only as far as the continuous coastline of experience reaches, a coastline that A396 we cannot leave without venturing out into a shoreless ocean, which, among always deceptive prospects, forces us in the end to abandon as hopeless all our troublesome and tedious efforts.

* * *

We still owe a distinct and general exposition of the transcendental and yet natural illusion in the paralogisms of pure reason, and also of a justification of their systematic ordering, running parallel to the table of categories. We could not have undertaken it at the beginning of this section without the danger of falling into obscurity or clumsily getting ahead of ourselves. Now we want to try to fulfill this obligation.

One can place all **illusion** in the taking of a **subjective** condition of thinking for the cognition of an **object**.^{b} In the Introduction to the Transcendental Dialectic we have further shown that pure reason concerns itself solely with totality in the synthesis of conditions for a given conditioned. Since now the dialectical illusion of pure reason cannot be any empirical illusion occurring along with determinate empirical cognitions, it must have to do with the universal conditions of thinking; and there are only three cases of the dialectical use of pure reason: A397

---

^{a} nothing farther
^{b} *Objects*

1. The synthesis of the conditions of a thought in general.
2. The synthesis of the conditions of empirical thinking.
3. The synthesis of the conditions of pure thinking.

In all three of these cases pure reason is concerned merely with the absolute totality of this synthesis, i.e., with that condition that is itself unconditioned. On this division is grounded the threefold transcendental illusion, which occasions the three sections of the Dialectic, and provides us with the idea for an equal number of putative sciences of pure reason: transcendental psychology, cosmology and theology. Here we have to do only with the first.

Because in thinking in general we abstract from every relation of the thought to any object*a* (whether of sense or of the pure understanding), the synthesis of conditions of a thought in general (No. 1) is not objective at all, but merely a synthesis of thought with the subject, which is, however, falsely taken to be a synthetic representation of an object.*b*

But it follows from this that the dialectical inference to the conditions of every thought in general, which is itself unconditioned, does not commit a mistake in content (for it abstracts from all content or objects),*c* but rather that it is mistaken in form alone, and would have to be called a paralogism.

A 398

Because, further, the only condition accompanying all thinking is the I, in the universal proposition "I think," reason has to do with this condition insofar as it is itself unconditioned. But it is only the formal condition, namely the logical unity of every thought, in which I abstract from every object; and yet it is represented as an object that I think, namely I itself, and its unconditioned unity.

If anyone were to pose the question to me: What is the constitution*d* of a thing that thinks? then I do not know the least thing to answer *a priori*, because the answer ought to be synthetic (for an analytic answer perhaps explains thinking, but gives no extended cognition of that on which thinking rests as to its possibility).*e* But for every synthetic solution, intuition is necessary; but this is entirely left out of so universal a problem. Likewise, no one can give a general answer to the question: Of what kind must a thing be in order to be movable? For then impenetrable extension (matter) is not given. But now although I know no general answer to that question, yet it seems to me that I could give it in the individual case, in the proposition that expresses self-conscious-

---

a Object
b Object
c Objecte
d Beschaffenheit
e Kant's text fails to close the parenthesis, but following Erdmann, we close it at this point.

ness: "I think." For this I is the primary subject, i.e., substance, it is simple, etc. But then these would have to be mere propositions of experience, which, in the absence of a universal rule expressing in general and *a priori* the conditions of the possibility of thinking, could[a] nevertheless contain no such predicates (since these are not empirical). In this way, my insight (so plausible at the start) into the nature of a thinking being, and indeed judged from mere concepts, becomes suspicious, even though I still have not discovered any mistake in it.

Further investigation, however, going back behind the origin of these attributes that I ascribe to Myself as a thinking being in general, can discover this error. They are nothing more than pure categories, through which I never think a determinate object, but rather only the unity of representations in order to determine their object. Without an intuition to ground it, the category alone cannot yield any concept of an object; for only through intuition is an object given, which is then thought in accordance with the category. If I declare a thing to be a substance in appearance, predicates of its intuition must be given to me previously, in which I distinguish the substratum (the thing itself) from that which merely depends on it. When I call a thing **simple in appearance**, then by that I understand that its intuition is of course a part of the appearance, but cannot itself be further divided, etc. But if something is cognized as simple only in the concept and not in appearance, then I really have no cognition of the object, but only of my concept, which I make of something in general that is not susceptible of any real intuition. I say only that I think something entirely simple, because I really do not know anything further to say about it than merely that it is something.

Now mere apperception ("I") is substance in concept, simple in concept, etc., and thus all these psychological theorems are indisputably correct. Nevertheless, one by no means thereby cognizes anything about the soul that one really wants to know, for all these predicates are not valid of intuition at all, and therefore cannot have any consequences that could be applied to objects of experience; hence they are completely empty. For that concept of substance does not teach me that the soul endures for itself, that it is not a part of outer intuitions that cannot be further divided and hence could not arise or perish through any natural alterations – pure[b] properties that could provide acquaintance with the soul in the connection of the experience, and disclosure concerning its origin and future state. Now if I say through the mere category: "The soul is a simple substance," then it is clear that since the understanding's naked concept of substance contains nothing beyond the fact

---

[a] Kant's verb is singular, but its subject appears to be plural, namely the relative pronoun referring to "propositions of experience."
[b] *lauter*

that the thing is to be represented as a subject in itself without in turn being the predicate of another subject, nothing about its persistence follows, and the attribute of simplicity certainly cannot be added to this persistence; hence one is not in the least instructed about what the soul can encounter in the alterations in the world. If one would tell us that it is a **simple part of matter,** then from what experience teaches us about this, we could derive its persistence and, together with its simple nature, its immortality. But the concept of the I, in the psychological principle ("I think"), tells us not one word about this.

But that the being that thinks in us supposes that it cognizes itself through pure categories, and indeed through those under each heading that express absolute unity, follows from this: Apperception is itself the ground of the possibility of the categories, which for their part represent nothing other than the synthesis of the manifold of intuition, insofar as that manifold has unity in apperception. Self-consciousness in general is therefore the representation of that which is the condition of all unity, and yet is itself unconditioned. Hence of the thinking I (the soul), which

A 402 [thus represents] itself as substance, simple, numerically identical in all time, and the correlate of all existence from which all other existence must be inferred, one can say **not so much** that it cognizes **itself through the categories,** but that it cognizes the categories, and through them all objects, in the absolute unity of apperception, and hence cognizes them **through itself.** Now it is indeed very illuminating that I cannot cognize as an object*a* itself that which I must presuppose in order to cognize an object*b* at all; and that the determining Self (the thinking) is different from the determinable Self (the thinking subject) as cognition is different from its object. Nevertheless, nothing is more natural and seductive than the illusion of taking the unity in the synthesis of thoughts for a perceived unity in the subject of these thoughts. One could call it the subreption of hypostatized consciousness (*apperceptionis substantiate*).*c*

If one wants to give a logical title to the paralogism in the dialectical syllogisms of the rational doctrine of the soul, insofar as they have correct premises, then it can count as *sophisma figurae dictionis,*d* in which the major premise makes a merely transcendental use of the category, in regard to its condition, but in which the minor premise and the conclusion, in respect of the soul that is subsumed under this condition,

A 403 make an empirical use of the same category. Thus e.g., the concept of substance in the paralogism of simplicity is a pure intellectual concept, which in the absence of conditions of sensible intuition is merely of

a *Object*
b *Object*
c "of substantized apperception." Kant's text reads *apperceptiones;* we follow Erdmann in correcting his Latin grammar.
d "sophistry of a figure of speech," or fallacy of equivocation. See *Logic* § 90, 9:135.

transcendental use, i.e., of no use at all. But in the minor premise the very same concept is applied to the object of all inner experience, yet without previously establishing it *in concreto* and grounding the condition of its application, namely its persistence; and hence here an empirical, though unreliable, use is being made of it.

In order, finally, to show the systematic connection of all these dialectical assertions in a sophistical*a* doctrine of the soul, in a connection of pure reason, and hence to show its completeness, one notes that apperception is carried through by all classes of categories, but only toward those concepts of the understanding which in each class ground the unity of the remaining ones in a possible perception, consequently, subsistence, reality, unity (not plurality), and existence; yet reason represents them all here as conditions of the possibility of a thinking being, which are themselves unconditioned. Thus in itself the soul cognizes:

A 404

1.
The unconditioned unity
of **relation,***b*
i.e.,
itself, not as inhering
but rather
subsisting

2.
The unconditioned unity
of **quality**
i.e.,
not as a real whole
but rather **simple***

3.
The unconditioned unity
in the **multiplicity** in time,
i.e.,
not numerically different
in different times,
but rather as
One and the very **same subject**

4.
The unconditioned unity
of **existence** in space
i.e.,
nothing as the consciousness of several things outside itself,
but rather
only of the existence of itself,
and of other things merely
as its representations.

---

* How the simple here once again corresponds to the category of reality, I now cannot yet show, but rather it will be proved in the following chapter, on the occasion of another use by reason of the very same concept.

a *vernünftelnden*
b *Verhältnisses*

A 405   Reason is the faculty of principles.[a] The assertions of pure psychology contain not empirical predicates of the soul, but rather those predicates which, if they exist, ought to determine the object in itself independently of experience, hence through mere reason. Thus they would properly have to be grounded on principles[b] and universal concepts of thinking nature in general. Instead, it turns out that one single representation, "I am," governs them all which, just because it expresses (indeterminately) what is purely formal in all my experience, proclaims itself as a universal proposition, valid for every thinking being, and which, since it is individual in all respects, brings with it the illusion of being an absolute unity of conditions of thought in general, and thereby extends itself farther than any possible experience could reach.

[a] *Principien*
[b] *Principien*

^a[*Paralogisms of Pure Reason*]³⁸

Now since the proposition **I think** (taken problematically) contains the B 406 form of every judgment of understanding whatever, and accompanies all categories as their vehicle, it is clear that the inferences from this proposition can contain a merely transcendental use of the understanding, excluding every admixture of experience; and of^b such a procedure, after what we have shown above, we cannot at the outset form any very favorable concept. Thus we will follow it through all the predications of the pure doctrine of the soul with a critical eye, <yet for the sake of brevity we will proceed to examine them in an uninterrupted exposition.^c

To begin with, the following general remarks can sharpen our attentiveness to this mode of inference. I do not cognize any object^d merely by the fact that I think, but rather I can cognize any object only by determining a given intuition with regard to the unity of consciousness, in which all thinking consists. Thus I cognize myself not by being conscious of myself as thinking, but only if I am conscious to myself of the intuition of myself as determined in regard to the function of thought. All *modi*^e of self-consciousness in thinking are therefore not yet them- B 407 selves concepts of the understanding of objects^f (categories), but mere functions, which provide thought with no object at all, and hence also do not present my self as an object to be cognized. It is not the consciousness of the **determining** self, but only that of the **determinable** self, i.e., of my inner intuition (insofar as its manifold can be combined in accord with the universal condition of the unity of apperception in thinking), that is the **object**.^g

1) Now in every judgment I am always the **determining** subject of

---

^a What follows is the portion of the "Paralogisms" chapter that was rewritten for the second edition. In the original, it follows the part of the text common to both editions without any interruption or new title. The new text actually begins with the last clause of the following paragraph.

^b In the first edition: "in."

^c *Zusammenhange;* with this final clause begins the second-edition version of the "Paralogisms."

^d *Object*

^e modes

^f *Objecte*

^g *Object*

that relation*^a* that constitutes the judgment. However, that the I that I think can always be considered as **subject,** and as something that does not depend on thinking merely as a predicate, must be valid – this is an apodictic and even an **identical proposition;** but it does not signify that I as **object**^b am for myself a self-**subsisting being** or **substance.** The latter goes very far, and hence demands data that are not encountered at all in thinking, and thus (insofar as I consider merely what thinks as such) perhaps demands more than I will ever encounter anywhere (in it).

2) That the I of apperception, consequently in every thought, is a **single thing** that cannot be resolved into a plurality of subjects, and hence a logically simple subject, lies already in the concept of thinking, and is consequently an analytic proposition; but that does not signify that the thinking I is a simple **substance,** which would be a synthetic proposition. The concept of substance is always related to intuitions, which in me cannot be other than sensible, and hence must lie wholly outside the field of understanding and its thinking, which is all that is really under discussion here if it is said that the I in thinking is simple. It would also be miraculous if what otherwise requires so much care in order to distinguish what is the substance and what is displayed in intuition, and even more to tell whether this substance could be simple (as in the parts of matter), were given here so directly, in the poorest representation of all, as if by a revelation.

3) The proposition of the identity of myself in everything manifold of which I am conscious is equally one lying in the concepts themselves, and hence an analytic proposition; but this identity of the subject, of which I can become conscious in every representation, does not concern the intuition of it, through which it is given as object,^c and thus cannot signify the identity of the person, by which would be understood the consciousness of the identity of its own substance as a thinking being in all changes of state; in order to prove that what would be demanded is not a mere analysis of the proposition "I think," but rather various synthetic judgments grounded on the given intuition.

4) [That] I distinguish my own existence, that of a thinking being, from other things outside me (to which my body also belongs) – this is equally an analytic proposition; for **other** things are those that I think of as **distinguished** from me. But I do not thereby know at all whether this consciousness of myself would even be possible without things outside me through which representations are given to me, and thus whether I could exist merely as a thinking being (without being a human being).

B408

B409

---

^a *Verhältnis*
^b *Object*
^c *Object*

Thus through the analysis of the consciousness of myself in thinking in general not the least is won in regard to the cognition of myself as object.[a] The logical exposition of thinking in general is falsely held to be a metaphysical determination of the object.[b]

It would be a great, or indeed the only stumbling block to our entire critique, if it were possible to prove *a priori* that all thinking beings are in themselves simple substances, thus (as a consequence of the same ground of proof) that personality is inseparable from them, and that they are conscious of their existence as detached from all matter. For in this way we would have taken a step beyond the sensible world, entering into the field of **noumena,**[c] and then no one could deny that we are entitled to extend ourselves farther into this field, settle in it, and, as far as each of us might be favored by an auspicious star, to take possession of it. For the proposition "Every thinking being as such is a simple substance" is a synthetic proposition *a priori*, first because it goes beyond the concept that grounds it by adding the **way of existing** to thinking in general and second because it adds to that concept a predicate (simplicity) that cannot be given in any experience whatever. Thus synthetic propositions *a priori* would not, as we have asserted, be feasible and accessible merely in relation to objects of possible experience, and in particular as principles[d] of the possibility of this experience itself, but rather they could reach as far as things in general and in themselves, which consequence would put an end to this whole critique and would bid us to leave things the same old way they were before. Yet that danger is not so great here if one approaches nearer to the matter. B410

The procedure of rational psychology is governed by a paralogism, which is exhibited through the following syllogism:

What cannot be thought otherwise than as subject does not exist otherwise than as subject, and is therefore substance.

Now a thinking being, considered merely as such, cannot be thought otherwise than as subject. B411

Therefore it also exists only as such a thing, i.e., as substance.

The major premise talks about a being that can be thought of in every respect, and consequently even as it might be given in intuition. But the minor premise talks about this being only insofar as it is considered as subject, relative only to thinking and the unity of consciousness, but not at the same time in relation to the intuition through which it is given as an object[e] for thinking. Thus the conclu-

---

[a] *Object*
[b] *Object*
[c] Not in roman type.
[d] *Principien*
[e] *Object*

sion is drawn *per Sophisma figurae dictionis,*[a] hence by means of a deceptive inference.*

B412   That this resolution of the famous argument into a paralogism is entirely correct shows itself clearly if one reviews in this connection the general remark to the systematic representation of the principles[b] and the section on noumena,[39] where it was proved that the concept of a thing that can exist for itself as subject but not as a mere predicate carries with it no objective reality at all, i.e., that one cannot know whether it applies to any object, since one has no insight into the possibility of such a way of existing, and consequently that it yields absolutely no cognition. Thus if that concept, by means of the term "substance," is to indicate an object[c] that can be given, and if it is to become a cognition, then it must be grounded on a persisting intuition as the indispensable condition of the objective reality of a concept, namely, that through

B413   which alone an object is given. But now we have in inner intuition nothing at all that persists, for the I is only the consciousness of my thinking; thus if we stay merely with thinking, we also lack the necessary condition for applying the concept of substance, i.e., of a subject subsisting for itself, to itself as a thinking being; and the simplicity of substance that is bound up with the objective reality of this concept completely falls away and is transformed into a merely logically qualitative unity of self-consciousness in thinking in general, whether or not the subject is composite.

B411   * "Thinking" is taken in an entirely different signification in the two premises: in the major premise, as it applies to an object[d] in general (hence as it may be given in intuition); but in the minor premise only as it subsists in relation to self-consciousness, where, therefore, no object[e] is thought, but only the relation to oneself as subject (as the form of thinking) is represented. In the first premise, things are talked about that cannot be thought of other than as subjects; the second premise, however, talks not about **things,** but about

B412   **thinking** (in that one abstracts from every object),[f] in which the I always serves as subject of consciousness; hence in the conclusion it cannot follow that I cannot exist otherwise than as subject, but rather only that in thinking my existence I can use myself only as the subject of judgment, which is an identical proposition, that discloses absolutely nothing about the manner of my existence.

[a] "by a sophism of a figure of speech," i.e., a fallacy of equivocation.
[b] That is, the Principles of Pure Understanding.
[c] *Object*
[d] *Object*
[e] *Object*
[f] *Object*

Refutation of Mendelssohn's proof
of the persistence of the soul.[40]

This acute philosopher soon noticed that the usual argument through which it is to be proved that the soul (if one grants that it is a simple being) cannot cease through **disintegration,** is insufficient for the aim of securing the soul's necessary continuing duration, since one could still assume cessation of its existence by **vanishing.** In his *Phaedo,* he sought to avoid this perishability, which would be a true annihilation, by attempting to prove that a simple being cannot cease to be at all because, since it cannot be diminished and thus lose more and more of its existence, and so be **gradually** transformed into nothing (since it has no $\quad$ B414 parts and thus no plurality in itself), there would be no time at all between a moment in which it is and another moment in which it is not, which is impossible. – Yet he did not consider that even if we allow the soul this simple nature, namely, that it contains no manifold [of parts] **outside one another,** and hence no extensive magnitude, one nevertheless cannot deny to it, any more than to any other existence, an intensive magnitude, i.e., a degree of reality in regard to all its faculties, indeed to everything in general that constitutes its existence, which might diminish through all the infinitely many smaller degrees; and thus the supposed substance (the thing whose persistence has not been otherwise established already) could be transformed into nothing, although not by disintegration, but by a gradual remission (*remissio*) of all its powers (hence, if I may be allowed to use this expression, through elanguescence). For even consciousness always has a degree, which can always be diminished;* consequently, so does the faculty of being conscious of oneself, and likewise with all other faculties. – Thus the persistence of the soul, merely as an object of inner sense, remains unproved and even unprovable, although its persistence in life, where the thinking being (as a human being) is at the same time an object of

---

* Clarity is not, as the logicians say, the consciousness of a representation;[41] for $\quad$ B414 a certain degree of consciousness, which, however, is not sufficient for memory, must be met with even in some obscure representations, because without any consciousness we would make no distinction in the combination of obscure representations; yet we are capable of doing this with the marks of some $\quad$ B415 concepts (such as those of right and equity, or those of a musician who, when improvising, hits many notes at the same time). Rather a representation is clear if the consciousness in it is sufficient for **a consciousness of the difference** between it and others. To be sure, if this consciousness suffices for a distinction, but not for a consciousness of the difference, then the representation must still be called obscure. So there are infinitely many degrees of consciousness down to its vanishing.

outer sense, is clear of itself; but this is not at all sufficient for the rational psychologist, who undertakes to prove from mere concepts the absolute persistence of the soul even beyond life.*

B415   * Those who believe that they have done enough to get a new possibility started properly when they defy one to show a contradiction in its presuppositions (as are all those who believe that they have insight into the possibility of think-

B416   ing even after life has ceased, though they have an example of thinking only through the empirical intuitions in human life) can be brought into great embarrassment through other possibilities that are not the least bit bolder. Such a possibility is the division of a **simple substance** into several substances, or conversely, the fusing together (coalition) of several substances into a simple one. For although divisibility presupposes a composite, what it requires is not necessarily a composite made up of substances, but merely a composite of degrees (of several faculties) of one and the same substance. Just as one can think of all the powers and faculties of the soul, even that of consciousness, as disappearing by halves, but in such a way that the substance always remains; so likewise one can without contradiction represent this extinguished half as preserved, yet not in it but outside it; only*a* since everything real in it, consequently having a degree, and so its whole existence, lacking in nothing, has been halved, another particular substance would arise outside it. For the multiplicity that was divided already existed previously, yet not as a multiplicity of substances, but rather of that reality as a quantum of existence in it,*b* and the unity of substance was only a way of existing, which through this division

B417   alone is transformed into a plurality of subsistence. But in this way too several simple substances could once again fuse together into one, and nothing would be lost except merely the plurality of subsistence, since the one substance would contain the degree of reality of all the previous ones together in itself; and perhaps the simple substance, which gives us the appearance of a matter (though of course not through a mechanical or chemical influence on each other, but through one unknown to us, of which these would be only the appearance) might produce offspring-souls through such a **dynamic** division of the parent-souls, as **intensive magnitudes,** which would meanwhile replace what had departed from them by a coalition with new material of the same kind. I am far from allowing any worth or validity to such figments of the brain, and the above principles*c* of the Analytic have sufficiently enjoined us to make none other than an experiential use of the categories (such as substance). But if the rationalist is keen to make the mere faculty of thinking into a self-subsisting being without any persisting intuition through which an object is given, merely because for him the unity of apperception in thinking

B418   allows of no explanation from something composite, instead of admitting, as would be better to do, that he does not know how to explain the possibility of

---

a Reading *nur* with the fourth edition; earlier editions have *und.*

b *in ihr,* whose referent is presumably *die Substanz;* however, the context would appear to require the pronoun to be plural: "in them" (*in ihnen*), sc. "in the substances."

c *Principien*

If we take the above propositions in a **synthetic** connection, as valid   B416
for all thinking beings, as they must be taken in rational psychology as
a system, and if from the category of relation,[a] starting with the proposition "All thinking beings are, as such, substances" we go backward   B417
through the series of propositions until the circle closes, then we finally
come up against the existence of thinking beings, which in this system
are conscious of themselves not only as independent of external things
but also as being able to determine themselves from themselves (in regard to the persistence belonging necessarily to the character of a sub-   B418
stance). But from this it follows that **idealism**, at least problematic
idealism, is unavoidable in that same rationalistic system, and if the existence of external things is not at all required for the determination of
one's own existence in time, then such things are only assumed, entirely
gratuitously, without a proof of them being able to be given.

If, on the contrary, we follow the **analytic** procedure, grounded on
the "I think" given as a proposition that already includes existence in itself, and hence grounded on modality, and then we take it apart so as to
cognize its content, whether and how this I determines its existence in
space or time merely through it, then the propositions of the rational
doctrine of the soul begin not from the concept of a thinking being in
general but from an actuality; and from the way this is thought, after
everything empirical has been detached from it, it is concluded what   B419
pertains to a thinking being in general, as the following table shows.

1.
I think,

2. **as subject,**		3. **as simple subject,**

4.
as identical subject
in every state of my thinking.

Now because in the second proposition here it is not determined
whether I **could** exist and be thought of only as subject and not as predicate of another thing, the concept of a subject is here taken merely logically, and it remains undetermined whether or not substance is to be
understood by it. Yet in the third proposition the absolute unity of ap-

---

a thinking nature, then why should not the **materialist,** even though he can
just as little present any experience in behalf of his possibilities, be justified in
an equal boldness, retaining the rationalist's formal unity while putting his
own principle to an opposite use?

[a] *Relation*

perception, the simple I, in the representation to which every combination or separation constituting thought is related, also becomes important for its own sake,[a] even if I have not settled anything about the subject's constitution or subsistence. Apperception is something real, and its simplicity lies already in its possibility. Now there is nothing real in space that is simple; for points (which constitute the only simple entities in space) are mere bounds, and not themselves something that serves to constitute space as parts. Thus from this follows the impossibility of explaining how I am constituted as a merely thinking subject on the basis of **materialism.** But because my existence in the first proposition is considered as given, since it does not say that every thinking being exists (which would at the same time predicate absolute necessity of them, and hence say too much), but only "**I exist** thinking," that proposition is empirical, and contains the determinability of my existence merely in regard to my representations in time. But since for this once again I first need something persisting, and, just insofar as I think myself, nothing of the sort is given to me in inner intuition, it is not possible at all through this simple self-consciousness to determine the way I exist, whether as substance or as accident. Thus if **materialism** will not work as a way of explaining my existence, then **spiritualism** is just as unsatisfactory for it, and the conclusion is that in no way whatsoever can we cognize anything about the constitution of our soul that in any way at all concerns the possibility of its separate existence.

B420

And how should it be possible to go beyond experience (of our existence in life) through the unity of consciousness with which we are acquainted only because we have an indispensable need of it for the possibility of experience, and even to extend our cognition to the nature of all thinking beings in general, through the empirical but in regard to all kinds of intuition indeterminate proposition "I think"?

B421

Thus there is no rational psychology as **doctrine** that might provide us with an addition to our self-consciousness, but only as **discipline,** setting impassable boundaries for speculative reason in this field, in order, on the one side, not to be thrown into the lap of a soulless materialism, or on the other side not to get lost wandering about in a spiritualism that must be groundless for us in life; on the contrary, it rather reminds us to regard this refusal of our reason to give an answer to those curious questions, which reach beyond this life, as reason's hint that we should turn our self-knowledge[b] away from fruitless and extravagant speculation toward fruitful practical uses, which, even if it is always directed only to objects of experience, takes its principles[c] from

[a] *für sich*
[b] *Selbsterkenntnis*
[c] *Principien*

somewhere higher, and so determines our behavior, as if our vocation[a] extended infinitely far above experience, and hence above this life.

From all this one sees that rational psychology has its origin in a mere misunderstanding. The unity of consciousness, which grounds the categories, is here taken for an intuition of the subject as an object,[b] and the category of substance is applied to it. But this unity is only the unity of thinking, through which no object[c] is given; and thus the category of substance, which always presupposes a given intuition, cannot be applied to it, and hence this subject cannot be cognized at all. Thus the subject of the categories cannot, by thinking them, obtain a concept of itself as an object[d] of the categories; for in order to think them, it must take its pure self-consciousness, which is just what is to be explained, as its ground. Likewise, the subject, in which the representation of time originally has its ground, cannot thereby determine its own existence in time, and if the latter cannot be, then the former as a determination of its self (as a thinking being in general) through categories can also not take place.*

B422

* The "I think" is, as has already been said, an empirical proposition, and contains within itself the proposition "I exist." But I cannot say "Everything that thinks, exists"; for then the property of thinking would make all beings possessing it into necessary beings. Hence my existence also cannot be regarded as inferred from the proposition "I think," as Descartes held (for otherwise the major premise, "Everything that thinks, exists" would have to precede it), but rather it is identical with it.[42] It expresses an indeterminate empirical intuition, i.e., a perception (hence it proves that sensation, which consequently belongs to sensibility, grounds this existential proposition), but it precedes the experience that is to determine the object[e] of perception through the category in regard to time; and here existence is not yet a category, which is not related to an indeterminately given object, but rather to an object of which one has a concept, and about which one wants to know whether or not it is posited outside this concept. An indeterminate perception here signifies only something real, which was given, and indeed only to thinking in general, thus not as appearance, and also not as a thing in itself (a noumenon), but rather as something that in fact exists and is indicated as an existing thing in the proposition "I think." For it is to be noted that if I have called the proposition "I think" an empirical proposition, I would not say by this that the I in this proposition is an empirical representation; for it is rather purely intellectual, because it belongs to thinking in general. Only without any empirical representation, which provides the material for thinking, the act I think would not take place, and the empirical is only the condition of the application, or use, of the pure intellectual faculty.[43]

B422

B423

---

[a] Bestimmung
[b] Object
[c] Object
[d] Object
[e] Object

453

B423

In this way, then, a cognition going beyond the bounds of possible experience yet belonging to the highest interests of humanity disappears,

B424 as far as speculative philosophy is concerned, in disappointed expectation; nevertheless the strictness of critique, by proving the impossibility of settling anything dogmatically about an object of experience beyond the bounds of experience, performs a not unimportant service for reason regarding this interest, in securing it likewise against all possible assertions of the contrary; this cannot be done otherwise than by proving one's proposition apodictically, or, if that does not succeed, then by seeking the sources of this incapacity, which, if they lie in the necessary limits of our reason, must then subject every opponent to exactly the same law of renunciation for all claims to dogmatic assertions.

Nevertheless, not the least bit is lost through this regarding the warrant, or indeed the necessity, for the assumption of a future life in accordance with principles of the practical use of reason, which is bound up with its speculative use; for in any case the merely speculative proof has never been able to have an influence on common human reason. It so turns on a hairsplitting point that even the schools can retain it only as long as they can keep it standing there spinning around ceaselessly like a top, and thus even in their own eyes it provides no persisting foundation on which anything could be built. Here all the proofs that

B425 the world can use preserve their undiminished worth, and rather gain in clarity and unaffected conviction through the removal of those dogmatic pretensions, since they place reason in its proper territory, namely the order of ends that is yet at the same time an order of nature; but then since reason exists at the same time as a practical faculty in itself, without being limited to the conditions of the latter order, it is justified in extending the former order, and with it our whole existence, beyond the bounds of experience and life. By **analogy with the nature** of living beings in this world, regarding which reason must assume as a necessary principle that no organ, no faculty, nothing superfluous, or disproportionate to its use, hence nothing purposeless is to be met with, but rather that everything is to be judged as precisely suitable to its function[a] in life, the human being, who alone can contain within himself the ultimate final end[b] of all this, would have to be the only creature excepted from it. For his natural predispositions, not only his talents and the drives to make use of them, but chiefly the moral law in

***

[a] *Bestimmung*
[b] *letzten Endzweck*

454

him, go so far beyond all the utility and advantage that he could draw from them in this life that the latter teaches him to esteem above all else the mere consciousness of a disposition to rectitude, even in the absence of any advantage, even of the phantom of posthumous fame, and he B426 feels himself called inwardly, through his conduct in this world, and the sacrifice of many advantages, to make himself a suitable citizen of a better one, which he has in its idea. This powerful ground of proof, which can never be refuted, accompanied by an ever increasing cognition of the purposiveness in everything we see and by a vision of the immensity of creation, hence also by the consciousness of a certain boundlessness in the possible extension of our knowledge,*a* along with a drive commensurate to it, always still remains, even if we must equally give up insight into the necessary continuation of our existence from the merely theoretical cognition of our self.

Conclusion of the solution of the psychological paralogism.

The dialectical illusion in rational psychology rests on the confusion of an idea of reason (of a pure intelligence) with the concept, in every way indeterminate, of a thinking being in general. I think of my self, in behalf of a possible experience, by abstracting from all actual experience, and from this conclude that I could become conscious of my existence even outside experience and of its empirical conditions. Consequently I B427 confuse the possible **abstraction** from my empirically determined existence with the supposed consciousness of a **separate** possible existence of my thinking Self, and believe that I cognize what is substantial in me as a transcendental subject, since I have in thought merely the unity of consciousness that grounds everything determinate as the mere form of cognition.

The problem of explaining the community of the soul with the body does not properly belong to the psychology that is here at issue, because it intends to prove the personality of the soul even outside this community (after death), and so it is **transcendent** in the proper sense, even though it concerns an object*b* of experience, but only to the extent that it ceases to be an object of experience. Meanwhile in accord with our doctrine*c* a sufficient reply can also be given to this problem. The difficulty presented by this problem consists, as is well known, in the presumed difference in kind between the object of inner sense (the soul) and

a Kenntnisse
b Object
c Lehrbegriff

455

the object of outer sense, since to the former only time pertains as the formal condition of its intuition, while to the latter space pertains also. But if one considers that the two kinds of objects are different not inwardly but only insofar as one of them **appears** outwardly to the other, B428 hence that what grounds the appearance of matter as thing in itself might perhaps not be so different in kind, then this difficulty vanishes, and the only difficulty remaining is that concerning how a community of substances is possible at all, the resolution of which lies entirely outside the field of psychology, and, as the reader can easily judge from what was said in the Analytic about fundamental powers and faculties, this without any doubt also lies outside the field of all human cognition.

General remark
concerning the transition from rational psychology to cosmology.

The proposition "I think," or "I exist thinking," is an empirical proposition. But such a proposition is grounded on empirical intuition, consequently also on the object thought, as an appearance; and thus it seems as if, according to our theory, the whole, even in thinking, is completely transformed into appearance, and in such a way our consciousness itself, as mere illusion, would in fact come down to nothing.*a*

Thinking, taken in itself,*b* is merely the logical function and hence the sheer*c* spontaneity of combining the manifold of a merely possible intuition; and in no way does it present the subject of consciousness as B429 appearance, merely because it takes no account at all of the kind of intuition, whether it is sensible or intellectual. In this way I represent myself to myself neither as I am nor as I appear to myself, but rather I think myself only as I do every object*d* in general from whose kind of intuition I abstract. If here I represent myself as **subject** of a thought or even as **ground** of thinking, then these ways of representing do not signify the categories of substance or cause, for these categories are those functions of thinking (of judging) applied to our sensible intuition, which would obviously be demanded if I wanted to **cognize** myself. But now I want to become conscious of myself only as thinking; I put to one side how my proper self is given in intuition, and then it could be a mere appearance that I think, but not insofar as I think; in the consciousness of myself in mere thinking I am the **being itself,** about which, however, nothing yet is thereby given to me for thinking.

---

a *auf nichts gehen*
b *für sich*
c *lauter*
d *Object*

But the proposition "I think," insofar as it says only that **I exist thinking,** is not a merely logical function, but rather determines the subject (which is then at the same time an object)*a* in regard to existence, and this cannot take place without inner sense, whose intuition always makes available the object*b* not as thing in itself but merely as appearance. Thus in this proposition there is already no longer merely spontaneity of thinking, but also receptivity of intuition, i.e., the thinking of my self applied to the empirical intuition of the very same subject. It is in this latter that the thinking self must now seek the conditions of the use of its logical functions for categories of substance, cause, etc., so as not merely to indicate itself as object*c* in itself through the "I," but also to determine its kind of existence, i.e., to cognize it as noumenon; which, however, is impossible, since inner empirical intuition is sensible, and makes available nothing but data of appearance, which affords nothing for knowledge of the separate existence of the object*d* of **pure consciousness,** but can serve merely in behalf of experience.

B430

But suppose there subsequently turned up – not in experience but in certain (not merely logical rules but) laws holding firm *a priori* and concerning our existence – the occasion for presupposing ourselves to be **legislative** fully *a priori* in regard to our own **existence,***e* and as self-determining in this existence;*f* then this would disclose a spontaneity through which our actuality is determinable without the need of conditions of empirical intuition; and here we would become aware that in the consciousness of our existence something is contained *a priori* that can serve to determine our existence, which is thoroughly determinable only sensibly, in regard to a certain inner faculty in relation to an intelligible world (obviously one only thought of).

B431

But this would nonetheless bring all the attempts of rational psychology not the least bit further. For through this admirable faculty, which for the first time reveals to me the consciousness of the moral law, I would indeed have a principle*g* for the determination of my existence that is purely intellectual; but through which predicates? Through none other than those that would have to be given to me in sensible intuition, and thus I would have landed right back where I was in rational psychology, namely in need of sensible intuitions in order to obtain significance for my concepts of the understanding, substance, cause, etc.; but those intuitions can never help me up beyond the field

a *Object*
b *Object*
c *Object*
d *Object*
e *Dasein*
f *Existenz*
g *Princip*

of experience. Meanwhile, I would still be warranted in applying these concepts in regard to their practical use, which is always directed to objects of experience, according to their analogical significance in their theoretical use, to freedom and the free subject, since by them I understand merely the logical functions of subject and predicate, ground and consequence, in accordance with which actions or effects are determined in conformity to those laws in such a way that they can at the same time always be explained conformably to the laws of nature and the categories of substance and cause, although they arise from a wholly different principle.[a] This should have been said only to guard against a misunderstanding that easily arises regarding this doctrine about our self-intuition as appearance. In the following there will be opportunity to make use of it.>

B432

[a] *Princip*

The
Transcendental Dialectic
Second Book
Second Chapter
The antinomy of pure reason[44]

We have shown in the introduction to this part of our work that every transcendental illusion of pure reason rests on dialectical inferences, whose schema is provided in general by logic in the three formal species of syllogisms, just as the categories find their logical schema in the four functions of all judgments. The **first species of these** sophistical inferences had to do with the unconditioned unity of the **subjective** conditions of all representations in general (of the subject or the soul), corresponding to the **categorical** syllogisms, whose major premise, as a principle,[a] states the relation of a predicate to a **subject**. Thus the **sec-** **ond species** of dialectical argument, by analogy with **hypothetical** syllogisms, will make the unconditioned unity of objective conditions in appearance its content, just as the **third species,** which will come forward in the following chapter, has as its theme the unconditioned unity of objective conditions of the possibility of objects in general.

It is remarkable, however, that the transcendental paralogism effects a merely one-sided illusion regarding the idea of the subject of our thought, and for the opposite assertion there is not the least plausibility[b] forthcoming from concepts of reason. The advantage is entirely on the side of pneumatism, even though pneumatism cannot deny that radical defect through which its entire plausibility dissolves into mere haze when put to the fiery test of critique.[45]

It turns out wholly otherwise when we apply reason to the **objective synthesis** of appearances, where reason thinks to make its principle[c] of unconditioned unity valid with much plausibility;[d] but it soon finds it-

---

[a] *Princip*
[b] *Schein*
[c] *Principium*
[d] *zwar mit vielem Scheine*

self involved in such contradictions that it is compelled to relinquish its demands in regard to cosmology.

Here a new phenomenon of human reason shows itself, namely a wholly natural antithetic, for which one does not need to ponder or to lay artificial snares, but rather into which reason falls of itself and even unavoidably; and thus it guards reason against the slumber of an imagined conviction, such as a merely one-sided illusion produces, but at the same time leads reason into the temptation either to surrender itself to a skeptical hopelessness or else to assume an attitude of dogmatic stubbornness, setting its mind rigidly to certain assertions without giving a fair hearing to the grounds for the opposite. Either alternative is the death of a healthy philosophy, though the former might also be called the **euthanasia** of pure reason.

Before we allow the divisions and dissensions occasioned by this contradiction in the laws (antinomy) of pure reason to make their entrance, we will offer certain elucidations that can classify and justify the method we will employ in treating our subject matter. I call all transcendental ideas, insofar as they concern absolute totality in the synthesis of appearances, **world-concepts,**[46] partly because of the unconditioned totality on which the concept of the world-whole also rests even though it is only an idea, and partly because they have to do merely with the synthesis of appearances, and hence with the empirical, whereas the absolute totality of the synthesis of the condition of all possible things in general will occasion an ideal of pure reason, which is wholly distinct from the world-concept, even though it stands in relation to it. Hence just as the paralogism of pure reason laid the ground for a dialectical psychology, so the antinomy of pure reason will put before our eyes the transcendental principles of an alleged pure (rational) cosmology, yet not in order to find it valid and to appropriate it, but rather, as is already indicated by terming it a contradiction of reason, in order to display it in its dazzling but false plausibility*a* as an idea that cannot be made to agree with appearances.

The
Antinomy of Pure Reason
First Section
The system of cosmological ideas.

Now in order to be able to enumerate these ideas with systematic precision according to a principle,*b* we must **first** note that it is only from the understanding that pure and transcendental concepts can arise, that reason really cannot generate any concept at all, but can at most only **free** a **concept of the understanding** from the unavoidable limitations

---

a *Schein*
b *Princip*

of a possible experience, and thus seek to extend it beyond the boundaries of the empirical, though still in connection with it. This happens $\quad$ B436 when for a given conditioned reason demands an absolute totality on the side of the conditions (under which the understanding subjects all appearances to synthetic unity), thereby making the category into a transcendental idea, in order to give absolute completeness to the empirical synthesis through its progress toward the unconditioned (which is never met with in experience, but only in the idea). Reason demands this in accordance with the principle: **If the conditioned is given, then the whole sum of conditions, and hence the absolutely unconditioned, is also given,** through which alone the conditioned was possible.[47] Thus **first,** the transcendental ideas will really be nothing except categories extended to the unconditioned, and the former may be brought into a table ordered according to the headings of the latter. **Second,** however, not all categories will work here, but only those in which the synthesis constitutes a **series,** and indeed a series of conditions subordinated (not coordinated) one to another for any conditioned. Absolute totality is demanded by reason only insofar as reason is concerned with the ascending series of conditions for a given condi- $\quad$ A410 tioned, hence not when dealing with the descending line of consequences, nor with the aggregate of coordinated conditions for these consequences. For in regard to the given conditioned, conditions are $\quad$ B437 regarded as already presupposed and given along with the conditioned; whereas, since the consequences do not make their conditions possible, but rather presuppose them, in proceeding to the consequences (or in descending from a given condition to the conditioned) one remains untroubled about whether or not in general the series stops, and the question about its totality is not at all a presupposition of reason.

Thus one necessarily thinks of the fully elapsed time up to the present moment as also given (even if not as determinable by us). But as to the future, since it is not a condition for attaining to the present, it is a matter of complete indifference for comprehending the present what we want to hold about future time, whether it stops somewhere or runs on to infinity. Let there be a series m, n, o, in which n is given as conditioned in respect of m, but at the same time as the condition of o, and the series ascends from the conditioned n to m (l, k, j, etc.); then I must presuppose the first series in order to regard n as given, and n is possible in accordance with reason (with the totality of conditions) only by means of that $\quad$ A411 series; but its possibility does not rest on the subsequent series o, p, q, r, which therefore cannot[a] be regarded as given, but only as *dabilis.*[b] $\quad$ B438

---

[a] *nicht . . . könne.* The fourth edition changes from the present to the imperfect subjunctive, reading "*nicht . . . konnte*" (could not).
[b] capable of being given

I will call the synthesis of a series on the side of the conditions, thus proceeding from the condition proximate to the given appearance toward the more remote conditions, the **regressive** synthesis, and the synthesis proceeding on the side of the conditioned, from its proximate consequence to the more remote ones, the **progressive** synthesis. The first proceeds *in antecedienta*,[a] the second *in consequentia*.[b] Thus the cosmological ideas are concerned with the totality of the regressive synthesis, and go *in antecedentia*, not *in consequentia*. If this latter happens, then that is an arbitrary and not a necessary problem of pure reason, because for the complete comprehensibility of what is given in appearance we need its grounds but not its consequences.

Now in order to set up a table of ideas according to the table of categories, we first take the two original *quanta* of all intuition, space and time. Time is in itself a series (and the formal condition of all series), and hence in it, in regard to a given present, the *antecedentia* are to be distinguished *a priori* as conditions (the past) from the *consequentia*[c] (the future). Consequently, the transcendental idea of an absolute totality of the series of conditions for a given conditioned applies only to all past time. According to the idea of reason, the whole elapsed past time is thought of as given necessarily as the condition for the given moment. But as for space, in it there is no difference between progress and regress, because it constitutes an **aggregate,** but **not** a **series,** since all its parts exist simultaneously. I could regard the present point in time only as conditioned in regard to past time but never as its condition, because this moment first arises only through the time that has passed (or rather through the passing of the preceding time). But since the parts of space are not subordinated to one another but are coordinated with one another, one part is not the condition of the possibility of another, and space, unlike time, does not in itself constitute a series. Yet the synthesis of the manifold parts of space, through which we apprehend it, is nevertheless successive, and thus occurs in time and contains a series.[48] And since in this series of aggregated spaces of a given space (e.g., the feet in a rod), the further spaces, starting with a given one, are each thought of as the **condition of the boundaries** of the previous ones, the **measurement** of a space is to be regarded as a synthesis of a series of conditions for a given conditioned; only the side of the conditions is not in itself distinguished from the side lying beyond the conditioned, consequently *regressus* and *progressus* in space appear to be one and the same.[49] Nonetheless, because a part of space is not given through an-

---

[a] toward antecedents

[b] toward consequents

[c] In Kant's text, this word is given in the ablative (*consequentibus*); when Kant uses Latin nouns he declines them as if he were writing the whole context in Latin.

other part but is only bounded by it, we must to that extent regard every bounded space as also conditioned, presupposing another space as the condition of its boundary, and so forth. Thus regarding boundedness, the progression is also a regress, and the transcendental idea of the absolute totality of a synthesis in the series of conditions also applies to space, and I can ask about the absolute totality of appearances in space as well as in past time. But whether an answer to any of these questions is possible will be determined in the future.

Second, reality in space, i.e., **matter,** is likewise something conditioned, whose inner conditions are its parts, and the parts of those parts are the remote conditions, so that there occurs here a regressive synthesis, whose absolute totality reason demands; and that cannot occur otherwise than through a complete division, in which the reality of matter disappears either into nothing or else into that which is no longer matter, namely the simple.[50] Consequently here too there is a series of conditions and a progress toward the unconditioned.

Third, as far as the categories of real relation among appearances are concerned, the category of substance and its accidents is not suited to a transcendental idea, i.e., in regard to this category reason has no ground to proceed regressively toward conditions. For accidents (insofar as they inhere in a single substance) are coordinated with one another, and do not constitute a series. In regard to substance, however, they are not really subordinated to it, but are rather the way substance itself exists. What might still seem to be an idea of transcendental reason here would be the concept of the **substantial.** Only since this signifies nothing other than the concept of a subsisting object in general, insofar as one thinks in it merely the transcendental subject without any predicates, but here only the unconditioned in a series of appearances is under discussion, it is clear that the substantial cannot constitute a member of that.[51] The same holds for substances in community, which are mere aggregates and have no exponents of a series, since they are not subordinated to one another as conditions of their possibility, which one could very well have said about spaces, whose boundaries were never determined in themselves, but always through another space. Thus there remains only the category of **causality,** which provides a series of causes for a given effect, in which one can ascend from the effect as the conditioned to the causes as conditions, and answer the question of reason.[52]

Fourth, the concepts of the possible, actual, and necessary lead to no series, except only insofar as the **contingent** in existence always has to be seen as conditioned and refers in accordance with the rule of the understanding to a condition under which it is necessary to refer this to a higher condition, until reason attains to unconditioned **necessity** only in the series in its totality.[53]

There are, accordingly, no more than four cosmological ideas, according to the four headings of the categories, if one selects those that necessarily carry with them a series in the synthesis of the manifold.

B443

1.
The absolute completeness
of the
composition
of a given whole of all appearances.*

2.
The
absolute
completeness
of the **division**
of a given whole
in appearance.

3.
The
absolute
completeness
of the **arising**
of an appearance in general.

4.
The absolute completeness
of the **dependence** of the **existence**
of the alterable in appearance.*

A416   The first thing to be noted here is that the idea of an absolute totality concerns nothing other than the exposition* of **appearances,** hence it does not concern the understanding's pure concept of a whole of things in general. Thus appearances are considered here as given, and reason demands the absolute completeness of the conditions of their possibility, insofar as these conditions constitute a series, hence an absolutely (i.e., in all respects) complete synthesis, through which appearance could be expounded* in accordance with laws of the understanding.

    Second, it is properly only the unconditioned that reason seeks in this
B444 synthesis of conditions, which proceeds serially, and indeed regressively, hence as it were the completeness in the series of premises that together presuppose no further premise. Now this **unconditioned** is always contained **in the absolute totality of the series** if one represents it in imagination. Yet this absolutely complete synthesis is once again only an idea; for with appearances one cannot know, at least not beforehand,

---

a   Added in Kant's copy: " 'Absolute totality' signifies the totality of the manifold of a thing in itself and is something contradictory in respect of appearances as mere representations, which are to be encountered only in the progression, not outside it in themselves." (E CLXV, p. 49; 23:40)

b   Added in Kant's copy: "That there is no difficulty in thinking of the form of the world, i.e., of the *commercii* of substances as phenomena, for they are in space and time; but as noumena substances do not [have] existence, and the possibility of a world is not explainable. But if it is assumed, then more worlds are possible." (E CLXVI, pp. 49–50; 23:40)

c   *Exposition*

d   *exponiert*

whether such a synthesis is even possible. If one represents everything through mere pure concepts of the understanding, without the conditions of sensible intuition, then one can say directly that for a given conditioned the whole series of conditions subordinated one to another is given; for the former is given only through the latter. But with appearances a special limitation is encountered in the way conditions are given, namely through the successive synthesis of the manifold of intu- A417 ition, which is supposed to be complete in the regress. Now whether this completeness is sensibly possible is still a problem. Yet the idea of this completeness still lies in reason, irrespective of the possibility or impossibility of connecting empirical concepts to it adequately. Thus, since the unconditioned is necessarily contained in the absolute totality B445 of the regressive synthesis of the manifold in appearance (following the categories, which represent appearance as a series of conditions for a given conditioned), one might also leave it undecided whether and how this totality is to be brought about; here reason thus takes the path of proceeding from the idea of a totality, even though it really has as its final intent the **unconditioned**, whether of the whole series or one part of it.

Now one can think of this unconditioned either as subsisting merely in the whole series, in which thus every member without exception is conditioned, and only their whole is absolutely unconditioned, or else the absolutely unconditioned is only a part of the series, to which the remaining members of the series are subordinated but that itself stands under no other condition.* In the first case the series is given *a parte priori* without bounds (without a beginning), i.e., it is given as infinite and A418 at the same time whole, but the regress in it is never complete and can be called only *potentialiter*[a] infinite. In the second case there is a first B446 [member] in the series, which in regard to past time is called the **beginning of the world**, in regard to space the **boundary of the world**, in regard to the parts of a whole given in its bounds the **simple**, in regard to causes absolute **self-activity** (freedom), in regard to the existence of alterable things absolute **natural necessity.**

We have two expressions, **world** and **nature**, which are sometimes run together. The first signifies the mathematical whole of all appear-

---

* The absolute whole of the series of conditions for a given conditioned is al-   A417/B445
ways unconditioned, because outside it there are no more conditions regard-   A418
ing which it could be conditioned. But the absolute whole of such a series is
only an idea, or rather a problematic concept, whose possibility has to be investigated, particularly in reference to the way in which the unconditioned
may be contained in it as the properly transcendental idea that is at issue.

[a] potentially

ances and the totality of their synthesis in the great as well as in the small, i.e., in their progress through composition*a* as well as through division. But the very same world is called nature* insofar as it is considered as a dynamic whole and one does not look at the aggregation in space or time so as to bring about a quantity, but looks instead at the unity in the **existence** of appearances. Now the condition of what happens is called the cause, and the unconditioned causality of the cause in appearance is called freedom; the conditioned cause in the narrower sense, on the contrary, is called the natural cause. The conditioned in existence in general is called contingent, and the unconditioned necessary. The unconditioned necessity of **appearances** can be called natural necessity.

Above I have called the ideas with which we are now concerned "cosmological ideas," partly because by "world" is understood the sum total of all appearances, and our ideas are also directed only toward the unconditioned among appearances, but partly too because in the transcendental sense the word "world" signifies the absolute totality of the sum total of existing things, and we are directing our attention only to the completeness of the synthesis (though properly only in the regress toward its conditions). Considering, moreover, that taken collectively these ideas are all transcendent and, even though they do not overstep the object,*b* namely appearances, **in kind,** but have to do only with the sensible world (not with *noumena*),*c* they nevertheless carry the synthesis to a **degree** that transcends all possible experience; thus in my opinion one can quite appropriately call them collectively **world-concepts.** In regard to the distinction between the mathematically and the dynamically unconditioned toward which the regress aims, I would call the first two world-concepts in a narrower sense (the world in great and

A419
B447

A420

B448

A418/B446
A419
* "Nature" taken adjectivally (*formaliter*)*d* signifies the connection of determinations of a thing in accordance with an inner principle*e* of causality. Conversely, by "nature" taken substantively (*materialiter*)*f* is understood the sum total of appearances insofar as these are in thoroughgoing connection through an inner principle*g* of causality. In the first sense one speaks of the "nature" of fluid matter, of fire, etc., and employs this word adjectivally; conversely, if one talks about the "things of nature," then one has in mind a subsisting whole.

a *Zusammensetzung*
b *Object*
c Kant declines the word in the Latin dative, as *Noumenis*.
d formally
e *Princip*
f materially
g *Princip*

small), but the remaining two **transcendent concepts of nature.** Up to now this distinction has been of no particular relevance, but as we proceed it may become more important.

The
Antinomy of Pure Reason
Second Section
Antithetic of pure reason.

If any sum total of dogmatic doctrines is a "thetic," then by "antithetic" I understand not the dogmatic assertion of the opposite but rather the conflict between what seem to be dogmatic cognitions (*thesin cum antithesi*),[a] without the ascription of a preeminent claim to approval of one side or the other. Thus an antithetic does not concern itself with one-sided assertions, but considers only the conflict between general cognitions of reason and the causes of this conflict. The transcendental antithetic is an investigation into the antinomy of pure reason, its causes and its result. If in using principles of the understanding we apply our reason not merely to objects of experience, for the use of principles of understanding, but instead venture also to extend these principles beyond the boundaries of experience, then there arise **sophistical** theorems,[b] which may neither hope for confirmation in experience nor fear refutation by it; and each of them is not only without contradiction in itself but even meets with conditions of its necessity in the nature of reason itself, only unfortunately the opposite has on its side equally valid and necessary grounds for its assertion.

A421

B449

The questions that are naturally presented by such a dialectic of pure reason are these: 1. In which propositions is pure reason inevitably really subjected to an antinomy? 2. On what causes does this antinomy rest? 3. In what way, if any, given this contradiction, does a path to certainty nevertheless remain open to reason?

A dialectical theorem of pure reason must accordingly have the following feature, distinguishing it from all sophistical[c] propositions: it does not concern an arbitrary question that one might raise only at one's option, but one that every human reason must necessarily come up against in the course of its progress; and second, this proposition and its opposite must carry with them not merely an artificial illusion that disappears as soon as someone has insight into it, but rather a natural and unavoidable illusion, which even if one is no longer fooled by it,

A422

B450

---

[a] "thesis with antithesis." The correct Latin would be *thesis;* Kant does not seem to have made up his mind whether the phrase is supposed to be in Latin or in Greek.
[b] **vernünftelnde** *Lehrsätze*
[c] *sophistischen*

still deceives though it does not defraud and which thus can be rendered harmless but never destroyed.

Such a dialectical doctrine will relate not to the unity of understanding in concepts of experience, but to the unity of reason in mere ideas, whose conditions, since, as a synthesis according to rules, must first be congruent with the understanding, and yet at the same time, as the absolute unity of this synthesis, must be congruent with reason, will be too large for the understanding if this unity is to be adequate to the unity of reason, and yet too small for reason if they are suited to the understanding; from this there must arise a contradiction that cannot be avoided no matter how one may try.

These sophistical^a assertions thus open up a dialectical battlefield, where each party will keep the upper hand as long as it is allowed to attack, and will certainly defeat that which is compelled to conduct itself^b merely defensively. Hence hardy knights, whether they support the good or the bad cause, are certain of carrying away the laurels of victory if only they take care to have the prerogative of making the last attack, and are not bound to resist a new assault from the opponent. One can easily imagine that from time immemorial this arena has often been entered, both sides gaining many victories, but that each time the final victory was decisive merely because care was taken that the champion of the good cause held the field alone, his opponent having been forbidden to take up his weapons again. As impartial referees we have to leave entirely aside whether it is a good or a bad cause for which the combatants are fighting, and just let them settle the matter themselves. Perhaps after they have exhausted rather than injured each other, they will see on their own that their dispute is nugatory, and part as good friends.

This method of watching or even occasioning a contest between assertions, not in order to decide it to the advantage of one party or the other, but to investigate whether the object of the dispute is not perhaps a mere mirage^c at which each would snatch in vain without being able to gain anything even if he met with no resistance – this procedure, I say, can be called the **skeptical method.** It is entirely different from **skepticism,** a principle of artful^d and scientific ignorance that undermines the foundations of all cognition, in order, if possible, to leave no reliability or certainty anywhere. For the skeptical method aims at certainty, seeking to discover the point of misunderstanding in disputes that are honestly intended and conducted with intelligence by both

A423

B451

A424

B452

---

^{a} *vernünftelnden*
^{b} *verfahren;* in the first edition, the word is *führen* (carry on).
^{c} *Blendwerk*
^{d} *kunstmäßig*

sides, in order to do as wise legislators do when from the embarrassment of judges in cases of litigation they draw instruction concerning that which is defective and imprecisely determined in their laws. The antinomy that reveals itself in the application of the law is for our limited wisdom the best way to test nomothetics,[a] in order to make reason, which does not easily become aware of its false steps in abstract speculation, attentive to the moments involved in determining its principles.

This skeptical method, however, is essentially suited only to transcendental philosophy, and can in any case be dispensed with in every other field of investigation, but not in this one. In mathematics its use would be absurd, because nowhere in mathematics do false assertions disguise themselves and make themselves invisible; for mathematical proofs always have to proceed along the lines of pure intuition, and indeed always through a self-evident synthesis. In experimental philosophy a doubt postponing judgment can be useful, but at least there is no possible misunderstanding that cannot be easily removed, and the ultimate means for deciding the controversy must at last lie in experience, whether it is found early or late. Morality can also give us its principles as a whole *in concreto*, along with their practical consequences in at least possible experiences, and thereby avoid misunderstandings due to abstraction. On the contrary, the transcendental assertions that presume to extend their insight beyond the field of all possible experience are neither in the case where their synthesis could be given in an *a priori* intuition, nor are they so constituted that a misunderstanding could be exposed by means of any experience. Transcendental reason thus permits no touchstone other than its own attempt to bring internal unification to its assertions, and this requires a free and unhindered contest of these assertions among themselves, which we will now initiate.*

A425

B453

---

* The antinomies follow according to the order of the transcendental ideas introduced above.

[a] *Prüfungsversuch der Nomothetik*

The Antinomy of Pure Reason
First Conflict of the Transcendental Ideas [54]

Thesis

The world has a beginning in time, and in space it is also enclosed in boundaries.

Proof

For if one assumes that the world has no beginning in time, then up to every given point in time an eternity has elapsed, and hence an infinite series of states of things in the world, each following another, has passed away. But now the infinity of a series consists precisely in the fact that it can never be completed through a successive synthesis. Therefore an infinitely elapsed world-series is impossible, so a beginning of the world is a necessary condition of its existence; which was the first point to be proved. [55]

Regarding the **second** point, again assume the opposite: then the world would be an infinite given whole of simultaneously existing things. Now we can think of the magnitude of a quantum[a] that is not

given as within certain boundaries of every intuition* in no other way than by the synthesis of its parts, and we can think of the totality of such a quantum[b] only through the completed synthesis, or through the repeated addition of units to each other.† Accordingly, in order to think

---

* We can intuit an indeterminate quantum as a whole, if it is enclosed within boundaries, without needing to construct its totality through measurement, i.e., through the successive synthesis of its parts. For the boundaries already determine its completeness by cutting off anything further.

† The concept of a totality is in this case nothing other than the representation of the completed synthesis of its parts, because, since we cannot draw the concept from an intuition of the whole (which is impossible in this case), we can grasp it, at least in the idea, only through the synthesis of the parts up to their completion in the infinite.

---

[a] Kant prints the word in German type but declines it in the Latin genitive: *Quanti*.
[b] Again, the genitive *Quanti* is used.

Antithesis

The world has no beginning and no bounds in space, but is infinite with regard to both time and space.

Proof

For suppose that it has a beginning. Since the beginning is an existence preceded by a time in which the thing is not, there must be a preceding time in which the world was not, i.e., an empty time. But now no arising of any sort of thing is possible in an empty time, because no part of such a time has, in itself, prior to another part, any distinguishing condition of its existence rather than its non-existence (whether one assumes that it comes to be of itself or through another cause). Thus many series of things may begin in the world, but the world itself cannot have any beginning, and so in past time it is infinite.[56]

As to the second point, first assume the opposite, namely that the world is finite and bounded in space; then it exists in an empty space, which is not bounded. There would thus be encountered not only a relation[a] between things in **space,** but also a relation of things **to space.** Now since the world is an absolute whole, besides which there is encountered no object of intuition, and hence no correlate of the world to A429/B457 which the world could stand in relation, the relation of the world to empty space would be a relation of the world to **no object.** Such a **relation,** however, and hence also the boundedness of the world by empty space, is nothing; therefore the world is not bounded at all in space, i.e., in its extension it is infinite.*

---

* Space is merely the form of outer intuition (formal intuition), but not a real A429/B457 object that can be outwardly intuited. Space, prior to all things determining (filling or bounding) it, or which, rather, give an **empirical intuition** as to its form, is, under the name of absolute space,[57] nothing other than the mere pos-

---

[a] *Verhältnis;* this will be the only word translated "relation" in Section 2 of the Antinomies unless otherwise noted.

the world that fills all space as a whole, the successive synthesis of the parts of an infinite world would have to be regarded as completed, i.e., in the enumeration of all coexisting things, an infinite time would have to be regarded as having elapsed, which is impossible. Accordingly, an infinite aggregate of actual things cannot be regarded as a given whole, hence cannot be regarded as given **simultaneously**. Consequently, a world is **not infinite** in its extension in space, but is rather enclosed within its boundaries, which was the second point.

A430/B458

Remark on the First Antinomy
I. On the Thesis

In these mutually conflicting arguments I have not sought semblances[a] in order to present (as one says) a lawyer's proof, which takes advantage of an opponent's carelessness and gladly permits a misunderstanding of the law in order to build the case for his own unjust claims on the refutation of the other side. Each of these proofs is drawn from the nature of the case, and any advantage that could be given to us by the fallacies of dogmatists on either side is to be set aside.

I could also have given a plausible[b] proof of the thesis by presupposing a defective concept of the infinity of a given magnitude, according to the custom of the dogmatists. A magnitude is **infinite** if none greater than it (i.e., greater than the multiple[c] of a given unit contained in it) is possible.[58] Now no multiplicity is the greatest, because one or more units can always be added to it. Therefore an infinite given magnitude, and hence also an infinite world (regarding either the past series or extension), is impossible; thus the world is bounded in both respects. I could have carried out my proof in this way: only this concept does not agree with what is usually understood by an infinite whole. It does not represent **how great** it is, hence this concept is not the concept of a

A432/B460

maximum; rather, it thinks only of the relation to an arbitrarily assumed unit, in respect of which it is greater than any number. According as the unit is assumed to be greater or smaller, this infinity would be greater or smaller; yet infinity, since it consists merely in the relation to this given unit, would always remain the same, even though in this way the absolute magnitude of the whole would obviously not be cognized at all, which is not here at issue.

The true (transcendental) concept of infinity is that the successive synthesis of unity in the traversal of a quantum can never be com-

---

[a] *Blendwerke*
[b] *dem Scheine nach*
[c] *Menge*

II. Remark
On the Antithesis.

The proof for the infinity of the world-series and of the sum total of the world rests on the fact that in the contrary case an empty time, and likewise an empty space, would have to constitute the boundary of the world. Now it is not unknown to me that attempts are made to avoid this consequence by alleging that a boundary of the world in space and time may quite well be possible without having to assume an absolute time before the world's beginning or an absolute space spreading beyond the real world, which is impossible. I am quite satisfied with the last part of this opinion of philosophers of the Leibnizian school. Space is merely the form of outer intuition, but not a real object that can be externally intuited, and it is not a correlate of appearances, but rather the form of appearances themselves. Thus space taken absolutely (simply by itself) alone cannot occur as something determining the existence of things, because it is not an object at all, but only the form of possible objects. Thus things, as appearances, do determine space, i.e., among all its possible predicates (magnitude and relation) they make it the case that this or that one belongs to reality; but space, as something subsisting in itself, cannot conversely determine the reality of things in regard to magnitude and shape, because it is nothing real in itself. A space,

sibility of external appearances, insofar as they either exist in themselves or can be further added to given appearances. Thus empirical intuition is not put together out of appearances and space (out of perception and empty intuition). The one is not to the other a correlate of its synthesis, but rather it is only bound up with it in one and the same empirical intuition, as matter and its form. If one would posit one of these two elements outside the other (space outside of all appearances), then from this there would arise all sorts of empty determinations of outer intuition, which, however, are not possible perceptions. E.g., the world's movement or rest in infinite empty space[59] is a determination of the relation of the two to one another that can never be perceived, and is therefore the predicate of a mere thought-entity.

pleted.* From this it follows with complete certainty that an eternity of actual states, each following upon another up to a given point in time (the present), cannot have passed away, and so the world must have a beginning.

In regard to the second part of the thesis, the difficulty of a series that is infinite and yet elapsed does not arise; for the manifold of an infinitely extended world is given **simultaneously.** Yet in order to think the totality of such a multiplicity, where we cannot appeal to boundaries which would of themselves constitute this totality in intuition, we have to give an account of our concept, since in such a case it cannot go from the whole to a determinate multiplicity of parts, but must establish the possibility of a whole through the successive synthesis of the parts. Now since this synthesis has to constitute a series that is never to be completed, one can never think a totality prior to it and thus also through it. For in this case the concept of the totality itself is the representation of a completed synthesis of the parts, and this completion, hence also its concept, is impossible.

A432 / B460　　* This [quantum] thereby contains a multiplicity^a (of given units) that is greater than any number, and that is the mathematical concept of the infinite.

^{a} *Menge*

therefore (whether it is full or empty),* may well be bounded by appearances, but appearances cannot be bounded **by an empty space** outside themselves. The same also holds for time. Admitting all this, it is nevertheless uncontroversial that one surely would have to assume these two non-entities, empty space outside the world and empty time before it, if one assumes a boundary to the world, whether in space or in time. A433/B461

For as to the attempt to escape this consequence by saying that if the world has boundaries (in time and space) then the infinite emptiness would have to determine the existence of things as to their magnitude, this consists in thinking surreptitiously of who knows what intelligible world in place of a **world of sense,** and, instead of a first beginning (an existence before which a time of non-existence precedes) one thinks of an existence in general that **presupposes no other condition** in the world, rather than the boundary of extension one thinks of the **limits** of the world-whole, and thus one gets time and space out of the way. But here we are talking only about the *mundus phaenomenon*[a] and its magnitude, where one can in no way abstract from the intended conditions of sensibility without removing the being itself. The world of sense, if it is bounded, necessarily lies in an infinite emptiness. If one wants to leave this out, and hence leave out space in general as the *a priori* condition of the possibility of appearances, then the whole world of sense is left out. But in our problem this alone is given to us. The *mundus intelligibilis*[b] is nothing but the concept of a world in general, abstracting from all conditions of intuiting it, and in regard to which, consequently, no synthetic proposition at all, whether affirmative or negative, is possible.[c]

---

* It is easy to notice what would be said here: that **empty space, insofar as it is bounded by appearances,** hence space **within the world,** does not contradict transcendental principles[d] at least, and thus could be allowed by them (even though its possibility would not be directly asserted). A431/B459 A433/B461

---

[a] world of appearance
[b] intelligible world
[c] In the first edition, Kant notes: "The cosmological proof of the existence of a necessary being is that from the first mover, or still more generally, from that which first begins. Now with this, causality must also begin; because the concept of a beginning always presupposes a time in which the series was not. In this time it still could not have causality, hence it would have had to begin first of all." (E CLXVIII, p. 50; 23:40)
[d] *Principien*

The Antinomy of Pure Reason
Second Conflict of the Transcendental Ideas[60]

Thesis

Every composite substance in the world consists of simple parts, and nothing exists anywhere except the simple or what is composed of simples.

Proof

For, assume that composite substances do not consist of simple parts: then, if all composition is removed in thought, no composite part, and (since there are no simple parts) no simple part, thus nothing at all would be left over; consequently, no substance would be given. Thus either it is impossible to remove all composition in thought or else after its removal something must be left over that subsists without any composition, i.e., the simple. In the first case, the composite would once again not consist of substances (because with substances composition is only a contingent relation,[a] apart from which, as beings persisting by themselves, they must subsist). Now since this case contradicts the pre-

supposition, only the second case is left: namely, that what is a substantial composite in the world consists of simple parts.[61]

From this it follows immediately that all things in the world are simple beings, that composition is only an external state of these beings, and that even though we can never put these elementary substances completely outside this state of combination and isolate them, reason must still think of them as the primary subjects of all composition and hence think of them prior to it as simple beings.[b]

---

[a] *Relation*

[b] In the first edition, Kant notes: "In the intellectual, if all division is brought to an end, the simple remains. In the sensible it can never be brought to an end. In thoughts, if it is cancelled, nothing remains." (E CLXVII, p. 50; 23:40)

Antithesis

No composite thing in the world consists of simple parts, and nowhere in it does there exist anything simple.

Proof

Suppose a composite thing (as substance) consists of simple parts. Because every external relation between substances, hence every composition of them, is possible only in space, there must exist as many parts of space as there are parts of the composite thing occupying it. Now space does not consist of simple parts, but of spaces. Thus every part of the composite must occupy a space. But the absolutely primary parts of the composite are simple. Thus the simple occupies a space. Now since everything real that occupies a space contains within itself a manifold of elements external to one another, and hence is composite, and indeed, as a real composite, it is composed not of accidents (for they cannot be external to one another apart from substance), but therefore of substances; thus the simple would be a substantial composite, which contradicts itself.

The second proposition of the antithesis, that in the world nothing at all exists that is simple, is here supposed to signify only this: The existence of the absolutely simple cannot be established by any experience   A437/B465
or perception, whether external or internal, and the absolutely simple is thus a mere idea, whose objective reality can never be established in any possible experience, and hence in the exposition*a* of appearances it has no application or object. For if we assumed that this transcendental idea could find an object in experience, then empirical intuition of some such object would have to be recognized, an intuition containing absolutely no manifold whose elements are external to one another and bound into a unity. Now since there is no inference from our not being conscious of <such a manifold to its> complete impossibility in any in-

---

a *Exposition*

A438/B466

Remark on the Second Antinomy
I. On the Thesis

When I talk about a whole which necessarily consists of simple parts, I understand thereby a substantial whole only as a proper composite, i.e., as a contingent unity of a manifold that, **given** as **separated** (at least in thought), is posited in a reciprocal combination and thereby constitutes one entity. Properly speaking, one should call space not a *compositum*[a] but a *totum*,[b] because its parts are possible only in the whole, and not the whole through the parts. In any case, it could be called a *compositum ideale*[c] but not a *compositum reale*.[d] Yet this is only a subtlety. For since space is not a composite of substances (not even of real accidents), if I remove all composition from it, then nothing, not even a point, might be left over; for a point is possible only as the boundary of a space (hence of a composite). Thus space and time do not consist of simple parts. What belongs only to the state of a substance, even if it has a magnitude (e.g., alteration), does not, therefore, consist of the simple, i.e., a certain degree of alteration does not arise through the accumulation of many simple alterations. Our inference from the composite to the simple is valid only for things subsisting by themselves.[e] But accidents of a state do not subsist by themselves. Thus one can easily ruin the proof for the necessity of simples as constituent parts of every substantial composite (and thus also the whole thesis), if one extends the proof too far and tries to make it valid for all composites without distinction, as has sometimes actually happened.

A440/B468

[a] composite
[b] whole
[c] ideal composite
[d] real composite
[e] *für sich*

tuition of an object,^{a} but this intuition is definitely required for absolute simplicity, it follows that this simplicity cannot be inferred from any perception, whatever it might be. Since, therefore, nothing can ever be given as an absolutely simple object^b in any possible experience, but the world of sense must be regarded as the sum total of all possible experiences, nothing simple is given anywhere in it.

This second proposition of the antithesis goes much further than the first, since the first banishes the simple only from the intuition of the composite, while the second, on the other hand, does away with the simple in the whole of nature; hence also it could not have been proved from the concept of a given object of outer intuition (of the composite), but only from its^c relation to a possible experience in general.

II. Remark
On the Antithesis

A439/B467

Against this proposition that matter is infinitely divisible, for which the ground of proof is merely mathematical, objections have been put forward by **monadists**,^{62} who already lay themselves open to suspicion by the fact that they would not allow even the clearest mathematical proofs to count as insights into the constitution of space, insofar as it is in fact the formal condition of the possibility of all matter, but would rather regard these proofs only as inferences from abstract but arbitrary^d concepts which could not be related^e to real things. It is as if it were possible to think up another kind of intuition than the one given in the original intuition of space, and to treat the determinations of space *a priori* as not at the same time applying to what is possible only insofar as it fills space. If one listens to them, then besides mathematical points, which are simple but are boundaries rather than parts of space, one would have to think of physical points too as being not only simple, but as also having, as parts of space, the privilege of filling it through their mere aggregation. Without repeating here the common and clear refutations of this absurdity, of which there are many, just as it is entirely pointless to try by merely discursive concepts to rationalize^f away the evidence of

---

^{a} *Object*; In the first edition: ". . . from the non-consciousness of a manifold to the complete impossibility of such a [manifold] in any intuition of the same object . . ."
^{b} *Object*
^{c} *desselben*; the grammatically possible antecedents for this possessive pronoun are: (1) "object" (in "a given object of outer intuition"); (2) "concept" (in "the concept of [the object (1)]"; and (3) "the composite." Given the argument of the previous paragraph, the most likely candidate seems to us to be (1), or possibly (2).
^{d} *willkürlichen*
^{e} *bezogen*
^{f} *vernünfteln*

Moreover, I am talking here only about the simple insofar as it is necessarily given in the composite, so that the latter can be resolved into the former as its constituent parts. The proper signification of the word **monas** (in Leibniz's usage)[63] refers only to the simple given **immediately** as simple substance (e.g., in self-consciousness) and not as element of the composite, which one could better call the atom. And since it is only in regard to composites that I want to prove simple substances, as their elements, I could call the antithesis[a] of the second antinomy "transcendental **atomistic**." But because this word has for some time already been used to indicate a special way of explaining corporeal appearances (*molecularum*),[b] and hence presupposes empirical concepts, it may be called the dialectical principle of **monadology.**

A442 / B470

[a] *Antithese;* following Erdmann, one should read *These.*
[b] of molecules

mathematics, I will remark only that when philosophy quibbles with
mathematics, this happens only because it forgets that this question has
to do only with **appearances** and their conditions. Here, however, it is
not enough to find the concept of the simple for the pure **concept of
the understanding** of the composite, but one must find the intuition
of the simple for the **intuition** of the composite (for matter), and this is
entirely impossible in accordance with the laws of sensibility, hence impossible with objects of sense. Thus for a whole made up of substances
thought through the pure understanding it might very well hold that
prior to all composition of such substances we must have a simple; but
this does not hold for a *totum substantiale phaenomenon,*[a] which, as empirical intuition in space, carries with it the necessary property that no
part of it is simple, because no part of space is simple. Meanwhile, the
monadists are subtle enough to try to escape from this difficulty by not
presupposing space as a condition of the possibility of objects of outer
intuition (bodies), but rather presupposing these objects and the dynamical relation of substances in general as the condition of the possibility of space. Now we have a concept of bodies only as appearances,
but as such they necessarily presuppose space as the condition of the
possibility of all external appearance; and so this dodge is futile, just as
it has also been sufficiently blocked above in the Transcendental
Aesthetic. If they were things in themselves, then the proof of the
monadists would of course hold.

A441 / B469

The second dialectical assertion has the peculiarity that it has against
it a dogmatic assertion that is the only one of all the sophistical[b] assertions that undertakes to provide visible proof, in an object of experience, of the reality of something we have ascribed above merely to
transcendental ideas, namely the simplicity[c] of substance: namely, that
the object of inner sense, the I that thinks, is an absolutely simple substance. Without going into this (since it was considered more completely above), I will remark only that if something is merely thought as
an object, without adding any synthetic determination of its intuition
(as happens in the completely bare representation "I"), then of course
nothing manifold and no composition can be perceived in such a representation. Since, further, the predicates through which I think this
object are mere intuitions of inner sense, nothing can occur in them
that could prove a manifold of elements external to one another, and
hence real composition. Thus self-consciousness is such that because
the subject that thinks is simultaneously its own object,[d] it cannot divide

A443 / B471

[a] substantial phenomenal whole
[b] *vernünftelnden*
[c] *Simplicität*
[d] *Object*

itself (though it can divide the determinations inhering in it); for in regard to its own self every object is absolute unity. Nonetheless, if this subject is considered **externally,** as an object of intuition, then it would indeed exhibit composition in its own appearance. This is the way in which it must be considered, however, if one wants to know whether or not there is in it a manifold of elements **external to** one another.

The Antinomy of Pure Reason
Third Conflict of the Transcendental Ideas[64]

Thesis

Causality in accordance with laws of nature is not the only one from which all the appearances of the world can be derived. It is also necessary to assume another causality through freedom in order to explain them.

Proof

Assume that there is no other causality than that in accordance with laws of nature: then everything **that happens** presupposes a previous state, upon which it follows without exception according to a rule. But now the previous state itself must be something that has happened (come to be in a time when it previously was not), since if it had been at every time, then its consequence could not have just arisen, but would always have been. Thus the causality of the cause through which something happens is always something **that has happened,** which according to the law of nature presupposes once again a previous state and its causality, and this in the same way a still earlier state, and so on. If, therefore, everything happens according to mere laws of nature, then at every time there is only a subordinate*a* but never a first beginning, and thus no completeness of the series on the side of the causes descending one from another. But now the law of nature consists just in this, that nothing happens without a cause sufficiently determined *a priori.* Thus the proposition that all causality is possible only in accordance with laws of nature, when taken in its unlimited universality, contradicts itself, and therefore this causality cannot be assumed to be the only one.

Accordingly, a causality must be assumed through which something happens without its cause being further determined by another previous cause, i.e., an **absolute** causal **spontaneity** beginning **from itself***b* a series of appearances that runs according to natural laws, hence transcendental freedom, without which even in the course of nature the series of appearances is never complete on the side of the causes.

a subaltern
b von selbst

====================

Antithesis

There is no freedom, but everything in the world happens solely in accordance with laws of nature.

Proof

Suppose there were a **freedom** in the transcendental sense, as a special kind of causality in accordance with which the occurrences of the world could follow, namely a faculty of absolutely beginning a state, and hence also a series of its consequences; then not only will a series begin absolutely through this spontaneity, but the determination of this spontaneity itself to produce the series, i.e., its causality, will begin absolutely, so that nothing precedes it through which this occurring action is determined in accordance with constant laws. Every beginning of action, however, presupposes a state of the not yet acting cause, and a dynamically first beginning of action presupposes a state that has no causal connection at all with the cause of the previous one, i.e., in no way follows from it. Thus transcendental freedom is contrary to the causal law, and is a combination between the successive states of effective causes in accor-   A447/B475
dance with which no unity of experience is possible, which thus cannot be encountered in any experience, and hence is an empty thought-entity.

Thus we have nothing but **nature** in which we must seek the connection and order of occurrences in the world. Freedom (independence) from the laws of nature is indeed a **liberation** from **coercion,** but also from the **guidance**[a] of all rules. For one cannot say that in place of the laws of nature, laws of freedom enter into the course of the world, because if freedom were determined according to laws, it would not be freedom, but nothing other than nature.[b] Thus nature and transcendental freedom are as different as lawfulness and lawlessness; the

---

[a] *Leitfaden*
[b] In the first edition: ". . . it would be not freedom, but nature."

Remark on the Third Antinomy
I. On the Thesis

The transcendental idea of freedom is far from constituting the whole content of the psychological concept of that name, which is for the most part empirical, but constitutes only that of the absolute spontaneity of an action, as the real ground of its imputability; but this idea is nevertheless the real stumbling block for philosophy, which finds insuperable difficulties in admitting this kind of unconditioned causality. Hence that in the question of freedom of the will which has always put speculative reason into such embarrassment is really only **transcendental,** and it concerns only whether a faculty of beginning a series of successive things or states **from itself** *a* is to be assumed. How such a faculty is possible is not so necessary to answer, since with causality in accordance with natural laws we likewise have to be satisfied with the *a priori* cognition that such a thing must be presupposed, even though we do not in any way comprehend how it is possible for one existence to be posited through another existence, and must in this case keep solely to experience. We have really established this necessity of a first beginning of a series of appearances from freedom only to the extent that this is required to make comprehensible an origin of the world, since one can take all the subsequent states to be a result of mere natural laws. But be-

cause the faculty of beginning a series in time entirely on its own *b* is thereby proved (though no insight into it is achieved), now we are permitted also to allow that in the course of the world different series may begin on their own as far as their causality is concerned, and to ascribe to the substances in those series the faculty of acting from freedom. One should not, however, be stopped here by a misunderstanding, namely, that since a successive series in the world can have only a comparatively first beginning, because a state of the world must always precede it, perhaps no absolutely first beginning of the series is possible

---

a *von selbst*
b *von selbst*

former burdens the understanding with the difficulty of seeking the ancestry of occurrences ever higher in the series of causes, because the causality in them is at every time conditioned, but it promises in compensation a thoroughgoing and lawful unity of experience, while the mirage[a] of freedom, on the contrary, though of course offering rest to the inquiring understanding in the chain of causes by leading it to an unconditioned causality that begins to act from itself, since it is itself blind, breaks away from the guidance of those rules by which alone a thoroughly connected experience is possible.

II. Remark
On the Antithesis

The defender of the omnipotence[b] of nature (transcendental **physiocracy**), in counteraction to the doctrine of freedom, would maintain his proposition against the sophistical[c] inferences of the latter, in the following way. **If you do not assume anything mathematically first in the world as far as time is concerned, then it is also not necessary for you to seek for something dynamically first as far as causality is concerned.** Whoever told you to think up an absolutely first state of the world, and hence an absolute beginning of the continuously elapsing series of appearances, and then, so that your imagination might find some point at which to rest, to set a boundary to limitless nature? Since the substances in the world have always existed – at least the unity of experience makes such a presupposition necessary – there is no difficulty in also assuming that the change of their states, i.e., the series of their alterations, has always existed, and hence that no first beginning, whether mathematical or dynamical, need be sought. The possibility of such an infinite descent, without any first member to which the rest is merely subsequent, cannot, as to its possibility, be made comprehensible.[d] But if you reject this riddle of nature on this account, then you will see yourself compelled to dispense with many fundamental properties (fundamental powers) which you can just as little comprehend, and even the possibility of an alteration in general must become a stumbling block for you. For if you did not find through experience that alteration really exists, then you would never be able to imagine[e] a priori how such an uninterrupted sequence of being and not-being is possible.

---

[a] *Blendwerk*
[b] *Allvermögenheit*
[c] *vernünftelnden*
[d] There is indeed an awkward redundancy in this sentence: "*Die Möglichkeit einer solchen unendlichen Abstammung . . . lasst sich, seiner Möglichkeit nach, nicht begreiflich machen.*"
[e] *ersinnen*

during the course of the world. For here we are talking of an absolute beginning not as far as time is concerned but as far as causality is concerned. If (for example) I am now entirely free, and get up from my chair without the necessarily determining influence of natural causes, then in this occurrence, along with its natural consequences to infinity, there begins an absolutely new series, even though as far as time is concerned this occurrence is only the continuation of a previous series. For this decision and deed do not lie within the succession of merely natural effects and are not a mere continuation of them; rather, the determining natural causes of that series entirely cease in regard to this event, which indeed follows upon that series, but does not follow from it;[a] and therefore it must be called, not as far as time is concerned but in regard to causality, an absolutely first beginning of a series of appearances.

The confirmation of the need of reason to appeal to a first beginning from freedom in the series of natural causes is clearly and visibly evident from the fact that (with the exception of the Epicurean school) all the philosophers of antiquity saw themselves as obliged to assume a **first mover**[65] for the explanation of motions in the world, i.e., a freely acting cause, which began this series of states first and from itself. For they did not venture to make a first beginning comprehensible on the basis of mere nature.

[a] *die zwar auf jene folgt, aber daraus nicht erfolgt*

Moreover, even if a transcendental faculty of freedom is conceded in order to begin alterations in the world, then this faculty would in any case have to be outside the world (although it always remains a bold presumption to assume an object outside the sum total of all possible intuitions, which cannot be given in any possible perception). Yet it can never be permitted to ascribe such a faculty to substances in the world itself, because then the connection of appearances necessarily determining one another in accordance with universal laws, which one calls nature, and with it the mark of empirical truth, which distinguishes experience from dreaming, would largely disappear. For alongside such a lawless faculty of freedom, nature could hardly be thought any longer, because the laws of the latter would be ceaselessly modified by the former, and this would render the play of appearances, which in accordance with mere nature would be regular and uniform, confused and disconnected.

The Antinomy of Pure Reason
Fourth Conflict of the Transcendental Ideas[66]

Thesis

To the world there belongs something that, either as a part of it or as its cause, is an absolutely necessary being.[a]

Proof

The world of sense, as the whole of all appearances, at the same time contains a series of alterations. For without these, even the temporal series, as a condition of the possibility of the world of sense, would not be given to us.* Every alteration, however, stands under its condition, which precedes it in time, and under which it is necessary. Now every conditioned that is given presupposes, in respect of its existence, a complete series of conditions up to the unconditioned, which alone is absolutely necessary. Thus there must exist something absolutely necessary, if an alteration exists as its consequence. This necessary being itself, however, belongs to the world of sense. For supposing it is outside it, then the series of alterations in the world would derive from it, without this necessary cause itself belonging to the world of sense.

Now this is impossible. For since the beginning of a time-series can be determined only through what precedes it in time, the supreme condition of the beginning of a series of changes must exist in the time[b] when the series was not yet (for the beginning is an existence, preceded by a time in which the thing that begins still was not). Thus the causal-

* Time, as formal condition of the possibility of alterations, indeed precedes it[c] objectively, yet subjectively and in the reality of consciousness, this representation is given, like any other, only through the occasion of perceptions.

[a] *. . . ein schlechthin notwendiges Wesen ist.* In the first edition: ". . . *ein schlechthin notwendig Wesen ist*" (. . . a being that is absolutely necessarily).

[b] Fourth edition: ". . . in the world"

[c] *dieser.* The antecedent of this singular dative feminine pronoun is unclear, and a matter of dispute; Erdmann prefers to read *diesen,* making the pronoun plural, and (by implication) referring it to "alterations"; on our reading, the singular pronoun refers to the *possibility* of alterations (thus requiring no textual emendation).

Antithesis

There is no absolutely necessary being existing anywhere, either in the world or outside the world as its cause.

Proof

Suppose that either the world itself is a necessary being or that there is such a being in it; then in the series of its alterations either there would be a beginning that is unconditionally necessary, and hence without a cause, which conflicts with the dynamic law of the determination of all appearances in time; or else the series itself would be without any beginning, and, although contingent and conditioned in all its parts, it would nevertheless be absolutely necessary and unconditioned as a whole, which contradicts itself, because the existence of a multiplicity cannot be necessary if no single part of it possesses an existence necessary in itself.

Suppose, on the contrary, that there were an absolutely necessary cause of the world outside the world; then this cause, as the supreme   A455/B483 member in the **series of causes** of alterations in the world, would first begin these changes and their series.* But it would have to begin to act then, and its causality would belong in time, and for this very reason in the sum total of appearances, i.e., in the world; consequently, it itself, the cause, would not be outside the world, which contradicts what was presupposed. Thus neither in the world nor outside it (yet in causal connection with it) is there any absolutely necessary being.

---

* The word "begin" is taken in two significations. The first is **active,** as when the cause begins (*infit*) a series of states as its effect. The second is **passive,** as when the causality in the cause itself commences (*fit*). I infer here from the former to the latter.

ity of the necessary cause of the alterations, hence the cause itself, belongs to time,[a] hence to appearance (in which alone time is possible, as its form); consequently, it cannot be thought as detached from the world of sense as the sum total of all appearances. Thus in the world itself there is contained something absolutely necessary (whether as the whole world-series itself or as a part of it).

A456/B484

Remark on the Fourth Antinomy
I. On the Thesis

In order to prove the existence of a necessary being, I am here obliged to use no argument except the **cosmological** one, which ascends from the conditioned in appearance to the unconditioned in concept by viewing the latter as the necessary condition for the absolute totality of the series. It belongs to another principle[b] of reason to attempt the proof using only the idea of a being that is supreme over all others, and such a proof will therefore have to be put forward separately.

Now the pure cosmological proof can establish the existence of a necessary being in no other way than by leaving it unsettled whether this being is the world itself or a thing distinct from it. For in order to ascertain the latter, principles would be required that are no longer cosmological and do not continue in the series of appearances, but proceed from concepts of contingent beings in general (insofar as they are considered merely as objects of understanding), and a principle connecting such beings with a necessary being through mere concepts; all this belongs to a **transcendent** philosophy, for which this is still not the place.

But if one begins the proof cosmologically, by grounding it on the series of appearances and the regress in this series in accordance with empirical laws of causality, then one cannot later shift from this and go over to something that does not belong to the series as one of its members. For something regarded as a condition must be taken in just the same significance as it has in the relation[c] of conditioned to its condition in the series, if it is to lead this series to its highest condition through a continuous progress. Now if this relation is sensible and belongs to a possible empirical use of the understanding, then the highest condition or cause can conclude the regress only in accordance with laws of sensibility, hence only as something belonging to the time-series, and the necessary being must be regarded as the supreme member of the world-series.

Nevertheless, some have taken the liberty of making such a shift

A458/B486

---

[a] Fifth edition: "to a time"
[b] *Princip*
[c] *Relation*

II. Remark
On the Antithesis

If one supposes that difficulties are to be encountered in ascending in a series of appearances to the existence of an absolutely necessary cause, then these difficulties must not be grounded on the mere concepts of the necessary existence of a thing, hence they cannot be merely ontological, but must arise from the causal connection with a series of appearances, when it tries to assume a condition which is itself unconditioned, thus they must be cosmological and based on empirical laws. It must be shown, however, that ascent in the series of causes (in the world of sense) could never end with an empirically unconditioned condition, and that the cosmological argument from the contingency of states of the world – from its alterations – comes out against the assumption of a first cause that primarily and absolutely initiates the series.

But an odd contrast shows itself in this antinomy: namely, that the same ground of proof from which the thesis of the existence of an original being was inferred, is used also in the antithesis to prove its non-existence, and indeed with equal rigor. First it is said **There is a necessary being** because the whole past time includes within itself the series of all conditions, and thus with it also the unconditioned (the necessary). Then it is said **There is no necessary being** just because the whole of the time that has elapsed includes within itself the series of all conditions (which therefore, taken all together, are once again conditioned). The cause is this. The first argument looks only to the **absolute totality** of the series of conditions, each determined by another in time, and from this it gets something unconditioned and necessary. The second argument, on the contrary, takes into consideration the **contingency** of everything determined in **the time-series** (because before each [member] a time must precede, in which its condition must once again be determined conditionally), and this completely gets rid of everything unconditioned and all absolute necessity. The mode of inference in both, moreover, is entirely suited to common human reason, which falls repeatedly into the trap of disagreeing with itself when it considers its object from two different standpoints. M. de Mairan took the controversy between two famous astronomers, arising from a similar difficulty in the choice of a standpoint, to be a sufficiently strange

($\mu\epsilon\tau\alpha\beta\alpha\sigma\iota\varsigma$ $\epsilon\iota\varsigma$ $\alpha\lambda\lambda o$ $\gamma\epsilon\nu o\varsigma$).[a] That is, from the alterations in the world they have inferred their empirical contingency, i.e., their dependence on empirically determining causes, and thus they obtained an ascending series of empirical conditions, which was quite right too. But since they could not find in this series a first beginning or a highest member, they suddenly abandoned the empirical concept of contingency and took up the pure category, which then occasioned a merely intelligible series, whose completeness rests on the existence of an absolutely necessary cause, which now, since it was no longer bound to sensible conditions, was also liberated from the time-condition that even its causality should begin. But this proceeding is entirely illegitimate, as one can conclude from the following.

In the pure sense of the category, the contingent is that whose contradictory opposite is possible. Now from empirical contingency one cannot at all infer this intelligible contingency. When something is altered, its opposite (the opposite of its state) is actual at another time, and hence possible; hence this is not the contradictory opposite of its previous state, for which it would be required that at the very time when the previous state was, its opposite could have been there in place of it, which cannot at all be inferred from the alteration. A body that was in motion (= A), comes to be in rest (= $not\text{-}A$). Now from the fact that an opposed state follows upon state A it cannot be inferred that the contradictory opposite of A is possible, and hence that A is contingent; for to have this it would be required that in the very time when there was motion, rest could have been there instead. Now we know nothing beyond the fact that rest was actual in the time that followed, and hence that it was possible too. But motion at one time and rest at another time are not contradictory opposites. Thus the succession of opposed determinations, i.e., alteration, in no way proves contingency in accordance with concepts of the pure understanding, and thus it also cannot lead to the existence of a necessary being in accordance with pure concepts of the understanding. Alteration proves only empirical contingency, i.e., that the new state could not at all have occurred on its own, without a cause belonging to the previous time, in accordance with the law of causality. This cause, even if it is assumed to be absolutely necessary, must yet be of such a kind as to be encountered in time and belong to the series of appearances.

A460/ B488

---

[a] change to another kind

phenomenon that he wrote a special treatise about it.[67] One inferred, namely, that **the moon turns on its axis** because it constantly turns the same side toward the earth; the other, that **the moon does not turn on an axis,** just because it constantly turns the same side toward the earth. Both inferences were correct, depending on the standpoint taken when observing the moon's motion.

The
Antinomy of Pure Reason
Third Section
On the interest of reason in these conflicts.

Now we have before us the entire dialectical play of the cosmological ideas, which do not permit an object congruent to them to be given in any possible experience, which, indeed, do not even permit reason to think them in agreement with the universal laws of experience, but which have not been thought up arbitrarily; reason, rather, in continuous progression of the empirical synthesis, has been led to them necessarily when it tries to liberate from every condition, and to grasp in its unconditioned totality, that which can always be determined only conditionally in accordance with rules of experience. These sophistical*a* assertions are only so many attempts to solve four natural and unavoidable problems of reason; there can be only so many of them, no more and no less, because there are no more series of synthetic presuppositions that bound the empirical synthesis *a priori.*

We have represented the glittering pretensions of reason to extend its territory beyond all the bounds of experience only in dry formulas, which contain merely the ground of reason's legal claims; and, as is fitting for a transcendental philosophy, we have divested these claims of everything empirical, even though the full splendor of reason's assertions can shine forth only in such a combination. But in this application, and in the progressive extension of the use of reason, since it commences with the field of experience and only gradually soars aloft to these sublime ideas, philosophy exhibits such a dignity that, if it could only assert its pretensions, it would leave every other human science far behind in value, since it would promise to ground our greatest expectations and prospects concerning the ultimate ends in which all reason's efforts must finally unite. The questions whether the world has a beginning and its extension in space a boundary; whether there is anywhere, perhaps in my thinking self, an indivisible and indestructible unity, or whether there is nothing but that which is divisible and perishable; whether my actions are free or, like those of other beings, controlled by the strings of nature and fate; whether, finally, there is a supreme cause of the world, or whether natural things and their order constitute the ultimate object, at which all our consideration of things must stop – these are questions for whose solution the mathematician would gladly give up his entire science; for that science cannot give him

any satisfaction in regard to the highest and most important ends of humanity. Even the proper dignity of mathematics (that pride of human

a *vernünftelnden*

reason) rests on the fact that since in the great as well as the small, in its order and regularity, and in the admirable unity of the forces moving nature, mathematics guides reason's insight into nature far beyond every expectation of any philosophy built on common experience, it gives occasion and encouragement even to the use of reason which extends beyond all experience, just as it provides to the philosophy[a] concerned with nature the most excellent materials for supporting its inquiries, as far as their character[b] allows, with appropriate intuitions.

Unfortunately for speculation (but perhaps fortunately for the practical vocation)[c] of humanity, reason sees itself, in the midst of its greatest expectations, so entangled in a crowd of arguments and counterarguments[d] that it is not feasible, on account either of its honor or even of its security, for reason to withdraw and look upon the quarrel with indifference, as mere shadow boxing, still less for it simply to command peace, interested as it is in the object of the dispute; so nothing is left except to reflect on the origin of this disunity of reason with itself, on whether a mere misunderstanding might perhaps be responsible for it, after the elucidation of which perhaps both sides will give up their proud claims, but in place of which reason would begin a rule of lasting tranquility over understanding and sense. A465/B493

For now we will postpone this fundamental inquiry a little longer, and first take into consideration on which side we would prefer to fight if we were forced to take sides. Since in this case we would consult not the logical criterion of truth but merely our interest, our present investigation, even though it would settle nothing in regard to the disputed[e] rights of both parties, will have the utility of making it comprehensible why the participants in this dispute have sooner taken one side than the other, even if no superior insight into the object has been the cause of it, and it likewise explains still other ancillary things, e.g., the zealous heat of the one side and the cold assurance of the other, and why they[f] hail the one party with joyful approval and are irreconcilably prejudiced against the other.

But there is something which, in this provisional estimate, determines the standpoint from which it can be carried out with appropriate thoroughness, and that is a comparison of the principles[g] from which

---

[a] *Weltweisheit*

[b] *Beschaffenheit*

[c] *Bestimmung*

[d] *Gründen und Gegengründen*

[e] *streitig;* the first edition reads "*strittig*" (disputable, questionable).

[f] This plural pronoun has no plausible nearby referent; both Müller and Kemp Smith translate it as "the world"; but probably its antecedent is supposed to be the "participants in this dispute" (who, Kant says, "have sooner taken one part than the other").

[g] *Principien*

the two parties proceed. In the assertions of the antithesis,[a] one notes a perfect uniformity in their manner of thought and complete unity in their maxims, namely a principle[b] of pure **empiricism,** not only in the explanation of appearances in the world, but also in the dissolution of the transcendental ideas of the world-whole itself. Against this the assertions of the thesis are grounded not only on empiricism within the series of appearances but also on intellectualistic starting points,[c] and their maxim is to that extent not simple. On the basis of their essential distinguishing mark, however, I will call them the **dogmatism** of pure reason.

A466/ B494

Thus in determining the cosmological ideas of reason, the side of **dogmatism** or the **thesis** exhibits:

First, a certain **practical interest,** in which every well-disposed person, once he understands its true advantage to him, heartily shares. That the world has a beginning, that my thinking self is of a simple and therefore incorruptible nature, that this self is likewise free and elevated above natural compulsion in its voluntary actions, and finally, that the whole order of things constituting the world descends from an original being, from which it borrows all its unity and purposive connectedness – these are so many cornerstones of morality and religion. The antithesis robs us of all these supports, or at least seems to rob us of them.[68]

Second, a **speculative interest** of reason is expressed on this side too. For if one assumes and employs the transcendental ideas in such a way, then one can grasp the whole chain of conditions fully *a priori* and comprehend the derivation of the conditioned, starting with the unconditioned, which the antithesis cannot do; this gives it a bad recommendation, since it can give no answers to questions about the conditions of their synthesis that do not leave something out, and with its answers further questions without any end are always left over. According to the antithesis, one must ascend from a given beginning to a still higher one, every part leads to a still smaller part, every event always has another event above it as its cause, and the conditions of existence in general are always supported again by others, without ever getting stability and support from a self-sufficient thing as an unconditioned original being.

A467/ B495

Third, this side also has the merit of **popularity,** which certainly constitutes no small part of what recommends it. The common under-

---

[a] the antithesis in each antinomy

[b] *Principium*

[c] *intellektuelle Anfänge;* cf. A853/B881, where those who hold that the essential object of cognition is supersensuous (Plato is taken as the paradigm and contrasted with Epicurus, just as is done here at A471/B500) are called "intellectualistic philosophers" or "intellectualists" (*Intellektualphilosophen, Intellektuellen*).

standing does not find the least difficulty in the idea of an unconditioned beginning for every synthesis, since in any case it is more accustomed to descending to consequences than to ascending to grounds; and in the concept of something absolutely first (about whose possibility it does not bother itself) it finds both comfort and simultaneously a firm point to which it may attach the reins guiding its steps, since otherwise, always having one foot in the air, it can never take any delight in the restless climb from the conditioned to the condition.

On the side of **empiricism** in determination of the cosmological A468/B496 ideas, or the **antithesis,** there is **first,** no such practical interest from pure principles *a* of reason as morality and religion carry with them. Mere empiricism seems rather to take all power and influence away from both. If there is no original being different from the world, if the world is without a beginning and also without an author, if our will is not free and our soul is of the same divisibility and corruptibility as matter, then **moral** ideas and principles lose all validity, and they collapse along with the **transcendental** ideas that constitute their theoretical support.

On the contrary, however, empiricism offers advantages to the speculative interests of reason, which are very attractive and far surpass any that the dogmatic teacher of the ideas of reason might promise. For with empiricism the understanding is at every time on its own proper ground, namely the field solely of possible experiences, whose laws it traces, and by means of which it can endlessly extend its secure and comprehensible *b* cognition. Here it can and should exhibit its object, in itself as well as in its relations, to intuition, or at least in concepts an image for which can be clearly and distinctly laid before it in similar given intuitions. Not only is it unnecessary for the understanding to abandon this chain of natural order so as to hang onto ideas with whose A469/B497 objects it has no acquaintance because, as thought-entities, they can never be given; but it is not even permitted to abandon its business, and, under the pretext that this has been brought to an end, to pass over into the territory of idealizing reason and transcendent concepts, where there is no further need to make observations and to inquire according to the laws of nature, but rather only to **think** and **invent,** certain that it can never be refuted by facts of nature because it is not bound by their testimony but may go right past them, or even subordinate them to a higher viewpoint, namely that of pure reason.

Hence the empiricist will never allow any epoch of nature to be assumed to be the absolutely first, or any boundary of his prospect to be

---

a *Principien*
b *fassliche*

regarded as the uttermost in its extent, or*a* that among the objects of nature that he can resolve through observation and mathematics and determine synthetically in intuition (the extended) there can be a transition to those which can never be exhibited *in concreto* either in sense or imagination (the simple); nor will he admit that one can take as fundamental **in nature** itself, a faculty (freedom) that operates independently of the laws of nature, and thereby restrict the business of the understanding, which is to trace the origin of appearances guided by

A470/B498   necessary rules; nor, finally, will he concede that the cause of anything should be sought outside nature (an original being), for we are acquainted with nothing beyond nature, since it is nature alone that provides us with objects and instructs us as to their laws.

Of course, if the empirical philosopher with his antithesis had no other intention than to strike down the impertinent curiosity and presumptuousness of those who so far mistake the true vocation*b* of reason that they make most of **insight** and **knowledge** just where insight and knowledge really cease, trying to pass off what one should base on practical interests as furthering speculative interests, in order, whenever seems comfortable to them, to break off the thread of their physical investigations and, with a pretense of extending cognition, to attach it to transcendental ideas, by means of which one really knows*c* only **that one knows*d* nothing;** if, I say, the empiricist were to content himself with this, then his principle would be a maxim for moderating our claims, for being modest in our assertions, and at the same time for the greatest possible extension of our understanding through the teacher really prescribed for us, namely experience. For in such a case, intellectual **presuppositions** and **faith** on behalf of our practical concern would not be taken from us; only one could not put them forward with

A471/B499   the title and pomp of science and rational insight, because real speculative **knowledge** can encounter no object anywhere except that of experience, and if one transgresses its boundary, then the synthesis that attempts cognitions which are new and independent of experience has no substratum of intuition on which it could be exercised.

But if empiricism itself becomes dogmatic in regard to the ideas (as frequently happens), and boldly denies whatever lies beyond the sphere of its intuitive cognitions, then it itself makes the same mistake of immodesty, which is all the more blamable*e* here, because it causes an irreparable disadvantage to the practical interests of reason.

---

a *oder;* the first edition reads "nor" (*noch*), the same word that, in both editions, introduces the last two main clauses of this sentence.

b *Bestimmung*

c *erkennt*

d *wisse*

e *tadelbar;* in the first edition, this word is *tadelhaft.*

This is the opposition of **Epicureanism*** and **Platonism.**[69]

Each of the two says more than it knows, but in such a way that the A472/B500 **first** encourages and furthers knowledge, though to the disadvantage of the practical, the **second** provides principles[a] which are indeed excellent for the practical, but in so doing allows reason, in regard to that of which only a speculative knowledge is granted us, to indulge in ideal explanations of natural appearances, and to neglect the physical investigation of them.

Finally, as to the **third** moment that can be seen in the provisional choice between the two conflicting parties, it is exceedingly strange that empiricism is completely contrary to everything popular, although one might have thought that the common understanding would eagerly take up a proposal promising to satisfy it through nothing but cognitions of experience and their rational connection, in place of transcendental dogmatism, which compels it to ascend to concepts far surpassing the insight and rational faculties even of those minds most practiced in thinking. But just this is its motive. For then it finds itself in a state in A473/B501 which even the most learned can take nothing away from it. If it understands little or nothing of these matters, neither can anyone else boast that they understand much more; and even if it cannot speak about them with as much scholastic correctness as others do, it can still ratiocinate[b] infinitely more about them, because it is wandering among

---

* There is still a question, however, whether Epicurus ever presented these A471/B499 principles as objective assertions. If they were perhaps nothing more than maxims of the speculative employment of reason, then in them he would have shown as genuine a philosophical spirit as any of the sages[c] of antiquity.[d] That in the explanation of appearances one must go to work as though the field of investigation were not cut off by any boundary or beginning of the world; that one must assume the material of the world as it has to be if we are to be taught about it by experience; that no other way of generating occurrences than their determination through unalterable natural laws, and finally that no cause distinct from the world are to be employed: even now these are principles, very A472/B500 correct but little observed, for extending speculative philosophy while finding out the principles[e] of morality independently of alien sources; if only those who demand that we **ignore** those dogmatic propositions, as long as we are concerned with mere speculation, might not also be accused of trying to **deny** them.

---

[a] *Principien*

[b] *vernünfteln*

[c] *Weltweisen*

[d] In the first edition the sentence does not end here but is separated from what follows by a colon.

[e] *Principien*

mere^a ideas, about which one can be at one's most eloquent just because one **knows nothing about them;** whereas regarding inquiries into nature, it would have to keep quiet and concede that it is ignorant. Comfort and vanity are therefore already a strong recommendation for these principles. Besides, even though for a philosopher it is very difficult to assume something as a principle without being able to give an account of it, or even to assume concepts into whose objective reality there can be no insight, there is nothing more usual for the common understanding. It wants to have something from which it can proceed with confidence. The difficulty of comprehending such a presupposition itself does not disturb it, because (in the case of one who does not know what it means to comprehend) this never crosses its mind, and it takes as known what has become familiar to it through repeated usage. Finally, for the common understanding every speculative interest vanishes before practical interest, and it imagines itself to have insight and knowledge into whatever its apprehensions or hopes impel it to assume or believe. In this way empiricism is robbed completely of all popularity by transcendentally idealizing reason; and for all the disadvantages it^b may contain regarding the supreme practical principles, we need have no apprehension that it will ever pass beyond the boundary of the schools, and acquire any considerable regard in the community or any favor among the great multitude.

B 502
A 474

Human reason is by nature architectonic, i.e., it considers all cognitions as belonging to a possible system, and hence it permits only such principles^c as at least do not render an intended cognition incapable of standing together with others in some system or other. But the propositions of the antithesis are of a kind that they do render the completion of an edifice of cognitions entirely impossible. According to them, beyond every state of the world there is another still older one; within every part there are always still more that are divisible; before every occurrence there was always another which was in turn generated by others; and in existence in general everything is always only conditioned, and no unconditioned or first existence is to be recognized. Thus since the antithesis nowhere allows a first or a starting point that would serve absolutely as the foundation for its building, a completed edifice of cognition on such presuppositions is entirely impossible. Hence the architectonic interest of reason (which is demanded not by empirical unity but by pure rational unity) carries with it a natural recommendation for the assertions of the thesis.

A 475 / B 503

---

^{a} *lauter*

^{b} *sie;* this pronoun, repeated in the next clause, refers grammatically to "transcendentally idealizing reason"; but as Erdmann implies, the sense requires that it be *er,* referring to "empiricism."

^{c} *Principien*

But if a human being could renounce all interests, and, indifferent to all consequences, consider the assertions of reason merely according to their grounds, then, supposing that he knows no way of escaping from the dilemma *a* except by confessing allegiance to one or the other of the conflicting doctrines, such a person would be in a state of ceaseless vacillation. Today it would strike him as convincing that the human will is **free**; tomorrow, when he considered the indissoluble chain of nature, he would side with the view that freedom is nothing but self-deception, and that everything is mere **nature**. But now if it came to be a matter of doing or acting, then this play of merely speculative reason would disappear like the phantom images *b* of a dream, and he would choose his principles *c* merely according to practical interest. But because mere honesty requires that a reflective and inquiring being should devote certain times solely to testing its own reason, withdrawing entirely from all partiality and publicly communicating his remarks to others for their judgment, *d* no one can be reproached for, still less restrained from, letting the propositions and counter-propositions, terrorized by no threats, come forward to defend themselves before a jury drawn from their own estate (namely the estate of fallible *e* human beings). A476/B504

The
Antinomy of Pure Reason
Fourth Section
The transcendental problems of pure reason,
insofar as they absolutely must be capable of a solution.

Wanting to solve all problems and answer all questions would be impudent boasting and such extravagant self-conceit that one would instantly forfeit all trust. Nevertheless, there are sciences whose nature entails that every question occurring in them must absolutely be answerable from what one knows, because the answer must arise from the same source as the question; and there it is in no way allowed to plead unavoidable ignorance, but rather a solution can be demanded. One must be able to know what is **just** or **unjust** in all possible cases in accordance with a rule, because our obligations are at stake, and we cannot have any obligation to do what **we cannot know**. *f* In the explanation of the ap-

---

a *Gedränge*
b *Schattenbilder*
c *Principien*
d *anderen zur Beurtheilung*
e *schwacher*
f In his copy of the first edition, Kant adds: "In the case of each antinomy, it must be shown that if objects of the senses are assumed as things in themselves, no resolution of this conflict would be possible. Consequently if the proposition were not proved above, it could be inferred from this." (E CLXIX, p. 50; 23:40)

A477/B505 pearances of nature, however, much must remain uncertain and many questions insoluble, because what we know about nature is in many cases far from sufficient for what we would explain. The question now is whether there is any question in transcendental philosophy dealing with an object*a* placed before us by reason that is unanswerable by this same pure reason, and whether one could have a right to avoid answering it decisively because one counts as absolutely uncertain (on the basis of what we can know)*b* that of which we have enough of a concept to be able to raise a question about it, but are so entirely lacking in means or faculties that we can never give the answer.

Now I assert that among all speculative cognition, transcendental philosophy has the special property that there is no question at all dealing with an object given by pure reason that is insoluble by this very same human reason; and that no plea of unavoidable ignorance and the unfathomable depth of the problem can release us from the obligation of answering it thoroughly*c* and completely; for the very same concept that puts us in a position to ask the question must also make us competent to answer it, since the object is not encountered at all outside the concept (as it is in the case of justice and injustice).

A478/B506 In transcendental philosophy, however, there are no questions other than the cosmological ones in regard to which one can rightfully demand a sufficient answer concerning the constitution of the object itself; the philosopher is not allowed to evade them by pleading their impenetrable obscurity, and these questions can have to do only with cosmological ideas. For the object must be given empirically, and the question concerns only its conformity with an idea. If the object is transcendental and thus in itself unknown, e.g., whether the something whose appearance (in ourselves) is thinking (the soul) is in itself a simple being, whether there is a cause of all things taken together that is absolutely necessary, etc., then we should seek an object for our idea, which we can concede to be unknown to us, but not on that account impossible.* The

---

* To the question, "What kind of constitution does a transcendental object have?" one cannot indeed give an answer saying **what it is,** but one can answer that the **question** itself **is nothing,** because no object for the question is given. Hence all questions of the transcendental doctrine of the soul are answerable and actually answered; for they have to do with the transcendental subject of all inner appearances, which is not itself an appearance and hence is not **given** as an object, and regarding which none of the categories (at which the question is really being aimed) encounter conditions of their application. Thus here is a case where the common saying holds, that no answer is an answer, namely that

A479/B507

---

a *Object*
b *erkennen*
c *gründlich*

cosmological ideas alone have the peculiarity that they can presuppose A479/B507 their object, and the empirical synthesis required for its concept, as given; and the question that arises from them has to do only with the progression of this synthesis, insofar as it is to contain an absolute totality, which, however, is no longer empirical, since it cannot be given in any experience. Now since we are here talking about a thing only as an object of a possible experience and not as a thing in itself, the answer to the transcendent cosmological question cannot lie anywhere outside the idea, for it does not have to do with any object in itself; and in regard to possible experience, the question asks not about what can be given *in concreto* in any experience, but rather about what lies in the idea which the empirical synthesis is merely supposed to approximate: therefore, this question must be able to be resolved from the idea alone; for this idea is merely a creature of reason, which therefore cannot refuse the responsibility and pass it on to the unknown object.

It is not as extraordinary as it initially seems that a science can de- A480/B508 mand and expect clear and certain solutions to all the questions belonging within it^a (*quaestiones domesticae*), even if up to this time they still have not been found. Besides transcendental philosophy, there are two pure sciences of reason, one with merely speculative, the other with practical content: **pure mathematics** and **pure morals.** Has it ever been proposed that because of our necessary ignorance of conditions it is uncertain exactly what relation, in rational or irrational numbers, the diameter of a circle bears to its circumference? Since it cannot be given congruently to the former, but has not yet been found through the latter, it has been judged that at least the impossibility of such a solution can be known^b with certainty, and Lambert gave a proof of this.[70] In the universal principles^c of ethics nothing can be uncertain, because the propositions are either totally nugatory and empty, or else they have to flow merely from our concepts of reason. On the other hand, in natural science^d there are an infinity of conjectures in regard to which certainty can never be expected, because natural appearances are objects that are given to us independently of our concepts, to which, therefore, the key lies not in us and in our pure thinking, but outside us, and for this reason in many cases it is not found; hence no certain account of these A481/B509

a question about the constitution of this something, which cannot be thought through any determinate predicate because it is posited entirely outside the sphere of objects that can be given to us, is entirely nugatory and empty.

---

^a *ihren Inbegriff*
^b *erkannt*
^c *Principien*
^d *Naturkunde*

matters can be expected. I do not include the questions of the transcendental analytic here, because now we are dealing only with the certainty of judgments in regard to objects, and not in regard to the origin of our concepts themselves.

Thus we cannot evade the obligation of giving at least a critical resolution of the questions of reason before us by lamenting the narrow limits of our reason and confessing, with the appearance of a modest self-knowledge,[a] that it lies beyond our reason to settle whether the world has existed from eternity or has a beginning, whether world-space is filled to infinity with beings or is enclosed within certain boundaries, whether there is anything simple in the world or everything has to be divided infinitely, whether there is a generating and producing through freedom or everything depends on the causal chain of the natural order, and finally, whether there is any being entirely unconditioned and in itself necessary or whether the existence of everything is conditioned and hence externally dependent and in itself contingent. For each of these questions concerns an object that can be given nowhere but in our thoughts, namely the absolutely unconditioned totality of the synthesis of appearances. If we cannot say or settle anything certain about these questions on the basis of our own concepts, then we must not pass the blame on to the subject matter,[b] as hiding itself from us; for such a subject matter (because it is encountered nowhere outside our idea) cannot be given to us at all, but rather we must seek the cause in our idea itself, as a problem permitting of no solution, about which, however, we stubbornly insist on an actual object corresponding to it. A clear presentation of the dialectic lying in our concept itself would soon bring us to complete certainty about what we have to judge in regard to such a question.

A482/B510

In response to your objection that these problems are uncertain one can counterpose this question, to which, at least, you must give a clear answer: Where do you get the ideas the solution to which involves you in such difficulties? Is it perhaps appearances, whose explanation you need here, and about which, owing to these ideas, you have to seek only the principles[c] or the rule of their exposition? Assume that nature were completely exposed to you; that nothing were hidden from your senses and to the consciousness of everything laid before your intuition: even then you still could not, through any experience, cognize *in concreto* the object of your ideas (for besides this complete intuition, a completed synthesis and the consciousness of its absolute totality would be re-

B511

---

[a] *Selbsterkenntnis*
[b] *Sache*
[c] *Principien*

quired, but that is not possible through any empirical cognition); hence   A483
your question cannot in any way be necessarily posed[a] in the course of
explaining any experience that might come before you, and thus posed,
as it were, through the object itself. For the object can never come before you, because it cannot be given in any possible experience. With all
possible perceptions, you always remain caught up among **conditions,**
whether in space or in time, and you never get to the unconditioned, so
as to make out whether this unconditioned is to be posited in an absolute beginning of the synthesis or in the absolute totality of the series
without a beginning. The whole,[b] in an empirical signification, is always
only comparative. The absolute whole of magnitude (the world-whole),
of division, of descent, of the conditions of existence in general, together with all the questions about whether these are to come about
through a finite or an endlessly continuing synthesis, has nothing to do
with any possible experience. For example, you will not be able to explain the appearance of a body the least bit better, or even any differently, whether you assume that it consists of simple parts or completely
of parts that are always composite; for no simple appearance can come
before you, and neither can any infinite composition. Appearances require to be explained only insofar as their conditions of explanation are
given in perception, but everything that can ever be given in it, taken   B512
together in an **absolute whole,**[c] is not itself any perception.[d] But it is   A484
really this whole[e] for which an explanation is being demanded in the
transcendental problems of reason.

Since, therefore, the solution to these problems can never occur in experience, you cannot say that it is uncertain what is to be ascribed to the
object regarding them. For your object is merely in your brain[f] and cannot be given at all outside it; hence all you have to worry about is agreeing with yourself, and avoiding the amphiboly that would make your
idea into a putative representation of something given empirically, and
thus of an object[g] to be cognized in accordance with the laws of experience. Thus the dogmatic solution is not merely uncertain, but impossible. The critical solution, however, which can be completely certain,
does not consider the question objectively at all, but instead asks about
the foundations of the cognition in which it is grounded.

---

[a] *kann eure Frage keineswegs . . . aufgegeben sein*
[b] *All*
[c] *absoluten Ganzen*
[d] *. . . ist selbst eine Warnehmung* (". . . is itself a perception"); but the sense seems to require *keine* rather than *eine*, and following Erdmann we have adopted this reading.
[e] *All*
[f] *Gehirne*
[g] *Object*

The
Antinomy of Pure Reason
Section Five
Skeptical representation of the cosmological questions raised by all four transcendental ideas.

We would gladly refrain from demanding to see our questions answered dogmatically if we comprehended right from the start that however the answer might come out, it would only increase our ignorance, removing one inconceivability only to replace it with another, taking us out of one obscurity only to plunge us into a still greater one, and perhaps even into contradictions. If our question is put merely in terms of affirmation or negation, then it is prudent to handle it by initially leaving aside the supposed grounds for each side and first taking into account what one would gain if the answer turned out on one side or on the opposite side. Now if it so happened that the result in both cases was something quite empty of sense (nonsense),*a* then we would have good grounds to summon our question itself to be critically examined and to see whether it does not itself rest on a groundless presupposition and play with an idea that better betrays its falsity in its application and consequences than in its abstract representation. This is the great utility of

the skeptical way of treating the questions that pure reason puts to pure reason; by means of it one can with little expense exempt oneself from a great deal of dogmatic rubbish, and put in its place a sober critique, which, as a true cathartic, will happily purge such delusions along with the punditry*b* attendant on them.

Accordingly, if I could antecedently see about a cosmological idea that whatever side of the unconditioned in the regressive synthesis of appearances it might come down on, it would **be either too big or too small** for every **concept of the understanding,** then I would comprehend that since it has to do with an object of experience,[71] which should conform to a possible concept of the understanding, this idea must be entirely empty and without significance because the object does not fit it no matter how I may accommodate the one to the other. And this is actually the case with all the world-concepts, which is why reason, as long as it holds to them, is involved in an unavoidable antinomy. For assume:

First, that **the world has no beginning;** then it is too **big** for your concept; for this concept, which consists in a successive regress, can never reach the whole eternity that has elapsed. Suppose **it has a beginning,** then once again it is **too small** for your concept of under-

standing in the necessary empirical regress. For since the beginning

---

a *lauter Sinnleeres (Nonsens)*
b *Vielwisserei*

always presupposes a preceding time, it is still not unconditioned, and the law of the empirical use of the understanding obliges you to ask for a still higher temporal condition, and the world is obviously too small for this law.

It is exactly the same with the two answers to the question about the magnitude of the world in space. For **if it is infinite** and unbounded, then it is **too big** for every possible empirical concept. **If it is finite** and bounded, then you can still rightfully ask: What determines this boundary? Empty space is not a correlate of things that subsists by itself, and it cannot be a condition with which you can stop, still less an empirical condition that constitutes a part of a possible experience. (For who can have an experience of what is absolutely empty?) But for the absolute totality of the empirical synthesis it is always demanded that the unconditioned be an empirical concept. Thus a **bounded** world is **too small** for your concept.

Second, if every appearance in space (matter) consists **of infinitely many parts,** then the regress of division is always **too big** for your concept; and if the **division** of space should **cease** at any one member of the division (the simple), then it is **too small** for the idea of the unconditioned. For this member always allows of still another regress to further parts contained in it.   A 488
B 516

Third, if you assume that in everything that happens in the world there is nothing but a sequence occurring according to laws of **nature,** then the causality of the cause is always once again something that happens, and that necessitates your regress to still higher causes, and hence the prolonging of the series of conditions *a parte priori* without cessation. Mere efficient*ª* **nature** in the synthesis of world-events is thus **too big** for all your concepts.

If you choose now and then to admit occurrences produced **from themselves,** hence generated **through freedom,** then by an unavoidable law of nature the question "Why?" will pursue you, and require you, in accord with the causal laws of experience, to go beyond this point; then you will find that such a totality of connection **is too small** for your necessary empirical concept.

Fourth: If you assume an **absolutely necessary** being (whether it be the world itself, or something in the world, or the cause of the world), then you must place it at a time infinitely far removed from every given point in time, because otherwise it would be dependent on another and an older existence. But then this existence is inaccessible and **too big** for your empirical concept, and you could never arrive at it through any regress, however far it might continue.

But if, in your opinion, everything that belongs to the world   A 489/ B 517

ª wirkende

(whether as conditioned or as condition) is **contingent,** then every existence given to you is **too small** for your concept. For this existence compels you to look around for yet another existence on which this one is dependent.

In all these cases, we have said that the **world-idea** is either too big for the empirical regress, hence for every possible concept of the understanding, or else too small for it. But why haven't we expressed ourselves in just the opposite way, and said that in the first case the empirical concept is always too small for the idea, and in the second too big for it – thus, as it were, holding the empirical regress responsible? Why have we instead accused the cosmological idea of falling short or exceeding its end, namely possible experience? The reason was this. It is possible experience alone that can give our concepts reality; without it, every concept is only an idea, without truth and reference to an object. Hence the possible empirical concept was the standard by which it had to be judged whether the idea is a mere idea and a thought-entity[a] or instead encounters its object within the world. For one says that one thing is too great or too small relative to another only when the former thing is assumed to exist for the sake of the latter, and hence has to be adapted to it. Among the conundrums[b] of the ancient dialectical schools was this question: If a ball does not pass through a hole, should one say that the ball is too big, or that the hole is too small? In this case, it is indifferent how you choose to express yourself; for you do not know which of the two is there for the sake of the other. By contrast, you will not say that the man is too tall for his clothing, but rather that the clothing is too short for the man.

Thus we have been brought at least to the well-grounded suspicion that the cosmological ideas, and all the sophistical assertions about them that have come into conflict with one another, are perhaps grounded on an empty and merely imagined concept of the way the object of these ideas is given to us; and this suspicion may already have put us on the right track for exposing the semblance that has so long misled us.[c]

---

[a] *Gedankending*

[b] *Spielwerke*

[c] In his copy of the first edition, Kant writes: "In the cosmological ideas, the first two propositions say too much for the opposition, the last two too little. The former say: 'Everything is either eternal in time or has a beginning,' while they should have said: 'or it is not eternal and exists as thing in itself in no time at all.'

"In the latter too little is said. Hence both can be true: e.g., everything in the world is either dependent or independent (everything necessary). The former is true of phenomena, the latter of noumena outside the world." (E CLXX, pp. 50-1; 23:40-1)

The
Antinomy of Pure Reason
Section Six
Transcendental idealism as the key to solving
the cosmological dialectic.

We have sufficiently proved in the Transcendental Aesthetic that everything intuited in space or in time, hence all objects of an experience
possible for us, are nothing but appearances, i.e., mere representations,   A491/B519
which, as they are represented, as extended beings or series of alterations, have outside our thoughts no existence grounded in itself. This
doctrine*a* I call **transcendental idealism.*** The realist, in the transcendental signification, makes these modifications of our sensibility into
things subsisting in themselves, and hence makes **mere representations** into things in themselves.

One would do us an injustice if one tried to ascribe to us that long-
decried empirical idealism that, while assuming the proper reality of
space, denies the existence of extended beings in it, or at least finds this
existence doubtful, and so in this respect admits no satisfactorily provable distinction between dream and truth. As to the appearances of
inner sense in time, it finds no difficulty in them as real things; indeed,
it even asserts that this inner experience and it alone gives sufficient
proof of the real existence of their object*b* (in itself) along with all this
time-determination.

Our transcendental idealism, on the contrary, allows that the objects   B520
of outer intuition are real too, just as they are intuited in space, along
with all alterations in time, just as inner sense represents them. For
since space is already a form of that intuition that we call outer, and
without objects in it there would be no empirical representation at all,   A492
we can and must assume extended beings in space as real; and it is precisely the same with time. Space itself, however, together with time,
and, with both, all appearances, are **not things,** but rather nothing but
representations, and they cannot exist at all outside our mind; and even
the inner and sensible intuition of our mind (as an object of conscious-

---

* <I have also occasionally called it **formal** idealism, in order to distinguish it
from **material** idealism, i.e., the common idealism that itself doubts or de-   B519
nies the existence of external things. In many cases it seems more advisable
to employ this rather than the expression given above, in order to avoid all
misinterpretation.>*c*

a *Lehrbegriff*
b Object
c This note was added in the second edition.

ness), the determination of which through the succession of different states is represented^a in time, is not the real self as it exists in itself, or the transcendental subject, but only an appearance of this to us unknown being, which was given to sensibility. The existence of this inner appearance, as a thing thus existing in itself, cannot be admitted, because its condition is time, which cannot be a determination of any thing in itself. In space and time, however, the empirical truth of appearances is satisfactorily secured, and sufficiently distinguished from its kinship with dreams, if both are correctly and thoroughly connected up according to empirical laws in one experience.

B521

Accordingly, the objects of experience are **never** given **in themselves,** but only in experience, and they do not exist at all outside it. That there could be inhabitants of the moon, even though no human being has ever perceived them, must of course be admitted; but this means^b only that in the possible progress of experience we could encounter them; for everything is actual that stands in one context with a perception in accordance with the laws of the empirical progression. Thus they are real when they stand in an empirical connection with my real consciousness, although they are not therefore real in themselves, i.e., outside this progress of experience.

A493

Nothing is really given to us except perception and the empirical progress from this perception to other possible perceptions. For in themselves, appearances, as mere representations, are real only in perception, which in fact is nothing but the reality of an empirical representation, i.e., appearance. To call an appearance a real thing prior to perception means^c either that in the continuation of experience we must encounter such a perception, or it has no meaning^d at all. For that it should exist in itself without relation to our senses and possible experience, could of course be said if we were talking about a thing in itself. But what we are talking about is merely an appearance in space and time, neither of which is a determination of things in themselves, but only of our sensibility; hence what is in them (appearances) are not something in itself, but mere representations, which if they are not given in us (in perception) are encountered nowhere at all.

B522

A494

The sensible faculty of intuition is really only a receptivity for being affected in a certain way with representations, whose relation to one another is a pure intuition of space and time (pure forms of our sensibility), which, insofar as they are connected and determinable in these

---

^{a} *vorgestellt wird;* Kant's sentence contains an extra verb, *ist;* thus the sentence as written doesn't parse, but it suggests that Kant had not decided whether to treat "is represented" as a passive verb or as an adjectival participle.
^{b} *bedeutet*
^{c} *bedeutet*
^{d} *Bedeutung*

relations*a* (in space and time) according to laws of the unity of experience, are called **objects**. The non-sensible cause of these representations is entirely unknown to us, and therefore we cannot intuit it as an object;*b* for such an object would have to be represented neither in space nor in time (as mere conditions of our sensible representation), without which conditions we cannot think any intuition. Meanwhile we can call the merely intelligible cause of appearances in general the transcendental object,*c* merely so that we may have something corresponding to sensibility as a receptivity. To this transcendental object*d* we can ascribe the whole extent and connection of our possible perceptions, and say that it is given in itself prior to all experience. But appearances are, in accordance with it, given not in themselves but only in this experience, because they are mere representations, which signify a real object only as perceptions, namely when this perception connects up with all others in accordance with the rules of the unity of experience. Thus one can say: The real things of past time are given in the transcendental object of experience, but for me they are objects and real in past time only insofar as I represent to myself that, in accordance with empirical laws, or in other words, the course of the world, a regressive series of possible perceptions (whether under the guidance of history or in the footsteps of causes and effects) leads to a time-series that has elapsed as the condition of the present time, which is then represented as real only in connection with a possible experience and not in itself; so that all those events which have elapsed from an inconceivable past time prior to my own existence signify nothing but the possibility of prolonging the chain of experience, starting with the present perception, upward to the conditions that determine it in time.

    If, accordingly, I represent all together all existing objects of sense in all time and all spaces, I do not posit them as being there in space and time prior to experience, but rather this representation is nothing other than the thought of a possible experience in its absolute completeness. In it alone are those objects (which are nothing but mere representations) given. But to say that they exist prior to all my experience means*e* only that they are to be encountered in the part of experience **to which** I, starting with the perception, must first of all progress. The cause of the empirical conditions of this progress, the cause, therefore, of which members of it I might encounter, and also the extent to which I may encounter them in the regress, is transcendental, and hence necessarily

B 523

A 495

B 524

A 496

---

a *Verhältnisse*
b *Object*
c *Object*
d *Object*
e *bedeutet*

unknown to me. We, however, have nothing to do with that, but only with the rule of the progress of experience, in which objects, namely appearances, are given. It is all the same to the outcome whether I say that in the empirical progress in space I could encounter stars that are a hundred times farther from me than the most distant ones I see, or whether I say that perhaps they are there to be encountered in world-space even if no human being has ever perceived them or ever will perceive them; for if they were given as things in themselves, without any reference to possible experience at all, then they would be nothing for me, hence they would not be objects contained in the series of the empirical regress. Only in another relation, when these same appearances are to

B525   be used on behalf of the cosmological idea of an absolute whole and having to do with a question that goes beyond the bounds of possible experience, is it important to distinguish between the ways one might take the reality of objects of sense when thinking them, so as to prevent

A497   a deceptive delusion that must inevitably arise if we misinterpret our own concepts of experience.

The
Antinomy of Pure Reason
Section Seven
Critical decision of the cosmological conflict of reason
with itself.

The entire antinomy of pure reason rests on this dialectical argument: If the conditioned is given, then the whole series of all conditions for it is also given; now objects of the senses are given as conditioned; consequently, etc. Through this syllogism, whose major premise seems so natural and evident, a corresponding number of cosmological ideas are introduced, in accordance with the difference of the conditions (in the synthesis of appearances), insofar as they constitute a series, which postulate an absolute totality of these series and thereby put reason into an unavoidable conflict with itself. But before we expose what is deceptive about this sophistical argument, we have to put in place certain of the

B526   concepts occurring in it, by correcting and determining them.

First, the following proposition is clear and undoubtedly certain: If

A498   the conditioned is given, then through it a regress in the series of all conditions for it is **given** to us **as a problem;**[a] for the concept of the conditioned already entails that something is related to a condition, and if this condition is once again conditioned, to a more remote condition, and so through all the members of the series. This proposition is therefore analytic and beyond any fear of a transcendental criticism. It is a

---

[a] *uns . . . aufgegeben sei*

logical postulate of reason to follow that connection of a concept with its conditions through the understanding, and to continue it as far as possible, which already attaches to the concept itself.

Further: If the conditioned as well as its condition are things in themselves, then when the first is given not only is the regress to the second **given as a problem,** but the latter is thereby really already **given** along with it; and, because this holds for all members of the series, then the complete series of conditions, and hence the unconditioned is thereby simultaneously given, or rather it is presupposed by the fact that the conditioned, which is possible only through that series, is given. Here the synthesis of the conditioned with its conditions is a synthesis of the mere understanding, which represents things **as they are** without paying attention to whether and how we might achieve acquaintance*[a]* with them. On the contrary, if I am dealing with appearances, which as mere representations are not given at all if I do not achieve acquaintance with them (i.e. to them themselves, for they are nothing except empirical cognitions),*[b]* then I cannot say with the same meaning*[c]* that if the conditioned is given, then all the conditions (as appearances) for it are also given; and hence I can by no means infer the absolute totality of the series of these conditions. For the **appearances,** in their apprehension, are themselves nothing other than an empirical synthesis (in space and time) and thus are given only **in this synthesis.** Now it does not follow at all that if the conditioned (in appearance) is given, then the synthesis constituting its empirical condition is thereby also given and presupposed; on the contrary, this synthesis takes place for the first time in the regress, and never without it. But in such a case one can very well say that a **regress** to the conditions, i.e., a continued empirical synthesis on this side is demanded or **given as a problem,***[d]* and that there could not fail to be conditions given through this regress.[72]

From this it is clear that the major premise of the cosmological syllogism takes the conditioned in the transcendental signification of a pure category, while the minor premise takes it in the empirical signification of a concept of the understanding applied to mere appearances; consequently there is present in it that dialectical deception that is called a *sophisma figurae dictionis.*[e] This deception is, however, not artificial, but an entirely natural mistake of common reason. For through common reason, when something is given as conditioned, we presuppose (in the major premise) the conditions and their series as it were **sight unseen,**

B527

A499

B528
A500

---

[a] *Kenntnis*
[b] *Kenntnisse*
[c] *Bedeutung*
[d] *aufgegeben*
[e] "sophism of a figure of speech," or fallacy of equivocation

because this is nothing but the logical requirement of assuming complete premises for a given conclusion, and no time-order is present in the connection of the conditioned with its condition; both are presupposed as given **simultaneously.** Further, it is likewise natural (in the minor premise) to regard appearances as things in themselves and likewise as objects given to the mere understanding, as was the case in the major premise, where I abstracted from all conditions of intuition under which alone objects can be given. But now in this we have overlooked a remarkable difference between the concepts. The synthesis of the conditioned with its condition and the whole series of the latter (in the major premise) carries with it no limitation through time and no concept of succession. The empirical synthesis, on the contrary, and the series of conditions in appearance (which are subsumed in the minor premise), is necessarily given successively and is given only in time, one member after another; consequently here I could not presuppose the absolute **totality** of synthesis and the series represented by it, as I could in the previous case, because there all members of the series are given in themselves (without time-condition), but here they are possible only through the successive regress, which is given only through one's actually completing it.

B529

A501

When such a fallacy has been shown to ground the common argument (for the cosmological assertions), the demands of both disputing parties could rightfully be dismissed as being based on no well-grounded title. But that does not put an end to their quarrel to the extent of winning them over to the view that one or both of them is wrong in what he actually asserts (in the conclusion), even if he does not know how to construct sound arguments [a] for it. Nothing seems clearer than that between the two, one of whom asserts that the world has a beginning, and the other that it has no beginning but has existed from eternity, one of them has to be right. But if this is so, then because there is equal evidence [b] on both sides, it is impossible ever to ascertain which side is right, and so the conflict drags on as before, even though the parties have been directed by the court of reason to hold their peace. Thus no means is left for ending the dispute in a well-grounded way and to the satisfaction of both sides, unless through the fact that they can do such a fine job of refuting each other they are finally won over to the view that they are disputing about nothing, and that a certain transcendental illusion has portrayed a reality to them where none is present. This is the path on which we will now set forth in settling a dispute that cannot be decided by a final judgment.

B530

A502

＊ ＊ ＊

[a] *Beweisgründe*
[b] *Klarheit*

Section VII. Critical decision of the cosmological conflict

Zeno the **eleatic,** a subtle dialectician, was already severely censured by Plato as a wanton sophist who, to show his art, would seek to prove some proposition through plausible arguments and then immediately to overthrow the same proposition through other arguments just as strong.[73] He asserted that God (presumably for him this was nothing but the world) is neither finite nor infinite, is neither in motion nor at rest, and is neither like nor unlike any other thing. To those who judged him, it appeared that he wanted entirely to deny two mutually contradictory propositions, which is absurd. But I do not find that this charge can be justly lodged against him. I will throw more light on the first of these propositions presently. As to the others, if by the word **God** he understood the universe, then he must of course say that neither is it persistingly present in its place (at rest) nor does it alter its place (move), because all places are only in the universe, hence this **universe** itself is in **no place.** If the world-whole includes in itself everything existing, then it is neither like nor unlike any **other thing,** because there is **no other thing** outside it, with which it might be compared. If two mutually opposed judgments presuppose an inadmissible condition, then despite their conflict (which is, however, not a real contradiction) both of them collapse, because the condition collapses under which alone either of them would be valid.

B 531
A 503

If someone said that every body either smells good or smells not good, then there is a third possibility, namely that a body has no smell (aroma) at all, and thus both conflicting propositions can be false. If I say the body is either good-smelling or not good-smelling (*vel suaveolens vel non suaveolens*), then both judgments are contradictorily opposed, and only the first is false, but its contradictory opposite, namely that some bodies are not good-smelling, includes also those bodies that **have no smell at all.** In the previous opposition (*per disparata*)[a] the contingent condition of the concept of body (of smell) **remained** in the case of the conflicting judgment, and hence it was not ruled out[b] by it; hence the latter judgment was not the contradictory opposite of the former.

Accordingly, if I say that as regards space either the world is infinite or it is not infinite (*non est infinitus*), then if the first proposition is false, its contradictory opposite, "the world is not infinite," must be true. Through it I would rule out only an infinite world, without positing another one, namely a finite one. But if it is said that the world is either infinite or finite (not-infinite), then both propositions could be false. For then I regard the world as determined in itself regarding its magnitude, since in the opposition I not only rule out its infinitude, and

A 504/ B 532

[a] through different things
[b] *aufgehoben*

517

with it, the whole separate*a* existence of the world, but I also add a determination of the world, as a thing active in itself, which might likewise be false, if, namely, the world were **not** given **at all as a thing in itself,** and hence, as regards its magnitude, neither as infinite nor as finite. Permit me to call such an opposition a **dialectical** opposition, but the contradictory one an analytical **opposition.**[b] Thus two judgments dialectically opposed to one another could both be false, because one does not merely contradict the other, but says something more than is required for a contradiction.

If one regards the two propositions, "The world is infinite in magnitude," "The world is finite in magnitude," as contradictory opposites, then one assumes that the world (the whole series of appearances) is a thing in itself. For the world remains, even though I may rule out the infinite or finite regress in the series of its appearances. But if I take away this presupposition, or rather this transcendental illusion, and

A 505 / B 533   deny that it is a thing in itself, then the contradictory conflict of the two assertions is transformed into a merely dialectical conflict, and because the world[c] does not exist at all (independently of the regressive series of my representations), it exists neither as **an in itself infinite** whole nor as **an in itself finite** whole. It is only in the empirical regress of the series of appearances, and by itself it is not to be met with at all. Hence if it*d* is always conditioned, then it is never wholly given, and the world is thus not an unconditioned whole, and thus does not exist as such a whole, either with infinite or with finite magnitude.[74]

What has been said here about the first cosmological idea, namely the absolute totality of magnitude in appearance, holds also for the others. The series of appearances is to be encountered only in the regressive synthesis itself, but is not encountered in itself in appearance, as a thing on its own given prior to every regress. Hence I will have to say: the multiplicity of parts in a given appearance is in itself neither finite nor infinite, because appearance is nothing existing in itself, and the parts are given for the very first time through the regress of the decomposing synthesis, and in this regress, which is never given absolutely **wholly** either as finite nor as infinite. The very same holds of the series of causes ordered one above another, or of conditioned exis-

A 506 / B 534   tence up to necessary existence, which can never be regarded in them-

---

a *abgesondert*

[b] In the two italicized phrases, the term used is *Opposition*, not Kant's usual term *Entgegensetzung.*

[c] In the first edition: ". . . and the world, because it . . ."

d *diese*, whose referent, on grammatical grounds, could be either "world" or "series" (but not "regress").

selves as either finite or infinite in their totality, because, as series of subordinated representations, they exist only in the dynamical regress; but prior to this regress, and as a series of things subsisting for themselves, they cannot exist at all in themselves.

Accordingly, the antinomy of pure reason in its cosmological ideas is removed by showing that it is merely dialectical and a conflict due to an illusion arising from the fact that one has applied the idea of absolute totality, which is valid only as a condition of things in themselves, to appearances that exist only in representation, and that, if they constitute a series, exist in the successive regress but otherwise do not exist at all. But one can, on the contrary, draw from this antinomy a true utility, not dogmatic but critical and doctrinal utility, namely that of thereby proving indirectly the transcendental ideality of appearances, if perhaps someone did not have enough in the direct proof in the Transcendental Aesthetic. The proof would consist in this dilemma. If the world is a whole existing in itself, then it is either finite or infinite. Now the first as well as the second alternative is false (according to the proof[a] offered above for the antithesis on the one side and the thesis on the other). Thus it is also false that the world (the sum total of all appearances) is a whole existing in itself. From which it follows that appearances in general are nothing outside our representations, which is just what we mean by their transcendental ideality.

B 535
A 507

This remark is of some importance. From it one sees that the above proofs of the fourfold antinomy are not semblances but well grounded, that is, at least on the presupposition that appearances, or a world of sense comprehending all of them within itself, are things in themselves. The conflict of the propositions drawn from it, however, uncovers a falsehood lying in this presupposition and thereby brings us to a discovery about the true constitution of things as objects of sense. Thus the transcendental dialectic by no means provides support for skepticism, though it does for the skeptical method, which can point to the dialectic as an example of the great utility of letting the arguments of reason confront one another in the most complete freedom; such arguments, although they may not deliver what one was seeking, nevertheless will always deliver something useful and serviceable for the correction of our judgments.[b]

---

[a] In the first edition: "proofs"

[b] Notes in Kant's copy of the first edition: "In the first class of antinomical propositions both are false, because they say more than is true, namely [that there is an] absolute totality of appearances.

"In the second [class] both can be true, because they will say less than is required for the opposition; [for] it can [happen] that intellectual [things] are posited in place of sensibles." (E CLXXI, p. 51; 23:41)

The
Antinomy of Pure Reason
Section Eight
The regulative principle[a] of pure reason in regard to the
cosmological ideas.

Since through the cosmological principle of totality no maximum in the series of conditions in a world of sense, as a thing in itself, is **given,** but rather this maximum can merely be **given as a problem**[b] in the regress of this series, the principle of pure reason we are thinking of retains its genuine validity only in a corrected significance:[c] not indeed as an **axiom** for thinking the totality in the object[d] as real, but as a **problem**[e] for the understanding, thus for the subject in initiating and continuing, in accordance with the completeness of the idea, the regress in the series of conditions for a given conditioned. For in sensibility, i.e., in space and time, every condition to which we can attain in the exposition of given appearances is in turn conditioned, because these appearances are not objects in themselves in which the absolutely unconditioned might possibly occur, but only empirical representations, which must always find in intuition their condition, which determines them as regards space or time. Thus the principle of reason is only a **rule,** prescribing a

regress in the series of conditions for given appearances, in which regress it is never allowed to stop with an absolutely unconditioned. Thus it is not a principle[f] of the possibility of experience and of the empirical cognition of objects of sense, hence not a principle of the understanding, for every experience is enclosed within its boundaries (conforming to the intuition in which it is given); nor is it a **constitutive principle**[g] of reason for extending the concept of the world of sense beyond all possible experience; rather it is a principle of the greatest possible continuation and extension of experience, in accordance with which no empirical boundary would hold as an absolute boundary; thus it is a principle[h] of reason which, as a **rule,** postulates what should be effected[i] by us in the regress, but **does not anticipate** what is given in itself **in the object**[j] prior to any regress. Hence I call it a **regulative**

---

[a] *Princip*
[b] *aufgegeben*
[c] *Bedeutung*
[d] *Object*
[e] *Problem*
[f] *Principium*
[g] **Princip**
[h] *Principium*
[i] *geschehen*
[j] *Object*

principle*a* of reason, whereas the principle of the absolute totality of the series of conditions, as given in itself in the object*b* (in the appearances), would be a constitutive cosmological principle,*c* the nullity of which I have tried to show through just this distinction, thereby preventing – what would otherwise unavoidably happen (through a transcendental subreption) – the ascription of objective reality to an idea that merely serves as a rule.

Now in order to determine the sense of this rule of pure reason appropriately, it must first be noted that it cannot say **what the object*d* is,** but only **how the empirical regress is to be instituted** so as to attain to the complete concept of the object.*e* For if the former were the case, then it would be a constitutive principle,*f* the likes of which is never possible on the basis of pure reason. Thus with it one can by no means have the intention to say that the series of conditions for a given conditioned is in itself finite or infinite; for in that way a mere idea of the absolute totality, which is produced only in the idea itself, would think an object that cannot be given in any experience, since an objective reality independent of empirical synthesis would be ascribed to a series of appearances. Thus the idea of reason will only prescribe a rule to the regressive synthesis in the series, a rule in accordance with which it proceeds from the conditioned, by means of all the conditions subordinated one to another, to the unconditioned, even though the latter will never be reached. For the absolutely unconditioned is not encountered in experience at all.

A510/B538

To this end, the first thing to do is to determine precisely the synthesis of a series insofar as it is never complete. With this aim one usually employs two expressions, which are supposed to draw a distinction, even though one does not know how to specify the ground of this distinction correctly. Mathematicians speak solely of a *progressus in infinitum.*g* But those who study concepts (philosophers) want, in place of this, to make the expression *progressus in indefinitum*b* the only valid one.75 Without stopping to examine the reservations to which this distinction has led, or to test whether their use has been good or fruitless, I will seek to determine these concepts precisely in relation to my own intentions.

A511/B539

One can rightly say of a straight line that it could be extended to in-

---

a *Princip*
b **Object**
c *Princip*
d *Object*
e *Object*
f *Principium*
g progress to infinity
h indefinite progress

finity, and here the distinction between the infinite and a progress of indeterminate length (*progressus in indefinitum*) would be an empty subtlety. For although when it is said, "Draw a line" it obviously sounds more correct to add *in indefinitum* than if it were said *in infinitum*, because the first means [a] no more than "Extend it as far as you **want**," but the second means [b] "You **ought** never to stop extending it" (which is not at all intended here); yet if we are talking only about what **can** be done, then the first expression is entirely correct, for you could always make it greater, to infinity. And this is also the situation in all cases where one is speaking only of a forward progress,[c] i.e., of a progress from the condition to the conditioned; this possible progress in the series of appearances goes to infinity. From one pair of parents you could progress in a descending line of generation without end, and you could also think

A 5 1 2 / B 5 4 0   that it might actually progress that way in the world. For here reason never needs an absolute totality in the series, because it is not presupposed as a condition as given (*datum*), but it is only added on as something conditioned, which is capable of being given (*dabile*), and this without end.

It is entirely otherwise with the problem how far does the regress extend when it ascends from the given conditioned to its conditions in the series: whether I can say here that there is **a regress to infinity** or only a regress extending **indeterminately far** (*in indefinitum*), and whether from human beings now living I can ascend to infinity in the series of their ancestors, or whether it can be said only that as far as I have gone back, there has never been an empirical ground for holding the series to be bounded anywhere, so that for every forefather I am justified in seeking, and at the same time bound to seek, still further for his ancestors, though not to presuppose them?

To this I say: If the whole was given in empirical intuition, then the regress in the series of its inner conditions goes to infinity. But if only one member of the series is given, from which the regress to an absolute totality is first of all to proceed, then only an indeterminate kind of

A 5 1 3 / B 5 4 1   regress (*in indefinitum*) takes place. Thus of the division of matter (of a body) that is given within certain boundaries, it must be said that it goes to infinity. For this matter is given in empirical intuition as a whole, and consequently with all its possible parts. Now since the condition of this whole is its part, and the condition of this part is a part made of parts, etc., and in this regress of decomposition an unconditioned (indivisible) member of this series of conditions is never encountered, not only is

---

[a] *bedeutet*
[b] *bedeutet*
[c] *Progressus*

there nowhere an empirical ground to stop the division, but the further members of the continuing division are themselves empirically given prior to this ongoing division, i.e., the division goes to infinity. On the contrary, the series of ancestors for a given human being is not given in its absolute totality in any possible experience, but the regress goes from each member of this generation to a higher one, so that no empirical boundary is to be encountered that would exhibit one member as absolutely unconditioned. But since the members that might supply the conditions for it nevertheless do not already lie in the empirical intuition of the whole prior to the regress, this regress does not go to infinity (by division of the given) but goes to an indeterminate distance, searching for more members for the given, which are once again always given only conditionally.

In neither of these two cases, that of the *regressus in infinitum* as well as in that of the *in indefinitum*, is the series of conditions regarded as being given as infinite in the object.*ᵃ* It is not things in themselves that are given, but only appearances, which, as conditions of one another, are given only in the regress itself. Thus the question is no longer how big this series of conditions is in itself – whether it is finite or infinite – for it is nothing in itself; rather, the question is how we are to institute the empirical regress and how far we are to continue it. And then there is a difference worth noting in regard to the rule to be followed in this progress. If the whole has been empirically given, then it is **possible** to go back **to infinity** in the series of its inner conditions. But if that whole is not given, but rather is first to be given only through an empirical regress, then I can say only that it is **possible** to progress to still higher conditions in the series **to infinity.** In the first case I could say: There are always more members there, and empirically given, than I reach through the regress (of decomposition); but in the second case I can say only: I can always go still further in the regress, because no member is empirically given as absolutely unconditioned, and thus a higher member may be admitted as possible and hence the inquiry after it may be admitted as necessary. In the former case it was necessary to **encounter** more members of the series, but in the latter case it is always necessary to **inquire** after more of them, because no experience is bounded absolutely. For you have either no perception that absolutely bounds your empirical regress, and then you must not hold your regress to be complete; or if you have such a perception bounding your series, then this cannot be a part of your regressive series (because that which **bounds** must be distinguished from **that which is bounded** by it), and so you have to continue your regress further to this condition, and so on.

A514/B542

A515/B543

ᵃ Object

The following section will place these remarks in a suitable light by giving them an application.

The Antinomy of Pure Reason
Section Nine
On the empirical use of the regulative principle[a] of reason, in regard to all cosmological ideas.

Since, as we have repeatedly shown, there is just as little transcendental use of pure concepts of understanding as there is of concepts of reason, because the absolute totality of series of conditions in the world of sense is based solely on a transcendental use of reason that demands this unconditioned completeness from what it presupposes is a thing in itself; and since the world of sense, however, contains nothing like that completeness, there can never again be an issue about the absolute magnitude of the series in this world, whether it might be bounded or **in itself** unbounded, but only about how far we should go back in the empirical regress when we trace experience back to its conditions, so that, following the rule of reason, we do not stop with any answer to its questions except that which is appropriate to the object.

Thus the only thing left to us is the **validity of the principle[b] of reason** as a rule for the **continuation** and magnitude of a possible experience, once its invalidity as a constitutive principle of appearances in themselves has been adequately demonstrated. If we can keep the former in view and beyond doubt, then the conflict of reason with itself will also be entirely at an end, since not only will the illusion that put reason at odds with itself have been done away with through its critical dissolution, but in place of it, that sense will have been uncovered in which reason agrees with itself, and whose misinterpretation was the sole cause of the conflict; and a principle that would otherwise be **dialectical** will be transformed into a **doctrinal** principle. In fact, if this principle can be preserved in its subjective signification for suitably determining the greatest possible use of the understanding in experience in regard to its objects, then that would be just as if the principle were (what it is impossible to get from pure reason) an axiom determining objects in themselves *a priori;* for even this could have no greater influence on the extension and correction of our cognition in regard to objects[c] of experience than by actively proving itself in the most extensive use of our understanding in experience.

A 516/ B 544

A 517/ B 545

[a] *Princip*
[b] *Princip*
[c] *Objecte*

I.
Resolution of the cosmological idea
of the totality of the composition of the appearances
of a world-whole.

Here, as well as in the case of the remaining cosmological questions, the ground of the regulative principle[a] of reason is the proposition that in the empirical regress there can be encountered **no experience of an absolute boundary,** and hence no experience of a condition as one that is **absolutely unconditioned empirically.** The reason for this, however, is that such an experience would have to contain in itself a bounding of appearance by nothing, or by the void, which the regress, carried on far enough, would have to encounter by means of a perception – which is impossible.

Now this proposition, which says only that in the empirical regress I can always attain only to a condition that must itself in turn be regarded as empirically conditioned, contains the rule *in termins*[b] that however far I may have come in the ascending series, I must always inquire after a higher member of the series, whether or not this member may come to be known to me through experience.   A 518/B 546

Now nothing further is required for the resolution of the first cosmological problem except to settle whether, in the regress to the unconditioned magnitude of the world-whole (in time and in space), this never bounded ascent can be called a **regress to infinity,** or only an **indeterminately continued regress** (*in indefinitum*).

The merely general representation of the series of all past states of the world, as well as of the things that simultaneously exist in the world's space, is nothing other than a possible empirical regress that I think, though still indeterminately, and through which alone there can arise the concept of such a series of conditions for a given perception.* Now I always have the world-whole only in concept, but by no means (as a whole) in intuition. Thus I cannot infer from its magnitude to the magnitude of the regress, and determine the latter according to the for-   A 519/B 547

---

* This world-series[c] can thus be neither bigger nor smaller than the possible empirical regress, on which alone its concept rests. And since this cannot yield a determinate infinite, nor yet something determinately finite (something absolutely bounded), it is clear from this that we can assume the magnitude of the world to be neither finite nor infinite, since the regress (through which this magnitude is represented) admits of neither of the two.   A 518/B 546

[a] *Princips*
[b] in its terms
[c] *Weltreihe*

mer, but rather it has to be through the magnitude of the empirical regress that I first make for myself a concept of the magnitude of the world. About this regress, however, I never know anything more than that from any given member of the series of conditions I must always proceed empirically to a higher (more remote) member. Thus by that means the magnitude of the whole of appearances is never determined absolutely; hence also one cannot say that this regress goes to infinity, because this would anticipate the members to which the regress has not yet attained, and would represent their multiplicity[a] as so great that no empirical synthesis can attain to it; consequently, it would **determine** (though only negatively) the magnitude of the world prior to the regress, which is impossible. For the latter (in its totality) is not given to me through any intuition, hence its magnitude is not given at all prior to the regress. Accordingly, we can say nothing at all about the magnitude of the world in itself, not even that in it there is the *regressus in infinitum*,[b] but rather we must seek the concept of its magnitude only according to the rule determining the empirical regress in it. But this rule says nothing more than that however far we may have come in the series of empirical conditions, we should never assume an absolute

A 520/ B 548   boundary, but rather we should subordinate every appearance as conditioned to another as its condition, and thus we must progress further to this condition; this is a *regressus in indefinitum*,[c] which, because it determines no magnitude in the object,[d] can be distinguished clearly enough from the regress *in infinitum*.

Accordingly, I cannot say the world is **infinite** in past time or in space. For such a concept of magnitude, as a given infinity, is empirical, hence it is absolutely impossible in regard to the world as an object of sense. I will also not say that the regress from a given perception to everything bounding it in a series, in space and in past time, goes **to infinity**; for this presupposes the infinite magnitude of the world; nor will I say that it is **finite**; for an absolute boundary is likewise empirically impossible. Accordingly, I will be able to say nothing about the whole object of experience (the world of sense), but only something about the rule in accord with which experience, suitably to its object, is to be instituted and continued.

Thus to the cosmological question about the magnitude of the world, the first and negative answer is: The world has no first beginning in time and no outermost boundary in space.

For in the opposite case, it would be bounded by empty time on the

A 521/ B 549   one side and by empty space on the other. Now since as appearance it

---

[a] *Menge*
[b] infinite regress
[c] indefinite regress
[d] *Object*

cannot in itself be either of these, because appearance is not a thing in itself, a perception of boundedness through absolutely empty time or empty space would have to be possible, through which these world-ends would have to be given in a possible experience. But such an experience, as completely empty of content, is impossible. Thus an absolute boundary of the world is empirically impossible, and hence also absolutely impossible.*

From this follows at the same time the **affirmative** answer: The regress in the series of appearances in the world, as a determination of the magnitude of the world, goes on *in indefinitum*, which is as much as to say that the world of sense has no absolute magnitude, but the empirical regress (through which alone it can be given on the side of its conditions) has its rule, namely always to progress from each member of the series, as a conditioned, to a still more remote member (whether by means of one's own experience, or the guiding thread of history, or the chain of effects and their causes), and nowhere to exceed the extension of the possible empirical use of one's understanding, since this extension is the sole and proper business of reason in its principles.*a* A 522 / B 550

What is not prescribed here is a determinate empirical regress that continues in a certain kind of appearance without ever ceasing, e.g., that from a living human being one must always ascend in the series of his ancestors without ever expecting a first pair, or in the series of bodies in the world without admitting an outermost sun; on the contrary, what is required is only the progress from appearances to appearances, even if they should not yield any actual perception (if this perception is too weak in degree to become an experience for our consciousness), because despite this they would still belong to possible experience.[76]

Every beginning is in time, and every boundary of the extended is in space. Space and time, however, are only in the world of sense. Hence appearances are **in the world** only conditionally, **the world** itself is neither conditioned nor bounded in an unconditional way.

Just for this reason, and since the world cannot be given **as a whole,** and even the series of conditions for a given conditioned, as a world-series, **cannot be given as a whole,** the concept of the magnitude of

---

* One will note that the proof is carried on here in an entirely different way A 521 / B 549 from the dogmatic one in the antithesis of the first antinomy. There, in accordance with the common and dogmatic way of representing it, we let the world of sense count as a thing whose totality is given in itself prior to any regress, and, if it did not occupy all space and all time, we denied it any determinate place in space and time. Hence the conclusion was different from this one too: namely, the actual infinity of the world was inferred.

a *Principien*

A 523/ B 551 the world is given only through the regress, and not given prior to it in a collective intuition. But the regress consists only in a **determining** of the magnitude, and thus it does not give a **determinate** concept, a concept of a magnitude that would be infinite in regard to a certain measure; thus it does not go to infinity (given, as it were), but goes only indeterminately far, so as to give a magnitude (of experience) that first becomes actual through this regress.

II.
Resolution of the cosmological idea of the totality of division of a given whole in intuition.

If I divide a whole that is given in intuition, then I go from a conditioned to the conditions of its possibility. The division of the parts (*subdivisio* or *decompositio*) is a regress in the series of these conditions. The absolute totality of this **series** would be given only when and if the regress could attain to **simple** parts. But if each of the parts in a continuously progressing decomposition is once again divisible, then the division, i.e., the regress from the conditioned to its condition, goes *in infinitum*;[a] for the conditions (the parts) are contained in the conditioned itself, and since this conditioned is given as a whole in an intuition enclosed within its boundaries, the conditions are all given along with it. The regress thus may not be called merely a regress *in indefinitum*, as only the previous cosmological idea allowed, where I was to proceed from the conditioned to conditions outside it, which were not given simultaneously with it, but were first added to it in the empirical regress. Despite this, it is by no means permitted to say of such a whole, which is divisible to infinity, that **it consists of infinitely many parts.** For though all the parts are contained in the intuition of the whole, the **whole division** is **not** contained in it; this division consists only in the progressive decomposition, or in the regress itself, which first makes the series actual. Now since this regress is infinite, all its members (parts) to which it has attained are of course contained in the whole as an **aggregate,** but the whole **series** of the **division** is not, since it is infinite successively and never is **as a whole;** consequently, the regress cannot exhibit any infinite multiplicity[b] or the taking together of this multiplicity into one whole.

A 524/ B 552

This general reminder is, first, very easily applied to space. Every space intuited within its boundaries is such a whole, whose parts in every decomposition are in turn spaces, and it is therefore divisible to infinity.

[a] to infinity
[b] *Menge*

Section IX. On the empirical use of the regulative principle

From this there also follows quite naturally the second application, to an external appearance enclosed within its boundaries (a body). Its division is grounded on the divisibility of space, which constitutes the possibility of the body as an extended whole. The latter is thus divisible to infinity, without, however, therefore consisting of infinitely many parts.

To be sure, it appears that since a body has to be represented as a substance in space, it is to be distinguished from a space as far as the law of the divisibility of space is concerned; for one can in any case concede that the decomposition of the latter could never do away with all composition, since then every space, having nothing else that is self-subsistent, would cease to be (which is impossible); yet it does not seem to be compatible with the concept of a substance – which is really supposed to be the subject of all composition, and has to remain in its elements even if its connection in space, by which it constitutes a body, were removed – that if all composition of matter were removed in thought, then nothing at all would remain. Yet with that which is called substance **in appearance** things are not as they would be with a thing in itself which one thought through pure concepts of the understanding. The former is not an absolute subject, but only a persisting image of sensibility, and it is nothing but intuition, in which nothing uncondi- tioned is to be encountered anywhere.

But now although this rule of progress to infinity applies without any doubt to the subdivision of an appearance as a mere filling of space, it cannot hold if we want to stretch it to cover the multiplicity of parts already detached with certainty in a given whole, constituting thereby a *quantum discretum.*[a,77] To assume that in every whole that is articulated into members[b] (organized), every part is once again articulated, and that in such a way, by dismantling the parts to infinity, one always encounters new complex parts[c] – in a word, to assume that the whole is articulated to infinity – this is something that cannot be thought at all, even though the parts of matter, reached by its decomposition to infinity, could be articulated. For the infinity of the division of a given appearance in space is grounded solely on the fact that through this infinity merely its divisibility, i.e., a multiplicity of parts, which is in itself absolutely indeterminate, is given, but the parts themselves are given and determined only through the subdivision – in short, on the fact that the whole is not in itself already divided up. Hence the division can determine a multiplicity as far as one wants to proceed in the regress of the division. In the case of an organic body articulated to infinity, on the contrary, the whole is represented through this very con-

[a] discrete quantity
[b] *gegliedert*
[c] *Kunstteile*

cept as already divided up, and a multiplicity of parts, determinate in itself but infinite, is encountered prior to every regress in the division – through which one contradicts oneself, since this infinite development is regarded as a series that is never to be completed (as infinite) and yet as one that is completed when it is taken together. The infinite division indicates only the appearance as *quantum continuum*,[a] and is inseparable from the filling of space; for the ground of its infinite divisibility lies precisely in that. But as soon as something is assumed as a *quantum discretum*,[b] the multiplicity of units in it is determined; hence it is always equal to a number. Thus only experience can settle how far the organization in an articulated body may go; and even if it was certain to attain to no inorganic parts, such parts must nevertheless at least lie within a possible experience. But how far the transcendental division of an appearance in general may reach is not a matter of experience at all, but it is rather a principle[c] of reason never to take the empirical regress in the composition of what is extended, in conformity with the nature of this appearance, to be absolutely complete.

A 528 / B 556

* * *

Concluding remark
on the resolution of the mathematical-transcendental
ideas, and preamble to the resolution of the
dynamic-transcendental ideas.[78]

When we represented the antinomy of pure reason in a table through all the transcendental ideas, where we showed the ground of this conflict and the only means of removing it – which consisted in declaring both of the opposed assertions to be false – we in all cases represented the conditions for their conditioned as belonging to relations of space and time, which is the usual presupposition of common human understanding, on which, therefore, the conflict entirely rested. In this respect all dialectical representations of totality in the series of conditions for a given conditioned were of the **same kind**[d] throughout. There was always a series, in which the condition was connected with the conditioned as a member of the series, and thereby was **homogeneous**,[e] since the regress is never thought of as completed, or else, if this were to happen, a member conditioned in itself would have to be falsely as-

---

[a] continuous quantity
[b] discrete quantity
[c] *Principium*
[d] *von gleicher Art*
[e] *gleichartig*

sumed to be a first, and hence unconditioned member. Thus it would not always be the object,[a] i.e., the conditioned, but the series of conditions for it, which was so considered merely in its magnitude; and then the difficulty – which could not be removed by any compromise, but only by completely cutting the knot – consisted in the fact that reason made it either **too long** or **too short** for the understanding, so that the understanding could never come out equal to reason's idea.

A529/B557

But in this we have overlooked an essential distinction governing the objects,[b] i.e., among the concepts of the understanding which reason aspires to raise to ideas, namely, that according to our table of categories two of them signify **mathematical,** but the other two a **dynamical** synthesis of appearances. Until now this was all right, since just as in the general representation of all transcendental ideas we always stayed only **within appearance,** so in the two mathematical-transcendental ideas we had no **object** other than one in appearance. Now, however, that we are progressing to **dynamical** concepts of the understanding, insofar as they are to be suited to the idea of reason, this distinction comes to be important, and opens up for us an entirely new prospect in regard to the suit in which reason has become implicated; whereas up to now it has been **dismissed** as based on false presuppositions on both sides, now perhaps in the dynamical antinomy there is a presupposition that can coexist with the pretensions of reason, and since the judge may make good the defects in legal grounds that have been misconstrued on both sides, the case can be **mediated** to the satisfaction of both parties, which could not be done in the controversy about the mathematical antinomy.

A530/B558

The series of conditions are obviously all homogeneous to the extent that one looks solely at how far they **reach:** whether they conform to the idea, or are too big or too small for it. Yet the concept of understanding grounding these ideas contains either solely a **synthesis of homogeneous things** (which is presupposed in the case of every magnitude, in its composition as well as its division), or else a synthesis of **things not homogeneous,** which must be at least admitted in the case of the dynamical synthesis, in causal connection as well as in the connection of the necessary with the contingent.

Hence it is that in the mathematical connection of series of appearances, none other than a **sensible** condition can enter, i.e., only one that is itself a part of the series; whereas the dynamic series of sensible conditions, on the contrary, allows a further condition different in kind, one that is not a part of the series but, as merely **intelligible,** lies outside the series; in this way reason can be given satisfaction and the unconditioned can be posited prior to appearances without confounding

A531/B559

[a] *Object*
[b] *Objecte*

the series of appearances, which is always conditioned, and without any violation of principles of the understanding.

Now by the fact that the dynamical ideas allow a condition of appearances outside the series of appearances, i.e., a condition that is not appearance, something happens that is entirely different from the result of the mathematical antinomy. In the latter it was the cause of the fact that both dialectically opposed assertions had to be declared false. The thoroughly conditioned character of what is in the dynamical series, on the contrary, which is inseparable from them as appearances, is connected with a condition that is empirically unconditioned, but also **nonsensible,** which gives satisfaction to the **understanding** on one side and to **reason** on the other,* and while the dialectical arguments that seek unconditioned totality on the one side or the other collapse, A532/B560 the rational propositions, on the contrary, taken in such a corrected significance, may **both be true;** which could never have occurred with the cosmological ideas dealing merely with mathematically unconditioned unity, because with them there is no condition of the series of appearances that is not itself also an appearance, constituting as such a further member of the series.

III.
Resolution of the cosmological idea*a*
of the totality of the derivation of occurrences in
the world
from their causes.

In respect of what happens, one can think of causality in only two ways: either according to **nature** or from **freedom.** The first is the connection of a state with a preceding one in the world of sense upon which that state follows according to a rule. Now since the **causality** of appearances rests on temporal conditions, and the preceding state, if it always existed, could not have produced any effect that first arose in time, the causality of the cause of what happens or arises has also

A531/B559 * For the understanding does not permit among **appearances** any condition that is itself empirically unconditioned. But if an **intelligible** condition, which therefore does not belong to the series of appearances as a member, may be thought for a conditioned (in appearance), without thereby interrupting in the least the series of empirical conditions, then such a condition could be admitted as **empirically unconditioned,** in such a way that no violation of the empirically continuous regress would occur anywhere.

a *Ideen* (plural); since the headings of the other three sections give this word in the singular, we do the same here.

arisen, and according to the principle of understanding it in turn needs a cause.*

By freedom in the cosmological sense, on the contrary, I understand A533/B561 the faculty of beginning a state **from itself,** *b* the causality of which does not in turn stand under another cause determining it in time in accordance with the law of nature. Freedom in this signification is a pure transcendental idea, which, first, contains nothing borrowed from experience, and second, the object of which also cannot be given determinately in any experience, because it is a universal law – even of the possibility of all experience – that everything that happens must have a cause, and hence that the causality of the cause, as **itself having happened** or arisen, must in turn have a cause; through this law, then, the entire field of experience, however far it may reach, is transformed into the sum total of mere nature. But since in such a way no absolute totality of conditions in causal relations*c* is forthcoming, reason creates the idea of a spontaneity, which could start to act from itself, without needing to be preceded by any other cause that in turn determines it to action according to the law of causal connection.

It is especially noteworthy that it is this **transcendental** idea of **freedom** on which the practical concept of freedom is grounded, and the former constitutes the real moment of the difficulties in the latter,*d* which have long surrounded the question of its possibility. **Freedom in** A534/B562 **the practical sense** is the independence of the power of choice from **necessitation** by impulses of sensibility. For a power of choice is **sensible** insofar as it is **pathologically affected** (through moving-causes of sensibility); it is called an **animal** power of choice (*arbitrium brutum*) if it can be **pathologically necessitated.** The human power of choice is indeed an *arbitrium sensitivum,e* yet not *brutumf* but *liberum,g* because sensibility does not render its action necessary, but in the human being there is a faculty of determining oneself from oneself, independently of necessitation by sensible impulses.[79]

It is easy to see that if all causality in the world of sense were mere nature, then every occurrence would be determined in time by another in accord with necessary laws, and hence – since appearances, insofar as they determine the power of choice, would have to render every action

---

a Kant notes: "The connection of effects and causes is not at all suited to things outside the world of sense; for how can God be a cause, be a being?" (E CLXXII, p. 51; 23:41)

b *von selbst*

c *Kausalverhältnisse*

d *dieser,* a feminine dative pronoun, which therefore agrees only with "freedom" in this context; if the text were emended to read *diesem,* it would refer to "concept."

e sensible power of choice

f animal

g free

necessary as their natural consequence – the abolition of transcendental freedom would also simultaneously eliminate all practical freedom. For the latter presupposes that although something has not happened, it nevertheless **ought** to have happened, and its cause in appearance was thus not so determining that there is not a causality in our power of choice such that, independently of those natural causes and even opposed to their power and influence, it might produce something determined in the temporal order in accord with empirical laws, and hence begin a series of occurrences **entirely from itself**.

A335/B363 Here, then, as is generally found in the conflicts of reason with itself when it ventures beyond the boundaries of possible experience, the problem is really not **physiological** but **transcendental**. Hence the question of the possibility of freedom does indeed beset psychology, but since it rests merely on dialectical arguments of pure reason, its solution must be solely the business of transcendental philosophy. Now in order[a] to put transcendental philosophy, which cannot decline to provide a satisfying answer here, in a position to give one, I must first seek, through the following remark, to determine more closely its procedure in dealing with this problem.

If appearances were things in themselves, and hence space and time were the forms of things in themselves, then the conditions would always belong to one and the same series as the conditioned, and from this there would also arise in the present case the antinomy common to all transcendental ideas, that this series must unavoidably turn out to be either too large or too small for the understanding. But the dynamical concepts of reason, with which we are concerned in this and the following number, have the peculiarity that since they do not consider their object as a magnitude but have to do only with its **existence**, one can thus abstract from the magnitude of the series of conditions, and

A336/B564 with them it is merely a matter of the dynamical relation[b] of condition to conditioned; thus the difficulty we encounter in the question about nature and freedom is only whether freedom is possible anywhere at all, and if it is, whether it can exist together with the universality of the natural law of causality, hence whether it is a correct disjunctive proposition that every effect in the world must arise **either** from nature **or** freedom, or whether instead **both**, each in a different relation, might be able to take place simultaneously in one and the same occurrence. The correctness of the principle of the thoroughgoing connection of all occurrences in the world of sense according to invariable natural laws is already confirmed as a principle of the transcendental analytic and will suffer violation. Thus the only question is whether, despite this, in re-

[a] Fifth edition: "And in order ... "
[b] *Verhältnis*

534

regard to the very same effect that is determined by nature, freedom might not also take place, or is this entirely excluded through that inviolable rule? And here the common but deceptive presupposition of the **absolute reality** of appearance immediately shows its disadvantageous influence for confusing reason. For if appearances are things in themselves, then freedom cannot be saved. Then nature is the completely determining cause, sufficient in itself, of every occurrence, and the condition for an occurrence is always contained only in the series of appearances that, along with their effect, are necessary under the law of nature. If, on the other hand, appearances do not count for any more A 537/ B 565 than they are in fact, namely, not for things in themselves but only for mere representations connected in accordance with empirical laws, then they themselves must have grounds that are not appearances. Such an intelligible cause, however, will not be determined in its causality by appearances, even though its effects appear and so can be determined through other appearances. Thus the intelligible cause, with its causality, is outside the series; its effects, on the contrary, are encountered in the series of empirical conditions. The effect can therefore be regarded as free in regard to its intelligible cause, and yet simultaneously, in regard to appearances, as their result according to the necessity of nature; this is a distinction which, if it is presented in general and entirely abstractly, must appear extremely subtle and obscure, but in its application it will be enlightening. Here I have only wanted to note that since the thoroughgoing connection of all appearances in one context of nature is an inexorable law, it necessarily would have to bring down all freedom if one were stubbornly to insist on the reality of appearances. Hence even those who follow the common opinion about this matter have never succeeded in uniting nature and freedom with one another.

The possibility of causality through freedom unified with   A 538/ B 566 the universal law of natural necessity.[80]

I call **intelligible** that in an object of sense which is not itself appearance. Accordingly, if that which must be regarded as appearance in the world of sense has in itself a faculty which is not an object of intuition through which it can be the cause of appearances, then one can consider the **causality** of this being in two aspects, as **intelligible** in its **action** as a thing in itself, and as **sensible** in the **effects** of that action as an appearance in the world of sense. Of the faculty of such a subject we would accordingly form an empirical and at the same time an intellectual concept of its causality, both of which apply to one and the same effect.[a] Think-

---

[a] Kant adds in his copy of the first edition: "Transcendental definitions: The causality of representations of a being in respect of the objects of them is life. The determinability of the power of representation to this causality is the faculty of desire. This power of

ing of the faculty of an object of sense in this double aspect does not contradict any of the concepts we have to form of appearances and of a possible experience. For since these appearances, because they are not things in themselves, must be grounded in a transcendental object determining them as mere representations, nothing hinders us from ascribing to this transcendental object, apart from the property through which it appears, also another **causality** that is not appearance, even though its **effect** is encountered in appearance. But every effective cause must have a **character,** i.e., a law of its causality, without which it would not be a cause at all. And then for a subject of the world of sense we would have first an **empirical character,** through which its actions, as appearances, would stand through and through in connection with other appearances in accordance with constant natural laws, from which, as their conditions, they could be derived; and thus, in combination with these other appearances, they would constitute members of a single series of the natural order. Yet second, one would also have to allow this subject an **intelligible character,** through which it is indeed the cause of those actions as appearances, but which does not stand under any conditions of sensibility and is not itself appearance. The first one could call the character of such a thing in appearance, the second its character as a thing in itself.

Now this acting subject, in its intelligible character, would not stand under any conditions of time, for time is only the condition of appearances but not of things in themselves.[81] In that subject no **action** would **arise** or **perish,** hence it would not be subject to the law of everything alterable in its time-determination that everything **that happens** must find its cause **in the appearances** (of the previous state). In a word, its causality, insofar as it is intellectual, would not stand in the series of empirical conditions that makes the occurrence in the world of sense necessary. This intelligible character could, of course, never be known[a] immediately, because we cannot perceive anything except insofar as it appears, but it would have to be **thought** in conformity with the empirical character, just as in general we must ground appearances in thought through a transcendental object, even though we know nothing about it as it is in itself.

In its empirical character, this subject, as appearance, would thus be

---

representation, if it is reason, hence is the determinability of its causality in respect of objects, i.e., its faculty of desire [is] will. If pure reason has causality, then the will is a pure will, and its causality is called freedom.

"[Now] we cannot cognize [*a priori*] any causes, nor in general any intuitions corresponding to the categories, or relationships between them, but we must take all these from experience. Hence whether freedom is possible cannot be settled." (E CLXXIII, pp. 51–2; 23:41)

[a] *gekannt*

subject to the causal connection, in accordance with all the laws of determination; and to that extent it would be nothing but a part of the world of sense, whose effects, like those of any other appearance, would flow inevitably from nature. Just as external appearances influence it, as far as its empirical character, i.e., the law of its causality, is known through experience, all its actions would have to admit of explanation in accordance with natural laws, and all the requisites for a perfect and necessary determination of them would have to be encountered in a possible experience.

But in its intelligible character (even though we can have nothing   A 541 / B 569
more than merely the general concept of it), this subject would nevertheless have to be declared free of all influences of sensibility and determination by appearances; and since, in it, insofar as it is a **noumenon,** nothing **happens,** thus no alteration requiring a dynamical time-determination is demanded, and hence no connection with appearances as causes is encountered in its actions, this active being would to this extent be independent and free of all the natural necessity present solely in the world of sense. Of it one would say quite correctly that it begins its effects in the sensible world **from itself,** without its action beginning **in it** itself; and this would hold without allowing effects in the world of sense to begin from themselves, because in this world they are always determined beforehand by empirical conditions in the preceding time, but only by means of the empirical character (which is a mere appearance of the intelligible character), and they are possible only as a continuation of the series of natural causes. Thus freedom and nature, each in its full significance, would both be found in the same actions, simultaneously and without any contradiction, according to whether one compares them with their intelligible or their sensible cause.

Clarification   A 542 / B 570
of the cosmological idea of a freedom in combination with
the universal natural necessity.*

I have found it good first to sketch the silhouette of a solution to our transcendental problem, so that one might better survey the course of reason in solving it. Now we will set out separately the decisive mo-

---

a Kant's notes: "What speculative philosophy could not succeed at, bringing reason out of the field of sensibility to something real outside it, practical reason is able to do, namely, giving an existence that is not sensible, [and] through laws that are grounded on reason. This is morality, if one admits it through freedom.

"Otherwise we would assume that there is no intuition at all without [the] senses and hence also no things outside the objects of sense belonging to intuition." (E CLXXIV, p. 52; 23:41–2)

ments on which the solution really depends, and take each particular moment into consideration.

The law of nature that everything that happens has a cause, that since the causality of this cause, i.e., the **action,** precedes in time and in respect of an effect that has **arisen** cannot have been always but must have **happened,** and so must also have had its cause among appearances, through which it is determined, and consequently that all occurrences are empirically determined in a natural order – this law, through which alone appearances can first constitute one **nature** and furnish objects of one experience, is a law of the understanding, from which under no pretext can any departure be allowed or any appearance be exempted; because otherwise one would put this appearance outside of all possible experience, thereby distinguishing it from all objects of possible experience and making it into a mere thought-entity and a figment of the brain.

A 543 / B 571

But although it looks as if there is solely a chain of causes, permitting no **absolute totality** at all in the regress to their conditions, this reservation does not detain us at all; for it has already been removed in our general judgment on the antinomy of reason occurring when reason proceeds to the unconditioned in the series of appearances. If we would give in to the deception of transcendental realism, then neither nature nor freedom would be left. Here the question is only: If in the whole series of all occurrences one recognizes purely[a] natural necessity, is it nevertheless possible to regard the same occurrence, which on the one hand is a mere effect of nature, as on the other hand an effect of freedom; or will a direct contradiction between these two kinds of causality be found?

Among the causes in appearance there can surely be nothing that could begin a series absolutely and from itself. Every action, as appearance, insofar as it produces an occurrence, is itself an occurrence, or event, which presupposes another state in which its cause is found; and thus everything that happens is only a continuation of the series, and no beginning that would take place from itself is possible in it. Thus in the temporal succession all actions of natural causes are themselves in turn effects, which likewise presuppose their causes in the time-series. An **original** action, through which something happens that previously was not, is not to be expected from the causal connection of appearances.

A 544 / B 572

But then if the effects are appearances, is it also necessary that the causality of their cause, which (namely, the cause) is also appearance, must be solely empirical?[82] Is it not rather possible that although for every effect in appearance there is required a connection[b] with its cause in accordance with laws of empirical causality, this empirical causality

[a] *lauter*
[b] *Verknüpfung*

538

itself, without the least interruption of its connection[a] with natural causes, could nevertheless be an effect of a causality that is not empirical, but rather intelligible, i.e., an original action of a cause in regard to appearances, which to that extent is not appearance but in accordance with this faculty intelligible, even though otherwise, as a link in the chain of nature, it must be counted entirely as belonging to the world of sense?

We need the principle[b] of the causality of appearances in order to be able to seek for and specify the natural conditions, i.e., causes in appearance, for natural occurrences. If this is conceded, and not weakened by any exceptions, then the understanding, which in its empirical use sees nothing but nature in all events and is justified in doing so, has everything it could demand, and physical explanations proceed on their own course unhindered. Now this is not in the least impaired, supposing also that it is in any case merely invented, if one assumes that among natural causes there are also some that have a faculty that is only intelligible, in that its determination to action never rests on empirical conditions but on mere grounds of the understanding, as long as the **action in the appearance** of this cause accords with all the laws of empirical causality. For in this way the acting subject, as *causa phaenomenon,*[c] would have all its actions linked with inseparable dependence to the natural chain of causes, and only the *phaenomenon* of this subject (with all its causality in appearance) would contain certain conditions that, if one would ascend from empirical objects to transcendental ones, would have to be regarded as merely intelligible. For if we follow the rule of nature only in that which might be the cause among appearances, then we need not worry about what sort of ground is thought for these appearances and their connection in the transcendental subject, which is empirically unknown to us. This intelligible ground does not touch the empirical questions at all, but may have to do merely with thinking in the pure understanding; and, although the effects of this thinking and acting of the pure understanding are encountered among appearances, these must nonetheless be able to be explained perfectly from their causes in appearance, in accord with natural laws, by following its merely empirical character as the supreme ground of explanation; and the intelligible character, which is the transcendental cause of the former, is passed over as entirely unknown, except insofar as it is indicated through the empirical character as only its sensible sign. Let us apply this to experience. The human being is one of the appearances in the world of sense, and to that extent also one of the natural causes whose

A545/B573

A546/B574

[a] *Zusammenhang*
[b] *Satzes*
[c] phenomenal cause

causality must stand under empirical laws. As such he must accordingly also have an empirical character, just like all other natural things. We notice it through powers and faculties which it expresses in its effects. In the case of lifeless nature and nature having merely animal life, we find no ground for thinking of any faculty which is other than sensibly conditioned. Yet the human being, who is otherwise acquainted with the whole of nature solely through sense, knows*a* himself also through pure apperception, and indeed in actions and inner determinations which cannot be accounted at all among*b* impressions of sense; he obviously is in one part phenomenon, but in another part, namely in regard to certain faculties, he is a merely intelligible object, because the actions of this object cannot at all be ascribed*c* to the receptivity of sensibility. We call these faculties understanding and reason; chiefly the latter is distinguished quite properly and preeminently from all empirically conditioned powers, since it considers its objects merely according to ideas and in accordance with them determines the understanding, which then makes an empirical use of its own concepts (even the pure ones).

A547/B575

Now that this reason has causality,*d* or that we can at least represent something of the sort in it, is clear from the **imperatives** that we propose*e* as rules to our powers of execution in everything practical.[83] The **ought** expresses a species of necessity and a connection with grounds which does not occur anywhere else in the whole of nature. In nature the understanding can cognize only **what exists,** or has been, or will be. It is impossible that something in it **ought to be** other than what, in all these time-relations,*f* it in fact is; indeed, the **ought,** if one has merely the course of nature before one's eyes, has no significance whatever. We cannot ask at all what ought to happen in nature, any more than we can ask what properties a circle ought to have; but we must rather ask what happens in nature, or what properties the circle has.

Now this "ought" expresses a possible action, the ground of which is nothing other than a mere concept, whereas the ground of a merely natural action must always be an appearance. Now of course the action must be possible under natural conditions if the ought is directed to it; but these natural conditions do not concern the determination of the power of choice itself, but only its effect and result in appearance. How-

A548/B576

---

a *erkennt*

b *gar nicht zum . . . zählen kann*

c *gar nicht zur . . . gezählt werden kann*

d Kant notes: "i.e., is the cause of actuality of its objects [*Objecte*]. This causality is called the will. But in transcendental philosophy one abstracts from the will." (E CLXXV, p. 52; 23:50)

e *aufgeben*

f *Zeitverhältnisse*

ever many natural grounds or sensible stimuli there may be that impel me to **will,** they cannot produce the **ought** but only a willing that is yet far from necessary but rather always conditioned, over against which the ought that reason pronounces sets a measure and goal, indeed, a prohibition and authorization.[a] Whether it is an object of mere sensibility (the agreeable) or even of pure reason (the good), reason does not give in to those grounds which are empirically given, and it does not follow the order of things as they are presented in intuition, but with complete spontaneity it makes its own order according to ideas, to which it fits the empirical conditions and according to which it even declares actions to be necessary that yet **have not occurred** and perhaps will not occur, nevertheless presupposing of all such actions that reason could have causality in relation to them; for without that, it would not expect its ideas to have effects in experience.

Now let us stop at this point and assume it is at least possible that reason actually does have causality in regard to appearances: then even though it is reason, it must nevertheless exhibit an empirical character, because every cause presupposes a rule according to which certain appearances follow as effects, and every rule requires a uniformity in its effects, grounding the concept of a cause (as a faculty), which, insofar as it must come to light from mere appearances, we could call the empirical character, which is constant, while its effects appear in alterable shapes, according to the differences among the conditions that accompany and in part limit it. A 549/ B 577

Thus every human being has an empirical character for his power of choice, which is nothing other than a certain causality of his reason, insofar as in its effects in appearance this reason exhibits a rule, in accordance with which one could derive[b] the rational grounds and the actions themselves according to their kind and degree, and estimate[c] the subjective principles[d] of his power of choice. Because this empirical character itself must be drawn from appearances as effect, and from the rule which experience provides, all the actions of the human being in appearance are determined in accord with the order of nature by his empirical character and the other cooperating causes; and if we could investigate all the appearances of his power of choice down to their basis, then there would be no human action that we could not predict with certainty, and recognize as necessary given its preceding conditions. Thus in regard to this empirical character there is no freedom, and according to this character we can consider the human being solely A 550/ B 578

[a] *Ansehen*
[b] *abnehmen*
[c] *beurtheilen*
[d] *Principien*

by **observing,** and, as happens in anthropology, by trying to investigate the moving causes of his actions physiologically.

But if we consider the very same actions in relation to reason, not, to be sure, in relation to speculative reason, in order to **explain** them as regards their origin, but insofar as reason is the cause of **producing** them by themselves – in a word, if we compare them with reason in a **practical** respect – then we find a rule and order that is entirely other than the natural order. For perhaps everything that **has happened** in the course of nature, and on empirical grounds inevitably had to happen, nevertheless **ought not to have happened.** At times, however, we find, or at least believe we have found, that the ideas of reason have actually proved their causality in regard to the actions of human beings as appearances, and that therefore these actions have occurred[a] not through empirical causes, no, but because they were determined by grounds of reason.

A551/B579 Suppose now that one could say reason has causality in regard to appearance; could reason's action then be called free even though in its empirical character (in the mode of sense)[b] it is all precisely determined and necessary? The empirical character is once again determined in the intelligible character (in the mode of thought).[c] We are not acquainted with the latter, but it is indicated through appearances, which really give only the mode of sense (the empirical character) for immediate cognition.* Now the action, insofar as it is to be attributed to the mode of thought as its cause, nevertheless does not follow from it in accord with empirical laws, i.e., in such a way that it is **preceded** by the conditions of pure reason, but only their effects in the appearance of inner sense **precede** it. Pure reason, as a merely intelligible faculty, is not subject to the form of time, and hence not subject to the conditions of the temporal sequence. The causality of reason in the intelligible character **does not arise** or start working at a certain time in producing an effect.

A552/B580 For then it would itself be subject to the natural law of appearances, to the extent that this law determines causal series in time, and its causal-

---

A551/B579 * The real morality of actions (their merit and guilt), even that of our own conduct, therefore remains entirely hidden from us. Our imputations can be referred only to the empirical character. How much of it is to be ascribed to mere nature and innocent defects of temperament or to its happy constitution (*merito fortunae*)[d] this no one can discover,[e] and hence no one can judge it with complete justice.

---

[a] *geschehen*
[b] *Sinnesart*
[c] *Denkungsart*
[d] to the merit of fortune
[e] *ergründen*

ity would then be nature and not freedom. Thus we could say that if reason can have causality in regard to appearances, then it is a faculty **through** which the sensible condition of an empirical series of effects first begins. For the condition that lies in reason is not sensible and does not itself begin. Accordingly, there takes place here what we did not find in any empirical series: that the **condition** of a successive series of occurrences could itself be empirically unconditioned. For here the condition is **outside** the series of appearances (in the intelligible) and hence not subject to any sensible condition or to any determination of time through any passing cause.

Nevertheless, this very same cause in another relation also belongs to the series of appearances. The human being himself is an appearance. His power of choice has an empirical character, which is the (empirical) cause of all his actions. There is not one of these conditions determining human beings according to this character which is not contained in the series of natural effects and does not obey the laws of nature according to which no empirically unconditioned causality is present among the things that happen in time. Hence no given action (since it can be perceived only as appearance) can begin absolutely from itself. A553/B581 But of reason one cannot say that before the state in which it determines the power of choice, another state precedes in which this state itself is determined. For since reason itself is not an appearance and is not subject at all to any conditions of sensibility, no temporal sequence takes place in it even as to its causality, and thus the dynamical law of nature, which determines the temporal sequence according to rules, cannot be applied to it.

Reason is thus the persisting condition of all voluntary actions under which the human being appears. Even before it happens, every one of these actions is determined beforehand in the empirical character of the human being. In regard to the intelligible character, of which the empirical one is only the sensible schema, no **before** or **after** applies, and every action, irrespective of the temporal relation in which it stands to other appearances, is the immediate effect of the intelligible character of pure reason; reason therefore acts freely, without being determined dynamically by external or internal grounds temporally preceding it in the chain of natural causes, and this freedom of reason can not only be regarded negatively, as independence from empirical conditions (for then the faculty of reason would cease to be a cause of appearances), but also indicated positively by a faculty of beginning a series of occur- A554/B582 rences from itself, in such a way that in reason itself nothing begins, but as the unconditioned condition of every voluntary action, it allows of no condition prior to it in time, whereas its effect begins in the series of appearances, but can never constitute an absolutely first beginning in this series.

In order to clarify the regulative principle*a* of reason through an example of its empirical use – not in order to confirm it (for such proofs are unworkable for transcendental propositions) – one may take a voluntary action, e.g. a malicious lie, through which a person*b* has brought about a certain confusion in society; and one may first investigate its moving causes, through which it arose, judging on that basis how the lie and its consequences could be*c* imputed to the person. With this first intent one goes into the sources of the person's empirical character, seeking them in a bad upbringing, bad company, and also finding them in the wickedness of a natural temper*d* insensitive to shame, partly in carelessness and thoughtlessness; in so doing one does not leave out of account the occasioning causes. In all this one proceeds as with any investigation in the series of determining causes for a given natural effect.

A555/B583   Now even if one believes the action to be determined by these causes, one nonetheless blames the agent, and not on account of his unhappy natural temper, not on account of the circumstances influencing him, not even on account of the life he has led previously; for one presupposes that it can be entirely set aside how that life was constituted, and that the series of conditions that transpired might not have been, but rather that this deed could be regarded as entirely unconditioned in regard to the previous state, as though with that act the agent had started a series of consequences entirely from himself. This blame is grounded on the law of reason, which regards reason as a cause that, regardless of all the empirical conditions just named, could have and ought to have determined the conduct of the person to be other than it is. And indeed one regards the causality of reason not as a mere concurrence with other causes,*e* but as complete in itself, even if sensuous incentives were not for it but were indeed entirely against it; the action is ascribed to the agent's intelligible character: now, in the moment when he lies, it is entirely his fault; hence reason, regardless of all empirical conditions of the deed, is fully free, and this deed is to be attributed entirely to its failure to act.*f*

In this judgment of imputation, it is easy to see that one has the thoughts that reason is not affected at all by that sensibility, that it does

---

a *Princip*

b *Mensch*

c *könne* (singular present subjunctive, indicating that the lie is the subject); in the first edition, the text reads *können* (plural, indicating that the consequences as well are included in the subject of the verb along with the lie).

d *Naturells*

e *Konkurrenz*. Although in modern German this means "competition" Kant used this term as an equivalent of *concursus*; in a theological context, it means divine assistance.

f *ihrer Unterlassung;* "reason" is the only grammatically possible antecedent of the possessive pronoun.

not alter (even if its appearances, namely the way in which it exhibits its
effects, do alter), that in it no state precedes that determines the following one, and hence that reason does not belong at all in the series of
sensible conditions which make appearances necessary in accordance
with natural laws. It, reason, is present to all the actions of human beings in all conditions of time, and is one and the same, but it is not itself in time, and never enters into any new state in which it previously
was not; in regard to a new state, reason is **determining** but not **determinable.** Therefore one cannot ask: Why has reason not determined
itself otherwise? But only: Why has it not determined **appearances**
otherwise through its causality? But no answer to this is possible. For
another intelligible character would have given another empirical one;
and if we say that regardless of the entire course of life he has led up to
that point, the agent could still have refrained from*a* the lie, then this
signifies only that it stands immediately under the power*b* of reason, and
in its causality reason is not subject to any conditions of appearance or
of the temporal series; the difference in time might be a chief difference
in appearances respecting their relations to one another, since these are
not things in themselves and hence not causes in themselves, but it
makes no difference to action in its relation to reason.

Thus in the judgment of free actions, in regard to their causality, we
can get only as far as the intelligible cause, but we cannot get **beyond
it;** we can know*c* that actions could be free, i.e., that they could be determined independently of sensibility, and in that way that they could
be the sensibly unconditioned condition of appearances. But why the
intelligible character gives us exactly these appearances and this empirical character under the circumstances before us, to answer this surpasses every faculty of our reason, indeed it surpasses the authority of
our reason even to ask it; it is as if one were to ask why the transcendental object of our outer sensible intuition gives precisely only the intuition of **space** and not some other one. Yet the problem which we had
to solve does not obligate us to answer these questions, for it was only
this: Do freedom and natural necessity in one and the same action contradict each other? And this we have answered sufficiently when we
showed that since in freedom a relation is possible to conditions of a
kind entirely different from those in natural necessity, the law of the latter does not affect the former; hence each is independent of the other,
and can take place without being disturbed by the other.

*** ***

---

a *unterlassen*
b *Macht*
c *erkennen*

A558/B586 It should be noted that here we have not been trying to establish the **reality** of freedom, as a faculty that contains the causes of appearance in our world of sense. For apart from the fact that this would not have been any sort of transcendental investigation having to do merely with concepts, it could not have succeeded, since from experience we can never infer something that does not have to be thought in accord with the laws of experience. Further, we have not even tried to prove the **possibility** of freedom; for this would not have succeeded either, because from mere concepts *a priori* we cannot cognize anything about the possibility of any real ground or any causality. Freedom is treated here only as a transcendental idea, through which reason thinks of the series of conditions in appearance starting absolutely through what is sensibly unconditioned, but thereby involves itself in an antinomy following its own laws, which it prescribes for the empirical use of the understanding. [To show] that this antinomy rests on a mere illusion, and that nature at least **does not conflict with** causality through freedom – that was the one single thing we could accomplish, and it alone was our sole concern.[a]

A559/B587

IV.
Solution of the cosmological idea
of the totality of dependence of appearances
regarding their existence in general.

In the preceding number we considered the changes in the world of sense in their dynamical series, where each is subordinated to another as its cause. Now this series of states serves only to lead us to an existence that could be the highest condition of everything alterable, namely to the **necessary being.** Here we deal not with unconditioned causality, but with the unconditioned existence of the substance itself. Thus the series we have before us is really only a series of concepts and not of intuitions, insofar as one intuition is the condition of another.

One easily sees, however, that since everything in the sum total of appearances is alterable, hence conditioned in its existence, there could not be any unconditioned member anywhere in the series of dependent existences whose existence would be absolutely necessary; and hence that if appearances were things in themselves, and so just for this reason their condition always belong to one and the same series of intuitions, then a necessary being could never occur as a condition of the existence of appearances in the world of sense.

A560/B588

But the dynamic regress has in itself this peculiar feature, distin-

---

[a] Kant notes: "Morality is that which, if it is correct, positively presupposes freedom.
"If the former is true, then freedom is proved." (E CLXXVI, p. 52; 23:42)

guishing it from the mathematical one: that since the latter really has to do only with the combination of parts into a whole, or with the dissolution of a whole into its parts, the conditions of this series always have to be seen as parts of it, hence as being of the same kind, and consequently as appearances, whereas in the former regress, which has to do not with the possibility of an unconditioned whole or an unconditioned part of a given whole but with the derivation of a state from its cause or of the contingent existence of a substance itself from the necessary existence of one, the condition need not necessarily constitute one empirical series along with the conditioned.

Therefore there remains only one way out of the apparent antinomy lying before us: since, namely, both the conflicting propositions can be true at the same time in a different relation in such a way that all things in the world of sense are completely contingent, hence having always only an empirically conditioned existence, there nevertheless occurs a non-empirical condition of the entire series, i.e., an unconditionally necessary being. For this, as an intelligible condition, would not belong to the series as a member of it (not even as the supreme member) at all, and would not make any member of the series unconditionally necessary, but it would leave the entire world of sense to the empirically conditioned existence which runs through all its members. Hence this way of grounding an unconditioned existence would be distinguished from the empirically unconditioned causality (of freedom) in the previous article in that in the case of freedom, the thing itself as cause (*substantia phaenomenon*)[a] would nevertheless belong to the series of conditions, and only **its causality** would be thought as intelligible, but here the necessary being would have to be thought of as entirely outside the series of the world of sense (as an *ens extramundanum*)[b] and merely intelligible; this is the only way of preventing it from being subjected to the law of the contingency and dependence of all appearances.[84]

A 561 / B 589

The **regulative principle**[c] **of reason** in regard to this problem of ours is therefore that everything in the world of sense has an empirically conditioned existence, and there cannot be an unconditioned necessity in it in regard to any of its properties, that there is no member of the series such that one does not always expect an empirical condition for it in a possible experience, and for which one must seek for such a condition as far as one can, and nothing justifies us in deriving any existence from a condition outside the empirical series, or indeed in taking anything in the series itself to be absolutely independent and self-sufficient; nevertheless, this is not in any way to deny that the entire series could

B 562 / B 590

---

[a] phenomenal substance
[b] a being outside the world
[c] *Princip*

be grounded in some intelligible being (which is therefore free of every empirical condition, containing, rather, the ground of the possibility of all these appearances).

But here it is not at all the intent[a] to prove the unconditionally necessary existence of any being, or even to ground the possibility of a merely intelligible condition of existence in the world of sense on it; rather, just as we limit reason so that it does not abandon the thread of the empirical conditions, and stray into **transcendent** grounds of explanation which do not admit of any exhibition *in concreto*, so on the other side we limit the law of the merely empirical use of the understanding, so that it does not decide the possibility of things in general, **nor** declare the intelligible, even though it is not to be used by us in explaining appearances, **to be impossible.** Thus it has been shown only that the thoroughgoing contingency of all natural things and all of nature's (empirical) conditions can very well coexist with the optional[b] presupposition of a necessary, even though merely intelligible condition, and thus that there is no true contradiction between these assertions, hence they can **both be true.** Such an absolutely necessary being of the understanding may always be impossible in itself, yet this can by A563/B591 no means be inferred from the universal contingency and dependence of everything belonging to the world of sense, nor can it be inferred from the principle[c] that we should not stop with any individual member of it and appeal to a cause outside the world. Reason goes its way in its empirical use, and a special way in a transcendental use.

The world of sense contains nothing but appearances, but these are mere representations, which are once again always sensibly conditioned, and, since here we never have to do with things in themselves as our objects, it is no wonder that we are never justified in making a leap from one member of the empirical series, whatever it might be, outside the connections of sensibility, just as if these members were things in themselves existing outside their transcendental ground, which one might leave behind in seeking the cause of their existence outside themselves; of course that would have to happen with contingent **things,** but not with mere **representations** of things, whose contingency itself is only a phenomenon, and can lead to no other regress but the one determining phenomena, i.e., the one which is empirical. But to think of an intelligible ground for appearances, i.e., for the world of sense, and of appearances freed from the contingency of the world of sense, is opposed neither to the unlimited empirical regress in the series of appearances nor to their thoroughgoing contingency. But that is also the

A564/B592 pearances nor to their thoroughgoing contingency. But that is also the

[a] *Meinung*
[b] *willkürlich*
[c] *Princip*

only thing we had to do to remove the apparent antinomy, and it could be done only in this way. For if for every conditioned the condition is always sensible (in its existence), and therefore something belonging to the series, then the condition is itself once again conditioned (as the antithesis of the fourth antinomy shows). Thus either reason, in demanding the unconditioned, must remain in conflict with itself, or else this unconditioned must be posited outside the series in the intelligible realm, where necessity is neither demanded nor permitted by any empirical condition, and thus in respect of appearances it is unconditionally necessary.

The empirical use of reason (in regard to the conditions of existence in the world of sense) is not affected by the admission of a merely intelligible being; rather it proceeds, according to the principle*a* of thoroughgoing contingency, from empirical conditions to higher ones, which are likewise always empirical. But just as little does this regulative principle exclude the assumption of an intelligible cause which is not in the series, when it is a matter of the pure use of reason (in regard to its ends). For here the intelligible cause signifies only the ground, for us transcendental and unknown, of the possibility of the sensible series in general, whose existence, independent of all conditions of the latter and unconditionally necessary in regard to it, is not at all opposed to the unbounded contingency of the former, and is therefore also not opposed to the regress, which is never ended, in the series of empirical conditions. A565/B593

Concluding remark
to the entire antinomy of pure reason.

As long as we, with our concepts of reason, have as our object merely the totality of the conditions in the world of sense, and what service reason can perform in respect of them, our ideas are transcendental but still **cosmological.** But as soon as we posit the unconditioned (which is what is really at issue) in that which lies outside the sensible world, and hence in that which is outside all possible experience, then the ideas come to be **transcendent;** they do not serve merely to complete the empirical use of reason (which always remains an idea, never to be completely carried out, but nevertheless to be followed), rather they separate themselves entirely from it and make themselves into objects whose matter is not drawn from experience, and whose objective reality rests not on the completion of the empirical series but on pure concepts *a priori.* Such transcendent ideas have a merely intelligible object, which

a Princip

one is of course allowed to admit as a transcendental object,[a] but about which one knows nothing; but for the assumption of such an object, in thinking it as a thing determinable by its distinguishing and inner predicates, we have on our side neither grounds of its possibility (since it is independent of all concepts of experience) nor the least justification, and so it is a mere thought-entity. Nevertheless, among the cosmological ideas, the one occasioning the fourth antinomy presses us to venture so far as to take this step. For the existence of appearances, not grounded in the least within itself but always conditioned, demands that we look around us for something different from all appearances, hence for an intelligible object, with which this contingency would stop. But if we once take the liberty of assuming a reality subsisting by itself[b] outside the entire field of sensibility, then appearances are regarded[c] only as contingent ways intelligible objects are represented by beings who are themselves intelligences; and because of this, nothing is left for us but the analogy by which we utilize concepts of experience in making some sort of concept of intelligible things, with which we have not the least acquaintance as they are in themselves. Because we cannot become acquainted with the contingent except through experience, but are here concerned with things which are not to be objects of experience at all, we have to derive our acquaintance[d] with them from what is necessary in itself, from pure concepts of things in general.[e] Thus the first step we take beyond the sensible world compels us, in acquiring new knowledge,[f] to begin with the investigation of the absolutely necessary being, and to derive from the concepts of it the concepts of all things insofar as they are merely intelligible; we will set about this attempt in the following chapter.

A 566/ B 594

A 567/ B 595

[a] *Object*

[b] *für sich*

[c] Reading, with Erdmann, *anzusehen sind* for *anzusehen.*

[d] *Kenntnis*

[e] Kant adds in his copy of the first edition: "Freedom makes for the greatest difficulty, because it simultaneously combines a being that belongs to the sensible world with the intellectual according to a given law, and thereby also with God." (E CLXXVII, p. 52; 23:42)

[f] *Kenntnisse*

The
Second Book of the Transcendental Dialectic
Chapter Three
The ideal of pure reason[85]

Section One
The ideal in general.

We have seen above that no objects at all can be represented through pure **concepts of the understanding** without any conditions of sensibility, because the conditions for the objective reality of these concepts are lacking, and nothing is encountered in them except the pure form of thinking. Nevertheless they can be exhibited *in concreto* if one applies them to appearances; for in the latter they have the proper material for a concept of experience, which is nothing but a concept of the understanding *in concreto*. **Ideas,** however, are still more remote from objective reality than **categories;** for no appearance can be found in which they may be represented *in concreto*. They contain a certain completeness that no possible empirical cognition ever achieves, and with them reason has a systematic unity only in the sense that the empirically possible unity seeks to approach it without ever completely reaching it.

But something that seems to be even further removed from objective reality than the idea is what I call the **ideal,** by which I understand the idea not merely *in concreto* but *in individuo,* i.e., as an individual thing which is determinable, or even determined, through the idea alone.

Humanity in its entire perfection contains not only the extension of all those properties belonging essentially to this nature and constituting our concept of it to the point of complete congruence with its ends, which would be our idea of perfect humanity, but also everything besides this concept that belongs to the thoroughgoing determination of the idea; for out of each [pair of] opposed predicates only a single one can be suited to the idea of the perfect human being. What is an ideal to us, was to **Plato an idea in the divine understanding,**[86] an individual object in that understanding's pure intuition, the most perfect thing of each species of possible beings and the original ground of all its copies in appearance.

Without venturing to climb as high as that, however, we have to admit that human reason contains not only ideas but also ideals, which do not, to be sure, have a creative power like the **Platonic** idea, but still have **practical** power (as regulative principles)*ᵃ* grounding the possibility of the perfection of certain **actions.** Moral concepts are not entirely pure concepts of reason, because they are grounded on something empirical (pleasure or displeasure). But in regard to the principle*ᵇ* through which reason places limits on a freedom which is in itself lawless, they can nevertheless serve quite well (if one attends merely to their form) as examples of pure concepts of reason. Virtue, and with it human wisdom in its entire purity, are ideas. But the sage (of the Stoics) is an ideal, i.e., a human being who exists merely in thoughts, but who is fully congruent with the idea of wisdom. Thus just as the idea gives the **rule,** so the ideal in such a case serves as the **original image**ᶜ for the thoroughgoing determination of the copy; and we have in us no other standard for our actions than the conduct of this divine human being, with which we can compare ourselves, judging*ᵈ* ourselves and thereby improving ourselves, even though we can never reach the standard. These ideals, even though one may never concede them objective reality (existence), are nevertheless not to be regarded as mere figments of the brain; rather, they provide an indispensable standard for reason, which needs the con-

cept of that which is entirely complete in its kind, in order to assess and measure the degree and the defects of what is incomplete. But to try to realize the ideal in an example, i.e., in appearance, such as that of the sage in a novel, is not feasible, and even has about it something nonsensical and not very edifying, since the natural limits which constantly impair the completeness in the idea render impossible every illusion in such an attempt, and thereby render even what is good in the idea suspect by making it similar to a mere fiction.

That is how it is with the ideal of reason, which always rests on determinate concepts and must serve as a rule and an original image, whether for following or for judging. It is entirely otherwise with the creatures of imagination, of which no one can give an explanation or an intelligible concept; they are, as it were, **monograms,** individual traits, though not determined through any assignable rule, constituting more a wavering sketch, as it were, which mediates between various appearances, than a determinate image, such as what painters and physiognomists say they have in their heads, and is supposed to be an incommunicable silhouette of their products or even of their critical judgments. These images can,

---

ᵃ Principien
ᵇ Princip
ᶜ Urbilde
ᵈ beurtheilen

552

though only improperly, be called ideals of sensibility because they are supposed to be the unattainable model for possible empirical intuitions, and yet at the same time they are not supposed to provide any rule capable of being explained or tested.

    A571/B579

The aim of reason with its ideal is, on the contrary, a thoroughgoing determination in accordance with *a priori* rules; hence it thinks for itself an object that is to be thoroughly determinable in accordance with principles,^{*a*} even though the sufficient conditions for this are absent from experience, and thus the concept itself is transcendent.^{*b*}

Chapter Three
Section Two
The transcendental ideal[87]
(*Prototypon transcendentale*)

Every **concept,** in regard to what is not contained in it, is indeterminate, and stands under the principle of **determinability:** that of **every two** contradictorily opposed predicates only one can apply to it, which rests on the principle of contradiction^{*c*} and hence is a merely logical principle,^{*d*} which abstracts from every content of cognition, and has in view nothing but the logical form of cognition.

Every **thing,** however, as to its possibility, further stands under the principle of **thoroughgoing determination;** according to which, among **all possible** predicates of **things,** insofar as they are compared with their opposites, one must apply to it.[88] This does not rest merely on the principle of contradiction, for besides considering every thing in relation^{*e*} to two contradictorily conflicting predicates, it considers every thing further in relation^{*f*} to **the whole of possibility,** as the sum total of all predicates of things in general; and by presupposing that as a condition *a priori*, it represents every thing as deriving its own possibility

    A572/B600

---

^{*a*} *Principien*

^{*b*} Kant adds: "Consequent way of thinking. We have proved all objects of experience only as appearances. There must, therefore, be something actual besides the objects of experience. No speculative way of cognition can attain to determining this something, because the latter is a mere form of thoughts, which with us are sensible; and the existence of that which we think through reason would not be able to be proved from mere concepts. But freedom in the practical furnishes an actual law of causality, which is not empirical, and therefore is the actuality which, concerning its quality, not only proves the actuality of something extrasensible but also determines it. The [a final word appears to be either 'unity' (*Einheit*) or 'insight' (*Einsicht*)] . . . " (E CLXXVIII, p. 53; 23:42)

^{*c*} *Satz des Widerspruchs*

^{*d*} *Princip*

^{*e*} *Verhältnis*

^{*f*} *Verhältnis*

from the share it has in that whole of possibility.* The principle[a] of thoroughgoing determination thus deals with the content and not merely the logical form. It is the principle of the synthesis of all predicates which are to make up the complete concept of a thing, and not merely of the analytical representation, through one of two opposed predicates; and it contains a transcendental presupposition, namely that of the material **of all possibility,** which is supposed to contain *a priori* the data for the **particular** possibility of every thing.

A573/B601

The proposition **Everything existing is thoroughly determined** signifies not only that of every **given** pair of opposed predicates, but also of every pair of **possible** predicates, one of them must always apply to it; through this proposition predicates are not merely compared logically with one another, but the thing itself is compared transcendentally with the sum total of all possible predicates. What it means is that in order to cognize a thing completely one has to cognize everything possible and determine the thing through it, whether affirmatively or negatively. Thoroughgoing determination is consequently a concept that we can never exhibit *in concreto* in its totality, and thus it is grounded on an idea which has its seat solely in reason, which prescribes to the understanding the rule of its complete use.

Now although this idea of the **sum total of all possibility,** insofar as it grounds every thing as the condition of its thoroughgoing determination in regard to the predicates which may constitute the thing, is itself still indeterminate, and through it we think nothing beyond a sum total of all possible predicates in general, we nevertheless find on closer investigation that this idea, as an original concept, excludes a multiplicity of predicates, which, as derived through others, are already given, or cannot coexist with one another; and that it refines itself to a concept thoroughly determined *a priori,* and thereby becomes the concept of an individual object that is thoroughly determined merely through the idea, and then must be called an **ideal** of pure reason.

A574/B602

If we consider all possible predicates not merely logically but transcendentally, i.e., as to their content which can be thought in them *a*

A572/B600

* Thus through this principle every thing is related to a common correlate, namely the collective possibility, which, if it (i.e., the matter for all possible predicates) were present in the idea of an individual thing, would prove an affinity of everything possible through the identity of the ground of its thoroughgoing determination. The **determinability** of every single **concept** is the **universality** (*universalitas*) of the principle of excluded middle between two opposed predicates; but the **determination** of a **thing** is subordinated to the **allness** (*universitas*) or the sum total of all possible predicates.

[a] *Principium*

priori, then we find that through some of them a being is represented, and through others a mere non-being. Logical negation, which is indicated solely by the little word "not," is never properly attached to a concept, but rather only to its relation*a* to another concept in a judgment, and therefore it is far from sufficient to designate a concept in regard to its content. The expression "non-mortal" cannot at all give the cognition that a mere non-being is represented in the object, but leaves all content unaffected. A transcendental negation, on the contrary, signifies non-being in itself, and is opposed to transcendental affirmation, which is a Something,*b* the concept of which in itself already expresses a being, and hence it is called reality (thinghood),*c* because through it alone, and only so far as it reaches, are objects Something (things); the opposed negation, on the contrary, signifies a mere lack, and where this alone is thought, the removal of every thing A575/B603 is represented.

Now no one can think a negation determinately without grounding it on the opposed affirmation. The person blind from birth cannot form the least representation of darkness, because he has no representation of light; the savage has no acquaintance with poverty, because he has none with prosperity.* The ignorant person has no concept of his ignorance, because he has none of science, etc. All concepts of negations are thus derivative, and the realities contain the data, the material, so to speak, or the transcendental content, for the possibility and the thoroughgoing determination of all things.

Thus if the thoroughgoing determination in our reason is grounded on a transcendental substratum, which contains as it were the entire storehouse of material from which all possible predicates of things can be taken, then this substratum is nothing other than the idea of an All of reality (*omnitudo realitatis*). All true negations are then nothing but A576/B604 **limits,** which they could not be called unless they were grounded in the unlimited (the All).

---

* The observations and calculations of astronomers have taught us much that is A575/B603 worthy of admiration, but most important, probably, is that they have exposed for us the abyss of our **ignorance,** which without this **information***d* human reason could never have imagined*e* to be so great; reflection on this ignorance has to produce a great alteration in the determination of the final aims*f* of the use of our reason.

---

a *Verhältnis*
b *Etwas* (Kant's capitalization)
c *Sachheit*
d *Kenntnisse*
e *vorstellen*
f *Endabsichten*

Through this possession of all reality, however, there is also represented the concept of a **thing in itself** which is thoroughly determined, and the concept of an *ens realissimum*[a] is the concept of an individual being, because of all possible opposed predicates, one, namely that which belongs absolutely to being, is encountered in its determination. Thus it is a transcendental **ideal** which is the ground of the thoroughgoing determination that is necessarily encountered in everything existing, and which constitutes the supreme and complete material condition of its possibility, to which all thinking of objects in general must, as regards the content of that thinking, be traced back. It is, however, also the one single genuine ideal of which human reason is capable, because only in this one single case is an – in itself universal – concept of one thing thoroughly determined through itself, and cognized as the representation of an individual.

A577/B605 The logical determination of a concept through reason rests on a disjunctive syllogism, in which the major premise contains a logical division (the division of the sphere of a general concept), the minor premise restricts this sphere to one part, and the conclusion determines the concept through this part. The general concept of a reality in general cannot be divided up *a priori*, because apart from experience one is acquainted with no determinate species of reality that would be contained under that genus. Thus the transcendental major premise for the thoroughgoing determination of all things is none other than the representation of the sum total of all reality, a concept that comprehends all predicates as regards their transcendental content not merely **under itself,** but **within itself;** and the thoroughgoing determination of every thing rests on the limitation of this **All** of reality, in that some of it is ascribed to the thing and the rest excluded from it, which agrees with the "either/or" of the disjunctive major premise and the determination of the object through one of the members of this division in the minor premise.[b] The use of reason through which it grounds its determination of all things in the transcendental ideal is, accordingly, analogous to its procedure in disjunctive syllogisms; that was the proposition on which I above[89] grounded the systematic division of all transcendental ideas, according to which they were generated parallel and corresponding to the three kinds of syllogisms.

---

[a] "most real being"; Kant declines the Latin phrase in the genitive.

[b] Kant adds in his copy of the first edition: "the principle [*Princip*] of determination says only that if a concept of a thing is to be determined, it could be determined only through one of the two: *A* or *non-A*. The principle [*Satz*] of thoroughgoing determination says that every thing (as existing, i.e., in respect of everything possible) is determined in respect of all possible predicates." (E CLXXIX, p. 53; 23:42)

Section II. On the transcendental ideal

It is self-evident that with this aim – namely, solely that of representing the necessary thoroughgoing determination of things – reason does not presuppose the existence of a being conforming to the ideal, but only the idea of such a being, in order to derive from an unconditioned totality of thoroughgoing determination the conditioned totality, i.e., that of the limited. For reason the ideal is thus the original image (*prototypon*) of all things, which all together, as defective copies (*ectypa*), take from it the matter for their possibility, and yet although they approach more or less nearly to it, they always fall infinitely short of reaching it.

Thus all the possibility of things (as regards the synthesis of the manifold of their content) is regarded as derivative, and only that which includes all reality in it is regarded as original. For all negations (which are the sole predicates through which everything else is to be distinguished from the most real being) are mere limitations of a greater and finally of the highest reality; hence they presuppose it, and as regards their content they are merely derived from it. All manifoldness of things is only so many different ways of limiting the concept of the highest reality, which is their common substratum, just as all figures are possible only as different ways of limiting infinite space. Hence the object of reason's ideal, which is to be found only in reason, is also called the **original being** (*ens originarium*); because it has nothing above itself it is called the **highest being** (*ens summum*), and because everything else, as conditioned, stands under it, it is called the **being of all beings** (*ens entium*). Yet all of this does not signify the objective relation of an actual object to other things, but only that of an **idea** to **concepts,** and as to the existence of a being of such preeminent excellence it leaves us in complete ignorance.

Because one also cannot say that an original being consists in many derivative beings, since each of the latter presupposes the former and so cannot constitute it, the ideal of the original being must also be thought of as simple.

The derivation of all other possibility from this original being, strictly speaking, also cannot be regarded as a **limitation** of its highest reality and as a **division,** as it were, of it; for then the original being would be regarded as a mere aggregate of derivative beings, which, according to the above, is impossible, even though we represented it in such a way at the beginning in our first crude outline.*a* Rather, the highest reality would ground the possibility of all things as a **ground** and not as a **sum total;** and the manifoldness of the former rests not on the limitation of the original being itself, but on its complete consequences; to which our whole sensibility, including all reality in appearance, would then belong, which cannot belong to the idea of a highest being as an ingredient.

---

a *Schattenriß*

557

A 580/ B 608   Now if we pursue this idea of ours so far as to hypostatize it, then we will be able to determine the original being through the mere concept of the highest reality as a being that is singular,[a] simple, all-sufficient, eternal, etc., in a word, we will be able to determine it in its unconditioned completeness through all predications.[b] The concept of such a being is that of **God** thought of in a transcendental sense, and thus the ideal of pure reason is the object of a transcendental **theology**, just as I have introduced it above.[90]

Meanwhile this use of the transcendental idea would already be overstepping the boundaries of its vocation[c] and its permissibility. For on it, as the **concept** of all reality, reason only grounded the thoroughgoing determination of things in general, without demanding that this reality should be given objectively, and itself constitute a thing. This latter is a mere fiction, through which we encompass and realize the manifold of our idea in an ideal, as a particular being; for this we have no warrant, not even for directly assuming the possibility of such a hypothesis, just as none of the consequences flowing from such an ideal have any bearing, nor even the least influence, on the thoroughgoing determination of things in general, on behalf of which alone the idea was necessary.

A 581/ B 609   It is not enough to describe the procedure of our reason and its dialectic; one must also seek to discover its sources, so as to be able to explain this illusion itself, as a phenomenon of the understanding; for the ideal we are talking about is grounded on a natural and not a merely arbitrary idea. Therefore I ask: How does reason come to regard all the possibility of things as derived from a single possibility, namely that of the highest reality, and even to presuppose these possibilities as contained in a particular original being?

The answer suggests itself on the basis of the discussions of the Transcendental Analytic themselves. The possibility of objects of sense is a relation[d] of these objects to our thought, in which something (namely, the empirical form) can be thought *a priori*, but what constitutes the material, the reality in appearance (corresponding to sensation) has to be given; without that nothing at all could be thought and hence no possibility could be represented.[91] Now an object of sense can be thoroughly determined only if it is compared with all the predicates of appearance and is represented through them either affirmatively or negatively. But because that which constitutes the thing itself (in appearance), namely the real, has to be given, without which it could not be thought at all, but

A 582/ B 610   that in which the real in all appearances is given is the one all-encom-

---

[a] *einig*

[b] *Prädicamente*, a term that (at A 82 / B 108) Kant seems to identify with the categories.

[c] *Bestimmung*

[d] *Verhältnis*

passing experience, the material for the possibility of all objects of sense has to be presupposed as given in one sum total; and all possibility of empirical objects, their difference from one another and their thoroughgoing determination, can rest only on the limitation of this sum total. Now in fact no other objects except those of sense can be given to us, and they can be given nowhere except in the context of a possible experience; consequently, nothing is an object **for us** unless it presupposes the sum total of all empirical reality as condition of its possibility.[92] In accordance with a natural illusion, we regard as a principle that must hold of all things in general that which properly holds only of those which are given as objects of our senses. Consequently, through the omission of this limitation we will take the empirical principle[a] of our concepts of the possibility of things as appearances to be a transcendental principle[b] of the possibility of things in general.

That we subsequently hypostatize this idea of the sum total of all reality, however, comes about because we dialectically transform the **distributive** unity of the use of the understanding in experience, into the **collective** unity of a whole of experience; and from this whole of appearance we think up an individual thing containing in itself all empirical reality,[93] which then – by means of the transcendental subreption we have already thought – is confused with the concept of a thing that stands at the summit of the possibility of all things, providing the real conditions for their thoroughgoing determination.*

A 583/B611

Chapter Three
Section Three
The grounds of proof of speculative reason for inferring the existence of a highest being.

In spite of its urgent need to presuppose something that the understanding could take as the complete ground for the thoroughgoing determination of its concepts, reason notices the ideal and merely fictive

---

* This ideal of the supremely real being, even though it is a mere representation, is first **realized**, i.e., made into an object,[c] then **hypostatized**, and finally, as we will presently allege, through a natural progress of reason in the completion of unity, it is even **personified**;[94] for the regulative unity of experience rests not on appearances themselves (of sensibility alone), but on the connection of its manifold by **understanding** (in one apperception); hence the unity of the highest reality and the thoroughgoing determinability (possibility) of all things seems to lie in a highest understanding, hence in an **intelligence**.

[a] *Princip*
[b] *Princip*
[c] *Object*

A 584/ B 612 character of such a presupposition much too easily to allow itself to be persuaded by this alone straightway to assume a mere creature of its own thinking to be an actual being, were it not urged from another source to seek somewhere for a resting place in the regress from the conditioned, which is given, to the unconditioned, which in itself and as regards its mere concept is not indeed actually given, but which alone can complete series of conditions carried out to their grounds. Now this is the natural course taken by every human reason, even the most common, although not everyone perseveres in it. It*a* begins not with concepts, but with common experience, and thus grounds itself on something existing. But this footing*b* gives way unless it rests on the immovable rock of the absolutely necessary. But this itself floats without a support if there is still only empty space outside it and under it, unless it itself fills everything, so that no room is left over for any further **Why?** – i.e., unless it is infinite in its reality.

If something, no matter what, exists, then it must also be conceded that something exists **necessarily.** For the contingent exists only under the condition of something else as its cause, and from this the same inference holds further all the way to a cause not existing contingently and therefore necessarily without condition. That is the argument on which reason grounds its progress to the original being.[95]

A 585/ B 613 Now reason looks around for the concept of a being suited for such a privileged existence, as the absolute necessity, yet not in order to infer its existence *a priori* from its concept (for if it were confident of that, then it might inquire only among mere concepts, and would not find it necessary to take a given existence as its ground), but rather only in order to find among all the concepts of possible things that one that has nothing within itself conflicting with absolute necessity. For in accordance with the first inference, reason takes it as already settled that something or other has to exist with absolute necessity. If it can now do away with everything that is not compatible with this necessity, except for one, then this is the absolutely necessary being, whether one can comprehend its necessity, i.e., derive it from its concept alone, or not.

Now that the concept of which contains within itself the "Because" to every "Why?" – that which is in no part or respect defective, that which is in all ways sufficient as a condition – seems to be the being suited to absolute necessity just because by itself possessing all the conditions for everything possible, it itself needs no condition, and is indeed not even susceptible of one; consequently, it satisfies the concept of unconditioned necessity on at least one point, in which no other concept can

---

a *Sie,* whose referent could grammatically be "reason" (or "every human reason"), but not "the natural course."

b *Boden*

equal it, since every other concept is defective and in need of comple- A586/B614
tion, not showing in itself any such mark of its independence of all further conditions. It is true that from this it still cannot be concluded with
certainty that what does not contain within itself the highest and in
every respect complete condition must therefore be conditioned in its
existence; but then it does not have in itself that single earmark of unconditioned existence which gives reason the power to cognize any
being as unconditioned through a concept *a priori.*

Thus among all the concepts of possible things the concept of a being
having the highest reality would be best suited to the concept of an unconditionally necessary being, and even if it does not fully satisfy this
concept, we still have no other choice, but see ourselves compelled to
hold to it, because we must not just throw the existence of a necessary
being to the winds; yet if we concede this existence, then in the entire
field of possibility we cannot find anything that could make a more
well-grounded claim to such a privilege in existence.[96]

This, therefore, is how the natural course of human reason is constituted. First it convinces itself of the existence of **some** necessary being.
In this it recognizes an unconditioned existence. Now it seeks for the
concept of something independent of all conditions, and finds it in that
which is the sufficient condition for everything else, i.e., in that which A587/B615
contains all reality. The All without limits, however, is absolute unity,
and carries with it the concept of one single being, namely the highest
being; and thus reason infers that the highest being, as the original
ground of all things, exists in an absolutely necessary way.

It cannot be disputed that this concept has a certain cogency[a] if it is
a matter of making **decisions,** that is, if the existence of some necessary
being is already conceded, and one agrees that one must take sides on
where one is to place it; for then one can make no more suitable choice
than – or rather, one has no other choice, but is compelled – to vote for
the absolute unity of complete reality as the original source of possibility. But if nothing impels us to come to a decision, and we would rather
let this entire matter be tabled until we are compelled to give our approval by the full weight of grounds of proof, i.e., if it is merely a matter of **estimating** how much we know about this problem and what we
merely flatter ourselves that we know – then the above inference does
not appear to be in anything like the same advantageous shape and
needs some special favor to make up for the defects in its rightful
claims.

For if we let everything stand just as it is here, namely: first, that from
any given existence (in any case merely my own) there is a valid infer- A588/B616
ence to the existence of an unconditionally necessary being; second,

---

[a] *Gründlichkeit*

that I have to regard a being that contains all reality, hence all conditions, as absolutely unconditioned, and consequently have found in it the concept of the thing which is suited for absolute necessity; then from this it still cannot be inferred that therefore the concept of a limited being, which does not have the highest reality, contradicts absolute necessity. For even if in its concept I do not find the unconditioned which the All of conditions already carries with it, still it cannot be concluded just from this that its existence must be conditioned; just as I cannot say in a hypothetical syllogism: Where a certain condition (here, namely, completeness according to concepts) is not, there too the conditioned thing is not. Rather we are still at liberty to count all the remaining limited beings equally as absolutely necessary, even though we cannot infer their necessity from the universal concept we have of them. Looked at in this way, however, this argument has not produced for us even the least concept of the properties of a necessary being, and has in fact not achieved anything at all.

Nevertheless there remains to this argument a certain importance and high regard of which it cannot straightway be divested simply on account of this objective insufficiency. For suppose there were obligations that were entirely correct in the idea of reason but would have no real application to us, i.e., would be without any incentives, if a highest being were not presupposed who could give effect and emphasis to the practical laws; then we would also have an obligation to follow those concepts, that even though they may not be objectively sufficient, are still preponderant in accordance with the measure of our reason, and in comparison with which we recognize nothing better or more convincing. The duty to choose would here tip the indecisiveness of speculation out of balance through a practical addition; indeed, reason, as the most circumspect judge, could not find any justification for itself if, under the pressure of urgent causes though with defective insight, its judgment were not to follow these grounds, than which we at least know none better.

This argument, although it is in fact transcendental, since it rests on the inner insufficiency of the contingent, is yet so simple and natural that it is suited to the commonest human understanding as soon as the latter is once led to it. One sees things alter, arise, and perish; therefore they, or at least their state, must have a cause. About every cause, however, that may be given in experience, the same thing may once again be asked. Now where could we more appropriately locate the **supreme** causality than right where the **highest** causality is, i.e., in that being, originally containing within itself what is sufficient for the possible effect, whose concept also comes about very easily through the single trait of an all-encompassing perfection. This highest cause we then take to be absolutely necessary, because we find it absolutely necessary to as-

A 589/B 617

A 590/B 618

cend to it and no ground for going still further beyond it. Therefore even through the blindest polytheism in all peoples we see shimmering a few sparks of monotheism, to which they have been led not by reflection and deep speculation, but only in accordance with a natural course of common understanding becoming gradually more intelligible.

There are only three kinds of proof for the existence of
God possible from speculative reason.

All paths on which one may set forth with this aim either begin from determinate experience and the special constitution of our world of sense known*a* through it, and ascend from that by means of laws of causality to the highest cause outside the world; or else they are empirically grounded on an experience that is only indeterminate, i.e., on some existence; or, finally, they abstract from all experience and infer the existence of a highest cause entirely *a priori* from mere concepts. The first proof is the **physico-theological,** the second the **cosmological,** and the third the **ontological** proof. There are no more of them, and there also cannot be any more. A591/B619

I will establish that reason accomplishes just as little on the one path (the empirical) as on the other (the transcendental), and that it spreads its wings in vain when seeking to rise above the world of sense through the mere might of speculation. As to the order in which these species of proof have to be presented for examination, however, it will be just the reverse of that taken by reason in gradually unfolding itself, and in which we have first placed them. For it will be shown that although experience has given the occasion for them, it is nevertheless merely the **transcendental concept** of reason that it has set forth for itself that directs these strivings and holds up the target in all such attempts. Thus I will begin by examining the transcendental proof, and later see what the addition of the empirical can do to increase the force of its proof.

Chapter Three A592/B620
Section Four
On the impossibility of an ontological proof of
God's existence.[97]

From the foregoing one easily sees that the concept of an absolutely necessary being is a pure concept of reason, i.e., a mere idea, the objective reality of which is far from being proved by the fact that reason needs it, since this only points to a certain though unattainable completeness, and properly serves more to set boundaries to the under-

---

a *erkannt*

standing than to extend it toward new objects. But here we find something strange and paradoxical, that the inference from a given existence in general to some absolutely necessary being seems to be both urgent and correct, and yet nevertheless in framing a concept of such a necessity, we have all the conditions of the understanding entirely against us.

In all ages one has talked about the **absolutely necessary** being, but has taken trouble not so much to understand whether and how one could so much as think of a thing of this kind as rather to prove its existence. Now a nominal definition*a* of this concept is quite easy, namely that it is something whose non-being is impossible; but through this one becomes no wiser in regard to the conditions that make it necessary*b* to regard the non-being of a thing as absolutely unthinkable, and that are really what one wants to know, namely whether or not through this concept we are thinking anything at all. For by means of the word **unconditional** to reject all the conditions that the understanding always needs in order to regard something as necessary, is far from enough to make intelligible to myself whether through a concept of an unconditionally necessary being I am still thinking something or perhaps nothing at all.

Still more: one believed one could explain this concept, which was ventured upon merely haphazardly, and that one has finally come to take quite for granted through a multiplicity of examples, so that all further demands concerning its intelligibility appeared entirely unnecessary. Every proposition of geometry, e.g., "a triangle has three angles," is absolutely necessary, and in this way one talked about an object lying entirely outside the sphere of our understanding as if one understood quite well what one meant by this concept.

All the alleged examples are without exception taken only from **judgments,** but not from **things** and their existence.*c* The unconditioned necessity of judgments, however, is not an absolute necessity of things.*d* For the absolute necessity of the judgment is only a conditioned necessity of the thing,*e* or of the predicate in the judgment. The above proposition does not say that three angles are absolutely necessary, but rather that under the condition that a triangle exists (is given), three an-

A593/B621

A594/B622

---

a *Namenerklärung*

b *unmöglich* (impossible); the sense, however, seems to require *notwendig.*

c Kant's note in his copy of the first edition: "'I am': is this an analytic or a synthetic judgment? 'A, an object [*Object*] in general, exists' is always a synthetic judgment and cannot be reached *a priori:* 'I am' is therefore not a cognition of the subject but merely the consciousness of the representation of an object [*Object*] in general." (E CLXXX, p. 53; 23:42–3)

d *Sachen*

e *Sache*

gles also exist (in it) necessarily. Nevertheless the illusion of this logical necessity has proved so powerful that when one has made a concept *a priori* of a thing that was set up so that its existence was comprehended within the range of its meaning, one believed one could infer with certainty that because existence necessarily pertains to the object*ᵃ* of this concept, i.e., under the condition that I posit this thing as given (existing), its existence can also be posited necessarily (according to the rule of identity), and this being itself, therefore, is necessarily, because its existence is thought along with a concept assumed arbitrarily and under the condition that I posit its object.

If I cancel the predicate in an identical judgment and keep the subject, then a contradiction arises; hence I say that the former necessarily pertains to the latter. But if I cancel the subject together with the predicate, then no contradiction arises; for there **is no longer anything** that could be contradicted. To posit a triangle and cancel its three angles is contradictory; but to cancel the triangle together with its three angles is not a contradiction. It is exactly the same with the concept of an absolutely necessary being. If you cancel its existence, then you cancel the A595/B623 thing itself with all its predicates; where then is the contradiction supposed to come from? Outside it there is nothing that would contradict it, for the thing is not supposed to be externally necessary; and nothing internally either, for by cancelling the thing itself, you have at the same time cancelled everything internal. God is omnipotent; that is a necessary judgment. Omnipotence cannot be cancelled if you posit a divinity, i.e., an infinite being, which is identical with that concept. But if you say, **God is not,** then neither omnipotence nor any other of his predicates is given; for they are all cancelled together with the subject, and in this thought not the least contradiction shows itself.

Thus you have seen that if I cancel the predicate of a judgment together with the subject, an internal contradiction can never arise, whatever the predicate might be. Now no escape is left to you except to say: there are subjects that cannot be cancelled at all and thus have to remain. But that would be the same as saying that there are absolutely necessary subjects – just the presupposition whose correctness I have doubted, and the possibility of which you wanted to show me. For I cannot form the least concept of a thing that, if all its predicates were cancelled, would leave behind a contradiction, and without a contradiction, A596/B624 I have through mere pure concepts *a priori* no mark of impossibility.

Against all these general inferences (which no human being can refuse to draw) you challenge me with one case that you set up as a proof through the fact that there is one and indeed only this one concept where the non-being or the cancelling of its object is contradictory

---

ᵃ Object

within itself, and this is the concept of a most real being. It has, you say, all reality, and you are justified in assuming such a being as possible (to which I have consented up to this point, even though a non-contradictory concept falls far short of proving the possibility of its object).* Now existence is also comprehended under all reality: thus existence lies in the concept of something possible. If this thing is cancelled, then the internal possibility of the thing is cancelled, which is contradictory.

A597/B625

I answer: You have already committed a contradiction when you have brought the concept of its existence, under whatever disguised name, into the concept of a thing which you would think merely in terms of its possibility. If one allows you to do that, then you have won the illusion of a victory, but in fact you have said nothing; for you have committed a mere tautology. I ask you: is the proposition, **This or that thing** (which I have conceded to you as possible, whatever it may be) **exists** – is this proposition, I say, an analytic or a synthetic proposition? If it is the former, then with existence you add nothing to your thought of the thing; but then either the thought that is in you must be the thing itself, or else you have presupposed an existence as belonging to possibility, and then inferred that existence on this pretext from its inner possibility, which is nothing but a miserable tautology. The word "reality," which sounds different from "existence" in the concept of the predicate, does not settle it. For if you call all positing (leaving indeterminate what you posit) "reality," then you have already posited the thing with all its predicates in the concept of the subject and assumed it to be actual, and you only repeat that in the predicate. If you concede, on the contrary, as in all fairness you must, that every existential proposition is synthetic, then how would you assert that the predicate of existence may not be cancelled without contradiction? – since this privilege pertains only in the analytic propositions, as resting on its very character.

A598/B626

I would have hoped to annihilate this over-subtle argumentation

A596/B624   * The concept is always possible if it does not contradict itself. That is the logical mark of possibility, and thereby the object of the concept is distinguished from the *nihil negativum*.*a* Yet it can nonetheless be an empty concept, if the objective reality of the synthesis through which the concept is generated has not been established in particular; but as was shown above,[98] this always rests on principles*b* of possible experience and not on the principles of analysis (on the principle*c* of contradiction). This is a warning not to infer immediately from the possibility of the concept (logical possibility) to the possibility of the thing (real possibility).

a negative nothing
b *Principien*
c *Satz*

without any digressions through a precise determination of the concept of existence, if I had not found that the illusion consisting in the confusion of a logical predicate with a real one (i.e., the determination of a thing) nearly precludes all instruction. Anything one likes can serve as a **logical predicate,** even the subject can be predicated of itself; for logic abstracts from every content. But the **determination** is a predicate, which goes beyond the concept of the subject and enlarges it. Thus it must not be included in it already.

Being is obviously not a real predicate, i.e., a concept of something that could add to the concept of a thing. It is merely the positing*a* of a thing or of certain determinations in themselves. In the logical use it is merely the copula of a judgment. The proposition **God is omnipotent** contains two concepts that have their objects:*b* God and omnipotence; the little word "**is**" is not a predicate in it, but only that which posits the predicate **in relation** to the subject. Now if I take the subject (God) together with all his predicates (among which omnipotence belongs), and say **God is,** or there is a God, then I add no new predicate to*c* the concept of God, but only posit the subject in itself with all its predicates, and indeed posit the **object** in relation to my **concept.** Both must contain exactly the same, and hence when I think this object as given absolutely (through the expression, "it is"), nothing is thereby added to the concept, which expresses merely its possibility. Thus the actual contains nothing more than the merely possible. A hundred actual dollars do not contain the least bit more than a hundred possible ones. For since the latter signifies the concept and the former its object and its positing*d* in itself, then, in case the former contained more than the latter, my concept would not express the entire object and thus would not be the suitable concept of it. But in my financial condition there is more with a hundred actual dollars than with the mere concept of them (i.e., their possibility). For with actuality the object is not merely included in my concept analytically, but adds synthetically to my concept (which is a determination of my state); yet the hundred dollars themselves that I am thinking of are not in the least increased through this being outside my concept.

A 599/ B 627

Thus when I think a thing, through whichever and however many predicates I like (even in its thoroughgoing determination), not the least bit gets added to the thing when I posit in addition that this thing **is.** For otherwise what would exist would not be the same as what I had thought in my concept, but more than that, and I could not say that the

A 600/ B 628

a *Position*
b *Objecte*
c *setze . . . zu*, which could also be translated: "posit . . . [in relation] to."
d *Position*

very object of my concept exists. Even if I think in a thing every reality except one, then the missing reality does not get added when I say the thing exists, but it exists encumbered with just the same defect as I have thought in it; otherwise something other than what I thought would exist. Now if I think of a being as the highest reality (without defect), the question still remains whether it exists or not. For although nothing at all is missing in my concept of the possible real content of a thing in general, something is still missing in the relation to my entire state of thinking, namely that the cognition of this object[a] should also be possible *a posteriori*. And here the cause of the predominant difficulty shows itself. If the issue were an object of sense, then I could not confuse the existence of the thing with the mere concept of the thing. For through its concept, the object would be thought only as in agreement with the universal conditions of a possible empirical cognition in general, but through its existence it would be thought as contained in the context of the entirety of experience; thus through connection with the content of the entire experience the concept of the object is not in the least increased, but our thinking receives more through it, namely a possible perception. If, on the contrary, we tried to think existence through the pure category alone, then it is no wonder that we cannot assign any mark distinguishing it from mere possibility.

A601/B629

Thus whatever and however much our concept of an object may contain, we have to go out beyond it in order to provide it with existence. With objects of sense this happens through the connection with some perception of mine in accordance with empirical laws; but for objects[b] of pure thinking there is no means whatever for cognizing their existence, because it would have to be cognized entirely *a priori*, but our consciousness of all existence (whether immediately through perception or through inferences connecting something with perception) belongs entirely and without exception to the unity of experience, and though an existence outside this field cannot be declared absolutely impossible, it is a presupposition that we cannot justify through anything.

The concept of a highest being is a very useful idea in many respects; but just because it is merely an idea, it is entirely incapable all by itself of extending our cognition in regard to what exists. It is not even able to do so much as to instruct us in regard to the possibility of anything more. The analytic mark of possibility, which consists in the fact that mere positings[c] (realities) do not generate a contradiction, of course, cannot be denied of this concept; since,[d] however, the connection of all

A602/B630

---

[a] *Object*
[b] *Objecte*
[c] *Positionen*
[d] *da;* the first edition reads *weil* (because).

real properties in a thing is a synthesis about whose possibility we cannot judge *a priori* because the realities are not given to us specifically – and even if this were to happen no judgment at all could take place because the mark of possibility of synthetic cognitions always has to be sought only in experience, to which, however, the object of an idea can never belong – the famous Leibniz was far from having achieved what he flattered himself he had done, namely, gaining insight *a priori* into the possibility of such a sublime ideal being.[99]

Thus the famous ontological (Cartesian) proof[100] of the existence of a highest being from concepts is only so much trouble and labor lost, and a human being can no more become richer in insight from mere ideas than a merchant could in resources if he wanted to improve his financial state by adding a few zeros to his cash balance.

Chapter Three
Section Five
On the impossibility of a cosmological proof of
God's existence.[101]

A 603 / B 631

It was entirely unnatural, and a mere novelty of scholastic wit, to want to take an idea contrived quite arbitrarily and extract from it the existence of the corresponding object itself. In fact one would never have tried this path if it had not been preceded by a need of our reason to assume for existence in general a basis in something necessary (with which one could stop the ascent), and if – since this necessity has to be unconditioned and certain *a priori* – reason were not compelled to seek a concept that, if possible, was sufficient to meet this demand by providing an existence that is supposed to be cognized fully *a priori*. It was believed that this had been found in the idea of a most real being, and this was therefore used only to provide more determinate acquaintance with something of which one was already convinced or persuaded on other grounds that it must exist, namely, the necessary being. Meanwhile this natural course of reason was concealed, and instead of ending with this concept one sought to begin with it in order to derive the necessity of the existence from it, which, however, this concept was fit only to augment.[a] From this arose the unfortunate ontological proof, which brings no satisfaction either to the natural and healthy understanding or to scholastically correct examination.

A 604 / B 632

The cosmological proof, which we will now investigate, retains the connection of absolute necessity with the highest reality, but instead of inferring as in the previous argument from the highest reality to necessity of existence, it rather infers from the previously given uncondi-

---

[a] . . . *die er doch nur zu ergänzen bestimmt war.*

tioned necessity of some being or other to the unbounded reality of this being, thus setting everything on the track of a species of inference that, whether reasonable or sophistical,*a* is at least natural, and has been the most persuasive one not only for the common but also for the speculative understanding; it is also the one that visibly draws the outlines*b* for all the proofs of natural theology, outlines which have always been followed and will be followed further, however one might try to embellish and disguise them with so much foliage and scrollwork. This proof, which Leibniz also called the proof *a contingentia mundi,*c* we will now place before our eyes and subject to examination.[102]

It goes as follows: If something exists, then an absolutely necessary being also has to exist. Now I myself, at least, exist; therefore, an absolutely necessary being exists. The minor premise contains an experience, the major premise an inference from an experience in general to the existence of something necessary.* Thus the proof really starts from experience, so it is not carried out entirely *a priori* or ontologically; and because the object of all possible experience is called "world," it is therefore termed the **cosmological** proof. Since it also abstracts from every particular property of objects of experience through which this world might differ from any other possible world, it is already distinguished by this terminology from the physico-theological proof, which uses observations about the particular constitution of this sensible world of ours for its grounds of proof.

A605 / B633

Now the proof further infers: The necessary being can be determined only in one single way, i.e., in regard to all possible predicates, it can be determined by only one of them, so consequently it must be **thoroughly** determined through its concept. Now only one single concept of a thing is possible that thoroughly determines the thing *a priori,* namely that of an *ens realissimum:*d* Thus the concept of the most real being is the only single one through which a necessary being can be thought, i.e., there necessarily exists a highest being.

A606 / B634

In this cosmological argument so many sophistical principles come together that speculative reason seems to have summoned up all its di-

A605 / B633

* This inference is too well known for it to be necessary to expound it in detail here. It rests on the allegedly transcendental natural law of causality that everything **contingent** must have a cause, which, if it in turn is contingent, must likewise have its cause, until the series of causes subordinated one to another has to end with an absolutely necessary cause, without which it would have no completeness.

a *ob vernünftigen oder vernünftelnden*
b *Grundlinien*
c from the contingency of the world
d "most real being"; Kant declines this phrase in the genitive.

alectical art so as to produce the greatest possible transcendental illusion. We will put off examining it for a while, so as in the meantime to make plain only one ruse through which it sets up an old argument in disguised form as a new one, and appeals to the agreement of two witnesses, namely a pure rational witness and another with empirical credentials, where only the first is there all alone, merely altering his clothing and voice so as to be taken for a second. In order to ground itself securely, this proof gets a footing in experience, and thereby gives itself the reputation that it is distinct from the ontological proof, which puts its whole trust solely in pure concepts *a priori*. But the cosmological proof avails itself of this experience only to make a single step, namely to the existence of a necessary being in general. What this being might have in the way of properties, the empirical ground of proof cannot teach; rather, here reason says farewell to it entirely and turns its inquiry back to mere concepts: namely, to what kinds of properties in general an absolutely necessary being would have to have, i.e., A607/B635 which among all possible things contains within itself the required conditions (*requisita*) for an absolute necessity.[103] Now reason believes it meets with these requisites solely and uniquely in the concept of a most real being, and so it infers: that is the absolutely necessary being. But it is clear that here one presupposes that the concept of a being of the highest reality completely suffices for the concept of an absolute necessity in existence, i.e., that from the former the latter may be inferred – a proposition the ontological proof asserted, which one thus assumes in the cosmological proof and takes as one's ground, although one had wanted to avoid it. For absolute necessity is an existence from mere concepts. Now if I say: the concept of the *ens realissimum*[a] is a concept, and indeed the one single concept, that fits necessary existence and is adequate to it, then I must admit that the latter could be concluded from it. Thus it is really only the ontological proof from mere concepts that contains all the force of proof in the so-called cosmological proof; and the supposed experience is quite superfluous – perhaps leading us only to the concept of a necessary being, but not so as to establish this concept in any determinate thing. For as soon as we have this intention, we have to abandon all experience at once and seek among pure concepts for the one that might contain the conditions for the possibility of an absolutely necessary being. But if there A608/B636 is insight into the possibility of such a being in such a way, then its existence is established too; for then what is meant is: among all possibles there is one that carries absolute necessity with it, i.e., this being exists with absolute necessity.[104]

All semblances in inferring are most easily discovered if one puts

***

[a] "most real being"; again Kant declines it in the genitive.

571

them before one's eyes in a scholastically correct way. Here is such a presentation.

If the proposition is correct: "Every absolutely necessary being is at the same time the most real being" (which is the *nervus probandi*[a] of the cosmological proof), then like any affirmative judgment, it must be convertible *per accidens*, thus: "Some most real beings are at the same time absolutely necessary beings." But now one *ens realissimum* does not differ the least bit from another, and thus what holds of **some** beings contained under this concept holds also of **all**. Hence I will also be able (in this case) to convert the proposition[b] **absolutely**, i.e., "Every most real being is a necessary being." Now because this proposition is determined merely from its concepts *a priori*, the mere concept of the most real being must also carry with it the absolute necessity of this being – which is just what the ontological proof asserts and the cosmological proof does not want to recognize, despite the fact that it underlies its inferences, though in a covert way.

A 609/ B 637

Thus the second way that speculative reason takes in order to prove the existence of the highest being is not only deceptive like the first, but it even has this further blamable feature in it, that it commits an *ignoratio elenchi*,[c] promising to put us on a new footpath, but after a little digression bringing us once again back to the old one, which for its sake we had left behind.

A short time ago[105] I said that in this cosmological argument an entire nest of dialectical presumptions is hidden, which transcendental criticism can easily discover and destroy. I will now only cite them, leaving it to the reader to investigate further their deceptive principles and remove them.

There is, for example: 1) The transcendental principle of inferring from the contingent to a cause, which has significance only in the world of sense, but which outside it does not even have a sense. For the merely intellectual concept of the contingent cannot produce any synthetic proposition, such as that of causality, and the principle of causality has no significance at all and no mark of its use except in the world of sense; here, however, it is supposed to serve precisely to get beyond the world

A 610/ B 638

of sense. 2) The inference from the impossibility of an infinite series of causes given one upon another to a first cause, which the principles[d] of the use of reason itself cannot justify our inferring within experience, still less our extending this principle to somewhere beyond it (into which the causal chain cannot be extended at all). 3) The false self-

[a] nerve of what is to be proved
[b] *ich's* added in the second edition.
[c] refutation by ignorance
[d] *Principien*

satisfaction reason finds in regard to the completion of this series by the fact that one finally does away with every condition – without which, however, there can be no concept of any necessity – and then since one cannot comprehend anything further, one assumes this to be the completion of one's concept. 4) The confusion of the logical possibility of a concept of all reality united (without internal contradiction) with its transcendental possibility, which requires a principle*a* of the feasibility of such a synthesis, but which once again can apply only to the field of possible experiences, etc.

The artifice of the cosmological proof is aimed merely at evading a proof of the existence of a necessary being *a priori* through mere concepts, which would have to be carried out ontologically, for which, however, we feel ourselves entirely incapable. In this respect, on the ground of an actual existence (an experience in general), we infer, as best we can, some absolutely necessary condition of that existence. Then we have no necessity of explaining the possibility of this condition. For, if it has been proved that it exists, then the question of its A611/B639 possibility is quite unnecessary. Now if we want to determine this necessary being more closely as to its constitution, then we do not seek what would suffice to comprehend from its concept the necessity of its existence; for if we could do that, then we would not have had the need of any empirical presupposition; no, we seek only the negative condition (*conditio sine qua non*) without which a being would not be absolutely necessary. Now that might very well get by in any other species of inference from a given consequence to its ground; but here, unfortunately, it so happens that the condition that one demands for absolute necessity can be encountered only in a single being, which therefore must contain everything in its concept that is required for absolute necessity, and thus makes possible an inference *a priori* to that; i.e., I have to be able to infer conversely that whatever thing this concept (of the highest reality) pertains to, that thing is absolutely necessary; and if I cannot so infer (as I must admit, if I want to avoid the ontological proof), then I have come to grief on my new path, and find myself once again right back where I started. The concept of the highest being satisfies all questions *a priori* that can be posed about the inner determinations of a thing, and it is therefore an ideal without equal, because the universal concept at the same time distinguishes*b* it A612/B640 as one individual among all possible things. But it does not deal at all satisfactorily with the question about its own existence, though that is really all that was at issue; and to those who assume the existence of a necessary being, and would only know which among all things had to

---

a *Principium*
b *auszeichnet*

be regarded as such a thing, one could not answer: This thing here is the necessary being.

It may well be allowed to **assume** the existence of a being of the highest sufficiency as the cause of all possible effects, in order to facilitate reason's search for the unity of its grounds of explanation. Yet to go so far as to say, **Such a being exists necessarily,** is no longer the modest expression of an allowable hypothesis, but rather the impudent presumption of an apodictic certainty; for if one proposes to cognize something as absolutely necessary, then that cognition must also carry absolute necessity with it.

The entire problem of the transcendental ideal comes to this: either to find a concept for the absolute necessity or to find the absolute necessity for the concept of some thing. If one can do the first, then one must be able to do the other too; for reason cognizes as absolutely necessary only what is necessary from its concept. But both entirely transcend all the utmost efforts to **satisfy** our understanding on this point, but also all attempts to make it **content** with its incapacity.

A613/B641

The unconditioned necessity, which we need so indispensably as the ultimate sustainer of all things, is for human reason the true abyss. Even eternity – however awful the sublimity with which a Haller[106] might portray it – does not make such a dizzying impression on the mind; for eternity only **measures** the duration of things, but it does not **sustain** that duration. One cannot resist the thought of it, but one also cannot bear it that a being that we represent to ourselves as the highest among all possible beings might, as it were, say to itself: "I am from eternity to eternity, outside me is nothing except what is something merely through my will; **but whence** then am I?" Here everything gives way beneath us, and the greatest perfection as well as the smallest, hovers without support before speculative reason, for which it would cost nothing to let the one as much as the other disappear without the least obstacle.

Many forces of nature that express their existence only through certain effects remain inscrutable for us, for we cannot trace them far enough through observation. The transcendental object[a] lying at the ground of appearances, and with it the ground why our sensibility has it rather than another supreme condition – these are and remain inscrutable for us, even though the thing itself[b] is given, only we have no insight into it. An ideal of pure reason, however, cannot be called **inscrutable,** because it has to display no further credentials for its reality than the need of reason to complete all synthetic unity by means of it. Since it is not even given as a thinkable object, it is also not inscrutable

A614/B642

[a] Object
[b] Sache selbst

as such an object; rather, as a mere idea it must find both its seat and its solution in the nature of reason, and so it can be investigated;[a] for reason consists just in the fact that we can give an account of all our concepts, opinions and assertions, either on objective grounds or, if they are a mere illusion, on subjective ones.

Discovery and explanation of the dialectical illusion in all transcendental proofs of the existence of a necessary being.

Both the proofs previously cited were attempted transcendentally, i.e., independently of empirical principles.[b] For although the cosmological proof is grounded on an experience in general, it is not carried out on the basis of any particular constitution of experience, but of pure principles of reason[c] in relation to an existence given through empirical consciousness in general; and even this introduction is an occasion for basing itself on entirely pure concepts. Now what in these transcendental proofs is the cause of the dialectical but natural illusion that connects the concepts of necessity and highest reality and that realizes and hypostatizes that which can be only an idea? What causes it to be unavoidable to assume something among existing things to be in itself necessary, and yet at the same time to shrink back from the existence of such a being as an abyss? And how is one to bring reason to an understanding of itself over this matter, so that from a vacillating state of different approval it may achieve one of calm insight?

A615/B643

There is something exceedingly remarkable in the fact that when one presupposes something existing, one can find no way around the conclusion that something also exists necessarily. It is on this entirely natural (though not for this reason secure) inference that the cosmological argument rested. On the contrary, if I assume the concept of anything I like, then I find that its existence can never be represented by me as absolutely necessary, and that whatever may exist, nothing hinders me from thinking its non-being; hence although for the existing in general I must assume something necessary, I cannot think any single thing itself as necessary in itself. That means: in going back to the conditions of existing I can never **complete** the existing without assuming a necessary being,[d] but I can never **begin** with this being.

A616/B644

If I must think something necessary for existing things in general but am not warranted in thinking any thing in itself as necessary, then it follows unavoidably from this that necessity and contingency do not per-

---

[a] *erforscht;* cf. *unerforschlich* (inscrutable).
[b] *Principien*
[c] *Vernunftprincipien*
[d] In the first edition: ". . . without necessarily assuming a being . . . "

tain to or concern the things themselves, because otherwise a contradiction would occur; hence neither of these two principles is objective, but they can in any case be only subjective principles[a] of reason, namely, on the one side, for everything given as existing to seek something that is necessary, i.e., never to stop anywhere except with an *a priori* complete explanation, but on the other side also never to hope for this completion, i.e., never to assume anything empirical as unconditioned, thereby exempting oneself from its further derivation. In such a significance both principles can very well coexist with one another, as merely heuristic and **regulative,** taking care of nothing but the formal interest of reason. For the one says that you should philosophize about nature **as if** there were a necessarily first ground for everything belonging to existence, solely in order to bring systematic unity into your cognition by inquiring after such an idea, namely an imagined first ground; but the other warns you

A617/B645 not to assume any single determination dealing with the existence of things as such a first ground, i.e., as absolutely necessary, but always to hold the way open to further derivation and hence always to treat it as still conditioned. But if everything perceived in things by us[b] has to be considered as necessarily conditioned, then no thing (which may be given empirically) can be regarded as absolutely necessary.

From this, however, it follows that you would have to assume the absolutely necessary being as **outside the world,** because it is supposed to serve only as a principle[c] of the greatest possible unity of appearances, as their supreme ground; and you can never reach it **within the world,** because the second rule bids you at every time to regard all empirical causes of unity as derivative.

The philosophers of antiquity regard[d] every form of nature as contingent, but the matter, in accordance with the judgment of common reason, as original and necessary. But if they had considered the matter not as a substratum respective to appearances but **in itself** as to its existence, then the idea of absolute necessity would have disappeared at once. For there is nothing that binds reason absolutely to this existence; on the contrary, it can, at any time and without conflict, give such a thing up in thoughts; but it is in thoughts alone that absolute necessity

A618/B646 lies. Hence a certain regulative principle[e] must be the ground of this persuasion. In fact extension and impenetrability (which together constitute the concept of matter) is also the highest empirical principle[f] of

---

[a] *Principien*

[b] *von uns;* the first edition reads "*vor uns*" (before us).

[c] *Princip*

[d] The first edition reads "regarded."

[e] *Princip*

[f] *Principium*

the unity of appearances, and has, insofar as it is empirically unconditioned, in itself the properties of a regulative principle.[a] Nevertheless,
since each determination of matter that constitutes what is real in it,
hence impenetrability too, is an effect (action) that must have its cause,
and hence is always derivative, matter is not suited to the idea of a necessary being as the principle[b] of all derivative unity, because each of its
real properties as derivative is only conditionally necessary and hence
can in itself be cancelled; but then the entire existence of matter would
be cancelled; but if this did not happen, we would have reached the
highest ground of unity empirically, which is forbidden by the second
regulative principle;[c] thus it follows that matter, and in general everything belonging to the world, is not suited to the idea of a necessary
original being as a mere principle[d] of the greatest empirical unity, but
this must be posited outside the world, since then we can always be confident of deriving the appearances of the world and their existence from
others, as though there were no necessary being, and nevertheless we
can strive ceaselessly toward completeness in this derivation, as though
such a being were presupposed as a highest ground.   A619/B647

The ideal of the highest being is, according to these considerations,
nothing other than a **regulative principle**[e] of reason, to regard all
combination in the world **as if it** arose from an all-sufficient necessary
cause, so as to ground on that cause the rule of a unity that is systematic and necessary according to universal laws; but it is not an assertion
of an existence that is necessary in itself. But at the same time it is unavoidable, by means of a transcendental subreption, to represent this
formal principle[f] to oneself as constitutive, and to think of this unity
hypostatically. For, just as with space, since it originally makes possible
all forms which are merely limitations of it, even though it is only a
principle[g] of sensibility, it is necessarily held to be a Something subsisting in itself with absolute necessity and an *a priori* object given in itself,
so it also comes about entirely naturally that since the systematic unity
of nature cannot be set up as a principle[b] of the empirical use of reason
except on the basis of the idea of a most real being as the supreme cause,
this idea is thereby represented as an actual object, and this object again,
because it is the supreme condition, is represented as necessary, so that

[a] *Princip*
[b] *Princip*
[c] *Princip*
[d] *Princip*
[e] *Princip*
[f] *Princip*
[g] *Principium*
[b] *Princip*

A620/B648 a **regulative** principle[a] is transformed into a **constitutive** one; this substitution reveals itself by the fact that if I now consider this supreme being, which was absolutely (unconditionally) necessary respective to the world, as a thing for itself, no concept is susceptible of this necessity; and thus it must have been encountered in my reason only as a formal condition of thought, and not as a material and hypostatic condition of existence.

Chapter Three
Section Six
On the impossibility of a physico-theological proof[107]

If, then, neither the concept of things in general nor the experience of any **existence in general** can achieve what is required, then one means is still left: to see whether a **determinate experience,** that of the things in the present world, their constitution and order, yields a ground of proof that could help us to acquire a certain conviction of the existence of a highest being. Such a proof we would call the **physico-theological** proof.[108] If this too should be impossible, then no satisfactory proof from speculative reason for the existence of a being that corresponds to our transcendental ideas is possible at all.

A621/B649 From all the above remarks one will soon see that to this inquiry a quite easy, concise, and conclusive reply can be expected. For how can any experience be given that is supposed to be adequate to an idea? For what is special about an idea is just that no experience can ever be congruent to it. The transcendental idea of a necessary all-sufficient original being is so overwhelmingly great, so sublimely high above everything empirical, which is at all times conditioned, that partly one can never even procure enough material in experience to fill such a concept, and partly if one searches for the unconditioned among conditioned things, then one will seek forever and always in vain, since no law of any empirical synthesis will ever give an example of such a thing, or even the least guidance in looking for it.

If the highest being were to stand in the chain of these conditions, then it would be a member of their series, and like the lower members, of which this is presupposed, a further investigation for a still higher ground would be required for it. If, on the contrary, one would separate it from this chain, and, as a merely intelligible being, not include it within the series of natural causes, then what bridge can reason build so as to reach it? For all laws of transition from effects to causes, indeed, all synthesis and extension of our cognition in general, are directed[b] to

[a] *Princip*
[b] *gestellt*

nothing other than possible experience, and hence merely to objects of the world of sense, and they can have a significance only in regard to A622/B650 them.

The present world discloses to us such an immeasurable showplace of manifoldness, order, purposiveness, and beauty, whether one pursues these in the infinity of space or in the unlimited division of it,[109] that in accordance with even the knowledge[a] about it that our weak understanding can acquire, all speech concerning so many and such unfathomable wonders must lose its power to express, all numbers their power to measure, and even our thoughts lack boundaries, so that our judgment upon the whole must resolve itself into a speechless, but nonetheless eloquent, astonishment.[110] Everywhere we see a chain of effects and causes, of ends and means, regularity in coming to be and perishing, and because nothing has entered by itself[b] into the state in which it finds itself, this state always refers further to another thing as its cause, which makes necessary just the same further inquiry, so that in such a way the entire whole[c] would have to sink into the abyss of nothingness if one did not assume something subsisting for itself originally and independently outside this infinite contingency, which supports it and at the same time, as the cause of its existence, secures its continuation. This highest cause (in regard to all things of the world) – how great should one think it is? We are not acquainted with the world in its whole content, still less do we know how to estimate its magnitude by A623/B651 comparison with everything possible. But since in respect to causality we need an ultimate and supreme being, what hinders us from at the same time positing in it a degree of perfection **exceeding everything else that is possible?** This we can easily effect, though to be sure only through the fragile outline of an abstract concept, if we represent all possible perfection united in it as a single substance – which concept is favorable to our reason in its parsimony of principles,[d] not subject to any contradictions, and even salutary for the extension of the use of our reason within experience, through the guidance such an idea gives to order and purposiveness, but is nowhere contrary to experience in any decisive way.

This proof always deserves to be named with respect. It is the oldest, clearest and the most appropriate to common human reason. It enlivens the study of nature, just as it gets its existence from this study and through it receives ever renewed force. It brings in ends and aims where they would not have been discovered by our observation itself, and ex-

---

[a] *Kenntnisse*
[b] *von selbst*
[c] *das ganze All*
[d] *Principien*

tends our information about nature through the guiding thread of a particular unity whose principle[a] is outside nature. But this acquaintance also reacts upon its cause, namely the idea that occasioned it, and increases the belief in a highest author to the point where it becomes an irresistible conviction.

Thus it would be not only discomfiting but also quite pointless to try to remove anything from the reputation of this proof. Reason, ceaselessly elevated by the powerful though only empirical proofs that are always growing in its hands, cannot be so suppressed through any doubt drawn from subtle and abstract speculation that it is not torn at once out of every brooding indecision, just as from a dream, by throwing a glance on the wonders of nature and the majesty of the world's architecture,[b] by which it elevates itself from magnitude to magnitude up to the highest of all, rising from the conditioned to the condition, up to the supreme and unconditioned author.

But although we have nothing to object against the rationality and utility of this procedure, but rather recommend and encourage it, we cannot on that account approve of the claims that this kind of proof may make to apodictic certainty and to having no need for approval based on any special favor or need of outside[c] support; it can in no way harm the good cause to tone down the dogmatic language of a scornful sophist[d] to the tone of moderation and modesty of a belief that is sufficient to comfort us, although not to command unconditional submission. Accordingly, I assert that the physico-theological proof can never establish the existence of a highest being alone, but must always leave it up to the ontological proof (to which it serves only as an introduction) in order to make good this lack; thus the latter still contains the **only possible argument**[111] (insofar as there is a merely speculative proof at all), which no human reason can bypass.

The chief moments of the physico-theological proof we are thinking of are the following: 1) Everywhere in the world there are clear signs of an order according to determinate aim, carried out with great wisdom, and in a whole of indescribable manifoldness in content as well as of unbounded magnitude in scope. 2) This purposive order is quite foreign to the things of the world, and pertains to them only contingently, i.e., the natures of different things could not by themselves[e] agree in so many united means to determinate final aims, were they not quite properly chosen for and predisposed to it through a principle[f] of rational

[a] *Princip*
[b] *Weltbau*
[c] *fremden*
[d] *Vernünftlers*
[e] *von selbst*
[f] *Princip*

order grounded on ideas. 3) Thus there exists a sublime and wise cause (or several), which must be the cause of the world not merely as an all-powerful nature working blindly through **fecundity,** but as an intelligence, through **freedom.** 4) The unity of this cause may be inferred from the unity of the reciprocal relation of the parts of the world as members of an artful structure, inferred with certainty wherever our observation reaches, but beyond that with probability in accordance with all principles of analogy.

A626/B654

Without quibbling with natural reason about the inference it draws from the analogy between natural products and those of human art, when it does violence to nature and constrains it not to proceed in accordance with its own ends but to bend to ours (the similarity of nature's ends to houses, ships, and clocks), just such a causality, namely understanding and will, is made a ground, when it derives the inner possibility of freely working nature (which makes all art, and perhaps even reason itself, possible) from another though superhuman art, which sort of inference perhaps might not stand up to the sharpest transcendental critique – one must nevertheless admit that once we are supposed to name a cause, we could not proceed more securely than by analogy with such purposive productions,[a] which are the only ones where we are fully acquainted with the causes and the way they act. Reason would not be able to justify[b] to itself an attempt to pass over from a causality with which it is acquainted to obscure and unprovable grounds of explanation, with which it is not acquainted.

According to this inference, the purposiveness and well-adaptedness of so many natural arrangements would have to prove merely the contingency of the form, but not of the matter, i.e., of substance, in the world; for the latter would further require that it be able to be proved that the things of the world would in themselves be unsuited for such an order and harmony according to universal laws if they were not **in their substance** the product of a highest wisdom; but entirely different grounds of proof from those provided by the analogy with human art would be required for this. Thus the proof could at most establish a highest **architect of the world,** who would always be limited by the suitability of the material on which he works, but not a **creator of the world,** to whose idea everything is subject, which is far from sufficient for the great aim that one has in view, namely that of proving an all-sufficient original being. If we wanted to prove the contingency of matter itself, then we would have to take refuge in a transcendental argument, which, however, is exactly what was supposed to be avoided here.

A627/B655

The inference thus goes from the thoroughgoing order and purpo-

---

[a] *Erzeugungen*
[b] *verantworten*

siveness that is to be observed in the world, as a thoroughly contingent arrangement, to the existence of a cause **proportioned to it.** The concept of this cause, however, has to give us something quite **determinate** to cognize about it, and thus it cannot be anything other than that of a being that possesses all power, wisdom, etc., in a word, all perfection, as an all-sufficient being. For the predicates **very great,** or "astonishing" or "immeasurable power" and "excellence" do not give any determinate concept at all, and really say nothing about what the thing in itself is, but are rather only relative representations, through which the observer (of the world) compares the magnitude of the object with himself and his power to grasp it, and they turn out to be terms of equally high praise whether one increases the magnitude of the object or makes the observing subject smaller in relation to it. Where it is a question of the magnitude (perfection) of a thing in general, there is no determinate concept except that which comprehends the whole of possible perfection, and only the All (*omnitudo*) of reality is thoroughly determinate in its concept.

A628/B656

Now I will not hope that anyone presumes to have insight into the relation of the magnitude of the world as he has observed it (in its scope as well as its content) to omnipotence, or the world-order to highest wisdom, or the unity of the world to the absolute unity of its author, etc. Thus physico-theology cannot give any determinate concept of the supreme cause of the world, and hence it cannot be sufficient for a principle[a] of theology, which is supposed to constitute in turn the foundation of religion.

The step to absolute totality is utterly impossible on the empirical path. But it is nevertheless made in the physico-theological proof. So what means are employed to get across such a wide gulf?

A629/B657

After one has gotten as far as admiring the magnitude of the wisdom, power, etc. of the world's author, and cannot get any farther, then one suddenly leaves this argument carried out on empirical grounds of proof and goes back to the contingency that was inferred right at the beginning from the world's order and purposiveness. Now one proceeds from this contingency alone, solely through transcendental concepts, to the existence of something absolutely necessary, and then from the concept of the absolute necessity of the first cause to its thoroughly determinate or determining concept, namely that of an all-encompassing reality. Thus the physico-theological proof, stymied in its undertaking, suddenly jumps over to the cosmological proof, and since this is only a concealed ontological proof, it really carries through its aim merely through pure reason, even though at the beginning this denied

---

[a] *Princip*

all kinship with it and had proposed to base everything on evident proofs from experience.

Thus the physico-theologians have no cause at all to be so coy when it comes to the transcendental kind of proof and to look down on it with the self-conceit of clearsighted students of nature looking down on the webs spun by gloomy quibblers.[a] For if they would only examine themselves, they would find that after they have made a certain amount of progress on the territory of nature and experience and seen themselves just as far removed as ever from the object with which their reason seems to confront them,[b] they suddenly leave this territory and pass over into the realm of mere possibilities, where on the wings of ideas they hope to approach that which has eluded all their empirical inquiries. After they finally suppose they have got firm footing through such a mighty leap, then they extend the now determinate concept (without knowing how they have come to be in possession of it) over the entire field of creation, and they elucidate the ideal, which was merely the product of pure reason – though shabbily enough and in a way far beneath the dignity of its object – through experience, though without being willing to concede that they have achieved their acquaintance with it, or their presupposition of it, while they were on a different footpath from that of experience.

A630/B658

Accordingly, the physico-theological proof of the existence of a single original being as the highest being is grounded on the cosmological, and the latter on the ontological; and since besides these three paths no more are open to speculative reason, the ontological proof from pure concepts of reason is the only possible one – if even one proof of a proposition elevated so sublimely above all empirical use of the understanding is possible at all.

Chapter Three
Section Seven
Critique of all theology from speculative principles[c]
of reason.[112]

A631/B659

If by "theology" I understand the cognition of the original being, then it is either from pure reason (*theologia rationalis*) or from revelation (*revelata*). Now the first of these thinks its object either merely through pure reason, by means of sheer transcendental concepts (as an *ens originarium, realissimum, ens entium*)[d] and is called **transcendental** theology,

---

[a] *finsterer Grübler*
[b] . . . *der ihrer Vernunft entgegen scheint*
[c] *Principien*
[d] original being, most real being, being of beings

or else through a concept which it borrows from nature (the nature of our soul) as the highest intelligence, and would have to be called **natural** theology. Someone who admits only a transcendental theology would be called a **deist;** but if he also accepts[a] a natural theology, he would be called a **theist.** The former concedes that we can in any case cognize the existence of an original being through mere reason, but our concept of it is merely transcendental – namely, only that of a being having all reality, but it cannot be determined more closely. The second asserts that reason is in a position to determine the object more closely by analogy with nature – namely as a being containing the original ground of all other things within itself through understanding and freedom. The deist represents this being merely as a **cause of the world** (whether through the necessity of its nature or through freedom remains undecided), the theist as an **author of the world.**

A 632 / B 660

Transcendental theology either thinks that the existence of an original being is to be derived from an experience in general (without more closely determining anything about the world to which this experience belongs), and is called **cosmotheology;** or it believes that it can cognize that existence through mere concepts, without the aid of even the least experience, and is called **ontotheology.**

Natural theology infers the properties and the existence of an author of the world from the constitution, the order and unity, that are found in this world, in which two kinds of causality and its rules have to be assumed, namely nature and freedom. Hence it ascends from this world to the highest intelligence, either as the principle[b] of all natural or of all moral order and perfection. In the first case it is called **physico-theology,** in the latter **moral theology.***

A 633 / B 661

Since one is accustomed to understanding by the concept of God not some blindly working eternal nature as the root of things, but rather a highest being which is supposed to be the author of things through understanding and freedom – and since this concept alone interests us – one could, strictly speaking, refuse all belief in God to the **deist,** and leave him solely with the assertion of an original being or a highest cause. However, since no one should be charged with wanting to deny something just because he does not have the confidence to assert it, it

A 632 / B 660   * Not theological morals; for that contains moral laws that **presuppose** the existence of a highest governor of the world, whereas moral theology, on the contrary, is a conviction of the existence of a highest being which grounds itself on moral laws.[c]

[a] *annimmt*
[b] *Princip*
[c] In the first edition: " . . . which is grounded on moral laws."

is gentler and fairer to say that the **deist** believes in a **God,** but the **theist** in a living **God** (*summa intelligentia*).[a] Now we want to seek out the possible sources of all these attempts of reason.

Here I content myself with defining theoretical cognition as that through which I cognize **what exists,** and practical cognition as that through which I represent **what ought to exist.** According to this, the theoretical use of reason is that through which I cognize *a priori* (as necessary) that something is; but the practical use is that through which it is cognized *a priori* what ought to happen. Now if it is indubitably certain, but only conditionally, that something either is or that it should happen, then either a certain determinate condition can be absolutely necessary for it, or it can be presupposed as only optional[b] and contingent. In the first case the condition is postulated (*per thesin*),[c] in the second it is supposed (*per hypothesin*).[d] Since there are practical laws that are absolutely necessary (the moral laws), then if these necessarily presuppose any existence as the condition of the possibility of their **binding** force, this existence has to be **postulated,** because the conditioned from which the inference to this determinate condition proceeds is itself cognized *a priori* as absolutely necessary. In the future we will show about the moral laws that they not only presuppose the existence of a highest being, but also, since in a different respect they are absolutely necessary, they postulate this existence rightfully but, of course, only practically; for now we will set aside this kind of inference.[113]

A634/B662

Since if it is merely a matter of what exists (not of what ought to be), the conditioned that is given to us in experience is also always thought of as contingent, then the condition that belongs to it cannot be cognized from this as absolutely necessary, but serves only as a relatively necessary – or rather as a **required** but in itself and *a priori* arbitrary – presupposition for the rational cognition of the conditioned. If, therefore, the absolute necessity of a thing is to be cognized in theoretical cognition, then this could happen only from concepts *a priori*, but never as a cause in relation to an existence that is given through experience.

A theoretical cognition is **speculative** if it pertains to an object or concepts of an object to which one cannot attain in any experience. It is opposed to the **cognition of nature,** which pertains to no objects, or their predicates, except those that can be given in a possible experience.

A635/B663

The principle of inferring from what happens (the empirically contingent) as effect to a cause, is a principle[e] of the cognition of nature,

---

[a] "highest intelligence"; Kant declines the Latin phrase in the accusative.
[b] *beliebig*
[c] by thesis
[d] by hypothesis
[e] *Princip*

but not of speculative cognition. For if one abstracts from it as a principle that contains the condition of possible experience in general, and, leaving out everything empirical, wants to assert it of the contingent in general, then not the least justification is left over for any synthetic proposition from which it can be discerned how I can go from what exists to something entirely different (called its cause); indeed, in such a speculative use the concept of a cause, like that of the contingent, loses all the significance that is made comprehensible by its objective reality *in concreto*.

Now if one infers from the existence of **things** in the world to their cause, this does not belong to the **natural** but to the **speculative** use of reason; for the former does not relate the things themselves (substances) to any cause, but relates to a cause only what **happens,** thus their **states,** as empirically contingent; that the substance itself (the matter) is contingent as to its existence would have to be a merely speculative cognition of reason. But if it were only a matter of the form of the world, the way it is combined and the changes of combination, yet I wanted to infer from this to a cause that is entirely distinct from the world, then this once again would be a judgment of merely speculative reason, because the object here is not any object^a of a possible experience. But then the principle of causality, which holds only within the field of possible experience and outside it is without any use or indeed without any meaning,^{b} would be completely diverted from its vocation.

A636/B664

Now I assert that all attempts of a merely speculative use of reason in regard to theology are entirely fruitless and by their internal constitution null and nugatory, but that the principles^c of reason's natural use do not lead at all to any theology; and consequently, if one did not ground it on moral laws or use them as guides, there could be no theology of reason at all. For all synthetic principles of understanding are of immanent use; but for the cognition of a highest being a transcendent use of them would be required, for which our understanding is not equipped at all. If the empirically valid law of causality is to lead to an original being, then this would have to belong to the causal chain in objects of experience; but then it, like all appearances, would have to be conditioned. But even if one were allowed to leap over the boundary of experience by means of the dynamical law of the relation of effects to their causes, what concept can this procedure obtain for us? Far from any concept of a highest being, because for us experience never offers us the greatest of all possible effects (such as would bear witness to this as its cause). If, merely so that nothing empty is left in our reason, we

A637/B665

---

^{a} *Object*
^{b} *Bedeutung*
^{c} *Principien*

are allowed to make good this lack of complete determination by means of a mere idea of the highest perfection and original necessity, then we could be permitted this only by special favor, but it cannot be demanded by the right of an irresistible proof. Thus the physico-theological proof could perhaps lend support to other proofs (if there were any), by connecting speculation with intuition; but by itself[a] it is more a preparation of the understanding for theological cognition, providing it with a straight and natural direction toward such cognition; it cannot complete the business **alone**.[114]

Thus from this one can very well see that transcendental questions admit only of transcendental answers, i.e., answers from pure[b] *a priori* concepts, without the least empirical admixture. But here the question is obviously synthetic and demands an extension of our cognition beyond all the boundaries of experience, namely to the existence of a being that is supposed to correspond to our mere idea, to which no experience can ever be equal. Now, according to the proofs we have given above, all synthetic cognition *a priori* is possible only by the fact that it expresses the formal conditions of a possible experience, and all principles are therefore only of immanent validity, i.e., they are related solely to objects of empirical cognition, or appearances. Thus through transcendental procedures aiming at a theology of mere speculative reason nothing is accomplished. $\qquad$ A638/B666

But if one would rather call all the above proofs of the Analytic into doubt than be robbed of the persuasion that these grounds of proof that have been used for so long are of great weight, even then one cannot refuse to satisfy me when I demand that one should at least explain how, and by means of what illumination, one is justified in confidently soaring above all possible experience through the power of mere ideas. New proofs, or improved reworkings of old ones, I would beg to be spared. For there is not much to choose here, since all merely speculative proofs finally amount to one single proof, namely the ontological, and I need not fear being overburdened by the fertility of the dogmatic champion of reason freed from sense; though without thinking myself very combative I will not refuse the challenge of discovering the fallacy $\qquad$ A639/B667 in every such attempt of this kind, and so frustrate its pretensions; yet in this way the hope for better luck on the part of those who have become accustomed to dogmatic persuasion will never be fully done away with, and so I confine myself to one single fair demand: that one should provide a general justification, based on the nature of human understanding, together with all remaining sources of cognition, for making a start at extending one's cognition entirely *a priori* and stretching it

---

[a] *für sich selbst*
[b] *lauter*

even to where no possible experience and hence no means suffices to secure objective reality for any of the concepts we have thought out. However the understanding may have obtained these concepts, the existence of their object cannot be found in them analytically, just because the cognition of the **existence** of the object[a] consists precisely in positing this existence in itself **outside the thought.** But it is entirely impossible to go from a concept by itself out beyond it and, without following its empirical connection (which, however, will at every time provide only appearances), to attain to the discovery of new objects and transcendent[b] beings.

But even though reason in its merely speculative use is far from adequate for such a great aim as this – namely, attaining to the existence of a supreme being – it still has in them a very great utility, that of **correcting** the cognition of this being by making it agree with itself and with every intelligible aim, and by purifying it of everything that might be incompatible with the concept of an original being, and of all admixture of empirical limitations.

Accordingly, despite all of its inadequacies, transcendental theology retains an important negative use, and is a constant censor of our reason when it has to do merely with pure ideas, which for this very reason admit of no standard but the transcendental one. For if in some other, perhaps practical relation, the **presupposition** of a highest and all-sufficient being, as supreme intelligence, were to assert its validity without any objection, then it would be of the greatest importance to determine this concept precisely on its transcendental side, as the concept of a necessary and most real being, to get rid of what is incompatible with the highest reality, what belongs to mere appearance (anthropomorphism, broadly understood), and at the same time to get out of the way all opposed assertions, whether they be **atheistic, deistic** or **anthropomorphic;** all this is very easy to do in such a critical treatment, since the same grounds for considering human reason incapable of asserting the existence of such a being, when laid before our eyes, also suffice to prove the unsuitability[c] of all counter-assertions. For where, by pure speculation of reason, will anyone acquire the insight that there is no highest being as the original ground of everything? Or that none of the properties apply to it that we represent, in accordance with their consequences, as analogical with the dynamic realities of a thinking being? Or that, in the latter case, they have to be subject to all the limitations inevitably imposed by sensibility on the intelligences with which experience acquaints us?[d]

A 640/ B 668

A 641/ B 669

---

[a] *Object*
[b] *überschwenglicher*
[c] *Untauglichkeit*
[d] Kant's sentence encompasses all three disjuncts and ends with a period.

Thus the highest being remains for the merely speculative use of reason a mere but nevertheless **faultless ideal,** a concept which concludes and crowns the whole of human cognition, whose objective reality cannot of course be proved on this path, but also cannot be refuted; and if there should be a moral theology that can make good this lack, then transcendental theology, up to now only problematic, will prove to be indispensable through determining its concept and by ceaselessly censoring a reason that is deceived often enough by sensibility and does not always agree with its own ideas. Necessity, infinity, unity, existence outside the world (not as soul of the world), eternity without all conditions of time, omnipresence without all conditions of space, omnipotence, etc.: these are purely transcendental predicates, and hence a purified A 642 / B 670 concept of them, which every theology needs so very badly, can be drawn only from transcendental theology.*a*

a In his copy of the first edition, Kant adds: "Whether, if there is no demonstration of the existence of God, there is not at least a great probability. This is not at all worthy of the object [*Objects*] also not possible on this path. Probability in the absolutely necessary is contradictory.

"All necessity of a thing as hypothesis is subjective, namely a need of reason of [our] speculation." (E CLXXXI, p. 54; 23:43)

Appendix
to the Transcendental Dialectic

On the regulative use of the ideas
of pure reason.[115]

The outcome of all dialectical attempts of pure reason not only confirms what we have already proved in the Transcendental Analytic, namely that all the inferences that would carry us out beyond the field of possible experience are deceptive and groundless, but it also simultaneously teaches us this particular lesson: that human reason has a natural propensity to overstep all these boundaries, and that transcendental ideas are just as natural to it as the categories are to the understanding, although with this difference, that just as the categories lead to truth, i.e., to the agreement of our concepts with their objects,[a] the ideas effect a mere, but irresistible, illusion, deception by which one can hardly resist even through the most acute criticism.

Everything grounded in the nature of our powers must be purposive and consistent with their correct use, if only we can guard against a certain misunderstanding and find out their proper direction. Thus the transcendental ideas too will presumably have a good and consequently **immanent** use, even though, if their significance is misunderstood and they are taken for concepts of real things, they can be transcendent in their application and for that very reason deceptive. For in regard to the whole of possible experience, it is not the idea itself but only its use that can be either **extravagant** (transcendent) or **indigenous** (immanent), according to whether one directs them straightway to a supposed object corresponding to them, or only to the use of the understanding in general regarding the objects with which it has to do; and all errors of subreption are always to be ascribed to a defect in judgment, never to understanding or to reason.

Reason never relates directly to an object, but solely to the understanding and by means of it to reason's own empirical use, hence it does not **create** any concepts (of objects)[b] but only **orders** them and gives

[a] *Objecte*
[b] *Objecte*

them that unity which they can have in their greatest possible extension, i.e., in relation to the totality of series; the understanding does not look to this totality at all, but only to the connection **through which series** of conditions always **come about** according to concepts. Thus reason really has as object only the understanding and its purposive applica- A644/B672 tion, and just as the understanding unites the manifold into an object[a] through concepts, so reason on its side unites the manifold of concepts through ideas by positing a certain collective unity as the goal of the un- derstanding's actions, which are otherwise concerned only with distrib- utive unity.

Accordingly, I assert: the transcendental ideas are never of constitu- tive use, so that the concepts of certain objects would thereby be given, and in case one so understands them, they are merely sophistical (dia- lectical) concepts. On the contrary, however, they have an excellent and indispensably necessary regulative use, namely that of directing the un- derstanding to a certain goal respecting which the lines of direction of all its rules converge at one point, which, although it is only an idea (*focus imaginarius*) – i.e., a point from which the concepts of the under- standing do not really proceed, since it lies entirely outside the bounds of possible experience – nonetheless still serves to obtain for these con- cepts the greatest unity alongside the greatest extension. Now of course it is from this that there arises the deception, as if these lines of direc- tion were shot out[b] from an object lying outside the field of possible empirical cognition (just as objects[c] are seen behind the surface of a mirror); yet this illusion (which can be prevented from deceiving) is nevertheless indispensably necessary if besides the objects before our A645/B673 eyes we want to see those that lie far in the background, i.e., when, in our case, the understanding wants to go beyond every given experience (beyond this part of the whole of possible experience), and hence wants to take the measure of its greatest possible and uttermost extension.

If we survey the cognitions of our understanding in their entire range, then we find that what reason quite uniquely prescribes and seeks to bring about concerning it is the **systematic** in cognition, i.e., its interconnection based on one principle.[d] This unity of reason always presupposes an idea, namely that of the form of a whole of cognition, which precedes the determinate cognition of the parts and contains the conditions for determining *a priori* the place of each part and its rela-

---

[a] *Object*
[b] The text reads "*ausgeschlossen . . . wären*" (were excluded). Editors have amended the text at this point in various ways. We follow Erdmann, substituting "*ausgeschossen . . . wären*"; a different but also eligible possibility is "*aus geschlossen*" (inferred from).
[c] *Objecte*
[d] *Zusammenhang aus einem Princip*

tion to the others. Accordingly, this idea postulates complete unity of the understanding's cognition, through which this cognition comes to be not merely a contingent aggregate but a system interconnected in accordance with necessary laws. One cannot properly say that this idea is the concept of an object,[a] but only that of the thoroughgoing unity of these concepts, insofar as the idea serves the understanding as a rule. Such concepts of reason are not created by nature, rather we question nature according to these ideas, and we take our cognition to be defective as long as it is not adequate to them. Admittedly, it is hard to find **pure earth, pure water, pure air,** etc. Nevertheless, concepts of them are required (though as far as their complete purity is concerned, have their origin only in reason) in order appropriately to determine the share that each of these natural causes has in appearance; thus one reduces[b] all materials to earths (mere weight, as it were), to salts and combustibles (as force), and finally to water and air as vehicles (machines, as it were, by means of which the aforementioned operate), in order to explain the chemical effects of materials in accordance with the idea of a mechanism. For even though it is not actually expressed this way, it is still very easy to discover the influence of reason on the classifications of students of nature.

A646/B674

If reason is the faculty of deriving the particular from the universal, then: Either the universal is **in itself certain** and given, and only **judgment** is required for subsuming, and the particular is necessarily determined through it. This I call the "apodictic" use of reason. Or the universal is assumed only **problematically,** and it is a mere idea, the particular being certain while the universality of the rule for this consequent is still a problem; then several particular cases, which are all certain, are tested by the rule, to see if they flow from it, and in the case in which it seems that all the particular cases cited follow from it, then the universality of the rule is inferred, including all subsequent cases, even those that are not given in themselves. This I will call the "hypothetical" use of reason.

A647/B675

The hypothetical use of reason, on the basis of ideas as problematic concepts, is not properly **constitutive,** that is, not such that if one judges in all strictness the truth of the universal rule assumed as a hypothesis thereby follows; for how is one to know all possible consequences, which would prove the universality of the assumed principle if they followed from it? Rather, this use of reason is only regulative, bringing unity into particular cognitions as far as possible and thereby **approximating** the rule to universality.

The hypothetical use of reason is therefore directed at the system-

---

[a] *Object*
[b] *bringt . . . auf*

atic unity of the understanding's cognitions, which, however, is the **touchstone of truth** for its rules. Conversely, systematic unity (as mere idea) is only a **projected** unity, which one must regard not as given in itself, but only as a problem;[a] this unity, however, helps to find a principle[b] for the manifold and particular uses of the understanding, thereby guiding it even in those cases that are not given and making it coherently connected.[c]

From this, however, one sees only that systematic unity or the unity of reason of the manifold of the understanding's cognition is a **logical** principle,[d] in order, where the understanding alone does not attain to rules, to help it through ideas, simultaneously creating unanimity among its various rules under one principle[e] (the systematic), and thereby interconnection, as far as this can be done. But whether the constitution of objects or the nature of the understanding that cognizes them as such are in themselves determined to systematic unity, and whether one could in a certain measure postulate this *a priori* without taking into account such an interest of reason, and therefore say that all possible cognitions of the understanding (including empirical ones) have the unity of reason, and stand under common principles[f] from which they could be derived despite their variety: that would be a **transcendental** principle of reason, which would make systematic unity not merely something subjectively and logically necessary, as method, but objectively necessary.

A648/B676

We will illustrate this through one case in which reason is used. Among the different kinds of unity according to concepts of the understanding belongs the causality of a substance, which is called "power."[g] At first glance the various appearances of one and the same substance show such diversity that one must assume almost as many powers as there are effects, as in the human mind there are sensation, consciousness, imagination, memory, wit, the power to distinguish, pleasure, desire, etc. Initially a logical maxim bids us to reduce this apparent variety as far as possible by discovering hidden identity through comparison, and seeing if imagination combined with consciousness may not be memory, wit, the power to distinguish, or perhaps even understanding and reason. The idea of a **fundamental power** – though logic does not at all ascertain whether there is such a thing – is at least the problem[h]

A649/B677

---

[a] *Problem*
[b] *Princip*
[c] *zusammenhängend*
[d] *Princip*
[e] *Princip*
[f] *Principien*
[g] *Kraft*
[h] *Problem*

set by a systematic representation of the manifoldness of powers. The logical principle*a* of reason demands this unity as far as it is possible to bring it about, and the more appearances of this power and that power are found to be identical, the more probable it becomes that they are nothing but various expressions of one and the same power, which can be called (comparatively) their **fundamental power.** One proceeds in just the same way with the rest of the powers.

These comparatively fundamental powers must once again be compared with one another, so as to discover their unanimity and thereby bring them close to a single radical, i.e., absolutely fundamental, power. But this unity of reason is merely hypothetical. One asserts not that such a power must in fact be found, but rather that one must seek it for the benefit of reason, namely for setting up certain principles*b* for the many rules with which experience may furnish us, and that where it can be done, one must in such a way bring systematic unity into cognition.

A650/B678

But if one attends to the transcendental use of the understanding, it is evident that this idea of a fundamental power in general does not function*c* merely as a problem*d* for hypothetical use, but pretends to objective reality, so that the systematic unity of a substance's many powers are postulated and an apodictic principle*e* of reason is erected. For even without our having attempted to find the unanimity among the many powers, or indeed even when all such attempts to discover it have failed, we nevertheless presuppose that such a thing will be found; and it is not only, as in the case cited, on account of the unity of substance that reason presupposes systematic unity among manifold powers, but rather reason does so even where many powers, though to a certain degree of the same kind, are found, as with matter in general, where particular natural laws stand under more general ones; and the parsimony of principles*f* is not merely a principle of economy for reason, but becomes an inner law of its nature.

In fact it cannot even be seen how there could be a logical principle*g* of rational unity among rules unless a transcendental principle*h* is presupposed, through which such a systematic unity, as pertaining to the object*i* itself, is assumed *a priori* as necessary. For by what warrant can reason in its logical use claim to treat the manifoldness of the powers

A651/B679

a *Princip*
b *Principien*
c *nicht . . . bestimmt sei*
d *Problem*
e *Princip*
f *Principien*
g *Princip*
h *Princip*
i *Object*

which nature gives to our cognition as merely a concealed unity, and to derive them as far as it is able from some fundamental power, when reason is free to admit that it is just as possible that all powers are different in kind, and that its derivation of them from a systematic unity is not in conformity with nature? For then reason would proceed directly contrary to its vocation, since it would set as its goal an idea that entirely contradicts the arrangement of nature. Nor can one say that it*a* has previously gleaned*b* this unity from the contingent constitution of nature in accordance with its principles*c* of reason. For the law of reason to seek unity is necessary, since without it we would have no reason, and without that, no coherent*d* use of the understanding, and, lacking that, no sufficient mark of empirical truth; thus in regard to the latter we simply have to presuppose the systematic unity of nature as objectively valid and necessary.

We also find this transcendental presupposition hidden in an admirable way in the principles of the philosophers, although they have not always recognized it or admitted it to themselves. That all the manifoldness of individual things does not exclude the identity of **species;** that the several species must be treated only as various determinations A652/B680 of fewer **genera,** and the latter of still higher **families,***e* etc.; that therefore a certain systematic unity of all possible empirical concepts must be sought insofar as they can be derived from higher and more general ones: this is a scholastic rule or logical principle,*f* without which there could be no use of reason, because we can infer from the universal to the particular only on the ground of the universal properties of things under which the particular properties stand.

But that such unanimity is to be encountered even in nature is something the philosophers presuppose in the familiar scholastic rule that one should not multiply beginnings (principles)*g* without necessity (*entia praeter necessitatem non esse multiplicanda*).*h* It is thereby said that the nature of things themselves offers material for the unity of reason, and the apparently infinite variety should not restrain us from conjecturing behind it a unity of fundamental properties, from which their manifoldness can be derived only through repeated determination. This unity, although it is a mere idea, has been pursued so eagerly in all ages that more often there has been cause to moderate than to encourage the de-

---

a i.e., reason
b *abgenommen*
c *Principien*
d *zusammenhängende*
e *Geschlechter*
f *Princip*
g *Principien*
h Entities are not to be multiplied without necessity.[116]

sire for it. The analysts had already done much when they were able to reduce all salts to two main genera, acidic and alkaline, but they even attempted to regard this distinction as merely a variety or varied expression of one and the same fundamental material. They sought to get the several species of earths (the material of stone and even of metal) gradually down to three, and finally to two; still not satisfied, they could not dismiss from their thought the conjecture that behind these varieties there is a single genus or even indeed a common principle*a* for both earths and salts. One might have believed that this is merely a device of reason for achieving economy, for saving as much trouble as possible, and a hypothetical attempt that, if it succeeds, will through this unity give probability to the grounds of explanation it presupposed. Yet such a selfish aim can easily be distinguished from the idea, in accordance with which everyone presupposes that this unity of reason conforms to nature itself; and here reason does not beg but commands, though without being able to determine the bounds of this unity.

If among the appearances offering themselves to us there were such a great variety – I will not say of form (for they might be similar to one another in that) but of content, i.e., regarding the manifoldness of existing beings – that even the most acute human understanding, through comparison of one with another, could not detect the least similarity (a case which can at least be thought), then the logical law of genera would not obtain at all, no concept of a genus, nor any other universal concept, indeed no understanding at all would obtain, since it is the understanding that has to do with such concepts. The logical principle*b* of genera therefore presupposes a transcendental one if it is to be applied to nature (by which I here understand only objects that are given to us). According to that principle, sameness of kind is necessarily presupposed in the manifold of a possible experience (even though we cannot determine its degree *a priori*), because without it no empirical concepts and hence no experience would be possible.

To the logical principle*c* of genera which postulates identity there is opposed another, namely that of **species,** which needs manifoldness and variety in things despite their agreement under the same genus, and prescribes to the understanding that it be no less attentive to variety than to agreement. This principle (of discrimination, or of the faculty of distinguishing) severely limits the rashness of the first principle (of wit);[117] and here reason shows two interests that conflict with each other: on the one side, an interest in the **domain** (universality) in regard to genera, on the other an interest in **content** (determinacy) in respect

a *Princip*
b *Princip*
c *Princip*

of the manifoldness of species; for in the first case the understanding thinks much **under** its concepts, while in the second it thinks all the more **in them.** This expresses itself in the very different ways of think- A655/B683 ing among students of nature; some of whom (who are chiefly speculative) are hostile to differences in kind, while others (chiefly empirical minds) constantly seek to split nature into so much manifoldness that one would almost have to give up the hope of judging its appearances according to general principles.[a]

This latter way of thinking is also obviously grounded on a logical principle[b] that has as its aim the systematic completeness of all cognitions, if, starting with the genus, I descend to whatever manifold may be contained under it, and thus in this way seek to secure extension for the system, just as in the first case I seek to secure simplicity by ascending to the genus. For from the sphere of the concept signifying a genus it can no more be seen how far its division will go than it can be seen from space how far division will go in the matter that fills it. Hence every **genus** requires different **species,** and these **subspecies,** and since none of the latter once again is ever without a sphere, (a domain as a *conceptus communis*),[c] reason demands in its entire extension that no species be regarded as in itself the lowest; for since each species is always a concept that contains within itself only what is common to different things, this concept cannot be thoroughly determined, hence it cannot be related to A656/B684 an individual, consequently, it must at every time contain other concepts, i.e., subspecies, under itself. This law of specification could be expressed thus: *entium varietates non temere esse minuendas.*[d]

But it is easy to see that even this logical law would be without sense or application if it were not grounded on a transcendental **law of specification,** which plainly does not demand an actual **infinity** in regard to the varieties of things that can become our objects – for the logical principle[e] asserting the **indeterminacy** of the logical sphere in regard to possible division would give no occasion for that; but it does impose on the understanding the demand to seek under every species that comes before us for subspecies, and for every variety smaller varieties. For if there were no lower concepts, then there would also be no higher ones. Now the understanding cognizes everything only through concepts; consequently, however far it goes in its divisions, it never cog-

---

[a] *Principien*
[b] *Princip*
[c] common concept
[d] "The varieties of entities are not to be diminished rashly." Clearly this is Kant's attempt to formulate a counter-principle to the principle of parsimony or "law of genera": *entia praeter necessitatem non esse multiplicanda* (Entities are not to be multiplied without necessity). See A652/B680 and endnote 116.
[e] *Princip*

nizes through mere intuition but always yet again through lower concepts. The cognition of appearances in their thoroughgoing determinacy (which is possible only through understanding) demands a ceaselessly continuing specification of its concepts, and a progress to the varieties that always still remain, from which abstraction is made in the concept of the species and even more in that of the genus.

A657/B685 Also this law of specification cannot be borrowed from experience; for experience can make no such extensive disclosures. Empirical specification soon stops in distinguishing the manifold, unless through the already preceding transcendental law of specification as a principle*a* of reason it is led to seek such disclosures and to keep on assuming them even when they do not immediately reveal themselves to the senses. That there are absorbent earths of different species (chalky earths and muriatic earths) needed for its discovery a foregoing rule of reason that made it a task for the understanding to seek for varieties, by presupposing nature to be so abundant that it presumes them. For we have an understanding only under the presupposition of varieties in nature, just as we have one only under the condition that nature's objects*b* have in themselves a sameness of kind, because it is just the manifoldness of what can be grasped together under a concept that constitutes use of this concept and the business of the understanding.

Reason thus prepares the field for the understanding: 1. by a principle*c* of **sameness of kind** in the manifold under higher genera, 2. by a principle of the **variety** of what is same in kind under lower species; and in order to complete the systematic unity it adds 3. still another law of the **affinity** of all concepts, which offers a continuous transition from A658/B686 every species to every other through a graduated increase of varieties. We can call these the principles*d* of the **homogeneity, specification** and **continuity** of forms. The last arises by uniting the first two, according as one has completed the systematic connection in the idea by ascending to higher genera, as well as descending to lower species; for then all manifolds are akin*e* one to another, because they are all collectively descended,*f* through every degree of extended determination, from a single highest genus.

Systematic unity under the three logical principles*g* can be made palpable*h* in the following way. One can regard every concept as a point,

---

a *Princip*
b *Objecte*
c *Princip*
d *Principien*
e *verwandt*
f *abstammen*
g *Principien*
h *sinnlich*

which, as the standpoint of an observer, has its horizon, i.e., a multiplicity of things that can be represented and surveyed, as it were, from it. Within this horizon a multiplicity of points must be able to be given to infinity, each of which in turn has its narrower field of view; i.e., every species contains subspecies in accordance with the principle[a] of specification, and the logical horizon consists only of smaller horizons (subspecies), but not of points that have no domain (individuals). But different horizons, i.e., genera, which are determined from just as many concepts, one can think as drawn out into a common horizon, which one can survey collectively from its middle point, which is the higher genus, until finally the highest genus is the universal and true horizon, determined from the standpoint of the highest concept and comprehending all manifoldness, as genera, species, and subspecies, under itself.

A659/B687

The law of homogeneity leads me to this highest standpoint, while the law of specification leads to all the lower ones and their greatest possible variety. Since, however, in such a way nothing in the entire domain of all possible concepts is empty, and outside it nothing can be encountered, there arises from the presupposition of that universal field of view and its thoroughgoing division the principle: *non datur vacuum formarum,*[b] i.e., there are no different original and primary genera, which would be, as it were, isolated and separated from one another (by an empty intervening space), but rather all the manifold genera are only partitionings[c] of a single supreme and universal genus; and from this principle its immediate consequence: *datur continuum formarum,*[d] i.e., all varieties of species bound one another and permit no transition to one another by a leap, but only through every smaller degree of distinction, so that from each one can reach another; in a word, there are no species or subspecies that are proximate (in the concept of reason), but intervening species are always possible, whose difference from the first and second species is smaller than their difference from each other.

A660/B688

The first law, therefore, guards against excess in the manifold variety of original genera, and recommends sameness of kind; the second, on the contrary, limits in turn this inclination to unanimity, and demands that one distinguish subspecies before one turns to the individuals with one's universal concepts. The third law unites the first two, prescribing even in the case of the highest manifoldness a sameness of kind through the graduated transition from one species[e] to others, which shows a

---

[a] *Princip*
[b] There is no vacuum of forms.
[c] *Abteilungen*
[d] There is a continuum of forms.
[e] *Species*

kind of affinity[a] of various branches, insofar as they have all sprouted from one stem.

This logical law of the *continuum specierum* (*formarum logicarum*)[b] presupposes, however, a transcendental law (*lex continui in natura*),[c] without which the use of the understanding through the former prescription would only mislead, since the prescription would perhaps take a path directly opposed to nature. This law must therefore rest on pure transcendental and not empirical grounds. For in the latter case it would come later than the systems; but it really first produced what is systematic in the cognition of nature. Behind these laws there is also nothing like a hidden intention to initiate probes, as mere experiments,

A 661 / B 689   though plainly this interconnection, where it applies, gives us a powerful reason to take as well grounded the unity that is hypothetically thought-out, and thus it has its utility in this respect; rather, one can see clearly that the laws judge the parsimony of fundamental causes, the manifoldness of effects, and the consequent affinity[d] of the members of nature in themselves reasonably and in conformity with nature, and these principles therefore carry their recommendation directly in themselves,[e] and not merely as methodological devices.

But it is easy to see that this continuity of forms is a mere idea, for which a corresponding object can by no means be displayed in experience, **not only** because the species[f] in nature are really partitioned and therefore in themselves have to constitute a *quantum discretum*,[g] and if the graduated progress in their affinity[h] were continuous, they would also have to contain a true infinity of intermediate members between any two given species, which is impossible; **but also** because we could make no determinate empirical use at all of this law, since through it there is indicated not the least mark of that affinity, or how and how far we are to seek the degrees of its variety; rather, we are given nothing more than a general indication that we are to seek for it.

A 662 / B 690   If we transpose the principles[i] we have adduced, so as to put them in an order which **accords with their experiential use**, then the principles[j] of systematic **unity** would stand something like this: **manifold-**

---

[a] *Verwandtschaft*
[b] "continuum of species (of logical forms)"; Kant declines the entire phrase in the genitive.
[c] law of the continuum in nature
[d] *Verwandtschaft*
[e] *bei sich*
[f] *Species*
[g] discrete quantum
[h] *Verwandtschaft*
[i] *Principien*
[j] *Principien*

ness, affinity, *ᵃ* **unity,** each taken, however, as idea*ᵇ* in the highest degree of their completeness. Reason presupposes those cognitions of the understanding which are first applied to experience, and seeks the unity of these cognitions in accordance with ideas that go much further than experience can reach. The affinity *ᶜ* of the manifold, without detriment to its variety, under a principle*ᵈ* of unity, concerns not merely the things, but even more the mere properties and powers of things. Hence if, e.g., the course of the planets is given to us as circular through a (still not fully corrected) experience, and we find variations, then we suppose these variations to consist in an orbit that can deviate from the circle through each of an infinity of intermediate degrees according to constant laws; i.e., we suppose that the movements of the planets that are not a circle will more or less approximate to its properties, and then we come upon the ellipse. The comets show an even greater variety in their paths, since (as far as observation reaches) they do not ever return in a circle; yet we guess at a parabolic course for them, since it is still akin*ᵉ* to the ellipse and, if the major axis of the latter is very long, it cannot be distinguished from it in all our observations. Thus under the guidance of those principles *ᶠ* we come to a unity of genera in the forms of these paths, but thereby also further to unity in the cause of all the laws of this motion (gravitation); from there we extend our conquests, seeking to explain all variations and apparent deviations from those rules on the basis of the same principle;*ᵍ* finally we even add on more than experience can ever confirm, namely in accordance with the rules of affinity,*ᵇ* even conceiving hyperbolical paths for comets in which these bodies leave our solar system entirely and, going from sun to sun, unite in their course the most remote parts of a world system, which for us is unbounded yet connected through one and the same moving force.*ⁱ*

A663/B691

What is strange about these principles,*ʲ* and what alone concerns us, is this: that they seem to be transcendental, and even though they contain mere ideas to be followed in the empirical use of reason, which reason can follow only asymptotically, as it were, i.e., merely by ap-

---

ᵃ Verwandtschaft
ᵇ jede derselben aber als Ideen . . . Kant's pronoun and noun do not agree in number; with Erdmann, we read *Idee* (singular).
ᶜ Verwandtschaft
ᵈ Principien
ᵉ verwandt
ᶠ Principien
ᵍ Princip
ᵇ Verwandtschaft
ⁱ Kraft
ʲ Principien

proximation, without ever reaching them, yet these principles,[a] as synthetic propositions *a priori*, nevertheless have objective but indeterminate validity, and serve as a rule of possible experience, and can even be used with good success, as heuristic principles, in actually elaborating it; and yet one cannot bring about a transcendental deduction of them, which, as has been proved above, is always impossible in regard to ideas.

A 664/ B 692

In the Transcendental Analytic we have distinguished among the principles of understanding the **dynamical** ones, as merely regulative principles[b] of **intuition,** from the **mathematical** ones, which are constitutive in regard to intuition. Despite this, the dynamical laws we are thinking of are still constitutive in regard to **experience,** since they make possible *a priori* the **concepts** without which there is no experience. Principles[c] of pure reason, on the contrary, cannot be constitutive even in regard to empirical **concepts,** because for them no corresponding schema of sensibility can be given, and therefore they can have no object *in concreto.* Now if I depart from such an empirical use of them, as constitutive principles, how will I nevertheless secure for them a regulative use, and with this some objective validity? And what sort of meaning[d] can that use have?

The understanding constitutes an object for reason, just as sensibility does for the understanding. To make systematic the unity of all possible empirical actions of the understanding is a business of reason, just as the understanding connects the manifold of appearances through concepts and brings it under empirical laws. The actions of the understanding, however, apart from the schemata of sensibility, are **undetermined;** likewise the **unity of reason** is also in itself **undetermined** in regard to the conditions under which, and the degree to which, the understanding should combine its concepts systematically. Yet although no schema can be found in **intuition** for the thoroughgoing systematic unity of all concepts of the understanding, an **analogue** of such a schema can and must be given, which is the idea of the **maximum** of division and unification of the understanding's cognition in one principle.[e] For that which is greatest and most complete may be kept determinately in mind,[f] because all restricting conditions, which give indeterminate manifolds, are omitted. Thus the idea of reason is an analogue of a schema of sensibility, but with this difference, that the application of concepts of the understanding to the schema of reason is not likewise a

A 665/ B 693

---

[a] *Principien*

[b] *Principien*

[c] *Principien*

[d] *Bedeutung*

[e] *Princip*

[f] *lässt sich bestimmt gedenken;* the first edition reads "*lässt sich bestimmt denken*" (may be thought determinately).

cognition of the object itself (as in the application of the categories to their sensible schemata), but only a rule or principle*a* of the systematic unity of all use of the understanding. Now since every principle that establishes for the understanding a thoroughgoing unity of its use *a priori* is also valid, albeit only indirectly, for the object of experience, the principles of pure reason will also have objective reality in regard to this object, yet not so as to **determine** something in it, but only to indicate the procedure in accordance with which the empirical and determinate use of the understanding in experience can be brought into thoroughgoing agreement with itself, by bringing it **as far as possible** into connection with the principle*b* of thoroughgoing unity; and from that it is derived.

A 666 / B 694

I call all subjective principles that are taken not from the constitution of the object*c* but from the interest of reason in regard to a certain possible perfection of the cognition of this object,*d* **maxims** of reason.[118] Thus there are maxims of speculative reason, which rest solely on reason's speculative interest, even though it may seem as if they were objective principles.*e*

If merely regulative principles are considered as constitutive, then as objective principles*f* they can be in conflict; but if one considers them merely as **maxims,** then it is not a true conflict, but it is merely a different interest of reason that causes a divorce between ways of thinking.*g* Reason has in fact only a single unified*b* interest, and the conflict between its maxims is only a variation and a reciprocal limitation of the methods satisfying this interest.

In this way the interest in **manifoldness** (in accordance with the principle*i* of specification) might hold more for **this** sophistical reasoner,*j* while **unity** (in accordance with the principle*k* of aggregation) holds more for **that** one. Each of them believes that his judgment comes from insight into the object,*l* and yet he grounds it solely on the greater or lesser attachment to one of the two principles, neither of which rests on any objective grounds, but only on the interest of reason, and that could better be called "maxims" than "principles."*m* If I see

A 667 / B 695

a *Princip*
b *Princip*
c *Object*
d *Object*
e *Principien*
f *Principien*
g *Trennung der Denkungsart*
b *einiges*
i *Princip*
j *Vernünftler*
k *Princip*
l *Object*
m *Principien*

insightful men in conflict with one another over the characteristics of human beings, animals or plants, or even of bodies in the mineral realm, where some, e.g., assume particular characters of peoples based on their descent or on decisive and hereditary distinctions between families, races, etc., while others, by contrast, fix their minds on the thought that nature has set up no predispositions at all in this matter, and that all differences rest only on external contingency, then I need only consider the constitution of the object in order to comprehend that it lies too deeply hidden for either of them to be able to speak from an insight into the nature of the object.[a] There is nothing here but the twofold interest of reason, where each party takes to heart one interest or the other, or affects to do so, hence either the maxim of the manifoldness of nature or that of the unity of nature; these maxims can of course be united, but as long as they are held to be objective insights, they occasion not only conflict but also hindrances that delay the discovery of the truth, until a means is found of uniting the disputed[b] interests and satisfying reason about them.

A 668/ B 696

It is the same with the assertion of, or the attack on, the widely respected law of the **ladder of continuity**[c] among creatures, made current by Leibniz[119] and excellently supported by Bonnet,[120] which is nothing but a pursuit of the principle of affinity resting on the interests of reason; for observation and insight into the arrangements of nature could never provide it as something to be asserted objectively. The rungs of such a ladder, such as experience can give them to us, stand too far apart from one another, and what we presume to be small differences are commonly such wide gaps in nature itself that on the basis of such observations (chiefly of the great manifoldness of things, among which it must always be easy to find certain similarities and approximations) nothing can be figured out about the intentions of nature. The method for seeking out order in nature in accord with such a principle,[d] on the contrary, and the maxim of regarding such an order as grounded in nature in general, even though it is undetermined where or to what extent, is a legitimate and excellent regulative principle[e] of reason, which, however, as such, goes much too far for experience or observation ever to catch up with it; without determining anything, it only points[f] the way toward systematic unity.

[a] *Object*
[b] *streitig;* the first edition reads "*strittig*" (dubious).
[c] *kontinuierlichen Stufenleiter*
[d] *Princip*
[e] *Princip*
[f] *vorzeichnen*

On the final aim of the natural dialectic
of human reason

The ideas of pure reason can never be dialectical in themselves; rather it is merely their misuse which brings it about that a deceptive illusion arises out of them; for they are given as problems for us by the nature of our reason, and this highest court of appeals for all rights and claims of our speculation cannot possibly contain original deceptions and semblances. Presumably, therefore, they have their good and purposive vocation in regard to the natural predisposition of our reason. But as usual the mob of sophists makes a hue and cry over absurdities and contradictions and rails at the regime whose inmost plans they are unable to penetrate, although they too have its benevolent influences to thank for their preservation and even for the culture which puts them in a position to blame and condemn.

One cannot avail oneself of a concept *a priori* with any security unless one has brought about a transcendental deduction of it. The ideas of reason, of course, do not permit any deduction of the same kind as the categories; but if they are to have the least objective validity, even if it is only an indeterminate one, and are not to represent merely empty thought-entities (*entia rationis ratiocinantis*),[a] then a deduction of them must definitely be possible, granted that it must also diverge quite far from the deduction one can carry out in the case of the categories. That deduction is the completion of the critical business of pure reason, and it is what we will now undertake.

It makes a big difference whether something is given to my reason as **an object absolutely** or is given only as an **object in the idea.** In the first case my concepts go as far as determining the object; but in the second, there is really only a schema for which no object is given, not even hypothetically, but which serves only to represent other objects to us, in accordance with their systematic unity, by means of the relation to this idea, hence to represent these objects indirectly. Thus I say the concept of a highest intelligence is a mere idea, i.e., its objective reality is not to consist in the fact that it relates straightway to an object (for in such a signification we would not be able to justify its objective validity); rather, it is only a schema, ordered in accordance with the conditions of the greatest unity of reason, for the concept of a thing in general, which

---

[a] *Gedankenwesen;* beings of sophistical reason

serves only to preserve the greatest systematic unity in the empirical use of our reason, in that one derives the object of experience, as it were, from the imagined object of this idea as its ground or cause. Then it is said, e.g., that the things in the world must be considered **as if** they had gotten their existence from a highest intelligence. In such a way the idea is only a heuristic and not an ostensive concept; and it shows not how an object is constituted but how, under the guidance of that concept, we ought to **seek after** the constitution and connection of objects of experience in general. Now if one can show that although the three kinds of transcendental ideas (**psychological,**[a] **cosmological** and **theological**) cannot be referred directly to any object corresponding to them and to its **determination,** and nevertheless that all rules of the empirical use of reason under the presupposition of such an **object in the idea** lead to systematic unity, always extending the cognition of experience but never going contrary to experience, then it is a necessary **maxim** of reason to proceed in accordance with such ideas. And this is the transcendental deduction of all the ideas of speculative reason, not as **constitutive** principles[b] for the extension of our cognition to more objects than experience can give, but as **regulative** principles[c] for the systematic unity of the manifold of empirical cognition in general, through which this cognition, within its proper boundaries, is cultivated and corrected[d] more than could happen without such ideas, through the mere use of the principles of understanding.

A 672 / B 700
I will make this clearer. Following the ideas named above as principles,[e] we will **first** (in psychology) connect all appearances, actions, and receptivity of our mind to the guiding thread of inner experience **as if** the mind were a simple substance that (at least in this life) persists in existence with personal identity, while its states – to which the states of the body belong only as external conditions – are continuously changing. Then **second** (in cosmology) we have to pursue the conditions of the inner as well as the outer appearances of nature through an investigation that will nowhere be completed, **as if** nature were infinite in itself and without a first or supreme member – although, without denying, outside of all appearances, the merely intelligible primary grounds for them, we may never bring these grounds into connection with explanations of nature, because we are not acquainted with them at all. Finally and **thirdly,** (in regard to theology) we have to consider every-

---

[a] The first edition reads "the psychological . . . "
[b] *Principien*
[c] *Principien*
[d] *berichtigt*; the first edition reads "*berechtigt*" (justified).
[e] *Principien*

thing that might ever belong to the context of possible experience **as if** this experience constituted an absolute unity, but one dependent through and through, and always still conditioned within the world of sense, yet at the same time **as if** the sum total of all appearances (the world of sense itself) had a single supreme and all-sufficient ground outside its range, namely an independent, original, and creative reason, as it were, in relation to which we direct every empirical use of **our** reason in its greatest extension **as if** the objects themselves had arisen from that original image of all reason. That means: it is not from a simple thinking substance that we derive the inner appearances of our soul, but from one another in accordance with the idea of a simple being; it is not from a highest intelligence that we derive the order of the world and its systematic unity, but rather it is from the idea of a most wise cause that we take the rule that reason is best off using for its own satisfaction when it connects up causes and effects in the world.

A673/B701

Now there is not the least thing to hinder us from **assuming** these ideas as objective and hypostatic, except only the cosmological ones, where reason runs up against an antinomy when it tries to bring this about (the psychological and theological ideas contain nothing of that sort at all). For there is no contradiction in them, so how could anyone dispute their objective reality, since he knows just as little about their possibility in denying it as we do in affirming it? Nevertheless, in order to assume something it is not enough that there is no positive hindrance to doing so, and we cannot be allowed to introduce mere thought-entities[a] that transcend all our concepts, though they contradict none of them, as real and determinate objects merely on credit, just so that speculative reason can complete its business as it likes. Thus they should not be assumed in themselves, but their reality should hold only as that of a schema of the regulative principle[b] for the systematic unity of all cognitions of nature; hence they should be grounded only as analogues of real things, but not as things in themselves. We remove from the object of an idea those conditions that limit our concept of the understanding, but that also make it possible for us to be able to have a determinate concept of any thing. And now we are thinking of a Something about which we have no concept at all of how it is in itself, but about which we think a relation to the sum total of appearances, which is analogous to the relation that appearances have to one another.

A674/B702

If, accordingly, we assume such ideal entities, then we do not really extend our cognition beyond the objects[c] of possible experience, but

[a] *Gedankenwesen*
[b] *Princip*
[c] *Objecte*

only extend the empirical unity of these objects^a through the systematic unity for which the idea gives us the schema; hence the idea holds not as a constitutive but merely as a regulative principle.^b For that we posit a thing corresponding to the idea, a Something or a real being – by this fact it is not said that we would extend our cognition of things with transcendental concepts; this being is grounded only in the idea and not in itself, hence only in order to express the systematic unity which is to serve us as the standard for the empirical use of reason, without settling anything about what the ground of this unity is, or about the inner property of such a being on which, as cause, it rests.

A675/ B703

Thus the transcendental and single determinate concept of God that merely speculative reason gives us is in the most precise sense **deistic,** i.e., reason does not furnish us with the objective validity of such a concept, but only with the idea of something on which all empirical reality grounds its highest and necessary unity, and which we cannot think except in accordance with the analogy of an actual substance that is the cause of all things according to laws of reason; of course this is insofar as we undertake to think it as a particular object at all, and do not, content with the mere idea of the regulative principle^c of reason, rather prefer to set aside the completion of all conditions of thought as too extravagant^d for human understanding; but that is not consistent with the aim of a perfect systematic unity in our cognition, to which reason at least sets no limits.

A676/ B704

Hence now it happens that if I assume a divine being, I do not have the least concept either of the inner possibility of such a highest perfection or of the necessity of its existence; but then I can deal satisfactorily with all other questions concerning the contingent, and reason can obtain the most perfect satisfaction in regard to the greatest unity for which it is searching in its empirical use, but not in regard to the presupposition itself; this proves that it is reason's speculative interest and not its insight which justifies it in starting from a point lying so far beyond its sphere in order to consider its objects in one complete whole.

Now here, regarding one and the same presupposition, a distinction reveals itself between ways of thinking which is rather subtle but nevertheless of great importance for transcendental philosophy. I can have a satisfactory reason for assuming something relatively (*suppositio relativa*) without being warranted in assuming it absolutely (*suppositio absoluta*). This distinction is pertinent when we have to do merely with a regula-

---

^a *Objecte*
^b *Princip*
^c *Princip*
^d *überschwenglich*

tive principle,[a] which we recognize as necessary, but whose source we do not know,[b] and for which we assume a supreme ground merely with the intention of thinking the universality of the principle[c] all the more determinately, as, e.g., when I think as existing a being that corresponds to a mere and indeed transcendental idea. For here I can never assume the existence of this thing in itself, because none of the concepts through which I can think any object determinately will attain to it, and the conditions for the objective validity of my concepts are excluded by the idea itself. The concepts of reality, substance, causality, even that of necessity in existence have, beyond their use in making possible the empirical cognition of an object, no significance at all which might determine any object.[d] They can therefore be used for explaining the possibility of things in the world of sense, but not the possibility of a **world-whole itself,** because this ground of explanation would have to be outside the world and hence it would not be an object of a possible experience. Now I can nevertheless assume such an incomprehensible being, the object of a mere idea, relative to the world of sense, though not in itself. For if the greatest possible empirical use of my reason is grounded on an idea (that of systematic complete unity, about which I will have more to say presently), which in itself can never be presented adequately in experience, even though it is unavoidably necessary for approximating to the highest possible degree of empirical unity, then I am not only warranted but even compelled to realize this idea, i.e., to posit for it an actual object, but only as a Something in general with which I am not acquainted at all and to which, as a ground of that systematic unity and in relation to that, I give such properties as are analogous to the concepts of the understanding in their empirical use. Thus according to the analogy of realities in the world, of substances, causality, and necessity, I will think of a being that possesses all of these in their highest perfection, and since this idea rests merely on my reason, I am able to think this being as **self-sufficient reason,** which is the cause of the world-whole through ideas of the greatest harmony and unity; thus I leave out all conditions limiting the idea, so as – under the auspices[e] of such an original ground – to make possible systematic unity of the manifold in the world-whole and, by means of this unity, the greatest possible empirical use of reason, by seeing all combinations **as if** they were ordained by a highest reason of which our reason is only a weak copy. Then I think this highest reason through mere concepts, which really have their application only in the

A677/ B705

A678/ B706

---

[a] *Princip*
[b] *erkennen*
[c] *Princip*
[d] *Object*
[e] *Schutze*

world of sense; but since I put that transcendental presupposition to no other use but a relative one – namely that it should give the substratum for the greatest possible unity of experience – I may very well think a being that I distinguish from the world through properties which belong solely to the world of sense. For by no means do I require, nor am I warranted in requiring, cognition of this object of my idea as to what it might be in itself; for I have no concepts for that, and even the concepts of reality, substance, causality, indeed even necessity in existence, lose all meaning[a] and are empty titles for concepts without any content when with them I venture outside the field of sense. I think only the relation[b] which a being, in itself unknown to me, has to the greatest systematic unity of the world-whole, and this is solely in order to make it into the schema of a regulative principle[c] for the greatest possible empirical use of my reason.

A679/ B707

If we now cast our glance over the transcendental object of our idea, then we see that we cannot presuppose its actuality in accordance with the concepts of reality, substance, causality, etc., **in itself,** because these concepts have not the least application to something that is entirely different from the world of sense. Thus reason's supposition[d] of a highest being as the supreme cause is thought merely relatively, on behalf of the systematic unity of the world of sense, and it is a mere Something in the idea, of which we have no concept of what it is **in itself.** This also explains why, in relation to that which is given to the senses as existing, we need the idea of a being which is **necessary** in itself, but can never have the least concept of this being and its absolute **necessity.**

A680/ B708

Now we can place the result of the entire Transcendental Dialectic clearly before our eyes, and precisely determine the final aim of the ideas of pure reason, which become dialectical only through misunderstanding and carelessness. Pure reason is in fact concerned with nothing but itself, and it can have no other concern, because what is given to it is not objects to be unified for the concept of experience, but cognitions of understanding to be unified for the concept of reason, i.e., to be connected in one principle.[e] The unity of reason is the unity of a system, and this systematic unity does not serve reason objectively as a principle, extending it over objects, but subjectively as a maxim, in order to extend it over all possible empirical cognition of objects. Nevertheless, the systematic connection that reason can give to the empirical use of the understanding furthers not only its extension but also

[a] *Bedeutung*
[b] *Relation*
[c] *Princip*
[d] *Supposition*
[e] *Princip*

guarantees its correctness, and the principle *a* of such a systematic unity is also objective but in an indeterminate way (*principium vagum*):*b* not as a constitutive principle*c* for determining something in regard to its direct object, but rather as a merely regulative principle and maxim for furthering and strengthening the empirical use of reason by opening up new paths into the infinite (the undetermined) with which the understanding is not acquainted, yet without ever being the least bit contrary to the laws of its empirical use.

But reason cannot think this systematic unity in any other way than $\qquad$ A681 / B709 by giving its idea an object, which, however, cannot be given through any experience; for experience never gives an example of perfect systematic unity. Now this being of reason (*ens rationis ratiocinatae*)*d* is, to be sure, a mere idea, and is therefore not assumed absolutely and **in itself** as something actual, but is rather taken as a ground only problematically (because we cannot reach it through any concepts of the understanding), so as to regard all the connection of things in the world of sense **as if** they had their ground in this being of reason; but solely with the intention of grounding on it the systematic unity that is indispensable to reason and conducive in every way to empirical cognition of the understanding but can never be obstructive to it.

One mistakes the significance of this idea right away if one takes it to be the assertion, or even only the presupposition, of an actual thing*e* to which one would think of ascribing the ground for the systematic constitution of the world; rather, one leaves it entirely open what sort of constitution in itself this ground, which eludes our concepts, might have, and posits an idea only as a unique standpoint from which alone one can extend the unity that is so essential to reason and so salutary to the understanding; in a word, this transcendental thing is merely the $\qquad$ A682 / B710 schema of that regulative principle*f* through which reason, as far as it can, extends systematic unity over all experience.

The first object*g* of such an idea is I myself, considered merely as thinking nature (soul). If I want to seek out the properties with which a thinking thing exists in itself, then I have to ask experience, and I cannot even apply any of the categories to this object except insofar as its schema is given in sensible intuition. By this means, however, I will never attain to a systematic unity of all the appearances of inner sense. Thus instead of the concept of experience (of that which the soul actu-

---

a *Princip*

b vague principle

c *Princip*

d "being of reason reasoned," i.e., an entity created by reason functioning rationally.

e *Sache*

f *Princip*

g *Object*

ally is), which cannot lead us very far, reason takes the concept of the empirical unity of all thought, and, by thinking this unity unconditionally and originally, it makes out of it a concept of reason (an idea) of a simple substance, unchangeable in itself (identical in personality), standing in community with other real things outside it – in a word, the concept of a simple self-sufficient intelligence. With this, however, reason has nothing before its eyes except principles^a of the systematic unity in explaining the appearances of the soul, namely by considering all determinations as in one subject, all powers, as far as possible, as derived from one unique fundamental power, all change as belonging to the states of one and the same persisting being, and by representing all **appearances** in space as entirely distinct from the actions of **thinking.** That simplicity of substance, etc., ought to be only the schema for this regulative principle,^b and it is not presupposed as if it were the real ground of properties of the soul. For these properties could rest on entirely different grounds, with which we are not acquainted at all, just as we might not really be able to cognize the soul at all through these assumed predicates even if we let them hold of it absolutely, since they constitute a mere idea that cannot be represented *in concreto* at all. Now nothing but advantage can arise from such a psychological idea, if only one guards against letting it hold as something more than a mere idea, i.e., if one lets it hold merely relative to the systematic use of reason in respect of the appearances of our soul. For then empirical laws of corporeal appearances, which are of an entirely different species, will not be mixed up in the explanation of what belongs merely to^c **inner sense;** then no windy hypotheses about the generation, destruction or palingenesis[121] of souls, etc., will be admitted; a consideration of this object of inner sense as a whole will^d therefore be instituted, and this will not be mixed up with properties of any different kind; moreover, the investigation of reason will be directed to carrying through the grounds of explanation in this subject as far as possible on the basis of a single principle;^e all of this is best effected through such a schema just **as if** it were an actual being – indeed, it can be effected only and solely in this way. The psychological idea can also signify nothing other than the schema of a regulative concept. For if I wanted only to ask whether the soul is not in itself of a spiritual nature, this question would have no sense at all. For through such a concept I would take away not merely corporeal nature, but all nature whatever, i.e., all predicates of any possible expe-

A683/B711

A684/B712

^a *Principien*
^b *Princip*
^c *für;* the first edition reads *"vor"* (before).
^d *wird;* this word is missing in the first edition.
^e *Princip*

rience, hence all conditions for thinking an object for such a concept, which alone and solely makes it possible for one to say that it has any sense.

The second regulative idea of merely speculative reason is the concept of the world in general. For nature is really the single given object*a* in regard to which reason needs regulative principles.*b* This nature is twofold: either thinking nature or corporeal nature. Yet to think of the latter as regards its inner possibility, i.e., to determine the application of the categories to it, we do not need any idea, i.e., any representation transcending experience; no such representation is possible in regard to it, because here we are guided merely by sensible intuition – not as with the fundamental psychological concept (the I), which contains *a priori* a certain form of thinking, namely its unity. Thus for pure reason there is nothing left to us except nature in general, and the completeness of   A685/B713 conditions in it in accordance with some one principle.*c* The absolute totality of the series of these conditions in the derivation of their members is an idea which of course can never come about fully in the empirical use of reason, but nevertheless serves as a rule for the way we ought to proceed in regard to them: namely that in the explanation of given appearances (in a regress or ascent), we ought to proceed **as if** the series were in itself infinite, i.e., proceed *in indefinitum;*[122] but where reason itself is considered as the determining cause (in the case of freedom), hence in the case of practical principles,*d* we should proceed as if we did not have before us an object*e* of sense but one of pure understanding, where the conditions can no longer be posited in the series of appearances, but are posited outside it, and the series of states can be regarded **as if** it began absolutely (through an intelligible cause); all this proves that the cosmological ideas are nothing but regulative principles,*f* and are far from positing, as it were constitutively, an actual totality in such series. The rest one can seek in its place in the Antinomy of Pure Reason.[123]

The third idea of pure reason, which contains a merely relative supposition*g* of a being as the sole and all-sufficient cause of all cosmological series, is the rational concept of **God.** We do not have the least   A686/B714 reason to assume absolutely (**to suppose**b **in itself**) the object of this idea; for what could enable or even justify us in believing or asserting a

a *Object*
b *Principien*
c *Princip*
d *Principien*
e *Object*
f *Principien*
g *Supposition*
h *supponieren*

613

being having the highest perfection, and its nature as necessarily existent, merely on the basis of its concept, were it not the world in relation to which alone this supposition*a* can be necessary? And that shows clearly that the idea of that being, like all speculative ideas, means nothing more than that reason bids us consider every connection in the world according to principles*b* of a systematic unity, hence **as if** they had all arisen from one single all-encompassing being, as supreme and all-sufficient cause. From this it is clear that here reason could aim at nothing except its own formal rule in the extension of its empirical use, but never at an extension of it **beyond all the boundaries of empirical use,** consequently, that under this idea there does not lie hidden any constitutive principle*c* for its use directed to possible experience.

A687/B715   This highest formal unity that alone rests on concepts of reason is the **purposive** unity of things; and the **speculative** interest of reason makes it necessary to regard every ordinance in the world as if it had sprouted from the intention of a highest reason. Such a principle,*d* namely, opens up for our reason, as applied to the field of experience, entirely new prospects for connecting up things in the world in accordance with teleological laws, and thereby attaining to the greatest systematic unity among them. The presupposition of a supreme intelligence, as the sole cause of the world-whole, but of course merely in the idea, can therefore always be useful to reason and never harmful to it. Thus if in regard to the shape*e* of the earth (which is round but somewhat flattened),* we presuppose the mountains, seas, etc., to be wise intentions of a world-author, then in this way we can make a lot of discoveries. As long as we keep to this presupposition as a **regulative** principle,*f* then even error cannot do us any harm. For then nothing

---

* The advantage created by the earth's spherical shape is well known; but few know that its flattening as a spheroid is the only thing preventing the elevations on the dry land, or even smaller mountains perhaps thrown up by earthquakes, from continuously displacing the earth's axis and perhaps appreciably so in not too long a time; this might happen if the swelling out of the earth at the equator were not such a mighty mountain that the centrifugal force*g* of every other mountain can never noticeably bring it out of place in regard to its axis. And yet without scruples we explain this wise arrangement from the equilibrium of the formerly fluid mass of the earth.

a *Supposition*
b *Principien*
c *Princip*
d *Princip*
e *Figur*
f *Princip*
g *Schwung*

more can follow from it in any case than that where we expected a teleological connection (*nexus finalis*), a merely mechanical or physical one
(*nexus effectivus*) is to be found; in such a case we only miss one more   A688/B716
unity, but we do not ruin the unity of reason in its empirical use. But
even this setback cannot at all affect the law itself, in its universal and
teleological aim. For although an anatomist can be convicted of error
when he relates some organ of an animal's body to an end which, as one
can clearly show, does not follow from it, it is nevertheless quite impossible to **prove** in any one case that a natural arrangement, whatever
it might be, has no end at all. Hence (medical) physiology extends its
very limited empirical acquaintance with the ends served by the structure of an organic body through a principle prompted merely by pure
reason – and this to such an extent that it is assumed confidently, and
with the agreement of all who understand the matter, that everything
in an animal has its utility and good aim; this presupposition, if it is
supposed to be constitutive, goes much further than previous observation can justify; from this it can be seen that it is nothing but a regulative principle*a* of reason for attaining to the highest systematic unity by
means of the idea of the purposive causality of the supreme cause of the
world, **as if** this being, as the highest intelligence, were the cause of
everything according to the wisest aim.

But if we depart from this restriction of the idea to a merely regulative   A689/B717
use, then reason will be misled in several ways, by forsaking the ground
of experience, which has to contain the markers for its course, and by
venturing beyond experience into the incomprehensible and inscrutable,
in whose heights it necessarily becomes dizzy because from this standpoint it sees itself entirely cut off from every use attuned to experience.

The first mistake that arises from using the idea of a highest being
not merely regulatively but (contrary to the nature of an idea) constitutively, is that of lazy reason (*ignava ratio*).* One can use this term for
any principle that makes one regard his investigation into nature, whatever it may be, as absolutely complete, so that reason can take a rest, as   A690/B718
though it had fully accomplished its business. Hence the psychological
idea too, if it is used as a constitutive principle*b* to explain the appear-

---

* This is what the ancient dialecticians called the sophism*c* which goes as fol-   A 689/B717
lows: If it is your fate to recover from this illness, then that will happen
whether you employ a physician or not.[124] Cicero says that this way of inferring gets its name from the fact that if one follows it, then that would leave
reason without any use in life.[125] This is why I record the sophistical argument
of pure reason using the same name.

a *Princip*
b *Princip*
c *Trugschluß* (deceptive inference).

ances of our soul, and then further to extend our cognition of this subject beyond all experience (to its state after death), makes things very convenient for reason, but also completely ruins and destroys every natural use of reason according to the guidance of experience. Thus the dogmatic spiritualist explains the unity of the person, which consists in remaining unaltered through all changes in its states, by the unity of a thinking substance, which he thinks he perceives immediately in the "I," and he explains the interest we take in things that are supposed to come to pass only after our death from the consciousness of the immaterial nature of our thinking subject, etc.; he presumes to dispense with all the natural investigation of the cause of these inner appearances of ours from physical grounds of explanation by, as it were, passing over the immanent sources of cognition in experience through an edict as it were of a transcendent reason, which makes things comfortable for him but also forfeits all insight. These disadvantageous consequences come to view even more clearly in the case of the dogmatism of our idea of a highest intelligence and the theological system of nature (physico-

A691/B719 theology) that is falsely grounded on it. For there all the ends showing themselves in nature, which are often only made up by us, serve only to make it extremely convenient for us in our search for causes, so that instead of seeking them in the universal laws of the mechanism of matter, we appeal right away to the inscrutable decree of the highest wisdom, and regard the toil of reason as completed when in fact the use of reason has been completely dispensed with – a use which finds its guiding thread nowhere unless it is provided to us by the order of nature and the series of alterations according to their internal and more general laws. This mistake can be avoided if we do not consider from the viewpoint of ends merely a few parts of nature, e.g., the distribution of dry land, its structure and the constitution and situation of mountains, or even only the organization of the vegetable and animal kingdoms, but if we rather make the systematic unity of nature **entirely universal** in relation to the idea of a highest intelligence. For then we make a purposiveness in accordance with universal laws of nature the ground, from which no particular arrangement is excepted, but arrangements are designated only in a way that is more or less discernible by us; then we have a regulative principle[a] of the systematic unity of a teleological connection, which, however, we do not determine beforehand, but may only

A692/B720 expect while pursuing the physical-mechanical connection according to universal laws. For only in this way can the principle[b] of purposive unity always extend the use of reason in regard to experience without doing damage to it in any individual case.

[a] *Princip*
[b] *Princip*

Section VII. Critique of all speculative theology

The second mistake that arises from the misinterpretation of the intended principle^a of systematic unity is that of perverted reason (*perversa ratio, ὕστερον πρότερον rationis*).^b The idea of systematic unity should only serve as a regulative principle^c for seeking this unity in the combination of things in accordance with universal laws of nature, and to the extent that something of the sort is encountered in an empirical way, one should believe oneself to have approximated to completeness in its use, though one obviously will never reach it. Instead of this, one reverses the matter and begins by grounding things hypostatically on the actuality of a principle^d of purposive unity; because it is entirely inscrutable, the concept of such a highest intelligence is determined anthropomorphically, and then one imposes ends on nature forcibly and dictatorially, instead of seeking for them reasonably on the path of physical investigation, so that teleology, which ought to serve only to supplement the unity of nature in accordance with universal laws, not only works to do away with it, but even deprives reason of its end, A693/B721 namely proving the existence of such an intelligent supreme cause from nature according to this end. For if one cannot presuppose the highest purposiveness in nature *a priori*, i.e., as belonging to the essence of nature, then how can one be assigned to seek it out and, following the ladder of purposiveness, to approach the highest perfection of an author of nature as a perfection which is absolutely necessary, hence cognizable *a priori?* The regulative principle^e demands that systematic unity be presupposed absolutely as a **unity of nature** that is recognized not only empirically but also *a priori*, though still indeterminately, and hence as following from the essence of things. But if I antecedently make a highest ordering being the ground, then the unity of nature will in fact be done away with. For then this unity is entirely foreign and contingent in relation to the nature of things, and it cannot be cognized from the universal laws thereof. Hence arises a vicious circle in one's proof, where one presupposes what really ought to have been proved.

To take the regulative principle^f of the systematic unity of nature for a constitutive one, and to presuppose hypostatically, as a cause, what is only in the idea as a ground for the harmonious use of reason, is only to confuse reason. The investigation of nature takes its own course, fol- A694/B722 lowing only the chain of natural causes according to their universal laws in conformity to the idea of an author, to be sure, yet not to derive from that idea the purposiveness it is seeking everywhere, but

^a *Princip*
^b perverse reason, later first of reason[126]
^c *Princip*
^d *Princip*
^e *Princip*
^f *Princip*

rather in order to cognize its existence from this purposiveness which it seeks in the essence of natural things, where possible in the essence of all things in general as well, and hence to cognize it as absolutely necessary. Whether or not this latter may succeed, the idea always remains correct, and so does its use, if it has been restricted to the conditions of a merely regulative principle.[a]

Complete purposive unity is perfection (absolutely considered). If we do not find this in the essence of the things which constitute the whole object of experience, i.e., all our objectively valid cognition, hence in universal and necessary laws of nature, then how will we infer straightaway from this to the idea of a highest and absolutely necessary perfection in an original being, which is the origin of all causality? The greatest systematic unity, consequently also purposive unity, is the school and even the ground of the possibility of the greatest use of human reason. Hence the idea of it is inseparably bound up with the essence of our reason. The very same idea, therefore, is legislative for us, and thus it is very natural to assume a corresponding legislative reason (*intellectus archetypus*) from which all systematic unity of nature, as the object of our reason, is to be derived.

A695/B723

In the Antinomy of Pure Reason, we took the opportunity to say that all questions that pure reason poses must absolutely be answerable,[127] and that the excuse of the limits of our cognition, which in many questions of nature is as unavoidable as it is proper, cannot be permitted here, because here the questions are not laid before us by the nature of things but only through the nature of reason, and they are solely about its internal arrangement. We can now confirm this assertion, which seemed bold at first glance, regarding the two questions in which pure reason has its greatest interest, and thereby bring our consideration of reason's dialectic to full completion.

A696/B724

Thus if one asks (in respect of a transcendental theology)* **first** whether there is anything different from the world which contains the ground of the world order and its connection according to universal laws, then the answer is: **Without a doubt.** For the world is a sum of appearances, and so there has to be some transcendental ground for it,

A695/B723

* What I have said earlier about the psychological idea and its proper vocation[b] as a principle[c] for the merely regulative use of reason exempts me from any particularly lengthy discussion of the transcendental illusion according to which that systematic unity of all manifoldness of inner sense is represented hypostatically. The procedure here is very similar to the one that the Critique observes in regard to the theological ideal.

[a] *Princip*
[b] *Bestimmung*
[c] *Princip*

i.e., a ground thinkable merely by the pure understanding. If the question is **second** whether this being is substance, of the greatest reality, necessary, etc., then I answer **that this question has no significance at all.** For all the categories through which I attempt to frame a concept of such an object are of none but an empirical use, and they have no sense at all when they are not applied to objects*a* of possible experience, i.e., to the world of sense. Outside this field they are mere titles for concepts, which one might allow, but through which one can also understand nothing. Finally, if the question is **third** whether we may not at least think this being different from the world in accordance with an **analogy** with objects of experience, then the answer is **by all means,** but only as object in the idea and not in reality, namely, only insofar as A 697 / B 725
it is a substratum, unknown to us, of the systematic unity, order, and purposiveness of the world's arrangement, which reason has to make into a regulative principle*b* of its investigation of nature. Still more, in this idea we can allow certain anthropomorphisms, which are expedient for the regulative principle*c* we are thinking of, without fear or blame. For it is always only an idea, which is by no means related directly to a being different from the world, but rather referred to the regulative principle*d* of the world's systematic unity, but only by means of a schema of that unity, namely of a supreme intelligence that is its author through wise intentions. What this original ground*e* of the world's unity is in itself ought not to have been thought through this, but rather only how we ought to use it, or rather its idea, in relation to the systematic use of reason in regard to things in the world.

But in this way (one will continue to ask) **can** we nevertheless assume a unique wise and all-powerful world author? **Without any doubt;** and not only that, but we **must** presuppose such a being. But then do we extend our cognition beyond the field of possible experience? **By no means.** For we have only presupposed a Something, of which we have no concept at all of what it is in itself (a merely transcendental object); A 698 / B 726
but, in relation to the systematic and purposive order of the world's structure, which we must presuppose when we study nature, we have thought this being, which is unknown to us, **in accordance with the analogy** with an intelligence (an empirical concept); i.e., in regard to the ends and the perfection on which those ends are grounded, we have given it just those properties that could contain the ground for such a systematic unity in accordance with the conditions of our reason. This

---

a *Objecte*
b *Princip*
c *Princip*
d *Princip*
e *Urgrund*, following the first edition; the second edition reads "*Ungrund*" (abyss).

idea is therefore grounded entirely **respective to the use** our reason makes of it **in the world.** But if we wanted to grant it absolute objective validity, then we would be forgetting that we are thinking solely of a being in the idea; and, since we began with a ground which is not determinable at all through considering the world, we would thereby place ourselves in no position to apply this principle*ᵃ* suitably to the empirical use of reason.

But (one will ask further) in such a way can I still make use of the concept and the presupposition of a highest being in rationally considering the world? Yes; that was really why things were grounded on this idea of reason. Yet may I regard purpose-like*ᵇ* orderings as intentions, by deriving them from the divine will, though of course mediately through predispositions toward them set up in the world? Yes, you can do that too, but only in such a way that it is all the same to you whether someone says that the divine wisdom has ordered everything to its supreme ends, or that the idea of the highest wisdom is a regulative one in the investigation of nature and a principle*ᶜ* of the systematic and purposive unity thereof in accordance with universal laws, even where we are not aware of it; i.e., where you do perceive purposive unity, it must not matter at all whether you say, "God has wisely willed it so" or "Nature has wisely so ordered it." For the greatest systematic and purposive unity, which your reason demands as a regulative principle*ᵈ* to ground all investigation of nature, was precisely what justified you in making the idea of a highest intelligence the ground as a schema of the regulative principle;*ᵉ* and however much purposiveness you encounter in the world in accordance with that principle,*ᶠ* so much confirmation do you have for the rightness of your idea; since, however, the principle*ᵍ* you are thinking of has no other aim than to seek out the necessary and greatest possible unity of nature, we will have the idea of a highest being to thank for this so far as we reach it, but we can never get around the universal laws of nature, so as to regard this purposiveness of nature as contingent and hyperphysical in its origin, without contradicting ourselves, since it was only by taking these laws as our aim that things were grounded on the idea; for we were not justified in assuming a being above nature with the properties we are thinking of, but only in grounding things on the idea of this being in order to regard ap-

A699/B727

A700/B728

ᵃ Princip
ᵇ zweckähnliche
ᶜ Princip
ᵈ Princip
ᵉ Princip
ᶠ Princip
ᵍ Princip

pearances*a* as systematically connected to one another in accordance with the analogy of a causal determination.

Just for this reason we are also justified in thinking of the world-cause in the idea not only according to a subtle anthropomorphism (without which nothing at all could be thought about it*b*), namely as a being that has understanding, liking and disliking, and desire and will in conformity with them, etc., but also in ascribing to that being infinite perfection far transcending what we could justify on the basis of our empirical acquaintance with the world-order. For the regulative law of systematic unity would have us study nature **as if** systematic and purposive unity together with the greatest possible manifoldness were to be encountered everywhere to infinity. For although we may light on or reach only a little of this perfection of the world, yet it belongs to the legislation of our reason to seek for it and presume it everywhere, and it must always be advantageous for us, and can never become disadvantageous, to institute our consideration of nature in accordance with this principle.*c* But under this way of representing the idea of a highest world-author as a ground, it is clear that I ground things not on the existence or acquaintance with this being, but only on its idea; thus I really derive nothing from this being, but only from the idea of it, i.e., from the nature of the things in the world in accordance with such an idea. It also seems to have been a certain, though to be sure undeveloped, consciousness of the genuine use of this rational concept of ours which occasioned the modest and reasonable*d* language used by philosophers of all ages in talking of the wisdom and providence of nature, and of divine wisdom, as if they were expressions with the same meaning*e* – preferring, indeed, the first expression as long as they have to do merely with speculative reason, because this restrains us from the presumption of making a bigger assertion than we are warranted in making, and at the same time points reason back to its proper field, which is nature.

Thus pure reason, which initially seemed to promise us nothing less than an extension of our knowledge*f* beyond all the boundaries of experience, if we understand it rightly contains nothing but regulative

A701/B729

---

a In Kant's text, this noun is preceded by *der*, an article that is either genitive or dative, leaving the verb "regard" with no direct object; with Erdmann, we read *die*, putting this noun in the accusative.

b *ihm*, whose only natural referent grammatically would be "anthropomorphism"; Wille suggests that the text be amended to read *ihr*, making the referent "the world cause."

c *Princip*

d *billige*

e *Bedeutung*

f *Kenntnisse*

principles,^a which certainly command greater unity than the empirical use of the understanding can reach, but just because they put the goal we are approaching so far off, they bring this goal to the highest degree of agreement with itself through systematic unity; but if one misunderstands them and takes them to be constitutive principles^b of transcendent cognition, then they produce a dazzling but deceptive illusion, persuasion and imaginary knowledge, and thus also eternal contradictions and controversies.

A 702 / B 730

* * *

Thus all human cognition begins with intuitions, goes from there to concepts, and ends with ideas. Although in regard to all three elements it has sources of cognition *a priori* which seem at first glance to scorn the boundaries of all experience, a completed critique convinces us that reason in its speculative use can with these elements never get beyond the field of possible experience, and that the proper vocation^c of this supreme faculty of cognition is to employ all its methods and principles only in order to penetrate into the deepest inwardness of nature[128] in accordance with all possible principles^d of unity, of which the unity of ends is the most prominent, but is never to fly across the boundaries of nature, outside which there is **for us** nothing but empty space. Of course the critical investigation, in the Transcendental Analytic, of all propositions that can extend our cognition beyond all actual experience has sufficiently convinced us that they can never lead to anything more than a possible experience, and if one were not mistrustful of even the clearest of abstract^e and general doctrines,^f and if charming and plausible prospects did not lure us to reject the compulsion of these doctrines, then of course we might have been able to dispense with our painstaking examination of the dialectical witnesses which a transcendent reason brings forward on behalf of its pretensions; for we already knew beforehand with complete certainty that all their allegations, while perhaps honestly meant, had to be absolutely null and void, because they dealt with information^g which no human being can ever get. Yet because there will never be an end to discussion unless one gets to the bottom of the illusion that can fool even the most rational, and also because the resolution of all our transcendental cognition into its ele-

A 703 / B 731

---

^a *Principien*
^b *Principien*
^c *Bestimmung*
^d *Principien*
^e The first edition reads " . . . even the clearest or abstract and general . . . "
^f *Lehrsätze*
^g *Kundschaft*

ments (as a study of our inner nature) not only has in itself no small value, but is even a duty for a philosopher, it was not only necessary to carry out an exhaustive examination of the vain elaborations of speculative reason in their entirety down to its primary sources, but also – since dialectical illusion is here not only deceptive for our judgment but also, owing to the interest we take in these judgments, is also alluring and natural, and so will be present in the future too – it was advisable to draw up an exhaustive dossier, as it were, of these proceedings and store it in the archives of human reason, so as to prevent future errors of a similar kind.

A 704
B 732

II.
Transcendental Doctrine of Method

^aIf I regard the sum total of all cognition of pure and speculative reason as an edifice for which we have in ourselves at least the idea, then I can say that in the Transcendental Doctrine of Elements we have made an estimate of the building materials and determined for what sort of edifice, with what height and strength, they would suffice. It turned out, of course, that although we had in mind a tower that would reach the heavens, the supply of materials sufficed only for a dwelling that was just roomy enough for our business on the plane of experience and high enough to survey it; however, that bold undertaking had to fail from lack of material, not to mention the confusion of languages that unavoidably divided the workers over the plan and dispersed them throughout the world, leaving each to build on his own according to his own design.[1] Now we are concerned not so much with the materials as with the plan, and, having been warned not to venture some arbitrary and blind project that might entirely exceed our entire capacity,^b yet not being able to abstain from the erection of a sturdy dwelling, we have to aim at an edifice in relation^c to the supplies given to us that is at the same time suited to our needs.

By the transcendental doctrine of method, therefore, I understand the determination of the formal conditions of a complete system of pure reason. With this aim, we shall have to concern ourselves with a **discipline,** a **canon,** an **architectonic,** and finally a **history** of pure reason,[2] and will accomplish, in a transcendental respect, that which, under the name of a **practical logic,**[3] with regard to the use of the understanding in general, the schools sought but accomplished only badly; for since general logic is not limited to any particular kind of cognition of the understanding (e.g., not to the pure cognition of the understanding) nor to certain objects, it cannot, without borrowing knowledge from other sciences, do more than expound titles for **possible methods** and technical expressions that are used in regard to that which is systematic in all sorts of sciences, which first makes the novice familiar with names the significance and use of which he will only learn in the future.

---

^a Throughout this part of the work there are minor changes in orthography between the two editions, very few of which affect the translation. Only the few that do will be noted.
^b *Vermögen*
^c *Verhältnis*

The Transcendental Doctrine of Method
First Chapter
The discipline of pure reason⁴

In humanity's general lust for knowledge, negative judgments, which are negative not merely on the basis of logical form but also on the basis of their content, do not stand in high regard: one regards them as jealous enemies of our unremitting drive straining for the expansion of our cognition, and it almost takes an apology to earn toleration for them, let alone favor and esteem.

To be sure, **logically** one can express negatively any propositions that one wants, but in regard to the content of our cognition in general, that is, whether it is expanded or limited by a judgment, negative judgments have the special job solely of **preventing error.** Hence even negative propositions, which are to prevent a false cognition, are often quite true yet empty where error is never possible, i.e., not appropriate for their purpose, and for this reason are often ridiculous, like the proposition of the scholastic orator that Alexander could not have conquered any lands without an army.

But where the limits of our possible cognition are very narrow, where the temptation to judge is great, where the illusion that presents itself is very deceptive, and where the disadvantage of error is very serious, there the **negative** in instruction, which serves merely to defend us from errors, is more important than many a positive teaching by means of which our cognition could be augmented. The **compulsion** through which the constant propensity to stray from certain rules is limited and finally eradicated is called **discipline.** It is different from **culture,** which would merely produce a **skill** without first canceling out another one that is already present. In the formation of a talent, therefore, which already has by itself a tendency to expression, discipline will make a negative contribution,* but culture and doctrine a positive one.

---

* I am well aware that in the language of the schools the name of **discipline** is customarily used as equivalent to that of instruction.ᵃ But there are so many

ᵃ *Unterweisung*

Everyone will readily grant that the temperament as well as the talents that would allow a free and unlimited movement (such as imagination and wit) require discipline in many respects. But that reason, which is properly obliged to prescribe its discipline for all other endeavors, should have need of one itself, may certainly seem strange, and in fact reason has previously escaped such a humiliation only because, given the pomp and the serious mien with which it appears, no one could easily come to suspect it of frivolously playing with fancies instead of concepts and words instead of things.

No critique of reason in empirical use was needed, since its principles were subjected to a continuous examination on the touchstone of experience; it was likewise unnecessary in mathematics, whose concepts must immediately be exhibited *in concreto* in pure intuition, through which anything unfounded and arbitrary instantly becomes obvious. But where neither empirical nor pure intuition keeps reason in a visible track, namely in its transcendental use in accordance with mere concepts, there it so badly needs a discipline to constrain its propensity to expansion beyond the narrow boundaries of possible experience and to preserve it from straying and error that the entire philosophy of pure reason is concerned merely with this negative use. Individual errors can be remedied through **censure** and their causes through critique. But where, as in pure reason, an entire system of delusions and deceptions is encountered, which are connected with each other and unified under common principles,[a] there a quite special and indeed negative legislation seems to be required, which under the name of a **discipline** erects, as it were, a system of caution and self-examination out of the nature of reason and the objects of its pure use, before which no false sophistical illusion can stand up but must rather immediately betray itself, regardless of all grounds for being spared.

But it is well to note that in this second main part of the transcendental critique I do not direct the discipline of pure reason to the content but rather only to the method of cognition from pure reason. The former has already taken place in the Doctrine of Elements. But there is so much that is similar in the use of reason, whatever object it may be

other cases where the first expression, as **correction,**[b] must carefully be contrasted to **teaching,**[c] and the nature of things itself also makes it necessary to preserve the only suitable expression for this difference, that I wish that this word would never be allowed to be used in anything but the negative sense.

[a] *Principien*
[b] *Zucht*
[c] *Belehrung*

A711/B739

A712/B740

applied to, and yet, insofar as it would be transcendental, it is so essentially different from all other uses, that without the admonitory negative doctrine of a discipline especially aimed at them the errors could not be avoided that must necessarily arise from the inappropriate pursuit of such methods, which might be suitable for reason elsewhere but not here.

First Chapter
First Section
The discipline of pure reason in dogmatic use.

Mathematics gives the most resplendent example of pure reason happily expanding itself without assistance from experience. Examples are contagious, especially for the same faculty, which naturally flatters itself that it will have the same good fortune in other cases that it has had in one. Hence pure reason hopes to be able to expand itself in as happy A 713/ B 741 and well grounded a way in its transcendental use as it succeeded in doing in its mathematical use, by applying the same method in the former case that was of such evident utility in the latter. It is therefore very important for us to know whether the method for obtaining apodictic certainty that one calls **mathematical** in the latter science is identical with that by means of which one seeks the same certainty in philosophy, and that would there have to be called **dogmatic.**

Philosophical cognition is **rational cognition** from **concepts,** mathematical cognition that from the **construction** of concepts.[5] But to **construct** a concept means to exhibit *a priori* the intuition corresponding to it. For the construction of a concept, therefore, a **nonempirical** intuition is required, which consequently, as intuition, is an **individual** object,[a] but that must nevertheless, as the construction of a concept (of a general representation), express in the representation universal validity for all possible intuitions that belong under the same concept. Thus I construct a triangle by exhibiting an object corresponding to this concept, either through mere imagination, in pure intuition, or on paper, in empirical intuition, but in both cases completely *a priori*, without having had to borrow the pattern for it from any expe- A 714/ B 742 rience. The individual drawn figure is empirical, and nevertheless serves to express the concept without damage to its universality, for in the case of this empirical intuition we have taken account only of the action of constructing the concept, to which many determinations, e.g., those of the magnitude of the sides and the angles, are entirely indifferent, and thus we have abstracted from these differences, which do not alter the concept of the triangle.

---

[a] *Object*

Philosophical cognition thus considers the particular only in the universal, but mathematical cognition considers the universal in the particular, indeed even in the individual, yet nonetheless *a priori* and by means of reason, so that just as this individual is determined under certain general conditions of construction, the object of the concept, to which this individual corresponds only as its schema, must likewise be thought as universally determined.

The essential difference between these two kinds of rational cognition therefore consists in this form, and does not rest on the difference in their matter, or objects. Those who thought to distinguish philosophy from mathematics by saying of the former that it has merely **quality** while the latter has **quantity** as its object *a* have taken the effect for the cause. The form of mathematical cognition is the cause of its pertaining solely to quanta. For only the concept of magnitudes can be constructed, i.e., exhibited *a priori* in intuition, while qualities cannot be exhibited in anything but empirical intuition. Hence a rational cognition of them can be possible only through concepts. Thus no one can ever derive an intuition corresponding to the concept of reality from anywhere except experience, and can never partake of it *a priori* from oneself and prior to empirical consciousness. The shape of a cone can be made intuitive without any empirical assistance, merely in accordance with the concept, but the color of this cone must first be given in one experience or another. I cannot exhibit the concept of a cause in general in intuition in any way except in an example given to me by experience, etc. Now philosophy as well as mathematics does deal with magnitudes, e.g., with totality, infinity, etc. And mathematics also occupies itself with the difference between lines and planes as spaces with different quality, and with the continuity of extension as a quality of it. But although in such cases they have a common object, the manner of dealing with it through reason is entirely different in philosophical than in mathematical consideration. The former confines itself solely to general concepts, the latter cannot do anything with the mere concepts but hurries immediately to intuition, in which it considers the concept *in concreto*, although not empirically, but rather solely as one which it has exhibited *a priori*, i.e., constructed, and in which that which follows from the general conditions of the construction must also hold generally of the object*b* of the constructed concept.

Give a philosopher the concept of a triangle, and let him try to find out in his way how the sum of its angles might be related to a right angle. He has nothing but the concept of a figure enclosed by three straight lines, and in it the concept of equally many angles. Now he may

A715/B743

A716/B744

a *Object*
b *Objecte*

reflect on this concept as long as he wants, yet he will never produce anything new. He can analyze and make distinct the concept of a straight line, or of an angle, or of the number three, but he will not come upon any other properties that do not already lie in these concepts. But now let the geometer take up this question. He begins at once to construct a triangle. Since he knows that two right angles together are exactly equal to all of the adjacent angles that can be drawn at one point on a straight line, he extends one side of his triangle, and obtains two adjacent angles that together are equal to two right ones. Now he divides the external one of these angles by drawing a line parallel to the opposite side of the triangle, and sees that here there arises an external adjacent angle which is equal to an internal one, etc.[6] In such a way, through a chain of inferences that is always guided by intuition, he arrives at a fully illuminating and at the same time general solution of the question.

A717/B745

But mathematics does not merely construct magnitudes (*quanta*), as in geometry, but also mere magnitude (*quantitatem*), as in algebra,[a] where it entirely abstracts from the constitution of the object that is to be thought in accordance with such a concept of magnitude.[7] In this case it chooses a certain notation for all construction of magnitudes in general (numbers), as well as addition, subtraction, extraction of roots, etc.,[b] and, after it has also designated the general concept of quantities in accordance with their different relations,[c] it then exhibits all the procedures through which magnitude is generated and altered in accordance with certain rules in intuition; where one magnitude is to be divided by another, it places their symbols together in accordance with the form of notation for division, and thereby achieves by a symbolic construction equally well what geometry does by an ostensive or geometrical construction (of the objects themselves), which discursive cognition could never achieve by means of mere concepts.

What might be the cause of the very different situations in which these two reasoners find themselves, one of whom makes his way in accordance with concepts, the other in accordance with intuitions that he exhibits *a priori* for the concepts? According to the transcendental fundamental doctrine expounded above, this cause is clear. At issue here are not analytic propositions, which can be generated through mere analysis of concepts (here the philosopher would without doubt have the advantage over his rival), but synthetic ones, and indeed ones that are to be cognized *a priori*. For I am not to see what I actually think

A718/B746

---

[a] *Buchstabenrechnung*

[b] Following Erdmann, closing the parenthesis after "numbers" instead of "subtraction"; also moving the "etc." following "subtraction" to its present position.

[c] *Verhältnissen*

in my concept of a triangle (this is nothing further than its mere definition), rather I am to go beyond it to properties that do not lie in this
concept but still belong to it. Now this is not possible in any way but
by determining my object in accordance with the conditions of either
empirical or pure intuition. The former would yield only an empirical
proposition (through measurement of its angles), which would contain
no universality, let alone necessity, and propositions of this sort are not
under discussion here. The second procedure, however, is that of
mathematical and here indeed of geometrical construction, by means
of which I put together in a pure intuition, just as in an empirical one,
the manifold that belongs to the schema of a triangle in general and
thus to its concept, through which general synthetic propositions must
be constructed.[a]

In vain, therefore, would I reflect on the triangle philosophically, i.e.,
discursively, without thereby getting any further than the mere definition with which, however, I had to begin. There is, to be sure, a transcendental synthesis from concepts alone, with which in turn only the
philosopher can succeed, but which never concerns more than a thing
in general, with regard to the conditions under which its perception
could belong to possible experience. But in mathematical problems the
question is not about this nor about existence[b] as such at all, but about
the properties of the objects in themselves, solely insofar as these are
combined with the concept of them.

    A 719/ B 747

In these examples we have only attempted to make distinct what a
great difference there is between the discursive use of reason in accordance with concepts and its intuitive use through the construction of
concepts. Now the question naturally arises, what is the cause that
makes such a twofold use of reason necessary, and by means of which
conditions can one know[c] whether only the first or also the second takes
place?

All of our cognition is in the end related to possible intuitions: for
through these alone is an object given. Now an *a priori* concept (a non-
empirical concept) either already contains a pure intuition in itself, in
which case it can be constructed; or else it contains nothing but the synthesis of possible intuitions, which are not given *a priori*, in which case
one can well judge synthetically and *a priori* by its means, but only discursively, in accordance with concepts, and[d] never intuitively through
the construction of the concept.

    A 720/ B 748

Now of all intuition none is given *a priori* except the mere form of ap-

---

[a] The word *construiert* is missing in the first edition.
[b] *Existenz*
[c] *erkennen*
[d] *und* in the second edition replaces *aber* in the first.

pearances, space and time, and a concept of these, as *quanta*, can be exhibited *a priori* in pure intuition, i.e., constructed, together with either their quality (their shape) or else merely their quantity (the mere synthesis of the homogeneous manifold) through number. The matter of appearances, however, through which **things** in space and time are given to us, can be represented only in perception, thus *a posteriori*. The only concept that represents this empirical content of appearances *a priori* is the concept of the **thing** in general, and the synthetic *a priori* cognition of this can never yield *a priori* more than the mere rule of the synthesis of that which perception may give *a posteriori*, but never the intuition of the real object, since this must necessarily be empirical.

Synthetic propositions that pertain to **things** in general, the intuition of which cannot be given *a priori*, are transcendental. Thus transcendental propositions can never be given through construction of concepts, but only in accordance with *a priori* concepts. They contain merely the rule in accordance with which a certain synthetic unity of that which cannot be intuitively represented *a priori* (of perceptions) should be sought empirically. They cannot, however, exhibit a single one of their concepts *a priori* in any case, but do this only *a posteriori*, by means of experience, which first becomes possible in accordance with those synthetic principles.

A721/B749

If one is to judge synthetically about a concept, then one must go beyond this concept, and indeed go to the intuition in which it is given. For if one were to remain with that which is contained in the concept, then the judgment would be merely analytic, an explanation of what is actually contained in the thought. However, I can go from the concept to the pure or empirical intuition corresponding to it in order to assess it *in concreto* and cognize *a priori* or *a posteriori* what pertains to its object. The former is rational and mathematical cognition through the construction of the concept, the latter merely empirical (mechanical) cognition, which can never yield necessary and apodictic propositions. Thus I could analyze my empirical concept of gold without thereby gaining anything more than being able to enumerate what I actually think by means of this word, which would certainly produce a logical improvement in my cognition, but no augmentation or supplementation of it. But I can take the matter that goes by this name and initiate perceptions of it, which will provide me with various synthetic though empirical propositions. The mathematical concept of a triangle I would construct, i.e., give in intuition *a priori*, and in this way I would acquire synthetic but rational cognition. However, if I am given the transcendental concept of a reality, substance, force, etc., it designates neither an empirical nor a pure intuition, but only the synthesis of empirical intuitions (which thus cannot be given *a priori*), and since the synthesis cannot proceed *a priori* to the intuition that corresponds to it, no determining synthetic proposition

A722/B750

but only a principle of the synthesis* of possible empirical intuitions can arise from it. A transcendental proposition is therefore a synthetic rational cognition in accordance with mere concepts, and thus discursive, since through it all synthetic unity of empirical cognition first becomes possible, but no intuition is given by it *a priori*.

There are thus two uses of reason, which, regardless of the universality of cognition and its *a priori* generation, which they have in common, are nevertheless very different in procedure, precisely because there are two components to the appearance through which all objects are given to us: the form of intuition (space and time), which can be cognized and determined completely *a priori*, and the matter (the physical), or the content, which signifies a something that is encountered in space and time, and which thus contains an existence and corresponds to sensation. With regard to the latter, which can never be given in a determinate manner except empirically, we can have nothing *a priori* except indeterminate concepts of the synthesis of possible sensations insofar as they belong to the unity of apperception (in a possible experience). With regard to the former we can determine our concepts *a priori* in intuition, for we create the objects themselves in space and time through homogeneous*ᵃ* synthesis, considering them merely as *quanta*. The former is called the use of reason in accordance with concepts, because we can do nothing further than bring appearances under concepts, according to their real content, which cannot be determined except empirically, i.e., *a posteriori* (though in accord with those concepts as rules of an empirical synthesis); the latter is the use of reason through construction of concepts, because these concepts, since they already apply to an *a priori* intuition, for that very reason can be determinately given in pure intuition *a priori* and without any empirical *data*. To decide about everything that exists (a thing in space or time) whether and how far it is or is not a quantum, whether existence or the lack thereof must be represented in it, how far this something (which fills space or time) is a primary substratum or mere determination, whether it has a relation of its existence to something else as cause or effect, and

A723/B751

A724/B752

---

* By means of the concept of cause I actually go beyond the empirical concept of an occurrence (that something happens), but not to the intuition that exhibits the concept of cause *in concreto*, rather to the time-conditions in general that may be found to be in accord with the concept of cause in experience. I therefore proceed merely in accordance with concepts, and cannot proceed through construction of concepts, since the concept is a rule of the synthesis of perceptions, which are not pure intuitions and which therefore cannot be **given** *a priori*.

A722/B750

ᵃ *gleichförmige*

finally whether with regard to its existence it is isolated or in reciprocal dependence with others; to decide about the possibility, actuality, and necessity of its existence or the opposites thereof: all of this belongs to **rational cognition** from concepts, which is called **philosophical.** But to determine an intuition *a priori* in space (shape), to divide time (duration), or merely to cognize the universal in the synthesis of one and the same thing in time and space and the magnitude of an intuition in general (number) which arises from that: that is a **concern of reason** through construction of the concepts, and is called **mathematical.**

The great good fortune that reason enjoys by means of mathematics leads entirely naturally to the expectation that, if not mathematics itself, then at least its method will also succeed outside of the field of magnitudes, since it brings all of its concepts to intuitions that it can give *a priori* and by means of which, so to speak, it becomes master over nature; while pure philosophy, on the contrary, fumbles around in nature with discursive *a priori* concepts without being able to make their reality intuitive *a priori* and by that means confirm it. Further, the masters of this art do not seem to lack any confidence in themselves, nor does the public seem to lack any great expectations of their talents, should they ever concern themselves about this at all. For since they have hardly ever philosophized about mathematics (a difficult business!), they have never given a thought to the specific difference between the two uses of reason. Rules used customarily and empirically, which they have borrowed from common reason, count as axioms with them. From whence the concepts of space and time with which they busy themselves (as the only original *quanta*) might be derived, they have never concerned themselves, and likewise it seems to them to be useless to investigate the origin of pure concepts of the understanding and the scope of their validity; rather, they merely use them. In all of this they proceed quite correctly, as long as they do not overstep their appointed boundaries, namely those of **nature.** But they slip unnoticed from the field of sensibility to the insecure territory of pure and even transcendental concepts, where they are allowed the ground neither to stand nor swim (*instabilis tellus, innabilis unda*),[a] and can make only perfunctory steps of which time does not preserve the least trace, while on the contrary their progress in mathematics is a high road on which even their most remote descendants can still stride with confidence.

A725/B753

A726/B754

---

[a] "Earth that cannot be stood upon, water that cannot be swum in" (Ovid, *Metamorphoses*, I.16). The line comes from Ovid's opening image of chaos, in which there are no fixed boundaries: "If there was land and sea, there was no discernible shoreline, no way to walk on the one, or swim or sail in the other. In the gloom and murk, vague shapes appeared for a moment, loomed, and then gave way, unsaying themselves and the world as well." (*The Metamorphoses of Ovid*, tr. David R. Slavitt [Baltimore: Johns Hopkins, 1994], p. 1)

Since we have made it our duty to determine the bounds of pure reason in transcendental use exactly and with certainty, but this sort of endeavor has the peculiarity that, in spite of the most pressing and clearest warnings, it still always lets itself hope that it can stave off having to give up entirely the effort to get beyond the bounds of experience into the charming regions of the intellectual, it is therefore necessary to cut away, as it were, the last anchor of a fantastical hope, and to show that the pursuit of the mathematical method in this sort of cognition cannot offer the least advantage, unless it is that of revealing its own nakedness all the more distinctly, and revealing that mathematics*a* and philosophy are two entirely different things, although they offer each other their hand in natural science, thus that the procedure of the one can never be imitated by that of the other.

Mathematics is thoroughly grounded on definitions, axioms, and demonstrations. I will content myself with showing that none of these elements, in the sense in which the mathematician takes them, can be achieved or imitated by philosophy;*b* and that by means of his method A727/B755 the mathematician can build nothing in philosophy except houses of cards, while by means of his method the philosopher can produce nothing in mathematics but idle chatter, while philosophy consists precisely in knowing its bounds, and even the mathematician, if his talent is not already bounded by nature and limited to his specialty, can neither reject its warnings nor disregard them.

1. On **definitions.***c,8* As the expression itself reveals, **to define** properly means just to exhibit originally*d* the exhaustive concept of a thing within its boundaries.* Given such a requirement, an **empirical** concept cannot be defined at all but only **explicated.** For since we have in it only some marks of a certain kind of objects of the senses, it is never certain whether by means of the word that designates the same object

---

* **Exhaustiveness** signifies the clarity and sufficiency of marks; **boundaries,** the precision, that is, that there are no more of these than are required for the exhaustive concept; **original,** however, that this boundary-determination is not derived from anywhere else and thus in need of a proof, which would make the supposed definition*e* incapable of standing at the head of all judgments about an object.

---

a *Meßkunst.*
b Substituting a semicolon for Kant's period.
c *Definitionen.* In this passage Kant prefers the Latinate *Definition* because it is, as he will argue, more precise in meaning than the German *Erklärung.* Throughout this paragraph "definition" will translate *Definition* and "define," *definiren,* unless otherwise noted.
d *urpsrünglich*
e *Erklärung*

one does not sometimes think more of these marks but another time fewer of them. Thus in the concept of **gold** one person might think, besides its weight, color, and ductility, its property of not rusting, while another might know nothing about this. One makes use of certain marks only as long as they are sufficient for making distinctions; new observations, however, take some away and add some, and therefore the concept never remains within secure boundaries. And in any case what would be the point of defining such a concept? – since when, e.g., water and its properties are under discussion, one will not stop at what is intended by the word "water" but rather advance to experiments, and the word, with the few marks that are attached to it, is to constitute only a **designation** and not a concept of the thing; thus the putative definition is nothing other than the determination of the word. Second, strictly speaking no concept given *a priori* can be defined, e.g., substance, cause, right, equity, etc. For I can never be certain that the distinct representation of a (still confused) given concept has been exhaustively developed unless I know that it is adequate to the object. But since the concept of the latter, as it is given, can contain many obscure representations, which we pass by in our analysis though we always use them in application, the exhaustiveness of the analysis of my concept is always doubtful, and by many appropriate examples can only be made **probably** but never **apodictically** certain. Instead of the expression "definition" I would rather use that of **exposition,**[a] which is always cautious, and which the critic can accept as valid to a certain degree while yet retaining reservations about its exhaustiveness. Since therefore neither empirical concepts nor concepts given *a priori* can be defined, there remain none but arbitrarily thought ones for which one can attempt this trick. In such a case I can always define my concept: for I must know what I wanted to think, since I deliberately made it up, and it was not given to me either through the nature of the understanding or through experience; but I cannot say that I have thereby defined a true object.[9] For if the concept depends upon empirical conditions, e.g., a chronometer,[b,10] then the object and its possibility are not given through this arbitrary concept; from the concept I do not even know whether it has an object, and my explanation[c] could better be called a declaration (of my project) than a definition of an object. Thus there remain no other concepts that are fit for being defined than those containing an arbitrary synthesis which can be constructed *a priori*, and thus only mathematics has definitions. For the object that it thinks it also exhibits *a priori* in intuition, and this can surely contain neither more nor less than

[a] *Exposition*
[b] *Schiffsuhr*
[c] *Erklärung*

638

the concept, since through the explanation[a] of the concept the object is originally given, i.e., without the explanation being derived from anywhere else. The German language has for the expressions **exposition, explication, declaration** and **definition**[b] nothing more than the one word "explanation,"[c,11] and hence we must somewhat weaken the stringency of the requirement by which we denied philosophical explanations the honorary title of "definition," and limit this entire remark to this, that philosophical definitions come about only as expositions of given concepts, but mathematical ones as constructions of concepts that are originally made, thus the former come about only analytically through analysis (the completeness of which is never apodictically certain), while the latter come about synthetically, and therefore **make** the concept itself, while the former only **explain** it. From this it follows:

a) That in philosophy one must not imitate mathematics in putting the definitions first, unless perhaps as a mere experiment. For since they are analyses of given concepts, these concepts, though perhaps only still confused, come first, and the incomplete exposition precedes the complete one, so that we can often infer much from some marks that we have drawn from an as yet uncompleted analysis before we have arrived at a complete exposition, i.e., at a definition; in a word, it follows that in philosophy the definition, as distinctness made precise, must conclude rather than begin the work.* On the contrary, in mathematics we do not have any concept at all prior to the definitions, as that through which the concept is first given; it therefore must and also always can begin with them.

b) Mathematical definitions can never err. For since the concept is first given through the definition, it contains just that which the defin-

---

* Philosophy is swarming with mistaken definitions, especially those that actually contain elements for definition but are not yet complete. If one would not know what to do with a concept until one had defined it, then all philosophizing would be in a bad way. But since, however far the elements (of the analysis) reach, a good and secure use can always be made of them, even imperfect definitions, i.e., propositions that are not really definitions but are true and thus approximations to them, can be used with great advantage. In mathematics definitions belong *ad esse*,[d] in philosophy *ad melius esse*.[e] Attaining them is fine, but often very difficult. Jurists are still searching for a definition of their concept of right.

---

[a] *Erklärung*
[b] All Latinate words: "*Exposition, Explikation, Deklaration und Definition.*"
[c] *Erklärung*
[d] to the being
[e] to the improvement of being

ition would think through it. However, although nothing incorrect can occur in its content, nevertheless sometimes, though to be sure only rarely, there can be a defect in the form (of its dress), namely with regard to precision. Thus the common explanation of the circle, that it is a **curved** line every point of which is the same distance from a single one (the center-point), contains the error of unnecessarily introducing the determination **curved.** For it must be a particular theorem, which can be deduced from the definition and easily proved, that every line each point of which is equally distant from a single one is curved (no part of it is straight). Analytical definitions, on the contrary, can err in many ways, either by bringing in marks that really do not lie in the concept or by lacking the exhaustiveness that constitutes what is essential in definitions, since one cannot be so entirely certain of the completeness of their analysis. For this reason the mathematical method of definition cannot be imitated in philosophy.

A732/B760

2. On **axioms.** These are synthetic *a priori* principles, insofar as they are immediately certain. Now one concept cannot be synthetically yet immediately combined with another, since for us to be able to go beyond a concept a third, mediating cognition is necessary. Now since philosophy is merely rational cognition in accordance with concepts, no principle is to be encountered in it that deserves the name of an axiom. Mathematics, on the contrary, is capable of axioms, e.g., that three points always lie in a plane, because by means of the construction of concepts in the intuition of the object it can connect the predicates of the latter *a priori* and immediately. A synthetic principle, on the contrary, e.g., the proposition that everything that happens has its cause, can never be immediately certain from mere concepts, because I must always look around for some third thing, namely the condition of time-determination in an experience, and could never directly cognize such a principle immediately from concepts alone. Discursive principles are therefore something entirely different from intuitive ones, i.e., axioms. The former always require a deduction, with which the latter can entirely dispense, and, since the latter are on the same account self-evident, which the philosophical principles, for all their certainty, can never pretend to be, any synthetic proposition of pure and transcendental reason is infinitely less obvious (as is stubbornly said) than the proposition that **Two times two is four.** To be sure, in the Analytic, in the table of the principles of pure understanding, I have also thought of certain axioms of intuition; but the principle that was introduced there was not itself an axiom, but only served to provide the principle[a] of the possibility of axioms in general, and was itself only a principle from concepts. For even the possibility of mathematics must be shown in

B761

A733

---

[a] *Principium*

transcendental philosophy. Philosophy thus has no axioms and can never simply offer its *a priori* principles as such, but must content itself with justifying their authority through a thorough deduction.

3. On **demonstrations.**[a] Only an apodictic proof, insofar as it is intuitive, can be called a demonstration. Experience may well teach us what is, but not that it could not be otherwise. Hence empirical grounds of proof cannot yield apodictic proof. From *a priori* concepts (in discursive cognition), however, intuitive certainty, i.e., self-evidence,[b] can never arise, however apodictically certain the judgment may otherwise be. Thus only mathematics contains demonstrations, since it does not derive its cognition from concepts, but from their construction, i.e., from the intuition that can be given *a priori* corresponding to the concepts. Even the way algebraists proceed with their equations, from which by means of reduction they bring forth the truth together with the proof, is not a geometrical construction, but it is still a characteristic construction,[12] in which one displays by signs in intuition the concepts, especially of relations[c] of quantities, and, without even regarding the heuristic, secures all inferences against mistakes by placing each of them before one's eyes. Philosophical cognition, on the contrary, must do without this advantage, since it must always consider the universal *in abstracto* (through concepts), while mathematics can assess the universal *in concreto* (in the individual intuition) and yet through pure *a priori* intuition, where every false step becomes visible. Since they can only be conducted by means of mere words (the object in thought), I would therefore prefer to call the former **acroamatic** (discursive) proofs rather than **demonstrations,** which, as the expression already indicates, proceed through the intuition of the object.

Now from all of this it follows that it is not suited to the nature of philosophy, especially in the field of pure reason, to strut about with a dogmatic gait and to decorate itself with the titles and ribbons of mathematics, to whose ranks philosophy does not belong, although it has every cause to hope for a sisterly union with it. These are idle pretensions that can never succeed, but that instead countermand its aim of revealing the deceptions of a reason that misjudges its own boundaries and of bringing the self-conceit of speculation back to modest but thorough self-knowledge[d] by means of a sufficient illumination of our concepts. In its transcendental efforts, therefore, reason cannot look ahead so confidently, as if the path on which it has traveled leads quite directly to the goal, and it must not count so boldly on the premises

---

[a] *Demonstrationen*
[b] *Evidenz*
[c] *Verhältnisse*
[d] *Selbsterkenntnis*

that ground it as if it were unnecessary for it frequently to look back and consider whether there might not be errors in the progress of its inferences to be discovered that were overlooked in its principles[a] and that make it necessary either to determine them further or else to alter them entirely.

I divide all apodictic propositions (whether they are demonstrable or immediately certain) into **dogmata** and **mathemata**. A direct synthetic proposition from concepts is a **dogma;** such a proposition through construction of concepts, on the contrary, is a **mathema.** Analytic judgments do not really teach us anything more[b] about the object than what the concept that we have of it already contains in itself, since they do not expand cognition beyond the concept of the subject, but only elucidate this concept. They cannot therefore properly be called dogmas (a word which one could perhaps translate as **theorems**).[c] But in accordance with ordinary usage, of the two types of synthetic *a priori* propositions only those belonging to philosophical cognition carry this name, and one would hardly call the propositions of arithmetic or geometry "dogmata." This usage thus confirms the explanation we have given that only judgments from concepts, and not those from the construction of concepts, can be called dogmatic.

Now all of pure reason in its merely speculative use contains not a single direct synthetic judgment from concepts. For through ideas, as we have shown, it is not capable of any synthetic judgments that would have objective validity; through concepts of the understanding, however, it certainly erects secure principles, but not directly from concepts, but rather always only indirectly through the relation of these concepts to something entirely contingent, namely **possible experience;** since if this (something as object of possible experience) is presupposed, then they are of course apodictically certain, but in themselves they cannot even be cognized *a priori* (directly) at all. Thus no one can have fundamental insight into the proposition "Everything that happens has its cause" from these given concepts alone. Hence it is not a dogma, although from another point of view, namely that of the sole field of its possible use, i.e., experience, it can very well be proved apodictically. But although it must be proved, it is called a **principle** and not a **theorem**[d] because it has the special property that it first makes possible its ground of proof, namely experience, and must always be presupposed in this.

Now if in the content of the speculative use of pure reason there are

---

[a] *Principien*
[b] Emphasized in the first edition.
[c] *Lehrsprüche*
[d] **Grundsatz und nicht Lehrsatz**

no dogmata at all, then any **dogmatic** method, whether it is borrowed from the mathematicians or is of some special kind, is inappropriate per se. For it merely masks mistakes and errors, and deceives philosophy, the proper aim of which is to allow all of the steps of reason to be seen in the clearest light. Nevertheless, the method can always be **systematic.** For our reason itself (subjectively) is a system, but in its pure use, by means of mere concepts, only a system for research in accordance with principles of unity, for which **experience** alone can give the matter. Of the special method of a transcendental philosophy, however, nothing can here be said, since we are concerned only with a critique of the circumstances of our faculty – whether we can build at all, and how high we can carry our building with the materials that we have (the pure *a priori* concepts). A738/B766

First Chapter
Second Section
The discipline of pure reason
with regard to its polemical use.

Reason must subject itself to critique in all its undertakings, and cannot restrict the freedom of critique through any prohibition without damaging itself and drawing upon itself a disadvantageous suspicion. Now there is nothing so important because of its utility, nothing so holy, that it may be exempted from this searching review and inspection, which knows no respect for persons. The very existence*a* of reason depends upon this freedom, which has no dictatorial authority, but whose claim is never anything more than the agreement of free citizens, each of whom must be able to express his reservations, indeed even his *veto*, without holding back. A739/B767

But now although reason can never **refuse** critique, it does not always have cause to **shrink** from it. Pure reason in its dogmatic (not mathematical) use is not, however, so conscious of the most exact observation of its supreme laws that it can appear before the critical eye of a higher and judicial reason except with modesty, indeed with a complete renunciation of all pretensions to dogmatic authority.

But it is quite different if it does not have to deal with the censure of a judge, but with the claims of its fellow citizens, against which it has merely to defend itself. For since the latter would be just as dogmatic, though in denial, as reason would be in its affirmation, there can be a justification κατ' ἄνθρωπον,*b* which secures it against all interference and provides it with a title to its possession that need shrink from no

---

a *Existenz*
b *ad hominem* (i.e., according to the person)

foreign pretensions, even though it cannot itself be sufficiently proved κατ᾽ ἀλήθειαν.[a]

Now by the polemical use of pure reason I understand the defense of its propositions against dogmatic denials of them. Here the issue is not whether its own assertions might perhaps also be false, but only that no one can ever assert the opposite with apodictic certainty (or even only with greater plausibility). For in this case we do not hold our possession merely by sufferance if we have a title to it, even if not a sufficient one, and it is completely certain that no one can ever prove the unlawfulness of this possession.

A 740 / B 768

It is worrisome and depressing that there should be an antithetic of pure reason at all, and that pure reason, though it represents the supreme court of justice for all disputes, should still come into conflict with itself. We had such an apparent antithetic of reason before us above,[13] to be sure, but it turned out that it rested on a misunderstanding, namely that of taking, in accord with common prejudice, appearances for things in themselves, and then demanding an absolute completeness in their synthesis, in one or another way (which were both equally impossible), which could hardly be expected in the case of appearances. There was thus in that case no real **contradiction of reason** with itself in the propositions "The series of appearances **given in themselves** has an absolutely first beginning" and "This series is absolutely and **in itself** without any beginning"; for both propositions are quite compatible, since **appearances,** as regards their existence (as appearances) **in themselves** are nothing at all, i.e., something contradictory, and thus their presupposition must naturally be followed by contradictory consequences.

A 741 / B 769

However, such a misunderstanding cannot be alleged and the conflict of reason thereby set aside if, say, it is asserted theistically **There is a highest being** and asserted atheistically, on the contrary, **There is no highest being,** or when it is asserted, in psychology, "Everything that thinks is of absolutely persistent unity and therefore distinct from all transitory material unity," against which someone else asserts, "The soul is not an immaterial unity and cannot be exempted from all transitoriness." For the object of the question is here free of anything foreign that contradicts its nature, and the understanding is concerned only with **things in themselves** and not with appearances. There would thus certainly be a genuine conflict here, if only pure reason had anything to say on the negative side that would approximate the ground for an assertion; for as far as the critique of the grounds of proof of the dogmatic affirmations is concerned, one can very well concede it without

---

[a] according to the truth

thereby giving up these propositions, which still have at least the interest of reason in their behalf, to which the opponent cannot appeal at all.

I am not, to be sure, of the opinion that excellent and thoughtful men (e.g., Sulzer),[14] aware of the weakness of previous proofs, have so often expressed, that one can still hope someday to find self-evident demonstrations of the two cardinal propositions of our pure reason: there is a God, and there is a future life. Rather, I am certain that this will never happen. For whence will reason derive the ground for such synthetic assertions, which are not related to objects of experience and their inner possibility? But it is also apodictically certain that no human being will ever step forward who could assert the **opposite** with the least plausibility, let alone assert it dogmatically. For since he could only establish this through pure reason, he would have to undertake to prove that a highest being or the thinking subject in us as pure intelligence is **impossible.** But whence will he derive the knowledge that would justify him in judging synthetically about things beyond all possible experience? We can therefore be entirely unconcerned that somebody will someday prove the opposite; we therefore do not have to think up scholastic proofs, but can always assume these propositions, which are quite consistent with the speculative interest of our reason in its empirical use and are, moreover, the only means for uniting this with the practical interest. For the opponent (who cannot here be considered a mere critic) we have our *non liquet*[a] ready, which must unfailingly confound him, while we do not need to refute his retort, for we always have in reserve the subjective maxims of reason, which he necessarily lacks, and under their protection we can regard all his shadow-boxing with tranquility and indifference.

A742/B770

A743/B771

Thus there is properly no antithetic of pure reason at all. For the only battleground for it would have to be sought in the field of pure theology and psychology; but this ground will bear no warrior in full armor and equipped with weapons that are to be feared. He can only step forward with ridicule and boasting, which can be laughed at like child's play. This is a comforting remark, which gives reason courage again; for on what else could it rely, if it, which is called to do away with all errors, were itself ruined, without any hope for peace and tranquil possession?

Everything that nature itself arranges is good for some aim. Even poisons serve to overpower other poisons which are generated in our own humors,[b] and therefore may not be omitted from a complete collection of cures (medicines). The objections against the suasions and the self-conceit of our purely speculative reason are themselves put

---

[a] I.e., the verdict "not proved."
[b] *Säften*, i.e., bodily liquids, or the four humors of premodern medicine.

forth by the nature of this reason, and they must therefore have their good vocation[a] and aim, which one must not cast to the wind. Why has providence set many objects, although they are intimately connected

with our highest interest, so high that it is barely granted to us to encounter them in an indistinct perception, doubted even by ourselves, through which our searching glance is more enticed than satisfied? Whether it is useful to venture determinate answers with regard to such views is at least doubtful, and perhaps even dangerous. But it is always and without any doubt useful to grant reason full freedom in its search as well as its examination, so that it can take care of its own interest without hindrance, which is promoted just as much by setting limits to its insights as by expanding them, and which always suffers if foreign hands intervene to lead it forcibly to aims contrary to its natural path.

Thus let your opponent speak only reason, and fight him solely with weapons of reason. For the rest, do not worry about the good cause[b] (of practical reason), for that never comes into play in a merely speculative dispute. In this case the dispute reveals nothing but a certain antinomy of reason, which, since it depends upon its nature, must necessarily be heard and examined. The conflict cultivates reason by the consideration of its object on both sides, and corrects its judgment by thus limiting it. What is here in dispute is not the **matter**[c] but the **tone.** For enough remains left to you to speak the language, justified by the sharpest reason,

of a firm **belief,** even though you must surrender that of **knowledge.**

If one were to ask the cool-headed David Hume, especially constituted for equilibrium of judgment, "What moved you to undermine, by means of reservations brooded on with so much effort, the persuasion, so comforting and useful for humans, that the insight of their reason is adequate for the assertion and determinate concept of a highest being?",[15] he would answer: "Nothing but the intention of bringing reason further in its self-knowledge,[d] and at the same time a certain aversion to the coercion which one would exercise against reason by treating it as great and yet at the same time preventing a free confession of its weaknesses, which become obvious to it in the examination of itself." But if, on the contrary, you were to ask Priestley,[16] who is devoted only to the principles of the **empirical** use of reason and is disinclined to all transcendental speculation, what sort of motives he had for tearing down two such pillars of all religion as the freedom and immortality of our soul (the hope of a future life is according to him merely the expectation of a miracle of resurrection), he, who is himself a pious and

---

[a] *Bestimmung*
[b] *Sache*, used in this sense throughout the remainder of this section.
[c] *Sache*
[d] *Selbsterkenntnis*

eager teacher of religion, would not be able to answer anything other than: the interest of reason, which is diminished by the exemption of certain objects from the laws of material nature, which are the only ones that we can know and determine with precision. It would seem unfair to decry the latter, who knew how to unite his paradoxical assertion with the aim of religion, and to do injury to a well-meaning man because he could not find his bearings as soon as he left the field of theory and nature. But this favor must likewise be shown to the no less well-intentioned Hume, unblemished in his moral character, who cannot forsake his abstract speculation because he rightly holds that its object lies entirely beyond the boundaries of natural science, in the field of pure ideas.

A 746/ B 774

Now what is to be done, especially in regard to the danger which seems to threaten the common good from this quarter? Nothing is more natural, nothing more equitable than the decision that you have to make. Let these people do what they want; if they exhibit talent, if they exhibit deep and new research, in a word, if only they exhibit reason, then reason always wins. If you grasp at means other than uncoerced reason, if you cry high treason, if you call together the public, which understands nothing of such subtle refinements, as if they were to put out a fire, then you make yourself ridiculous. For the issue is not what is advantageous or disadvantageous to the common good in these matters, but only how far reason can get in its speculation in abstraction from all interest, and whether one can count on such speculation at all or must rather give it up altogether in favor of the practical. Thus instead of charging in with a sword, you should instead watch this conflict peaceably from the safe seat of critique, a conflict which must be exhausting for the combatants but entertaining for you, with an outcome that will certainly be bloodless and advantageous for your insight. For it is quite absurd to expect enlightenment from reason and yet to prescribe to it in advance on which side it must come out. Besides, reason is already so well restrained and held within limits by reason itself that you do not need to call out the guard to put up civil resistance against that party whose worrisome superiority seems dangerous to you. In this dialectic there is no victory about which you would have cause to worry.

A 747/ B 775

Reason also very much needs such a conflict, and it is to be wished that it had been undertaken earlier and with unlimited public permission. For then a mature critique would have come about all the earlier, at the appearance of which all of this controversy would have had to disappear, since the disputants would have learned insight into the illusion and prejudices that have disunited them.

There is a certain dishonesty *a* in human nature, which yet in the end,

---

a *Unlauterkeit*

A748/B776 like everything else that comes from nature, must contain a tendency to good purposes, namely an inclination to hide its true dispositions and to make a show of certain assumed ones that are held to be good and creditable. It is quite certain that through this propensity to conceal themselves as well as to assume an appearance that is advantageous for them humans have not merely **civilized** themselves but gradually **moralized** themselves to a certain degree, since no one could penetrate the mask of respectability, honorableness, and propriety, and one therefore found a school for self-improvement in the supposedly genuine examples of the good which he saw around himself. Yet this tendency[a] to pretend to be better than one is and to express dispositions[b] that one does not have serves as it were only **provisionally** to bring the human being out of his crudeness and first allow him to assume at least the **manner** of the good, which he recognizes; for later, when the genuine principles have finally been developed and incorporated into his way of thought, that duplicity must gradually be vigorously combated, for otherwise it corrupts the heart, and good dispositions cannot grow among the rampant weeds of fair appearance.[c]

I am sorry to perceive the very same dishonesty, misrepresentation, and hypocrisy even in the utterances of the speculative way of thinking, where human beings have far fewer hindrances to and no advantage at all in forthrightly confessing their thoughts openly and unreservedly.

A749/B777 For what can be more disadvantageous to insight than falsely communicating even mere thoughts, than concealing doubts which we feel about our own assertions, or giving a semblance of self-evidence to grounds of proof which do not satisfy ourselves? As long as these machinations arise merely from private vanity (which is usually the case in speculative judgments, which have no special interest and are not readily liable to apodictic certainty), then the vanity of others resists them **with public approval,** and in the end things end up at the same point to which they would have been brought, though much earlier, by the most honest disposition and sincerity. But where the public holds that subtle sophists[d] are after nothing less than to shake the foundation of the public welfare, then it seems not only prudent but also permissible and even creditable to come to the aid of the good cause with spurious grounds rather than to give its putative enemies even the advantage of lowering our voice to the modesty of a merely practical conviction and necessitating us to admit the lack of speculative and apodictic certainty. I should think, however, that there is nothing in the

[a] *Anlage*
[b] *Gesinnungen*
[c] *des schönen Scheins*
[d] *Vernünftler*

world less compatible with the aim of maintaining a good cause than duplicity, misrepresentation, and treachery. That in weighing up the rational grounds of a mere speculation everything must proceed honorably seems to be the least that one can demand. If one could securely count even on this minimum, however, then the dispute of speculative reason about the important questions of God, immortality (of the soul), and freedom would either have long been decided or else would be brought to an end very soon. Thus honesty of disposition often stands in an inverse relation[a] to the goodness of the cause itself, and the latter has perhaps more upright and sincere opponents than defenders.

A750/B778

I therefore presuppose readers who would not want a just cause to be defended with injustice. Now with regard to them it is already decided that, in accordance with our principles of critique, if one looks not to what happens but to what properly should happen, then there really must not be any polemic of pure reason. For how can two people conduct a dispute about a matter the reality of which neither of them can exhibit in an actual or even in a merely possible experience, about the idea of which he only broods in order to bring forth from it something **more** than an idea, namely the actuality of the object itself? By what means would they escape from the dispute, since neither can make his cause directly comprehensible and certain, but rather can only attack and refute that of his opponent? For this is the fate of all assertions of pure reason: that since they go beyond the conditions of all possible experience, outside of which no document of truth is ever to be encountered, yet at the same time must make use of the laws of the understanding, which are destined merely for empirical use but without which no step may be taken in synthetic thought, they must always be exposed to the enemy, and each can take advantage of the exposure of his enemy.

A751/B779

One can regard the critique of pure reason as the true court of justice for all controversies of pure reason; for the critique is not involved in these disputes, which pertain immediately to objects,[b] but is rather set the task of determining and judging what is lawful[c] in reason in general in accordance with the principles of its primary institution.

Without this, reason is as it were in the state of nature, and it cannot make its assertions and claims valid or secure them except through **war.** The critique, on the contrary, which derives all decisions from the ground-rules of its own constitution, whose authority no one can doubt, grants us the peace of a state of law,[d] in which we should not conduct

[a] *Verhältnisse*
[b] *Objecte*
[c] *die Rechtsame*
[d] *eines gestzlichen Zustandes*

our controversy except by **due process.** What brings the quarrel in the state of nature to an end is a **victory,** of which both sides boast, although for the most part there follows only an uncertain peace, arranged by an authority in the middle; but in the state of law it is the **verdict,** which, since it goes to the origin of the controversies themselves, must secure a perpetual peace. And the endless controversies of a merely dogmatic reason finally make it necessary to seek peace in some sort of critique of this reason itself, and in a legislation grounded upon it; just as Hobbes asserted, the state of nature is a state of injustice and violence, and one must necessarily leave it in order to submit himself to the lawful coercion which alone limits our freedom in such a way that it can be consistent with the freedom of everyone else and thereby with the common good.[17]

To this freedom, then, there also belongs the freedom to exhibit the thoughts and doubts which one cannot resolve oneself for public judgment without thereupon being decried as a malcontent and a dangerous citizen. This lies already in the original right of human reason, which recognizes no other judge than universal human reason itself, in which everyone has a voice; and since all improvement of which our condition is capable must come from this, such a right is holy, and must not be curtailed. It is also very unwise to denounce as dangerous certain daring assertions or audacious attacks upon that which already has on its side the approval of the greatest and best part of the public: for that would be to give them an importance that they should not have at all. When I hear that an uncommon mind has demonstrated away the freedom of the human will, the hope of a future life, and the existence of God, I am eager to read the book, for I expect that his talent will advance my insights. I am completely certain in advance that he will not have accomplished any of this, not because I believe myself already to be in possession of incontrovertible proofs of these important propositions, but rather because the transcendental critique, which has revealed to me the entire stock of our pure reason, has completely convinced me that just as pure reason is entirely inadequate for affirmative assertions in this field, even less will it know what to do in order to be able to assert something negative about these questions. For where would the supposed free-thinker derive his knowledge that, there is, e.g., no highest being? This proposition lies outside the field of possible experience, and therefore also beyond the boundaries of all human insight. The dogmatic defender of the good cause against this enemy I would not read at all, because I know in advance that he will only attack the illusory grounds of the other in order to gain entry for his own, and that an everyday illusion does not give as much material for new observations as an alien one that is sensibly thought out. The enemy of religion, on the contrary, who is dogmatic in his own way, would give my

A752/B780

A753/B781

A754/B782

critique desirable occupation and occasion for some refinement of its principles, without his principles being anything to fear in the least.

But should not the young, at least, who are entrusted to academic instruction, be warned about writings of that sort, and be protected from premature acquaintance with such dangerous propositions, until their power of judgment has matured or rather the doctrine that one would ground in them has become firmly rooted, in order vigorously to resist all persuasion to the contrary, from wherever it might come?

If matters of pure reason had to be left to dogmatic procedures, and if the opponents really had to be disposed of polemically, i.e., in such a way that one must enter into battle armed with grounds of proof against opposed assertions, then nothing would be more advisable **in the short run,** but at the same time nothing more vain and fruitless **in the long run,** than to place the reason of the young under tutelage for a long time and protect it against seduction for at least as long. But when, subsequently, either curiosity or the fashion of the age should put writings of that sort in their hands, would that youthful persuasion then hold fast? He who brings with him nothing but dogmatic weapons to resist the attacks of his opponent, and who does not know how to develop the hidden dialectic which lies no less in his own breast than in that of his counterpart, sees illusory grounds that have the advantage of novelty step forth against illusory grounds that no longer have that advantage but which instead arouse the suspicion of having abused the credulity of the young. He believes that he cannot better show that he has outgrown the discipline of childhood than by setting himself above those well-intended warnings, and, accustomed to dogmatism, he takes long drafts of the poison that dogmatically corrupts his principles. A755/B783

Exactly the opposite of that which has just been recommended must take place in academic education, although, to be sure, only under the presupposition of a thorough instruction in the critique of pure reason. For in order to put the principles*a* of the latter into practice as early as possible and to show their adequacy against the greatest dialectical illusion, it is absolutely necessary to direct the attacks that would be so fearsome for the dogmatist against the reason of the student, which is still weak but is enlightened by critique, and allow him to make the experiment of examining the groundless assertions of his opponents one by one in light of those principles. It cannot be difficult for him to dissolve those arguments into thin air, and thus he feels early his own power to defend himself fully against harmful deceptions of that sort, which must in the end lose all their plausibility*b* for him. But now whether the very same blows that bring down the edifice of the enemy A756/B784

a *Principien*
b *Schein*

must also be just as damaging to his own speculative structure, should he think of erecting anything of the sort: about that he is entirely unconcerned, because he does not need to dwell in that, but rather still has before him a prospect in the practical field, where with good ground he can hope for a firmer terrain on which to erect his rational and salutary system.

There is accordingly no real polemic in the field of pure reason. Both parties fence in the air and wrestle with their shadows, for they go beyond nature, where there is nothing that their dogmatic grasp can seize and hold. Fight as they may, the shadows that they cleave apart grow back together in an instant, like the heroes of Valhalla, to amuse themselves anew in bloodless battles.

However, there is also no permissible skeptical use of pure reason, which one could call the principle of its **neutrality** in all controversies. To incite reason against itself, to hand it weapons on both sides, and then to watch its heated struggle quietly and scornfully is not seemly from a dogmatic point of view, but rather has the look of a spiteful and malicious cast of mind. If, however, one takes regard of the inexorable deception and bragging of the sophists, who will not be moderated by any critique, then there is really no other course but to set the boasting of one side against another, which stands on the same rights, in order at least to shock reason, by means of the resistance of an enemy, into raising some doubts about its pretensions and giving a hearing to the critique. But for reason to leave just these doubts standing, and to set out to recommend the conviction and confession of its ignorance, not merely as a cure for dogmatic self-conceit but also as the way in which to end the conflict of reason with itself, is an entirely vain attempt, by no means suitable for arranging a peaceful retirement for reason; rather it is at best only a means for awaking it from its sweet dogmatic dreams in order to undertake a more careful examination of its condition. Since, however, this skeptical manner of withdrawing from a tedious quarrel of reason seems to be the shortcut, as it were, for arriving at enduring philosophical tranquility, or at least the high road that is happily recommended by those who would give a philosophical appearance to a scornful contempt for all investigations of this kind, I find it necessary to exhibit this manner of thought in its true light.

A757/B785

A758/B786

On the
impossibility of a skeptical satisfaction
of pure reason that is divided against itself.[18]

The consciousness of my ignorance (if this is not at the same time known to be necessary) should not end my inquiries, but is rather the proper cause to arouse them. All ignorance is either that of things[a] or of the determination and boundaries of my cognition. Now if the ignorance is contingent, then in the first case it must drive me to investigate the things (objects) **dogmatically,** in the second case to investigate the boundaries of my possible cognition **critically.** But that my ignorance is absolutely necessary and hence absolves me from all further investigation can never be made out empirically, from **observation,** but only critically, by **getting to the bottom of**[b] the primary sources of our cognition. Thus the determination of the boundaries of our reason can only take place in accordance with *a priori* grounds; its limitation, however, which is a merely indeterminate cognition of an ignorance that is never completely to be lifted, can also be cognized *a posteriori*, through that which always remains to be known even with all of our knowledge. The former cognition of ignorance, which is possible only by means of the critique of reason itself, is thus **science,** the latter is nothing but **perception,** about which one cannot say how far the inference from it might reach. If I represent the surface of the earth (in accordance with sensible appearance)[c] as a plate, I cannot know how far it extends. But experience teaches me this: that wherever I go, I always see a space around me in which I could proceed farther; thus I cognize the limits of my actual knowledge of the earth[d] at any time, but not the boundaries of all possible description of the earth. But if I have gotten as far as knowing that the earth is a sphere and its surface the surface of a sphere, then from a small part of the latter, e.g., from the magnitude of one degree, I can cognize its diameter and, by means of this, the complete boundary, i.e., surface of the earth, determinately and in accordance with *a priori* principles;[e] and although I am ignorant in regard to the objects that this surface might contain, I am not ignorant in regard to the magnitude and limits of the domain that contains them.

A759/B787

The sum total of all possible objects for our cognition seems to us to be a flat surface, which has its apparent horizon, namely that which comprehends its entire domain and which is called by us the rational concept of unconditioned totality. It is impossible to attain this empirically, and all attempts to determine it *a priori* in accordance with a certain principle[f] have been in vain. Yet all questions of our pure reason pertain to that which might lie outside this horizon or in any case at least on its borderline.

A760/B788

[a] *Sachen*
[b] ***Ergründung***
[c] *Schein*
[d] *Erdkunde* (i.e., geography)
[e] *Principien*
[f] *Princip*

The famous David Hume was one of these geographers of human reason, who took himself to have satisfactorily disposed of these questions by having expelled them outside the horizon of human reason, which however he could not determine. He dwelt primarily on the principle of causality, and quite rightly remarked about that that one could not base its truth (indeed not even the objective validity of the concept of an efficient cause in general) on any insight at all, i.e., *a priori* cognition, and thus that the authority of this law is not constituted in the least by its necessity, but only by its merely general usefulness in the course of experience and a subjective necessity arising therefrom, which he called custom.[19] Now from the incapacity of our reason to make a use of this principle that goes beyond all experience, he inferred the nullity of all pretensions of reason in general to go beyond the empirical.

One can call a procedure of this sort, subjecting the *facta* of reason to examination and when necessary to blame, the **censorship** of reason. It is beyond doubt that this censorship inevitably leads to **doubt** about all

A 761 / B 789 transcendent use of principles. But this is only the second step, which is far from completing the work. The first step in matters of pure reason, which characterizes its childhood, is **dogmatic.** The just mentioned second step is **skeptical,** and gives evidence[a] of the caution of the power of judgment sharpened by experience. Now, however, a third step is still necessary, which pertains only to the mature and adult power[b] of judgment, which has at its basis firm maxims of proven universality, that, namely, which subjects to evaluation not the *facta* of reason but reason itself, as concerns its entire capacity[c] and suitability for pure *a priori* cognitions; this is not the censorship but the **critique** of pure reason, whereby not merely **limits** but rather the determinate **boundaries** of it – not merely ignorance in one part or another but ignorance in regard to all possible questions of a certain sort – are not merely suspected but are proved from principles.[d] Thus skepticism is a resting-place for human reason, which can reflect upon its dogmatic peregrination and make a survey of the region in which it finds itself in order to be able to choose its path in the future with greater certainty, but it is not a dwelling-place for permanent residence; for the latter can only be found in a complete certainty, whether it be one of the cognition of the objects themselves or of the boundaries within which all of our cog-

A 762 / B 790 nition of objects is enclosed.

Our reason is not like an indeterminably extended plane, the limits of

---

[a] *zeugt;* in A, *zeigt.* If *zeugt* is a misprint introduced in B, then the translation would be "shows."
[b] *männlichen*
[c] *Vermögen*
[d] *Principien*

which one can cognize only in general, but must rather be compared with a sphere, the radius of which can be found out from the curvature of an arc on its surface (from the nature of synthetic *a priori* propositions), from which its content and its boundary can also be ascertained with certainty. Outside this sphere (field of experience) nothing is an object[a] for it; indeed even questions about such supposed objects concern only subjective principles[b] of a thoroughgoing determination of the relations[c] that can obtain among the concepts of understanding inside of this sphere.

We are really in possession of synthetic *a priori* cognition, as is established by the principles of understanding, which anticipate experience. Now if someone cannot even make the possibility of these comprehensible to himself, he may certainly begin to doubt whether they are really present in us *a priori;* but he cannot declare this to be an impossibility through the mere power of the understanding, and declare to be nugatory all of the steps that reason takes in accordance with their guidance. He can only say: If we had insight into their origin and authenticity, then we would be able to determine the domain and the boundaries of our reason; but until this has happened, all assertions of the latter are   A763/B791 shots in the dark. And in such a way a thoroughgoing doubt of all dogmatic philosophy that goes its way without any critique of reason itself would be entirely well founded; yet reason cannot on that account be entirely denied such a progress, if it is prepared and secured through better groundwork.[d] For one thing, all the concepts, indeed all the questions that pure reason lays before us, lie not in experience but themselves in turn only in reason, and they must therefore be able to be solved and their validity or nullity must be able to be comprehended. We are, also, not justified in repudiating these problems under the excuse of our incapacity, as if their solution really lay in the nature of things, and in rejecting further investigation, since reason has given birth to these ideas from its own womb alone, and is therefore liable to give account of either their validity or their dialectical illusion.

All skeptical polemicizing is properly directed only against the dogmatist, who continues gravely along his path without any mistrust of his original objective principles,[e] i.e., without critique, in order to unhinge his concept[f] and bring him to self-knowledge.[g] In itself it settles nothing at all about what we can know and what by contrast we cannot

---

[a] *Object*
[b] *Principien*
[c] *Verhältnisse*
[d] *Grundlegung*
[e] *Principien*
[f] *Concept*
[g] *Selbsterkenntnis*

A 764/ B 792   know. All failed dogmatic attempts of reason are *facta*, which it is always useful to subject to censure. But this cannot decide anything about reason's expectations of hoping for better success in its future efforts and making claims to that; mere censure can therefore never bring to an end the controversy about what is lawful*^a* in human reason.

Since Hume is perhaps the most ingenious of all skeptics, and is incontrovertibly the preeminent one with regard to the influence that the skeptical procedure can have on awakening a thorough examination of reason, it is well worth the trouble to make clear, to the extent that is appropriate to my aim, the path of his inferences and the aberrations of such an insightful and valuable man, which nevertheless began on the trail of truth.

Hume perhaps had it in mind, although he never fully developed it, that in judgments of a certain kind we go beyond our concept of the object. I have called this sort of judgment **synthetic**. There is no difficulty about how, by means of experience, I can go beyond the concepts that I possess thus far. Experience is itself a synthesis of perceptions that augments my concept which I have by means of one perception by the addition of others. But we also believe ourselves to be able to go beyond

A 765/ B 793   our concepts *a priori* and to amplify our cognition. We attempt to do this either through pure understanding, with regard to that which can at least be an **object**^{*b*} **of experience,** or even through pure reason, with regard to such properties of things, or even with regard to the existence of such objects, that can never come forth in experience. Our skeptic did not distinguish these two kinds of judgments, as he should have, and for that reason held this augmentation of concepts out of themselves and the parthenogenesis, so to speak, of our understanding (together with reason), without impregnation by experience, to be impossible; thus he held all of its supposedly *a priori* principles^{*c*} to be merely imagined, and found that they are nothing but a custom arising from experience and its laws, thus are merely empirical, i.e., intrinsically contingent rules, to which we ascribe a supposed necessity and universality. However, for the assertion of this disturbing proposition he referred to the universally acknowledged principle of the relationship of cause to effect. Since in that case no faculty of understanding can lead us from the concept of a thing to the existence of something else which is thereby universally and necessarily given, he believed that he could infer from this that without experience we have nothing that could augment our concept and justify us in making such a judgment, which amplifies itself *a priori*. That the sunlight

A 766/ B 794   that illuminates the wax also melts it, though it hardens clay, under-

---

^a die Rechtsame
^b **Object**
^c Principien

standing could not discover let alone lawfully infer from the concepts that we antecedently have of these things, and only experience could teach us such a law. In the transcendental logic, on the contrary, we have seen that although of course we can never **immediately** go beyond the content of the concept which is given to us, nevertheless we can still cognize the law of the connection with other things completely *a priori*, although in relation to a third thing, namely **possible** experience, but still *a priori*. Thus if wax that was previously firm melts, I can cognize *a priori* that something must have preceded (e.g., the warmth of the sun) on which this has followed in accordance with a constant law, though without experience, to be sure, I could **determinately** cognize neither the cause from the effect nor the effect from the cause *a priori* and without instruction from experience. He therefore falsely inferred from the contingency of our determination **in accordance with the law** the contingency of **the law** itself, and he confused going beyond the concept of a thing to possible experience (which takes place *a priori* and constitutes the objective reality of the concept) with the synthesis of the objects of actual experience, which is of course always empirical; thereby, however, he made a principle*a* of affinity, which has its seat in the understanding and asserts necessary connection, into a rule of association, which is found merely in the imitative imagination and which can present only contingent combinations, not objective ones at all.

The skeptical aberrations of this otherwise extremely acute man, however, arose primarily from a failing that he had in common with all dogmatists, namely, that he did not systematically survey all the kinds of *a priori* synthesis of the understanding. For had he done so, he would have found, not to mention any others here, that e.g., **the principle of persistence** is one that anticipates experience just as much as that of causality. He would thereby have been able to mark out determinate boundaries for the understanding that expands itself *a priori* and for pure reason. But since he merely **limits** our understanding without **drawing boundaries** for it, and brings about a general distrust but no determinate knowledge*b* of the ignorance that is unavoidable for us, by censuring certain principles of the understanding without placing this understanding in regard to its entire capacity*c* on the scales of critique, and, while rightly denying to understanding what it really cannot accomplish, goes further, and disputes all its capacity*d* to expand itself *a priori* without having assessed this entire capacity, the same thing happens to him that always brings down skepticism, namely, he is himself doubted, for his objections

A 767 / B 795

a *Princip*
b *Kenntnis*
c *Vermögen*
d *Vermögen*

A 768/ B 796 rest only on *facta*, which are contingent, but not on principles[a] that could effect a necessary renunciation of the right to dogmatic assertions.

Further, since he does not know the difference between the well founded claims of the understanding and the dialectical pretensions of reason, against which his attacks are chiefly directed, reason, whose entirely peculiar momentum is not in the least disturbed, but only hindered, does not feel that the room for its expansion is cut off, and although it is annoyed here and there it can never be entirely dissuaded from its efforts. For it is armed to parry attacks, and is all the more obstinate in attempting to carry out its demands. But a complete overview of its entire capacity and the conviction arising from that of the certainty of a small possession, even in case of the vanity of higher claims, put an end to all dispute, and move it to rest satisfied with a limited but undisputed property.

Against the uncritical dogmatist, who has not measured the sphere of his understanding and thus has not determined the boundaries of his possible cognition in accordance with principles,[b] who therefore does not already know in advance how much he is capable of but thinks he can find it out through mere experiments, these skeptical attacks are not merely dangerous but are even disastrous. For if he is hit in a single assertion that he cannot justify or make plausible by means of principles,[c] then suspicion falls upon all of them, however persuasive they might otherwise be.

A769/B797 And thus the skeptic is the taskmaster of the dogmatic sophist for a healthy critique of the understanding and of reason itself. When he has gotten this far he does not have to fear any further challenge, for he then distinguishes his possession from that which lies entirely outside it, to which he makes no claims and about which he cannot become involved in any controversies. Thus the skeptical procedure is not, to be sure, itself **satisfying** for questions of reason, but it is nevertheless **preparatory** for arousing its caution and showing it fundamental means for securing it in its rightful possessions.

First Chapter
Third Section
The
discipline of pure reason with regard
to hypotheses.

Since, then, through the critique of our reason we finally know that we cannot in fact know anything at all in its pure and speculative use,

---

[a] *Principien*
[b] *Principien*
[c] *Principien*

should it not then open up an all the wider field for **hypotheses,** since it is at least granted to reason to invent[a] and to opine, if not to assert?

If the imagination is not simply **to enthuse** but is, under the strict oversight of reason, **to invent,**[b] something must always first be fully certain and not invented,[c] or a mere opinion, and that is the **possibility** of the object itself. In that case it is permissible to take refuge in opinion concerning the actuality of the object, which opinion, however, in order not to be groundless, must be connected as a ground of explanation with that which is actually given and consequently certain, and it is then called an **hypothesis.**[20]

A 770/ B 798

Now since we cannot construct *a priori* the least concept of the possibility of dynamical connection, and the category of the pure understanding does not serve for thinking up such a thing but only for understanding it where it is encountered in experience, we cannot originally cook up,[d] in accordance with these categories, a single object with any new and not empirically given property and ground a permissible hypothesis on it; for this would be to found reason on empty figments of the brain rather than concepts of things. Thus we are not allowed to think up any sort of new original forces, e.g., an understanding that is capable of intuiting its object without sense or an attractive force without any contact, or a new kind of substance, e.g., one which would be present in space without impenetrability; consequently we also cannot conceive of any community of substances that would be different from anything that experience provides;[21] no presence except in space, no duration except merely in time. In a word: it is only possible for our reason to use the conditions of possible experience as conditions of the possibility of things; but it is by no means possible for it as it were to create new ones, independent of these conditions, for concepts of this sort, although free of contradiction, would nevertheless also be without any object.

A 771 / B 799

The concepts of reason are, as we have said, mere ideas, and of course have no object in any sort of experience, but also do not on that account designate objects that are invented[e] and at the same time thereby assumed to be possible. They are merely thought problematically, in order to ground regulative principles[f] of the systematic use of the understanding in the field of experience in relation to them (as heuristic fictions). If one departs from this, they are mere thought-entities, the

[a] *dichten*
[b] *dichten*
[c] *erdichtet*
[d] *aussinnen*
[e] *gedichtete*
[f] *Principien*

possibility of which is not demonstrable, and which thus cannot be used to ground the explanation of actual appearances through an hypothesis. It is entirely permissible to **think** the soul as simple in order, in accordance with this **idea,** to make a complete and necessary unity of all powers of the mind, even though one cannot have insight into it *in concreto,* into the principle[a] of our judgment of its inner appearances. But to **assume** the soul as simple substance (a transcendent concept) would be a proposition that would not only be indemonstrable (as is the case

A 772 / B 800   with many physical hypotheses), but which would also be hazarded entirely arbitrarily and blindly, since the simple cannot come forth in any experience at all, and, if one here understands by substance the persistent object[b] of sensible intuition, there can be no insight at all into the possibility of a **simple appearance.** Merely intelligible beings or merely intelligible properties of the things of the sensible world cannot be assumed as opinions with any well-founded authority of reason, although (since one has no concept of either their possibility or their impossibility) they also cannot be dogmatically denied on the basis of any supposedly better insight.

For the explanation of given appearances no other things and grounds of explanation can be adduced than those which are connected to the given appearances by already known laws of appearances. A **transcendental hypothesis,** in which a mere idea of reason would be used for the explanation of things in nature, would thus be no explanation at all, since that which one does not adequately understand on the basis of known empirical principles[c] would be explained by means of something about which one understands nothing at all. And the principle[d] of such an hypothesis would really serve only for the satisfaction of reason and not for the advancement of the use of the understanding in regard to objects. Order and purposiveness in nature must in turn be explained from natural grounds and in accordance with laws of nature, and here

A 773 / B 801   even the wildest hypotheses, as long as they are physical, are more tolerable than a hyperphysical hypothesis, i.e., the appeal to a divine author, which one presupposes to this end. For that would be a principle[e] of lazy reason (*ignava ratio*), at once bypassing all causes, of whose objective reality, at least as far as possibility is concerned, one could still learn through continued experience, in order to take refuge in a mere idea, which is very comforting to reason. As far as the absolute totality of the ground of explanation in the series of those causes is concerned,

---

[a] *Princip*
[b] *Object*
[c] *Principien*
[d] *Princip*
[e] *Princip*

however, that can create no difficulty with regard to the objects of the world,[a] for since these are nothing but appearances, nothing that is completed in the synthesis of the series of conditions can be hoped for from them.

Transcendental hypotheses of the speculative use of reason and a freedom to make good the lack of physical grounds of explanation by using all sorts of hyperphysical ones can never be permitted at all, partly because reason is not advanced by them but rather cut off from all progress in their use, and partly because this license must ultimately destroy all fruits of the cultivation of its own proper soil, namely experience. For whenever the explanation of nature becomes difficult, we always have at hand a transcendental ground of explanation that spares us that inquiry, and our research is concluded not through insight but through the total incomprehensibility of a principle[b] which was thought up so far in advance that it must have contained the concept of that which is absolutely first.

A 774/B 802

The second point which is requisite to make an hypothesis worthy of being assumed is its adequacy for determining *a priori* the consequences these are given. If for this purpose auxiliary hypotheses need to be called in, they arouse the suspicion of being a mere invention, since each of them requires the same justification which the underlying thought needed, and hence can give no reliable testimony. If on the presupposition of an unlimitedly perfect cause there is no lack of grounds of explanation for all the purposiveness, order, and greatness[c] that is found in the world, then the deviations from these and the evils that reveal themselves, at least according to our concepts, require still further hypotheses in order to save the first from these objections. If the simple self-sufficiency of the human soul, which has been laid at the ground of its appearances, is impugned by difficulties because these are phenomena similar to the alterations of matter (growth and decay), then new hypotheses must be called in to help, which are not without plausibility but are still without any confirmation, except that which is given to them by the opinion assumed as the primary ground, which they were supposed to explain.

A 775/B 803

If the assertions of reason that have here been adduced as examples (incorporeal unity of the soul and existence of a highest being) are not to count as hypotheses, but as dogmata proven *a priori*, then they are not even an issue. In that case, however, one would indeed take care that the proof have the apodictic certainty of a demonstration. For to make the actuality of such ideas merely **probable** is an absurd proposal, just

[a] *Weltobjecte*
[b] *Princips*
[c] *Größe*

as if one thought to prove a proposition of geometry as merely probable. Reason in abstraction from all experience can cognize everything
only *a priori* and necessarily, or not at all; hence its judgment is never an
opinion, but either abstention from all judgment or apodictic certainty.
Opinions and probable judgments about what pertains to things can
occur only as grounds of explanation of that which is actually given or
as consequences in accordance with empirical laws of that which actually grounds what is actually given; thus they can occur only in the series of objects of experience. **To form opinions** outside this field is the
same as to play with thoughts, unless one merely has the opinion that
an uncertain path of judgment can perhaps lead to truth.

A 776/ B 804   However, although in merely speculative questions of pure reason no
hypotheses are allowed to ground propositions, they are nevertheless
entirely admissible for defending them, i.e., not in dogmatic but in
polemical use. By defense, however, I understand not the augmentation
of grounds of proof for its assertion, but rather the mere frustration of
the opponent's illusory insights, which would demolish our own asserted propositions. But now all synthetic propositions from pure reason have the peculiarity that if he who asserts the reality of certain ideas
never knows enough to make his proposition certain, on the other side
his opponent can just as little know enough to assert the contrary. This
equality in the lot of human reason favors neither of them in speculative cognitions, and there is thus the true battleground of feuds that can
never be resolved. It will be shown in what follows, however, that in regard to its **practical use** reason still has the right to assume something
which it would in no way be warranted in presupposing in the field of
mere speculation without sufficient grounds of proof; for all such presuppositions injure the perfection of speculation, about which, however,
the practical interest does not trouble itself at all. There it thus has a
possession the legitimacy of which need not be proved, and the proof of
A 777/ B 805 which it could not in fact give. The opponent should therefore prove.
But since he no more knows something about the object that is doubted
which would establish its non-being than does the former, who asserts
its actuality, here an advantage on the side of he who asserts something
as a practically necessary presupposition (*melior est conditio possidentis*)[a] is
revealed. He is, namely, free to use, as it were in an emergency, the very
same means for his good cause[b] as his opponent would use against it,
i.e., to use the hypotheses that do not serve to strengthen the proof of
it but serve only to show that the opponent understands far too little
about the object of the dispute to be able to flatter himself with an advantage in speculative insight over us.

---

[a] The condition of the possessor is the better.
[b] *Sache*

Hypotheses are therefore allowed in the field of pure reason only as weapons of war, not for grounding a right but only for defending it. However, we must always seek the enemy here in ourselves. For speculative reason in its transcendental use is dialectical **in itself.** The objections that are to be feared lie in ourselves. We must search them out like old but unexpired claims, in order to ground perpetual peace on their annihilation. External quiet is only illusory. The seed of the attacks, which lies in the nature of human reason, must be extirpated; but how can we extirpate it if we do not give it freedom, indeed even nourishment, to send out shoots, so that we can discover it and afterwards eradicate it with its root? Thus, think up for yourself the objections which have not yet occurred to any opponent, and even lend him the weapons or concede him the most favorable position that he could desire. There is nothing in this to fear, though much to hope, namely that you will come into a possession that can never be attacked in the future. A778/B806

Now to your complete armament there also belong the hypotheses of pure reason, which, although they are merely leaden weapons (for they have not been steeled through any law of experience), are nevertheless just as capable as those which any opponent might use against you. If, therefore, you come up against the difficulty for the immaterial nature of the soul which is not subjected to any corporeal transformation (assumed in some other, non-speculative context), the difficulty, namely, that experience seems to prove that both the elevation as well as the derangement of our mental powers are merely different modifications of our organs, you can weaken the power of this proof by assuming that our body is nothing but the fundamental appearance to which the entire faculty of sensibility and therewith all thinking are related, as their condition, in our present state (in life). Separation from the body would be the end of this sensible use of your cognitive power and the beginning of the intellectual. The body would thus be not the cause of thinking but a merely restricting condition on it, thus it would be regarded as furthering the sensible and animal but for that reason all the more as hindering the pure and spiritual life, and the dependence of the former on the corporeal constitution would prove nothing about the dependence of life in its entirety on the state of our organs. But you could go even further, and indeed raise new doubts, which have either not been suggested before or else have not been driven far enough. A779/B807

The contingency of conception, which in humans as well as in irrational creatures depends on opportunity, but besides this also on nourishment, on government, on its moods and caprices, even on vices, presents a great difficulty for the opinion of the eternal duration of a creature whose life has first begun under circumstances so trivial and so entirely dependent on our liberty. As far as the duration of the entire species (here on earth) is concerned, this difficulty amounts to little, since the contingency in the individual[a] is nonetheless subjected to a rule in the whole; but with regard to each individual[b] it certainly seems questionable to expect such a powerful effect from such inconsequential causes. Against this, however, you could propose a transcendental hypothesis: that all life is really only intelligible, not subject to temporal alterations at all, and has neither begun at birth nor will be ended through death;[c] that this life is nothing but a mere appearance, i.e., a sensible representation of the purely spiritual life, and the entire world of the senses is a mere image, which hovers before our present kind of cognition and, like a dream, has no objective reality in itself; that if we could intuit the things and ourselves **as they are** we would see ourselves in a world of spiritual natures with which our only true community had not begun with birth nor would not cease with bodily death (as mere appearances), etc.

A 780/ B 808

Now although we do not know or seriously assert the least thing about all of this which we have here pleaded against the attack, and it is all not even an idea of reason but merely a concept **thought up** for self-defense, nevertheless we proceed quite rationally here, showing the opponent who thinks he has exhausted all of the possibilities by falsely representing the lack of their empirical conditions as a proof of the complete impossibility of that which is believed by us, that he can span the entire field of possible things in themselves through mere laws of experience just as little as we can acquire anything for our reason in a well-grounded manner outside of experience. He who turns such hypothetical countermeasures against the pretensions of his rashly negative opponent must not be considered to hold them as his own genuine opinions. He abandons them as soon as he has finished off the dogmatic self-conceit of his opponent. For as modest and as moderate as it may be for someone merely to refuse and deny the assertions of another, as soon as he would make these objections valid as proof of the opposite his claim would be no less proud and conceited than if he had seized hold of the affirmative party and its assertion.

A 781/ B 809

Thus one sees that in the speculative use of reason hypotheses have no validity as opinions in themselves, but only relative to opposed transcendent pretensions. For the extension of the principles[d] of possible experience to the possibility of things in general is just as transcendent as the assertion of the objective reality of such concepts, which can never find their objects anywhere but outside the boundary of all possible experience. What pure reason judges assertorically must be neces-

[a] *im Einzeln*
[b] *jeden Individuum*
[c] Following Erdmann, using a semicolon instead of Kant's period here.
[d] *Principien*

sary (like everything cognized by reason), or it is nothing at all. Thus in fact it contains no opinions at all. The hypotheses in question are, however, only problematic judgments, which at least cannot be refuted, though of course they cannot be proved by anything, and they are therefore not private opinions, though against reigning scruples they A782/B810 cannot be dispensed with (even for inner tranquility). But one must preserve them in this quality, and indeed carefully make sure that they are not believed in themselves and as having an absolute validity, and that they do not drown reason in fictions and deceptions.

First Chapter
Fourth Section
The discipline of pure reason in regard
to its proofs.

The proofs of transcendental and synthetic propositions are unique among all proofs of synthetic *a priori* cognition in that in their case reason may not apply itself directly to the object by means of its concepts, but must first establish the objective validity of the concepts and the possibility of their synthesis *a priori*. This is not merely a necessary rule of caution, but concerns the essence and the possibility of the proofs themselves. It is impossible for me to go beyond the concept of an object *a priori* without a special clue which is to be found outside of this concept. In mathematics it is *a priori* intuition that guides my synthesis, and there all inferences can be immediately drawn from[a] pure intuition. In transcendental cognition, as long as it has to do merely with concepts A783/B811 of the understanding, this guideline is possible experience. The proof does not show, that is, that the given concept (e.g., of that which happens) leads directly to another concept (that of a cause), for such a transition would be a leap for which nothing could be held responsible; rather it shows that experience itself, hence the object[b] of experience, would be impossible without such a connection. The proof, therefore, had to indicate at the same time the possibility of achieving synthetically and *a priori* a certain cognition of things which is not contained in the concept of them. Without attention to this the proofs, like water breaking its banks, run wildly across the country, wherever the tendency of hidden association may happen to lead them. The illusion of conviction, which rests on subjective causes of association and is taken for the insight of a natural affinity, cannot balance the misgiving to which steps risked in this way properly give rise. Hence all attempts to prove the principle of sufficient reason have also, according to the

---

[a] Following the second edition, which reads "*von*"; the first has "*an*."
[b] *Object*

A784/B812

general consensus of experts, been in vain, and, since one still could not abandon this principle, until the transcendental critique came onto the scene one preferred obstinately to appeal to healthy human understanding (a refuge, which always proves that the cause of reason is in despair) rather than to attempt new dogmatic proofs.

But if the proposition of which a proof is to be given is an assertion of pure reason, and if I would even go beyond my concepts of experience by means of mere ideas, then all the more must this proof contain the justification of such a step of synthesis (if it would otherwise be possible) as a necessary condition of its probative force. Hence as plausible as the supposed proof of the simple nature of our thinking substance from the unity of apperception may be, yet it is unavoidably faced with the difficulty that, since absolute simplicity is not a concept that can be immediately related to a perception, but rather as an idea must be merely inferred, there can be no insight at all into how the mere consciousness that is contained or at least can be contained **in all thinking** should, even though it is to this extent a simple representation, lead to the consciousness and knowledge*a* of a thing **in which** alone thinking can be contained.[22] For if I represent to myself the force of my body in motion, it is to that extent absolute unity for me, and my representation of it is simple; hence I can also express it through the motion of a point, since its volume is not relevant, and without diminution of the force it can be represented as being as small as one wants and can even be con-

A785/B813

ceived of as being located in one point. But I would not infer from this that if nothing is given to me except the moving force of a body then the body can be conceived of as a simple substance just because its representation abstracts from all magnitude of the content of space and is therefore simple. Now I discover a paralogism in the fact that the simple in the abstract is entirely different from the simple in the object*b* and that the I, which taken in the first sense*c* comprises no manifold **within itself,** if taken in the second sense, in which it signifies the soul itself, can be a very complex concept, namely containing **under itself** and designating quite a lot. Only in order to have any presentiment of this paralogism (for without such a provisional conjecture one would hardly have any suspicion of the proof), it is always necessary to have at hand an enduring criterion of the possibility of such synthetic propositions, which prove more than experience can yield, which criterion consists in the fact that the proof leads to the required predicate not directly but only by means of a principle*d* of the possibility of expand-

a *Kenntnis*
b *Object*
c *im ersteren Verstande*
d *Princip*

ing our given concepts *a priori* to ideas and realizing these. If this caution is always used, and if before one even attempts the proof one wisely considers how and with what basis for hope one could expect such an expansion through pure reason, and whence, in cases of this sort, one would derive these insights, which are not developed from concepts and which also cannot be anticipated in relation to possible experience, then one can be spared many difficult and nevertheless fruitless efforts, since one would not attribute to reason anything which obviously exceeds its capacity,[a] but would rather subject reason, which does not gladly suffer constraint in the paroxysms of its lust for speculative expansion, to the discipline of abstinence. A786/B814

The first rule, therefore, is this: to attempt no transcendental proofs without having first considered whence one can justifiably derive the principles on which one intends to build and with what right one can expect success in inferences from them. If they are principles of the understanding (e.g., of causality), then it is in vain to try to arrive by their means at ideas of pure reason; for those principles are valid only for objects of possible experience. If they are to be principles from pure reason, then again all effort is in vain. For reason has principles, to be sure, but as objective principles they are all dialectical, and can only be valid as regulative principles[b] of the systematically coherent use of experience. But if such ostensible proofs are already given, then oppose the *non liquet*[c] of your mature power of judgment against their deceptive conviction, and even if you cannot yet penetrate their deception you still have a perfect right to demand the deduction of the principles that are used in them, which, if they are supposed to have arisen from pure reason, will never be provided for you. And thus it is not even necessary for you to concern yourself with the development and refutation of each groundless illusion, but you can dispose of the entire heap of these inexhaustible tricks of dialectic at once in the court of a critical reason, which demands laws. A787/B815

The second peculiarity of transcendental proofs is this: that for each transcendental proposition only **a single** proof can be found. If I am to draw an inference not from concepts but rather from the intuition which corresponds to a concept, whether it be a pure intuition, as in mathematics, or an empirical intuition, as in natural science, the intuition that grounds the inference offers me a manifold of material for synthetic propositions that I can connect in more than one way, thus allowing me to reach the same proposition by different paths since I may start out from more than one point.

[a] *Vermögen*
[b] *Principien*
[c] The verdict "not proved."

Every transcendental proposition, however, proceeds solely from one concept, and states the synthetic condition of the possibility of the object in accordance with this concept. The ground of proof can therefore only be unique, since outside this concept there is nothing further by means of which the object could be determined, and the proof can therefore contain nothing more than the determination of an object in general in accordance with this concept, which is also unique. In the transcendental analytic we drew, e.g., the principle "Everything that happens has a cause" from the unique condition of the objective possibility of a concept of that which happens in general, namely that the determination of an occurrence in time, and consequently this (occurrence) as belonging to experience, would be impossible if it did not stand under such a dynamical rule. Now this is also the only possible ground of proof; for only through the fact that an object is determined for the concept by means of the law of causality does the represented occurrence have objective validity, i.e., truth. To be sure, still other proofs of this principle, e.g., from contingency, have been attempted;[23] but if this is considered clearly, one cannot discover any characteristic of contingency except that of **happening**, i.e., existence which is preceded by a not-being of the object, and one therefore always comes back to the same ground of proof. If the proposition "Everything that thinks is simple" is to be proved, one does not dwell on the manifoldness of thinking, but sticks solely with the concept of the I, which is simple and to which all thinking is related. It is just the same with the transcendental proof of the existence of God, which depends solely on the reciprocality of the concepts of the most real being and the necessary being, and cannot be sought anywhere else.

Through this cautionary remark the critique of the assertions of reason is very much reduced. Where reason would conduct its business through mere concepts, only a single proof is possible if any proof is possible at all. Thus if one sees the dogmatist step forth with ten proofs, one can be sure that he has none at all. For if he had one that proved apodictically (as must be the case in matters of pure reason), for what would he need the rest? His intention is only that of every parliamentary advocate: one argument for this one, another one for that, in order to take advantage of the weakness of his judges who, without getting into the business deeply and in order to get rid of it quickly, just grasp at the first argument that occurs to them and decide accordingly.

The third special rule of pure reason, if it is subjected to a discipline in regard to transcendental proofs, is that its proofs must never be **apagogic** but always **ostensive**. The direct or ostensive proof is, in all kinds of cognition, that which is combined with the conviction of truth and simultaneously with insight into its sources; the apagogic proof, on the contrary, can produce certainty, to be sure, but never comprehensibility of the truth in regard to its connection with the grounds of its possibility. Hence the latter are more of an emergency aid than a pro- A790/B818 cedure which satisfies all the aims of reason. Yet they have an advantage in self-evidence over the direct proofs in this: that a contradiction always carries with it more clarity of representation than the best connection, and thereby more closely approaches the intuitiveness of a demonstration.

The real cause for the use of apagogic proofs in various sciences is probably this. If the grounds from which a certain cognition should be derived are too manifold or lie too deeply hidden, then one tries whether they may not be reached through their consequences. Now *modus ponens*, inferring the truth of a cognition from the truth of its consequences, would be allowed only if all of the possible consequences are true; for in this case only a single ground of this is possible, which is therefore also the true one.[24] But this procedure is unusable, because to have insight into all possible consequences of any proposition that is assumed exceeds our powers; yet one uses this kind of inference, though to be sure with a certain degree of care, if it is merely a matter of proving something as an hypothesis, since there an inference by analogy is allowed: that, namely, if as many consequences as one has tested agree with an assumed ground then all other possible ones will also agree with it. But for this reason an hypothesis can never be transformed into a A791/B819 demonstrated truth by this path. The *modus tollens* of rational inferences,[a] which infers from the consequences to the grounds, proves not only entirely strictly but also in all cases easily. For if even only a single false consequence can be derived from a proposition, then this proposition is false.[25] Now instead of having to run through the entire series of the grounds in an ostensive proof that can lead to the truth of a cognition, by means of complete insight into its possibility, one need only find a single false one among the consequences flowing from its contrary, and then the contrary is also false, thus the cognition that one had to prove is true.

Apagogic proof, however, can be allowed only in those sciences where it is impossible **to substitute** that which is subjective in our representations for that which is objective, namely the cognition of what is in the object. Where the latter is the dominant concern, however, then it must frequently transpire that the opposite of a certain proposition either simply contradicts the subjective conditions of thought but not the object, or else that both propositions contradict each other only under a subjective condition that is falsely held to be objective, and that since the condition is false, both of them can be false, without it being possible to infer the truth of one from the falsehood of the other.

---

[a] *Vernunftschlüsse*, which could also be translated "syllogisms."

A 792 / B 820   In mathematics this subreption is impossible; hence apagogic proof has its proper place there. In natural science, since everything there is grounded on empirical intuitions, such false pretenses can frequently be guarded against through the comparison of many observations; but this kind of proof itself is for the most part unimportant in this area. The transcendental attempts of pure reason, however, are all conducted within the real medium of dialectical illusion, i.e., the subjective which offers itself to or even forces itself upon reason as objective in its premises. Now here it simply cannot be allowed that assertions of synthetic propositions be justified by the refutation of their opposites. For either this refutation is nothing other than the mere representation of the conflict of the opposed opinion with the subjective conditions of comprehensibility through our reason, which does nothing by way of rejecting the thing itself (just as, e.g., unconditional necessity in the existence of a being cannot be conceived by us at all, and hence every speculative proof of a necessary highest being is therefore rightfully opposed **subjectively,** but the possibility of such an original being **in itself** is not rightfully opposed), or else both, the affirmative as well as the negative part, taken in by transcendental illusion, have as their ground

A 793 / B 821   an impossible concept of the object, and then the rule holds that *non entis nulla sunt predicata,*[a] i.e., both what one asserts affirmatively as well as what one asserts negatively of the object are incorrect, and one cannot arrive at cognition of the truth apagogically through the refutation of its opposite. So, for example, if it is presupposed that the sensible world is given in its totality **in itself,** then it is false that it must be **either** infinite in space or[b] finite and bounded, just because both of these are false. For appearances (as mere representations), which would yet be given **in themselves** (as objects)[c] are something impossible, and the infinity of this imagined whole would, to be sure, be unconditioned, but would nevertheless (since everything in appearances is conditioned) contradict the unconditioned determination of magnitude that is presupposed in the concept.

Apagogic proof is also the real deception with which the admirers of the thoroughness of our dogmatic sophists have always been held off; it is the champion, as it were, who would prove the honor and the indisputable right of his chosen party by his pledge to take on anyone who would doubt it, although through such boasting nothing is settled about the real issue but only the relative strength of the opponents, and indeed only that of the one who is on the attack. The observers, seeing

A 794 / B 822   that each is in turn first victor then vanquished, often take the occasion

---

[a] Nothing is to be predicated of any non-being.
[b] The "or" is emphasized in the first edition but not in the second.
[c] *Objecte*

to have skeptical doubts about the object[a] of the dispute itself. However, they do not have cause for this, and it is sufficient to declare to them: *non defensoribus istis tempus eget.*[b] Each must conduct his affair by means of a legitimate proof through the transcendental deduction of its grounds of proof, i.e., directly, so that one can see what his claim of reason has to say for itself. For if his opponent stands on subjective grounds, it is of course easy to refute him, but without any advantage to the dogmatist, who commonly depends in just the same way on subjective causes of judgment and who can in the same way be driven into a corner by his opponent. But if both sides would only proceed directly, then either they themselves must notice the difficulty, indeed the impossibility of discovering a title for their assertions, and will in the end be able to appeal only to their antiquity, or else the critique will easily reveal the dogmatic illusion, and compel pure reason to surrender its exaggerated pretensions in its speculative use, and to draw back within the boundaries of its proper territory, namely practical principles.

---

[a] *Object*

[b] "The time does not need these defenses." The complete quotation is *"Non tali auxilio, nec defensoribus istis tempus eget"* (Virgil, *Aeneid* II.5, 21); in the translation by Robert Fitzgerald, "The time is past for help like this, for this kind of defending" (Virgil, *The Aeneid*, tr. Robert Fitzgerald [New York: Random House, 1981], p. 51). The line is spoken by Hecuba to Priam as the aged king of Troy arms himself against the Greeks in the final death throes of his city.

The Transcendental Doctrine of Method
Second Chapter
The canon of pure reason

It is humiliating for human reason that it accomplishes nothing in its pure use, and even requires a discipline to check its extravagances and avoid the deceptions that come from them. But, on the other side, that reason can and must exercise this discipline itself, without allowing anything else to censor it, elevates it and gives it confidence in itself, for the boundaries that it is required to set for its speculative use at the same time limit the sophistical pretensions of every opponent, and thus it can secure against all attacks everything that may still be left to it from its previously exaggerated demands. The greatest and perhaps only utility of all philosophy of pure reason is thus only negative, namely that it does not serve for expansion, as an organon, but rather, as a discipline, serves for the determination of boundaries, and instead of discovering truth it has only the silent merit of guarding against errors.

Nevertheless, there must somewhere be a source of positive cognitions that belong in the domain of pure reason, and that perhaps give occasion for errors only through misunderstanding, but that in fact constitute the goal of the strenuous effort of reason. For to what cause should the unquenchable desire to find a firm footing beyond all bounds of experience otherwise be ascribed? Pure reason has a presentiment of objects of great interest to it. It takes the path of mere speculation in order to come closer to these; but they flee before it. Presumably it may hope for better luck on the only path that still remains to it, namely that of its **practical** use.

I understand by a canon the sum total of the *a priori* principles of the correct use of certain cognitive faculties in general. Thus general logic in its analytical part is a canon for understanding and reason in general, but only as far as form is concerned, since it abstracts from all content. Thus the transcendental analytic was the canon of the pure **understanding;** for it alone is capable of true synthetic *a priori* cognitions. But where no correct use of a cognitive power is possible there is no canon. Now according to the proofs that have previously been given, all synthetic cognition of pure **reason** in its speculative use is entirely impossible. There is thus no canon for its speculative use at all (for this is through and through dialectical); rather all transcendental logic is in this respect nothing but a discipline. Consequently, if there is to be any legitimate use of pure reason at all, in which case there must also be a **canon** of it, this will concern not the speculative but rather the **practical use of reason,** which we will therefore now investigate.[26]   A797/B825

On the Canon of Pure Reason
First Section
On the ultimate end of the pure use
of our reason.

Reason is driven by a propensity of its nature to go beyond its use in experience, to venture to the outermost bounds of all cognition by means of mere ideas in a pure use, and to find peace only in the completion of its circle in a self-subsisting systematic whole. Now is this striving grounded merely in its speculative interest, or rather uniquely and solely in its practical interest?

I will set aside the good fortune of reason in a speculative regard, and ask only about those problems the solution of which constitutes its ultimate end, whether it may reach this or not, and in respect to which all other ends have merely the value of means. These highest ends must, in accordance with the nature of reason, in turn have unity, in order to advance, in a united manner, that interest of humanity which is subordinated to no higher one.   A798/B826

The final aim to which in the end the speculation of reason in its transcendental use is directed concerns three objects: the freedom of the will,[a] the immortality of the soul, and the existence of God. With regard to all three the merely[b] speculative interest of reason is very small, and with respect to this an exhausting labor of transcendental research, hampered with unceasing hindrances, would be undertaken only with difficulty, since one would not be able to make any use of the discoveries that might be made which would prove its utility *in concreto,* i.e., in the investigation of nature. The will may well be free, yet this can concern only the intelligible cause of our willing. For, in accordance with an inviolable fundamental maxim without which we could not exercise any reason in empirical use, we must explain the phenomena of its manifestations, i.e., actions, no differently than all other appearances of nature, namely in accordance with its unalterable laws. Second, we

---

[a] *des Willens.* In what follows, *Wille* will be translated as "will" and *Willkühr* as "choice" or "faculty of choice."

[b] Following the second edition, which has *das bloß* instead of *bloß das.*

might be able to have insight into the spiritual nature of the soul (and with that into its immortality), yet that cannot be counted on either as an explanatory ground of the appearances in this life or for the special constitution of the future state, because our concept of an incorporeal nature is merely negative, and does not in the least expand our cognition nor offer any suitable material for any conclusions except merely fictional ones, which cannot be sanctioned by philosophy. Third, even if the existence of a highest intelligence were proved, we would, to be sure, be able to make that which is purposive in the arrangement and order of the world comprehensible in general, but would by no means be authorized to derive from it any particular arrangement and order, or boldly to infer one where it is not perceived, for it is a necessary rule of the speculative use of reason not to bypass natural causes and abandon that about which we could be instructed by experience in order to derive something that we know from something that entirely surpasses all our knowledge.*ᵃ* In a word, these three propositions always remain transcendent for speculative reason, and have no immanent use, i.e., one that is permissible for objects of experience and therefore useful for us in some way, but are rather, considered in themselves, entirely idle even though extremely difficult efforts of our reason.

A799/B827

If, then, these three cardinal propositions are not at all necessary for our **knowing,** and yet are insistently recommended to us by our reason, their importance must really concern only the **practical.**

A800/B828

Everything is practical that is possible through freedom. But if the conditions for the exercise of our free choice*ᵇ* are empirical, then in that case reason can have none but a regulative use, and can only serve to produce the unity of empirical laws, as, e.g., in the doctrine of prudence the unification of all ends that are given to us by our inclinations into the single end of **happiness** and the harmony of the means for attaining that end constitute the entire business of reason, which can therefore provide none but **pragmatic** laws of free conduct for reaching the ends recommended to us by the senses, and therefore can provide no pure laws that are determined completely *a priori.* Pure practical laws, on the contrary, whose end is given by reason completely *a priori,* and which do not command under empirical conditions but absolutely, would be products of pure reason. Of this sort, however, are the **moral** laws; thus these alone belong to the practical use of reason and permit a canon.

Thus the entire armament of reason, in the undertaking that one can call pure philosophy, is in fact directed only at the three problems that have been mentioned. These themselves, however, have in turn their

---

ᵃ *Kenntnis*
ᵇ *Willkühr*

more remote aim, namely, **what is to be done** if the will is free, if there is a God, and if there is a future world. Now since these concern our conduct in relation to the highest end, the ultimate aim of nature which provides for us wisely in the disposition of reason is properly directed only to what is moral.

A 801 / B 829

However, since we now cast our attention upon an object that is foreign* to transcendental philosophy, caution is necessary in order not to digress into episodes and injure the unity of the same system, but on the other side also in order not to say too little about the new material, thus allowing it to fail in clarity or conviction. I hope to achieve both by keeping as close as possible to the transcendental and setting aside entirely what might here be psychological, i.e., empirical.

And here the first thing to note is that for the present I will use the concept of freedom only in a practical sense*a* and set aside, as having been dealt with above, the transcendental signification of the concept, which cannot be empirically presupposed as an explanatory ground of the appearances but is rather itself a problem for reason.[27] A faculty of choice, that is, is merely **animal** (*arbitrium brutum*) which cannot be determined other than through sensible impulses, i.e., **pathologically.** However, one which can be determined independently of sensory impulses, thus through motives*b* that can only be represented by reason, is called **free choice** (*arbitrium liberum*), and everything that is connected with this, whether as ground or consequence, is called **practical.** Practical freedom can be proved through experience. For it is not merely that which stimulates the senses, i.e., immediately affects them, that determines human choice, but we have a capacity*c* to overcome impressions on our sensory faculty of desire by representations of that which is useful or injurious even in a more remote way; but these considerations about that which in regard to our whole condition is desirable, i.e., good and useful, depend on reason. Hence this also yields laws that are imperatives, i.e., objective **laws of freedom,** and that say **what ought to happen,** even though perhaps it never does happen, and that are thereby

A 802 / B 830

---

* All practical concepts pertain to objects of satisfaction or dissatisfaction,*d* i.e., of pleasure or displeasure, and thus, at least indirectly, to objects of our feeling. But since this is not a power for the representation of things, but lies outside the cognitive power altogether, the elements of our judgments, insofar as they are related to pleasure or displeasure, thus belong to practical philosophy, and not to the sum total of transcendental philosophy, which has to do solely with pure *a priori* cognitions.

A 801 / B 829

a *Verstande*
b *Bewegursachen*
c *Vermögen*
d *Wohlgefallens, oder Mißfallens*

distinguished from **laws of nature,** which deal only with that **which does happen,** on which account the former are also called practical laws.

A803/B831 But whether in these actions, through which it prescribes laws, reason is not itself determined by further influences, and whether that which with respect to sensory impulses is called freedom might not in turn with regard to higher and more remote efficient causes be nature – in the practical sphere this does not concern us, since in the first instance we ask of reason only a **precept** for conduct; it is rather a merely speculative question, which we can set aside as long as our aim is directed to action or omission.*a* We thus cognize practical freedom through experience, as one of the natural causes, namely a causality of reason in the determination of the will, whereas transcendental freedom requires an independence of this reason itself (with regard to its causality for initiating a series of appearances) from all determining causes of the world of the senses, and to this extent seems to be contrary to the law of nature, thus to all possible experience, and so remains a problem. Yet this problem does not belong to reason in its practical use, so in a canon of pure reason we are concerned with only two questions that pertain to the practical interest of pure reason, and with regard to which a canon of its use must be possible, namely: Is there a God? Is there a future life? The question about transcendental freedom concerns merely speculative knowledge, which we can set A804/B832 aside as quite indifferent if we are concerned with what is practical, and about which there is already sufficient discussion in the Antinomy of Pure Reason.

On the Canon of Pure Reason
Second Section
On the ideal of the highest good,
as a determining ground
of the ultimate end of pure reason.

In its speculative use reason led us through the field of experiences, and, since it could never find complete satisfaction for itself there, it led us on from there to speculative ideas, which in the end, however, led us back again to experience, and thus fulfilled its aim in a way that is quite useful but not quite in accord with our expectation. Now yet another experiment remains open to us: namely, whether pure reason is also to be found in practical use, whether in that use it leads us to the ideas that attain the highest ends of pure reason which we have just adduced, and thus whether from the point of view of its practical interest reason may

---

a *Thun oder Lassen,* the standard eighteenth-century German phrase for behavior subject to moral regulation and evaluation.

not be able to guarantee that which in regard to its speculative interest it entirely refuses to us.

All interest of my reason (the speculative as well as the practical) is united in the following three questions:

1. What can I know? A 805 / B 833

2. What should I do?

3. What may I hope?

The first question is merely speculative. We have (as I flatter myself) already exhausted all possible replies to it, and finally found that with which reason must certainly satisfy itself and with which, if it does not look to the practical, it also has cause to be content; but from the two great ends to which this entire effort of pure reason was really directed we remain just as distant as if, out of a concern for comfort, we had declined this labor at the outset. If, therefore, the issue is knowledge, then this much at least is certain and settled, that we can never partake of knowledge with respect to those two problems.

The second question is merely practical. As such, to be sure, it can belong to pure reason, but in that case it is not transcendental, but moral, and thus it cannot be in itself a subject for our critique.

The third question, namely, "If I do what I should, what may I then hope?" is simultaneously practical and theoretical, so that the practical leads like a clue to a reply to the theoretical question and, in its highest form, the speculative question. For all **hope** concerns happiness, and with respect to the practical and the moral law it is the very same as what knowledge and the natural law is with regard to theoretical cognition of things. The former finally comes down to the inference that A 806 / B 834 something **is** (which determines the ultimate final end) **because something ought to happen;** the latter, that something **is** (which acts as the supreme cause) **because something does happen.**

Happiness is the satisfaction of all of our inclinations (*extensive,*[a] with regard to their manifoldness, as well as *intensive,*[b] with regard to degree, and[c] also *protensive,*[d] with regard to duration). The practical law from the motive of **happiness** I call pragmatic (rule of prudence); but that which is such that it has no other motive than the **worthiness to be happy** I call moral (moral law).[e] The first advises us what to do if we want to partake of happiness; the second commands how we should behave in order even to be worthy of happiness. The first is grounded on

---

[a] extensively
[b] intensively
[c] In the first edition, "as."
[d] protensively
[e] *moralisch (Sittengesetz)*

empirical principles;^a for except by means of experience I can know neither which inclinations there are that would be satisfied nor what the natural causes are that could satisfy them. The second abstracts from inclinations and natural means of satisfying them, and considers only the freedom of a rational being in general and the necessary conditions under which alone it is in agreement with the distribution of happiness in accordance with principles,^b and thus it at least **can** rest on mere ideas of pure reason and be cognized *a priori*.

A807/B835   I assume that there are really pure moral laws, which determine completely *a priori* (without regard to empirical motives, i.e., happiness) the action and omission, i.e., the use of the freedom of a rational being in general, and that these laws command **absolutely** (not merely hypothetically under the presupposition of other empirical ends), and are thus necessary in every respect.[28] I can legitimately presuppose this proposition by appealing not only to the proofs of the most enlightened moralists but also to the moral judgment of every human being, if he will distinctly think such a law.

Pure reason thus contains – not in its speculative use, to be sure, but yet in a certain practical use, namely the moral use – principles^c of the **possibility of experience,** namely of those actions in conformity with moral precepts which **could** be encountered in the **history** of humankind. For since they command that these actions ought to happen, they must also be able to happen, and there must therefore be possible a special kind of systematic unity, namely the moral, whereas the systematic unity of nature **in accordance with speculative principles^d of reason** could not be proved, since reason has causality with regard to freedom in general but not with regard to the whole of nature, and moral principles of reason^e can produce free actions but not laws of nature. Thus the principles^f of pure reason have objective reality in their practical use, that is, in the moral use.

A808/B836   I call the world as it would be if it were in conformity with all moral laws (as it **can** be in accordance with the **freedom** of rational beings and **should** be in accordance with the necessary laws of **morality**) a **moral world.**^g This is conceived thus far merely as an intelligible world, since abstraction is made therein from all conditions (ends) and even from all hindrances to morality in it (weakness or impurity^h of human nature).

---

^a *Principien*
^b *Principien*
^c *Principien*
^d ***Principien***
^e *Vernunftprincipien*
^f *Principien*
^g Here Kant uses even larger type than his ordinary emphasis.
^h *Unlauterkeit*

Thus far it is therefore a mere, yet practical, idea, which really can and should have its influence on the sensible world, in order to make it agree as far as possible with this idea. The idea of a moral world thus has objective reality, not as if it pertained to an object of an intelligible intuition (for we cannot even think of such a thing), but as pertaining to the sensible world, although as an object of pure reason in its practical use and a *corpus mysticum* of the rational beings in it, insofar as their free choice under moral laws has thoroughgoing systematic unity in itself as well as with the freedom of everyone else.

This was the reply to the first of the two questions of pure reason that concern the practical interest: **Do that through which you will become worthy to be happy.** Now the second question asks: Now if I behave so as not to be unworthy of happiness, how may I hope thereby to partake of it? For the answer to this question, the issue is whether the principles^a of pure reason that prescribe the law *a priori* also necessarily connect this hope with it.

A809/B837

I say, accordingly, that just as the moral principles^b are necessary in accordance with reason in its **practical** use, it is equally necessary to assume in accordance with reason in its **theoretical** use^c that everyone has cause to hope for happiness in the same measure as he has made himself worthy of it in his conduct, and that the system of morality is therefore inseparably combined with the system of happiness, though only in the idea of pure reason.

Now in an intelligible world, i.e., in the moral world, in the concept of which we have abstracted from all hindrances to morality (of the inclinations), such a system of happiness proportionately combined with morality can also be thought as necessary, since freedom, partly moved and partly restricted by moral laws, would itself be the cause of the general happiness, and rational beings, under the guidance of such principles,^{d} would themselves be the authors of their own enduring welfare and at the same time that of others. But this system of self-rewarding morality is only an idea, the realization of which rests on the condition that **everyone** do what he should, i.e., that all actions of rational beings occur as if they arose from a highest will that comprehends all private choice in or under itself. But since the obligation from the moral law remains valid for each particular use of freedom even if others do not conduct themselves in accord with this law, how their consequences will be related to happiness is determined neither by the nature of the things in the world, nor by the causality of actions themselves and their rela-

A810/B838

---

^{a} *Principien*
^{b} *Principien*
^{c} The second occurrence of "use" is added in the second edition.
^{d} *Principien*

tion^a to morality; and the necessary connection of the hope of being happy with the unremitting effort to make oneself worthy of happiness that has been adduced cannot be cognized through reason if it is grounded merely in nature, but may be hoped for only if it is at the same time grounded on a **highest reason,** which commands in accordance with moral laws, as at the same time the cause of nature.

I call the idea of such an intelligence, in which the morally most perfect will, combined with the highest blessedness, is the cause of all happiness in the world, insofar as it stands in exact relation^b with morality (as the worthiness to be happy), **the ideal of the highest good.**[29] Thus only in the ideal of the highest **original** good can pure reason find the ground of the practically necessary connection of both elements of the highest derived good, namely of an intelligible, i.e., **moral** world. Now since we must necessarily represent ourselves through reason as belonging to such a world, although the senses do not present us with anything except a world of appearances, we must assume the moral world to be a consequence of our conduct in the sensible world; and since the latter does not offer such a connection to us, we must assume the former to be a world that is future for us. Thus God and a future life are two presuppositions that are not to be separated from the obligation that pure reason imposes on us in accordance with principles^c of that very same reason.

Morality in itself constitutes a system, but happiness does not, except insofar as it is distributed precisely in accordance with morality. This, however, is possible only in the intelligible world, under a wise author and regent. Reason sees itself as compelled either to assume such a thing, together with life in such a world, which we must regard as a future one, or else to regard the moral laws as empty figments of the brain, since without that presupposition their necessary success, which the same reason connects with them, would have to disappear. Hence everyone also regards the moral laws as **commands,** which, however, they could not be if they did not connect appropriate consequences with their rule *a priori*, and thus carry with them **promises** and **threats.** This, however, they could not do if they did not lie in a necessary being, as the highest good, which alone can make possible such a purposive unity.

Leibniz called the world, insofar as in it one attends only to rational beings and their interconnection in accordance with moral laws under the rule of the highest good, the **realm**[30] **of grace,** and distinguished it from the **realm of nature,** where, to be sure, rational beings stand

A811 / B839

A812 / B840

^a *Verhältnisse*
^b *Verhältnisse*
^c *Principien*

under moral laws but cannot expect any successes for their conduct except in accordance with the course of nature in our sensible world.[31] Thus to regard ourselves as in the realm of grace, where every happiness awaits us as long as we do not ourselves limit our share of it through the unworthiness to be happy, is a practically necessary idea of reason.

Practical laws, insofar as they are at the same time subjective grounds of actions, i.e., subjective principles, are called **maxims.** The **judgment**[a] of morality concerning its purity and consequences takes place in accordance with **ideas,** the **observance** of its laws, in accordance with **maxims.**[32]

It is necessary that our entire course of life be subordinated to moral maxims; but it would at the same time be impossible for this to happen if reason did not connect with the moral law, which is a mere idea, an efficient cause which determines for the conduct in accord with this law an outcome precisely corresponding to our highest ends, whether in this or in another life. Thus without a God and a world that is now not visible to us but is hoped for, the majestic ideas of morality are, to be sure, objects of approbation and admiration but not incentives for resolve and realization, because they would not fulfill the whole end that is natural for every rational being and determined *a priori* and necessarily through the very same pure reason.   A813/B841

Happiness alone is far from the complete good for our reason. Reason does not approve of it (however much inclination may wish for it) where it is not united with the worthiness to be happy, i.e., with morally good conduct. Yet morality alone, and with it, the mere **worthiness** to be happy, is also far from being the complete good. In order to complete the latter, he who has not conducted himself so as to be unworthy of happiness must be able to hope to partake of it. Even reason free from all private aims cannot judge otherwise if, without taking into account an interest of its own, it puts itself in the place of a being who would have to distribute all happiness to others; for in the practical idea both elements are essentially combined, though in such a way that the moral disposition, as a condition, first makes partaking in happiness possible, rather than the prospect of happiness first making possible the moral disposition. For in the latter case the disposition would not be moral and would therefore also be unworthy of complete happiness,   A814/B842 which knows[b] no other limitation before reason except that which is derived from our own immoral conduct.

Thus happiness in exact proportion with the morality of rational beings, through which they are worthy of it, alone constitutes the highest

---

[a] *Beurtheilung*
[b] *erkennt*

good of a world into which we must without exception transpose ourselves in accordance with the precepts of pure but practical reason, and which, of course, is only an intelligible world, since the sensible world does not promise us that sort of systematic unity of ends, the reality of which can be grounded on nothing other than the presupposition of a highest original good, since self-sufficient reason, armed with all of the sufficiency of a supreme cause, in accordance with the most perfect purposiveness, grounds, conserves and completes the order of things that is universal though well hidden from us in the sensible world.

Now this moral theology has the peculiar advantage over the speculative one that it inexorably leads to the concept of a **single, most perfect,** and **rational** primordial being, of which speculative theology could not on objective grounds give us even a **hint,** let alone **convince** us. For neither in speculative nor in natural theology, as far as reason may lead us, do we find even a single significant ground for assuming a single*a* being to set before all natural causes, on which we would at the same time have sufficient cause to make the latter dependent in every way. On the contrary, if, from the standpoint of moral unity, we assess the cause that can alone provide this with the appropriate effect*b* and thus obligating force for us, as a necessary law of the world, then there must be a single supreme will, which comprehends all these laws in itself. For how would we find complete unity of purposes among different wills? This will must be omnipotent, so that all of nature and its relation to morality in the world are subject to it; omniscient, so that it cognizes the inmost dispositions and their moral worth; omnipresent, so that it is immediately ready for every need that is demanded by the highest good for the world; eternal, so that this agreement of nature and freedom is not lacking at any time, etc.

But this systematic unity of ends in this world of intelligences, which, though as mere nature it can only be called the sensible world, as a system of freedom can be called an intelligible, i.e., moral world (*regnum gratiae*),*c* also leads inexorably to the purposive unity of all things that constitute this great whole, in accordance with universal laws of nature, just as the first does in accordance with universal and necessary moral laws, and unifies practical with speculative reason. The world must be represented as having arisen out of an idea if it is to be in agreement with that use of reason without which we would hold ourselves unworthy of reason, namely the moral use, which depends throughout on the idea of the highest good. All research into nature is thereby directed toward the form of a system of ends, and becomes, in its fullest extension,

A815/B843

A816/B844

---

a Emphasized in the first edition.
b *Effekt*
c realm of grace

physico-theology. This, however, since it arises from moral order as a unity which is grounded in the essence of freedom and not contingently founded through external commands, brings the purposiveness of nature down to grounds that must be inseparably connected *a priori* to the inner possibility of things, and thereby leads to a **transcendental theology** that takes the ideal of the highest ontological perfection as a principle[a] of systematic unity, which connects all things in accordance with universal and necessary laws of nature, since they all have their origin in the absolute necessity of a single original being.

What sort of **use** can we make of our understanding, even in regard to experience, if we do not set ends before ourselves? The highest ends, however, are those of morality, and only pure reason can grant us cognition of these. But though equipped and guided with these, we still cannot even make any purposive use of our acquaintance[b] with nature for cognition[c] unless nature itself has introduced purposive unity; for A817/B845 without this we would not even have any reason, since we would have no school for it and no culture through objects that would offer the material for such concepts. That purposive unity is necessary, however, and grounded in the essence of the faculty of choice itself, and therefore this one, which contains the condition of the application of that unity *in concreto*, must also be necessary, and thus the transcendental improvement of our rational cognition is not the cause but rather merely the effect of the practical purposiveness which pure reason imposes on us.

Hence we also find in the history of human reason that before the moral concepts were adequately purified and determined and the systematic unity of purposes was understood in accordance with them and from necessary principles,[d] the knowledge of nature and even a considerable degree of culture of reason in many other sciences could, on the one hand, produce only rudimentary and vague concepts of the deity, and, on the other, leave a remarkable indifference with regard to this question in general. A greater refinement of moral ideas, which was made necessary by the extremely pure moral law of our religion, made reason attend more sharply to its object by means of the interest that it required reason to take in this object, and, without a contribution from either more ample acquaintance with nature or correct and reliable transcendental insights (which have been lacking at all times), produced A818/B846 a concept of the divine being that we now hold to be correct, not because speculative reason convinces us of its correctness but because it is

---

[a] *Princip*
[b] *Kenntnis*
[c] *Erkenntnis*
[d] *Principien*

in perfect agreement with the moral principles of reason.[a] And thus, in the end, only pure reason, although only in its practical use, always has the merit of connecting with our highest interest a cognition that mere speculation can only imagine but never make valid, and of thereby making it into not a demonstrated dogma but yet an absolutely necessary presupposition for reason's most essential ends.

But now when practical reason has attained this high point, namely the concept of a single original being as the highest good, it must not undertake to start out from this concept and derive the moral laws themselves from it, as if it had elevated itself above all empirical conditions of its application and soared up to an immediate acquaintance with new objects. For it was these laws alone whose **inner** practical necessity led us to the presupposition of a self-sufficient cause or a wise world-regent, in order to give effect[b] to these laws, and hence we cannot in turn regard these as contingent and derived from a mere will, especially from a will of which we would have had no concept at all had we not formed it in accordance with those laws.[33] So far as practical reason has the right to lead us, we will not hold actions to be obligatory because they are God's commands, but will rather regard them as divine commands because we are internally obligated to them.[34] We will study freedom under the purposive unity in accordance with principles[c] of reason, and will believe ourselves to be in conformity with the divine will only insofar as we hold as holy the moral law that reason teaches us from the nature of actions themselves, believing ourselves to serve this divine will only through furthering what is best for the world[d] in ourselves and others. Moral theology is therefore only of immanent use, namely for fulfilling our vocation here in the world by fitting into the system of all ends, not for fanatically or even impiously abandoning the guidance of a morally legislative reason in the good course of life in order to connect it immediately to the idea of the highest being, which would provide a transcendental use but which even so, like the use of mere speculation, must pervert and frustrate the ultimate ends of reason.

A819/B847

A820/B848

On the Canon of Pure Reason
Third Section
On having an opinion, knowing, and believing.[35]

Taking something to be true[e] is an occurrence in our understanding that may rest on objective grounds, but that also requires subjective causes in

[a] *moralischen Vernunftprincipien*
[b] *Effect*
[c] *Principien*
[d] *das Weltbeste*
[e] *Das Fürwahrhalten*

the mind of him who judges. If it is valid for everyone merely as long as he has reason, then its ground is objectively sufficient, and in that case taking something to be true is called **conviction.**[a] If it has its ground only in the particular constitution of the subject, then it is called **persuasion.**[b]

Persuasion is a mere semblance,[c] since the ground of the judgment, which lies solely in the subject, is held to be objective. Hence such a judgment also has only private validity, and this taking something to be true cannot be communicated. Truth, however, rests upon agreement with the object,[d] with regard to which, consequently, the judgments of every understanding must agree (*consentientia uni tertio, consentiunt inter se*).[e] The touchstone of whether taking something to be true is conviction or mere persuasion is therefore, externally, the possibility of communicating it and finding it to be valid for the reason of every human being to take it to be true; for in that case there is at least a presumption that the ground of the agreement of all judgments, regardless of the difference among the subjects, rests on the common ground, namely the object,[f] with which they therefore all agree and through which the truth of the judgment is proved.

A821/B849

Accordingly, persuasion cannot be distinguished from conviction subjectively, when the subject has taken something to be true merely as an appearance of his own mind; but the experiment that one makes on the understanding of others, to see if the grounds that are valid for us have the same effect on the reason of others, is a means, though only a subjective one, not for producing conviction, to be sure, but yet for revealing the merely private validity of the judgment, i.e., something in it that is mere persuasion.

If, moreover, one can unfold the subjective **causes** of the judgment, which we take to be objective **grounds** for it, and thus explain taking something to be true deceptively as an occurrence in our mind, without having any need for the constitution of the object,[g] then we expose the illusion and are no longer taken in by it, although we are always tempted to a certain degree if the subjective cause of the illusion depends upon our nature.

I cannot **assert** anything, i.e., pronounce it to be a judgment necessarily valid for everyone, except that which produces conviction. I can preserve persuasion for myself if I please to do so, but cannot and should not want to make it valid beyond myself.

A822/B850

[a] *Überzeugung*
[b] *Überredung*
[c] *Schein*
[d] *Objekte*
[e] [Because of] agreement with a third thing, they agree among themselves.
[f] *Objecte*
[g] *Objects*

Taking something to be true, or the subjective validity of judgment, has the following three stages in relation to conviction (which at the same time is valid objectively): **having an opinion, believing,** and **knowing. Having an opinion** is taking something to be true with the consciousness that it is subjectively **as well as** objectively insufficient. If taking something to be true is only subjectively sufficient and is at the same time held to be objectively insufficient, then it is called **believing.** Finally, when taking something to be true is both subjectively and objectively sufficient it is called **knowing.** Subjective sufficiency is called **conviction** (for myself), objective sufficiency, **certainty** (for everyone). I will not pause for the exposition of such readily grasped concepts.

I must never undertake **to have an opinion** without at least **knowing** something by means of which the in itself merely problematic judgment acquires a connection with truth which, although it is not complete, is nevertheless more than an arbitrary invention. Furthermore, the law of such a connection must be certain. For if in regard to this too I have nothing but opinion, then it is all only a game of imagination without the least relation to truth. In judging from pure reason, **to have an opinion** is not allowed at all. For since it will not be supported on grounds of experience, but everything that is necessary should be cognized *a priori*, the principle*a* of connection requires universality and necessity, thus complete certainty, otherwise no guidance to the truth is forthcoming at all. Hence it is absurd to have an opinion in pure mathematics: one must know, or else refrain from all judgment. It is just the same with the principles of morality, since one must not venture an action on the mere opinion that something is **allowed,** but must know this.

In the transcendental use of reason, on the contrary, to have an opinion is of course too little, but to know is also too much. In a merely speculative regard, therefore, we cannot judge at all here, for subjective grounds for taking something to be true, such as those that can produce belief, deserve no approval in speculative questions, where they neither remain free of all empirical assistance nor allow of being communicated to others in equal measure.

Only in a **practical relation,** however, can taking something that is theoretically insufficient to be true be called believing.[36] This practical aim is either that of **skill** or of **morality,** the former for arbitrary and contingent ends, the latter, however, for absolutely necessary ends.

Once an end is proposed, then the conditions for attaining it are hypothetically necessary. This necessity is subjectively but still only comparatively sufficient if I do not know of any other conditions at all under which the end could be attained; but it is sufficient absolutely and for

A823/B851

A824/B852

a Princip

686

everyone if I know with certainty that no one else can know of any other conditions that lead to the proposed end. In the first case my presupposition and taking certain conditions to be true is a merely contingent belief, in the second case, however, it is a necessary belief. The doctor must do something for a sick person who is in danger, but he does not know[a] the illness. He looks to the symptoms,[b] and judges, because he does not know of anything better, that it is consumption. His belief is merely contingent even in his own judgment; someone else might perhaps do better. I call such contingent beliefs, which however ground the actual use of the means to certain actions, **pragmatic beliefs.**

The usual touchstone of whether what someone asserts is mere persuasion or at least subjective conviction, i.e., firm belief, is **betting.** Often someone pronounces his propositions with such confident and inflexible defiance that he seems to have entirely laid aside all concern for error. A bet disconcerts him. Sometimes he reveals that he is persuaded enough for one ducat but not for ten. For he would happily bet one, but at ten he suddenly becomes aware of what he had not previously noticed, namely that it is quite possible that he has erred. If we entertain the thought that we should wager the happiness of our whole life on something, our triumphant judgment would quickly disappear, we would become timid and we would suddenly discover that our belief does not extend so far.[37] Thus pragmatic belief has only a degree, which can be large or small according to the difference of the interest that is at stake.

A825/B853

Since, however, even though we might not be able to undertake anything in relation to an object,[c] and taking something to be true is therefore merely theoretical, in many cases we can still conceive and imagine an undertaking for which we would suppose ourselves to have sufficient grounds if there were a means for arriving at certainty about the matter; thus there is in merely theoretical judgments an **analogue** of practical judgments, where taking them to be true is aptly described by the word **belief,** and which we can call **doctrinal beliefs.**[d] If it were possible to settle by any sort of experience whether there are inhabitants of at least some of the planets that we see, I might well bet everything that I have on it. Hence I say that it is not merely an opinion but a strong belief (on the correctness of which I would wager many advantages in life) that there are also inhabitants of other worlds.

[a] *kennt*

[b] *Erscheinungen*, here used in a non-technical sense.

[c] *Object*

[d] ***Glaube.*** While it would be natural to translate *Glaube* as "faith" when Kant is writing specifically about belief in the existence of God, in what follows there are numerous occurrences of the term which can only be translated by "belief," so it seems better to use that translation throughout. This also allows us to translate the verb *glauben* as "believe."

A826/B854   Now we must concede that the thesis of the existence of God belongs to doctrinal belief. For although with regard to theoretical knowledge of the world I have nothing **at my command** that necessarily presupposes this thought as the condition of my explanations of the appearances of the world, but am rather obliged to make use of my reason as if everything were mere nature, purposive unity is still so important a condition of the application of reason to nature that I cannot pass it by, especially since experience liberally supplies examples of it. But I know no other condition for this unity that could serve me as a clue for the investigation of nature except insofar as I presuppose that a highest intelligence has arranged everything in accordance with the wisest ends. Consequently, the presupposition of a wise author of the world is a condition of an aim which is, to be sure, contingent but yet not inconsiderable, namely that of having a guide for the investigation of nature. The outcome of my experiments also so often confirms the usefulness of this presupposition, and nothing can be decisively said against it, so that I would say too little if I called my taking it to be true merely having an opinion, but rather even in this theoretical relation[a] it can be said that I firmly believe in God; but in this case this belief must not strictly be called practical, but must be called a doctrinal belief, which the **the-**
A827/B855   **ology** of nature (physico-theology) must everywhere necessarily produce. In regard to this same wisdom, in respect of the magnificent equipment of human nature and the shortness of life which is so ill suited to it, there is likewise to be found sufficient ground for a doctrinal belief in the future life of the human soul.

The expression of belief is in such cases an expression of modesty from an **objective** point of view, but at the same time of the firmness of confidence in a **subjective** one. If here too I would call merely theoretically taking something to be true only an hypothesis that I would be justified in assuming, I would thereby make myself liable for more of a concept of the constitution of a world-cause and of another world than I can really boast of; for of that which I even only assume as an hypothesis I must know at least enough of its properties so that I need invent **not its concept** but **only its existence.** The word "belief," however, concerns only the direction that an idea gives me and the subjective influence on the advancement of my actions of reason that holds me fast to it, even though I am not in a position to give an account of it from a speculative point of view.

But there is something unstable about merely doctrinal belief; one is often put off from it by difficulties that come up in speculation, al-
A828/B856   though, to be sure, one inexorably returns to it again.

It is entirely otherwise in the case of **moral belief.** For there it is ab-

---

[a] *Verhältnisse*

solutely necessary that something must happen, namely, that I fulfill the moral law in all points. The end here is inescapably fixed, and according to all my insight there is possible only a single condition under which this end is consistent with all ends together and thereby has practical validity, namely, that there be a God and a future world; I also know with complete certainty that no one else knows of any other conditions that lead to this same unity of ends under the moral law. But since the moral precept is thus at the same time my maxim (as reason commands that it ought to be), I will inexorably believe in the existence of God and a future life, and I am sure that nothing can make these beliefs unstable, since my moral principles themselves, which I cannot renounce without becoming contemptible in my own eyes, would thereby be subverted.[38]

In this way enough is left to us, even after the frustration of all the ambitious aims of a reason that wanders about beyond the boundaries of all experience, that we have cause to be satisfied with it from a practical point of view. Of course, no one will be able to boast that he **knows** that there is a God and a future life; for if he knows that, then he is precisely the man I have long sought. All knowing (if it concerns an object of reason alone) can be communicated, and I would therefore also be able to hope to have my knowledge extended to such a wonderful degree by his instruction. No, the conviction is not **logical** but **moral** certainty, and, since it depends on subjective grounds (of moral disposition) I must not even say "**It is** morally certain that there is a God," etc., but rather "**I am** morally certain" etc. That is, the belief in a God and another world is so interwoven with my moral disposition that I am in as little danger of ever surrendering the former as I am worried that the latter can ever be torn away from me. A829/B857

The only reservation that is to be found here is that this rational belief is grounded on the presupposition of moral dispositions. If we depart from that, and assume someone who would be entirely indifferent in regard to moral questions, then the question that is propounded by reason becomes merely a problem for speculation, and in that case it can be supported with strong grounds from analogy but not with grounds to which even the most obstinate skepticism[a] must yield.* But

---

* The human mind takes (as I believe is necessarily the case with every rational being) a natural interest in morality, even though this is not undivided and practically overwhelming. Strengthen and magnify this interest, and you will find reason very tractable and even enlightened for uniting the speculative with the practical interest. But if you do not take care to make human beings first at least half-way good, you will never be able to make sincere believers out of them! A830/B858

[a] *Zweifelsucht*

A830/B858 no human being is free of all interest in these questions. For although he might be separated from the moral interest by the absence of all good dispositions, yet even in this case there is enough left to make him **fear** a divine existence and a future. For to this end nothing more is required than that he at least cannot pretend to any **certainty** that there is **no** such being and **no** future life, which would have to be proved through reason alone and thus apodictically since he would have to establish them to be impossible, which certainly no rational human can undertake to do. That would be a **negative** belief, which, to be sure, would not produce morality and good dispositions, but would still produce the analogue of them, namely it could powerfully restrain the outbreak of evil dispositions.

But is that all, one will say, that pure reason accomplishes in opening up prospects beyond the bounds of experience? Nothing more than two articles of belief? This much common understanding could also have

A831/B859 accomplished without taking advice from the philosophers!

I will not boast here of the merit that philosophy has on account of the laborious effort of its critique of human reason, supposing even that this should be found in the end to be merely negative, for something more about that will be forthcoming in the next section. But do you demand then that a cognition that pertains to all human beings should surpass common understanding and be revealed to you only by philosophers? The very thing that you criticize is the best confirmation of the correctness of the assertions that have been made hitherto, that is, that it reveals what one could not have foreseen in the beginning, namely that in what concerns all human beings without exception nature is not to be blamed for any partiality in the distribution of its gifts, and in regard to the essential ends of human nature even the highest philosophy cannot advance further than the guidance that nature has also conferred on the most common understanding.

The Transcendental Doctrine of Method
Third Chapter
The
architectonic of pure reason

By an **architectonic** I understand the art of systems. Since systematic unity is that which first makes ordinary cognition into science, i.e., makes a system out of a mere aggregate of it, architectonic is the doctrine of that which is scientific in our cognition in general, and therefore necessarily belongs to the doctrine of method.

Under the government of reason our cognitions cannot at all constitute a rhapsody but must constitute a system, in which alone they can support and advance its essential ends. I understand by a system, however, the unity of the manifold cognitions under one idea. This is the rational concept of the form of a whole, insofar as through this the domain of the manifold as well as the position of the parts with respect to each other is determined *a priori*. The scientific rational concept thus contains the end and the form of the whole that is congruent with it. The unity of the end, to which all parts are related and in the idea of which they are also related to each other, allows the absence of any part to be noticed in our knowledge of the rest, and there can be no contingent addition or undetermined magnitude of perfection that does not have its boundaries determined *a priori*. The whole is therefore articulated (*articulatio*) and not heaped together (*coacervatio*);[a] it can, to be sure, grow internally (*per intus susceptionem*)[b] but not externally (*per appositionem*),[c] like an animal body, whose growth does not add a limb but rather makes each limb stronger and fitter for its end without any alteration of proportion.

For its execution the idea needs a **schema**, i.e., an essential manifoldness and order of the parts determined *a priori* from the principle[d] of the end. A schema that is not outlined in accordance with an idea,

---

[a] Literally, "heaped up."
[b] from an internal cause
[c] by juxtaposition
[d] *Princip*

i.e., from the chief end of reason, but empirically, in accordance with aims occurring contingently (whose number[a] one cannot know in advance), yields **technical** unity, but that which arises only in consequence of an idea (where reason provides the ends *a priori* and does not await them empirically) grounds **architectonic** unity. What we call science, whose schema contains the outline (*monogramma*) and the division of the whole into members in conformity with the idea, i.e., *a priori*, cannot arise technically, from the similarity of the manifold or the contingent use of cognition *in concreto* for all sorts of arbitrary external ends, but arises architectonically, for the sake of its affinity and its derivation from a single supreme and inner end, which first makes possible the whole; such a science must be distinguished from all others with certainty and in accordance with principles.[b]

A834/B862

Nobody attempts to establish a science without grounding it on an idea. But in its elaboration the schema, indeed even the definition of the science which is given right at the outset, seldom corresponds to the idea; for this lies in reason like a seed, all of whose parts still lie very involuted and are hardly recognizable even under microscopic observation. For this reason sciences, since they have all been thought out from the viewpoint of a certain general interest, must not be explained and determined in accordance with the description given by their founder, but rather in accordance with the idea, grounded in reason itself, of the natural unity of the parts that have been brought together. For the founder and even his most recent successors often fumble around with an idea that they have not even made distinct to themselves and that therefore cannot determine the special content, the articulation (systematic unity) and boundaries of the science.

It is too bad that it is first possible for us to glimpse the idea in a clearer light and to outline a whole architectonically, in accordance with the ends of reason, only after we have long collected relevant cognitions haphazardly[c] like building materials and worked through them technically with only a hint from an idea lying hidden within us. The systems seem to have been formed, like maggots, by a *generatio aequivoca*[39] from the mere confluence of aggregated concepts, garbled at first but complete in time, although they all had their schema, as the original seed, in the mere self-development of reason, and on that account are not merely each articulated for themselves in accordance with an idea but are rather all in turn purposively united with each other as members of a whole in a system of human cognition, and allow an architectonic to all human knowledge, which at the present time, since so much mater-

A835/B863

[a] *Menge*
[b] *Principien*
[c] *rhapsodistisch*

ial has already been collected or can be taken from the ruins of collapsed older edifices, would not merely be possible but would not even be very difficult. We shall content ourselves here with the completion of our task, namely, merely outlining the **architectonic** of all cognition from **pure reason,** and begin only at the point where the general root of our cognitive power divides and branches out into two stems, one of which is **reason.** By "reason" I here understand, however, the entire higher faculty of cognition, and I therefore contrast the rational to the empirical.

If I abstract from all content of cognition, objectively considered, then all cognition, considered subjectively, is either historical or ratio- A836/B864 nal. Historical cognition[40] is *cognitio ex datis,*[a] rational cognition, however, *cognitio ex principiis.*[b] However a cognition may have been given originally, it is still historical for him who possesses it if he cognizes it only to the degree and extent that it has been given to him from elsewhere, whether it has been given to him through immediate experience or told to him or even given to him through instruction (general cognitions). Hence he who has properly **learned** a system of philosophy, e.g., the Wolffian system, although he has in his head all of the principles, explanations, and proofs together with the division of the entire theoretical edifice, and can count everything off on his fingers, still has nothing other than a complete **historical** cognition of the Wolffian philosophy; he knows and judges only as much as has been given to him. If you dispute one of his definitions, he has no idea where to get another one. He has formed himself according to an alien reason, but the faculty of imitation is not that of generation, i.e., the cognition did not arise **from** reason for him, and although objectively it was certainly a rational cognition, subjectively it is still merely historical. He has grasped and preserved well, i.e., he has learned, and is a plaster cast of a living human being. Rational cognitions that are objectively so (i.e., could have arisen originally only out of the reason of human beings themselves), may also bear this name subjectively only if they have been drawn out of the universal sources of reason, from which critique, in- A837/B865 deed even the rejection of what has been learned, can also arise, i.e., from principles.[c]

Now all rational cognition is either cognition from concepts or cognition from the construction of concepts; the former is called philosophical, the latter mathematical. I have already dealt with the inner difference between the two in the first chapter.[41] A cognition can accordingly be objectively philosophical and yet subjectively historical, as

---

[a] cognition from data, or from what is given.
[b] cognition from principles
[c] *Principien*

is the case with most students and with all of those who never see beyond their school and remain students their whole lives. But it is strange that mathematical cognition, however one has learned it, can still count subjectively as rational cognition, and that the difference present in the case of philosophical cognition is not present in this case. The cause of this is that the sources of cognition on which alone the teacher can draw lie nowhere other than in the essential and genuine principles[a] of reason, and consequently cannot be derived from anywhere else by the student, nor disputed in any way, precisely because reason is here used *in concreto* though nevertheless *a priori*, founded, that is, in pure and therefore error-free intuition, and excludes all deception and error.[42] Among all rational sciences (*a priori*), therefore, only mathematics can be learned, never philosophy (except historically); rather, as far as reason is concerned, we can at best only learn **to philosophize.**

A 838/ B 866 Now the system of all philosophical cognition is **philosophy.** One must take this objectively if one understands by it the archetype for the assessment[b] of all attempts to philosophize, which should serve to assess[c] each subjective philosophy, the structure of which is often so manifold and variable. In this way philosophy is a mere idea of a possible science, which is nowhere given *in concreto*, but which one seeks to approach in various ways until the only footpath, much overgrown by sensibility, is discovered, and the hitherto unsuccessful ectype, so far as it has been granted to humans, is made equal to the archetype. Until then one cannot learn any philosophy; for where is it, who has possession of it, and by what can it be recognized? One can only learn to philosophize, i.e., to exercise the talent of reason in prosecuting its general principles[d] in certain experiments that come to hand, but always with the reservation of the right of reason to investigate the sources of these principles themselves and to confirm or reject them.[43]

Until now, however, the concept of philosophy[e] has been only **a scholastic concept,**[f] namely that of a system of cognition that is sought only as a science without having as its end anything more than the systematic unity of this knowledge, thus the **logical** perfection of cognition. But there is also a **cosmopolitan concept**[g] (*conceptus cosmicus*) that has always grounded this term, especially when it is, as it were, personified and represented as an archetype in the ideal of the **philosopher.**

A 839/ B 867 From this point of view philosophy is the science of the relation of all

---

[a] *Principien*
[b] *Beurtheilung*
[c] *beurtheilen*
[d] *Principien*
[e] Added in Kant's copy of the first edition: "Idealist, idea" (E CLXXXII, p. 54; 23:50).
[f] **Schulbegriff**
[g] *Weltbegriff*

cognition to the essential ends of human reason (*teleologia rationis humanae*),[a] and the philosopher is not an artist of reason but the legislator of human reason. It would be very boastful to call oneself a philosopher in this sense[b] and to pretend to have equaled the archetype, which lies only in the idea.

The mathematician, the naturalist, the logician are only artists of reason, however eminent the former may be in rational cognitions and however much progress the latter may have made in philosophical cognition. There is still a teacher in the ideal, who controls all of these and uses them as tools to advance the essential ends of human reason. Him alone we must call the philosopher; however, since he himself is still found nowhere, although the idea of his legislation is found in every human reason, we will confine ourselves to the latter and determine more precisely what philosophy, in accordance with this cosmopolitan concept,* prescribes for systematic unity from the standpoint of ends.   A 840/ B 868

Essential ends are on this account not yet the highest, of which (in the complete systematic unity of reason) there can be only a single one. Hence they are either the final end,[c] or subalternate ends, which necessarily belong to the former as means. The former is nothing other than the entire vocation[d] of human beings, and the philosophy of it is called moral philosophy. On account of the preeminence which moral philosophy had over all other applications of reason, the ancients understood by the name of "philosopher" first and foremost the moralist, and even the outer appearance of self-control through reason still suffices today for calling someone a philosopher after a certain analogy, in spite of his limited knowledge.

Now the legislation of human reason (philosophy) has two objects, nature and freedom, and thus contains the natural law as well as the moral law, initially in two separate systems but ultimately in a single philosophical system. The philosophy of nature pertains to everything that **is;** that of morals only to that which **should be.**

All philosophy, however, is either cognition from pure reason or rational cognition from empirical principles.[e] The former is called pure philosophy, the latter empirical.

---

* A **cosmopolitan concept** here means one that concerns that which necessarily interests everyone; hence I determine the aim of a science in accordance with **scholastic concepts** if it is regarded only as one of the skills for certain arbitrary ends.   A 839/ B 867

[a] teleology of human reason
[b] *Bedeutung*
[c] *Endzweck*
[d] *Bestimmung*
[e] *Principien*

A841/B869 Now the philosophy of pure reason is either **propaedeutic** (preparation), which investigates the faculty of reason in regard to all pure *a priori* cognition, and is called **critique,** or, second, the system of pure reason (science), the whole (true as well as apparent) philosophical cognition from pure reason in systematic interconnection, and is called **metaphysics;** this name can also be given to all of pure philosophy including the critique, in order to comprehend the investigation of everything that can ever be cognized *a priori* as well as the presentation of that which constitutes a system of pure philosophical cognitions of this kind, but in distinction from all empirical as well as mathematical use of reason.

Metaphysics is divided into the metaphysics of the **speculative** and the **practical** use of pure reason, and is therefore either **metaphysics of nature** or **metaphysics of morals.** The former contains all rational principles*a* from mere concepts (hence with the exclusion of mathematics) for the **theoretical** cognition of all things; the latter, the principles*b* which determine **action and omission** *a priori* and make them necessary. Now morality is the only lawfulness of actions which can be derived entirely *a priori* from principles.*c* Hence the metaphysics of morals is really the pure morality, which is not grounded on any an-

A842/B870 thropology (no empirical condition). The metaphysics of speculative reason is that which has customarily been called metaphysics **in the narrower sense;**d but insofar as the pure doctrine of morals nevertheless belongs to the special stem of human and indeed philosophical cognition from pure reason, we will retain this term for it, although we set it aside here as not **now** pertaining to our end.

It is of the utmost importance to **isolate** cognitions that differ from one another in their species and origin, and carefully to avoid mixing them together with others with which they are usually connected in their use. What chemists do in analyzing materials, what mathematicians do in their pure theory of magnitude, the philosopher is even more obliged to do, so that he can securely determine the proper value and influence of the advantage that a special kind of cognition has over the aimless use of the understanding. Hence human reason has never been able to dispense with a metaphysics as long as it has thought, or rather reflected,*e* though it has never been able to present it in a manner sufficiently purified of everything foreign to it. The idea of such a science is just as old as speculative human reason; and what reason does

---

a *Principien*
b *Principien*
c *Principien*
d *Verstande*
e *nachgedacht*

not speculate, whether in a scholastic or a popular manner? One must nevertheless admit that the distinction of the two elements in our cognition, one of which is in our power completely *a priori* but the other of which can be derived only from experience *a posteriori*, has remained very indistinct, even among professional thinkers, and hence the determination of the bounds of a special kind of cognition, and thus the genuine idea of a science with which human reason has so long and so intensively occupied itself, has never been accomplished. When it was said that metaphysics is the science of the first principles*a* of human cognition,[44] an entirely special kind of cognition was not thereby marked off, but only a rank in regard to generality, through which, therefore, it could not be clearly differentiated from empirical cognition; for even among empirical principles*b* some are more general and therefore higher than others, and in the series of such a subordination (where one does not differentiate that which can be cognized completely *a priori* from that which can be cognized only *a posteriori*), where is one to make the cut that distinguishes the **first** part and highest members from the **last** part and the subordinate members?[45] What would one say if chronology could designate the epochs of the world only by dividing them into the first centuries and the rest that follow them? One would ask, Do the fifth century, the tenth century, and so on also belong among the first ones?; likewise I ask, Does the concept of that which is extended belong to metaphysics? You answer, Yes! But what about that of body? Yes! And that of fluid body? You are stumped, for if it goes on this way, then everything will belong to metaphysics. From this one sees that the mere degree of subordination (the particular under the universal) cannot determine any boundaries for a science, but rather, in our case, only the complete heterogeneity and difference of origin can. But what obscured the fundamental idea of metaphysics from yet another side was that, as *a priori* cognition, it shows a certain homogeneity with mathematics, to which, as far as *a priori* origin is concerned, it is no doubt related; but the comparison between the kind of cognition from concepts in the former with the manner of judging *a priori* through the mere construction of concepts in the latter requires a difference between philosophical and mathematical cognition – thus a decided heterogeneity is revealed, which was always felt, as it were, but was never able to be brought to distinct criteria. Thus it has been the case until now that since philosophers themselves erred in the development of the idea of their science, its elaboration could have no determinate end and no secure guideline, and philosophers, with such arbitrarily designed projects, ignorant of the path they had to take, and

a Principien
b Principien

always disputing among themselves about the discoveries that each would like to have made on his own, have brought their science into contempt first among others and finally even among themselves.

A845/B873 Thus all pure *a priori* cognition, by means of the special faculty of cognition in which alone it can have its seat, constitutes a special unity, and metaphysics is that philosophy which is to present that cognition in this systematic unity. Its speculative part, to which this name has been especially appropriated, namely that which we call **metaphysics of nature** and which considers everything insofar as it **is** (not that which ought to be) on the basis of *a priori* concepts, is divided in the following way.[a]

Metaphysics in this narrower sense[b] consists of **transcendental philosophy** and the **physiology** of pure reason. The former considers only the **understanding** and reason itself in a system of all concepts and principles that are related to objects in general, without assuming objects[c] that **would be given** (*Ontologia*); the latter considers **nature,** i.e., the sum total **of given** objects (whether they are given by the senses or, if one will, by another kind of intuition), and is therefore **physiology** (though only *rationalis*).[46] Now, however, the use of reason in this rational consideration of nature is either physical or hyperphysical, or, better, either **immanent** or **transcendent.** The former pertains to nature so far as its cognition can be applied in experience (*in concreto*), the latter to that connection of the objects of experience which surpasses all

A846/B874 experience. Hence this **transcendent** physiology has either an **inner** connection to its object or an **outer** one, both of which, however, go beyond possible experience; the former is the physiology of nature in its entirety, i.e., the **transcendental cognition of the world,** the latter that of the connection of nature in its entirety to a being beyond nature, i.e., the transcendental **cognition of God.**[47]

Immanent physiology, on the contrary, considers nature as the sum total of all objects of the senses, thus considers it as it is given **to us,** but only in accordance with *a priori* conditions, under which it can be given to us in general. There are, however, only two sorts of objects for this. 1. Those of outer sense, thus the sum total of these, **corporeal nature.** 2. The object of inner sense, the soul, and, in accordance with the fundamental concepts of this in general, **thinking nature.** The meta-

---

[a] Inserted in Kant's copy of the first edition:
"I would divide it in accordance with the classes of the categories, so that in each class the third category, which contains the other two, yields the idea of the science:
"1. General ontology [*Allgemeine Wesenlehre*]; 2. Theory of nature; 3. Cosmology [*Weltwissenschaft*]; 4. Theology." (E CLXXXIII, p. 54; 23:43). This is the last emendation Kant made in his copy of the first edition.
[b] *Verstande*
[c] *Objecte*

physics of corporeal nature is called **physics,** but, since it is to contain only the principles of its *a priori* cognition, **rational physics.** The metaphysics of thinking nature is called **psychology,** and because of the cause that has just been adduced only the **rational cognition** of this is here meant.

Accordingly, the entire system of metaphysics consists of four main parts. **1. Ontology. 2. Rational Physiology. 3. Rational Cosmology. 4. Rational Theology.** The second part, namely the doctrine of nature of pure reason, contains two divisions, *physica rationalis** and *psychologia rationalis.*[48]   A847/B875

The original idea of a philosophy of pure reason itself prescribes this division; it is therefore **architectonic,** in conformity with its essential ends, and not merely **technical,** in accordance with contingently perceived affinities and, as it were, established by good luck; and for that very reason it is unchangeable and legislative. However, there are several points here which could arouse reservations and weaken the conviction of its lawfulness.

First, how can I expect an *a priori* cognition and thus a metaphysics of objects that are given to our senses, thus given *a posteriori?* And how is it possible to cognize the nature of things in accordance with *a priori* principles[a] and to arrive at a **rational** physiology? The answer is: We   A848/B876 take from experience nothing more than what is necessary to **give** ourselves an object,[b] partly of outer and partly of inner sense. The former is accomplished through the mere concept of matter (impenetrable lifeless extension), the latter through the concept of a thinking being (in the empirically inner representation "I think"). Otherwise, we must in the entire metaphysics of these objects abstain entirely from any empirical principles[c] that might add any sort of experience beyond the concept in order to judge something about these objects.

* One should not think, indeed, that I understand by this what is commonly   A847/B875 called *physica generalis,* which is more mathematics than philosophy of nature. For the metaphysics of nature abstracts entirely from mathematics, and has nowhere near as many ampliative insights to offer as the latter, yet it is still very important with regard to the critique of the pure cognition of understanding that is to be applied to nature in general; in its absence even mathematicians, depending on certain common but in fact metaphysical concepts, have without noticing it burdened the doctrine of nature with hypotheses that disappear in a critique of these principles[d] without doing the least damage to the use of mathematics in this field (which is entirely indispensable).

[a] *Principien*
[b] *Object*
[c] *Principien*
[d] *Principien*

Second: Once one gives up the hope of achieving anything useful *a priori*, where does that leave **empirical psychology,** which has always asserted its place in metaphysics, and from which one has expected such great enlightenment in our own times?[49] I answer: It comes in where the proper (empirical) doctrine of nature must be put, namely on the side of **applied** philosophy, for which pure philosophy contains the *a priori* principles,[a] which must therefore be combined but never confused with the former. Empirical psychology must thus be entirely banned from metaphysics, and is already excluded by the idea of it. Nevertheless, in accord with the customary scholastic usage one must still concede it a little place (although only as an episode) in metaphysics, and indeed from economic motives, since it is not yet rich enough to comprise a subject on its own and yet it is too important for one to expel it entirely or attach it somewhere else where it may well have even less affinity than in metaphysics. It is thus merely a long-accepted foreigner, to whom one grants refuge for a while until it can establish its own domicile in a complete anthropology (the pendant to the empirical doctrine of nature).

A849/B877

This is, therefore, the general idea of metaphysics, which, since we initially expected more from it than could appropriately be demanded and long amused ourselves with pleasant expectations, in the end fell into general contempt when we found ourselves deceived in our hopes. From the whole course of our critique we will have been sufficiently convinced that even though metaphysics cannot be the foundation of religion, yet it must always remain its bulwark, and that human reason, which is already dialectical on account of the tendency of its nature, could never dispense with such a science, which reins it in and, by means of a scientific and fully illuminating self-knowledge,[b] prevents the devastations that a lawless speculative reason would otherwise inevitably perpetrate in both morality and religion. We can therefore be sure that however obstinate or disdainful they may be who know how to judge a science not in accord with its nature, but only from its contingent effects, we will always return to metaphysics as to a beloved from whom we have been estranged, since reason, because essential ends are at issue here, must work without respite either for sound insight or for the destruction of good insights that are already to hand.

A850/B878

Thus the metaphysics of nature as well as morals, but above all the **preparatory** (propaedeutic) critique of reason that dares to fly with its own wings, alone constitute that which we can call philosophy in a genuine sense.[c] This relates everything to wisdom, but through the path of

[a] *Principien*
[b] *Selbsterkenntnis*
[c] *Verstande*

science, the only one which, once cleared, is never overgrown, and never leads to error. Mathematics, natural science, even the empirical knowledge of humankind, have a high value as means, for the most part to contingent but yet ultimately to necessary and essential ends of humanity, but only through the mediation of a rational cognition from mere concepts, which, call it what one will, is really nothing but metaphysics.

Just for this reason metaphysics is also the culmination of all **culture** of human reason, which is indispensable even if one sets aside its influ-   A851/B879 ence as a science for certain determinate ends. For it considers reason according to its elements and highest maxims, which must ground even the **possibility** of some sciences and the **use** of all of them. That as mere speculation it serves more to prevent errors than to amplify cognition does no damage to its value, but rather gives it all the more dignity and authority through its office as censor, which secures the general order and unity, indeed the well-being of the scientific community, and prevents its cheerful and fruitful efforts from straying from the chief end, that of the general happiness.

The Transcendental Doctrine of Method
Fourth Chapter
The history of pure reason

This title stands here only to designate a place that is left open in the system and must be filled in the future. I will content myself with casting a cursory glance from a merely transcendental point of view, namely that of the nature of pure reason, on the whole of its labors hitherto, which presents to my view edifices, to be sure, but only in ruins.

It is remarkable enough, although it could not naturally have been otherwise, that in the infancy of philosophy human beings began where we should now rather end, namely, by studying first the cognition of God and the hope or indeed even the constitution of another world. Whatever crude concepts of religion the old customs, which were left over from the rude state of the nations, may have introduced, these still did not prevent their more enlightened part from dedicating themselves to free investigations of this object, and it was readily understood that there could be no more fundamental and reliable way of pleasing the invisible power who rules the world, in order to be happy at least in another world, than the good conduct of life. Hence theology and morality were the two incentives, or better, the points of reference*a* for all the abstract inquiries of reason to which we have always been devoted. The first, however, was really that which gradually drew purely speculative reason in its train, which subsequently became so famous under the name of metaphysics.

I will not now distinguish the times in which this or that alteration of metaphysics occurred, but will present in a cursory outline only the difference of the ideas which occasioned the chief revolutions. And here I find three points of view on which the most notable changes on this stage of conflict have been founded.

1. **With regard to the object** of all of our rational cognitions, some were merely **sensual philosophers,** others merely **intellectual philosophers.** Epicurus can be called the foremost philosopher of sensibility, and Plato that of the intellectual. This difference of schools,

---

a Beziehungspunkte

702

however, as subtle as it is, had already begun in the earliest times, and has long preserved itself without interruption. Those of the first school asserted that reality is in the objects of the senses alone, and that everything else is imagination; those of the second school, on the contrary, said that in the senses there is nothing but semblance,[a] and that only the A854/B882 understanding cognizes that which is true. The former, however, did not on this account dispute the reality of the concepts of the understanding, but they were only **logical** for them, though they were **mystical** for the others. The former admitted **intellectual concepts,** but accepted only sensible **objects.** The latter demanded that the true objects be merely **intelligible,** and asserted an **intuition** through pure understanding not accompanied by any senses, which in their opinion only confused it.

2. **With regard to the origin** of pure cognitions of reason, whether they are derived from experience or, independent of it, have their source in reason. Aristotle can be regarded as the head of the **empiricists,** Plato that of the **noologists.** Locke, who in recent times followed the former, and Leibniz, who followed the latter (although with sufficient distance from his mystical system), have nevertheless not been able to bring this dispute to any decision.[50] Epicurus on his part at least proceeded more consistently in accord with his sensual system (for in his inferences he never exceeded the bounds of experience) than Aristotle and Locke (especially, however, the latter), who, after he had derived all concepts and principles from experience, goes so far in their use as to assert that one can prove the existence of God and the immortality of the soul (though both objects lie entirely outside of the bounds of possible experience) just as self-evidently as any mathematical theorem.[51] A855/B883

3. **With regard to method.** If something is to be called a method, it must be a procedure in accordance with **principles.** Now one can divide the methods currently dominant in this department of natural inquiry into the **naturalistic** and the **scientific.** The **naturalist** of pure reason takes as his principle that through common understanding without science (which he calls "healthy reason") more may be accomplished with regard to the most sublime questions that constitute the task of metaphysics than through speculation. He asserts, therefore, that one can determine the magnitude and breadth of the moon more securely by eye than by mathematical rigmarole. This is mere misology brought to principles, and, what is most absurd, the neglect of all artificial means is recommended as a **method of its own** for expanding cognition. For one cannot with good cause blame the naturalists for what follows from the **lack** of greater insight. They follow common reason, without boast-

---

[a] *Schein*

ing of their ignorance as a method that would contain the secret of drawing the truth out of the deep well of Democritus. *Quod sapio, satis est mihi; non ego curo, esse quod Arcesilas aerumnosique Solones*[a] is their motto, with which they can lead a contented and praiseworthy life without troubling themselves with science or confusing their business.

Now as far as the observers of a **scientific** method are concerned, they have here the choice of proceeding either **dogmatically** or **skeptically,** but in either case they have the obligation of proceeding **systematically.** If I here name with regard to the former the famous Wolff, and with regard to the latter David Hume, then for my present purposes I can leave the others unnamed. The **critical** path alone is still open. If the reader has had pleasure and patience in traveling along in my company, then he can now judge, if it pleases him to contribute his part to making this footpath into a highway, whether or not that which many centuries could not accomplish might not be attained even before the end of the present one: namely, to bring human reason to full satisfaction in that which has always, but until now vainly, occupied its lust for knowledge.

---

[a] "What I know is enough for me; I don't care for the labors of Arcesilas or Solon" (Persius, *Satires*, iii, 78–9).

EDITORIAL NOTES

Editors' introduction

1 References to Kant's works other than the *Critique of Pure Reason* will be cited throughout this volume by giving the volume and page number of their location in the standard German edition of Kant's works, *Kant's gesammelte Schriften*, edited by the Royal Prussian (later German) Academy of Sciences (Berlin: Georg Reimer, later Walter de Gruyter & Co., 1900–), the so-called *Akademie* edition. Throughout these notes, the abbreviation "R" refers to Kant's *Reflexionen*, the notes from his *Handschriftliche Nachlaß* (handwritten remains), as printed in Vols. 14–19 of the *Akademie* edition (edited by Erich Adickes and Friedrich Berger from 1911 to 1934). Unless otherwise noted, all translations will be our own. References to the *Critique of Pure Reason* will be given by the pagination of the first ("A") and/or second ("B") edition, which are reproduced in the margins of the present translation. The present citation is at 5:151.

2 For a general characterization of the philosophies of Wolff and Baumgarten, see Lewis White Beck, *Early German Philosophy: Kant and his Predecessors* (Cambridge, Mass.: Harvard University Press, 1969), chs. XI and XII, pp. 256–96. For an account of the continuing viability of Wolffianism and its reaction to Kant, see Frederick C. Beiser, *The Fate of Reason* (Cambridge, Mass.: Harvard University Press, 1987), ch. 7, pp. 193–225.

3 In the twentieth century, Hume has often been held not to have advocated skepticism, but rather to have used skepticism about traditional metaphysics to prepare the way for his own naturalistic explanation of central human beliefs. See Norman Kemp Smith, *The Philosophy of David Hume* (London: Macmillan, 1941), and Barry Stroud, *Hume* (London: Routledge & Kegan Paul, 1977).

4 On both Lockean and popular philosophers – there was some overlap between the philosophers Kant characterizes in these two ways – see Beiser, *The Fate of Reason*, ch. 6, pp. 165–92. For the influence of the "common sense" philosophy of Thomas Reid in Germany during Kant's lifetime, see Manfred Kuehn, *Scottish Common Sense in Germany, 1768–1800* (Kingston and Montreal: McGill-Queen's University Press, 1987).

5 To borrow a metaphor from Lewis White Beck; see his article "Kant's Strategy," in his *Essays on Kant and Hume* (New Haven: Yale University Press, 1978), pp. 3–19.

6   See Giorgio Tonelli, *Kant's Critique of Pure Reason within the Tradition of Modern Logic*, ed. David H. Chandler (Zürich and New York: Georg Olms, 1994), p. 6.

7   See Alexander Gottlieb Baumgarten, *Meditationes philosophicae de nonnullis ad poema pertinentibus* (1735), §§ 115–16; *Metaphysica* (1739), § 533; and *Aesthetica* (1750–58), § 1. The first text may be found in A. G. Baumgarten, *Philosophische Betrachtungen über einige Bedingungen des Gedichtes*, ed. Heinz Paetzold (Hamburg: Felix Meiner, 1983), pp. 84–7, and the other two in A. G. Baumgarten, *Texte zur Grundlegung der Ästhetik*, ed. Hans Rudolf Schweizer (Hamburg: Felix Meiner, 1983), pp. 17, 79.

8   See Kant's note at A21/B35–6. Kant tacitly retracted this criticism of Baumgarten when he decided, after 1787, that there was an *a priori* principle if not science for judgments of taste, and characterized judgments of natural and artistic beauty and sublimity as "aesthetic judgments" in his 1790 *Critique of Judgment*. This work made Baumgarten's original term "aesthetics" the canonical name for the philosophical discussion of natural and artistic beauty and related properties.

9   See Tonelli, p. 6.

10 Kant used this traditional distinction, found in such texts as Georg Friedrich Meier's *Auszug aus der Vernunftlehre* (1752), on which he lectured, in his own logic lectures; see the text published from his logic by Gottlob Benjamin Jäsche, *Immanuel Kant's Logic: A Manual for Lectures* (1800), in Immanuel Kant, *Lectures on Logic*, ed. J. Michael Young (Cambridge: Cambridge University Press, 1992), especially pp. 589–629.

11 On the origins of these terms, see again Tonelli, *passim.*

12 See Locke's *Essay concerning Human Understanding*, book I, chs. 2–4.

13 A century ago, the great Kant scholar Hans Vaihinger published a two-volume commentary of 1066 pages that deals only with the introduction and the "Transcendental Aesthetic" of the *Critique*! See Hans Vaihinger, *Commentar zu Kants Kritik der reinen Vernunft*, 2 vols. (Stuttgart: Spemann and Union Deutsche Verlagsgesellschaft, 1881–92).

14 The classical presentation of this dispute is in the correspondence between Leibniz and the Newtonian Samuel Clarke, published by Clarke in 1717 after Leibniz's death the previous year; see H. G. Alexander, ed., *The Leibniz-Clarke Correspondence* (Manchester: Manchester University Press, 1956).

15 For recent alternative interpretations, see Henry E. Allison, *Kant's Transcendental Idealism* (New Haven: Yale University Press, 1983) and Paul Guyer, *Kant and the Claims of Knowledge* (Cambridge: Cambridge University Press, 1987).

16 Early critiques of Kant's "metaphysical deduction" came from successors such as J. G. Fichte and G. W. F. Hegel. A classical modern critique of the metaphysical deduction can be found in J. F. Bennett, *Kant's Analytic* (Cambridge: Cambridge University Press, 1966). Recent defenses of the metaphysical deduction can be found in Béatrice Longuenesse, *Kant et la pouvoir de juger* (Paris: PUF, 1993) and Reinhard Brandt, *The Table of Judgment*, trans. Eric Watkins, North American Kant Society Studies in Philosophy, Volume 4 (Atascadero, Cal.: Ridgeview, 1995).

17 For some discussion of the complexities of the "Transcendental Deduc-

tion," see Paul Guyer, "The Transcendental Deduction of the Categories," in Paul Guyer, ed., *The Cambridge Companion to Kant* (Cambridge University Press, 1992), pp. 123–60.

18 See *Prolegomena*, Remarks II and III following § 13, 4:288–94.

19 Richard Rorty used this phrase in a well-known attack upon the essentially pre-Kantian conception of human knowledge in his *Philosophy and the Mirror of Nature* (Princeton: Princeton University Press, 1979).

20 See Lewis White Beck, *The Actor and the Spectator* (New Haven: Yale University Press, 1975).

21 *Prolegomena*, 4:260. Lewis White Beck has conjectured that this "recollection" of Hume – a recollection because Kant had read Hume before this time but not previously felt his full impact – must have occurred in 1772 (see his edition of the *Prolegomena* [Indianapolis: Bobbs-Merrill, 1950], p. 8n., and his *Early German Philosophy: Kant and His Predecessors* [Cambridge, Mass.: Harvard University Press, 1969], p. 457). In a note in his own copy of his classroom metaphysics text, Alexander Gottlieb Baumgarten's *Metaphysica*, which has been widely cited for at least a century, Kant also wrote that "The year '69 gave me great light" (R 5037, 18:68). This remark suggests that Kant's intellectual revolution may have begun in 1769 and only culminated in 1772. There has been much discussion about just how Kant's thought changed during those years (see Lothar Kreimendahl, *Kant – Der Durchbruch von 1769* [Cologne: Jürgen Dinter Verlag, 1990]). We will return to some of the issues involved below.

22 A selection from these manuscripts has been edited by Eckart Förster and translated by Förster and Michael Rosen in Immanuel Kant, *Opus postumum* (Cambridge: Cambridge University Press, 1993).

23 This phrase is borrowed from the title of Leibniz's essay "The Principles of Nature and Grace, based on Reason," written in 1714 and posthumously published in 1718. When considering the influence of Leibniz on his contemporaries and on most of the eighteenth century, it must be kept in mind that he was not known by the works that have been most influential in the twentieth century, the "Discourse on Metaphysics" and other writings from the period around 1686, but was instead known almost exclusively by the *Theodicy* of 1710, "The Principles of Nature and Grace," and the contemporary "Monadology" (first published in 1720), and by the posthumously published *Leibniz-Clarke Correspondence* (1717). Thus what Leibniz was best known for in his own time and through the first half of Kant's life was his vision of the preestablished harmony of the monads on the one hand and his dispute with the Newtonians about the nature of space and time on the other. The *New Essays concerning Human Understanding*, Leibniz's lengthy commentary on Locke's *Essay concerning Human Understanding*, was left unpublished when Locke died in 1704 and not published until 1765. Although it then certainly became of great interest to Kant, it did not change Kant's fundamental image of Leibniz or the basic character of Leibniz's lasting influence on Kant.

24 *Nova dilucidatio*, 1:388. Translation by David Walford from Immanuel Kant, *Theoretical Philosophy 1755–1770* (Cambridge: Cambridge University Press, 1992), p. 6.

25 *Nova dilucidatio*, 1:389; Walford, p. 7.
26 *Nova dilucidatio*, 1:397; Walford, p. 19.
27 *Nova dilucidatio*, 1:393–4; Walford, pp. 13–14.
28 *Nova dilucidatio*, 1:394–5; Walford, p. 15.
29 See the section entitled "The Ideal of Pure Reason," particularly A567–83/B595–611.
30 *Nova dilucidatio*, 1:410; Walford, p. 37.
31 *Nova dilucidatio*, 1:411–12; Walford, p. 39.
32 *Nova dilucidatio*, 1:398–406; Walford, pp. 20–31.
33 See *Nova dilucidatio*, 1:398; Walford, p. 20.
34 *Nova dilucidatio*, 1:402; Walford, p. 25.
35 *Critique of Practical Reason*, 5:97.
36 *Nova dilucidatio*, 1:412–13; Walford, p. 40.
37 *False Subtlety*, 2:58–9; Walford, pp. 102–3.
38 *False Subtlety*, 2:59; Walford, p. 103.
39 The argument from design was already criticized briefly in Hume's published works, e.g., the *Enquiry concerning the Human Understanding* (1748), section XI, and was criticized extensively in Hume's as yet unpublished *Dialogues concerning Natural Religion* (originally drafted as early as 1751, but not to be published until 1779). But although the *Enquiry* had been translated into German as early as 1755, it does not seem to have had a major impact on Kant by 1762, and of course the *Dialogues* were not yet known to Kant at this point. When they were published and translated into German, they had a tremendous influence on him, and are constantly alluded to though not explicitly cited in the *Critique of Judgment*.
40 *Only Possible Basis*, 2:79; Walford, p. 126.
41 *Only Possible Basis*, 2:83–7; Walford, pp. 128–31.
42 *Only Possible Basis*, 2:110; Walford, p. 152.
43 *Only Possible Basis*, 2:113; Walford, p. 155.
44 See *Critique of Judgment*, introduction, IV, 5:180.
45 A translation of the Academy's official abridgement of Mendelssohn's essay can be found in Walford, pp. 276–86. The full essay can be found in Moses Mendelssohn, *Gesammelte Schriften*, ed. Fritz Bamberger and Leo Strauss, vol. 2 (Berlin: Akademie Verlag, 1931), pp. 267–330. A detailed contrast between Mendelssohn's and Kant's essays can be found in Paul Guyer, "Mendelssohn and Kant: One Source of the Critical Philosophy," *Philosophical Topics* **19** (1991): 119–52.
46 *Inquiry*, 2:276; Walford, p. 248.
47 *Inquiry*, 2:285–6; Walford, pp. 258–9.
48 *Inquiry*, 2:289; Walford, p. 262.
49 *Inquiry*, 2:292; Walford, p. 265.
50 *Inquiry*, 2:295; Walford, p. 268.
51 *Inquiry*, 2:297; Walford, p. 271. As suggested above, Kant was later to reverse this assessment, arguing that only morally necessary predicates could be determinately attributed to God (A814/B842).
52 *Inquiry*, 2:298–300; Walford, pp. 272–4.
53 See, for instance, Hobbes's explanation of the difference in *De Corpore*, ch. 6, § 7.

54 Thus Kant's detailed discussion of the contrast between mathematics and philosophy in the *Critique*, which is found not just in the "Transcendental Aesthetic" but also in the "Doctrine of Method" (especially A712–38/B740–66), should be carefully compared to but not identified with his treatment of the distinction in the earlier *Inquiry*.

55 *Negative Magnitudes*, 2:202; Walford, p. 239.

56 *Negative Magnitudes*, 2:203; Walford, p. 240.

57 *Negative Magnitudes*, 2:203–4; Walford, p. 241.

58 See Walford, p. lxxii, and Kant's correspondence with J. H. Lambert in letters 33 and 34, 13 November and 31 December 1765, 10:51–7.

59 Kant uses the Latin word *intuitus* to signify the immediate and singular representations offered by the senses; see the inaugural dissertation, *De mundi sensibilis atque intelligibilis forma et principiis* (On the Form and Principles of the Sensible and Intelligible World), § 1, 2:387; § 10, 2:396; § 14.3, 2:399; and § 15.C, 2:402. In the *Critique of Pure Reason*, he will employ the analogously formed German word *Anschauung* for the same purpose. In view of Kant's original Latin word, his German word has traditionally been translated as "intuition." Some have objected to this because of some of the connotations of "intuition" in English, but it seems better to us to preserve the traditional Latinate translation, reminding the reader that whatever associations this and other terms might suggest, their meaning in Kant's argument must be defined by what he says about them and not by such antecedent associations.

60 *De mundi*, § 1, 2:388; Walford, p. 378.

61 *De mundi*, §§ 3–4, 2:392; Walford, p. 384.

62 Thus Kant originally uses the term "noumena" in what the *Critique* proscribes as its "positive" rather than permissible "negative" sense (B 307). Whether Kant fully purges the positive sense of "noumena" from the *Critique*, especially from his argument in the "Antinomy of Pure Reason," is a difficult question of interpretation.

63 Pierre Bayle had made a number of such paradoxes prominent in his article on "Zeno of Elea" in his widely read *Historical and Critical Dictionary*, first published in 1687 (a translation can be found in Pierre Bayle, *Historical and Critical Dictionary*, trans. Richard H. Popkin [Indianapolis: Hackett Publishing Co., 1991], pp. 350–88). Bayle's article was influential for Berkeley; see his *Principles of Human Knowledge*, e.g., § 118 (in *The Works of George Berkeley*, ed. A. A. Luce and T. E. Jessop [Edinburgh: Thos. Nelson, 1949), Vol. 2, pp. 94–5). Berkeley's treatment of the paradoxes of the infinite may in turn have influenced Hume; see *Enquiry concerning Human Understanding*, section XII, part II (in Hume's *Enquiries*, ed. L. A. Selby-Bigge, 3rd. ed. revised by P. H. Nidditch [Oxford: Oxford University Press, 1975], pp. 155–7).

64 See especially B xxiv–xxx in the second-edition preface to the *Critique*.

65 *De mundi*, § 1, 2:387; Walford, p. 377.

66 *De mundi*, § 1, 2:388; Walford, p. 378.

67 *De mundi*, § 3, 2:393; Walford, p. 384.

68 *De mundi*, § 5, 2:393; Walford, p. 385.

69 *De mundi*, § 4, 2:393; Walford, p. 384.

70 *De mundi*, § 4, 2:392–3; Walford, pp. 384–5.

71 *De mundi*, § 5, 2:394; Walford, p. 386.

72 *De mundi*, §§ 8–9, 2:395–6; Walford, p. 388.

73 It will be used in as late a passage as the "Refutation of Idealism" added to the second edition; see B 276–7n.

74 In the *Critique of Judgment*, Kant will add the power of judgment, which itself has both determinant and reflective forms, as another fundamental cognitive faculty; see *Critique of Judgment*, Introduction, IV, 5:179.

75 See *Critique of Pure Reason*, A 633–7 / B 661–5. It is important to recognize that the inaugural dissertation represents a milestone in the development of Kant's moral philosophy in its suggestion that the paradigm of moral perfection is a product of pure rationality; see Manfred Kuehn, "The Moral Dimension of Kant's Inaugural Dissertation," in Hoke Robinson, ed., *Proceedings of the Eighth International Kant Congress* (Milwaukee: Marquette University Press, 1995), vol. I, part 2, pp. 373–89. However, it is also important to recognize that he had not yet arrived at his mature view that the practical use of reason is the *only* legitimate pure yet real use of reason.

76 *De mundi*, § 13, 2:398; Walford, p. 391.

77 E.g., *De mundi*, § 14.7, 2:402; Walford, p. 395.

78 E.g., *De mundi*, § 14.3, 2:399; Walford, p. 392.

79 *De mundi*, § 12, 2:397–8; Walford, p. 390.

80 *De mundi*, § 13, 2:398; Walford, p. 391.

81 All in *De mundi*, § 14, 2:398–402; Walford, pp. 391–5.

82 See A 30–2 / B 46–8.

83 See A 46–9 / B 64–7.

84 These are all to be found in *De mundi*, § 15, 2:402–5; Walford, pp. 395–8.

85 In the *Critique*, Kant will explain the ideality of space and time by referring both to their subjectivity and to their universality and necessity; see A 28 / B 44 for both senses.

86 *De mundi*, § 16, 2:407; Walford, p. 402.

87 *De mundi*, § 19, 2:408; Walford, pp. 402–3.

88 *De mundi*, § 22, 2:409; Walford, pp. 403–4.

89 A 211–15 / B 256–62.

90 *De mundi*, § 23, 2:410–11; Walford, pp. 406–7.

91 *De mundi*, § 24, 2:412; Walford, p. 407.

92 *De mundi*, § 26, 2:413; Walford, p. 409.

93 *De mundi*, § 27, 2:213–14; Walford, pp. 409–10.

94 *De mundi*, § 28, 2:415; Walford, p. 411.

95 *De mundi*, § 29, 2:417; Walford, p. 413.

96 *De mundi*, § 30, 2:418; Walford, pp. 414–15.

97 These include one book review, a brief essay on the "Different Races of Mankind" that was an advertisement for Kant's lectures on physical geography, and a pair of essays appearing in a local journal promoting a progressive school in Dessau.

98 Herz published a little book in 1772 that was an odd amalgam of what he had learned from Kant's dissertation and more Wolffian views he was then acquiring from Moses Mendelssohn; see Marcus Herz, *Betrachtungen aus*

der spekulativen Weltweisheit, ed. E. Conrad, H. P. Delfosse, and B. Nehren (Hamburg: Felix Meiner, 1990).

99 The primary sources are notes in Kant's copy of Baumgarten's *Metaphysica*, which was the basis for his course on metaphysics, that were transcribed first by Benno Erdmann in *Reflexionen Kants zur Kritik der reinen Vernunft* (Leipzig: Fues, 1884) and then by Erich Adickes in volumes 17 and 18 of the *Akademie* edition, which first appeared in 1926 and 1928 (Reflections 4273–5635 in Adickes's numbering, plus a few subsequent ones, cover the period of the 1770s). Adickes's edition also includes a number of loose sheets or drafts which tend to be more informative than the marginalia. The most important of these come from the so-called *Duisburg Nachlaß*, named after a nineteenth-century owner; the material from this group pertaining to the development of the *Critique* is found in Reflections 4674–84 in the *Akademie* edition. There is no evidence that Kant preserved all his notes at any time in his life, and many papers that did survive the remainder of his life after the publication of the *Critique* may have been dispersed upon his death in 1804 and thereafter lost. So our information about the 1770s remains fragmentary.

100 Kant was finally to publish the *Groundwork for the Metaphysics of Morals* in 1785, and the work actually entitled *The Metaphysics of Morals*, his detailed exposition of political and moral duties, not until 1797.

101 Letter 57, 2 September 1770, 10:96–9; translation in Arnulf Zweig, *Kant: Philosophical Correspondence 1759–99* (Chicago: University of Chicago Press, 1967), pp. 58–60.

102 See letter 61 from Lambert, 13 October 1770, 10:103–11; letter 62 from Sulzer, 8 December 1770, 10:111–13; and letter 63 from Mendelssohn, 25 December 1770, 10:113–16; translations of the letters from Lambert and Mendelssohn in Zweig, pp. 60–70.

103 10:105; Zweig, p. 61.

104 10:107; Zweig, p. 63.

105 10:112.

106 10:115; Zweig, p. 69.

107 10:121–4, at 121.

108 10:123.

109 10:129; Zweig, p. 71.

110 A36–7/ B53–4.

111 10:130; Zweig, p. 71.

112 10:130–1; Zweig, p. 72.

113 10:132; Zweig, p. 73.

114 10:143–6; Zweig, pp. 76–9. This is the next surviving letter to Herz; Kant's tone suggests he had not written to Herz for some time, so the letter is probably the first one he wrote to Herz after the letter of February 1772.

115 10:144–5; Zweig, pp. 77–8.

116 10:198–200; Zweig, p. 86. In this letter Kant thanks Herz for sending him a copy of Herz's newly published *Essay on Taste and the Causes of its Diversity* (Berlin: F. C. Voß, 1776), but then rather lamely apologizes for not discussing some points in more detail on the ground that he cannot

remember to whom he has lent the book (10:198). This would suggest
that Herz's book had no influence on the later development of Kant's
own aesthetic theory in the period from 1787 to 1790, culminating in the
publication of the *Critique of Judgment* in 1790 (a second edition of Herz's
book was also published in 1790, too late to be available to Kant during
his own composition). In fact, Kant's criticism of the "empirical interest
in the beautiful" in § 41 of the *Critique of Aesthetic Judgment* may have
been a veiled attack upon Herz's theory, which Kant had by no means
forgotten.

117 R 4673, 17:636–7.
118 R 4673, 17:638.
119 R 4673, 17:640.
120 R 4676, 17:653–4.
121 R 4676, 17:654.
122 R 4674, 17:644.
123 R 4676, 17:655.
124 R 4674, 17:645–6.
125 R 4684, 17:671.
126 R 4674, 17:643.
127 R 4678, 17:660.
128 R 4677, 17:658.
129 See A80/B106.
130 R 4674, 17:646–7.
131 R 4675, 17:652.
132 R 4681, 17:665–6.
133 R 4756, 17:698–702.
134 R 4756, 17:701.
135 R 4756, 17:699–701.
136 R 4756, 17:699–700.
137 R 4756, 17:700.
138 R 4756, 17:702.
139 R 4757, 17:703–4.
140 A426–60/B454–88.
141 R 4757, 17:704–5.
142 R 4758, 17:706.
143 R 4759, 17:709–10.
144 R 5203, 18:116–17.
145 A137–47/B176–87.
146 In the note immediately preceding the one just cited, Kant states that
    "*Principium rationis* is the principle of the determination of things in tem-
    poral sequence" (R 5302, 18:116).
147 R 5552, 18:220.
148 *Prolegomena*, §§ 14–23, 4:294–306.
149 *Metaphysical Foundations*, introduction, 4:474–6n.
150 See especially R 5923, 18:385–7, and R 5930–4, 18:390–3.
151 *Real Progress*, 20:271–7.
152 The problem lies behind the "patchwork theory" asserted by Hans
    Vaihinger in 1902 – see his "The Transcendental Deduction of the Cate-

gories in the First Edition of the *Critique of Pure Reason*," translated by Moltke S. Gram in his *Kant: Disputed Questions* (Chicago: Quadrangle Books, 1967), pp. 23–61 – and carried over into English-language scholarship by Norman Kemp Smith, *A Commentary to Kant's 'Critique of Pure Reason*,' second ed. (London: Macmillan, 1923). It was resisted by H. J. Paton, in articles such as "Is the Transcendental Deduction a Patchwork?" (1929) and "The Key to Kant's Deduction of the Categories" (1931), both reprinted in Gram, pp. 62–91 and pp. 247–68, and in his *Kant's Metaphysic of Experience* (London: Allen and Unwin, 1936). But versions of it have been revived in Robert Paul Wolff, *Kant's Theory of Mental Activity* (Cambridge, Mass.: Harvard University Press, 1963) and Paul Guyer, *Kant and the Claims of Knowledge* (Cambridge: Cambridge University Press, 1987). The question of whether or not Kant had a unitary strategy for the deduction remains open.

153 R 5553, 18:223.
154 R 5553, 18:221.
155 R 5552, 18:220.
156 R 5552, 18:220.
157 R 5553, 18:222–3. In the *Critique*, see A 307–8/B 364.
158 R 5553, 18:226.
159 E.g., A 306/B 363.
160 A 323/B 380.
161 R 5553, 18:226.
162 See again R 4747, 17:705.
163 R 5553, 18:223–4.
164 R 5637, 18:273.
165 Letter 164, 10:266–7; Zweig, p. 93.
166 Letter 166, 10:268–70; Zweig, p. 95.
167 For an account of Feder's transformation of Garve's draft, see Frederick C. Beiser, *The Fate of Reason: German Philosophy from Kant to Fichte* (Cambridge, Mass.: Harvard University Press, 1987), pp. 172–7. A translation of the Göttingen review appears in Johann Schultz, *Exposition of Kant's Critique of Pure Reason*, trans. James C. Morrison (Ottawa: University of Ottawa Press, 1995), pp. 171–7. After attempting to pacify Kant, Garve published his original version of the review in the friendlier *Allgemeine deutsche Bibliothek* in 1783; translation in Morrison, pp. 179–99.
168 See *Prolegomena*, § 13, remarks II and III (4:288–93), and appendix, 4:374–5.
169 *Prolegomena*, § 13, remark III, 4:290–1.
170 *Prolegomena*, appendix, 4:373n.
171 *Prolegomena*, appendix, 4:374–5, and § 13, remark I, 4:287–8.
172 *Prolegomena*, appendix, 4:381.
173 *Prolegomena*, preface, 4:263–4.
174 See *Prolegomena*, § 4, 4:274–5.
175 *Prolegomena*, §§ 18–20, 4:297–302; see especially p. 300.
176 *Metaphysical Foundations of Natural Science*, preface, 4:475n.
177 See especially R 5637, 18:271–6; R 5643, 18:282–4; R 5923, 18:385–7; and R 5929–34, 18:389–94.

178 For this chronology, see the notes by Benno Erdmann at 3:555–8.

179 Garve's original and altogether more sympathetic review, which had in the meantime been published in its original form, also raised the concern that Kant's theory of the positive use of only practical reason would "find acceptance in the heart and mind of only a few men" (Morrison, p. 193).

180 B 14–19; cf. *Prolegomena*, 4:267–9.

181 See R 5653–4, 18:306–13; R 5709, 18:332; R 6311–17, 18:607–29; and R 6323, 18:643–4.

Dedication

1 Karl Abraham Baron von Zedlitz (1731–1793) was an important educational reformer in the government of Frederick the Great. He joined the justice ministry in 1755, and in 1770 (the same year Kant was appointed to his professorship at the University of Königsberg) Zedlitz became Minister of Justice in charge of ecclesiastical and scholastic affairs. He held this post until 1788 (two years after Frederick's death). Because Zedlitz had the reputation of being a religious freethinker, Frederick William II then replaced him with J. C. Wöllner, with whose attempts to enforce religious orthodoxy among clergy and educators Kant soon came into conflict. As minister in charge of education, Zedlitz was important in establishing new schools throughout Prussia in the late eighteenth century. He was also author of *Sur le patriotisme, considéré comme objet d'éducation dans les états monarchiques* (On patriotism considered as an object of education in monarchical states) (Berlin, 1776). In 1778, Zedlitz offered Kant a professorial chair at the University of Halle (letter of 28 February 1778, 10: 224–5), which, however, he declined.

Prefaces

1 This preface was omitted in the second edition of 1787.

2 Christian Wolff (1679–1754) was the central figure in the German Enlightenment. Wolff's most prominent follower, Alexander Gottlieb Baumgarten (1714–1762), was author of *Metaphysica* (Halle, 1738; fourth edition, 1757; seventh edition, 1779), the text used most often in Kant's academic lectures (2:308–10). Baumgarten's text is reprinted in the *Akademie* edition at 17:5–226.

3 Notably, of course, David Hume (1711–1776), who had a considerable following in Germany.

4 The avowed aim of John Locke (1632–1704) was to discover "the original, certainty and extent of human knowledge" by tracing the genesis of all knowledge to its origin in experience (*An Essay concerning Human Understanding* [1690] book I, chapter I, § 2). Additional references to Locke as "physiologist of reason" may be found at R 4866 (1776–78, 18:21). See also R 4894 (1776–78, 18:21–2) for a related comment.

5 This is a reference to popular Enlightenment philosophy, such as that of Johann August Eberhard (1739–1809), J. G. Feder (1740–1821), Christian Garve (1742–1798), Christoph Friedrich Nicolai (1733–1811), and Moses

Mendelssohn (1729–1786). It emphasized appeals to healthy common sense over rigorous argument, and the popular dissemination of progressive ideas with practical import over the investigation of metaphysical questions, toward which they often expressed contempt.

6 The term "critique" or "criticism" (*Kritik*) was apparently first derived by Kant from Henry Home, Lord Kames (1696–1762), *Elements of Criticism* (1762), in which he referred to judgments in matters of beauty or taste (see 9:15). Kant's first use of it is in an announcement of lectures for 1765–66 (see 2:311). As early as 1769, Kant defines "critique as a science not for bringing forth but for assessing certain things in accordance with rules of perfection; thus metaphysics is a science for assessing cognitions from pure reason" (R 4148, 17:434).

7 To this paragraph, compare R 4945 (1776–78, 18:37).

8 See R 4900–1 (1776–78, 18:23).

9 Jean Terrasson (1670–1750), *Philosophie nach ihrem allgemeinen Einflusse auf alle Gegenstände des Geistes und der Sitten*, tr. Frau Gottsched (Berlin, 1762), p. 117. The original (French) edition was: *La philosophie éxplicable à tous les objets de l'esprit et de la raison. Precédé des reflexions de M. d'Alembert, d'une lettre de M. Moncrif & d'une autre lettre de M. *** sur la personne et les ouvrages de l'auteur*. Paris: Chez Prault & Fils, 1754.

10 See also Kant's comments about the length and style of his work at R 5015 (1776–78, 18:60–61) and R 5031 (1776–78, 18:67).

11 The Cape of Good Hope, the southernmost point in Africa.

12 In his letter to Schütz of 25 June 1787, Kant says he has in mind the demonstration in Euclid, *Elements*, bk. I, prop. 5 (10:466). Diogenes Laertius actually reports that Thales learned geometry from the Egyptians, but also that he taught them to measure the height of the pyramids using the lengths of their shadows (*Lives of Eminent Philosophers* [London: Heinemann, 1924] 1.24,27).

13 Galileo Galilei (1564–1642) described these experiments concerning acceleration in his *De Motu Accelerato* and the "Third Day" of *Dialogues on the Two World Systems* (1632).

14 Evangelista Torricelli (1608–1647), a follower of Galileo, invented the barometer, described here, in 1643. His findings were first published posthumously in the edition of his academic lectures (1715).

15 Georg Ernst Stahl (1660–1734) performed experiments with combustion and the smelting of metals which led to his formulation of the phlogiston theory in 1702. Antoine Lavoisier's discoveries, which eventually led to the replacement of the phlogiston theory, were first made in 1777, but were unavailable to Kant in 1781. The phlogiston theory was still accepted by many chemists, such as Joseph Priestley, for many years afterward. Kant followed the revolution in chemistry very closely and in 1796 attended a replication of Lavoisier's crucial experiments by his colleague Carl Gottfried Hagen (as reported by A. F. Gehlen, *Neues allgemeines Journal der Chemie* 2 [1804], p. 240). Kant's acceptance of Lavoisier's oxidation theory is evident in the *Opus postumum* (22:508).

16 "All apprehended change of place is due to movement either of the observed object or of the observer, or to differences in movements that are

occurring simultaneously in both. For if the observed object and the observer are moving in the same direction with equal velocity, no motion will be detected. Now it is from the earth that we visually apprehend the revolution of the heavens. If, then, any movement is ascribed to the earth, that motion will generate the appearance of itself in all things which are external to it, though as occurring in the opposite direction, as if everything were passing across the earth. This will be especially true of the daily revolution. For it seems to seize upon the whole universe, and indeed upon everything that is around the earth, though not the earth itself . . . As the heavens, which contain and cover everything, are the common locus of things, it is not at all evident why it should be to the containing rather than to the contained, to the located rather than to the locating, that motion is ascribed" (Nicolaus Copernicus [1473–1543], *De revolutionibus orbium coelestium* [Nuremberg, 1543] 1:5).

17   The claim that metaphysics has only a negative theoretical use but a positive practical use will be one of Kant's most fundamental philosophical theses. In addition to the "Canon of Pure Reason" below and the *Critique of Practical Reason* and *Critique of Judgment*, see the following notes: R 4284 (1770–71? 1773–75? 1776–78? 18:45); R 4892 (1776–78, 18:50); R 5112 (1776–78, 18:93), where Kant uses the same metaphor as the present passage and says that "Metaphysics is as it were the police of our reason with regard to the public security of morals and religion"; R 5073 (1776–78, 18:79–80), where Kant uses instead a medical metaphor; R 5119 (1776–78, 18:96–7); and Kant's important comment on the character of his own idealism, perhaps written shortly after the publication of the first edition of the *Critique*, R 5642 (1780–81, 18:279–82).

18   For further discussion of what this means, see R 5962 (1785–89, 18:401–5) at p. 401.

19   Kant's dissatisfaction with the exposition of the new "Refutation of Idealism," which he had added to the second edition of the *Critique* (B 274–9) is evident from this further attempt at getting it right. This footnote is in fact only the beginning of further attempts, in 1788 and 1790, to perfect this crucial argument; see the note to B 274 for references to these attempts.

Introduction

1   In R 2740, Kant defines experience as "perception with rules." In R 2741, he defines experience as "the agreement of perceptions (of empirical representations) to the cognition of an object" (both notes from 1775–79; at 16:494). These two definitions may seem distinct, but will turn out to be identical when cognition of an object is subsequently reduced to agreement with rules (e.g., A 104, B 137).

2   An argument that the distinction between *a priori* and *a posteriori* cognition precedes all other philosophical distinctions can be found in R 4851 (18:8–10), from 1776–78, which also offers a sketch of the systematic division of the whole of philosophy as Kant saw it at this point.

3   At R 4851 (1776–78), Kant asserts that the distinction between *a priori* and *a posteriori* precedes that between the sensible and intelligible, giving rise to

the distinction between two different types of *a priori* knowledge that escaped Plato and Leibniz (18:8–10).

4 Although Kant had introduced a distinction between the analytic *method* of philosophy and the synthetic *method* of mathematics as early as the *Inquiry concerning the distinctness of the principles of natural theology and morality*, written in 1762 and published in 1764 (see its First Reflection, § 1, 2:276), his distinction between analytic and synthetic *judgments* was publicly introduced for the first time in the following passage of the *Critique of Pure Reason*. However, the appearance of the distinction in the *Critique* was the product of a long gestation. The distinction appears in Kant's marginalia to his copy of Baumgarten's *Metaphysica* as early as 1764–66, e.g., R 3738 (17:278–9), and recurs throughout the years in which the *Critique* was evolving, as in 1769, e.g., R 3923 (17:348) and R 3928 (17:350–1), and again in 1772, e.g., R 4477 (17:566). An extensive discussion of the distinction appears in R 4634 (17:616–19), a note from 1773–76. Extensive use of the distinction is also to be found in the loose sheets of the so-called *Duisburg Nachlaß* of 1774–75, e.g., R 4674 (17:643–7), R 4675 (17:648–53), R 4767 (17:653–7), R 4683 (17:669–70), and R 4684 (17:670–3). In Kant's notes in Georg Friedrich Meier's logic textbook (*Auszug aus der Vernunftlehre*), see also R 3127 (1764–68) and 3128 (1769–70) (16:671), R 3042 (1773–75?; 16:629), and 3136 (1776–78 or 1780s, 16:674). After the publication of the *Critique*, the distinction was at the center of the debate between Kant and the neo-Leibnizian J. A. Eberhard; see Henry E. Allison, *The Kant-Eberhard Controversy* (Baltimore: Johns Hopkins University Press, 1973), especially his translation from Kant's *On a discovery according to which any new Critique of Pure Reason has been made superfluous by an earlier one*, 20:228–33 (Allison, pp. 141–5). Even in his latest writings, Kant was still exploring the distinction; see, e.g., *Opus postumum*, VII.IV.1, 22:40–1 (in Immanuel Kant, *Opus postumum*, edited by Eckart Förster [Cambridge: Cambridge University Press, 1993], pp. 177–78).

5 With this paragraph, compare specifically R 4634 (1772–76, 17:616–19) and R 4676 (1773–75, 17:653–7).

6 Compare this with the definition at R 4851 (1776–78, 18:10): "Cognition is called transcendental with regard to its origin, transcendent with regard to the object [*Objects*] that cannot be encountered in any experience." See also R 4890 (1776–78, 18:20).

7 R 2740 and 2741 (16:494).

8 See R 4851 (18:8–10).

9 In *Metaphysik Mrongovius*, Kant draws a similar distinction between the *a priori simpliciter* and the *a priori secundum quid*, where the latter is "cognized through reason but from empirical principles" (29:751).

10 Compare R 3955 (17:364), from 1769. At R 4993 (1776–78; 18:54–5), Kant suggests that philosophy has both pure and empirical parts, a claim crucial to his eventual distinction between the critiques of theoretical and practical reason on the one hand and the metaphysics of nature and morals on the other, so the present suggestion that there is such a thing as impure but *a priori* cognition should not be overlooked. See also R 5048 (1776–78; 18:72).

11 Compare the ensuing discussion with Leibniz's comments in the preface to the *New Essays concerning Human Understanding*, translation by Jonathan Bennett and Peter Remnant (Cambridge: Cambridge University Press, 1981), pp. 49–51.

12 For a similar suggestion, see Kant's inaugural dissertation, "*On the form and principles of the sensible and intelligible worlds,*" § 29 (2:417).

13 Kant refers, of course, to Hume's famous discussion of causation in the *Enquiry concerning Human Understanding* (1748). Hume discusses "skeptical doubts" about causal *reasoning* in section IV, and provides his "skeptical solution" to these doubts in section V; he then discusses "the idea of necessary connexion" and provides his psychological account of the origin of that idea in section VII. Kant's reference to the concepts of "cause" and of a "necessity of connection" would seem to refer primarily to the latter section. The first *Enquiry* was translated into German as early as 1755.

14 See note 4 to the first-edition introduction, above.

15 See note 5 above.

16 Kant's attempt to characterize the difference between mathematical and philosophical propositions goes back to his response to the 1762 Berlin Academy of Science essay competition, his *Inquiry concerning the distinctness of the principles of natural theology and morality*, written in 1762 and published in 1764 (2:273–301; *Theoretical Philosophy 1755–1770*, ed. Walford, pp. 243–75). The synthetic character of mathematical propositions was also a central issue in Kant's polemics with Eberhard; see *On a Discovery*, 8:191–3, 210–13 (Allison, *Kant-Eberhard Controversy*, pp. 110–12, 126–8).

17 Kant refers to Johann Andreas Segner, *Elementa Arithmeticae, Geometriae et Caluculi* (Halle, 1756; second edition, 1767), translated into German by J. W. Segner, *Anfangsgründe der Arithmetik, Geometrie und der geomtrischen Berechnung* (Halle, 1764; second edition, 1773). Hans Vaihinger refers Kant's example specifically to figures on pp. 27 and 79 of the 1773 edition of Segner's work; Hans Vaihinger, *Commentar zu Kant's Kritik der reinen Vernunft*, Vol. I (Stuttgart: W. Spemann, 1881), p. 299.

18 For another example, see R 4922 (18:29), from the early 1780s: "That the radius can be carried over into the circumference 6 times cannot be derived from the concept of the circumference" ("6 times" is obviously Kant's approximation for $2\pi r$).

19 Vaihinger argues (*Commentar*, vol. I, pp. 303–4) that the following sentences, which continue the paragraph just concluded, should actually complete the previous paragraph, and Kemp Smith accordingly transposes it. However, the disputed lines occur in the same position in the *Prolegomena*, so in order to make this transposition here one must also make it in the *Prolegomena* (as does Lewis White Beck in his edition of that work [Kant, *Prolegomena to any Future Metaphysics* (Indianapolis: Bobbs-Merrill, 1950), p. vi]), thereby assuming that Kant twice allowed the same misprint to stand. Given the rapidity with which Kant made his revisions for the second edition of the *Critique*, this is hardly impossible; but we leave the text as originally printed, although it does seem that what follows should be read as a comment on the whole discussion of mathematical propositions rather than on the first part of the present paragraph.

20 For several earlier formulations of this point, see R 5115 and 5116 (1776–78, 18:94–6).

21 The first five paragraphs of this section are loosely based on *Prolegomena*, § 5 (2:275–80), but, unlike the preceding paragraphs on mathematics, not directly copied from it.

22 In the *Treatise of Human Nature*, Hume *does* argue that "the ideas which are most essential to geometry, *viz.* those of equality and inequality, of a right line and a plain surface, are far from being exact and determinate . . . As the ultimate standard of these figures is deriv'd from nothing but the senses and imagination, 'tis absurd to talk of any perfection beyond what these faculties can judge of . . ." (book I, part II, section IV; in the edition by L. A. Selby-Bigge, revised by P. H. Nidditch [Oxford, 1978], pp. 50–1). In other words, he here denies the possibility of pure mathematics, precisely what Kant supposes his "sound understanding" would have prevented him from doing. Kant's ignorance of Hume's assertion of the empirical foundation and limitation of mathematics in the *Treatise*, which is not repeated in the first *Enquiry*, is good evidence for the traditional assumption that Kant had no firsthand acquaintance with most of the *Treatise*, which was not translated into German until 1791.

23 See note 6 to the first-edition introduction, above.

Transcendental aesthetic

1 After having begun to distinguish the methods of mathematics and philosophy in the *Inquiry concerning the distinctness of the principles of natural theology and morality* written in 1762 and published in 1764, Kant first publicly distinguishes between the cognitive faculties of sensibility and intellect in his inaugural dissertation, "On the form and principles of the sensible and intelligible world," defended and published in 1770. His argument there anticipates the argument of the present section of the *Critique* that space and time are the necessary conditions of outer and inner sense, and as such are principles of "phenomena" or things as they appear rather than of "noumena" or things as they are in themselves (§ 13, 2:398). The detailed arguments that space and time are *a priori* forms of intuition are anticipated in §§ 14 and 15 of the inaugural dissertation (2:399–405). However, Kant did not begin to use the *name* "Transcendental Aesthetic" as his term for the science of the *a priori* conditions of sensibility until several years after 1770. The term "aesthetic" is used as the designation for the "philosophy of sensibility" as early as 1769 in R 1584 (16:25), but the term "transcendental aesthetic" seems to appear first in R 4643 (17:622–3), a note ascribed to the period 1772–76. Other important anticipations of the "Transcendental Aesthetic" include R 4673, notes Kant made on a letter dated 28 April 1774 (17:636–42), and the loose sheet R 4756 (17:699–703), an important draft of an outline for the emerging *Critique* in which Kant deals with the matter of the "Transcendental Aesthetic" under the rubric of a "Transcendental Theory of Appearance," and also heads other sections of his outline as a "Transcendental Theory of Experience" and a "Dialectic of Sensibility."

2 Elsewhere, Kant defines an intuition as the "immediate relation of the

power of representation to an individual object" (R 5643, 1780–88, 18:282). For earlier accounts of intuition, see R 3955, 3957, 3958, and 3961 (1769, 17:364–7).

3 On the contrast between intuition and sensation, see R 4636 (1772–76, 17:619–20). More generally, on Kant's classification of the various forms of cognitive states, see the inaugural dissertation, § 5 (2:394); R 619–20 (1769, 15:268); R 2835–6 (1773–77, 16:536–40); and the scheme given at A 320/B 367 below, as well as the further reflections noted there.

4 Kant refers in this note to Alexander Gottlieb Baumgarten (1711–1762), who was not only the author of the textbooks on metaphysics and ethics on which Kant based his lecture courses in those subjects, but also the author of the two works which introduced and gave currency to the term "aesthetics" used in its modern sense, i.e., as the name for the philosophy of art and/or beauty; these works were Baumgarten's dissertation *Meditationes philosophicae de nonnullis ad poema pertinentibus* (Halle, 1735), and the two-volume though uncompleted *Aesthetica* (Halle, 1750 and 1758). It is not clear whether Kant was acquainted with Baumgarten's aesthetic theory firsthand or through the three-volume work in German published by Baumgarten's disciple Georg Friedrich Meier, *Die Anfangsgründe aller schönen Künste und Wissenschaften* (Halle, 1748–50) (Meier was also the author of the textbook used in Kant's logic courses). In any case, although in the present footnote Kant evinced a hostility to Baumgarten's new usage which he modified only slightly in the revisions of this note in the second edition, by 1790 Kant had accepted Baumgarten's usage, and so entitled the section of the *Critique of Judgment* of that year dealing with what he here says should be called the "critique of taste" the "Critique of Aesthetic Judgment." For comments on Baumgarten, see R 5081 (1776–78, 18:81–2). For further critical comments about the status of aesthetics in Baumgarten's (and the modern) sense, see R 1578, 1579, 1587, 1588 (1760s, 16:16–23, 26–7), R 4276 (1770–71, 17:492), and R 5063 (1776–78, 18:76–7).

5 Compare R 5298 (1776–78 or 1780s, 18:146–8).

6 With this paragraph compare R 4188 and 4189 (1769–70, 17:449–50).

7 See R 4199 (1769–70, 17:453).

8 Compare R 5315 (1776–1780s, 18:151).

9 For a contrasting assertion, see R 4511 (1772–75, 17:578). For further discussion, see R 5636 (1780s, 18:267–8).

10 See R 5637 (1780s, 18:271–6, especially p. 271).

11 See R 4071 (1769, 17:404), R 4315 (1769–71, 17:503–4), R 4425 (1771, 17:541), and R 4673 (1773–75, 17:636–42, especially p. 638).

12 Kant suggests a quite different argument for this point in the *Opus postumum*, where he states that it is *because* space is a form of intuition that it must be infinite; the unstated premise is presumably that no matter how much is given to us, we must always be able to represent it spatially because space is the form of intuition of outer objects. Of course, this might be thought to presuppose the proof that space is a form of intuition which is still being given here. See *Opus postumum*, 22:12, 43–4, 415, 417, 419–20; in Kant, *Opus postumum*, edited by Eckart Förster (Cambridge: Cambridge

University Press, 1993), pp. 170–1, 178–9, 181–3. See also R 6338 and 6338a (1794–98, 18:658–65).

13 A large number of reflections bear on the argument of this paragraph. See R 4077–8 (1769, 17:405–6), R 4191 (1769–70, 17:451), R 4673 (1773–75, 17:536–42), R 4674 (1773–75, 17:643–7, especially p. 645), R 5329 (1776–78, 18:153), R 5552 (1778–79? 1780s?, 18:218–20, especially p. 220), R 5637 (1780s, 18:271–6, especially pp. 271–2), R 5876 (1783–84, 18:374–5), and, even as late as 1797, R 6342 (18:667), R 6346 (18:670–1), R 6348 (18:671–2), R 6349 (18:672–5), R 6350 (18:676–7), R 6351 (18:677–8), and 6352 (18:678–9). Kant's interest in this long-settled matter may have been revived at this late date by an essay competition of the Royal Academy of Sciences intended to call forth defenses of the anti-Kantian position that all knowledge is of empirical origin; see R 6351.

14 Kant describes this as hypothetical correctness at R 4976 (1776–78, 18:46–7).

15 For alternative versions of the metaphysical exposition of time, see, in addition to the inaugural dissertation § 14, R 4673 (1774, 17:636–42, especially pp. 636–7) and R 4756 (1775–77, 17:699–703, especially p. 700).

16 See R 4071 (1769, 17:404).

17 Compare R 4319 (1770–71, 17:504–5).

18 See note 13 above.

19 See R 5317, 5319, 5320 (1776–78, 18:151), and R 5325 (1776–78, 18:152).

20 Kant refers here to objections that had been brought against his inaugural dissertation by two of the most important philosophers of the period, Johann Heinrich Lambert and Moses Mendelssohn, as well as by the then well-known aesthetician and member of the Berlin Academy of Sciences, Johann Georg Sulzer. Lambert objected that even though Kant was correct to maintain that "Time is indisputably a *conditio sine qua non*" of all of our representations of objects, it does not follow from this that time is unreal, for "*If alterations are real then time is also real*, whatever it might be" (letter 61 to Kant, of 18 October 1770, 10:103–11, at 106–7). Mendelssohn also wrote that he could not convince himself that time is "something merely subjective," for "Succession is at least a necessary condition of the representations of finite spirits. Now finite spirits are not only subjects, but also objects of representations, those of both God and their fellow spirits. Hence the sequence [of representations] on one another is also to be regarded as something objective" (letter 63 to Kant, of 25 December 1770, 10:113–16, at 115). (The objection that time cannot be denied to be real just because it is a necessary property of our representations, since our representations themselves are real, has continued to be pressed against Kant; see, for instance, P. F. Strawson, *The Bounds of Sense* [London: Methuen, 1966], pp. 39 and 54.) Sulzer took an only slightly more conciliatory line: he insisted that "Duration and extension are absolutely simple concepts, which cannot be explained, although they have in my opinion a true reality," even though he was prepared to concede that "Time and space, however, are composite concepts," which may thus be regarded as subjective although grounded in an objectively valid experience of duration and extension (letter 62 to Kant, of 8 December 1770, 10:110–12, at 111). Sulzer

describes himself as having been an adherent of Leibniz's view of time and space, but his view that time is a composite concept grounded on the simple concept of duration is also reminiscent of Locke's treatment of the idea of time as a complex idea (specifically, a simple mode) formed from the experience of duration (*Essay concerning Human Understanding*, book II, chapter XIV).

21 See again R 5320 (1776–78, 18:151).

22 This is somewhat disingenuous: Lambert at least made it clear that his reservations about Kant's account of time apply equally to the case of space. He wrote: "The reality of time and of space appears to have something so simple and so heterogeneous from everything else that one can only think it but not define it . . . I therefore cannot say that time and also space are merely an aid in behalf of human representation" (letter of 13 October 1770, at 10:107).

23 To the whole of this paragraph, compare R 4673 (1773–75, 17:636–42).

24 Here Kant refers to the theory of absolute space of Newton and his followers such as Samuel Clarke. Newton's view of absolute space and time is presented in *Philosophiae Naturalis Principia Mathematica* (London, 1687), Scholium to Definition VIII, book I, and discussed by Clarke in his contributions, beginning with Clarke's First Reply, to the Leibniz-Clarke correspondence, *A Collection of Papers which Passed between the Late Learned Mr. Leibnitz and Dr. Clarke, in the Years 1715 and 1716* (London, 1717); a German edition of the correspondence, translated by Heinrich Köhler, with an introduction by Christian Wolff and a posthumous reply to Clarke's fifth letter by L. P. Thümmig, was published in 1720 (Frankfurt and Leipzig), as was a French edition, edited by Des Maiseaux (Amsterdam). There is no doubt about Kant's familiarity with this famous controversy.

25 Here Kant refers to the view of Leibniz and his followers. He had already anticipated his striking objection, which focuses on this epistemological problem with Leibniz's position rather than its ontology (which Kant essentially shares), in the inaugural dissertation, § 15D (2:404). See also R 5298 (1776–1780s, 18:146–7), R 5327 (1776–1780s, 18:153), and R 5876 (1783–84, 18:374–5).

26 See R 4652 (1772–78, 17:626). See also *Metaphysical Foundations of Natural Science*, 4:476–7.

27 For a classical statement of the view to which Kant is objecting, see G. W. Leibniz, *New Essays on Human Understanding*, book I, chapter I, § 11: "But the ideas that come from the senses are confused; and so too, at least in part, are the truths which depend on them; whereas intellectual ideas, and the truths depending on them, are distinct, and neither [the ideas nor the truths] originate in the senses; though it is true that without the senses we would never think of them" (translation by Jonathan Bennett and Peter Remnant [Cambridge: Cambridge University Press, 1981], p. 81).

28 For a parallel passage, also using the example of a triangle, see Kant's letter to Marcus Herz of 26 May 1789 (letter 362, 11:48–55; translation in Arnulf Zweig, *Kant: Philosophical Correspondence 1759–99* [Chicago: University of Chicago Press, 1967], pp. 150–6).

29 Compare to this whole section R 5637 (1780–83 or 1785–88, 18:268–76),

probably a draft for the first edition of the *Critique* but possibly a draft for the second edition.

30 On the argument of this section, see also R 5805 (1783–84, 18:358–9); R 5811 (1783–84, 18:360); R 5813 (1785–89, 18:361); R 6329 (1793, 18:650–1); and *Metaphysik Volckmann*, 28:419–20. In the first draft of the introduction to the *Critique of Judgment*, however, Kant suggests that there is little content to the "general theory of time" (20:237).

31 See note 20 above.

32 See note 22 above.

33 See note 24 above.

34 See note 25 above.

35 See note 27 above.

36 For related arguments, see R 5655 (1788–89, 18:313–16, especially pp. 314–15); Kant's essay "Some remarks to Ludwig Heinrich Jakob's *Examination of Mendelssohn's Morgenstunden*" (8:149–55, at pp. 153–4); and the argument against Leibniz's monadology in *Metaphysik Mrongovius*, 29:827.

37 On the contrast between appearance and illusion, see also R 4999 (1776–78, 18:56).

38 Berkeley typically attacks the reality of *matter* rather than of space and time themselves; thus Kant would appear to be closer to the mark in the last part of this sentence than in the earlier part, in which he seems to suggest that Berkeley's idealism results from the supposition that there are contradictions inherent in the idea of space and time themselves as self-subsisting entities. In *The Principles of Human Knowledge* §§ 98–9, however, Berkeley does object to the "attempt to frame a simple idea of *time*, abstracted from the succession of ideas in my mind, which flows uniformly, and is participated in by all beings," and likewise to the attempt to "abstract extension and motion from all other qualities" (*The Works of George Berkeley, Bishop of Cloyne*, ed. A. A. Luce and T. E. Jessop [Edinburgh: Nelson, 1949], vol. II, pp. 83–4). Here Berkeley comes closer to the reasoning Kant imputes to him.

39 On the argument of this paragraph, see also R 5781 (1780s, 18:353), R 5797 (1780s, 18:357), R 5962 (1785–89, 18:401–5), and R 6317 (1790–91, 18:623–9, especially p. 626).

Transcendental analytic ("Analytic of concepts")

1 For related comments, see R 5087 and 5089 (1776–78, 18:83–4).

2 An early account of the restrictions on what Kant was later to call "general logic" may be found at R 1599 (1769–70, 16:29–30); see also R 1608 (1776–78, 16:34). Other precursors of the present passage from the same period are R 3946 (17:350–60) and R 3949 (17:361). For later comments, see R 1624 (1780s, 16:42) and R 1647 (1790s, 16:43). See also Kant's *Logic*, edited by Benjamin Gottlob Jäsche, introduction I (9:12; in Immanuel Kant, *Lectures on Logic*, tr. J. Michael Young [Cambridge: Cambridge University Press, 1992], p. 528).

3 Kant would appear to have derived this figure from the Greek satirist Lucian of Samosata (b. ca. 120 A.D.), who writes in his dialogue *Demonax*,

section 28, line 5: "Once when he [Demonax, a supposed Cynic sage] came upon two uncouth philosophers inquiring and wrangling with one another – one of them putting absurd questions, the other answering perfectly irrelevantly – he said 'Don't you think, my friends, that one of these guys is milking a he-goat and the other putting a sieve underneath it?'" (reference and translation by John M. Cooper). Kant cites "*Lucians Schriften. Erster Theil. Zürich bey Geßner. 1769.*" at R 5553 (1778–79? 1780–81? 18:221–9, at p. 225).

4   See R 2129 (1769–70, 16:245–6); R 2131–3 (1772–78, 16:247); R 2147 (1776–78, 16:252); R 2155 (1776–78, 16:254); R 2162 (1776–78, 16:256); and R 2177 (1780s, 16:259). See also the Jäsche *Logic*, introduction VII (9:50–7; *Lectures on Logic*, pp. 557–64).

5   For earlier statements of this doctrine, see R 3920–1 (1769, 17:344–6).

6   For an earlier sketch, see R 3063 (1776–78, 16:636–8).

7   On this paragraph, see R 3063 (1776–78, 16:636–8, especially p. 638); R 3065–6 (1776–1780s, 16:639); R 3069 (1780s, 16:640).

8   See R 3104–6 (1776–78, 16:660–1).

9   Compare R 4288 (1770–71? 1776–78? 17:497) and R 5228 (1776–78, 18:125–6).

10 See R 4679 (1776–78, 17:662–4, especially p. 664: "All appearances belong under titles of understanding").

11 For related claims, see R 4285 (1770–71? 1776–78? 17:496) and R 4520 (1772–76, 17:580).

12 The history of the evolution of Kant's list of categories is long and complicated, and only a selection of the relevant documents can be listed here. The main feature of this development was the only gradual connection of the three categories of relation, on which Kant focused early and often, especially in the documents of 1774–75, with the quadripartite scheme reflected in the previous table of the logical functions of judgment. A prime example of the latter tendency is R 3941 (1769, 17:356–7); an early example of the former tendency is R 4493 (1772–76, 17:571–2). One of the first clear statements of the conjunction of the two analyses is R 4656 (1772–76, 17:623–4); see also R 5055 (1776–78, 18:74). Among other early statements, see also R 4276 (1770–71, 17:492–3) and R 4215 (1775–78, 17:684–5). For an interesting late restatement of the whole doctrine, see R 6338a (1794–95, 18:659–65). Among the large number of notes focusing primarily on the categories of relation, see R 4385 (1771, 17:528); R 4496 (1772–76, 17:573); R 5284 and 5286 (1776–78, 18:143); R 5289–90 (1776–78, 18:144); and R 5854 (1783–84, 18:369–70).

13 See, however, R 4276 (1770–71, 17:492–3), where the categories are defined as "the general actions of reason."

14 For Kant's first formulations of the problem of a transcendental deduction of the categories, see his famous letter to Marcus Herz of 21 February 1772 (letter 70, 10:129–35; translation in Zweig, *Philosophical Correspondence*, pp. 70–6). For contemporaneous reflections, see R 4473 (1772, 17:564–5) and R 4633–4 (1773–76, 17:615–19).

15 For other passages using the same distinction, see R 5636 (1780–81, 18:267–8) and *Metaphysik Mrongovius*, 29:764.

16 Kant calls Locke a "physiologist of reason" at a number of places, including R 4866 (1776–78, 18:14–15) and R 4893 (1776–78, 18:21).

17 For a similar passage, in which Kant formulates a possibility he ultimately means to reject without using the subjunctive mood, but then more explicitly rejects it, see R 5221 (1776–78, 18:122–3).

18 See R 4634 (1776–78, 17:616–19).

19 In addition to R 4634, just cited, see also R 4383 (1776–78, 17:527–8) and R 5184 (1776–1770s, 18:111–12).

20 There are a number of notes in which Kant uses this formulation; see R 4672 (1773, 17:635–6), R 5643 (1780–84, 18:282–4), R 5854 (1783–84, 18:369–70), and R 5931–2 (1783–84, 18:390–2).

21 An anticipation of this doctrine of threefold synthesis, which clearly shows that its importance is to explain how appearances are subject to the laws of both intuition and understanding, can be found at R 5216 (1776–78, 18:121). Although Kant will not explicitly refer to this doctrine in the second-edition deduction, R 6358, a major sketch of "the whole of the critical philosophy" from as late as the end of 1797 (18:682–5), shows that he continued to hold the view then (see especially p. 684) and presumably had never given it up.

22 For other statements of the claim of this paragraph, see R 4676 (1773–75, 17:653–7, at p. 656); R 4678 (1773–75, 17:660–2, at p. 660); R 5221 (1776–78, 18:122–3), R 5390 (1776–78? 1778–79? 18:169–70); and R 5636–7 (1780–81, 18:266–76, especially pp. 267–8 and 271).

23 For similar treatments of the significance of the thought of an object, see R 4642 (1772–76, 17:622), R 4679 (1773–75, 17:662–4, at p. 663), R 4681 (1773–75, 17:665–8, at pp. 666–7), R 5213 (1776–78, 18:120), and R 5643 (1780–88, 18:282–4, at p. 283). For an early statement that gives this analysis of relation of cognition to an object and then takes the next step by adducing the "unity of the mind" as its ground, see R 5203 (1776–78, 18:116–17). See also R 4679, at 17:664.

24 In addition to R 5203, cited in the previous note, see also R 4674 (1773–75, 17:643–7) and R 4677 (1773–75, 17:657–60).

25 Compare R 4678 (1773–75, 17:660–2, at p. 660), R 5203 (1776–78, 18:116–17), R 5213 (1776–78, 18:120), and R 5216 (1776–78, 18:121).

26 On the concept of the transcendental object, see the important R 5554 (1778–81, 18:229–31), where Kant states that the transcendental object "is no real object or given thing, but a concept, in relation to which appearances have unity" (p. 230).

27 See the parallel passage at R 5636 (1780–81, 18:267–8, at p. 257).

28 Compare R 4676 (1773–75, 17:653–7, at p. 656). See also the loose sheet B 12 (undated) (23:17–20, at p. 19).

29 For further comments on the contrast between productive and reproductive imagination and on the relation between apperception and productive imagination, see the undated loose sheet B 12 (23:17–20, at p. 18).

30 Compare the accounts given at R 4674 (1773–75, 17:643–7, at p. 647), R 4676 (17:653–7, at p. 656), and R 4677 (1773–75, 17:657–60, especially p. 658).

31 On the concept of nature, see R 5607–8 (1778–81, 18:248–51) and R 5904 (1780s? 1776–78? 18:380).

32 Kant's thought about the best way to accomplish the task of the "Transcendental Deduction" was in constant ferment between 1781 and 1787; and although he claims in the preface to the second edition that he changed nothing fundamental in his proofs, only in the style of his exposition, it is clear that he considered a number of alternative strategies for the deduction in the period between the two editions and that the version finally published in 1787 differs from that of 1781 in many ways. Two published documents from the intervening period are *Prolegomena to any future Metaphysics* (1783), §§ 16–22, in which the argument turns on a distinction between mere judgments of perception and judgments of experience, with the latter but not the former being held to have *a priori* concepts of the understanding as necessary conditions; and the long footnote in the preface to the *Metaphysical Foundations of Natural Science* (1786) (4:474–6n.), in which Kant suggests by contrast that the deduction could be grounded entirely on the "precisely determined definition of a judgment in general" (4:475n.). It is notable that there is no reference to the unity of apperception or self-consciousness in either of these attempted deductions. Other important documents on the development of the deduction, many of which date from the period 1783–84, would thus seem to postdate the composition of the *Prolegomena*, which Kant seems to have finished in the summer of 1782, and would thus be either afterthoughts on the *Prolegomena* or notes toward the next edition of the *Critique*. Several notes including extensive sketches of a deduction which may or may not postdate the first edition of the *Critique* include: R 5637, which may be from 1780–81 or later (18:271–6); R 5642, which is univocally assigned to 1780–81 (18:279–82); and R 5643, which may be from anywhere between 1780 and 1788 (18:282–4). Those univocally assigned to the period 1783–84 include: R 5923 (18:385–7), R 5926 (18:388), R 5927 (18:388–9), and R 5930–4 (18:390–3).

33 Although he presumably presents here only an outline of the strategy for the ensuing deduction, in a later manuscript Kant suggested that the inference that any combination requires an *a priori* concept is virtually the whole of the deduction. See the manuscripts, written in 1793 or later, entitled *What Real Progress Has Metaphysics Made in Germany since the Time of Leibniz and Wolff?* (20:271, 275–6; in the translation by Ted Humphrey [New York: Abaris Books, 1983], pp. 75, 83–5).

34 To this note compare especially R 5930 (1783–84, 18:390).

35 To this paragraph compare also the loose sheet B 12 (23:18–20, especially p. 19).

36 The singularity or unity of space and time play no role in the argument of § 25, but do play a crucial role in that of § 26. Kant's reference to § 25 here should therefore presumably be replaced by a reference to § 26.

37 This is the key premise in a number of Kant's sketches of the deduction from 1783–84, including R 5927 (18:388–9) and R 5932 (18:391–2), as well as R 5643, assigned to the broader period 1780–88 (18:282–4). From the same period, see also *Metaphysik Volckmann*, 28:405–6. For Kant's later thought on the concept of an object, see R 6350 (1797, 18:675–7).

38 To the argument of this and the following section, compare especially R 5923 (18:385–7).

39 Kant is here summing up the argument of his 1762 essay *Die falsche Spitz-findigkeit der vier syllogistischen Figuren;* translated as "The False Subtlety of the Four Syllogistic Figures" in David Walford, ed., *Immanuel Kant: Theoretical Philosophy, 1755–1770* (Cambridge: Cambridge University Press, 1992), pp. 85–105.

40 Compare especially R 5933 (18:392–3).

41 Erdmann, following Vaihinger, substitutes "§ 10" for the original "§ 13." This reflects the fact that Kant derives the table of categories from the table of the logical functions of judgment in § 10 (as numbered in the second edition). However, it is in § 13 that Kant raises the question of whether the categories necessarily apply to all of our possible experience in the way that space and time as the forms of intuition do; his reference to § 13 here is presumably intended to show that here is where he has finally answered the question raised in that earlier section. Thus we leave Kant's reference as it stands.

42 For an important note on the problem of inner sense, see R 5655 (1788–89, 18:313–16).

43 Kant continued to worry about the problem of inner sense until the end of his career; for late reflections, see R 6349 (1797, 18:672–5), R 6350 (1797, 18:675–7, especially p. 675), and R 6354 (1797, 18:680). The claim that the unidimensionality of time must be represented by the spatial figure of a line, although it does not figure in the "Refutation of Idealism" added at B 274–9 below, does figure in the version of the "Refutation" found at R 5653 (1788, 18:306–12, at pp. 308–9). The distinct claim that *changes* in time and the determinate duration of intervals between changes in time can only be empirically known on the basis of periodic changes in objects in space is emphasized throughout the drafts of the "Refutation" found in R 6311–17 (1790, 18:607–29). See also B 288–92 below.

44 To this note, compare the draft of an essay entitled "Answer to the question, Is it an experience that I think?" at R 5661 (1788–90, 18:318–20). See also A 402 and Kant's long footnote at B 422–3n., below.

45 By this term, here first introduced, Kant refers back to the derivation of the categories from the logical functions of judgment (§§ 9–12). This new designation for that argument is widely used in the literature on Kant.

46 To this note, compare R 5926 (1783–84, 18:388).

47 On this conception of nature, see R 5406–11 (1776–1780s, 18:174–5).

48 This term alludes to the biological theory that the germ cells of the two parents give rise to the embryo as a new product, rather than as the evolution of something preformed; the theory of epigenesis is the antithesis of the theory of preformation, and not just a contrast to the concept of *generatio aequivoca.* For another instance of Kant's use of this and the related biological terms to classify philosophical theories, see his classification of theories of reproduction at *Critique of Judgment,* § 81 (5:421–4).

49 This alludes to the biological theory, the antithesis of epigenesis, that the embryo exists completely formed in the germ cell of one parent and that the other parent's germ cell only stimulates it to growth.

Transcendental analytic ("Analytic of principles")

50   Kant's view that judgment may be taught by examples but that there is a
     limit to the efficacy of principles has deep roots in this thought; see R 1580
     (1769–70, 16:23). This paragraph's opening suggestion that there would be
     an infinite regress if judgment needed rules to apply rules becomes even
     more prominent in *Critique of Judgment*, preface, 5:169.

51   The first mention of the doctrine of schematism seems to be at R 5552
     (1778–79, 18:218–21, at p. 220). This late origin of the concept is consis-
     tent with the absence of any separation between the tasks of a transcenden-
     tal deduction and of a theory of principles of judgment in the reflections of
     the mid-1770s, especially R 4674–84 from the *Duisburg Nachlaß*; only once
     the two tasks had been separated would it have been necessary to invent the
     bridge between them, and so the final form of the "Transcendental Analy-
     tic," in which the "Schematism" forms a bridge between the "Analytic of
     Concepts" and "Analytic of Principles" ("Doctrine of Judgment"), though
     it is formally the first chapter of the latter, does not appear to have taken
     shape in Kant's mind before 1778. The next mention of the "schematistic"
     is from the immediate period of the composition of the first edition of the
     Critique, in R 5636 (1780–81, 18:267–8). The doctrine of the schematism
     is also prominent in three reflections from the period 1783–84, R 5932–4
     (18:391–4), although it is mentioned by name only in R 5933 (18:392–3).
     Finally, there is a late note in which Kant holds the chapter on the schema-
     tism "for one of the most important" even though his own disciple Jakob
     Sigismund Beck could not understand it; see R 6369 (1797, 18:685–7).

52   The distinction between a mere image and a rule which Kant will make in
     this paragraph in order to undermine any empiricist criticism of abstract
     mathematical ideas such as Berkeley's (see *A Treatise concerning the Principles
     of Human Knowledge*, introduction, § 18) had already been suggested by
     Leibniz in his discussion of Locke's resolution of the Molyneux problem;
     see *New Essays on Human Understanding*, book II, chapter IX, § 8, where
     Leibniz says "how essential it is to distinguish *images* from *exact ideas* which
     are composed of definitions" (Bennett and Remnant, p. 137).

53   For several reflections clarifying Kant's concepts of quantity, see R 5583,
     5585, and 5589 (1778–1780s, 18:240–2).

54   To these three paragraphs, compare R 5763 (1783–84, 18:347). See also R
     5764 (1783–84, 18:347–8).

55   On the distinction between the principles of analytic and synthetic judg-
     ments in this and the following section, see R 3919–23 (1769, 17:344–8),
     R 3925–6 (1769, 17:349), and especially R 3928 (1769, 17:350–1).

56   In addition to the reflections cited in the previous note, see also R 4476–8,
     4480, and 4482 (1772, 17:565–9).

57   Compare with this *Critique of Judgment*, introduction V, 5:184–5.

58   See R 5585 (1779–81, 18:241–2), where Kant suggests that the mathemat-
     ical principles are so called because they are the conditions of the possibil-
     ity of applied mathematics.

59   For some light on these terms, see R 4675 (1775, 17:648–53, at pp. 648–9)
     and R 4681 (1773–5, 17:665–8, at pp. 667–8).

60 This distinction is already well worked out in R 5758 (1775–77, 17:705–8, at p. 706).

61 On this section, see R 5583, 5585, and 5589 (1778–80s, 18:240–2). See also *Opus postumum*, 21:454–7.

62 See R 5726–7 (1785–89, 18:336–8) and R 5832–50 (1780s, 18:365–9). See also *Metaphysik Volckmann*, 28:424–5.

63 On Kant's definition of intensive magnitude, see R 5331 (1776–78, 18:154). See also R 5582 (1778–79, 18:239–40) and R 5587 (1778–1780s, 18:241).

64 See R 4719 (1773–79, 17:686) and especially R 5341 (1776–1780s, 18:156). See also *Metaphysik Mrongovius*, 29:834.

65 Thought to have been introduced by Epicurus, a preconception in the form of a general concept or notion, formed from prior experience, used to anticipate properties of newly encountered objects; not an entirely apt comparison for Kant, since there is nothing clearly *a priori* in the Epicurean conception.

66 See note 15 above.

67 Although the principle of their proof was suggested as early as 1769–70 in R 4174 (17:444), the "Analogies of Experience" were at the heart of Kant's original argument for the *a priori* objective validity of the relational categories as well as the forms of intuition in the mid-1770s, and there are numerous anticipations of the following material among Kant's notes from this period, especially among the so-called *Duisburg Nachlaß* from 1774–75 (R 4674–84, 17:643–73). Among other passages, see R 4674 (at pp. 646–7), R 4678 (at pp. 660–1), R 4681 (at p. 666), and R 4684 (at pp. 670–1). See also R 4756, where Kant introduces the theses of the three analogies under the title of a "Transcendental Theory of Experience" (1775–77, 17:699–703, at pp. 702–3). See also R 5088 (1776–78, 18:84), R 5214 (1776–78, 18:120), and especially R 5221 (1776–78, 18:122–3), where Kant argues that the rules furnished by the analogies are the basis for distinguishing objective truth from merely subjective play or fiction in a way that seems most closely related to the following exposition of the second analogy.

68 A quite different explanation for the use of the term "analogy" as the designation for the principles of substance, causation, and community is given at R 4675 (1775, 17:648–53, at p. 648).

69 For some of the more important of Kant's notes on the concept of substance and the arguments for its permanence, see R 4039 (1769, 17:393–4); R 4052–60 (1769, 17:398–401); R 4681 (1773–75, 17:665–8, at p. 666); R 4684 (1773–5, 17:670–3, at p. 671); R 4699–703 (1773–77, 17:679–81); R 5278–98 (1776–78, 18:141–7); R 5348 (1776–78, 18:158), which clearly anticipates the opening argument of both versions of the first analogy; and R 5871 (1780–81, 18:373), which more clearly bears on the argument of the final three paragraphs of the first analogy. For interesting comments on the empirical use of the concept of substance, see *Metaphysik L₁* (28:208–9).

70 The point at which Kant is driving here, that accidents are not something separate from the substance but rather simply the positive determinations of the substance and therefore the way in which it is known, would appear to be directed against Locke's concern that even if we know the qualities of

a substance something about it necessarily still remains unknown (*Essay concerning Human Understanding*, book II, chapter XXIII, §§ 3–4). Kant recurs to this point often: see R 4053 (1769–70, 17:399), R 5855 (1780s, 18:370), R 5861 (1783–84, 18:371), and *Metaphysik Volckmann*, 28:429–30.

71 See R 5291 (1776–78, 18:144). In several places, Kant suggests that the argument for the permanence of substance can be derived from the present definition of substance; see R 5297 (1776–77, 18:146), R 5791 (1783–84, 18:356), and R 5873 (1783–84?, 18:373). A later reflection, however, makes it clear that a synthetic *a priori* proposition like the principle of conservation cannot be derived from a mere definition; see R 6305 (1790–98, 18:706), and tries to construct an argument for the permanence of substance different from any suggested in the text.

72 To this epistemological argument for the permanence of substance, compare R 5871 (1780–81? 18:373).

73 As this remark suggests, permanence and therefore substantiality is not itself something that is directly perceived. See R 4054 (1769, 17:399) and R 5358 (1776–77, 18:160). The later discussion to which Kant refers is at A204–6/B249–51.

74 The earliest statement of the underlying principle of Kant's argument for this principle appears to be R 4174 (1769, 17:444), which states quite explicitly that things need to stand in a "real connection" in order to be placed in a series of succession because there is no perception of their position in absolute time. In the *Duisburg Nachlaß* of 1774–75, there are important anticipations of the argument of the second analogy at R 4675 (17:648–53, at p. 648), R 4682 (17:668–9), and R 4684 (17:670–3, at pp. 670–1). Important later reflections include R 5189 (1776–78, 18:112–13), R 5202 (1776–1780s, 18:116), and R 5699 (1780–84, 18:329), where Kant explicitly says, "The *principium rationis* is valid only of experience." See also the discussion in *Metaphysik Volckmann*, 28:407–9.

75 On the connection between substance and action, see R 5289–90 (1776–78? 18:144), and the later R 5650 (1785–88, 18:298–302, at p. 298).

76 This thesis can be considered the capstone of Kant's long struggle against the idea that distinct substances are related merely by preestablished harmony, which began in his *New Elucidation of the Primary Principles of Metaphysical Cognition* (1755), proposition XII (2:39; in *Theoretical Philosophy 1755–1770*, p. 39). An important note on this theme from the early 1760s is R 3730 (17:272). From the 1770s, relevant notes include R 4704 (1773–77, 17:681), R 5429 (1776–79, 18:179), and R 5598 (1778–79 18:246). From approximately the same period, see also the discussion in *Metaphysik L₁*, 28:212–13.

77 To this paragraph, compare similar discussions in several of Kant's versions of the "Refutation of Idealism" from 1790, especially R 6312 (18:612–13) and R 6313 (18:613–15, at p. 614).

78 The following postulates and their discussion bring to a head Kant's contrast between logical and real relations, especially between logical and real possibility, which had been the basis of his critique of rationalism since the 1763 *Attempt to Introduce the Concept of Negative Magnitude into Philosophy*. For an anticipation of the mature doctrine from as early as 1764–66, see R

3756 (17:284–5). For notes from the 1770s, see R 4288 (1771–72, 17:497), R 4298–9 (1770–71, 17:499–500), R 4302 (1770–75, 17:500), and R 4682 (1773–75, 17:668–9). For notes from the 1780s, see R 5710–23 (various dates, 18:332–5), R 5754 and 5757 (1785–89, 18:345), R 5763 (1783–84, 18:347), and R 5772 (1785–89, 18:349). From the 1780s, see also *Metaphysik Volckmann*, 28:412–13 and 416–18.

79 For Kant's contrast between non-contradictoriness as the condition of merely logical or "analytical" possibility and the stronger notion of the objective reality of the concept or real or "synthetic" possibility of the object, see also R 5184 (1776–1780s, 18:111–12), R 5556 (1778–81, 18:232), R 5565 (1778–1780s, 18:235), R 5569 (1778–1780s, 18:235–6), R 5572 (1778–1780s, 18:237), and R 5772 (1785–89, 18:349–50).

80 This could appear to be a reference to the existence of an ether as the condition of the possibility of perception which Kant argues for in his *Opus postumum*, especially in the sections known as *Übergang 1–14* (see 22: 609–15). However, since Kant goes on to say that the possibility of this third thing is entirely groundless because it has no basis in experience while he subsequently argues that the existence of the ether is actually a condition of the possibility of experience, it would seem that he is here considering (and denying) the possibility of a third kind of substance in addition to matter and mind, rather than the extremely refined form of matter, which is how he later conceives of the ether.

81 This would appear to be a reference to the Swedenborgian supposition of a world of spirits capable of communicating with each other without the benefit of any material medium that Kant lampooned in the *Dreams of a Spirit-Seer* (1766); see 2:329–34, in *Theoretical Philosophy, 1755–1770*, pp. 316–21.

82 See R 5181 (1776–78, 18:110–11) and R 5185–6 (1776–1780s, 18:112).

83 Kant was obviously dissatisfied with this new section of the second edition, for in addition to the modification of the argument already suggested in the preface at b xxxix–xli, numerous sketches of the argument from the years *after* the publication of the second edition also survive. These include, from late in 1788, R 5653–4 (18:305–13) and the related R 5655 (18:313–16), and from 1790, apparently written in conjunction with a visit by Kant's disciple J. G. C. Kiesewetter, R 6311 (18:606–12, in Kiesewetter's hand) and R 6312–17 (18:613–29). Other relevant notes include R 5709 (1785–89, 18:332) and R 6323 (1793, 18:641–4, at p. 643). From the period *prior* to the publication of the first edition of the *Critique*, two interesting notes are R 5399 and 5400 [1776–78?, 18:172].)

84 Kant already made this distinction between problematic and dogmatic idealism in the later 1770s; see *Metaphysik L₁*, 28:206–9.

85 See also R 5661, the draft of an essay entitled "Answer to the question, is it an experience that we think?" (1788–90, 18:318–20).

86 See b 156 above and b 288–94 below.

87 In addition to the reflections cited in note 83, on this paragraph see also the late R 6345 (1797, 18:670).

88 On this contrast, see among other notes R 4030–9 (1769, 17:390–4), R 5196 (1776–78, 18:115), R 5565–72 (1778–81, 18:235–7), R 5755–61 (1783–84, 18:345–7), and R 5768 (1783–84, 18:348–9).

89 To this paragraph, compare R 5719 (1780s? 18:334), R 5723 (1785–89, 18:335), and R 5769 (1783–84, 18:349).

90 Kant may be referring here to Johann Heinrich Lambert, who made much use of the term "postulate" in his philosophy and was generous in his conception of the grounds on which postulates could be admitted, apparently believing that if a proposition was of use in a scientific inquiry its mere possibility was adequate for postulating its truth; for example, he writes that "that which, considered in itself, is possible, can be presupposed as a postulate in a practical problem" (*Dianoiologie*, § 530, in *Neues Organon, oder Gedanken über die Erforschung und Bezeichnung des Wahren und dessen Unterscheidung vom Irrthum und Schein*, vol. I [Leipzig, 1764; in the edition by Günter Schenk (Berlin: 1990), vol. I, p. 263]). By "practical," here, Lambert means experimental, not moral; but in spite of his criticism in the present context, Kant's later use of "postulate" as a term in his practical philosophy may not be unconnected to Lambert's use of the term.

91 Here again Kant refers to the distinction between real and logical opposition first introduced in *The Attempt to Introduce the Concept of Negative Magnitudes into Philosophy*, where the relation between motions in opposite directions is one of his primary examples of real rather than logical opposition, and where rest is thus treated not as a logical contradiction but as a real state resulting from real opposition between equal motions or forces in opposite directions. See *Negative Magnitudes*, 2:171–2, 179–80; in Walford, ed., *Theoretical Philosophy, 1755–1770*, pp. 211, 218.

92 For statements of this Leibnizian thesis that would have been known to Kant, see *Principles of Nature and Grace*, § 13; *Monadology*, §§ 78–90; and *Leibniz-Clarke Correspondence*, Leibniz's Fifth Paper, § 87. A classical statement of the doctrine not available to Kant is in *Discourse on Metaphysics*, § 14.

93 Kant alludes here to the section of the "Transcendental Dialectic" entitled "The Paralogisms of Pure Reason," A 341–404 and B 399–432.

Transcendental analytic ("Phenomena and Noumena" and "Amphiboly")

94 Kant's geographical imagery goes back a long way: see R 4458 (1772, 17:559). This note is found in a series of interesting notes (R 4445–76, 17:552–66), which show Kant working out the situation of his emerging philosophy in both historical (R 4446–51) and systematic (R 4452–76) terms; Kant's mature position that pure reason has only a negative use in the theoretical context and a positive use only in the practical context can already be seen emerging (R 4453, 4457, 4459). The present chapter's distinction between negative and positive senses of the concept of the noumenon is an important step in Kant's larger argument for this position.

95 See R 5554 (1778–81, 18:229–30), where Kant writes that "Noumenon properly signifies something which is always the same, namely the transcendental object [*Object*] of sensible intuition. However, it is not a real object [*object*] or given thing, but rather a concept, in relation to which appearances have unity" (p. 230).

96 Here Kant refers to B 288–9 in the "General Remark on the System of Principles" added in B.

97 The view that "pure ideas of reason are ideas of reflection" that "do not represent objects, but only laws for comparing the concepts which are given to us through the senses" goes back to 1769; see R 3917 (17:342–4). More immediate precursors of the present section can be found at R 5051 (1776–78, 18:73); R 5552 (1778–81, 18:218–21), clearly a draft for the present section, which lists the specific pairs of concepts discussed below at A 263–6/ B 319–22 as well as the classification of concepts of something and nothing (A 290–2/ B 346–9); and R 5554 (1778–81, 18:229–30). See also R 5907 (1785–88? 1776–79? 18:381). On the critique of Leibniz, see *Real Progress*, 20:281–5.

98 See also *Metaphysik Mrongovius*, 29:838–43.

99 Leibniz illustrated his principle of the identity of indiscernibles, the principle that two things could never differ solely in spatiotemporal location without also having internal differences, which Kant is here attacking, with the example of two drops of water or milk, in his Fourth Letter to Samuel Clarke, § 4, first published in the Leibniz-Clarke correspondence in 1717, the year after Leibniz's death.

100 For us, evidence for the ascription of such a view to Leibniz would be an essay like "Primary Truths," in which Leibniz infers the identity of indiscernibles from the analytical nature of all proof of truth, an inference which depends upon the assumption that the analysis of concepts is the source of all truth (in G. W. Leibniz, *Philosophical Essays*, ed. Roger Ariew and Daniel Garber [Indianapolis: Hackett, 1989], pp. 31–2). But since Kant could not have been familiar with this essay, not published until 1905, he must have based his characterization of Leibniz's reasoning on other sources, such as the derivation of the identity of indiscernibles from the claim that all differences in nature are founded on "intrinsic denominations" at *Monadology*, § 9. Leibniz's discussion of the principle in his Fifth Paper in the *Leibniz-Clarke Correspondence*, §§ 21–5, does not make its origins as opposed to its implications particularly clear, although the following §§ 26–9 do suggest that the principle is connected with Leibniz's denial of the fundamentality of spatial and temporal predicates, which by implication leaves only conceptual considerations as the basis of truth.

101 The introduction of an arithmetical example in this context is another reference to the argument of *Negative Magnitudes*, where Kant uses the mathematical concept of subtraction rather than the logical notion of contradiction to provide a framework for understanding opposition in real entities such as forces, emotions, and so on. See 2:172–4; in *Theoretical Philosophy, 1755–1770*, pp. 212–14.

102 Among sources available to Kant, see, e.g., *A New System of Nature*, in Ariew and Garber, p. 139; *Principles of Nature and Grace*, § 2; and *Monadology*, §§ 3–11.

103 See the *Leibniz-Clarke Correspondence*, Leibniz's Fifth Paper, § 47.

104 Aristotle's *Topics* begins with the proposal "to find a line of inquiry whereby we shall be able to reason from reputable opinions about any subject presented to us, and also shall ourselves, when putting forward an argument, avoid saying anything contrary to it" (100a20–3; translation by

W. A. Pickard-Cambridge, in *The Complete Works of Aristotle*, ed. Jonathan Barnes [Princeton: Princeton University Press, 1984], vol. i, p. 167). In the words of W. D. Ross, the object of the *Topics* "is to study the dialectical syllogism," where "The dialectical syllogism is distinguished from the scientific by the fact that its premises are not true and immediate but are merely probable, i.e., such as commend themselves to all men, to most men, or to wise men" (*Aristotle*, fifth edition, revised [London: Methuen, 1949], p. 56). Kant seems to be suggesting that the *Topics* was used to suggest arguments that would appear credible because of their form without regard to the plausibility of their premises at all.

105   Presumably Kant here has in mind Locke's claim that sensation and reflection are the two sources of all our ideas (*Essay concerning Human Understanding*, bk. II, ch. i, §§ 3–4), and is understanding Locke's reflection to be reflection on ideas of sensation only. This would be a misunderstanding of Locke, since Locke says that we can get simple ideas from reflection on the "operations of our own Mind," a doctrine which is actually a precursor to Kant's view that the laws of our own intuition and thinking furnish the forms of knowledge to be added to the empirical contents furnished by sensation, although of course Locke did not go very far in developing this doctrine; in particular, he did not see that mathematics and logic could be used as sources of information about the operations of the mind.

106   See *Negative Magnitudes*, 2:176–7; in *Theoretical Philosophy, 1755–1770*, pp. 216–17.

107   Here Kant is referring to Leibniz's doctrine that all the properties of things are perfections in virtue of which they have a claim to existence, with those that actually exist being those that have the most perfection and thus comprise the most perfect world; on this account, there are no actually negative properties, but only limitations to the positive perfections of things (see, e.g., *The Principles of Nature and Grace*, §§ 9–10). This was a doctrine with which Kant had been arguing since the essay on *Negative Magnitudes*; see especially its section 3, 2:189–93; in *Theoretical Philosophy, 1755–1770*, pp. 227–30.

108   Here Kant is alluding to Leibniz's emendation of Descartes's ontological argument, where Leibniz argued that the latter is sound as long as it is preceded by a proof that the concept of God is internally non-contradictory, a proof easily supplied since the concept of an all-perfect being contains nothing but positive determinations which cannot conflict with each other (see the third paragraph of *Meditations on Knowledge, Truth and Ideas*, originally published in 1684, as well as many later expositions of the claim).

109   For some of the many statements of this doctrine with which Kant would have been familiar, see *A New System of Nature* (1695) (in Ariew and Garber, eds., *Philosophical Essays*, pp. 143–4); *Principles of Nature and Grace*, §§ 12–13; and *Monadology*, §§ 56–9.

110   See *Leibniz-Clarke Correspondence*, Leibniz's Third Letter, § 4, and Leibniz's Fifth Letter, §§ 29, 33.

111 This is a misquotation from the poem "*Die Falschheit menschlicher Tugenden*" by Viktor Albrecht von Haller, *Gedichte* (Bern, 1732); Haller's lines are:

Ins Innere der Natur dringt kein erschaffener Geist.
Zu glücklich, wenn sie noch die äußere Schale weist.

(No created spirit penetrates into the inner in nature. / It is already too much good luck if it knows the outer shell.)

112 In his *Logic*, Kant defines this as the rule that "What belongs to or contradicts the genus or species belongs to or contradicts all the objects that are contained under that genus or species," a rule which in turn he derives from the "Principle of categorical inferences of reason," namely "What belongs to the mark of a thing belongs also to the thing itself; and what contradicts the mark of a thing contradicts also the thing itself" (Jäsche *Logic*, § 63; in J. Michael Young, ed., *Lectures on Logic* [Cambridge: Cambridge University Press, 1992], pp. 617–18). The inference from the general principle of categorical inferences to the *dictum de omni et nullo* is based on the fact that a concept is a subset of the marks of an object, typically a proper subset since the Leibnizian idea of a complete concept of a particular is only an ideal of reason.

113 See, e.g., Leibniz's *Principles of Nature and Grace*, § 2.

114 Here Kant refers to the fact that Wolff's and Baumgarten's systems of general ontology begin by defining the distinction between the possible and the impossible, excluding from the sphere of the possible only that which is logically self-contradictory; see e.g. Baumgarten, *Metaphysica*, *Pars* I, *Caput* I, *Sectio* I, §§ 7–18, 17:24–30.

115 As noted above, there is a draft of the following material at R 5552 (1778–79? 1780–81? 18:218–21, at pp. 218–19). See also R 5726 (1785–89, 18:336–8, at p. 336).

Transcendental dialectic

1 Kant introduced very early the term "dialectic" as the title for "the theory of the subjective laws of the understanding, insofar as they are held to be objective" (see R 1579, 1760–64?, 1769–70? 16:17–23 at p. 23). Kant appears to have discovered the antinomies of pure reason in particular, which he expounded in the middle of the three sections of the second book of the "Dialectic," "The Dialectical Inferences of Pure Reason," by 1769; see, for example, R 3922 (1769, 17:346–7), R 3928–9 (1769, 17:350–2), R 3936–7 (1769, 17:354–5), R 3942 (1769? 1764–8? 17:357), R 3954 (1769, 17:363), R 3974 (1769, 17:371–2), and R 3976 (1769, 17:372–3). It may be the discovery of the antinomies that Kant refers when he later says that "the year '69 gave me great light," R 5307 (1776–78, 18:69). However, in Kant's first published treatment of some of the material of the "Dialectic," §§ 23–9 of the inaugural dissertation of 1770, he argues that metaphysical error arises from unduly restricting pure reason by the conditions of sensibility rather than from failing to recognize that ideas of pure reason alone cannot give theoretical knowledge, as the notes of the 1769 and the comments of R 5307

already suggest. The first extensive outlines for the eventual "Dialectic" of the published *Critique* are found at R 4756–60 (1775–77, 17:699–713). A striking feature of these outlines is that at this point Kant foresaw the presentation of the "Dialectic" in terms of a tripartite contrast between "immanent principles of the empirical use of the understanding" and "transcendent principles of the pure use of reason" (R 4757, 17:703) or a quadripartite contrast between "the principles of the exposition of appearances" and the "principles of rationality" (R 4759, 17:709–10), in which, in particular, competing claims about the simplicity of the self would be treated under the general issue of the decomposition of the complex into the simple, and all issues about God would be treated under the heading of necessity; in other words, at this point the subject matter of the eventual "Paralogisms of Pure Reason" and the "Ideal of Pure Reason" were to be treated under the second and fourth antinomies respectively, and there was no division of the "Dialectic" into three main parts. R 5109 (1776–78, 18:90–92) does not yet suggest any departure from this plan, although R 4849, from the same period, does suggest the division between the "Paralogisms" and the "Antinomies" (18:5–8). By the time of the important R 5553 (1778–79, 18:221–9), however, the threefold division of the whole "Dialectic" and the fourfold subdivision of each of its three main parts was clearly in place (see 18:223); this note is the single most important draft of the "Dialectic." For later comments, see also R 5642 (dated 1780–81, but clearly written after the publication of the first edition of the *Critique*; 18:279–82) and R 5962 (1785–89, 18:401–5).

2 For Kant, "probability" is the holding of a proposition for true on insufficient ground, whether the insufficiency is objective or subjective. See A820–3/B848–51 and *Logic* 9:81–6.

3 Kant discusses the understanding as a law-governed power, comparing the laws of the understanding with the rules of grammar in the *Logic* 9:11–13.

4 Compare Kant's discussion of sensory illusion in the *Anthropology* § 8, 7:146.

5 See R 4930 (1776–78, 18:31–2), where Kant draws a distinction between *Anschein* or *apparentia* as error due to lack of judgment and unavoidable *natürliche Schein* or *species*, of which *transcendentale Schein* is an instance.

6 Inference is the derivation of one judgment from another (*Logic* § 41, 9:114). In immediate inferences, which Kant calls "inferences of the understanding," the judgment is derived directly, without the aid of any other inference. Such inferences include those from the universal affirmative to the particular affirmative (*Logic* § 46, 9:116), the denial of the contradictory, contrary, and subcontrary (*Logic* §§ 47–50, 9:116–18), the rules of conversion (*Logic* §§ 51–3, 9:118–9), and contraposition (*Logic* §§ 54–5, 9:119). Mediate inferences, or "inferences of reason," infer one proposition from another by means of a third. Under this heading, Kant includes the theory of syllogisms (*Logic* §§ 56–9, 120–1).

7 This contrast between understanding and reason is anticipated at R 5553 (1778–79, 18:221–9, at p. 224).

8 See previous note.

9 Kant's threefold division of syllogisms according to the form of the major premise is presented in *Logic* §§ 60–1, 9:121–2.

10   In addition to the passage previously cited from R 5553 (18:224), see also
      R 5596 (1778–79? 1780–81, 18:245).

11   For further comments on Plato, see R 6050 (1780s? 1776–79? 18:434–7)
      under the title "On philosophical enthusiasm"; R 6051 (1780s? 1776–79?
      18:437–9); and R 6055 (1783–84, 18:439).

12   On Plato's doctrine of recollection (*anamnesis*), see *Meno* 81, *Phaedo* 73–7,
      Phaedrus 243–57. Also see an allusion to it at *Republic* 518c, which speaks of
      turning the eye of the soul toward the forms.

13   Johann Jakob Brucker (1696–1770), author of *Historia critica philosophica*
      (Leipzig: Breitkopf, 1742–44); the section on Plato is volume 1, pp.
      627–728, and the disparaging remarks about the political applications of
      Plato's theory of ideas are on p. 726.

14   Plato never asserts that punishment would be unnecessary in the perfect
      state, in the *Republic* or anywhere else. On the contrary, he often empha-
      sizes the educational value of punishment in making people more just (*Re-
      public* 591b; cf. *Gorgias* 476–9).

15   Plato did hold that forms or ideas are causes (*aitiai*) of natural things. See
      Phaedo 100c–102a, *Republic* 508e, *Timaeus* 29a–30b.

16   There are a number of reflections that should be compared to this classi-
      fication of kinds of representation. These include R 1705 (1776–79, 16:88–
      9); R 2834–6 (1769–70? 1764–68? 16:536), R 2835 (1773–75? 1762–64?
      1769? 16:536–7), and R 2836 (1775–77? 1776–78? 16:538–9), and R 4073
      (1769, 17:404–5).

17   To this paragraph, compare R 5093 (1776–78, 18:85).

18   The foundation of the ideas of reason in the categories of relation is clearly
      sketched at R 5555 (1778–1780s, 18:231–2).

19   The argument of the preceding paragraph, which differs from that of the
      previous section by grounding the tripartite division of the "Dialectic" on
      a tripartite division of kinds of objects rather than on the three relational
      categories (as at A 323/ B 379), is anticipated at R 5553 (1778–79? 1780–81?
      221–9, at pp. 225–6 and 229). In R 5642 (1780–81, 18:279–82), Kant not
      only uses this new foundation but even connects it instead of the three re-
      lational categories to the three forms of rational inference (categorical, hy-
      pothetical, disjunctive; see 18:281).

20   The Wolffian system of metaphysics, as expounded by Baumgarten in
      Metaphysica (Halle, 1738), is divided into the general science of "ontology"
      (*Metaphysica* §§ 4–350), followed by the three special sciences of "cosmol-
      ogy" (*Metaphysica* §§ 351–500), "psychology" (*Metaphysica* §§ 501–799),
      and "natural theology" (*Metaphysica* §§ 800–1000).

21   Kant defines a paralogism as "an inference which is false in its form (al-
      though its matter (the premises) are correct)" at R 5552 (1778–79? 1780s?
      18:218–21, at p. 218).

22   Kant expounds in several places the traditional rational psychology which
      is criticized here: Among them are R 4230 (1769–70? 17:467–69), *Meta-
      physik L₁* (28:265–8); the lengthiest treatment in the later *Metaphysik Mron-
      govius* (29:903–20) refers to many criticisms made in the *Critique*. Kant
      treats the subject of rational psychology as part of the antinomies at R
      4758–9 (1775–77, 17:705–11). He is clearly working out further details of

his critique of rational psychology at R 5451–61 (1776–78, 18:186–9). He finally outlines the critique of rational psychology at R 5553 (1778–79, 18:221–9 at pp. 227–8).

23 Compare Kant's account of the "subreption of the power of judgment" at R 5059 (1776–78, 18:75). The foundation of Wolffian rational psychology was the doctrine of the soul as a "monad" or simple substance (Baumgarten, *Metaphysica* §§ 402–5, 742, 755). Compare also Leibniz, *Principles of Nature and Grace* §§ 1–2. Leibniz, *Die philosophische Schriften*, ed. C. I. Gerhardt (Berlin: Akademie Verlag, 1875–90), 6:509–606. (References to Leibniz will be to the Gerhardt edition, cited either by section [§] number within a given work or by volume:page.)

24 Here Kant refers to the arguments for the soul's simplicity put forward in the Wolffian tradition. The simplicity of the soul was also central to its claim to immortality, since natural perishability was taken to consist in the dissolution of a composite. See Wolff, *Psychologia rationalis* § 3, *Gesammelte Werke* (Hildesheim: Olms, 1972) II.6; Baumgarten, *Metaphysica* §§ 745–7, 756–7. At this point Wolff and Baumgarten were following Leibniz, *Monadology* (6:607–23) §§ 1–6, 14. But Adickes and Kemp Smith (*A Commentary to Kant's Critique of Pure Reason* [New York: Humanities, 1962], pp. 458–9) have argued that Kant was thinking of the arguments used by Moses Mendelssohn (1729–1786) in his dialogue *Phädon* (1767), *Gesammelte Schrifte*. Jubiläumsausgabe. (Berlin: Akademie Verlag, 1932) 3:69–73. See note 40 below.

25 For other treatments of this argument, see R 4234 (1769–70? 17:470–1) and *Metaphysik Mrongovius*, 29:905.

26 Important discussions of the immortality of the soul include R 4238–40 (1769–70, 17:472–5) and *Metaphysik Mrongovius*, 29:910–20.

27 For a precursor of Kant's sense of "person" here, see Leibniz, *New Essays Concerning Human Understanding*, preface G 6:58, and James Beattie, *An Essay on the Nature and Immutability of Truth*, chapter II, section 2 (Edinburgh: William Creech, 1776), p. 50. Because the German translation of the latter work was the source for Kant's knowledge of Hume's views about the self, he can be presumed to be familiar with this passage. A clear statement of the paralogism here analyzed can be found at R 4933 (1776–78, 18:32). R 5646 (1785–88, 18:295) suggests that only morality can provide a secure basis for identity of the self. The most famous modern discussion of personal identity was John Locke, *Essay concerning Human Understanding* (1690), ed. P. Nidditch (Oxford: Clarendon, 1975) Book II, ch. 27, §§ 9–29, pp. 335–48. Locke held that personal identity depends on "sameness of consciousness," but distinguished this from sameness of substance. A purer example of the position Kant is criticizing is articulated by Leibniz in his discussion of Locke in the *New Essays on Human Understanding* (first published in 1765). Leibniz agrees with Locke that "consciousness or the sense of *I* proves moral or personal identity," but criticizes Locke for holding that it proves only "apparent identity" and thinking that "apparent identity could be preserved in the absence of any real identity," i.e. identity of substance (Leibniz, *New Essays on Human Understanding*, G 6:236). Leibniz insists that immaterial beings or spirits necessarily perceive their existence

through time and hence that the memory which provides an epistemic guarantee of personal identity also provides a guarantee of substantial identity as well. Awareness of the substantial continuity of oneself is for him so immediate that doubting the veracity of memory regarding it would be tantamount to skepticism about every matter of fact, a doubt so extreme as to render skepticism itself pointless (Leibniz, *New Essays on Human Understanding* 6:238–9). Baumgarten presents two accounts of personal identity, the first grounding it on "intellectual memory" (*Metaphysica* § 641), the second on free will (*Metaphysica* § 756).

28 See the related argument at R 5650 (1785–89, 18:298–302).

29 The reference is to those, such as Cratylus, who followed the famous sayings of Heraclitus, *panta rhei* ("Everything flows") (Fragment 40) and "You can't step into the same river twice, for other waters are always flowing on" (Fragment 48). Cf. Plato, *Cratylus* 402a; Aristotle, *Metaphysics* 1010a7.

30 This refers to Descartes's thesis that objects of the senses may be doubted though my existence as a thinking thing cannot be (*Oeuvres de Descartes*, ed. C. Adam and P. Tannery [Paris: Cerf, 1897–1913] 6:17–21, 25–6). But Kant may also have in mind Descartes's insistence that he does not perceive bodies with his senses, but with his mind (*Meditations, Oeuvres de Descartes* 6:31–3).

31 Compare this analysis with R 5400 (1776–78? 1773–75? 18:189).

32 This is the postulate of empirical thought regarding actuality (A218/B266).

33 According to the second-edition "Refutation of Idealism" (B 274), Kant associates "dogmatic" idealism with Berkeley and "skeptical" or "problematic" idealism with Descartes. Cf. also *Prolegomena to Any Future Metaphysics*, 4:375. Baumgarten defines an "idealist" as someone "admitting only spirits into this world" (*Metaphysica* § 402, cf. § 438).

34 A reference to the antinomies, probably in particular to the second antinomy, which threatens us with a contradiction regarding the divisibility of matter (A434–45/B462–73).

35 See R 5457 (1776–78, 18:187–8) and especially R 5461 (1776–78? 18:189).

36 Regarding mind–body interaction, there were three main systems discussed in the Wolffian tradition, and mentioned here by Kant. (1) The system of physical influence held that minds and bodies causally influence one another by their natural powers. It was associated with Descartes, adopted by Locke, and endorsed by Wolff (*Psychologia rationalis* [1728], *Gesammelte Schriften* II.6 §§ 558–88) and Baumgarten (*Metaphysica* §§ 763–6); it was defended by Kant's teacher, Martin Knutzen, in *Commentatio philosophica de commercio mentis et corporis per influxum physicum explicando* (Philosophical Treatise concerning the Interaction between Mind and Body Explained by Physical Influence) (1735). Kant criticizes this system in the inaugural dissertation (1770) §§ 16–22 (2:406–10). (2) The system of preestablished harmony is that of Leibniz; it maintains that bodies and minds each follow their own laws, but their actions are coordinated by God in his choice of a maximally harmonious world (see *Monadology* §§ 78–81). It is critically discussed by Wolff (*Psychologia rationalis* §§ 612–42) and Baumgarten (*Metaphysica* § 768). (3) The "system of supernatural assistance" probably

refers to the occasionalism of some later Cartesians, such as Arnold Geulincx (1624–1669) and Geraud Cordemoy (d. 1684), but developed most fully and originally by Nicolas Malebranche (1638–1715) (*On the Search for Truth* [(1675)], tr. T. M. Lennon and P. J. Olscamp [Columbus: Ohio University Press, 1980] 6.2.3, pp. 446–52). It holds that bodies and minds have no natural power to influence one another, but each influences the other through the mediation of God's causality. Occasionalism was rejected by Wolff (*Psychologia rationalis* §§ 589–611) and Baumgarten (*Metaphysica* § 767).

37   "Pillars of Hercules" was the name commonly given in antiquity to the headlands, Gibraltar to the north and Jebel Musa to the south, at the eastern end of the Strait of Gibraltar, which opens on the Atlantic Ocean.

38   Reflections bearing on the revision of the "Paralogisms" for the second edition include R 5650 (1785–88, 18:298–302) and R 5811 (1783–84, 18:360).

39   See B 288–94 and A 235–60/ B 294–315.

40   Moses Mendelssohn, *Phädon oder über die Unsterblichkeit der Seele* (Berlin: Fr. Nicolai, 1767). Mendelssohn, *Gesammelte Schriften.* Jubiläumsausgabe. (Berlin: Akademie Verlag, 1932) 3:5–129. In the first edition of this work, Mendelssohn's reasoning in favor of immortality of the soul is presented in the following representative passage:

"If we say," Socrates went on, "that the soul dies, then we must suppose one of the following: Either all its powers and faculties, its actions and passions, suddenly cease, they vanish suddenly in an instant; or the soul, like the body, suffers gradual transformations, countless changes of dress, proceeding in a constant series, and in this series there is an epoch where it is no longer a human soul, but has become something other than that, becoming dust, air, plant or a part of another animal. Is there a third case, another way in which the soul can die, besides *suddenly* or *gradually?*"

"No," replied Cebes. "This division completely exhausts the possibilities."

"Good," said Socrates, "then those who still doubt whether the soul is mortal may choose, if they care to, between its suddenly vanishing or its ceasing bit by bit to be what it was . . .

"*Perhaps the soul perishes suddenly, vanishes in an instant.* In itself this kind of death is possible. But can it be produced by nature?

"Not at all, if what we have admitted is true, that nature can produce no annihilation. And have we rightly admitted this?" asked Socrates. "Between *being* and *non-being* there is a terrible gap, which can never be leapt over by nature, which works gradually . . . No, Cebes, let us sooner fear that the sun will change into ice, than fear a fundamentally evil action, *annihilation through a miracle,* from the Self-sufficient Good . . .

"But now we have seen that there is no determinate moment when one can say, 'The animal dies *now.*' The dissolution of the animal machine has long since begun before its effects become visible; for there never fail to be animal movements opposing the preservation of the whole; only they decrease bit by bit until finally the movements of the parts no longer harmonize in a single final end, but each of them has taken on its particular final end, and then the machine has dissolved . . .

"Thus if the death of the body is also to be the death of the soul, then there must be no moment in which one can say 'Now the soul vanishes,' but the soul must decrease in force and effectiveness bit by bit, just as the movements in the parts of the machine cease to harmonize to a single final end . . .

"Thus we only have to investigate whether the inner powers of the soul could not perish gradually, just as the parts of a machine separate . . .

"The body dies: that means, all movements now no longer appear to aim at life and the preservation of the whole . . . And the soul? my Cebes, where will we put it? Its machine is corrupted. The parts left over from it no longer belong to *it* and do not constitute a whole that could have a soul. Here there are no longer any organs for sensing or tools for feeling, through which the soul could attain to any sensation. Is everything in it therefore to be empty and desolate? Are all its sensations, imaginings, desires and abhorrences, its inclinations and passions vanished, without leaving behind the least trace?"

"Impossible," said Cebes. "What would that be except complete annihilation? And no annihilation, as we have seen, belongs to the faculties of nature . . ." (*Phädon*. *Gesammelte Schriften* 3:69–73)

Yet the precise argument against the annihilation of the soul which Kant seems to have in mind was apparently added by Mendelssohn in an appendix to the third edition of *Phädon* in 1769:

A natural action, it has been said from time immemorial, must have a beginning, a middle and an end, that is, it must occupy a stretch of time before it is completed. This part of time may be as small as you like, but to be consistent with the nature of time, it must have moments following one after another. If the powers of nature are to produce an effect, they must approach this effect gradually and prepare for it, before it follows. But an effect that cannot be prepared, which must follow in only one instant, ceases to be natural, and cannot be produced by powers which must do everything in time. All these propositions were not unknown to the ancients, and they appear to me to be present, not without clarity, in the reasoning of Plato *about opposed states and the transition from one to the other*. Therefore I sought to put them before my readers in Plato's way, but with the clarity suitable to our time. They are quite evident to healthy reason; yet through the *doctrine of continuity* they achieve, in my opinion, a high degree of certainty. It was not reluctantly that I embraced the opportunity to acquaint my readers with this important doctrine, because they lead to correct concepts concerning the alterations of the body and the soul, without which death and life, mortality and immortality, cannot be considered from the right standpoint. (*Phädon, Gesammelte Schriften* 3:147–8)

41   This is, however, the account of clarity given by Kant himself (*Logic*, 9:33). But there he was expounding Georg Friedrich Meier (1718–1777), *Auszug aus der Vernunftlehre* (Extract from the Theory of Reasoning) (Halle, 1752), which he had used as a text since 1765 (2:310–11). Meier is presumably the sort of logician Kant has in mind here.

42   In fact, Descartes *denies* that we may infer "I exist" from "I think" by way of the general proposition "Whatever thinks exists," for precisely the reason Kant mentions here. See "Reply to Second Objections," *Oeuvres de Descartes* 7:140.

43   To this note, compare R 5661 (1788–90, 18:318–20), *Nachtrag* CLXXX to A592/B620 below (E 53, 23:42–3), and the discussion of Descartes at *Metaphysik Mrongovius*, 29:876–7. See also Leibniz's discussion of the *cogito* in *New Essays*, book IV, chapter VII § 7, G 6:411, and the treatment by Nicolaus Tetens (1736 or 1737–1807), *Philosophische Versuche über die menschliche Natur und ihre Entwicklung* (1777–78; reprint Berlin, Kant-Gesellschaft, 1913), pp. 552, 555. Wolff divided psychology into *psychologia empirica* and *psychologia rationalis*. *Psychologia empirica* begins by treating of

the soul's existence, which he grounds on the Cartesian *cogito* (*Psychologia empirica* §§ 12–15, *Gesammelte Werke* II.5 [Hildesheim: Olms, 1968]). *Psychologia rationalis* deals with the "nature and essence" of the soul, and especially the functions of the intellect (*Psychologia rationalis, Gesammelte Werke* II.6). See also Baumgarten, *Metaphysica* §§ 504–18.

44   As mentioned in note 1 above, there are a number of Kant's reflections giving evidence of his discovery of the antinomies in 1769 (e.g. R 3936–37, 17:355) and the antinomies predominate in Kant's first outlines of the "Dialectic" in R 4756–60 (1775–77, 17:699–713). Other important notes from this period are R 4742 (17:694) and R 4780 (17:725). From the 1780s, important reflections on the antinomies include R 5959–61 (18:399–401), R 5962 (1785–89, 18:401–5), R 5970 (1783–84, 18:408–9), R 5973 (1783–84, 18:411–12) and R 5979 (1785–88, 18:413–14).

45   With these two paragraphs, compare R 4454 (1772? 1773–75? 17:557).

46   "A WORLD is a series (multitude, whole) of actual finite things which are not parts of one another" (Baumgarten, *Metaphysica* § 354); "In every world there are actual parts, which are singulars connected into a whole" (*Metaphysica* § 357).

47   For the source of this principle in Wolffian cosmology, see following note.

48   "Because the parts of the world are either simultaneous or successive, if they are posited outside one another, they are connected in the world either by time or by space or by both" (Baumgarten, *Metaphysica* § 374; cf. § 238). In four successive paragraphs, Baumgarten considers the parts of the world connected in space and time (first antinomy) (*Metaphysica* § 374), connected causally (third antinomy) (*Metaphysica* § 375), connected as actual parts (second antinomy) (*Metaphysica* § 376), and as possibles forming a contingent whole (fourth antinomy) (*Metaphysica* § 377). He concludes that either there is no world, or that it must consist in a multitude or series forming a unity (*Metaphysica* § 379). This says, in effect, that if the (conditioned) members of each of the identified series are given, then the whole (the unconditioned) must also be given. At the same time, Baumgarten notes that because it is so constituted, the unity of the world is a "hypothetical unity" (*Metaphysica* § 362) as distinct from an "absolute" unity (*Metaphysica* § 76).

49   "A PROGRESS (regress) TO INFINITY is a series of contingent entities posited outside one another, of which one is the cause of the other" (Baumgarten, *Metaphysica* § 380).

50   Baumgarten argues that the world must consist of simple parts or monads (Baumgarten, *Metaphysica* §§ 392–405). Compare Leibniz, *Monadology* § 1.

51   Compare Baumgarten, *Metaphysica* §§ 388–90, which argues (no doubt with Spinoza in mind) that the world is not a substance, its parts are not accidents, and an infinite substance is not a unique substance.

52   Compare Baumgarten, *Metaphysica* §§ 358, 380–1.

53   Baumgarten emphasizes the contingency both of the parts of the world and of the world as a whole (*Metaphysica* §§ 361–64). He argues that if we suppose the world to be necessary, then we must suppose that the determination of its parts is also necessary, hence that the parts themselves must be necessary and therefore infinite (which contradicts the nature of parts) (*Metaphysica* § 361).

54 In addition to the reflections already cited in notes 1 and 44, see also R
    4090 (1769–70, 17:412), R 4134 (1769–70, 17:428–30), R 4210 (1770–77,
    17:457), R 4522 (1772–76, 17:580–1), R 4525 (1772–76, 17:582), R 4529
    (1772? 1773–75? 17:583–4), R 4708 (1773–79, 17:682–3) and R 4717
    (1773–75? 1775–77? 17:685).

55 This argument has a long history in the Western philosophical-theological
    tradition, where a number of Christian philosophers used it to demon-
    strate the origin of the world at a finite past time, contrary to the pagan
    (especially Aristotelian) view that the world had no beginning in time. But
    it is not clear from what source Kant derived it (or whether he reinvented
    it himself). The argument appears to have been first invented by John
    Philoponus (c.490–c.570). In the middle ages, it was most closely associ-
    ated with the name of St. Bonaventure (c.1217–1274). But Bonaventure
    seems to have gotten it from his older Franciscan contemporary Richard
    Rufus of Cornwall (d. after 1259), who does not seem to have known the
    works of Philoponus and may have devised the argument anew around
    1235. The argument was criticized by a number of medieval philosophers
    (notably St. Thomas Aquinas and William of Ockham) who held that the
    creation of the world at a finite past time was indemonstrable by reason
    and knowable only through revelation. Kant, however, does not appear to
    have been directly acquainted with any of these medieval sources, nor do
    we know of any specific source through which such knowledge might have
    been mediated. One early modern proponent of the argument with whose
    works Kant might have been (directly or indirectly) acquainted was the
    Cambridge theologian Richard Bentley (1662–1742): "For, consider the
    present revolution of the Earth . . . God Almighty, if he so pleaseth, may
    continue this motion to perpetuity in infinite revolutions to come; because
    futurity is inexhaustible, and can never be spent or run out by *past and pres-
    ent* moments. But then, if we look backwards from this present revolution,
    we may apprehend the impossibility of infinite revolutions on that side; be-
    cause all are *already* past, and so were once actually *present*, and conse-
    quently are finite . . . For surely we cannot conceive a preteriteness (if I
    may say so) still backwards *in infinitum*, that never was present, as we can
    endless futurity that never will be present. So that one is potentially infi-
    nite, yet nevertheless the other is actually finite" (Bentley, *Sermons Preached
    at Boyle's Lecture* [1692], ed. A. Dyce [London, 1838], p. 134).

56 Compare Kant's argument for the "First Analogy " (especially A188/B231)
    and the second-edition "Refutation of Idealism" (B275–8 and Bxxxix–xli
    note). The conclusion of this argument is the same as that of an *ad hominem*
    argument Leibniz presents against the Newtonian concept of absolute
    space (Leibniz, *Correspondence with Clarke*, 7:373).

57 "Absolute space" is an allusion to the Newtonian theory of space (cf.
    "Transcendental Aesthetic," A23/B38, B 69–72, and *Metaphysical First
    Grounds of Natural Science*, 4:481).

58 This "dogmatic" formulation is close to the negation of Baumgarten's de-
    finition of "comparative magnitude" at *Metaphysica* § 161.

59 Leibniz criticized the apparent implication of the Newtonian view, that there
    could be infinite empty space (Leibniz, *Correspondence with Clarke*, 7:368).

60 On the second antinomy, see especially R 4534 (1772–78, 17:585–6).

61 This argument bears close comparison with the opening sections of Leibniz's *Monadology:* "1. The Monad, which we shall discuss here, is nothing but a simple substance that enters into composites – simple, that is, without parts. 2. And there must be simple substances, since there are composites; for the composite is nothing more than a collection, or aggregate, of simples" (Leibniz, *Monadology* §§ 1–2).

62 This term is no doubt intended to include Leibniz (see the two previous notes) and the Wolffians (see Baumgarten, *Metaphysica* §§ 230–45, 396–405). It might also be applied to the view put forward in the *Theoria philosophiae naturalis* (Vienna, 1758) by the Ragusan Jesuit Rudjer Boscović (1711–1787). But the view criticized here actually seems closest to that held by Kant himself in his *Physical Monadology* of 1756 (1:473–88; see also *Metaphysical First Grounds of Natural Science,* 4:504).

63 The term "monad" had been used earlier by Henry More (1614–1687). But it is likely that Leibniz's most direct source was More's student Lady Anne (Finch), Viscountess Conway (1631–1679), with whose philosophy Leibniz was acquainted through her physician and publicist, and Leibniz's correspondent, Francis Mercurius van Helmont (1614–1698).

64 Numerous reflections bear specifically on the third antinomy. These include R 3922 (17:346–7), R 3976 (1769, 17:372–3), R 4225–7 (1769–70, 17:464–6), R 4338 (1770–71, 17:510–11), R 4723 (1773–75, 17:688), R 5413 (1776–78, 18:176), R 5612–19 (1778–79, 18:252–8), R 5829 (1783–84, 18:365), R 5964 (1783–84, 18:405–6), R 5972 (1780s, 18:410), and R 5976–8 (1783–84, 18:412–13).

65 The best-known doctrine of a first mover was that of Aristotle (*Physics,* book 8 (256a1–267b27), *Metaphysics,* book 12 (1071b3–1076a5)). Compare Baumgarten, *Metaphysica* § 300.

66 See R 4039 (1769–70, 17:393–4), R 4117 (1769, 17:423), R 4179–80 (1769–70, 17:445–6), R 4242–53 (1769–70, 17:476–83), R 5263 (1776–78, 18:135–6) and R 5949 (1780s, 18:397).

67 Jean-Jacques Dortous de Mairan (1678–1771) succeeded Fontenelle as perpetual secretary of the Royal Academy of Sciences in Paris in 1740 and remained in that post until his death. He wrote on a variety of subjects in physics and natural sciences, including his *Dissertation on Ice* (1715), *Physical and Historical Treatise on the Aurora Borealis* (1733), *Dissertation on the Estimation of Moving Forces of Bodies* (1741), and *Letter to Mme Chatelet on the Question of Living Forces* (1741). Mairan also published many papers in the *Journal des Scavans* and the *Recueil de l'Académie royale des sciences,* both of which he also edited. According to Ferdinand Alquié, *Oeuvres philosophiques de Emanuel Kant* (Paris: Gallimard, 1980–86), 1:1692, the treatise referred to here was published in the *Recueil* in 1747. However, we have been unable to verify this reference.

68 One of the first reflections to connect theoretical propositions and the interest of practical reason in this way is R 5109 (1776–78, 18:90–2).

69 Kant opposes Plato and Epicurus again regarding the object of knowledge (A853–4/B881–2). Cf. *Logic,* 9:29–30.

70 J. H. Lambert (1728–1777), "Memoir to the Berlin Academy on Transcen-

dental Magnitudes" (1768), in *Beiträge zum Gebrauch der Mathematik und deren Anwendung* (Contributions to the Use of Mathematics and its Application) (1766–72).

71 Kant also uses this formulation at R 5639 (1780–81? 1778–89? 1785–88? 18:276–9).

72 To this paragraph, compare R 5961 (1780s? 1776–79? 18:400–1) and R 5962 (1785–89, 18:401–5).

73 Zeno of Elea (c. 500–440 B.C.), reportedly a younger contemporary of Parmenides of Elea (Plato, *Parmenides* 127a–b). Zeno is best known for the four paradoxes of continuity, infinity, and motion discussed by Aristotle (*Physics* 9, 239b5–240a9). For Plato's remark, referred to here by Kant, see *Parmenides* 127d–128c (cf. *Phaedrus* 261d).

74 See R 5902 (1785–89, 18:379) and R 5903 (1780s? 1776–79? 18:379–80).

75 The distinction between infinite and indefinite is drawn by Baumgarten (*Metaphysica* § 248). Cf. Descartes, *Principles of Philosophy* 1.26–7 (*Oeuvres de Descartes* 8:14–15). For both Baumgarten and Descartes, the point is to reserve the property of true infinity for God alone.

76 In addition to A225/B273–4 above, see R 4618 (1772, 17:610).

77 See Baumgarten, *Metaphysica* § 159.

78 The distinction between the mathematical and dynamical antinomies and their solutions is discussed in a number of reflections: see R 5368–9 (1776–78, 18:163), R 5608 (1778–81, 18:249–51), R 5817 (1783–84, 18:362), R 5962 (1785–89, 18:401–5), R 5964 (1783–84, 18:405–6), R 5967–8 (1783–84, 18:407–8), R 6337 (1794–95, 18:657–8) and R 6421 (1790–95, 18:711).

79 Compare Baumgarten on the brute soul (*Metaphysica* §§ 792–3) and the free power of choice (*Metaphysica* §§ 712–19).

80 See note 64 above.

81 See R 5413 (1776–80s, 18:176).

82 See R 4548 (1772–75, 17:589), R 5413 (1776–80s, 18:176), R 5441 (1776–78, 18:182–3), R 5608 (1779–81, 18:249–51), R 5612–14, 5616 (1778–79, 18:252–6) and R 5618–19 (1778–79, 18:257–8).

83 This claim, which will be a major claim of Kant's *Groundwork of the Metaphysics of Morals* (1785) and *Critique of Practical Reason* (1788), is suggested as early as R 4336 (1770–71? 1769? 17:509–10). See also R 5441 (1776–78, 18:182–3) and R 5608 (1779–81, 18:249–51).

84 To this paragraph, compare R 5368–9 (1776–78, 18:163), R 5962 (1785–89, 401–5) and R 5968 (1783–84, 18:407–8).

85 In his 1763 work *The Only Possible Ground of Proof for a Demonstration of the Existence of God* (2:63–163, translation in Walford [ed.], *Theoretical Philosophy 1755–1770*, pp. 107–201), Kant had already worked out much of the criticism of the three arguments for the existence of God presented in section III of this chapter. Section II, however, criticizes a theistic argument akin to one Kant had proposed in 1763. In spite of this early origin of much of the material expounded in this chapter, however, Kant had apparently intended to discuss rational arguments for the existence of God only within the framework of the antinomies as late as the drafts of the "Dialectic" from 1775 (R 4756–60, 17:699–713), which would have meant

in effect discussing only the cosmological argument. The extensive outline of the "Dialectic" at R 5553 (1778–79? 1780–81? 221–9), however, shows that by two years later Kant had formulated the idea of a tripartite dialectic with a separate "Ideal of Pure Reason" (p. 223), thereby leading to the reincorporation into the *Critique* of the 1763 criticisms of the ontological and physico-theological arguments. In addition to the many particular reflections, especially on the ontological argument, that will be mentioned below, the reader interested in Kant's critique of rational theology should also consult the extensive set of notes on Johann August Eberhard's *Vorbereitung zur natürlichen Theologie*, preserved as R 6206–310 (1783–88, 18:489–606), and the *Lectures on the Philosophical Doctrine of Religion*, tr. A. Wood, in Di Giovanni and Wood (eds.), *Writings on Religion and Rational Theology* (New York: Cambridge University Press, 1996), pp. 335–451.

86   It was not Plato's doctrine that the ideas are the thoughts of God, but this doctrine did originate in syncretistic Platonism from the period of the Middle Academy, through the combination of Platonism with Stoicism in such thinkers as Albinus (second century B.C.). The theory of divine ideas was later adopted by Platonists as diverse as Philo of Alexandria, Plotinus, and St. Augustine, and became fundamental to later Christian interpretations of Platonism. See A. H. Armstrong (ed.), *The Cambridge History of Later Greek and Early Medieval Philosophy* (Cambridge: Cambridge University Press, 1967), pp. 64–6, 142, 245, 621.

87   A large number of reflections bear on the argument of this section. Expositions of the argument that thoroughgoing determination of the concept of any individual requires a thoroughly determinate *ens realissimum*, offered largely without criticism, can be found at R 4244–9 (1769–70, 17:477–81), R 4253 (1769–70, 17:482–3), R 4255 (1769–70, 17:484), R 4262 (1769–70? 1772–76? 17:486–7), R 4255 (1772–75, 17:695–6), R 4569–70 (1772–75, 17:597–8), R 4729 (1773–75, 17:619–20), R 5270–74 (1776–78, 18:138–40), R 5500 (1776–78, 18:199–200), R 5502–5 (1776–78, 18:200–2) and R 5522 (1776–78, 18:207–8). Criticisms of the argument turn up only in reflections subsequent to the first publication of the *Critique:* see R 6248–56 (1785–88, 18:530–3), R 6290 (1783–84, 18:558–9), R 6293 (1783–84, 18:561–2) and R 6298 (1783–84, 18:565).

88   Following Leibniz, the Wolffians held that each individual thing is individuated through its complete concept, which is determined by one and only one of every possible pair of contradictorily opposed predicates. Thus they distinguish a universal concept (which applies in principle to indefinitely many individual things) from an individual concept (which individuates an individual thing) through the fact that the former is undetermined with respect to some pairs of contradictorily opposed predicates, whereas the latter is subject to what Baumgarten calls the "principle of thoroughgoing determination" (*principium omnimodae determinatio*) (*Metaphysica* § 148). See also Wolff, *Ontologia, Gesammelte Werke* II.3, pp. 187–9; Baumgarten, *Metaphysica* §§ 53, 151, and Kant, *Logic* § 15, 9:99.

89   See A304/B 360–1; and recall that *Vernunftschluß*, here translated as "syllogism," could also be translated (more etymologically) as "inference of reason."

90　See A334–5/B391–2.

91　See A220–4/B266–72.

92　This was the line of thinking Kant himself developed in *The Only Possible Ground of Proof for a Demonstration of God's Existence* (1763), 2:77–83.

93　In *The Only Possible Ground of Proof*, Kant immediately follows his argument for a necessary being with arguments that a necessary being must be unique and wholly simple, hence one in the highest degree (2:83–4).

94　This was Kant's procedure in *The Only Possible Ground of Proof*, 2:87–92.

95　This line of argument is a form of the standard modern cosmological argument and not the novel proof in Kant's 1763 essay (see previous note). It closely resembles the proofs of a necessary God from the contingency of the world given by Wolff and his followers.

96　On this paragraph, see R 5760–4 (1783–88, 18:346–7).

97　Kant's critique of the ontological argument is in a sense the oldest part of his critical philosophy, already having been expressed *in nuce* in his 1755 *New Elucidation of the Primary Principles of Metaphysical Cognition* (1:394–5; *Theoretical Philosophy 1755–1770*, p. 15). In addition to that discussion and the one in *The Only Possible Ground of Proof*, there are many reflections to which the present section might be compared: see R 3706 (1760–64, 17:240–3), R 4659 (1772–76, 17:628–9), R 4729 (1773–75, 17:689–90), R 5231 (1776–80s, 18:126: "all existential propositions are synthetic"), R 5255 (1776–78, 18:133), R 5506 (1776–78, 18:202, which refers explicitly to "the Cartesian proof"), R 5507 (1776–78, 18:203), R 5523 (1776–79, 18:207), R 5716 (1780s? 1776–79? 18:351–2), R 5783 (1783–84, 18:353–4), R 6276 (1785–88, 18:543) and R 6389 (1790–95, 18:700–2). See also *Metaphysik Volckmann*, 28:413.

98　See note 91 above.

99　Leibniz attempted to prove that God is possible by arguing that impossibility requires a contradiction between a reality and its negation, which cannot occur in the case of a most real being. See Leibniz, *Philosophischen Schriften* 4:295–6, 7:261.

100　The ontological argument is found in Descartes, *Meditations on First Philosophy*, meditation five. See *Oeuvres de Descartes* 6:65–71, cf. 7:150, 166–7.

101　Like his criticism of the ontological argument, Kant's criticism of the cosmological argument is anticipated in *The Only Possible Ground of Proof*. In addition, see the following reflections: R 4117 (1769, 17:423), R 4587–8 (1772–76, 17:602–3), R 4597 (1772–78, 17:605), R 5505 (1776–78, 18:202), R 5530 (1776–79, 18:209), R 6378 (1785–88, 18:544–6; this is a detailed critique of Mendelssohn's attempt to revive the cosmological argument in his *Morgenstunden* [1785], section XII), R 6320 (1792–94, 18:634–5) and R 6322–4 (1792–94, 18:637–47).

102　Leibniz comes close to stating this argument at times (for example, see *Monadology* § 45). But it is more characteristic of him to argue for the necessity of God independently of the need to explain contingent things (for example, *Monadology* § 44). Kant's source for the cosmological argument seems to be not Leibniz but Wolff and his followers: Wolff, *Theologia Naturalis* (Frankfurt and Leipzig, 1730) § 69, 1:55, and *Metaphysik* (Halle, 1751) § 928, 1:574–5; Baumgarten, *Metaphysica* §§ 308–10,

Friedrich Christian Baumeister (1709–1785), *Institutiones metaphysicae* (1738) § 78, and Joachim Georg Darjes (1714–1791), *Elementa metaphysica* (1754), *Elementa theologiae naturalis* § 44. Kant's first critique of this argument is to be found in *The Only Possible Ground of Proof* (2:157–9).

103   See R 6331 (1793–94, 18:651–4 at p. 653).

104   See R 6297 (1783–84, 18:563–5).

105   See A606/ B634.

106   "But in that earnest place / Him who holds nothing back / Eternity holds fast in its strong arms." Viktor Albrecht von Haller (1708–1777), Swiss physiologist and poet. "Unvollkommenes Gedicht über Ewigkeit" (Imperfect Poem on Eternity) (1736), *Hallers Gedichte*, ed. Ludwig Hirzel (Bibliothek älterer Schriftwerke der deutschen Schweitz, 1882), 3:151. The above lines from the poem are quoted by Kant in "The End of All Things" (1794), 8:327; cf. also 2:151.

107   There are fewer reflections on the criticism of the argument from design than on the others; see R 5631 (1778–80s, 18:262–3). However, the *Critique of Judgment*'s discussion of moral theology is based on an antecedent critique of physico-theology; see especially § 84 (5:436–42).

108   In *The Only Possible Ground of Proof*, Kant refuses to regard physico-theology as any sort of *demonstration* of God's existence (2:159–62). He rather considers physico-theology as a way of considering nature, and subjects "the usual method of physico-theology" to extensive criticism (2:116–23), suggesting another method, better suited to the needs of natural science, in its place (2:123–37).

109   Compare Leibniz, *Monadology* §§ 66–9. In *The Only Possible Ground of Proof*, Kant was also impressed by the microscopic researches of John Hill (c. 1716–1775), which had discovered "numerous animal species in a single drop of water, predatory kinds equipped with instruments of destruction, . . . ; when I contemplate the intrigues, the violence, the scenes of commotion in a single part of matter, and when I direct my gaze upwards to the immeasurable spaces of the heavens teeming with worlds as with specks of dust, . . . no human language can express the feelings aroused by such a thought" (2:117 note). Hill's chief work was *A General Natural History* (1748–52), but the research Kant would have known was published in the *Hamburger Magazin* between 1753 and 1758.

110   Compare the presentation of the argument from design by Hume's Cleanthes:

> "Look round the world, contemplate the whole and every part of it: you will find it to be nothing but one great machine, subdivided into an infinite number of lesser machines, which again admit of subdivisions to a degree beyond what human senses and faculties can trace or explain. All these various machines, and even their most minute parts, are adjusted to each other with an accuracy which ravishes into admiration all the men who have ever contemplated them." (Hume, *Dialogues concerning Natural Religion*, ed. A. W. Colver and J. V. Price, part II [Oxford: Clarendon Press, 1976], pp. 161)

Kant became acquainted with the German translation of Hume's *Dialogues* about the time of the composition of the *Critique of Pure Reason*, but it is not clear whether he was acquainted with it by the time he wrote this section. He was certainly acquainted with it by the time of his *Lectures on the Philosophical Doctrine of Religion* (probably 1783), 27:1062–4.

111 Surely this is an allusion to the title of Kant's own *The Only Possible Ground of Proof* (1763), which, however, not only intends that the title describe an argument different from the ontological argument, but even contains Kant's first statement of his critique of the ontological argument (2:72–7, 156–7).

112 See R 4113 (1769? 1770–71? 17:420–2) for an early sketch of the several options for theology discussed in this section.

113 Of course, Kant will explore the idea of a practical foundation for theology much more fully in the "Canon of Pure Reason" below, as well as in the *Critique of Practical Reason* and *Critique of Judgment*. But see also R 5624 (1778–79? 1780–81? 259–60) and R 6086–117 (1783–88, 18:445–60).

114 Kant's assessment of physico-theology now seems to agree more with that found in *The Only Possible Ground of Proof*. See note 108 above.

115 There are few notes bearing on this appendix; for one, see R 5602 (1778–80s, 18:247).

116 This principle is now commonly called "Ockham's razor" after William of Ockham (c.1288–1350). Ockham certainly did employ some such principle often, but the closest formulation to the one Kant quotes is *"pluralitas non est ponenda sine necessitate"* (plurality is not to be posited without necessity). The wording quoted by Kant is derived from the later scholastic Ioannes Poncius (d. 1660), who refers to *"axioma vulgare . . . frequenter un-untur Scholastici: Non sunt multiplicanda entia sine necessitate"* (the common axiom frequently enunciated by the scholastics: Entities are not to be multiplied without necessity), *Commentarii Theologici quibus Io. Duns Scoti Quaestiones in libros Sent.* III d.34 (Paris, 1661), IV:387. As this citation (to a commentary on John Dun Scotus) would suggest, the principle was enunciated and employed by Scotus before it was ever used by Ockham. But it became especially associated with Ockham's name, doubtless because he was well known for his ontological parsimony and reductionist analyses – since he even frequently used the principle he derived from Scotus to criticize Scotus himself. The original source of the principle was Aristotle (*Physics* I:4 [188a17–18], I:6 [189a14–15], *Topics* VIII:11 [162a24–5]). Cf. Rega Wood, *Ockham on the Virtues* (West Lafayette, In: Purdue, 1997), pp. 20, 36.

117 Wit (*Witz, ingenium*) is an innate talent of the mind. It takes two forms: *ingenium comparans*, a talent for comparing and assimilating things that are superficially different, and *ingenium argutans*, a talent for making subtle distinctions. In this passage, he seems to have the former sort of wit in mind, since it is the power of discrimination which sets limits to it. Cf. *Anthropology* § 54, 7:220.

118 This formulation occurs already at R 5080 (1776–78, 18:81).

119 "The **Law of Continuity** states that nature leaves no gaps in the orderings she follows, though not all individuals belong to the same orderings"

(Leibniz, *New Essays on Human Understanding* G 6:307). This principle is closely related to the formula saying that God always does things in the most perfect way, involving the greatest variety combined with the greatest order. See *Discourse on Metaphysics* §§ 5–6, 4:430–2; *Principles of Nature and Grace* §§ 3, 10; *Monadology* § 58.

120 Charles Bonnet (1726–1793) was a Swiss naturalist. The work referred to is *Contemplation de la nature* (Amsterdam: Chez Marc-Michel Ray, 1764), which Kant probably knew in its German version: *Betrachtungen über die Natur*, tr. Johann Daniel Titus (Leipzig: Junius, 1766), pp. 29–85.

121 In biology, "palingenesis" was used to refer to the process by which an organism metamorphoses from one stage to another in the course of its life cycle. (The term was used in this sense, for example, by Bonnet, see previous note.) But it also meant "metempsychosis," or the transmigration of a soul from one life to another, and it appears to be in this sense that Kant uses the term here. The relation between the two senses was discussed by Leibniz, *New System of Nature*, 4:479–80, *Monadology* §§ 72–74. See also Baumgarten, *Metaphysica* § 704.

122 For the explanation of this phrase, see A510–12/B538–40.

123 See "Antinomy of Pure Reason," section eight, A508–16/B536–44.

124 Compare: "As for the future, we must not, with the quietists, stand ridiculously with arms folded, awaiting that which God will do, according to the sophism which the ancients called λογον ἀεργον, the lazy reason" (Leibniz, *Discourse on Metaphysics* § 4, G 4:430). "Quietism" is a form of Christian spirituality, influential in the seventeenth century, which urges the wickedness and futility of all human effort and advocates complete resignation to the will of God. Its best-known advocates were Miguel de Molinos (1640–1697), Jeanne Marie Guyon (1648–1717), and François de Salignac de la Mothe Fénelon (1650–1715), Archbishop of Cambrai. Quietism was a consistent target of Leibniz's criticism. For the source of the term *ignava ratio* and its condemnation by "the ancients," see the following note.

125 "This kind of reasoning is justly called lazy or inert, because with the same reasoning one would suppress every activity in life" (*De fato* 12–13 [28–30]). Cicero is objecting to Chrysippus's Stoic doctrine of fate. This allusion is employed in Leibniz, *Theodicy* § 55. Leibniz's use of the Greek λογον ἀεργον, suggests an earlier (Greek) source, but apparently only the target (Stoicism), and not the epithet itself, was Greek.

126 ὑστηρον προτερον refers broadly to the error of putting first that which should come later ("putting the cart before the horse"), or more narrowly, in logic, to the methodological error of proving first what should have been proved later.

127 See "Antinomy of Pure Reason," section four, A476–84/B504–12.

128 See above, notes to "Analytic of Principles," note 111.

Doctrine of method

1 Kant alludes, of course, to the biblical story of Babel (Genesis 11.1–9).

2 On these divisions of the transcendental doctrine of method, see R 4858

(1776–78, 18:11), R 4865 (1776–78, 18:14), R 4986 (1776–78, 18:52), R 4988–9 (18:1776–78, 18:52–3), R 5039 (1776–78, 18:70), R 5044 (1776–78, 18:71), and R 5074 (1776–78, 18:180).

3   There is an ambiguity in the definition of "practical logic" in Kant's paradigm of a scholastic logic textbook, Georg Friedrich Meier's *Auszug aus der Vernunftlehre* (Halle, 1752), which foreshadows the complex agenda of the present "Doctrine of Method." Meier initially defines *logica practica* or "the practical doctrine of reason" as concerning the "particular ways in which the rules of learned cognition and learned presentation are applied" (§ 7, 17:72–3), which Kant is here arguing is not a part of logic proper but rather calls for philosophical reflection on the applicability of concepts of the understanding and reason. This is the initial concern of the "Doctrine of Method." Later, however, Meier writes that "**A cognition is practical** (*cognitio practica*) insofar as it can move us in a noticeable way to do or omit an action" (§ 216, 17:516). This suggests that "practical logic" has to do not with the application of theoretical concepts but rather with rules for action, or what Kant comes to call practical rather than theoretical reason; and Kant will also broach the foundations of his moral theory in the "Doctrine of Method," above all in the section entitled the "Canon of Pure Reason," thus suggesting that it is ultimately his moral philosophy and not merely his transcendental reflection which is the proper successor to the "practical logic" of the schools.

4   On the general concept of a "discipline," see R 5089 (1776–78, 18:80).

5   The contrast between mathematical and philosophical method was one of Kant's oldest themes, and a major element in his campaign against previous forms of rationalism. For a major early statement, see the 1764 prize essay *Inquiry concerning the Distinctness of the Principles of Natural Theology and Morals* (2:273–301). In this work, Kant argued that mathematics yields synthetic propositions and philosophy analytic ones, a view which the "Transcendental Aesthetic" of this *Critique* has revoked; but in the present section he retains another main claim of the earlier work, that mathematical proofs proceed by the construction of particular mathematical objects while philosophical arguments are not constructive and determinate, but yield only more general principles and procedures for cognitive inquiry (see also the contrast between mathematical and philosophical analogies at A179–80/B222–3). For other statements of the contrast between mathematical and philosophical methods, see R 1634 (1752–56, 16:53–5); R 4445 (1772, 17:552–4); R 5583 (1778–80s, 18:241), R 5593 (1778–80s, 18:243–4), and R 5645 (1785–88? 1780–84? 18:287–95, at pp. 290–1).

6   The proof Kant is describing is found in Euclid's *Elements*, book I, proposition 32.

7   Kant is not here distinguishing between the *concept* of quantity and specific magnitudes, as he often does, but rather between the more determinate magnitudes of geometry (e.g., 180°) and the abstract magnitudes of algebra (e.g., $5x$ or x^n).

8   On Kant's theory of definition, see the Jäsche *Logic*, §§ 99–109 (*Lectures on Logic*, pp. 631–6), and corresponding passages in the lectures on logic, including *Blomberg Logic* (*Lectures on Logic*, pp. 211–19), *Vienna Logic* (*Lectures on Logic*, pp. 356–66), and *Dohna-Wundlacken Logic* (*Lectures on Logic*, pp.

489–93). Among Kant's notes, see R 2911–68 (various periods, 16:572–89) and R 2993–3008 (1769–80s, 16:606–11).

9   Kant's conception of "arbitrarily thought" concepts here is similar to Locke's conception of ideas of mixed modes, which are always "adequate," because "not being intended for Copies of Things really existing, but for Archetypes made by the Mind," a mixed mode is "referred to nothing else but it self" (*Essay concerning Human Understanding*, book II, chapter xxxi, § 3).

10 Kant is referring to the technological challenge in the eighteenth century of making a clock precise enough for computation of longitude, a task so difficult that the prize of £20,000 offered for its successful accomplishment by the British parliament in 1714 was not fully awarded until 1773. For a detailed account, see John Noble Wilford, *The Mapmakers* (New York: Knopf, 1981), pp. 130–6.

11 See R 2920–8 (1769–75, 16:576–9) and R 2950 (1778–80s, 16:585).

12 Here Kant is using "characteristic" (*characteristisch*) in the sense of a computational method in which concepts are assigned numerical values, the sense underlying Leibniz's project of a "universal characteristic," in which all questions could be solved by analysis by assigning a numerical value to all concepts (see, e.g., Leibniz's draft "Preface to a Universal Characteristic" of 1678–79, in Ariew and Garber, pp. 5–10).

13 Kant here refers to the "Antinomy of Pure Reason," of course.

14 Johann Georg Sulzer (1720–1779), Wolffian philosopher and director of the philosophical section of the Berlin Academy of Sciences, now remembered primarily for his work in aesthetics, especially *Unterredungen über die Schönheit der Natur* (Berlin, 1750) and *Allgemeine Theorie der schönen Künste* (Leipzig, 1771–74), where he extended Baumgarten's approach into an even more psychological theory that the primary object of enjoyment in aesthetic experience is the state of our own cognitive condition. Sulzer was the translator of Hume's first *Enquiry* (1755), and also the author of the Berlin Academy prize question for 1763 in response to which Kant's 1764 *Inquiry* was written, as well as one of the original critics of Kant's theory of the ideality of time in the inaugural dissertation. The present reference is to Sulzer's *Vermischte Schriften* of 1773.

15 Kant is obviously referring to the arguments of Hume's posthumously published *Dialogues concerning Natural Religion* (1779). The *Dialogues* were published in German in 1781, in a translation by the Königsberg writer Johann Georg Hamann (1730–1788) who, like his follower Friedrich Heinrich Jacobi (1743–1819), enlisted Hume in the cause of his own dogmatic fideism. Because of his earlier connection with Hamann as well as his interest in Hume, Kant would certainly have read Hamann's translation immediately upon publication, if not indeed prior to it.

16 Joseph Priestley (1733–1804), English dissenting minister, teacher, scientist, and philosopher. As a scientist, Priestley's major accomplishment was the isolation of oxygen, although it was left to Cavendish and Lavoisier to interpret the theoretical significance of Priestley's discovery. As a philosopher, he was a defender of the associationism of David Hartley (1705–57), and defended materialism, with the consequence that immortality could not be a natural condition of mankind, and determinism, especially in two works of

1777, *Disquisitions Relating to Matter and Spirit* and *The Doctrine of Philosophical Necessity Illustrated*. The first of Priestley's works to appear in German was apparently his *History of the Corruptions of Christianity* in 1782, so Kant presumably knew about his philosophical views from reviews when writing the *Critique*. However, Kant had already mentioned Priestley in R 5021 (1776–78, 18:63), characterizing him along with Locke as an empiricist.

17 Here Kant first alludes to Hobbes's diagnosis of the state of nature as given in *Leviathan*, book I, chap. XIII (see also *De Cive*, chap. I, § XII) and to Hobbes's formulation of the second "Fundamental Law of Nature" in chap. XIV, and then anticipates his own formulation of the "Universal Principle of Right" in the introduction to the "Doctrine of Right" in the *Metaphysics of Morals*, § C (6:230).

18 To this section compare the long note R 5645 (1785–88? 1780–84? 18:287–95).

19 Hume's assertion that the principle of our causal inferences is "Custom or Habit" would have been best known to Kant from *An Enquiry concerning Human Understanding*, section V ("Skeptical Solution of these Doubts"), part I. The *Enquiry* was first translated into German by J. G. Sulzer in 1755.

20 For some comments on the necessary conditions for an hypothesis, see R 5560 (1778–81, 18:233–4) and R 5570 (1778–81, 18:236).

21 Here Kant may be alluding to his ironic attack on Swedenborgian spiritualism in *Dreams of a Spirit-Seer* (1766), e.g., 2:332–4; in *Theoretical Philosophy, 1755–1770*, pp. 319–21, as well as to his attack on the Leibnizian conception of substances as monads in the "Amphiboly of the Concepts of Reflection" above.

22 Here Kant recapitulates his criticism of the inference from the simplicity of the representation of the self to the simplicity of the self as object in the second "Paralogism of Pure Reason"; see A 355–6 and B 407–8.

23 See Kant's own proof in *The New Elucidation of the First Principles of Metaphysical Cognition*, prop. VIII, 1:396; in *Theoretical Philosophy, 1755–1770*, p. 17.

24 Kant defines *modus ponens* in the *Heschel Logic* as inferring *a positione antecedens ad positionem consequentis*, or inferring from the positing of the antecedent to the positing of the consequence (*Lectures on Logic*, p. 405). This seems to be the same as the usual modern definition of *modus ponens* as the rule of inference that if p and $p \rightarrow q$ then q. However, the modern formulation is not understood to have the consequence that Kant imputes to it, namely that a proposition p can be known to be true only if all of its consequences ($q, r, \ldots$) are known to be true.

25 Here Kant's definition is incomplete but he does not seem to be departing from the customary interpretation of *modus tollens*. This is usually understood as the rule of inference that if $p \rightarrow q$ and *not-q* then *not-p*, which is precisely what Kant takes it to imply. Kant defines *modus tollens* as inferring *a remotione consequentis ad remotionem antecedentis*, i.e., from the removal (or denial) of the consequent to that of the antecedent, in *Heschel Logic* (*Lectures on Logic*, p. 405).

26 At this late stage in the book, the claim that reason may have a canon in its practical but not in its theoretical use may seem like an afterthought, but at

least in the second edition Kant's preface reveals that one of the chief objectives of the entire enterprise has been to prepare the ground for this claim (see B xxv). Numerous notes also reveal the important position of this claim: see, for example, R 4241 (1770–71? 17:475–6), R 4459 (1772, 17:559–60), R 4461 (1772, 17:560–1), R 4849 (1776–78, 18:5–8, at p. 6), and R 5637 (1780–81, 18:268–78, especially p. 273). See also the series of notes from 1783–84 labeled by Kant "On moral theology" at R 6086–917 (18:445–60).

27 On the different concepts of freedom, see *Groundwork of the Metaphysics of Morals*, section III (4:446–8), and R 4225–7 (1769–70, 17:444–6), R 4548–50 (1772–75, 17:589–90), and R 6076–7 (1785–88, 18:443). On the claim that transcendental freedom is necessarily incomprehensible, which is of quite early origin, see R 4334 (1770–71? 1769? 1773–75? 17:508–9) and R 4338 (1770–71? 1769? 1773–75? 17:510–11).

28 Of course, the content of the moral law will be discussed at length in the *Groundwork of the Metaphysics of Morals*, section II, and the *Critique of Practical Reason*, §§ 1–8. But see also the interesting notes at R 5445–6 (1776–78, 18:184).

29 This will be discussed at length in Kant's subsequent works, including the "Dialectic" of the *Critique of Practical Reason* (5:107–141), the "Doctrine of Method" of the "Critique of Teleological Judgment" in the *Critique of Judgment*, §§ 83–4, 86–7, (5:429–36, 442–53), and *Religion within the Boundaries of Pure Reason*, preface (6:6–8n.). See also Kant's notes from 1783–89 at R 6108–9 (18:456–7), R 6113 (18:459), R 6132–3 (18:464–5), and, from the 1790s, R 6443 (19:718–19).

30 *Reich*; usually translated as "kingdom," the translation by "realm" (or "empire") better connotes the idea of a body of subjects who are themselves autonomous under the leadership of a higher rules who does not undermine their autonomy.

31 Here Kant refers to Leibniz's essay *On the Principles of Nature and Grace, based on Reason*, written in 1714 and first published posthumously in the French journal *L'Europe savante* in 1718.

32 Compare this definition of a maxim with that offered in the *Groundwork*, 4:420–1n. The present definition makes it clearer than the *Groundwork* does that an agent can adopt an objectively valid law as his subjectively valid maxim, which any coherent interpretation of Kant's ethical theory requires.

33 See R 4996 (1776–78, 18:55), R 5495 (1776–78, 18:198–9), and R 6314 (1790–91, 18:616–17).

34 The anti-voluntarist argument expressed here was long a part of Kant's moral philosophy, and central to the conception of morality that he conveyed to his students in his lectures on ethics; see, for instance, *Moralphilosophie Collins*, 27:274–9; in Immanuel Kant, *Lectures on Ethics*, edited by Peter Heath and J. B. Schneewind (Cambridge: Cambridge University Press, 1997), pp. 65–69. The rejection of voluntarism, that is, the view that moral laws are such simply because they are willed by God rather than because of their inherent rationality, was a centerpiece of the Enlightenment in both Germany (where it was advanced by Christian Wolff) and Britain, where it was argued by Anthony Ashley Cooper, third earl of Shaftesbury, prior to 1699, when John Toland published a pirated edition of Shaftes-

bury's *An Inquiry Concerning Virtue, or Merit;* see book I, part III, section II (in the edition by David Walford [Manchester: Manchester University Press, 1971], p. 30).

35 There are numerous texts bearing on the argument of this section. First of all, see the Jäsche *Logic,* introduction section IX (*Lectures on Logic,* pp. 570–88); then see R 2450 and 2451 (1764–68, 16:373–5), R 2452 and 2454 (1769–70, 16:375–6), R 2457–62 (1770–75, 16:377–81), R 2477 (1780s, 16:387), R 2479–80 (1780s, 16:388), R 2486 (1780s, 16:389), R 2492 (1780s, 16:392–3), R 2493 (1790s, 16:393), R 2793 (1790s, 16:513–15), and R 5645 (1785–88? 1780–84? 18:287–95).

36 In a number of notes, Kant makes clear that practical believing cannot be equated with theoretical belief in a mere probability: see R 6108–10 (1783–89, 18:456–8), R 6280 (1785–88, 18:546–8), and R 2495 (1790s, 16:393–4).

37 Here Kant presumably alludes to Pascal's wager; see his *Pensées,* nos. 223, 418 (Lafuma numbering).

38 See R 2630 (1780s, 16:443), R 2692 (1780s, 16:472), R 2714 (1773–76, 16:480–1), and R 2793 (1790s, 16:513–15).

39 I.e., spontaneous generation; here Kant is again using a biological theory that still retained credence for his simile.

40 The ensuing conception of historical cognition, together with the claim that someone may have only historical cognition of a rational body of truths if he himself has only learned it from another, derives from Wolff; see *Discursus praeliminaris de philosophia in genere* (1728), e.g., §§ 3, 8, 22–4; translation by Richard J. Blackwell, *Preliminary Discourse on Philosophy in General* (Indianapolis: Bobbs-Merrill, 1963), pp. 3, 5, 13–14.

41 By this Kant means the first chapter of the "Doctrine of Method," i.e., the "Discipline of Pure Reason."

42 Here Kant is obviously alluding to Plato's theory of mathematical learning in the *Meno* (82b–86a), although of course he has replaced Plato's theory of recollection with his own view that the source of mathematical knowledge is *a priori* intuition.

43 In *Emile,* book III, Rousseau argues that the child learns philosophy best by solving practical tasks and not by being glued to books (in the translation by Allan Bloom [New York: Basic Books, 1979], p. 177). Perhaps Kant had this thought in mind in the present paragraph.

44 For the classical formulation of this characterization of metaphysics, see Aristotle, *Metaphysics,* I (A), 1 (981b25–982a2); Kant himself characterized the subject-matter of metaphysics in these terms in *A New Elucidation of the First Principles of Metaphysical Cognition* of 1755 (1:387); in *Theoretical Philosophy, 1755–1770,* p. 5.

45 Here Kant again seems to have Wolff in mind, who sometimes suggests that philosophical knowledge is just more general than specific historical knowledge; see *Discursus praeliminaris,* § 43; Blackwell, pp. 26–7.

46 Here Kant is referring to the Wolffian distinction between ontology or general metaphysics as the general science of what is possible, i.e., the categories of things, and special metaphysics or rational theology, cosmology, and psychology, as the most general science of what actually exists. See *Discursus praeliminaris,* § 29; Blackwell, p. 17.

47   Here Kant is referring to the Wolffian distinction between rational cosmology and rational theology. See *Discursus praeliminaris*, §§ 56, 47, 59; Blackwell, pp. 33–5.

48   Here Kant is subsuming rational physics and rational psychology under the general title of rational physiology, suggesting that there are constructive doctrines of rational physics and psychology, expounding the *a priori* conditions of empirical judgments in physics and psychology, that can replace the merely dialectical transcendent doctrines of rational cosmology and rational psychology (as well as rational theology) which he has already rejected in the "Dialectic." However, although Kant was to go on to produce his "rational physics" in the *Metaphysical Foundations of Natural Science* of 1786, there he would deny that any rational psychology (*Seelenwissenschaft*) at all is possible, on the ground that inner sense, unlike outer sense, does not yield to mathematization, and thus there can be no genuine science of inner sense (see 4:471). But that oft-cited argument is undercut by the present paragraph, especially Kant's footnote, which distinguishes between the *a priori* principles of *rational* physics and the mathematical principles of *general* physics, which are in fact underwritten by the principles of rational physics; for there could still be *a priori* principles of inner sense, underwriting the *a priori* application of concepts of causation and interaction to psychological phenomena without yielding any mathematically interesting principles for these phenomena – indeed, that is precisely what the "Analogies of Experience" and "Refutation of Idealism" have done.

49   In the systems of Wolff and Baumgarten, empirical psychology was included as a separate chapter alongside rational psychology; the latter dealt primarily with the immateriality and immortality of the soul, while the former tried to describe the experience of thought and passion. But here Kant seems to have in mind the philosophical project of Locke, in which the "original, certainty, and extent of human knowledge" were to be determined by the "historical, plain method" of introspective psychology (see *An Essay concerning Human Understanding*, bk. I, ch. i, § 2), as well as Locke's successors, both British, such as Hume, but also Germans influenced by Lockean and Humean psychology, such as Sulzer and Johann Nicolaus Tetens (1736?–1807), whose *Philosophische Versuche* (Leipzig: 1777) provided Kant with the model of empirical cognitive psychology that Kant undergirded with this transcendental psychology in the "subjective" side of the transcendental deduction of the categories, especially in the first edition.

50   Leibniz constructed this comparison between himself and Locke on the one hand and Plato and Aristotle on the other at the opening of the preface to his *New Essays concerning Human Understanding* (p. 47 in the translation by Bennett and Remnant), a book that made a deep impression on Kant at the time of its posthumous publication in 1765.

51   Kant refers here to *An Essay concerning Human Understanding*, book IV, chapter X, § 1, where Locke says of the existence of God that "its Evidence be (if I mistake not) equal to mathematical Certainty." Locke does not make the same claim about knowledge of the immortality of the mind or spirit, although this chapter does include an argument that *matter* is *not* eternal (§ 18).

GLOSSARY *

German-English

Abfolge	succession (cf. *Folge, Sukzession, Nacheinander; Reihenfolge*)
abhängig	dependent
Ablauf	lapse
ableiten	derive
Absicht	aim; intention; respect
absondern	separate
abstammen	descend
Abstammung	ancestry
absteigen	descend
abstrahieren	to abstract
abweisen	dismiss
Affinität	affinity
All	(the) all
allgemein	general; universal
Allheit	totality (cf. *Totalität*)
an sich	in itself
analytisch	analytic
Anfang	beginning
anhängend	dependent
Anlage	predisposition
annehmen	assume
anschauen	intuit
anschaulich	intuitive
Anschauung	intuition (*intuitus*)
Ansehung	regard
Anspruch	claim
anstellen	institute
antreffen	encounter; find
Anwendung	application
Art	way, species, kind, manner
Aufgabe	problem (cf. *Problem*)

* This is not meant as a complete guide to Kant's vocabulary, but only as a guide to our translation of philosophically significant terms. The vast number of obvious cognates (e.g., *Apperzeption*= apperception) are omitted.

757

aufgegeben	given as a problem
Auflösung	solution; resolution; dissolution
aufhören	cease
aufsteigen	ascend
Ausdehnung	extension
Ausdruck	expression
ausführlich	exhaustive
ausmachen	constitute; make out; settle
außer	outside; external
Äußeres	external (thing)
äußerlich	external
bedeuten	signify
Bedeutung	significance; meaning
bedingt	conditioned
Bedingung	condition
Begebenheit	occurrence (cf. *Ereignis*)
begreifen	comprehend (*comprehendere*)
begrenzen	bound (cf. *einschränken*)
Begriff	concept (*conceptus*)
beharren	persist
beharrlich	persistent
Beharrlichkeit	persistence
behaupten	assert
beilegen	ascribe
bejahen	affirm
Belehrung	teaching
Benennung	term
Beobachtung	observation
berichtigen	correct
Beschaffenheit	constitution; property
beschäftigen (*sich*)	be concerned
besonder	particular; special
beständig	constant
bestätigen	confirm
bestehen	subsist; exist; consist
bestimmen	determine
Bestimmung	determination (*determinatio*), vocation
Betrachtung	consideration
beurteilen	assess; judge
Beurteilung	estimation; judgment
Bewegung	motion
Bewegungsgrund	motive (cf. *Triebfeder*)
Beweis	proof

Beweisgrund	ground of proof
Bewußtsein	consciousness
Bezeichnung	designation
Beziehung	relation (cf. *Verhältnis, Relation*)
Bild	image
bleiben	remain; endure
bleibend	abiding; lasting
Blendwerk	semblance; mirage (cf. *Schein, Illusion*)
bloß	mere, merely
Boden	terrain
Cultur	culture
darstellen	exhibit; present
dartun	demonstrate
Dasein	existence (cf. *Existenz*)
Dauer	duration
Demonstration	demonstration
denken	think, conceive
Denk(ungs)art	way of thinking
deutlich	distinct; clear (cf. *klar*)
Ding	thing (cf. *Sache*)
dunkel	obscure
durch	through; by
durchgängig	thorough(going)
Eigenschaft	property
eigentümlich	peculiar
Einbildungskraft	(power of) imagination
Eindruck	impression
Einerleiheit	identity (cf. *Identität*)
einfach	simple
Einfluß	influence *(influx)*
einheimisch	indigenous
Einheit	unity
einsehen	have insight into; see (into); understand *(perspicere)*
einschränken	limit (cf. *begrenzen*)
Einstimmung	agreement
Einteilung	division
Empfindung	sensation *(sensatio)*
empirisch	empirical
endlich	finite
Entgegensetzung	opposition
enthalten	contain

759

Entschließung	decision
entstehen	arise
Ereignis	event (cf. *Begebenheit*)
Erfahrung	experience
Erfahrungs-	experiential
erkennen	cognize; recognize (*cognoscere*)
Erkenntnis	cognition (*cognitio*) (cf. *Kennen, Wissen*)
Erklärung	explanation, definition, declaration
Erläuterung	clarification, elucidation
Erörterung	exposition (*expositio*)
Erscheinung	appearance
Erste	first member (of a series)
erwägen	consider
Erweiterung	amplification; expansion
erzeugen	produce, generate
Existenz	existence (cf. *Dasein*)
Fähigkeit	capacity (*capacitas*)
Fertigkeit	skill
figürlich	figurative (*speciosum*)
Fläche	surface
Folge	sequel; sequence
folgen	follow
folgern	conclude (cf. *schließen*)
Folgerung	consequence
Form	form
Fortgang	progression; progress (*progressus*)
Fortschritt	progress
Fortsetzung	continuation
Fruchtbarkeit	fecundity
Fürwahrhalten	taking to be true
Ganze	whole; entirety
gänzlich	entirely
Gattung	genus
Gebrauch	use
Gedankending	thought-entity (*ens rationis*)
Gefühl	feeling
Gegenstand	object (cf. *Object*)
Gegenwirkung	counter-effect
gegliedert	articulated
Geist	mind, spirit (cf. *Gemüt*)
gemein	common

760

Glossary

Gemeinschaft	community
Gemüt	mind
Geschäft	concern, business
geschehen	happen
Gesetz	law
Gestalt	shape
Gewicht	weight
Gewohnheit	habit; custom
Glaube	belief; faith
gleichartig	homogeneous
Glied	member
Glückseligkeit	happiness
Grad	degree
Grenze	bound(ary) (cf. *Schranke*)
Größe	magnitude (cf. *Quantität, Quantum*)
grund	ground; basis
Grundkraft	fundamental power
Grundsatz	principle (cf. *Princip, Principium*)
gründlich	well-grounded; thorough
gültig	valid
hinabgehen	descend
hinzufügen	add
hinzusetzen	add
Idealismus	idealism
Idee	idea
Inbegriff	sum total
Inhalt	content
Kennen	know; be acquainted with (*noscere*)
Kenntnis	acquaintance; information; knowledge
Körper	body
körperlich	corporeal
Kraft	force, power
Kriterium	criterion
Lage	position
Läuterung	purification
lediglich	solely, strictly
Lehre	doctrine
Lehrsatz	theorem
Lehrspruch	theorem

Leit-	guiding
Leitfaden	guiding thread; clue
Lust	pleasure
mannigfaltige	manifold (*adj.*)
Mannigfaltige	manifold (*n.*), manifold of elements
Mannigfaltigkeit	manifold (*n.*); manifoldness
Materie	matter
Meinung	opinion
Menge	multitude; multiplicity; amount
Mensch	human being
Merkmal	mark (*nota*)
Mittel	means
möglich	possible
nach	in accordance (with); according to; after
Nacheinandersein	succession (cf. *Folge, Sukzession*)
nachfolgen	succeed
nähern	approximate
Naturanlage	natural predisposition
Naturell	natural temper
nichtig	nugatory
notwendig	necessary, necessarily
notwendigerweise	necessarily
Nutzen	utility; usefulness
nützlich	useful
Obersatz	major premise
oberst	supreme
Object	object (cf. *Gegenstand*)
Ort	place
Perzeption	perception (cf. *Wahrnehmung*)
Probierstein	touchstone
Quelle	source
Raum	space
Realismus	realism
Reihe	series
Reihenfolge	succession (cf. *Folge, Nacheinander, Abfolge; Sukzession*); successive series
rein	pure (cf. *lauter*)
Relation	relation (cf. *Beziehung, Verhältnis*)

Rückgang	regress (*regressus*)
Ruhe	rest
Sache	thing (cf. *Ding*)
Satz	proposition; sentence; principle
Schätzung	appraisal
Schein	illusion (cf. *Erscheinung, Illusion, Blendwerk*)
schickanieren	quibble
schlechthin	absolutely
schließen	infer (cf. *folgern*)
Schluß	inference, conclusion (cf. *Vernnunftschluß*)
Schranke	limitation
Schwärmerei	enthusiasm
schwer	heavy
Schwere	gravity
Schwerkraft	gravitational force
selbständig	self-sufficient; independent
Selbstbewußtsein	self-consciousness
Selbsterkenntnis	self-knowledge
Selbsttätigkeit	self-activity
setzen	posit; place; put
Sinn	sense (*n.*)
sinnlich	sensible
Sinnlichkeit	sensibility
Steigerung	increase
Stoff	material, matter
subaltern	subordinate
synthetisch	synthetic
Teil	part
teilbar	divisible
Teilung	division
Triebfeder	incentive
überfliegend	extravagant
Übergang	transition
übergehen	pass (into)
Überlegung	reflection (cf. *Reflexion*)
Überredung	persuasion
Überzeugung	conviction
Umfang	domain
Undurchdringlichkeit	impenetrability
unendlich	infinite
unerforschlich	inscrutable

unerweislich	indemonstrable
ungereimt	absurd
Unlust	displeasure
unmittelbar	immediate, immediately
Untersatz	minor premise
Unterscheidung	distinction
Unterschied	difference
Unterweisung	instruction
Urbild	archetype (*prototypon*)
Ursache	cause (*causa*)
ursprünglich	original
Urteil	judgment
urteilen	judge
Urteilskraft	(power of) judgment
Urwesen	original being (*ens originarium*)
Veränderung	alteration (cf. *Wechsel*)
veranlassen	occasion
Verbindung	combination (*combinatio*) (cf. *Verknüpfung, Zusammenhang*)
verfließen	elapse
Verhältnis	relation (cf. *Beziehung, Relation*)
Vergleichung	comparison
Verknüpfung	connection (*connexio*) (cf. *Verbindung, Zusammenhang*)
vermittelst	by means of
Vermögen	faculty, capacity (*facultas*)
verneinen	deny; negate
Vernnunftschluß	syllogism; inference of reason
Vernunft	reason
vernünfteln	ratiocinate; rationalize
vernünftelnd	sophistical
Verschiedenheit	difference (cf. *Unterschied, Differenz*)
verschwinden	vanish
Verstand	understanding (*intellectus*)
verstehen	understand (*intelligere*)
verwandeln	transform
Verwandtschaft	affinity (cf. *Affinität*)
verweisen	refer
Vielheit	plurality
vollkommen	perfect
vollständig	complete
Voraussetzung	presupposition
vorherbestimmt	preestablished
vorhergehen	precede

vorstellen (sich)	represent; imagine
Vorstellung	representation (*repraesentatio*)
Wahn	delusion
Wahrnehmung	perception (*perceptio*) (cf. *Perzeption*)
Wahrscheinlichkeit	probability
Wandelbar	changeable
Wechsel	change (cf. *Veränderung*)
wechselseitig	reciprocal
wechselsweise	reciprocally
Wechselwirkung	interaction
wegfallen	disappear
Welt	world
Weltall	world-whole
Weltbesgriff	cosmological concept, cosmopolitan concept
Weltganze	world-whole
Weltkörper	heavenly body
Weltreihe	world-series
Weltweisheit	philosophy
Weltwissenschaft	cosmology
Wesen	being; essence
Widerlegung	refutation
Widerspruch	contradiction
Widerstand	resistance
Widerstreit	conflict; opposition
Wiederholung	repetition
Wirken	effect (*v.*); produce
Wirklichkeit	actuality; reality
Wirkung	effect
Wissen	knowledge (*scientia*)
Wissenschaft	science (*scientia*)
Zahl	number
Zeit	time
Zeitfolge	temporal sequence
Zergliederung	analysis
Zerteilung	disintegration
Zucht	correction
zufällig	contingent
zugleich	simultaneous; at the same time
Zugleichsein	simultaneity
Zurechnung	imputation
zureichend	sufficient

Glossary

Zusammengesetztes	(a) composite
Zusammenhang	connection, interconnection; nexus (*nexus, conjunctio*) (cf. *Verbindung, Verknüpfung*)
Zusammensetzung	composition
Zusammenstellung	juxtaposition
Zustand	state; condition
Zwang	coercion; compulsion
Zweck	end; purpose
zweckmäßig	purposive; suitable

English-German

abiding	*bleibend*
absolute(ly)	*absolut, schlechthin*
abstract (*v.*)	*abstrahieren*
absurd	*ungereimt, absurd*
actual	*wirklich*
add	*hinzufügen, hinzusetzen*
affinity	*Affinität, Verwandtschaft*
affirm	*bejahen*
agreement	*Einstimmung*
aim	*Absicht*
all (*n.*)	*All*
alteration	*Veränderung*
ampliative	*erweitende*
amplification	*Erweiterung*
analysis	*Analyse, Zergliederung*
analytic	*analytisch*
ancestry	*Abstammung*
appearance	*Erscheinung*
application	*Anwendung*
appraisal	*Schätzung*
approximate (*v.*)	*nähern*
archetype	*Urbild*
arise	*entstehen*
articulated	*gegliedert*
ascribe	*beilegen*
assert	*behaupten*
assess	*beurteilen*
assume	*annehmen*
beginning (*n.*)	*Anfang*
being (*n.*)	*Sein; Wesen*
belief	*Glaube*

believe	*glauben*
belong	*gehören*
body	*Körper*
bound(ary)	*Grenze*
capacity	*Fähigkeit* (capacitas), *Vermögen*
cause	*Ursache*
cease	*aufhören*
change (*n.*)	*Wechsel*
changeable	*wandelbar*
claim	*Anspruch*
clarification	*Erläuterung*
clear	*klar; deutlich*
clue	*Leitfad*
coercion	*Zwang*
cognition	*Erkenntnis* (cognitio)
cognize	*erkennen* (cognoscere)
combination	*Verbindung* (combinatio)
common	*gemein*
community	*Gemeinschaft*
comparison	*Vergleichung*
complete	*vollständig*
composite (*n.*)	*Zusammengesetztes*
composition	*Zusammensetzung*
comprehend	*begreifen* (comprehendere)
compulsion	*Zwang*
conceive	*denken*
concept	*Begriff* (conceptus)
concern	*Geschäft*
conclude	*folgern*
conclusion	*Schluß*
condition	*Bedingung, Zustand*
conditioned	*bedingt*
confirm	*bestätigen*
conflict	*Widerstreit*
connection	*Verknüpfung* (connexio), *Zusammenhang* (nexus, conjunctio)
consciousness	*Bewußtsein*
consequence	*Folgerung*
consider	*betrachten, erwägen*
consist (of)	*bestehen (aus)*
constant	*beständig*
constitute	*ausmachen*
constitution	*Beschaffenheit, Verfassung*
contain	*enthalten*

767

content	*Inhalt, Gehalt*
contingent	*zufällig*
continuation	*Fortsetzung*
contradiction	*Widerspruch*
conviction	*Überzeugung*
corporeal	*körperlich*
correct (*v.*)	*berichtigen*
correction	*Berichtigung, Zucht*
cosmology	*Kosmologie, Weltwissenschaft*
counter-effect	*Gegenwirkung*
criterion	*Kriterium*
culture	*Cultur*
custom	*Gewohnheit*

decision	*Entschließung*
definition	*Definition, Erklärung*
degree	*Grad*
delusion	*Wahn*
demonstrate	*demonstrieren, dartun, darlegen*
demonstration	*Demonstration*
deny	*verneinen*
dependent	*abhängig, anhängend*
derive	*ableiten*
descend	*abstammen; absteigen; hinabgehen*
designation	*Bezeichnung*
determination	*Bestimmung*
determine	*bestimmen*
difference	*Unterschied, Verschiedenheit, Differenz*
disappear	*wegfallen*
disintegration	*Zerteilung*
dismiss	*abweisen*
displeasure	*Unlust*
distinct	*deutlich*
distinction	*Unterscheidung*
divisible	*teilbar*
division	*Teilung, Einteilung*
doctrine	*Lehre, Doktrin*
domain	*Umfang*
duration	*Dauer*

effect	*Wirkung*
elapse	*verfließen, ablaufen*
elucidation	*Erläuterung*

empirical	*empirisch*
encounter	*antreffen*
end	*Zweck*
endure	*bleiben, dauern*
enduring	*bleibend*
enthusiasm	*Schwärmerei*
entirely	*gänzlich*
essence	*Wesen*
estimation	*Beurteilung*
event	*Ereignis*
exhaustive	*ausführlich*
exhibit	*darstellen*
existence	*Dasein, Existenz*
expansion	*Erweiterung*
experience	*Erfahrung*
experiential	*Erfahrungs-*
explanation	*Erklärung*
exposition	*Erörterung, Exposition*
expression	*Ausdruck*
extension	*Ausdehnung, Erweiterung*
external (thing)	*äußerlich; Äußeres*
extravagant	*überfliegend*
faculty	*Vermögen* (facultas)
faith	*Glaube*
fecundity	*Fruchtbarkeit*
feeling	*Gefühl*
figurative	*figürlich* (speciosum)
finite	*endlich*
follow	*folgen*
force	*Kraft*
form	*Form*
fundamental power	*Grundkraft*
general	*allgemein*
genus	*Gattung*
given	*gegeben*
given as a problem	*aufgegeben*
gravitational force	*Schwerkraft*
gravity	*Schwere*
ground	*Grund*
guide	*leiten*
guiding thread	*Leitfaden*

habit	*Gewohnheit*
happen	*geschehen*
happiness	*Glückseligkeit*
heavenly body	*Weltkörper*
heavy	*schwer*
homogeneous	*gleichartig; homogen*
human being	*Mensch*

idea	*Idee*
identity	*Identität, Einerleiheit*
illusion	*Schein, Illusion*
image	*Bild*
imagination	*Einbildung, Einbildungskraft*
imagine	*einbilden, sich vorstellen*
immediate(ly)	*unmittelbar*
impenetrability	*Undurchdringlichkeit*
impression	*Eindruck*
imputation	*Zurechnung*
in itself	*an sich (selbst)*
incentive	*Triebfeder*
increase	*Steigerung*
indemonstrable	*unerweislich*
independent	*selbständig, unabhängig*
indigenous	*einheimisch*
infer	*schließen*
inference	*Schluß*
infinite	*unendlich*
influence	*Einfluß* (influx)
inscrutable	*unerforschlich*
insight	*Einsehen* (perspicere)
institute	*anstellen*
instruction	*Unterweisung*
intention	*Absicht*
interaction	*Wechselwirkung*
interconnection	*Zusammenhang*
intuit	*anchauen*
intuitable	*anschaubar, anschaulich*
intuition	*Anschauung* (intuitus)
intuitive	*anschaulich*

judge (v.)	*urteilen*
judgment	*Urteil, Urteilskraft*
juxtaposition	*Zusammenstellung*

know	*wissen* (scire); *kennen* (noscere)
knowledge	*Wissen* (scientia); *Kenntnis*
lapse	*Ablauf*
lasting	*bleibend*
law	*Gesetz*
limit(ation)	*einschränken, Einschränkung, Schranke*
magnitude	*Größe*
major premise	*Obersatz*
manifold (*adj.*)	*mannigfaltig*
manifold (*n.*)	*Mannigfaltige; Mannigfaltigkeit*
mark	*Merkmal* (nota)
material	*Stoff*
matter	*Materie*
means	*Mittel*
member	*Glied*
mere(ly)	*bloß*
mind	*Gemüt, Geist*
minor premise	*Untersatz*
mirage	*Blendwerk*
motion	*Bewegung*
motive	*Bewegungsgrund*
multiplicity	*Menge*
multitude	*Menge*
necessarily	*notwendig, notwendigerweise*
necessary	*notwendig*
need (*n.*)	*Bedürfnis*
negate	*verneinen*
nexus	*Zusammenhang* (nexus)
nugatory	*nichtig*
number	*Zahl*
object	*Gegenstand, Object*
observation	*Beobachtung*
occasion	*veranlassen*
occurrence	*Begebenheit*
opinion	*Meinung*
opposition	*Entgegensetzung, Opposition, Widerstreit*
original	*ursprünglich*
original being	*Urwesen* (ens originarium)
outer	*äußerlich*
outside	*außer*

part	*Teil*
particular	*besonder*
peculiar	*eigentümlich*
perception	*Wahrnehmung* (perceptio)
perfect	*vollkommen*
perfection	*Vollkommenheit*
persist	*beharren*
persistence	*Beharrlichkeit*
persuasion	*Überredung*
philosophy	*Philosophie, Weltweisheit*
place	*Ort*
pleasure	*Lust*
plurality	*Vielheit*
posit	*setzen*
position	*Lage, Position, Setzung*
possible	*möglich*
power	*Kraft, Macht*
precede	*vorhergehen*
predisposition	*Anlage*
preestablished	*vorherbestimmt*
present	*darstellen*
presupposition	*Voraussetzung*
principle	*Grundsatz, Prinzip, Prinzipium; Satz*
probability	*Wahrscheinlichkeit*
problem	*Aufgabe, Problem*
produce	*erzeugen; wirken*
progress	*Fortschritt, Fortgang*
progression	*Fortgang*
proof	*Beweis*
property	*Eigenschaft, Beschaffenheit*
proposition	*Satz*
pure	*rein; lauter*
purification	*Läuterung*
purpose	*Zweck*
purposive	*zweckmäßig*
ratiocinate	*vernünfteln*
rationalize	*vernünfteln*
real	*real, wirklich*
reality	*Realität; Wirklichkeit*
reason	*Vernunft*
reciprocal	*wechselseitig, wechselsweise*
refer	*verweisen*
refutation	*Widerlegung*

regress	*Rückgang, Regressus*
relation	*Beziehung, Verhältnis, Relation*
remain	*bleiben*
represent	*vorstellen*
representation	*Vorstellung* (repraesentatio)
rest	*Ruhe*
science	*Wissenschaft* (scientia)
self-activity	*Selbsttätigkeit*
self-consciousness	*Selbstbewußtsein*
self-knowledge	*Selbsterkenntnis*
self-sufficient	*selbständig*
semblance	*Blendwerk*
sensation	*Empfindung* (sensatio)
sense (*n.*)	*Sinn*
sensibility	*Sinnlichkeit*
sensible	*sinnlich*
sentence	*Satz*
separate	*absondern*
sequence	*Folge*
series	*Reihe*
settle	*ausmachen*
shape	*Gestalt*
significance	*Bedeutung*
signify	*bedeuten*
simple	*einfach*
simultaneity	*Zugleichsein*
simultaneous	*zugleich*
skill	*Fertigkeit*
solely	*lediglich*
solution	*Auflösung*
sophistical	*vernünftelnd*
source	*Quelle*
space	*Raum*
species	*Art, Species*
state	*Zustand*
subordinate	*untergeordnet, subaltern*
subsist	*bestehen*
succeed	*nachfolgen*
succession	*Abfolge, Nacheinandersein, Sukzession*
sufficient	*zureichend*
sum	*Summe*
sum total	*Inbegriff*
supreme	*oberst*

surface   *Fläche*
syllogism   *Vernunftschluß, Syllogismus*
synthetic   *synthetisch*

take (to be true)   *Fürwahrhalten*
teaching   *Belehrung*
temporal sequence   *Zeitfolge*
term   *Benennung*
terrain   *Boden*
theorem   *Lehrsatz, Lehrspruch*
thing   *Ding, Sache*
thorough   *gründlich*
thorough(going)   *durchgängig*
thought-entity   *Gedankending* (ens rationis)
through   *durch*
time   *Zeit*
totality   *Totalität, Allheit*
touchstone   *Probierstein*
transform   *verwandeln*
transition   *Übergang*

understand   *verstehen* (intelligere)
understanding   *Verstand* (intellectus)
unity   *Einheit*
universal   *allgemein*
use (*n.*)   *Gebrauch*
use (*v.*)   *brauchen*
useful   *nützlich*
utility   *Nutzen*

valid   *gültig*
vanish   *verschwinden*

weight   *Gewicht*
well-grounded   *gründlich*
whole   *Ganze*
world   *Welt*
world-series   *Weltreihe*
world-whole   *Weltganze, Weltall*

INDEX

absolute, 400–401

absolute possibility, 401, 553–56

absolute whole, 507; *see also* conditions, and unconditioned; totality; whole

accidents, 301–2

action, 313, 535–40; *see also* freedom

actuality: postulate of, 321, 325, 333n, 430; relation to possibility and necessity, 330–32; schema of, 275; *see also* reality

aesthetic, transcendental, 4, 7–8, 14, 62, 70, 155–92 (in first edition, 155–71; in second edition, 172–92), 248, 261, 326, 347, 348, 479, 511, 519, 719–23; meaning of, 156, 173, 720

affection, 512, 533; and self, 257–60

affinity: law of, 598–601, 657; transcendental, 235–36, 240

agreement and opposition, 367, 369

Albinus, 746

Alexander the Great, 628

algebra, 641, 751

Allison, Henry E., 717

Alquié, Ferdinand, 744

alteration, 303–5, 314–16; continuity of, 292–93, 315–16; reality of, 165–66, 182–83; requires perception of motion, 335–36; and time, 179–80

amphiboly of concepts of reflection, 13, 366–83

analogies of experience, 11–12, 55–56, 295–321, 729–30; separation from transcendental deduction, 61

analogy, 602, 619, 729

analytic and synthetic judgments, *see* judgment

analytic and synthetic methods, 32–33, 68–69, 451, 717

analytic, transcendental, 4–5, 8–13, 14, 62–63, 201–383, 345, 358; distinction from dialectic, 197–200; division into analytic of concepts and principles, 201–3

Anselm, Saint, 17, 26

anthropology, 14, 542, 696, 700

anticipations of perception, 11, 290–95, 729

antinomy of pure reason, 5, 14, 16–17, 56, 459–550, 613, 743–45; arrangement of,

105; in inaugural dissertation, 37–38; in 1770s, 57–60, 63–64; mathematical and dynamical, 16–17, 530–32; meaning of, 410, 467–69; solution to, 479–95. *See also* conditions; God; infinity; simplicity; soul; space; time

appearance: contrast to illusion, 190–91; contrast to things in themselves, 36, 38–40, 115–16, 159–62, 163–71, 176–78, 180–92, 230, 276–77, 305–6, 340, 347–48, 352, 356, 364, 375, 381, 511, 515; meaning of, 155, 172; only object of *a priori* cognition, 235–36, 243–44, 263–64, 345, 358; *see also* Phenomena

apperception (transcendental, transcendental unity of): as condition of possibility of experience, 225, 434–6; in deduction, as ground of all necessity, 71, 231–38, 240–44, 246–52, 725, 726; early theory of, 54–5; eliminated from *Prolegomena*, 69; empirical and pure, 237, 246–7, 250–1; and inner sense, 189–90, 250, 257–60, 276, 281, 296–97; and interaction, 319; and judgment, 251–52; objective contrasted to subjective, 250–52; in paralogism of pure reason, 419, 423–24, 441, 451–52, 666; presupposes a manifold, 250; principle of is analytic, 248–49; and synthetic judgment, 281–82; and time-determination, 296–97, 320; *see also* consciousness

apprehension, synthesis of, 228–29, 261–62, 289, 291; is always successive, 300, 305, 306–8, 311–12

a priori (cognition): criteria of, 137–38; meaning of, 136–37, 716–17; *see also* cognition; judgment

Aquinas, Saint Thomas, 743

architectonic: of pure reason, 19, 502, 627, 691–701; and structure of *Critique*, 3–6

Arcesilas, 704

Aristotle, 106, 212, 213, 371, 395, 703, 733–34, 739, 745, 749, 755, 756

arithmetic: method of, 631–43; as synthetic *a priori* cognition, 144

Index

assistance, supernatural, *see* occasionalism

association, 229–30, 235–36, 239–40, 657, 659

astronomy, 351, 363, 715–16

atheism, 119, 558, 644

Attempt to Introduce the Concept of Negative Magnitudes into Philosophy, 28, 34–5

axioms: in mathematics, 288–89, 640–41; none in philosophy, 640; subreptic, 44–45, 58

axioms of intuition, 11, 286–89, 729

Babel, Tower of, 627, 750

Bacon, Francis, 91, 108

Baumeister, Friedrich Christian, 748

Baumgarten, Alexander, 2, 4, 5, 14, 25, 26, 156n, 173n, 705, 706, 707, 711, 714, 720, 737, 738, 739, 742, 743, 744, 745, 746, 747, 752, 756

Bayle, Pierre, 709

beauty, 708, 711–12

Beck, Jakob Sigismund, 728

Beck, Lewis White, 705, 707, 718

Beiser, Frederick C., 705, 713

belief, 684–90; contrast to knowledge and opinion, 646, 684–90; doctrinal, 687; moral, 688; negative, 690; pragmatic, 687; *see also* faith

Bennett, Jonathan F., 706

Bentley, Richard, 743

Berkeley, George, 67–68, 70, 72, 709, 723, 728, 739; dogmatic idealism of, 326

biology, 612, 692, 727, 750, 755

body, 130–31, 141–42, 529, 663, 698; relation to soul, 16, 432–39

Bonnet, Charles, 604, 750

Boscović, Rudjer, 744

Brandt, Reinhard, 706

Brucker, Johann Jakob, 397, 737

canon of pure reason, 5, 19, 65, 672–90, 753–54

categories (pure concepts of understanding), 201–66; as conditions of the possibility of experience, 48–55, 226–28, 234–36, 238, 241, 244, 264–65, 345–46, 358–59; definition and meaning of, 4, 8–9, 213–14, 226, 252, 256, 342, 344, 357; discovery of problem of, 48; and ideas of reason, 399–400, 402, 406, 413, 445, 459, 461, 464; as laws for nature, 263–44; mathematical contrasted to dynamical, 215, 531; metaphysical deduction of, 210–12, 261, 727; and non-being, 382–83; and principles of pure understanding, 278–79; of relation, 724; schematism of, 10–11, 271–77; table of, 8, 212; transcendental

deduction of, 60–63, 68–70, 103, 219–66, 734–35, 727; and unity of space and time, 261–62; and unity, truth, and perfection, 216–18; use restricted to appearances, 276–77, 298, 334, 339–42, 345–46, 348–49, 350–52, 355–65, 379–81, 659–60

causality, 21–22, 35, 304–16, 463, 484–90, 654–58, 667–68, 718, 730; *a priori* concept of needs deduction, 223; category of, 212, 214, 215, 235, 262–63, 265, 343, 357; first, 475, 484–90; and freedom, 463–64, 484–90, 532–46; not property of things in themselves, 115; particular laws of, 30–31; and perception of motion, 335–36; and postulate of necessity, 329–30; proof of, 11, 304–16, 730; schema of, 10, 272, 275; simultaneous with effect, 312–13, 730; and synthetic judgment, 131–32; universal law of, 4, 45, 304, 654, 730

certainty, 684–90; in mathematics, 630–31, 641

character, empirical versus intelligible, 535–37, 541, 544–45

chemistry, 591–92, 715, 742–53

chronometer, 638, 752

Chrysippus, 750

Cicero, 615, 750

Clarke, Samuel, 706, 707, 722, 733

coexistence, *see* simultaneity

cogito, see 'I think'

cognition: *a priori*, 2–3, 70, 102, 110–13, 127–29, 132, 221–23, 235–36, 243–44, 399, 716, 717–18; contrast to belief and opinion, 684–90; contrast between empirical and *a priori*, 136–37, 193; empirical, 695, 700–1, 716; historical, 693; limits of, 13, 622, 636; in mathematics, synthetic *a priori*, 143–45; objective reality of, 282; rational, 92–96, 702–3; requires both intuitions and concepts, 13, 155, 172, 193–94, 199, 224, 253–56, 260, 264, 334–35, 344, 352–53, 364–65; requires synthesis, 210–11; of self, 62, 259–60, 337, 412–15, 421, 423, 442, 445, 453; time and space as sources of, 166–67, 170–71, 183–84, 187–88; transcendental, 133, 196, 717

color, 161, 178, 292, 295

combination, 245–49, 258, 262, 285–86n

community, 316–19, 336; category of, 212, 215–16, 343, 358; proof of, 316–19, 730; schema of, 275; between soul and body, 433–34, 436–37, 611–12; between substances, 463, 659; *see also* interaction

concepts: deduction of *a priori*, 219–23,

Index

Plotinus, 746
Poncius, Ioannes, 749
possibility: and ideal of reason, 553–59; ontology as science of, 755; postulate of, 321–25, 330–31; real as opposed to logical, 30, 34–35, 323–25, 343–44, 358, 361, 571–72, 731; relation to necessity, 330–323; schema of, 275; *see also* modality; necessity
postulates: of empirical thinking, 298, 321–33; meaning of, 332; of pure practical reason, 116–17, 585–89, 681–82, 688
practical use of reason, 114–17, 458, 498–501, 662, 672–90, 749
predication and existence, 563–69
pre-established harmony, 30, 374, 436, 739
preformation system of pure reason, 265, 727
Priestley, Joseph, 646, 715, 752–53
principles: constitutive versus regulative, 45, 297–98, 520–25, 547, 552, 576–78, 591, 602–4, 606–23; dynamical versus mathematical, 11, 284–86, 297–99, 487, 530–32, 547, 745; of empirical thinking, 10–13, 278–337; theoretical versus practical, 672–90; *see also* laws; maxims
probability, 384, 589, 638, 661–62, 736, 755
Prolegomena to Any Future Metaphysics, 9, 12, 23, 62, 66–71
proof: kinds of, 19, 641–43, 668–71; in mathematics and philosophy, 641–43, 665–71; *see also* God, proofs of the existence of
psychology: empirical, 415, 606, 611–13, 699–700; rational, 14, 15–16, 31, 64–65, 411–25, 432–43, 451–58, 606, 611–13, 618, 634–45, 698–99, 737–42, 755–56
purpose, 673–84; in nature, 578–83, 613–22, 645–46, 660–61

quality, categories of, 9, 11, 212, 285, 295, 631
quantity: categories of, 9, 11, 212, 215, 285, 631; discrete and continuous, 529–30, 600; schema of, 274
quietism, 750

Real Progress of Metaphysics from the Time of Leibniz and Wolff, 62
realism, transcendental and empirical, 425–430
reality: category of, 212, 344, 382, 555, 558, 568, 564–69; empirical, 425–30; noumenal and phenomenal, 369; objective, 282, 335; schema of, 274–75, 290–95, 342–43, 357; *see also* actuality

reason, 101–2, 104–5, 109, 387–93, 444, 543, 691–701; apodictic use of, 592; concepts of, 394–405; and dialectic, 5, 14–15, 387–405, 496–503; history of, 702–4; lazy (*ignava ratio*, λογον ἀεργον), 615–16, 660, 750; maxims of, 594–604; perverse (ὕστερον πρότερον rationis), 617–18, 750; necessarily systematic, 113–14; polemical use of, 643–45, 663; practical as opposed to speculative, 5, 14, 70, 107, 112–15, 117, 458, 498–501, 662, 672–90, 749; relation to understanding, 40–1, 508–10, 736
recognition, synthesis of, 228, 230–34, 236
reflection, transcendental, 366–68, 371
refutation of idealism, 70–72, 121–22n, 326–29; *see also* idealism, refutations of
regulative principles, opposed to constitutive, 14, 18, 45, 297–98, 520–24, 547, 552, 567–78, 591, 602–4, 606–23, 659–60
Reid, Thomas, 705
relations: categories of, 9, 11, 15, 55, 212, 215–16; of judgments, 208–9; logical and real, 730–31; space and time as, 188–89, 378–79; *see also* causality; community; space; time
religion, 101n, 498–99, 582, 647, 700
representation, 398–99; *see also* appearance, concepts; ideas; intuition
reproduction, synthesis of, 228, 229–30, 236
right, concept of, 397, 639
Rorty, Richard, 707
Ross, W. David, 734
Rousseau, Jean-Jacques, 24, 755
Rufus, Richard, 743
rules: 636, 750; in causality, 307–11; in time-determination, 61; understanding as faculty of, 242–43; *see also* concepts; imperatives; laws; maxims; schemata

schemata: of concepts of the understanding, 271–77, 631; definition of, 273; of ideas, 691–92; *see also* Schematism
schematism of categories, 10–11, 61, 271–77, 728; definition of, 273
Schmidt, Raymund, 74–5
Schultz, Johann, 713
Schütz, Christian Gottfried, 715
Scotus, John Duns, 749
sciences, 627, 691–701
Segner, Johann Andreas, 144, 718
self: cognition of, 257–60, 327–29, 337, 412–15, 421, 423, 444, 445, 463; consciousness of, 61–62, 411–25, 445–48; *see also* apperception; consciousness; inner self; soul